Organizational Communication

Second Edition

Dennis:
To the memory of Grace Mortimer Mumby
1925–2018
A long life well lived

Tim:
To Sophia Hinojosa
Mi bonita . . . te amo siempre

Organizational Communication

A Critical Introduction
Second Edition

Dennis K. Mumby
University of North Carolina at Chapel Hill

Timothy R. Kuhn
University of Colorado Boulder

Los Angeles | London | New Delhi
Singapore | Washington DC | Melbourne

FOR INFORMATION:

SAGE Publications, Inc.
2455 Teller Road
Thousand Oaks, California 91320
E-mail: order@sagepub.com

SAGE Publications Ltd.
1 Oliver's Yard
55 City Road
London EC1Y 1SP
United Kingdom

SAGE Publications India Pvt. Ltd.
B 1/I 1 Mohan Cooperative Industrial Area
Mathura Road, New Delhi 110 044
India

SAGE Publications Asia-Pacific Pte. Ltd.
18 Cross Street #10-10/11/12
China Square Central
Singapore 048423

Acquisitions Editor: Lilly Norton
Editorial Assistant: Sarah Wilson
Content Development Editor: Jennifer Jovin
Production Editor: Karen Wiley
Copy Editor: Renee Willers
Typesetter: C&M Digitals (P) Ltd.
Proofreader: Ellen Brink
Cover Designer: Anupama Krishnan
Marketing Manager: Allison Henry

Printed in the United States of America

Library of Congress Cataloging-in-Publication Data (on file)

ISBN 978-1-4833-1706-9

SUSTAINABLE FORESTRY INITIATIVE
Certified Chain of Custody
Promoting Sustainable Forestry
www.sfiprogram.org
SFI-01268

SFI label applies to text stock

18 19 20 21 22 10 9 8 7 6 5 4 3 2 1

Brief Contents

Detailed Contents

2. Developing a Critical Approach to Organizational Communication   31

5. Communication, Culture, and Organizing   119

PART III. CRITICAL PERSPECTIVES ON ORGANIZATIONAL COMMUNICATION AND THE NEW WORKPLACE   145

6. Post-Fordism and Organizational Communication   147

7. Power and Resistance at Work

8. Communicating Gender at Work

14. Communication, Meaningful Work, and Personal Identity

Preface

It's been quite a while (decades, in fact) since we were students, taking the sort of course you're in now. And though our memories of those days may be a little fuzzy, we recall never really liking the textbooks we were assigned. They were dry and uninteresting attempts to capture large bodies of theory and research, which reduced the complex scholarly literature into lists that we had to regurgitate on exams. As professors, those frustrations grew only stronger. Although there are several terrific organizational communication textbooks (a few of them written by scholars we deeply respect), finding a textbook that fits with the way we approach this course proved challenging. Specifically, the typical textbook is written as if from nowhere. It's hard to tell from reading the book if the author has a particular perspective or set of assumptions that he or she brings to the study of the topic. In other words, most textbooks read as though they're offering an objective, authoritative account of a particular body of knowledge; the author's voice almost never appears. But the truth is that every theory and every program of research you've ever read about in your college career operates according to a set of principles—a perspective, if you like—that shapes the very nature of the knowledge claims made by that research.

Now this does not mean that all research is biased in the sense of simply being the expression of a researcher's opinions and prejudices; all good research is rigorous and systematic in its exploration of the world around us. Rather, all researchers are trained according to the principles and assumptions of a particular academic community (of which there are many), and academic communities differ in their beliefs about what makes good research. That's why there are debates in all fields of research. Sometimes those debates are over facts (this or that is or isn't true), but more often those debates are really about what assumptions and theoretical perspectives provide the most useful and insightful way to study a particular phenomenon.

Certainly, the field of organizational communication is no different. In the 1980s, our field went through paradigm debates in which a lot of time was spent arguing over the "best" perspective from which to study organizations—a debate in which Dennis was a key participant (Corman & Poole, 2000; Mumby, 1997, 2000). Fortunately, the result of these debates was a richer and more interesting field of study; some disciplines are not so lucky and end up divided into oppositional camps, sometimes for many decades.

As you can probably see, we're not going to try to overview, in objective fashion, the many perspectives and stances characterizing the organizational communication field over its history. Our interpretation of the literature, as well as our selection of which literature to include, is shaped by our shared critical orientation. We describe what that means in Chapter 2, but here we should position ourselves: We should address what brought us to this field and how our experiences shape the critical stance from which this book is written. How we got here matters.

For the past 30 years or so Dennis has been writing about organizations from what can broadly be described as a critical perspective. But he didn't start out as an organizational communication scholar. In the late 1970s as an undergraduate at Sheffield Hallam University, Dennis pursued a BA in communication studies—the first such degree of its kind in the United Kingdom. There, exposed to the cultural studies perspective that we'll discuss in Chapter 2, Dennis developed a strong interest in how communication and power work in the context of everyday life. How does communication shape people's realities, and how do some people or groups have more influence over the shaping of reality than others? As an undergraduate, Dennis had never heard of organizational communication, but when he moved to the United States to pursue a PhD, he discovered that some scholars were beginning to think about how we could study organizations as important sites of power and control that shape societal meanings and human identities in significant ways. Thus, he realized that he could apply his broad-based interest in communication and power to an important social context—the organization. Over 35 years later, he still finds organizations endlessly fascinating as communication contexts for examining how people's social realities of identities are shaped. Thus, Dennis is less interested in things such as how efficient organizations are (a perspective that some researchers would take) and more interested in how they function as communication phenomena that have a profound—sometimes good, sometimes bad—impact on who we are as people. We spend almost all our time in organizations of one kind or another, and certainly our entire work lives are spent as members of organizations, so it's extremely important to understand the implications of our organizational society of various kinds for who we are as people.

For Tim, the path was a little different. He traces his early interest in organizational communication to conversations around his family's dinner table, when his father would regale the family with stories of the workplace that day. As a mid-level manager in charge of juice production for a well-known health products company, he regularly complained about the managers above him, who were inevitably shortsighted and petty. During Tim's senior year of high school, his father was fired from that job, and the conversations around the dinner table made it clear that Dad's strong distrust of (and lack of respect for) authority was at the root of his firing. When the same thing happened at two similar positions over the next few years, questions of power and identity in the workplace became fascinating. Around the same time that his father lost his job, his mother resumed her career as a kindergarten teacher (until then, Tim's mother was a homemaker—an occupation that, sadly, rarely registers as "work"). The amount of effort she devoted to her classroom was astounding. She worked late into the evening, almost every evening, commenting on students' work, creating lesson plans, and producing materials for the classroom. She earned a fraction of the salary Tim's father did for work that seemed even more important and didn't seem to deal with the same shortsighted managers as her husband did, and her passion extended the workday well past when he had finished. A different set of questions about power, identity, and the workplace entered Tim's mind. He didn't know it then, but the seeds were planted for understanding organizations, and organizing processes, as shot through with power; he also started wondering about how workers' (i.e., his parents') identities were constructed so differently and how those identities produced rather different outcomes. He eventually came around to seeing communication processes as key to establishing (and displaying and modifying) identities, coordinating with others, negotiating authority, and enacting resistance—and his research has revolved around how communication constitutes the very organizations in which those processes are accomplished.

⚙ OVERVIEW OF THE BOOK

But what does this have to do with writing a textbook? We believe that a textbook should not only adequately reflect the breadth of different perspectives in a field, but it should also adopt its own perspective from which a field is studied. It makes no sense that an author should have to check his or her theoretical perspective at the door when he or she becomes a textbook author—the pretense of neutrality and objectivity we mentioned above. In fact, from a student perspective, reading a textbook that's explicit about its theoretical orientation makes for a much richer educational experience. It's hard to engage in an argument with someone when that person refuses to state his or her position; when you know where someone is coming from, you are better able to engage with his or her reasoning, as well as articulate your own perspective. Dialogue is possible!

So it's important to us that you know up front who you're dealing with here.

Furthermore, the way we've structured this textbook does not mean that it is only about the critical perspective. In some ways it is a "traditional" textbook in its coverage of the major research traditions that have developed in the field over the past 100 years. The difference from other textbooks lies in our use of the critical perspective as the lens through which we examine these traditions. Thus, the critical perspective gives us a particular—and powerful—way of understanding both organizational life and the theories and research programs that have been developed to understand it. So as you are reading this book, keep reminding yourself "These guys are working from the perspective of critical theory—how does that shape the way they think about organizations? What conclusions does it lead them to, and how might other assumptions lead in different directions?" Also ask yourself "When do I agree with Dennis and Tim, and when do I disagree with them? Why do I agree or disagree, where did my own beliefs come from, and what does that tell me about my own view of the world?"

In addition to the critical perspective we adopt in this book, we're also bringing a particular communication approach. Rather than thinking of this book as exploring theories of organizational communication, you can think of it as developing a communicative mode of explanation that enables us to understand organizations as communicative phenomena. Organizations can (and have) been studied from psychological, sociological, and business perspectives (among others), but to study them from a communication perspective means something distinctive and, we think, unique. From this perspective, communication is not just something that happens "in" organizations; rather, it is the very lifeblood of organizations. Organizations, and organizing practices, *are* communication. It is what makes organizations meaningful places that connect people together to engage collectively in meaningful activity. The implications of this communication perspective will become clearer as we move through the chapters of the book.

🪣 NEW FOR THE SECOND EDITION

There are a number of innovations in this new edition. Indeed, almost every chapter has been extensively revised to reflect developments in the field of organizational communication and work over the last few years. New to this edition are as follows:

- A new chapter on "Information and Communication Technologies in/at Work." This chapter includes discussions of new developments such as platform capitalism and algorithmic management, mobile communication and the extension of the workplace, and extensive discussion of issues related to knowledge management

- A new chapter on "Fordism and Organization Communication" that provides a comprehensive critical review of early theories of management, including scientific management, bureaucracy, human relations theory, and human resource management

- A new chapter on "Post-Fordism and Organizational Communication," including discussions of the rise of the gig economy, neoliberal capitalism, the enterprise self, and immaterial labor.

- A new discussion of organizations and corporate social responsibility (Chapter 13)

- A new discussion of the "new science" of complexity and chaos theory (Chapter 4)

- A chapter on "Branding, Work, and Consumption" that is completely updated from the first edition.

🪣 PEDAGOGICAL AIDS

We've also updated the pedagogical aids in this new edition that will assist you in getting to grips with the various and sometimes complex issues that we'll be addressing. First, each chapter contains at least one **Critical Case Study** that enables you to apply the issues discussed in that chapter to a real-world situation. Think of these case studies as an effort to demonstrate the fact that there's nothing as practical as a good theory. Second, each chapter contains a **Critical Research** box that provides some insight into the material in the chapter by interpreting a key study that exemplifies some topic of the chapter. Finally, each chapter highlights **key terms** in bold throughout the text and lists the key terms at the end of each chapter, along with definitions in the **glossary** at the end of the book.

🪣 ANCILLARIES

In addition to the text, a full array of ancillary website materials for instructors and students is available at www.sagepub.com/mumbyorg.

The password-protected Instructor Teaching Site at www.sagepub.com/mumbyorg contains a test bank, PowerPoint presentations, chapter summaries, and web resources for use in the classroom.

The open-access Student Study Site at www.sagepub.com/mumbyorg contains web resources, quizzes, and interactive flashcards for key terms to enhance student learning.

THE CRITICAL PERSPECTIVE OF THE BOOK

We'd like to say one last thing about the perspective we adopt in this book. This textbook (and indeed, any textbook) is political in the sense suggested by organizational communication scholars Karen Ashcraft and Brenda Allen (2003):

> As they orient students to the field and its defining areas of theory and research, textbooks perform a political function. That is, they advance narratives of collective identity, which invite students to internalize a particular map of central and marginal issues, of legitimate and dubious projects. (p. 28)

As we suggested above, knowledge is far from neutral. The ways authors produce, frame, and claim value for knowledge shapes our understandings of it in particular ways. The map we lay out in this book will, we hope, enable you to negotiate organizational life as more engaged and thoughtful organizational citizens (as both members and critical analysts of organizations of all sorts). As such, we hope this book will better equip you to recognize the subtle and not-so-subtle ways organizations shape human identities—both collective and individual.

Acknowledgments

We are all familiar with the philosophical question, "If a tree falls in the forest, and no one is around to witness it, does it make a sound?" Academics face a similar conundrum, which is something like, "If a book is written but no one reads it, does it still express important ideas?" When Dennis wrote the first edition of this textbook a few years ago, he wanted to write a book that brought together academic ideas that he had been working on for a number of years but also engaged a broader audience. A "critical" organizational communication textbook that covered all the traditional bases along with thematic issues of power and ideology had never been written before and so he was unsure if anyone would "hear" it. Gratifyingly, the first edition was a success, hence this second edition. So, Dennis would first like to thank all those instructors who took a chance with a non-traditional textbook, and who reported back to him their positive experiences using this text to teach courses in organizational communication. He is grateful to them all.

This is the seventh book that Dennis has published with SAGE and he continues to appreciate the professional relationship he has with them. The personnel may have changed over the years, but their commitment to high quality academic work has not. For this second edition, acquisitions editor Terri Accomazzo showed infinite patience during the many delays in delivery of the manuscript (who knew a second edition would be so hard?). Production editor Karen Wiley worked hard to keep the production process moving along and meet the publication deadline. Editorial assistant Sarah Wilson worked with great enthusiasm and expertise on the photo program. And last but not least, Renee Willers was a fabulous copy editor, improving the manuscript greatly with her keen editorial eye.

Dennis would also like to thank his family for their continued support. The summer of 2018 (when this book was being completed) was a tough one, with his mother passing away in late June. But everyone in the extended Mumby clan rallied around each other to collectively demonstrate what family is all about. Special thanks to Al and Pol for providing the space for a couple of weeks of quiet contemplation (plus the occasional rowdy World Cup game).

Tim would like to thank the many students he's had the privilege to teach—more accurately, to learn alongside—at several universities. In addition to academic mentors and colleagues at those universities, he has been fortunate to have some amazing conversational partners over the years. Those conversations encouraged him to embrace thinking that explored new territory compared to where his academic career began and he is grateful to those who helped him make the intellectual move (especially the students who had to suffer through some pretty poor lectures along the way).

Also crucial in the development of this book was a series of PhD seminars Dennis and Tim co-taught at Copenhagen Business School between 2008 and 2014. We would like to thank the faculty at CBS, especially Robyn Remke (who has since moved on from CBS), for bringing us in. This course was an opportunity to test the themes we pursue in this book. For Tim, these seminars showed how intellectually stimulating (and, perhaps even more important, fun) working with Dennis would be. It's exceedingly rare to find a scholar who can bring together deep theoretical knowledge, combine it with an exhaustive understanding of contemporary scholarship, hone it against everyday experiences and events, and discuss it with simultaneous wit and humility—but Dennis pulled off that rare combination in that course, as well as in the first edition of this book. When Dennis invited him to collaborate on this edition, Tim jumped at the chance.

Finally, Dennis would like to thank Tim for being willing to join him as co-author for this second edition. Dennis and Tim have been friends for over 20 years, and he could not have chosen a smarter and more adept partner-in-crime for this text.

PART I

Studying Organizations Critically

CHAPTER 1

What Is Organizational Communication?

Humans are organizational animals; modern life is defined by organizations and corporations.

"Everything communicates."
—Sergio Zyman, former Chief Marketing Officer, Coca-Cola.

We are organizational beings. We go to work, attend college and church, do volunteer work, join social groups, shop at numerous stores, internalize thousands of commercials from large corporations, and participate in social media. Human beings are communicating, organizing creatures, and we define ourselves largely through our various organizational memberships and communicative connections.

As simple as this assertion is, it hides a rather complex reality. The organizations that define who we are—and our relationships to them—have become increasingly complicated. Indeed, as systems of communication, we largely take for granted organizations and their roles in our lives. In a 2005 commencement address at Kenyon College titled "What is Water?," the late author David Foster Wallace told the following story: Two young fish are swimming along and run into an older fish, who nods at them in passing and says, "Mornin', boys. How's the water?" The two young fish swim along for a while until one turns to the other and says, "What the hell is water?" In many ways our relationships to organizations and the communication processes that create them is a bit like a fish's relation to water—they are essential to our self-definition and sense of being-in-the-world, but we navigate them without really paying much attention to how they give meaning to our lives.

One purpose of this book, then, is to provide you with a map to navigate the water we all swim in and to figure out the complexities of organizational communication processes. This map is important because in the last 30 years the influence of organizations and corporations in our lives has increased considerably. Indeed, some have argued that corporations in particular have become more powerful and influential than governments. With the advent in the 1980s of an economic and political system called neoliberalism and an organizational form called post-Fordism (both of which we will discuss in detail in Chapter 6), corporations significantly expanded their spheres of influence such that work and consumption increasingly define people's lives. As the quotation from former CEO of Coca-Cola Sergio Zyman at the beginning of the chapter indicates, corporations have understood for a long time that much of that influence depends on the sophisticated use of communication processes to shape the world we live in. "Everything communicates" is not just a lame slogan that every communication major hears in her or his first introductory course. Rather, it reflects corporations' recognition that, especially in the 21st century, communication is their lifeblood. Moreover, they recognize that their ability to shape meaning and social reality through communication processes is fundamental to their continued success. Thus, if corporations take communication seriously as a complex process, then as students of organizational communication we must take it just as seriously and explore how organizations and corporations function as complex communication phenomena.

Given the power and influence of organizations in contemporary society, it is important to understand organizational communication as a process that is inescapably linked to the exercise of power. As we will argue throughout this book, power is a defining feature of everyday organizational life, and an issue with which all perspectives on organizational communication must grapple. Indeed, so fundamental is power to our understanding of how organizations function that management researchers Stewart Clegg, David Courpasson, and Nelson Phillips (2006) claim, "Power is to organizations as oxygen is to breathing" (p. 3). What does it mean to make this claim, and what are its implications for how we live our lives as organizational beings?

First, let's briefly discuss how the modern organization developed. The emergence of capitalism as the dominant economic system in the late 18th century required work to be organized in a quite different manner than in precapitalist systems. In the next section, we address the emergence of this new organization that transformed both work and society.

❀ TIME, SPACE, AND THE EMERGENCE OF THE MODERN ORGANIZATION

The idea of working for an organization and earning a wage is an idea of fairly recent invention. Indeed, early capitalism had a great deal of difficulty persuading people that regular employment was a good thing, with resistance to this idea extending well into the 20th century. In one sense, then, "The history of capitalism is a history involving the gradual reconciliation of individuals with the sacrifices of the working day" (Frayne, 2015, p. 29). As late as the middle of the 19th century, working for an employer rather than for oneself was called "wage slavery." For the average U.S. citizen, such a notion directly contradicted the principles of freedom and independence on which the United States was established. In fact, in the early 19th century around 80% of U.S. citizens were self-employed; by 1970, this number had decreased to a mere 10% (Braverman, 1974). To be described as an "employee"—a term that came into widespread use only in the late 19th century and was originally used exclusively to describe railroad workers—was definitely not a compliment. As management scholar Roy Jacques (1996) argues, "Before the late nineteenth century in the U.S., there were workers, but the employee did not exist" (p. 68).

This shift from a society consisting of "workers" to one consisting of "managers" and "employees" is key to understanding the historical transformations that led to the emergence of an "organizational society." This shift involves both a change in the kinds of jobs people held and a more fundamental transformation of collective beliefs, values, and cultural practices involved in the transformation from an agrarian to an industrial society. Moreover, a change occurred in the forms of discipline and control to which people were willing to consent. In Foucault's (1979a) terms, the employee as a particular "subject" (i.e., an object of scrutiny about whom knowledge is produced) was created as a definable and measurable entity. Similarly, managers as an identifiable social group were also created to administer and control the newly emergent employee. To understand our origins as corporate or organizational beings, we will explore the elements of this creation process.

The transformation from an agriculturally based, agrarian society (in which most people worked for themselves to produce goods for self-consumption) to an industrial society required workers who embodied different work habits. The development of these new work habits can be traced in good part to the emergence of a new understanding and measurement of time. British historian E. P. Thompson (1967) identifies the shift from task time to clock time as being a defining feature in the emergence of industrial capitalism. Task time refers to an organic sense of time where work is shaped by the demands of the tasks to be performed. For example, the lives of the people living and working in a seaport are shaped by the ebb and flow of the tides, regardless of the "objective" clock time. Life in a farming community is shaped by the seasons; working long hours in the harvest season contrasts with the more limited amount of labor in the winter months. Similarly, the lives of independent craftspeople and artisans are oriented around the tasks they perform and are not dictated by the hands of the clock.

Thompson (1967) shows how in preindustrial Britain little of life was subject to routine, with work involving "alternate bouts of intense labour and of idleness" (p. 73). For the most part, people worked when they needed to and thought nothing of mixing leisure with labor. Thompson argues that this task orientation toward time is more humanly comprehensible than labor dictated by the clock and represents a lack of demarcation between work and life in general. From the perspective of clock time, however, such an orientation toward work appears wasteful.

In the struggle between employers and employees in early industrial capitalism, time proved to be *the* significant point of contention. As more and more people shifted from self-employment to working for others, employers attempted to impose a new sense of time—clock time—that was alien to most workers but essential to the development of systematic and synchronized forms of mass production. As such, under the employer–employee industrial relationship, time was transformed from something that was passed to something that was spent—time became *a form of currency*. In this new relationship, it is not the task that is dominant but the value of the time for which the employer is paying the worker.

However, the introduction of clock time into the workplace marked a period of considerable struggle between employers and employees, in which the former attempted to erode the old customs and habits of preindustrial life rooted in task time. For example, in the late 1700s pottery factory owner Josiah Wedgwood was the first employer to introduce a system of "clocking in" for workers (Thompson, 1967, p. 83), dictating the precise time that employees started and finished work. In addition, early industrialists recognized that schooling could socialize future workers into the discipline of industrial time. Thus, a number of late 18th-century social commentators viewed education as "training in the habit of industry," referring not to specific skills but to the discipline required for industrial work (Thompson, 1967, p. 84).

The introduction of clock time, then, was not only crucial for the development of mass-production techniques but also as a means of controlling a workforce for whom independent work was the norm. As Thompson (1967, p. 80) points out, the shift to clock time was not simply a technological advancement, but more significantly, it made possible the systematic exploitation of labor. Once time became a commodity—something that was paid for in purchasing labor power—then employers used all possible means to extract as much labor as possible from their workers. In fact, much of the workplace conflict in the 19th and early 20th centuries revolved around the length of the working day, with workers' unions playing a significant role in reducing the number of hours employees were required to work. Indeed, in the struggle to reduce the length of the working day, a common late 19th-century labor union slogan was "Eight hours for work, eight hours for sleep, and eight hours for what we will." Nevertheless, the basic principle that workers could be required by employers to work a certain number of hours was accepted relatively early in the Industrial Revolution.

Even today, clock time is still the defining feature of work for many people. An employee's level of power and prestige is at least partly reflected by how independent he or she is from the clock. Generally speaking, the more one is considered a professional, the less one is tied to clock time and the more one is invested in the nature of the tasks one performs (Ciulla, 2000). For example, as university professors, we have a considerable amount of discretion over how we organize our time. As long as we fulfill our professional obligations (teaching, advising, committee work, research, etc.), how and where we spend that time is entirely up to us. We don't have to clock in when we come to work or clock out when we leave. On the other hand, for an assembly line or fast-food worker, the clock and speed of the "assembly line" dictate the entire working day. Such a worker has little or no control over how his or her time is spent.

In the first part of this chapter, we have been establishing the historical context for the emergence of the modern organizational form. As we can see, the issue of control figures prominently, as factory owners increasingly tried to dictate employees' relationship to work. In order for organizations to function as collective, coordinated, goal-oriented social structures, fundamental shifts had to occur in the experience and meaning of work. While it took a number of decades, the average worker was disciplined to internalize the idea of working for someone else in a synchronized, coordinated manner for a specified time period. However, this transition from task time to clock time and from agrarian to industrial work was by no means smooth. Indeed, workers who in precapitalist times were used to a good deal of autonomy and independence in terms of how they worked did not take easily to the new regimes of control imposed by the industrial organization. In the next section, then, we will explore how the modern organization developed strategies and structures for managing the autonomy of its workers. Thus, we will examine organizations as communicative structures of power.

ORGANIZATIONS AS COMMUNICATIVE STRUCTURES OF POWER

Beginning in the late 19th century, as industrial capitalism became the dominant economic system, the new corporate organization and its employees became a focal point of study for social scientists in various academic fields. In the 150 years since then, researchers have developed various theories to explain how people can be motivated to come together to perform specific tasks when, more often than not, they would rather be somewhere else doing something different. Such has been the centrality of this problem for social scientists that sociologist Charles Perrow (1986) has claimed, "The problems advanced by social scientists have been primarily the problems of human relations in an authoritarian setting" (p. 53). For Perrow, the primary "authoritarian setting" is the workplace.

This problem of human relations in organizations is a complex one, as we will see in the course of this book. One of the defining features of an organization is that it coordinates the behaviors of its members so that they can work collectively. But while coordination is a nice concept in theory, it is surprisingly complicated to achieve in practice. Particularly in for-profit organizations (where most people work), one of the principal factors that limits such coordination is the tension between a human desire for autonomy and agency on the one hand, and organizational efforts to shape the will of employees to serve its goals on the other. Philosopher of work Joanne Ciulla (2000) nicely expresses this tension when she states, "The struggle for freedom and power or control has long been the struggle between masters and slaves, lords and serfs, and employers and employees. It is the central problem of work" (p. 70). Table 1.1 below summarizes some of the ways in which, in the modern workplace, this tension between employee autonomy and organizational control is manifested.

As the table suggests, there is an inherent tension between an employee's desire to maximize her or his salary and a company's desire to minimize costs and maintain profitability. The proliferation of companies that outsource many of their manufacturing jobs to other countries that provide cheaper labor is testament to this fact. Similarly, most workers would prefer job stability and be able to rely on a consistent paycheck, but this stability goes against the trend over the last 30 years of companies maintaining flexibility

Table 1.1 Some Tensions Between Employee Autonomy and Organizational Control

Employee Goals		Organizational Goals
Maximizing salary	←----------------------→	Minimizing costs
Job stability	←----------------------→	Organizational flexibility and change
Maximizing leisure time	←----------------------→	Maximizing work time
Behaving spontaneously	←----------------------→	Behaving predictably
Asserting individual values	←----------------------→	Asserting collective values
Developing personal relationships	←----------------------→	Developing professional relationships
Creativity	←----------------------→	Efficiency
Relaxing the labor process	←----------------------→	Intensifying the labor process

by re-engineering, getting rid of nonessential jobs (e.g., outsourcing janitorial work), and focusing on core competencies (Weil, 2014). Thus, job instability has become the order of the day for millions of workers.

Of course, not all of these tensions exist in simple opposition to each other. For example, while organizations largely function as rational systems, employee expression of emotions at work is hardly taboo; if you have ever worked in retail, you know that providing customers with a positive experience involves expressions of warmth, positivity, and happiness. However, employee emotional expression is usually carefully prescribed by organizations in order to meet their goals (a phenomenon called emotional labor, which we will discuss in Chapter 7). In this sense, then, the tension derives from the ways in which a natural human trait (emotional expression) is co-opted by the organization to increase profits. In other words, human emotions are rationalized (i.e., made to serve the instrumental and efficiency goals of the organization) in ways that may not be comfortable for the employee (as anyone will attest who is required to smile throughout an 8-hour shift, regardless of how customers treat him or her).

Our point here is that these tensions have to be resolved in some way and that, generally speaking, they are resolved in ways that are consistent with organizational rather than individual goals. Telephone company executive Chester Barnard (1938) was among the first to argue that organizations are successful to the extent that they can subordinate the goals and beliefs of individual organization members to those of the larger organization. All organizational and management theories thus implicitly pose the question "How do we get organization members to behave in ways that they may not spontaneously engage in and that may even be against their best interests?" In many ways, the history of management thought is the history of efforts to develop more and more sophisticated answers to this question.

However, organization members do not passively accept these various efforts to control their behavior. On the contrary, the history of management thought is also a history of struggle, as employees have individually and collectively resisted management efforts to limit their autonomy in the workplace (Fleming, 2014a; Mumby, Thomas, Martí, & Seidl, 2017; Paulsen, 2014). These forms of resistance run the gamut from striking, sit-ins, and sabotage (called Luddism in the 19th century), to more creative acts of resistance. In the early days of industrial capitalism, for example, workers fought for safer working conditions and an 8-hour workday by striking and picketing. In more recent times, corporate efforts to engineer organizational culture and instill certain values in employees are sometimes hijacked by employees for their own ends, or else employees create their own countercultures in the organization, rejecting the values communicated by management (e.g., Ezzamel, Willmott, & Worthington, 2001; R. Smith & Eisenberg, 1987). Thus, it is important to think about power as a dynamic process of struggle that rests on a complex relationship between control and resistance. That is, organizational control is never a simple cause-effect phenomenon (like one billiard ball hitting another); it often produces creative employee responses that produce unintended outcomes for the organization. Thus, when we describe organizations as communicative structures of power, we are talking about how the tensions between employee autonomy and organizational control efforts play out dynamically through various communication processes.

Before we can examine these different organization theories through the lens of power, however, we need to develop a coherent and clear notion of what organizational communication means. Let's address this below.

⚙ DEFINING ORGANIZATIONAL COMMUNICATION

In this section, we'll explore what it means to talk about organizational communication. W. Charles Redding (1988)—widely regarded as the founder of the field of organizational communication—argues that all complex organizations (i.e., social structures large enough to make face-to-face communication among all members impossible at all times) exhibit the following four essential features: (1) interdependence, (2) differentiation of tasks and functions, (3) goal orientation, and (4) control. Oddly, he did not include communication as a defining feature of organizations. However, we will examine that feature via a fifth element: the communication–organization relationship. Let's examine each of these elements in turn, beginning with the communication–organization relationship.

The Communication–Organization Relationship

One of the problems in defining the term *organizational communication* is that we are dealing with two phenomena—*organization* and *communication*—that are individually extremely complex. While there are a number of different ways to think about the organization–communication relationship (R. Smith, 1992), two have been particularly influential in the history of organizational communication: (1) The "communication in organizations" perspective, and (2) the "organizations as communication" perspective. Let's discuss these two perspectives below.

Communication in Organizations

This perspective views organizations as relatively stable, physical structures within which communication occurs. In this sense, organizations are containers for communication processes, and people send information to each other from their various positions in the organization. In many respects, this has been the dominant model of organizational communication for much of the history of the field. Its approach is largely technical, focusing on questions of efficiency and clarity. Some of the main questions at issue here are as follows: (1) How can communication be made more accurate? (2) How do communication breakdowns occur? (3) How can we make sure that the message sent is the message that is received? and (4) What is the most appropriate medium through which to send messages? Here, issues related to noise (factors that distort message reception), channel (the medium of communication) information content (what is new in the message?), and redundancy (repetitive elements that increase the possibility of accurate message reception) are seen as key factors to take into account when thinking about effective organizational communication. In this approach, we can think about the communication–organization relationship as one in which communication occurs *in* organizations.

This perspective on the organization–communication relationship has its place, especially if one is primarily interested in questions of clarity and accuracy, but it also has serious limitations. First, by treating communication simply as an information transmission process within an already established organizational structure, it tends to downplay the significance of communication in the optimal performance of organizations. Communication becomes one organizational variable among many, and thus is easy to overlook. Indeed, management scholar Stephen Axley (1984) has argued that the information transfer model (what he calls the "conduit" model of communication) is fairly dominant among managers, leading them to think of good communication as relatively easy to accomplish and thus not deserving of much attention or adequate resources.

Second, it overlooks the complexity of the communication process. The reality is that communication is not just a means for transferring information from one person or location to another; rather, it is the process through which we create meaning. When we think of communication merely as information transfer, we are unable to recognize and take into account the complexity and ambiguity that is inherent in communication as a meaning creation process. If we are to be good communicators (as organization members or otherwise), we need to be able to appreciate the multiple meanings that can be present in any communication context.

Third, we have a sense of who we are, our connections to others, and our place in the world because we are communicating beings. When Sergio Zyman says that "everything communicates," he is acknowledging the fundamentally symbolic nature of reality; that is, everything—words, stories, the shape of a building, or even a rainy day—has the potential to be meaningful to us (and meaningful in potentially multiple ways). Finally, this information transmission view of communication is a problem because it tends to treat organizations as given. When we think of organizational communication as the process of communicating in organizations, then the organizations themselves tend to be taken for granted. They become relatively fixed, unproblematic structures that exist independently from the communication process that occurs within them. A useful video titled

"What Is Organizational Communication?" (produced by organizational communication scholar Matt Koschmann, 2012) that critiques this "container" view of the organization–communication relationship is available on YouTube.

Organizations as Communication

The second perspective, and the one that we will adopt throughout this book, has a much more "muscular" conception of communication in framing the organization–communication relationship. This perspective argues that communication constitutes organization—an idea referred to by some organizational communication scholars as the CCO approach to organizations (Ashcraft, Kuhn, & Cooren, 2009; Cooren, 2000; Putnam & Nicotera, 2009). Put simply, this means that communication activities are the basic, defining "stuff" of organizational life. Without communication, organizations cease to exist as meaningful human collectives. In this sense, organizations are not simply physical containers within which people communicate; rather, organizations exist because people communicatively create the complex systems of meaning that we call organizations. From this perspective, communication is more than simply one factor among many of organizational life; rather, organizations are seen as fundamentally communicative phenomena.

A useful way of thinking about organizations from this perspective is to view them as complex patterns of communication habits. Just as individuals develop habitual, routine behaviors that enable them to negotiate daily life, so large groups of people develop patterns of communication behavior that enable coordination and collective, goal-oriented activity. A meeting, for example, is a communication phenomenon that is meaningful and significant precisely because it is structured around rules for what counts as a meeting and features more formal and ritualized communication patterns regarding things such as turn taking, decision making, and so forth, all of which differentiate it from a casual hallway conversation.

Although there are multiple definitions and conceptions of communication, in this book we will adopt a meaning-centered perspective, viewing communication as the basic, constitutive process through which people come to experience and make sense of the world in which they live. In other words, communication does not just describe an already existing reality but actually *creates* people's social reality. For example, organization members who talk about themselves as a "family" create a quite different social reality from that of an organization where a "machine" metaphor is dominant and organization members see themselves simply as cogs in that machine (R. Smith & Eisenberg, 1987).

From such a perspective, we can define communication as follows: *the dynamic, ongoing process of creating and negotiating meanings through interactional symbolic (verbal and nonverbal) practices, including conversation, metaphors, rituals, stories, dress, and space.* As we will see in later chapters, this definition is not accepted by all theories of organizational communication. However, it provides a useful benchmark against which we can examine and critique other perspectives.

Following from the above definition of communication, we can define organizational communication in the following way: *the process of creating and negotiating collective, coordinated systems of meaning through symbolic practices oriented toward the achievement of organizational goals.* This definition moves away from the idea of organizations as objective structures within which people communicate and emphasizes the notion that organizations are, in many respects, nothing but the collective communication behaviors of their members. Of course, these collective communication behaviors do not just occur arbitrarily and spontaneously, but are rather coordinated in particular ways. Organizations are, after all, complex entities, often with hundreds or thousands of employees (so we also shouldn't assume that those collective, coordinated systems of meaning are fully shared by all members). So, let's unpack this definition of organizational communication further by examining the other defining features of organizations.

Interdependence

Organizations exhibit interdependence insofar as no member can function without affecting, and being affected by, other organization members. All complex organizations consist of intricate webs of interconnected communication activities, the integration of which determines the success or failure of the organization. Universities, for example, consist of complex webs of students, faculty, departments, schools, staff, and administrators, each group shaping and being shaped by all the others. While students may seem to be the group with the least agency (i.e., ability to influence others), they nevertheless heavily shape the behavior of the other groups (e.g., by making courses popular or unpopular through enrollment), especially given their role as the primary "customers" of universities (McMillan & Cheney, 1996).

As organizations have become increasingly complex and global in the past 20 or 30 years, interdependence has become an even more significant and defining feature of organizational life. Many large organizations depend on a complicated array of subsidiaries, outsourcing processes, communication technologies, and leveraged financial structures in order to flourish. Any change in one aspect of this complex system of interdependence can create changes in the entire system. For example, disruption of microchip production in South Korea (where 50% of the world's microchips are made), could lead to delays in the launch of the latest iPhone.

Differentiation of Tasks and Functions

All organizations, however large or small, operate according to the principle of division of labor, in which members specialize in particular tasks and the organization as a whole is divided into various departments. As the 18th century economist Adam Smith illustrated through his description of pin manufacture, many more pins can be produced when the manufacturing process is divided into many specialized tasks than if all the tasks are performed by a single individual (A. Smith, 1776/1937). This feature of organizations truly came into its own in the late 19th and early 20th centuries with the introduction of two complementary systems for organizing work: scientific management (developed by Fredrick Taylor) and bureaucracy (developed as a universal set of organizing principles by German sociologist Max Weber). We will discuss these two developments in Chapter 3, but together they had a profound effect on the organization of work for much of the 20th century. Scientific management analyzed each organizational task to determine the most efficient and productive way to work, and bureaucracy made sure that each person knew his or her place in the organization by creating a rational system of "offices" that defined each work role. Indeed, for much of the 20th century these two theories of organization were the defining features of 20th-century capitalism. As we will see in Chapter 6, in the late 20th century this system of classifying and differentiating tasks started to decline in influence as organizations turned to more "post-bureaucratic" arrangements that integrated tasks and focused more on skilled "knowledge workers."

Goal Orientation

Whether nonprofit or for-profit, organizations are oriented toward particular goals. Indeed, one could argue that the goals of an organization are what provide it with its particular character, coalescing its members into something more than a random group of individuals. Barnard (1938) makes this goal orientation explicit in his definition of an organization: "An organization comes into being when (1) there are persons able to communicate with each other (2) who are willing to contribute to action (3) to accomplish a common purpose" (p. 82). Universities have education and research as their overarching goals; for-profit companies aim for excellence in their products and thus a large market share.

© iStockphoto.com/gerenme

The control of employees has been a focus of management research for more than 100 years.

Of course, organizations often have multiple and competing goals, making Barnard's idea of a "common purpose" a complex one. Within a large software company, for example, there may be conflict between the respective goals of the research and development (R&D) and marketing departments. The former might want to spend extra months perfecting a new software program, while the latter might be more interested in getting it to customers quickly and working the bugs out in later versions. At a large research university, students may want an educational experience that involves small class sizes and lots of contact time with professors, while the research focus of the institution tends to produce large classes (which are more efficient and cost-effective from the university administration's perspective) and little face-to-face contact with professors.

Sometimes company goals can conflict with those of other interest groups, such as community members, employees, or shareholders. In its goal to increase profits, a company might pollute the environment, lay off workers, overlook safety regulations, or move its production facilities to countries where labor is cheaper and workplace safety regulations are more lax. In recent years, shareholder groups have increased their power in publicly traded organizations; in consequence, the quarterly report has become a key marker of corporate success, with significant pressure on organizations to produce quick results. In her study of Wall Street investment banking, anthropologist Karen Ho (2009) shows how increased shareholder power has caused many corporations to move away from long-term planning and toward short-term returns on investment—a shift that has had negative consequences for the stability of the economy.

Control Processes

Control is a central, defining feature of complex organizations. As we discussed earlier, the goals and interests of employees and the larger organization frequently conflict, and so various forms of control are necessary to achieve coordinated, goal-oriented behavior. Organizational control is not, by definition, problematic; however, it can often have negative consequences for employees, as we will see below and in later chapters. While Redding (1988) presents two forms of control (hierarchy of authority, as well as rules, plans, and roles), we will outline five different control processes that have evolved since the emergence of the industrial capitalist organization in the late 19th century.

It is important to note that these forms of organizational control generally emerged as a response to employee efforts to exercise autonomy (Edwards, 1979). As such, each form of control can be thought of as an attempt to overcome the limitations of earlier control methods; to the degree that certain forms of control were unable to adequately corral worker autonomy and resistance (at least to the satisfaction of owners and managers), they were superseded by newer, more sophisticated forms of control. Direct control was superseded by technological control, technological control by bureaucratic control, and so forth.

Direct Control

The simplest way to control employees is to direct them in explicit ways and then monitor their behavior to make sure they are performing adequately. As such, many organizations function through superior–subordinate relations, where the former has the authority to coerce the latter into working in specific ways. Since the beginning of the industrial revolution, supervisors have been employed to make sure that workers diligently perform their tasks rather than take long breaks or talk to coworkers. As we will see in Chapter 3, in the early stages of industrialization such coercive forms of control were deployed to direct workers who were not used to working in factory settings where clock time ruled.

Such close supervision, however, is hardly a relic of 19th and early 20th century factories. You have probably had jobs where your work was closely monitored by a supervisor. In their cleverly titled book, *Void Where Prohibited*, Marc Linder and Ingrid Nygaard (1998) document restrictions on factory workers' rest and toilet breaks, arguing that such restrictions are more widespread now than they were in the early 20th century. The authors even document cases of workers wearing adult diapers on the production line because of the company's tight restrictions on toilet breaks! Indeed, in 2014 a call center worker in the United Kingdom had £50 deducted from his or her pay for using the bathroom—a case that become known as the "toilet tax" and raised questions in the U.K. parliament about fair treatment of workers. Direct supervisory control of workers, then, is still very much a feature of the modern organization.

However, one of the limitations of this form of control is that supervisors are not always able to directly control worker productivity. Certainly, supervisors can monitor the presence and absence of workers and reward or punish them accordingly, but getting them to work faster is not as easy as it might appear. For example, particularly in the early days of capitalism, workers often knew more about the work than their supervisors did and were able to disguise their level of productivity. Indeed, many groups of workers deliberately engaged in output restriction (partly as a way of preserving their jobs or preventing their piece rate from being cut—an issue we will discuss on depth in Chapter 3). Moreover, as organizations grew in size, it became increasingly difficult to directly monitor and control the work of employees. Technological control, then, was in part an effort to overcome the problems with direct forms of control.

Technological Control

As the name suggests, technological control involves the implementation of various forms of organizational technology to control worker productivity (Edwards, 1979). Henry Ford's introduction of the moving production line in automobile manufacturing in 1913 is the classic and most important example of such control. Indeed, this innovation revolutionized the production process in early industrial capitalism and helped usher in an era that we now refer to as "Fordism" (Chapter 3 will discuss this important development). Certainly, the moving production line was a more efficient system of production, but it also had the additional benefit (at least from a management perspective) of limiting workers' autonomy and their ability to control the rate of production; workers became largely an appendage to the assembly line at which they worked.

As our economy has shifted from heavy production to a service economy, the forms of technological control have changed. The fast-food industry is a good example of a modern form of technological control, where computer technology carefully regulates (down to the second) every task performed by the employee. At McDonald's, for example, even the dispensing of soda is controlled to make sure exactly the right quantity is released into the cup—the employee has no room at all to exercise discretion (Ritzer, 2015). A more recent innovation is the introduction of scheduling software that allows companies to schedule employees to work shifts exactly when and where they are needed (Kantor, 2014). Big box stores like Walmart use such software to schedule more workers when there's a surge in sales, or send them home when sales are flagging. While this system is efficient and cost saving (employees aren't being paid when there's little work for them to do), it can have a damaging effect on the personal lives of the workers who are subject to this software. For example, scheduling child care can be difficult if one is called in to work at short notice, and making plans with friends or loved ones becomes difficult (not to mention planning on a consistent paycheck). Moreover, many of the employees subject to this software tend to be low-wage service industry workers who have little job security, making complaints about such a system difficult or dangerous to one's employment status.

In a service-oriented economy, customers, too, are subject to technological control. In fast-food restaurants, hard seats encourage customers to "eat and run," and menu items are placed in highly visible locations so the customers are ready to deliver their orders as soon as they arrive at the head of the line (Leidner, 1993). In addition, customers are "trained" to line up to place orders and to bus their own trays in order to increase efficiency and productivity. Many fast-food restaurants, including McDonald's, now provide touch screens that enable customers to place orders without even speaking to a live person. Airport check-in is now mostly self-service, with customers doing the work that used to be done by airline employees—a significant cost savings for the airlines. And many companies (e.g., AT&T and

Bloomberg/Bloomberg/Getty Images

Technological forms of control often shift work from employees to customers

Comcast) use online customer discussion forums that enable customers to solve technical problems for each other, thus significantly reducing customer service expenses. Even restaurant chains like Chili's and Applebee's that have servers now feature electronic tablets at diners' tables, enabling customers to browse the menu, order items, and keep noisy children quiet with electronic games (Colt, 2014). The cost of investing in these tablets is more than offset by the extra items that customers order. Indeed, the purpose of introducing the tablets is precisely to drive up revenue—perhaps an indication that people are sometimes more comfortable interacting with electronic interfaces than real people. If you are a server in a restaurant, this change might lead to a decline in wait staff!

Finally, technological control in the form of electronic surveillance is widespread in organizations. With such technology, employees can never be certain when they are being monitored and thus are forced to behave at all times *as if* they are under surveillance. The philosopher Michel Foucault (1979a) has referred to this form of control as *panopticism*, after the Panopticon—a prison designed by the 19th century utilitarian thinker Jeremy Bentham. Bentham's prison was designed in a circular fashion so a guard in the central watchtower could observe all the prisoners without being visible himself. As such, the prisoners engaged in a form of self-policing. People working in telemarketing, for example, are subject to such surveillance by an invisible supervisor who can monitor their calls. Similarly, employees doing data-entry jobs often have their keystrokes counted, allowing employers to collect data on their productivity remotely.

Bureaucratic Control

Bureaucratic control has been a feature of organizations since the early 20th century and despite the recent shift to post-bureaucratic structures, it is still common in many organizations (Edwards, 1979). It emerged in part as a mechanism to counter some of the excesses of early capitalism, characterized by boom and bust cycles in which little long-range planning occurred (Sennett, 2006). As we will see in Chapter 3, the bureaucratic form is a central—perhaps defining—feature of Western democratic societies, enabling organization members to gain advancement on merit rather than based on one's connections. Indeed, one of the problems with technological control (particularly assembly line work at places like Ford) was that it brought thousands of workers together under one roof in difficult and alienating working conditions; many of these workers agitated for unionization of the workforce to improve pay and working conditions. The creation of bureaucratic control mechanisms—systems of formal rules, structures, job descriptions, merit systems, and so forth—thus promoted a more democratic workplace where employees were less subject to the arbitrary whims of supervisors.

In addition, bureaucracies tend to promote taken for granted ways of behaving—a very effective mechanism of control. By and large we don't think too much about the rules and regulations that shape our organizational lives, but they can be a highly effective means of coordinating and controlling organizational activity (Du Gay, 2000; Perrow, 1986). For example, the smooth running of your day on campus as you move from class to class would be impossible without an efficient bureaucratic system that carefully coordinates the schedule—timed to the minute—of every student and faculty member. In this sense, organizational life is unimaginable without at least some level of bureaucracy.

Of course, as we all know, bureaucratic systems can also be very alienating. It is very easy to feel like a number when we are trying to accomplish goals but are constantly thwarted by the red tape of bureaucracy. While bureaucratic forms of control were particularly dominant in the three decades after World War II, both workers and managers alike began to experience them as oppressive, constraining, and often inflexible. Bureaucratic organizations tended to be hierarchical, slow to change, and unsuited to an increasingly volatile global environment. Indeed, the 1970s was a period of stagnation for large U.S. and European corporations, and many workers engaged in industrial action against reduced benefits, layoffs, and the lack of a voice at work. This time period led to the emergence of a new form of control.

Ideological Control

As a response to the failure of bureaucratic control and the increasing employee resistance that it faced, ideological control refers to the corporate development of a system of values, beliefs, and meanings with which employees are expected to identify strongly. From a management perspective, the beauty of ideological control is that it requires little direct supervision of employees. Instead, if employees have been appropriately socialized into the organization's system of beliefs and values, then they have internalized what it means to work in the best interests of the organization. The focus of ideological control, then, is not the behavior of employees per se, but rather their sense of self. Some researchers have even referred to the development of this form of control as an effort to develop "designer selves" in employees; that is, identities that are connected to the goals and values of the company for which they work (Casey, 1995). For example, Nike employees who get a "swoosh" tattoo might be said to have a strong connection between their personal and corporate sense of self (such an employee calls himself or herself an "Ekin"—Nike spelled backwards!).

Ideological control emerged along with the corporate culture movement that became popular in U.S. organizations in the 1980s (Peters & Waterman, 1982). This movement developed as an effort to charge work with meaning and overcome the sense of alienation that bureaucratic organizations had promoted. Companies that promote a strong corporate culture often carefully vet potential employees to make sure they "fit" the culture and then make explicit and carefully calibrated efforts to indoctrinate new employees through training programs such as "culture boot camp." For example, Disney employees are put through an intensive training program where they learn how to maintain the seamless fantasy that is the hallmark of Disney theme parks. Disney keeps a tight rein on its corporate culture; the Disney employee handbook even dictates the appropriate length and style of sideburns! Similarly, companies such as IBM, Whole Foods, and Southwest Airlines are recognized for their distinctive cultures. The success of Southwest as a low-cost airline has been attributed in no small part to management's cultivation of a culture of fun among employees at all levels (Freiberg & Freiberg, 1996).

One of the interesting features of corporate culture and ideological control is that it often focuses more on the values, meanings, and emotions connected to work than it does on the technical aspects of work. While direct, technological, and bureaucratic forms of control all attempt to shape how work actually gets done, ideological control tends to focus more on cultivating in employees a set of feelings that will connect them emotionally to the organization. In this sense, ideological control aims to develop strong "corporate clans," with employees having a strong sense of connection to the clan's belief system.

While this form of control can be an effective means of creating an engaged, energized workforce, it can also be quite oppressive to many organization members, particularly as it often asks the employee to invest his or her very identity, or sense of self, in the company. However, it is a form of oppression that is often disguised as something else—for example, being a "team" or "family" member. Employees who don't fit with the team or family may feel alienated from their work. Management scholar John Van Maanen's (1991) account of his experience working at Disneyland is a great example of someone who resists the ideological control to which he is subjected—and loses his job as a result! In fact, one of the main problems with ideological control and corporate culture was precisely that employees often saw through these thinly veiled efforts to manipulate their feelings. Management scholar Gideon Kunda's (1992) famous study, *Engineering Culture*, for example, shows how seasoned employees viewed the strong culture of a high-tech corporation with a great deal of cynicism. And David Collinson's (1988) study of a U.K. engineering firm shows how the shop-floor workers dismissed management efforts to introduce a new corporate culture as a "let's be pals" act aimed at co-opting workers.

Thus, while ideological control and corporate culture were introduced as a way to revitalize the workplace and tap into employees' desire for more meaningful work, it ended up imposing a new system of conformity that tried to get all employees to share the same values and beliefs. Interestingly, the corporate culture model emerged at the time when a new organizational form—post-Fordism—was beginning to emerge, and it also signaled a shift to a new form of organizational control.

Biocratic Control

While ideological control rests on the assumption that a company needs to create a strong internal culture with which employees identify, **biocratic control** shifts the focus away from such conformity, instead attempting to capture the diversity of its workforce. Thinking of organizations as "biocracies" (Fleming, 2014b) focuses on the idea that in the current, post-Fordist organization, it is "life itself" (bios) that companies are attempting to capture. What do we mean by this? For most of the history of industrial capitalism there has been a fairly clear separation between work and other aspects of people's lives. Indeed, Fordist capitalism pretty much insisted that the two realms were kept separate (although Henry Ford himself did take a strong interest in his employees' private lives, only hiring workers who abided by his strict moral code of sobriety and fidelity in marriage). For example, sociologist Hugh Beynon's (1973) study, *Working for Ford*, reports the following workplace motto: "When we are at work, we ought to be at work. When we are at play, we ought to be at play. There is no use trying to mix the two." Today's post-Fordist organization has, in many respects, overturned this principle, introducing work into home and play, and home and play into the workplace. Many people work from home, and play has become a serious business; in turn, companies are increasingly creating organizational environments that draw on the creative energies and leisure activities that people have typically reserved for life away from work.

Management scholar Peter Fleming (2014b) coined the term *biocracy* to capture this new form of organizational control. Drawing from philosopher Michel Foucault's (2008) notion of "biopower" (or power over life itself), Fleming argues that today's organizations have largely erased the distinction between work and home or leisure, capturing parts of our lives not typically associated with work. Now, rather than attempting to limit worker autonomy through various forms of control, companies aim to enlist the whole employee, asking workers to "just be yourself" while at work (Fleming, 2014a, p. 87). However, this strategy does not mean only bringing personal authenticity to work but also thinking of one's entire life as framed by work.

Think, for example, about your own day-to-day life as a college student. With adjustment for your own particular college context, we imagine that many of you have schedules similar to the ones reported by journalist David Brooks (2001) in an article called "The Organization Kid," in which he interviewed students at Princeton University: "crew practice at dawn, classes in the morning, resident-adviser duty, lunch, study groups, classes in the afternoon, tutoring disadvantaged kids in Trenton, a cappella practice, dinner, study, science lab, prayer session, hit the StairMaster, study a few hours more." Brooks indicates that some students even make appointments to meet with friends, lest they lose touch. Does this kind of daily schedule sound familiar to you?

Brooks's point is that students willingly (and happily) pursue these punishing schedules because they see it as necessary for the continual process of career advancement; they are basically spending 4 years as professional, goal-oriented students whose goal is continuous self-improvement. But this self-improvement is less about shaping one's intrinsic sense of well-being, and more about preparing oneself for a highly competitive market in which one's "brand" must be distinguishable from all the others. We suspect that a high percentage of you are engaged in precisely this kind of self-disciplinary activity in an effort to distinguish yourselves from one another and make yourselves more marketable to potential employers.

Biocratic control has emerged as the relationship between organizations and employees has shifted away from the post–World War II social contract of stable, lifetime employment and toward free agency and a climate of much greater instability in the job market. This instability is reflected not only in people's high mobility in the job market but also in the fact that "the self" (the identity of each employee) has become a project each individual must constantly work on—and not just at work. Because the project of the self is never finished and must be continuously monitored and improved (in order to meet an ever more competitive work environment), people live in a persistent state of anxiety about the value of their individual brand. Thus, individuals constantly engage in behaviors where the creation and continual improvement of an "entrepreneurial self" is the goal (Holmer Nadesan & Trethewey, 2000). Our entire lives are therefore framed through work in the sense that everything we do becomes an extension of our desire to be economically competitive. As Lair and Wieland (2012) show, college students even have to strategically defend their choices of major to justify how employable it makes them (have you had to defend your choice of major to family and friends?). As such, we become our own entrepreneurial projects in which career is a defining construct around which life decisions are made. In its most extreme form, the constant efforts to manage and maintain an entrepreneurial self has led to a concern with "instafame" (Marwick, 2015) in which everyone is trying to develop a presence in the "attention economy." People post YouTube videos of themselves, tweet, write blogs, and engage in whatever behavior might attract eyeballs and hence add to one's brand (Duffy, 2017; Duffy & Hund, 2015).

Fleming argues that within the current system of biocratic control, the employee "is probably one of the most micro-managed of all time" (2014a, p. 37). While the previous forms of control we discussed provide opportunities for resistance and autonomy, biocratic control is more difficult to escape precisely because it encompasses all aspects of life and is largely taken for granted. We now live in an economic and political system—neoliberalism—in which the individual (rather than the social) reigns supreme, and every behavior is evaluated in terms of its potential to be marketized (i.e., turned into economic value). It's hard for us to leave our unfinished tasks at work, and it's difficult to ignore the email from a coworker or supervisor that arrives in our inbox at 9 p.m. Our work identities and social identities are increasingly inseparable, leading some scholars to speak of the "social factory" (Gill & Pratt, 2008); that is, the notion that work has spilled outside of the organization, and economic value is created no longer only *in* organizations but also by the everyday activities in which we routinely engage. For example, every time we post something on our Facebook accounts, we create data points for Facebook that can be analyzed and sold to marketers so that they can target us with advertising that fits our tastes (Cote & Pybus, 2011). While this idea of biocratic power might be difficult to grasp at the moment, don't despair—we will discuss it in more detail in Chapter 6 when we talk about post-Fordism.

Summarizing the Five Forms of Control

Given the centrality of the ideas of power and control in this book, it is important to keep several issues in mind. First, many organizations use multiple forms of control at the same time. For example, an employee might be subject to direct control and bureaucratic control and also be heavily indoctrinated into the company's ideology. Furthermore, while analytically distinct, these forms of control overlap in practice in the workplace; for example, an organization's culture (ideological control) might emphasize a value system based on the importance of hierarchy and rule following (bureaucratic control), as is the case with military organizations.

Second, these forms of control operate with decreasing levels of direct coercion and increasing levels of participation by employees—in other words, control occurs via active consent. Thus, direct control is the most coercive (telling someone exactly what to do), while biocratic control is the least coercive (autonomous employee behavior and decision making). However, the development of less explicit and coercive forms of control does not mean that control is no longer an important issue in daily organizational life. Indeed, the development of more sophisticated forms of control suggests a greater need to understand the everyday dynamics of such control and its impact on our lives as organization members.

Third, as we indicated above, each form of control tends to develop in response to the failure of earlier forms of control to adequately deal with employee autonomy and resistance. In this sense, we can view each new form of control as building on earlier forms.

Finally, the increasingly sophisticated forms of organizational control require a similarly sophisticated understanding of the role of communication in these control processes. Direct, technological, and bureaucratic forms of control rely mainly on a fairly simple understanding of communication as information transmission, while ideological and bio-cratic forms of control depend on a view of communication as complex and central to the construction of employee identities and organizational meaning systems—issues that figure prominently in this book. In other words, ideological and biocratic forms of control can only be properly understood through the constitutive conception of the communication-organization relationship that we discussed above.

In the final section of the chapter we turn to a discussion of the relationships among communication, organization, and work. Because most of you reading this book are at the beginning of your professional careers and are probably thinking less about organizations per se and more about jobs, it is important that the topics discussed in this book take into account the changes in the nature of work that have occurred over the last 30 years. In this sense, the work world that you will be entering is quite different from the one that your parents or grandparents entered.

⟡ COMMUNICATION, ORGANIZATIONS, AND WORK

All societies have had work at their centre; ours is the first to suggest that it could be something much more than a punishment or a penance

—Alain De Botton (2009, p. 106)

This book is about organizational communication, but it's also about work and its place in our lives. After all, unless we are independently wealthy, most of us take for granted that we must work for a living. Work is what enables us to pay the bills and put food on the table. Work provides us with the resources we need to purchase both life's necessities and the little luxuries that make life more palatable. Moreover, work gives us a sense of self-worth and achievement. In other words, work—and particularly working for a living—is very much a defining feature of our lives (think about one of the first questions you ask when you meet someone). It is a dominant part of the social imaginary (the ideas, values, and institutions that define us as a society) that shapes who we are and our connection to the broader society in which we live (Weeks, 2011). At the same time, however, work in the 21st century is increasingly both insecure and unsatisfying. As much as work defines who we are, however, many of us are unhappy with our jobs. Consider the following statistics:

- The Conference Board's 2016 annual report on job satisfaction among U.S. workers indicates that only 49.6% of workers are satisfied with their jobs—down from a 61.1% job satisfaction rate when the annual survey began in 1987 (although the 2016 figure is the highest since 2005).

- A 2013 Gallup poll of 230,000 full- and part-time workers in 142 countries indicated that only 13% of these workers felt engaged by their jobs (i.e., found work interesting, with opportunities for participation in decision making).

- A 2015 Gallup survey indicated that only 32% of U.S. workers felt engaged by their jobs (Adkins, 2016).

- A 2018 Gallup survey reports that while 69% of Germans report being satisfied with their jobs, only 15% feel engaged by their work (Nink & Schumann, 2018).

- A 2018 Gallup report states that engaged and talented workers with at least 10 years of tenure at one company constitute only 5% of the workforce.

We are faced, then, with an interesting contradiction—most of us are heavily invested in and defined by our work, but a majority of us are dissatisfied with the work we do. We often experience it as alienating, meaningless, and—increasingly in the last 20 years—insecure and in flux. In addition, as the last statistic suggests, few people are staying in one job for a long time. Work is therefore a taken for granted aspect of modern society, and yet it is a condition that many of us struggle with and against.

It is important, then, that we think carefully about our relationship to work. Yes, we are by definition organizational beings, but to what degree does that mean that we are, therefore, defined by our work? The sociologist Max Weber pointed out that in traditional, precapitalist societies, people worked to live; that is, they worked only to the degree that they could produce or earn what they needed to maintain themselves and their families. Today, however, we live to work. Our jobs have become much more than the means through which we reproduce ourselves and have instead become invested with all kinds of symbolic value, levels of prestige, and psychological motivations (Gini, 2001). We are consumed by work and committed to an ethic that says that if we are not working hard and pursuing successful careers, then we are failing to realize our potential as human beings. As Alain de Botton's quote at the beginning of this section points out, work used to be a form of punishment that only the lowest classes in society (slaves, peasants, etc.) performed. Now work holds an exalted place in our imaginations.

But in the 21st century, work has become more problematic as a defining feature of life. While everyone is expected to pursue jobs and careers (and will experience negative sanctions by society if they don't), the economic system that dominated much of the 20th century has undergone changes that render the place of work in our social imaginary more problematic. Recently two articles appeared on the front page of the *New York Times* on the same day. One article reported that since 2010 fully half of the jobs created in the European Union have been temporary work, with young job seekers stuck in a constant cycle of seeking jobs (Alderman, 2017). The other article reports that around 40% of U.S. workers in their 20s receive some kind of financial support from their parents—the product of an increasingly insecure work environment, exacerbated by the fact that skilled knowledge work is increasingly concentrated in urban areas, where rent and living expenses are high. When you are moving around from one temporary job to another, it's difficult to establish financial stability (Bui, 2017). Taken together, these two stories capture much about the nature of contemporary work and the shift toward what some refer to as a gig economy—a term coined at the height of the financial crisis in 2009, when many people were forced to take multiple, typically low-paying jobs with few or no benefits.

Currently there are about 57 million people in the United States who work in the gig economy—around 34% of the working population. It is predicted that by 2027, this figure will increase to over 50%; in other words, the majority of the workforce will be freelance (Freelance Union & Upwork, 2017). Companies like Uber, TaskRabbit, Airbnb, and Etsy offer the opportunity for people to be their own bosses and work when they want (opening up possibilities for greater work–life balance). But while the possibility of greater work autonomy and lifestyle flexibility is a potential positive effect, there are a number of problems with this kind of work. For example, workers in the gig economy do not get the benefits typically associated with full-time employment—health care, pension plan, vacation days, and so forth. Indeed, people who work for companies like Uber are not actually employed by Uber; they are independent contractors who work for themselves and pay Uber a commission on each fare. Moreover, gig economy work tends to be low paid, and so such workers tend to have multiple jobs, thus undermining the idea that the gig economy leads to more balance between work and life

Some authors (e.g., Livingston, 2016) have argued that the labor market in 21st century capitalism has broken down to the point where it no longer provides opportunities for productive and fulfilled lives, and thus we need to radically rethink our relationship to work. The ongoing effects of technology, outsourcing, globalization processes, and the shifts away from manufacturing to service and knowledge work mean that, in many respects, the "job" as we traditionally know it is disappearing. Mulcahy (2016), for example, argues that many companies now see hiring full-time employees as an act of last resort and instead develop business models that rely heavily on contract and part-time workers. Recognizing this economic reality, Mulcahy says that she tells her MBA students that they should stop looking for a job and instead look for work; in other words, they should develop an independent mindset and a repertoire of critical skills that are flexible and applicable to a wide array of work opportunities rather than honed for a specific job or career trajectory. However, a recent *Harvard Business Review* article makes the significant point that the hardest thing about working in the gig economy for which Mulcahy coaches her students is that it's difficult to create a cohesive sense of self. Because our identities are so closely tied to our work, "those engaged in multiple jobs may find themselves plagued with issues of authenticity: who am 'I' really, if I'm all these things at once?" (Caza, Vough, & Moss, 2017).

So many workers today face a basic contradiction: On the one hand, work in the gig economy is, by definition, insecure; on the other hand, we want work to be meaningful, satisfying and provide us with a strong sense of identity. How do we develop this strong and coherent sense of self when the work we invest in is insecure and contingent? Social philosopher André Gorz (1999) has argued that we live an age of "generalized insecurity," in which the traditional touchstones of stability and identity—family, community, work, religious affiliation, and so on—have become increasingly unstable. This issue is becoming particularly acute because the topic of meaningful work has exploded in the last few years. Most people don't just want a job; they want work that is meaningful and rewarding.

CRITICAL RESEARCH 1.1

Kristen Lucas (2011). The working class promise: A communicative account of mobility-based ambivalences. *Communication Monographs, 78*, 347–369.

Kristen Lucas's study is based on interviews with 62 people who identify as working class, and provides fascinating insight into how people make sense of their class positioning in society. Lucas argues that while the American Dream of individual success is a pervasive and empowering discourse in U.S. society, for working class people, their relationship to this discourse is quite complex. On the one hand, the American Dream speaks to possibilities for social mobility; on the other, for members of the working class, loyalty to one's class roots is also a powerful and compelling discourse. In her interviewees' talk about work, Lucas identifies a discourse that she calls the "working class promise." This discourse, she argues, has four prominent themes: (1) a strong work ethic, (2) provision for one's family, (3) the dignity of all work and workers, and (4) humility—never becoming arrogant or pretentious and forgetting one's roots. Lucas argues that this working class promise discourse complicates the relationship of working class people to the American Dream discourse because the former treats class as a socially constructed value system, while the latter treats class as an objective structure. Thus, within the constructed value system of the working class promise, interviewees created a value hierarchy in which working class values were elevated above those of the elite or upper class, middle class, and nonworking poor—a social construction that is in conflict with the American Dream class hierarchy of upper class, middle class, working class, and lower class. As Lucas shows, this conflict between the values of the working class promise and the ideals of the American Dream creates a paradox for members of the working class: "Whereas the goal of the American Dream is to rise out of the ranks of the lower social class . . . the goal of the Working Class Promise is to maintain membership of the class by upholding a shared, work-related value system" (p. 364). Members of the working class (especially those who are socially mobile) "must negotiate culturally contradictory mandates of both maintaining *and* rising above their social class origin. Consequently, feelings of ambivalence should be expected as straddlers must engage in complex negotiations of identity work to align their class-based identities in such ways to position themselves as both achievers of the American Dream and keepers of the Working Class Promise" (p. 365). In general, Lucas effectively illustrates the degree to which class is, at least in part, a communicatively constructed phenomenon that has a profound effect on how we view ourselves.

Discussion Questions

1. What class do you identify with? Why? What are markers of your class membership? Do you even believe that class exists is U.S. society? Why or why not?

2. Have you experienced anything similar to the respondents in Lucas's study? Have you experienced a transition from one class to another (e.g., through getting an education and improving your job prospects)? How do you negotiate this straddling of cultures and classes?

3. Would you identify any additional themes to the ones that Lucas identifies as making up the discourse of the working class promise? Is there a similar discourse of the middle class promise or the upper class promise?

How is this discussion of contemporary work connected to communication issues? Our position in this book will be that just as organizations are communicatively constructed, so is work. Indeed, we would argue that in 21st century capitalism, work and communication are intimately connected (Kuhn, Ashcraft, & Cooren, 2017). We both make sense of work through communicative processes and do work through communication. As we will see in the chapter on branding, today communication (rather than manufacturing products) is the primary medium of profit for companies. How we understand work and our relationship to it is intimately related to our connections to others—friends, family, community, and so forth. Work as a social imaginary is communicated to us through group, cultural, and societal discourses that shape its place in our lives and how it figures in our sense of self. As Lucas's (2011) study of members of the working class shows (see "Critical Research" above), people draw on and enact prominent discourses that circulate in their communities as they attempt to make sense of themselves as workers. Regardless, however, of whether you view yourself as working, middle, or upper class (a recent Pew Research Center report shows that the U.S. middle class is shrinking, down from 61% of adults in 1971 to 50% in 2015 (Pew, 2015), we all construct and negotiate our relationships to work, largely through the cultural and societal discourses that are available to us—discourses that, as we will see in the course of this book, change over time.

Thus, as you work through this book, it's important to keep in mind that while work and organizations are a ubiquitous and defining feature of our lives, the ways in which we experience them are not natural and inevitable. Organizations and work in the 21st century are the product of centuries of human struggle over what society and our place in it should be like. This book is an effort to help you understand the complexities of that struggle, the better to engage with it.

CRITICAL CASE STUDY 1.1

A Conduit Model of Education

In a very real sense, how we *think about* communication has consequences for how we *behave and communicate* with others. Stephen Axley (1984) illustrates this powerfully in an argument regarding the dominance of the "conduit metaphor" in organizations. Following linguist Michael Reddy, Axley suggests that everyday talk about communication is dominated by an information transmission model that operates according to four implicit assumptions: (1) Language transfers thoughts and feelings between people, (2) speakers and writers insert thoughts and feelings into words, (3) words contain those thoughts and feelings, and (4) listeners and readers extract those thoughts and feelings from the words (p. 429). This model is implicit in everyday expressions such as "He couldn't get his ideas across" and "She tried hard to put her thoughts into words." Let's look at the consequences of this model for the education process.

In U.S. colleges and universities, there is an increasing tendency toward large classes with enrollments of 400 to 500 students. The educational principles embedded in this tendency operate according to a conduit, transmission model of communication. Large class sizes mean that any interaction between professor and students is highly limited, with the dominant discourse being a monologue by the professor. In keeping with this monologue, students view themselves as the passive recipients of information transmitted by the professor. Knowledge consists of information inserted into words and transmitted from the professor's mouth to the students' brains, with lecture notes operating as the repository of such information. Professors try to ensure effective transmission of information by introducing redundancy into the system via the use of PowerPoint, repeating main issues, creating podcasts, putting lectures on iTunes, and so forth.

But the conduit model completely undermines any conception of education as an active and dynamic process in which students and professors engage in dialogues about interpretive possibilities. With pedagogy reduced to the transmission of hard, nonnegotiable facts, we are unable to recognize the extent to which knowledge production is actually a highly contested, contingent, and ever-changing process. The unhappy result is that by the time students do finally get to participate in classes of 20 or 30 (usually in their senior years), they have become little more than efficient note takers. They simply want to know what the truth (at least in test-taking terms) is so they can write it down. Many students have thus been trained to apply a monologic model to a dialogic context.

Moreover, one might argue that the dialogic model is inefficient and unproductive in a context where students have become professional self-entrepreneurs who view education as a means to improving their personal brand equity. The knowledge acquired in courses is useful only if translated into a stellar GPA and well-rounded transcript.

Discussion Questions

1. In groups or individually, develop a definition of communication. In what sense is it similar to or different from the conduit model of communication?

2. To what extent has your experience of college education been similar to the one described here? How has it been different?

3. If you were to create the ideal educational environment, what would it look like? Identify some principles of organizational communication discussed in this chapter that might help you formulate this ideal.

4. Do you agree or disagree with the view of today's students as discussed under biocratic control? Why or why not? How would you describe your own student identity?

CONCLUSION

In this first chapter, we have tried to raise some questions about our commonsense understandings of organizations and work. By adopting a critical communication perspective, we can move away from thinking of organizations as formal structures within which we communicate and toward thinking of organizations as existing only because of the collective communication processes in which people engage. In this sense, *communication constitutes organization*—a principle that will guide us throughout this book, and which is foundational to the critical communication perspective on organizations and work that this book adopts.

As we have discussed in this first chapter, such a critical communication perspective views organizations as communicative structures of control in which organizations attempt to manage the tension between individual and organizational goals and values. Indeed, one of the claims that underlies this book is the idea that all management theories from the early 20th century to the present are premised on the understanding of the need to manage this crucial tension.

However, while this chapter has provided us with a sense of the big picture, we do not yet have a detailed sense of the specific lens or perspective we will use to examine these different management and organization theories and bodies of research. As will become clear in the course of this book, it is impossible to examine theory and research without adopting a position oneself (even though many textbooks tend to adopt a "God's-eye view," a view from "nowhere and everywhere"). As we mentioned earlier in this chapter, this book is written explicitly from a critical communication perspective, and so Chapter 2 will be devoted to a detailed discussion of this approach. We will discuss the history of the critical perspective and its underlying assumptions, goals, and values. By the end of the chapter, we will have a useful set of principles with which to make sense of the complex terrain that constitutes the field of organizational communication studies.

CRITICAL APPLICATIONS

1. Individually or in groups, identify the different forms of control addressed in this chapter. Think about instances where you have experienced these forms of control. Some will be routine and everywhere; others will be more unusual. How did they make you feel? What were your responses to these experiences? To what degree do you take these control mechanisms for granted? Are there situations where you have tried to resist or circumvent organizational control mechanisms?

2. Choose a news story that features some aspect of organizational life and explore how you might take a communication perspective on the issue that the news story explores.

KEY TERMS

biocratic control   19

bureaucratic control   17

clock time   6

communication   11

direct control   14

ideological control   18

organizational communication   11

organizational control   14

task time   5

technological control   15

STUDENT STUDY SITE

Visit the student study site at **www.sagepub.com/mumbyorg** for these additional learning tools:

- Web quizzes
- eFlashcards
- SAGE journal articles

- Video resources
- Web resources

CHAPTER 2

Developing a Critical Approach to Organizational Communication

The critical approach can enable you to navigate the complexities of organizational life.

In Chapter 1 we addressed the question "What is organizational communication?" In this chapter we will discuss the perspective that informs the answer we gave to that question—the critical approach. By the end of this chapter, you will have the analytic tools that will enable you to understand and critique the various theories, research traditions, and organizational processes we will be examining in the remaining chapters of this book. In developing these analytic tools, our goal is to help you become organizationally literate and thus better understand the expanding role of organizations in creating the world in which we live. Being organizationally literate enables us to become better organizational citizen-scholars, attending more critically to the important organizational processes and practices that shape both our working and leisure activities.

In this chapter, then, we develop in detail the perspective that provides the guiding assumptions for this book. You may have noticed that the subtitle of this book is "A Critical Introduction." In this context, the term *critical* refers not to the everyday, negative sense of that term but rather to a perspective on organizations that has emerged in the past three or four decades. From this perspective, organizations are viewed as political systems where different interest groups compete for organizational resources (Morgan, 2006). The critical approach highlights the goal of making organizations more participatory and democratic structures that are more responsive to the needs of their multiple stakeholders (Deetz, 1995). As we examine different organizational and management theories through the course of this book, we will assess them with this critical approach as our guidepost.

The first goal of this chapter, then, is to provide you with a sense of what it means to take a critical approach to the study of organizations; what does theory look like from a critical perspective? As such, we will examine the various influences and schools of thought that have helped establish a body of critical research in the field of organizational communication. A second goal of this chapter is to explain in some detail the principal elements of the critical approach. What are its assumptions? How does it view organizational communication and organizing practices? What are its goals and purposes? A third and final goal of this chapter is to show how the critical approach can be used as a way to examine and critique other ways of understanding organizations. As we move forward in the book, each perspective we address will be examined critically.

First, let's turn to an examination of why theory—despite its frequent complexity—is an important tool for understanding organizations and their place in the world around us.

⚙ UNDERSTANDING THEORY IN THE CRITICAL ANALYSIS OF ORGANIZATIONAL COMMUNICATION

For many of you the term *theory* is likely to send you running for cover. Theories typically seem abstract and largely inapplicable to everyday life (as reflected in the phrase "That's all well and good in theory, but . . ."). However, theories are actually indispensable to everyday life, and we would be unable to get along without them. As the psychologist Kurt Lewin (1951) once said, "There's nothing so practical as good theory" (p. 169). At an everyday level, we operate with implicit or commonsense theories that enable us to navigate the world. We do not typically subject these theories to careful reflection, except in instances where they fail us in some way.

For example, many people operate with the implicit theory that success is an individual thing; achievement is due to individual abilities and hard work. This theory may be partly true, but it overlooks the fact that everyone is positioned in societies and social structures that both enable and constrain their opportunities and shape their worldviews. For example, women are more likely to attribute their success to external factors such as mentors, supportive friends, and plain luck; men, on the other hand, are more likely to attribute their success to their own abilities. Does this difference tell us more about men's and women's psychological makeup, or more about the broader social structures that shape men's and women's life chances (and which may indeed shape psychological makeup)? The point is that while our implicit theories enable us to negotiate the world around us, they are often not very good at getting us to rethink our relationship to the world or, indeed, getting us to question how the world itself is structured.

Thus, implicit theories tend to maintain taken for granted, commonsense understandings of the world. However, we suggest that theory can also be understood as the systematic development of a particular mode of inquiry that enables the examination and critique of the commonsense understandings of the world that become taken for granted. Cultural studies scholars Stuart Hall and Alan O'Shea (2013) define common sense in the following way:

> A form of "everyday thinking" which offers frameworks of meaning with which to make sense of the world. It is a form of popular, easily-available knowledge which contains no complicated ideas, requires no sophisticated argument and does not depend on deep thought or wide reading. It works intuitively, without forethought or reflection. It is pragmatic and empirical, giving the illusion of arising directly from experience, reflecting only the realities of daily life and answering the needs of the "common people" for practical guidance and advice. (p. 1)

Commonsense thinking is often uncritical, reflecting tradition and reproducing the status quo. Part of the challenge of good theory, then, is to help people develop their critical communication capacities so that they can question commonsense thinking and interrogate our "direct" experience of the world. We never really have direct access to the world around us because it is shaped by communication processes that are both the medium and expression of different institutional structures, including class, education, mass and social media, organizations, religion, family, and so forth. In this sense, all of our experience is mediated in some fashion. Systematically developed theory, then, enables us to explore *how* our world is communicationally mediated and constructed and helps us understand the consequences of that construction process for ourselves and others.

Let's begin the case for this view of theory by making a "commonsense" argument that largely reflected "reality" 100 or more years ago: Women are influenced by their emotions rather than by their intellect and, as such, should not be allowed to do important things such as vote, hold high office, or have jobs with lots of responsibility (other than those that involve looking after children). Ideally, they should stay away from public life and focus on what they were born to do—looking after their husbands, caring for households, and raising children. From our "enlightened" 21st century perspective, it's hard to imagine that anyone in their right senses would still hold such a view of women and their abilities. But the reality is that well into the 20th century (and even for some people today) this opinion was the prevailing commonsense view of women's place in the world. At the turn of the 20th century, women could not vote, were barred from most colleges (there were—and still are—special women-only colleges), and had little access to occupations other than the most menial (domestic work, factory work, etc.). This so-called Cult of Domesticity, or Cult of True Womanhood—rooted in the four womanly ideals of purity, piety, submissiveness, and domesticity—did not emerge naturally but was part of a systematic effort during the 19th century by cultural and political elites to maintain an ideology of separate spheres, in which men ruled the public sphere, and women were confined to the domestic sphere. Women who challenged this "natural" division (e.g., 19th century feminist reformists such as Susan B. Anthony and Lucretia Mott) were described as "only semi-women, mental hermaphrodites" (Welter, 1966, p. 173).

It's really only with the benefit of 20/20 historical hindsight that we can see the absurdity of an economic and political system that effectively disenfranchised 50% of the population. But imagine being part of that reality. If you were a 19th century man, this view of the world would be reproduced all around you. For example, if you were a lawyer, your colleagues, including your personal secretary, would be all male (secretarial work had a high status in the early 19th century and wasn't feminized until the 1930s), and you would likely work with an exclusively male clientele. At your club (lots of men—working, middle, and upper class—belonged to male-only private social clubs at this time), you would hear opinions expressed about those crazy and militant suffragettes who were holding marches and handcuffing themselves to railings outside government buildings as a way to agitate for the vote. You might even have some sympathy for those women, but it would be extremely hard to express such sympathy in the male-dominated world in which you moved; indeed, your professional success might depend heavily on your ability to present yourself as an upstanding, reliable fellow who held no "radical" political beliefs. Even if you were a woman during this period, you might actually have agreed that a woman's place is in the home and be completely opposed to women's suffrage (a good example of how dominant ideologies and views of the world are often accepted and espoused by those who have the most to lose from that ideology). As absurd as this ideology of separate spheres seems to us today, it is worth noting that we are still living with the legacy of it, given the degree to which women are still underrepresented in many professions.

The way things are, then, is both socially constructed and difficult to change; it's created by humans, but it also endures for a long time as it becomes sedimented in institutions and organizations. It's therefore easy to hold intuitive, commonsense views of the world, in part because it takes less effort than challenging institutional forms and social structures that many people accept as natural. Change does occur, however, but typically only with the emergence of social movements (the labor movement, feminism, civil rights, gay rights, etc.) rooted in an alternate critical theory about how the world might work that over time produce a critical mass of people who internalize this theory in a way that enables them to envision a different reality. Thus, it took 72 years between the launching of the first wave of the feminist movement at the Seneca Falls, NY, conference in 1848 and the granting of the vote for women in 1920 (at least in the United States; see "Women's Suffrage," n.d., a Wikipedia link that tells you when women received the vote in other nations).

By and large, then, commonsense assumptions about the world tend to reflect the existing structures of power and privilege in society. What we think of as direct experience is heavily rooted in and mediated by those structures and institutions of power, which are difficult to transform. One of the ways that these transformations can occur is by the systematic questioning of commonsense assumptions about the world through the development of critical communication capacities in each of us. Such capacities can be nurtured by the careful development of systematic forms of inquiry in questioning common sense. The more we understand how theory and systematic inquiry work, the better sense we have of the multiple ways the world around us gets constructed. For example, in this book we will examine a number of different organization and management theories, many of which have had a profound effect on the nature of work in organizational life. As such, it is important that we have the tools that will enable us to understand and critique the implications of these theories for how work is carried out, as well as for how each theory constructs us as human beings in relationship to work.

We want you to think of this entire book, then, as an effort to challenge your common-sense understandings of the world of work and organizations through the development of a critical approach to organizational communication. By the end of the book, our hope is that you will possess a set of critical communication capacities—what we might call a "communication imagination" (Kuhn, 2017)—that will enable you to interrogate your relationship to work and organizational life. In the rest of this chapter, we will unpack the principles and concepts that make up the critical approach.

UNPACKING THE CRITICAL APPROACH

While there are a number of different historical influences on the critical approach, one common thread tends to run through all these influences—the work of Karl Marx (Marx, 1961, 1967; Marx & Engels, 1947). In the past 100 years or so, Marx's large body of writings has profoundly influenced modern social thought. Indeed, along with sociologists Emile Durkheim and Max Weber, Marx is considered to be a foundational thinker in our understanding of how society functions culturally, politically, and economically. However, the complexity of Marx's work has led over the decades to a number of different interpretations of his ideas. These different interpretations have, in turn, resulted in the establishment of different research traditions and schools of thought that expand on Marx's original ideas and attempt to make them relevant to contemporary society.

In this section we will first discuss some of the basic elements of Marx's theory of society. Then we will take a look at two schools of thought that are strongly influenced by Marx but that, at the same time, critique some of the limitations of his work and attempt to provide alternative views of society. These two schools of thought are (1) The Institute for Social Research (commonly known as the Frankfurt School) and (2) cultural studies.

Karl Marx

During his life (1818–1883), **Marx** was witness to major economic and political upheaval in Europe, as **capitalism** became the dominant economic and political system. Unlike earlier theorists such as Adam Smith (author of *The Wealth of Nations*, whom we will talk about more in Chapter 3), Marx did not celebrate the emergence of capitalism but rather criticized the ways in which it exploited working people. As Marx (1967) showed in his most famous work, *Capital*, despite the 19th century's unprecedented growth in production and hence in wealth, most of this wealth was concentrated in the hands of a very small minority of people he called capitalists. Even more significantly, Marx showed that this wealth was not directly produced by capitalists but was generated through the exploitation of the laborers who worked for the capitalists in their factories.

How does Marx arrive at this analysis of capitalism as an exploitative system? Let's identify some basic issues.

Marx's Key Issues

First, Marx provides a detailed analysis of the historical development of different economic systems, or forms of ownership. He describes these as tribal, ancient, feudal, and capitalist.

Karl Marx's writings have significantly influenced how we understand capitalist organizations.

Each of these periods represents increasing levels of societal complexity in terms of how goods are produced, the forms of property ownership that exist, and the system of class relations—or social hierarchy—in place. For example, tribal societies featured a hunter–gatherer system of production, little division of labor, and no class system insofar as tribal property was communal. Ancient societies, such as Greece and Rome, were city-states organized around agriculture, with a developed civil and political system. In addition, the class structure consisted of male citizens, noncitizen women, and slaves, with slaves doing all the direct labor. In the feudal system, production was concentrated in agriculture, ownership was in the hands of an aristocratic class that had stewardship over the land, and the class system consisted of serfs who performed labor and the aristocrats who had rights over the serfs.

It was in capitalism, however, that the economic system took on its most complex—and most exploitative—form. Here, production shifted from the countryside to the town, and due to the passing of a series of "enclosure" laws that privatized common land (which everyone could use) for the exclusive use of the aristocracy, commoners were coercively removed from this land (where they kept livestock, hunted game, and grew produce) and forced to migrate to the developing cities, thus creating a large pool of wage labor for the new factories. An anonymous 18th-century poem helps to capture the massive impact of these enclosure laws on the lives of ordinary people:

> *The law locks up the man or woman*
> *Who steals the goose from off the common*
> *But leaves the greater villain loose*
> *Who steals the common from the goose*

The law demands that we atone
When we take things we do not own
But leaves the lords and ladies fine
Who take things that are yours and mine

(as cited in Boyle, 2003, p. 33)

Marx is famous for developing a theory called **historical materialism**—an approach that analyzes history according to different modes of production, each involving shifting forms of property ownership and class relations. Marx identifies these different forms as common ownership (tribal society), citizen–slave (ancient society), aristocrat–serf (feudal society), and capitalist–wage laborer (capitalist society). In the last three cases, Marx shows that each system consists of an exploiting and an exploited class, with the former living off and dependent on the labor of the latter.

But what does Marx identify as being particularly exploitative about capitalism? Certainly, in the context of early 21st-century society, capitalism is usually associated with democracy and freedom, and it has certainly been a driving force behind huge increases in our standard of living over the past 100 years or more. What was it, then, that Marx critiqued about this economic and political system?

In his analysis of capitalism, Marx identifies four elements peculiar to this particular economic system.

1. Under capitalism, workers are no longer able to produce for themselves what they need to live. In Marx's terms, they do not possess their own means of production (land, tools, animals, machinery, etc.). Because the advent of capitalism in Europe saw the forcible removal of large populations from common land, these dislocated people were forced to sell at the going market rate the only thing that remained to them—their labor power. In this sense, the nonowners of the means of production (workers) are forced to satisfy their own economic needs by selling their labor power to the dominant group (the capitalists). Thus, workers actually perform the economic maintenance of the capitalist class and are reduced to commodities in the process.

2. Marx identifies capitalism as the only system of economic production in which the very foundation of the system is not to make goods in order to produce even more goods but rather to turn money into even more money. In this sense, the product a particular company makes is largely irrelevant, as long as that company continues to make a strong return on its capital investment. Thus, the actual use value (the benefit you enjoy from consuming a good or service) of the product is much less important than its exchange value (the commodities, such as money, you could get for the product if you sold or traded it). This shift is even truer today than it was in Marx's time. For example, companies such as Virgin (originally just a record store) include the following businesses: mobile phones, airlines, rail service, books, insurance, casinos, fitness gyms, and many others. The only connection among these various enterprises is the Virgin brand (a topic we will get to in Chapter 10). Moreover, financial service companies (Citigroup, for example) do not even make tangible products as such but manage money itself in order to make more money. As

Marx shows, this means that under capitalism, everything—including workers—can become a commodity, a good with exchange value, to be bought and sold.

3.   The exploitative nature of capitalism is hidden. That is, when workers sell their labor power to capitalists they are not selling a specific amount of labor but rather, a certain capacity to labor for a particular period of time. For example, a worker may be hired to work 10 hours a day at a particular hourly rate (say, $10). The capitalist's goal is to extract as much labor as possible from the worker during that 10-hour period (e.g., by constant supervision, speeding up the work process, etc.). Thus as Marx points out, the labor of the worker produces more value than that at which it is purchased (indeed, the value of the labor is infinitely expandable, limited only by technology, machine efficiency, and the worker's physical capacity). Marx refers to this difference between the value of the labor power, as purchased by the capitalist, and the actual value produced by the laborer as **surplus value**. This surplus value is the source of profit for the capitalist. Surplus value is hidden because the worker appears to be paid for a full day's work. However, as Marx shows, the worker is paid for only that portion of the working day that is necessary to maintain the worker; that is, feed and clothe him or her—what Marx calls necessary labor. The rest of the working day is surplus labor and is actually unpaid.

4.   Related, Marx pointed out that because capitalists were not purchasing a fixed amount of labor but a capacity to labor through the purchase of labor time, the actual amount that workers worked during that time (e.g., an 8-hour day) was largely indeterminate. As such, the capitalist labor process always involves an ongoing process of struggle (still part of work today) between capitalists who try to intensify the labor process as much as possible and workers who try to maintain at least some sense of autonomy and control over how much and how fast they work. Thus, the forms of control that we discussed in Chapter 1 (direct, technological, etc.) are very much about managerial efforts to turn the indeterminacy of labor power into a determinate amount of productivity, often in the face of resistance on the part of workers.

Perhaps Marx's most important point is that because workers under capitalism must sell their labor power and work for someone else, they experience **alienation** from both themselves and their own labor. As Marx states:

> In his work . . . [the worker] does not affirm himself but denies himself, does not feel content but unhappy, does not develop freely his physical and mental energy but mortifies his body and ruins his mind. The worker therefore only feels himself outside his work, and in his work feels outside himself. (Marx, 1961, p. 37)

As we saw in Chapter 1 and will see in subsequent chapters, the whole question of worker alienation is a key issue in how organizations manage work and employees. For Marx, good, fulfilling work is free from alienation, but work under capitalism work is inherently alienating because it deprives workers of the ability to experience work as an embodiment of their own creativity and skills; they are forced to work for someone else and largely become appendages to the machines at which they work.

While Marx was obviously addressing the conditions that existed in 19th-century facto-ries, the same principles—and in some cases working conditions—still exist today (indeed, one of the reasons many companies move production overseas is that labor laws regard-ing minimum wage, length of working day, workplace safety, and so on, are less strict or even nonexistent, thus creating more surplus value). As we reported in Chapter 1, a 2013 Gallup survey of workers worldwide reported that only 13% of workers feel engaged at work—a statistic that suggests that alienation is still a significant problem over a century after Marx's death.

In her participant-observation study of Subaru-Isuzu Automotive, for example, sociolo-gist Laurie Graham (1993) shows how contemporary capitalist organizations attempt to increase the amount of surplus value that workers produce. Graham discusses how work-ers are grouped into teams (in an effort to improve worker engagement) and required to perform a long list of tasks on a moving production line. When the plant first opened, the workers struggled to complete the tasks (22 in all) in the designated 5-minute time period. However, through increased efficiency and line speed up, the same tasks were soon per-formed in 3 minutes and 40 seconds. As Graham indicates, "Everyone was expected to con-tinually make his or her job more efficient, striving to work to maximum capacity" (p. 160). In Marx's terms, we can say that the workers produced an increasing amount of surplus value, while the value they accrued to themselves in the form of wages remained the same.

This example is interesting because the workers were apparently happy to work ever harder while receiving no reward for this extra work (except perhaps a pat on the back, although there is a long history of companies firing employees as they become more efficient—hence, paradoxically, it is not always in employees' best interests to work hard!). This apparent willingness to put up with a system of exploitation brings us to the next crucial aspect of Marx's critique of capitalism—his theory of **ideology**.

Marx uses the notion of ideology to show how the economic structure of society directly impacts the system of ideas that prevails at particular points in history. True to his materialist and economic orientation, Marx saw ideas as the outcome of economic activ-ity. Marx argues that not only does our social existence shape how we see the world, but also how we see reality depends on the ideas of those who control the means of produc-tion. In capitalism, of course, those in control are the ruling capitalist class. In one of his most famous passages, Marx says the following:

> The ideas of the ruling class are in every epoch the ruling ideas: i.e., the class, which is the ruling material force of society, is at the same time its ruling intellectual force. The class which has the means of material production at its disposal, has control at the same time over the means of mental production, so that thereby generally speaking, the ideas of those who lack the means of mental production are subject to it. (Marx & Engels, 1947, p. 39)

Ideology, then, is the system of attitudes, beliefs, ideas, perceptions, and values that shape the reality of people in society. However, ideology does not simply reflect reality as it exists—it is not *merely* an outcome of economic activity—but shapes reality to favor the interests of the dominant class (while standing in a relationship of opposition, or contradiction, to the working class). What does this mean? In the case of capitalism, it means that, for example, framing the labor process as "a fair day's work for a fair day's pay" ideologically legitimates the accumulation of surplus value by capitalists. As we have seen, however, capitalism obscures the exploitative features of the labor process.

Other examples of ideologies that operate in society include (1) continuous attempts through the 19th and 20th centuries to construct a perception of women (The "Cult of Domesticity/True Womanhood," as mentioned above) as unable to do "men's work" (except during times of war, of course), and (2) the development of a myth of individualism in which success is seen as purely the product of hard work and intelligence (the Horatio Alger myth) and failure becomes the responsibility of the individual. There are many more such examples, but all function to structure reality in a way that serves the interests of the dominant class. Thus, while Marx shows that economic interests structure ideologies, he also shows that such ideologies take on a life of their own, inverting reality in a way that marginalizes some groups and privileges other, dominant groups.

In sum, Marx's writings have had a profound impact on our understanding of the relationships among economics, social reality, and the class structure of society. Taken together, his ideas of historical materialism, worker exploitation, and ideology demonstrated the importance of looking beneath mere appearances to examine the underlying social relations in capitalist society. In this sense, he provided an incisive critique of how capitalism turned everything into commodities (including workers themselves) and alienated people from natural productive activity.

Critiquing Marx

While Marx's work is central to an understanding of the critical approach, his work also has significant limitations that have led scholars to revise his ideas over the past 100 years.

The first criticism is his belief in the evolutionary nature of the economic model of history. Marx believed that he had developed a set of universal principles that, much like Darwin's theory of the evolution of species, explained the inevitable development of political and economic systems around the world. Thus, for Marx and his followers, just as feudalism had naturally evolved into capitalism, so capitalism would evolve into socialism.

The belief in the inevitability of this process was rooted partly in Marx's contention that capitalism was so exploitative and so beset with problems and paradoxes that it was bound to fail. Like slavery and feudalism before it, an economic system that kept the vast majority of people in poverty for the benefit of a few surely could not continue to survive. Marx argued that the basic contradictions of capitalism (e.g., that while the working class produced wealth directly through their labor, the capitalist class accumulated the vast majority of that wealth for itself) would eventually become so apparent that people would revolt. Indeed, in the middle of the 19th century, conditions in English factories had become so appallingly oppressive and poverty was so widespread that strong revolutionary movements (e.g., the Chartists) gained considerable support amongst the general population. Similarly, in the United States, the late 19th and early 20th centuries saw massive wealth, poverty, and social unrest existing side by side. Trade unionism had strongly increased its membership, and the women's movement was actively demanding social and political reform.

However, as we all know, capitalism did not collapse (at least not in Western Europe and in the United States). In fact, the one major revolution of the early 20th century took place in a country—Russia—that was relatively underdeveloped industrially (thus violating Marx's principle that revolution would occur only in advanced capitalist countries). Despite a number of crises, including the Depression of the 1930s, capitalism continued to be the dominant economic system. So, from a historical point of view, Marx's "evolutionary" position has proven problematic.

A second—and related—criticism of Marx is his almost exclusive focus on the economic features of capitalism. While his development of an economic, materialist view of society is important, he tends to overemphasize the extent to which the economic structure of a society determines its cultural, political, and ideological features. As later scholars showed, there is no easy one-to-one correspondence between economics and social reality. One cannot say, for example, that all members of the working class will develop a similar ideological point of view. As we know, there are many working-class people who share a conservative ideology and many upper-class people who have radical ideologies (the billionaire businessman George Soros would be a good current example). In this sense, while Marx's model suggests that economics determines class, which in turn determines ideology, later scholars have shown this position to be extremely suspect.

Finally, because he was writing in the middle of the 19th century, Marx was unable to foresee the significant changes that capitalism would go through in the next 100 years or so. As we have said, capitalism did not collapse as Marx predicted, and later scholars would have to account for how capitalism was able to adapt to changing economic and political circumstances. While subsequent generations of Marxist scholars would not abandon principles of social change, they nevertheless needed to develop theories that would explain why capitalism continued to reign supreme despite the continued existence of poverty and exploitation.

In the next two sections, we will discuss two neo-Marxist schools of thought that have strongly influenced both social theory generally and critical organizational communication studies more specifically. Both schools have critiqued Marx's original writings and attempted to adapt his work to the analysis of modern capitalism.

The Institute for Social Research (the Frankfurt School)

The Institute for Social Research, founded in Frankfurt, Germany, in 1923, has had a major impact on European and U.S. theory and research over the past several decades (Jeffries, 2016). In the past 30 years, it has grown in importance for scholars in the field of communication, particularly those studying mass media, rhetoric, and organizational communication. Established by a group of radical German Jewish intellectuals, most of whom came from well-to-do backgrounds, the work of this school was an attempt to reinterpret Marxist thought in the light of 20th-century changes in capitalism. In particular, Frankfurt School members were interested in understanding capitalism not only as an economic system (which as we have seen was Marx's main focus) but also as a cultural and ideological system that had a significant impact on the way people thought about and experienced the world. Important Frankfurt School members included Max Horkheimer (who was the school's most influential director), Theodor Adorno, Herbert Marcuse (who became a significant figure in the 1960s student movement), and Walter Benjamin.

These researchers were concerned that in the 40 years since Marx's death, Marxist theory had become overly dogmatic. Indeed, the basic tenets of Marxist thought had become akin to a system of religious principles seen as universally and indisputably true. For Frankfurt School members, "the true object of Marxism . . . was not the uncovering of immutable truths, but the fostering of social change" (Jay, 1973, p. 46). In broad terms, then, the work of the Frankfurt School was an attempt to make Marxist theory relevant to the changing nature of capitalism in the 20th century (Kellner, 1989).

In responding to Marxism's apparent failure to predict the demise of capitalism, the scholars of the Frankfurt School embarked on a research agenda that attempted both to retain the spirit of Marxism and to move beyond its rather simplistic model of inevitable economic evolution. In short, the Frankfurt School wanted to continue the examination and critique of capitalism that Marx had begun, but it decided to take this project in a different direction than that pursued by Marx and his followers.

What was this new direction? While the scholars of the Frankfurt School pursued many diverse research agendas, there are two themes around which much of their work tended to coalesce. First, the Frankfurt School researchers believed that orthodox Marxism was in error in focusing principally on the economic aspects of capitalism. While the economic foundations of a society strongly influence the structure and processes of that society, Frankfurt Schoolers believed it was just one element in a more complex model of society. As such, they rejected the model of **economic determinism** (which argued that the nature of society was causally determined by its economic foundation) of orthodox Marxism. In its place, Frankfurt Schoolers developed a **dialectical theory** through which they viewed society as the product of the interrelationships among its cultural, ideological, and economic aspects. This theory became known as **critical theory**—a term still used today to describe a great deal of neo-Marxist theory and research.

Second, Frankfurt School members were interested more broadly in the nature of knowledge itself and in examining the course that modernist, Enlightenment thought was taking in the 20th century. While they believed in the Enlightenment-inspired ideals of human emancipation and happiness, many were concerned that the 20th century had witnessed the perversion of these ideals. As we will see below, many Frankfurt School researchers developed a profound skepticism about the possibilities for fulfilling the goals of the Enlightenment project. Both of these themes are discussed next.

Critical Theory and the Critique of Capitalism

Given the failure of classical Marxism to predict the demise of capitalism, the Frankfurt School turned its attention to studying the processes by which capitalism was able to legitimate and sustain itself despite the existence of paradoxes and contradictions that Marx argued would lead to its overthrow. This shift in focus involved turning away from the traditional Marxist base-superstructure model of society (in which the economic base, the capitalist–laborer relations of production, is portrayed as determining the ideological and political superstructure). In its place, the Frankfurt School developed a dialectical model, arguing for an interdependent relationship between the cultural and ideological elements of society on the one hand and the economic foundations of society on the other.

In their examination of the cultural and ideological aspects of society, Frankfurt School researchers were particularly interested in the then recent emergence of various forms of mass media such as radio, television, film, and popular music. Frankfurt School scholars made the claim that these media functioned as control mechanisms through which general consent to capitalism was maintained. Horkheimer and Adorno (Horkheimer & Adorno, 1988) coined the term **culture industry** to describe the coming together of popular forms of mass culture, the media, and advertising to create a "totally administered society" that left individuals little room for critical thought. According to Horkheimer and Adorno (1988), the development of the culture industry was one of the principal means by which capitalism could simultaneously perpetuate itself through the continuous creation of new needs and produce a mass consciousness that buys into the ideological beliefs of capitalist consumer society. As Jacques (1996, p. 153) states, "The same industrial processes which have resulted in the mass production of goods and services have been applied to the mass production of needs themselves."

Thus, the term *culture industry* suggests three ideas: (1) popular culture is mass-produced just like cars, laundry detergent, and candy; (2) it is administered from above and imposed on people rather than generated by them spontaneously; and (3) it creates needs in people that would not otherwise exist but are nevertheless essential for the continued survival and expansion of capitalism and maintenance of the status quo. These ideas will be taken up in much more detail in Chapter 10 on branding.

Critical Theory and the Critique of Enlightenment Thought

In addition to developing a critical theory of society and capitalism, Frankfurt School members sought to analyze the relationship between Enlightenment thought and 20th-century forms of science and rationality. Although they saw themselves very much working in the tradition of Enlightenment rationality, they considered that the confluence of capitalism, science, and instrumental forms of thinking had led to the perversion of the Enlightenment project. In one of their most famous statements on the 20th century's "fall from grace," Horkheimer and Adorno (1988) comment, "In the most general sense of progressive thought, the Enlightenment has always aimed at liberating men from fear and establishing their sovereignty. Yet the fully enlightened earth radiates disaster triumphant" (p. 3).

Critical theory thus involves an examination of why—particularly in the 20th century—humankind, "instead of entering into a truly human condition, is sinking into a new kind of barbarism" (Horkheimer & Adorno, 1988, p. xi). For Frankfurt School researchers, the main answer to this question lies with the emergence of science and technology and the dominance of instrumental reasoning. While Adorno and Horkheimer do not argue that science and technology are bad per se, they suggest that society's focus on objectification and quantification has led to an extremely narrow conception of knowledge that is unreflective. In this sense, Horkheimer and Adorno claim that Enlightenment thought has become totalitarian, serving the interests of domination and supplanting more radical forms of thought (Kellner, 1989, p. 89). Indeed, where the Enlightenment supposedly stands for progress and greater freedom, Horkheimer and Adorno see a logical progression from factories to prisons to the concentration camps of Nazi Germany (keep in mind that they are writing as Jewish intellectuals in the immediate aftermath of World War II).

In summary, we can say that the critical theory of the Frankfurt School is both a critique of the existing conditions of capitalist society and an instrument of social transformation aimed at increasing human freedom, happiness, and well-being (Kellner, 1989, p. 32). However, like the classical Marxism it critiques, the Frankfurt School version of critical theory also possesses some limitations. We will briefly address these limitations next.

Critiquing the Frankfurt School

The most problematic element in Frankfurt School research is its narrow conception of the role of mass culture in society. It is probably fair to say that Adorno and many of his colleagues had a rather elitist notion of what counted as culture, developing a rather rigid distinction between high and mass culture. For Adorno, only high culture was authentic, being able to produce the kind of insight and critical reflection that would result in social transformation. On the other hand, he saw the mass-produced culture of the culture industry as completely without redeeming value and as simply reproducing the status quo in capitalist society.

But this rigid separation of high and mass culture ironically ran counter to Adorno's (1973) espousal of a dialectical approach to the study of society. Through this polar opposition, Adorno and his colleagues overlooked the possibility that mass, popular culture could function as other than an instrument of social control. Missing from the Frankfurt School's approach to popular culture was the idea that perhaps the consumers of the culture industry were more than simply unwitting dupes who accepted at face value everything the mass media produced. As later scholars show, there is no single culture industry, nor is there only one way in which people interpret the products of that industry. Indeed, one could argue that popular culture is a contested terrain in which conservative and radical meanings and interpretations compete for dominance. This complexity is even more true in today's social media environment, where anyone with a smartphone and an Internet connection can participate in the creation of media products; people are no longer simply passive consumers of carefully marketed media messages.

Thus, Frankfurt School researchers both overestimated the power of the culture industry to create a totally administered society in support of capitalism and underestimated the ability of the average person to develop interpretations that contest administered meanings. However, there is little doubt that the culture industry represents an extremely powerful and dominant force in modern society. In Chapter 10, for example, we will examine the emergence of corporate branding over the last 30 years and explore how strategically companies use branding as a way to shape people's experience of themselves and the world. In this sense, while the Frankfurt School certainly overestimated the power of the culture industry, we should not underestimate its ability to influence social reality and shape meaning in society.

In sum, the Frankfurt School represents an important contribution to our understanding of the relationships among capitalism, culture, and power. It is central to our attempts to understand how people's experiences of the world are shaped at an everyday level. As we will see in later chapters, modern organizations have become extremely adept at shaping our perceptions, feelings, and identities, both as organization members and as consumers of corporate products. The reality is that we live and work in a corporate world, and very little of who we are is not affected in some fashion by corporate structures, processes, and systems of communication.

Cultural Studies

The research tradition known as **cultural studies** has had a major impact on scholars in a wide variety of fields, including English, media studies, and communication. In this section, we will examine some of the principal elements of this work and discuss its implications for a critical approach to organizational communication.

As we saw earlier, Frankfurt School scholars used the term *culture industry* to describe the emergence and negative effects of popular culture in society, but scholars associated with cultural studies—an interdisciplinary academic movement that traces its birth to a group of scholars associated with the University of Birmingham in the United Kingdom, beginning in the mid-1960s—use the term *culture* in a different way. They critique the distinction between high and low culture (R. Williams, 1983), arguing that such an opposition was not only elitist but also limited the ways in which everyday culture could be conceptualized. Thus, over the past several decades researchers in the cultural studies tradition have taken everyday culture as a serious object of study, examining the complex ways in which it structures experience. Indeed, Stuart Hall, one of the founders of cultural studies, defines culture simply as "experience lived, experience interpreted, experience defined" (Hall, 2016, p. 33). Researchers have studied the everyday sense-making experiences of people as they engage with various cultural phenomena including soap operas (Gledhill, 1997), teenage girls' magazines (McRobbie, 2000), shopping malls (Fiske, 1989), and many others as ways to try to understand how people live, interpret, and define their experience.

In studying everyday experience, then, cultural studies researchers explore the systems of shared meanings that connect members of a particular group or community. Such shared meanings are developed through "systems of representation" (Hall, 1997a, 1997b) that enable communities to make sense of the world in particular ways. Systems of representation involve not only language (spoken and written) but also clothing, music, nonverbal behaviors, space (architects construct buildings to convey particular meanings), and so forth. Because of their tendency to focus on often marginalized subcultures, many cultural studies researchers have focused on how such subcultures make sense of their conditions of marginality through resistant and oppositional representational practices. For example, Dick Hebdige's (1979) well-known study of 1960s and 1970s U.K. youth subcultures (groups he called mods, rockers, skinheads, and punks) focused on the importance of dress as a system of representation that distinguished these groups, from both each other and from the mainstream culture. Another cultural studies researcher, Paul Willis (1977) studied a subculture of working class kids at a U.K. high school who developed their own jargon and ways of behaving (fighting, stealing, pulling pranks) as a way of resisting the middle-class culture of the school. More recently, Angela McRobbie (2016) has studied the way workers in the "new culture industries" (jobs in media design, advertising, PR, etc.) use the idea of creativity as a way of making sense of and coming to terms with the insecurity and marginality of the employment environment that confronts them. Defining themselves as creative enables the workers to make sense of their continuous gig work (short-term, temporary jobs—see Chapter 6) as a necessary sacrifice in developing their personal brands.

In each of these studies, culture is examined as both an ongoing, routine everyday practice and as consisting of various systems of representation that enable people to collectively make meaning. People appropriate signs and symbols in ways that enable them to construct a sense of identity that provides security in contexts that are not always secure: Hebdige's and Willis's subcultures exist on the margins of society, and McRobbie's workers try to construct stable work identities in an economy where the work environment is insecure. In each case (and in the cultural studies tradition generally), the focus is typically on how people make sense of and negotiate life—both individually and collectively—in the context of systems of power and resistance. From a cultural studies perspective, this involves a focus on ideology and processes of ideological struggle. While Marx argued, "The ideas of the ruling class are in every epoch the ruling ideas," cultural studies researchers focus more on how such "ruling ideas" play out in everyday life, as people conform to, accommodate, resist, and challenge them. The notion that the "ruling class" (whatever that might mean) simply imposes its ideology on an unwitting, oppressed population is thus rejected by cultural studies researchers as they try to unpack how social groups make meaning in the face of dominant ideologies. For example, Hebdige's and Willis's groups clearly reject the dominant 1970s ideology (of middle-class jobs and conspicuous consumption) and create their identities in explicit opposition to it, while McRobbie's workers try to make sense of and accommodate the dominant 21st-century ideology of neoliberalism and enterprise selves (which we will discuss in Chapter 6). Thus, while the Frankfurt School paid little attention to the possibilities for culture as a site of struggle, cultural studies takes up this possibility in a systematic way.

CRITICAL RESEARCH 2.1

David Collinson (1988). "Engineering humor": Masculinity, joking and conflict in shop-floor relations. *Organization Studies, 9*, 181–199.

Critical management scholar David Collinson's study is an excellent example of how adopting a critical lens moves us beyond commonsense understandings of organizational communication processes. The essay takes us inside Slavs—a truck manufacturing plant in the industrial north of the United Kingdom. The plant is characterized by a hostile and divided workplace where the workers express a deep distrust of management. The shop-floor workers are a good example of what Marx called "alienated labor"; they feel little connection to the work they do and see themselves as having no voice in the factory. Collinson's study explores how the workers have developed an informal shop-floor culture in which (often crude) humor is a defining feature, functioning to help the workers regain a sense of agency in the factory.

Collinson's analysis shows that the workers employ humor in three ways: (1) as resistance, (2) as conformity, and (3) as control. First, humor is used to resist both workplace alienation and boredom and to resist management efforts to impose a new corporate culture. Much of the workers' humor is directed at management, making fun of them for not doing "real work" (i.e., hard, physical labor). Second, humor is used to create a culture of conformity on the shop floor. To be accepted, all workers must participate in the informal culture of pranks and "piss-taking" (i.e., making fun of other workers); otherwise, they are viewed as not "real men." Finally, humor is used as control to make sure that all the workers pull their weight equally (the group incentive pay system means that one slacker can affect everyone's pay). Workers are made fun of mercilessly if they are viewed as lazy.

What is particularly interesting about Collinson's analysis (and what gives it its critical orientation) is his exploration of how this shop-floor humor is deeply rooted in working class, heterosexual masculine values. Members of management are "nancy boys" (slang for homosexual) because they don't do real work. Women are either sex objects to be exploited or wives to take care of kids and have the dinner on the table (but definitely should not be in the workplace). Collinson is very sympathetic to the workers' plight as alienated labor, while at the same time he recognizes that their efforts to create meaning in their work is rooted in deeply problematic commonsense (in the sense critiqued above) views of gender and sexuality. In this sense, Collinson effectively highlights the contradictions in the workers' culture; on the one hand, they collectively attempt to resist their exploitation by capitalism, while on the other hand, they employ exploitive views of gender and sexuality.

Discussion Questions

1. Have you ever worked in an organization where humor was a feature of work? How was it used?

2. Have you ever felt exploited in a job you held? What was the source of that feeling? Did you try to do anything about it?

3. Have you ever felt alienated from a job you have had? What was it about the work that left you feeling alienated? What about the job would have needed to change for you to feel more connected to the work?

Critiquing Cultural Studies

In many respects, the cultural studies tradition is quite compatible with the critical approach to organizational communication that we adopt in this book. Its focus on everyday processes of sense making and identity management in the context of relations of power and resistance fits well with how we think about work and organizational communication. Work and organizations are sites of meaning and identity production (Deetz, 1992); people spend much of their lives thinking about, engaging in, and constructing personal identities in relation to work. In this sense, organizations are important contexts in which social actors engage with and make sense of the world.

Ironically, however, the cultural studies tradition has tended to ignore work and organizations as important sites of "experience lived, experience interpreted, experience defined" (Hall, 2016, p. 33). Like the Frankfurt School, their research has tended to study people and their experiences when they are not at work, analyzing popular culture and mass media, and with some exceptions (e.g., McRobbie, 2016), they have overlooked work as a significant site for the communicative construction of meaning, identity, and ideological struggle. This oversight is somewhat ironic, of course, given the extent to which the cultural studies tradition is rooted in Marx's writings, and much of Marx's work (particularly *Capital*) focused on the centrality of work and the labor process in capitalist relations of production.

Thus, while strictly speaking we would not define ourselves as cultural studies researchers, we have great affinity with that work and want to bring much of its insights to the study of work and organizational communication. In the final section of this chapter, then, we lay out what it means to understand organizations from a critical perspective. Below, we provide a handy table that summarizes the differences and similarities among Marx, the Frankfurt School, and Cultural Studies.

CRITICAL CASE STUDY 2.1

Making Sense of Traffic Lights

Drawing on the work of Swiss linguist Ferdinand de Saussure (1960) and French philosopher Roland Barthes (1972), cultural studies researchers show that the elements or signs that make up systems of representation are both arbitrary and conventional. In other words, there is no natural or intrinsic meaning associated with a particular sign, and its meaning rests on an agreed on set of rules, or conventions, that govern how the signs are coded. Saussure further showed that the meaning of a sign does not depend on what that sign refers to (e.g., "tree" and the object that grows in your garden) but on its relationship to other signs in the same system of representation. In this sense, meaning arises out of *difference*. Saussure referred to this scientific study of systems of representation as semiology (today, the term *semiotics* is most used to describe this area of study).

Let's take a simple, everyday example to illustrate this principle. As drivers, we are all dependent on traffic lights to regulate our driving behavior, and our understanding of traffic lights depends on our ability to learn the coding system that translates the lights into meaningful signs. Thus, red means "stop," yellow means "get ready to stop" (or, to some people, "drive faster"!), and green means "go." However, there is nothing natural about these meanings or about the relationship between the colors and what they refer to. Such meanings are arbitrary and conventional and work only because everyone agrees on their meanings. If everyone agreed to use a blue light to mean "stop," then this system of representation would work just as well. But there's another important principle at work here. Not only is the connection between the lights and what they refer to arbitrary, but also their meaning is determined by the lights' relationship to, and difference from, one another. Thus, red means, or signifies, "stop" only because it can be differentiated from yellow and green. In this sense, meaning arises within a system of differences. This principle is borne out by the fact that in Britain the representational system of traffic lights is slightly more complex. Even though the same colors are used, an extra element of difference is added through the lighting of red and yellow together after the red—this combination of colors means "get ready to go" and prepares drivers for the appearance of the green light. Again, however, this combination is meaningful only in its difference from red, yellow, and green as they appear separately.

One of Saussure's great achievements was to show that language—or any system of representation—is not something that arises from within us but instead, is fundamentally social, requiring that we participate in the system of rules and conventions in order to be understood and share meaning. In this sense, systems of representation are what create the very possibility for culture and society and what—in a very real and concrete sense—create who we are as people (i.e., they create our identities).

Cultural studies researchers have taken up and explored these basic principles in studying the various systems of representation that constitute culture and society. However, as their work illustrates, most systems are much more complex than the traffic light example above. One of their findings has been that the meaning of particular signs or the combination of signs is not fixed but can change over time or can function simultaneously with multiple meanings, depending on the ways in which signs are combined. Hall (1985), for an example, shows how black as a signifier of race meant very different things in his native Jamaica compared with his adopted nation of Britain, and he had to learn a whole new system of racial representation when he moved there in the 1950s (when Britain was still very racially homogeneous and experiencing the arrival of its first group of immigrants from the West Indies). Thus, we are not passive receivers of representational processes; instead, we have to interpret and make sense of them actively. Indeed, signs are not meaningful until they occur in a specific cultural context and have been interpreted in some fashion.

Discussion Questions

1. Beyond traffic lights, what other systems of representation can you think of? What elements of difference do they rely on to generate meaning?

2. In our society, what are the differences that make a difference? In other words, what differences count and are ascribed meaning in ways that affect our lives?

3. What systems of representation and forms of difference are important in work and organizational contexts?

Sutthipong Kongtrakool/Moment/Getty Images

Capitalism needs to expand continually into new markets to survive.

Table 2.1 Comparing Marx, the Frankfurt School, and Cultural Studies			
Issue	**Marx**	**Frankfurt School**	**Cultural Studies**
View of capitalism	• System of exploitation through wage labor • Mode of production that will fail, to be replaced by socialism • Exchange value privileged over use value	• Economic, political, and cultural system of exploitation • Highly adaptable to change • Creates narrow, instrumental view of knowledge that serves status quo	• Close relation between economics and systems of representation • Capitalism neither inevitable nor bound to fail; contested through alternative meanings and subcultures
Conception of culture	• Determined by economic system • Ideology works to create dominant meanings/ ideas that serve ruling class (capitalists)	• Popular culture administered from above through culture industry • Only high culture has meaning and can resist capitalism	• High/low culture distinction rejected • Culture produced through everyday life and creative activity of knowing actors
Role of ideology	• Maintains status quo: Ideas of ruling class are ruling ideas	• Works through culture industry to maintain status quo	• Place where meanings are contested; change can occur
Possibilities for resistance and/or social change	• Inevitable because of contradictions in capitalism • Workers will unite and overthrow capitalism, creating socialist system	• Unlikely because of capitalist culture industry and its ideology administered from above • Proletariat reduced to cultural "dopes"	• Resistance occurs at everyday level in subcultures • Capitalism not overthrown but reformed through incremental change

⬡ UNDERSTANDING ORGANIZATIONAL COMMUNICATION FROM A CRITICAL PERSPECTIVE

The critical approach adopts a number of assumptions about organizations as communicative phenomena. In this section we will examine those assumptions in detail.

Organizations Are Socially Constructed Through Communication Processes

In the past 30 years or so, there has been wide acceptance of the idea that organizations are not objective structures but rather, exist as a result of the collective and coordinated communication processes of its members. Communication is not something that happens *in* organizations; rather, organizations come into being through communication processes (Ashcraft, Kuhn, & Cooren, 2009; Kuhn, Ashcraft, & Cooren, 2017; Putnam, 1983). Such a position is often referred to as a social constructionist approach because of its belief that language and communication do not simply reflect reality but actually create the realities in which we live.

From this perspective, scholars study various forms of symbolic practice such as story-telling, metaphors, and humor in an attempt to understand the role they play in creating the reality that organization members experience (e.g., Brown, 2006; Browning, 1992; Lynch, 2002; Mumby, 2009). Like the cultural studies tradition, this work is concerned with the ways in which people collectively create systems of meaning. Thus, an underlying premise of this research is that social actors are active participants in the communicative construction of reality. As we mentioned in Chapter 1, in recent years, a group of organizational communication scholars have developed what is called the CCO approach—the communicative construction of organization—that looks at how routine organizational conversations and texts (reports, mission statement, etc.) shape organizational reality (Ashcraft et al., 2009; Cooren, 2015). From this perspective, documents are understood not as simple providers of information, but as themselves having the power to shape people's behaviors in significant ways (Brummans, 2007; Brummans, Cooren, Robichaud, & Taylor, 2014). So when we say that social actors are active participants constructing social reality, we're pointing not merely to people but to the range of elements making up systems of meaning.

Organizations Are Political Sites of Power

Not only are organizations communicatively constructed, but such construction processes are influenced by processes of power and control. In other words, organizational meanings do not simply arise spontaneously but are shaped by the various actors and stakeholder interests. In this context, the critical approach to organizations explores the relationship between the social construction process discussed above and the exercise of power.

There are many ways to conceive of organizational power (e.g., Bachrach & Baratz, 1962; Clegg, 1989; Courpasson, 2006; Lukes, 1974), and we will examine some of these in more detail in Chapter 7. However, the critical approach views power as the dynamic process by which various stakeholders struggle to secure and maintain their interests in particular contexts. Thus, the critical approach's view of power is consistent with Italian philosopher Antonio Gramsci's (1971) concept of **hegemony**. For Gramsci, the notion of hegemony referred to the struggle over the establishment of certain meanings and ideas in society. He suggested that the process by which reality was shaped was always a contested process and that the hegemony of a particular group depended on its ability to articulate ideas that are actively taken up and pursued by members of other groups. In his own words, Gramsci defines hegemony as

> the "spontaneous" consent given by the great masses of the population to the general direction imposed on social life by the dominant fundamental group; this consent is "historically" caused by the prestige (and consequent confidence) which the dominant group enjoys because of its position and function in the world of production. (p. 12)

As we saw in discussing control in Chapter 1, organizations for the most part do not exercise power coercively but rather through developing consensus about various work issues. According to organizational communication scholars Phil Tompkins and George Cheney, organizations engage in "unobtrusive control" in which members come to accept the value premises on which their organization operates and actively adopt those premises in their organizational behavior (Cheney, 1991; Cheney & Tompkins, 1987). Another way to think of this process is that organizational power is exercised when members experience strong identification with that organization (Barker, 1993, 1999).

However, the critical approach does not argue that processes such as unobtrusive control and identification are by definition problematic. Clearly, collective action and members' identification with an organization are necessary for that organization to thrive. Rather, the concern is with the extent to which the assumptions upon which identification are based is both open to examination and freely arrived at. Whose interests do these assumptions serve? Are organization members identifying with and taking on value systems that, when closely examined, work against their own best interests?

As communication scholar Stan Deetz has shown, organizations consist of multiple stakeholders (managers, workers, shareholders, community members, customers, etc.), but rarely do these multiple and competing interests enter organizational decision making processes (Deetz, 1995; Deetz & Brown, 2004). For example, while a corporation may reap huge profits from moving its operations to a country where labor is cheap, such a move can be devastating (economically, culturally, and psychologically) for the community left behind. Who gets to define the premises on which such a decision is made? What right do host communities have to expect responsible behavior from resident corporations? Who gets to define responsible behavior, and how does that notion shape decision making?

Thus, the conception of power with which the critical approach operates is one that emphasizes the "deep structure" of organizational life (Giddens, 1979). That is, the critical approach is interested in identifying the underlying interests, values, and assumptions that make some forms of organizational reality and member choices possible and foreclose the possibility of other choices and realities. The critical approach thus asks "How are the underlying interests, values, and assumptions shaped through the communication practices of the organization?"

Therefore, when we say organizations are political sites, we mean that they consist of different underlying vested interests, each of which has different consequences for organizational stakeholders. The dominant interests are those that are consistently best able to utilize political, cultural, and communicative resources to shape organizational reality in a way that supports those interests. These dominant interests often engage in forms of "discursive closure" (Deetz, 1992) that limit the ways in which people can think, feel, experience, speak, and act in their organizations. This leads us to the third critical assumption about organizations.

Organizations Are Key Sites of Human Identity Formation in Modern Society

Following a number of scholars in management and organization studies, we can argue that organizations are not just places where people work but, more fundamentally, they function as important sites for the creation of personal identity (Beech, 2011; Deetz, 1992; Kenny, Whittle, & Willmott, 2011; Kuhn, 2006; Wieland, 2010; Wrzesniewski, LoBuglio, Dutton, & Berg, 2013). Deetz, for example, argues that the modern corporation has become the primary institution for the development of our identities, surpassing the family, church, government, and education system in this role. In this sense, we are all subject to processes of **corporate colonization**—a concept that reflects the extent to which corporate ideologies and discourses pervade our lives.

Several researchers have examined how the boundaries between work and other aspects of our lives are becoming increasingly blurry and thus, harder to manage. The emergence of "no-collar" work (usually creative "knowledge work" that occurs in decentralized organizations with flexible but highly demanding work schedules) in the past 15 to 20 years has put even more pressure on a coherent, stable sense of identity because it breaks down the boundaries between work and other spheres of life almost completely. As Andrew Ross (2003) has shown, while such no-collar work often occurs in humane, participative organizational environments, the hidden costs to our sense of self (in terms of losing any sense of identity independent from work) can be high. We will look more closely at this issue in Chapters 6 and 14.

Organizations Are Important Sites of Collective Decision Making and Democracy

The above three defining features of the modern organization situate it as a central institution of contemporary society. As such, we can argue that the workplace not only is an important context in which people's identities are constructed but also represents one of the principal—if not *the* principal—social and political realms within which decisions that affect our daily lives get made. There are two ways in which the critical approach examines issues of decision making and organizational democracy.

First, several researchers in organizational communication and related fields question traditional, hierarchical organizational structures, arguing that the quality of organizational life is enhanced with the development of more participatory structures (Cheney, 1999; Rothschild-Whitt, 1979; Stohl & Cheney, 2001). Joyce Rothschild-Whitt (1979), for example, compares the traditional, bureaucratic organization with what she calls the "collectivist" organization—a structure that emphasizes shared power and widely dispersed decision-making responsibilities. And George Cheney (1999) has conducted field research on the Mondragón system of worker-owned cooperatives in the Basque region of Spain, examining the democratic decision processes by which they operate. Most of this research emphasizes both the need to develop more humane and democratic workplace practices and also argues that greater democracy can be more effective for the organization in its utilization of human resources.

Second, the critical approach moves beyond the immediate workplace and examines how organizations shape the meaning systems with which we make sense of the world. In this sense, the critical study of organizations is not only about the cultures of organizations but also about the organization of culture (Carlone & Taylor, 1998). Similar to Deetz's notion of corporate colonization, this work examines how the modern corporation has shaped people's values, interests, and beliefs well beyond the corporation's boundaries. Understanding the organization of culture leads us to ask questions such as How do organizations structure our experience of the world? How do they structure our needs and wants? What are the consequences of these structuring processes for our identities as human beings? Communication scholar Alex Lyon (2011), for example, has studied the pharmaceutical industry (specifically, Merck) and shown how its communication practices have led to a massive increase in the number of opioids that doctors prescribe to patients. As we know, such communication practices have contributed to an opioid epidemic in the United States, with prescribed drugs perceived as the default way to deal with many problems.

CONCLUSION

The purpose of this chapter has been to provide you with an overview of the major characteristics of the critical approach to organizational communication—an approach that is the foundation for the rest of the book. As such, we discussed some of the major theorists and traditions associated with the critical approach. First, we examined the writings of the most famous exponent of the critical approach, Karl Marx, focusing mainly on his critique of 19th-century capitalism. Second, we explored the limitations of Marx's ideas and suggested the need to modernize his perspective to account for 20th-century changes in the capitalist system. Third, we saw how such changes are reflected in the writings of two later critical traditions—the Institute for Social Research (better known as the Frankfurt School) and the cultural studies tradition.

Both of these schools of thought shift their attention to the cultural and ideological features of capitalism, examining the relationships between capitalism and popular culture. While the Frankfurt School adopted a rather elitist perspective, clearly distinguishing between high and mass culture (the culture industry), the cultural studies school focused more on the radical potential of popular culture and its possibilities for resisting the dominant values of commodity capitalism. We also brought our discussion back to focus more directly on organizational issues, examining the features of organizational communication as viewed from a critical perspective.

We are now in a position to examine the various theories and bodies of research that make up the field of organizational communication. Armed with the analytic tools we have discussed in these first two chapters, we can begin to get to grips with the history of organizational communication as a field of study and to understand the historical, cultural, and political forces that have shaped the role of organizations in our society.

CRITICAL APPLICATIONS

1. Reflect on your relationship to popular culture. What are some of the ways you participate in and/or consume it? How invested are you in various aspects of popular culture (music, fashion, etc.)? Would you describe your relationship to popular culture as better described by the Frankfurt School perspective or the cultural studies perspective? Why?

2. Develop as complete a list as possible of the various organizations to which you belong. How would you describe your membership and participation in each? To what extent do they shape your identity as a person?

3. Examine the series of dots below. Try to connect them all with no more than four straight lines and without taking your pencil off the paper. How difficult was this to accomplish? How does this exercise reflect the way in which ideology works?

$$\begin{matrix} \bullet & \bullet & \bullet \\ \bullet & \bullet & \bullet \\ \bullet & \bullet & \bullet \end{matrix}$$

KEY TERMS

alienation   38

capitalism   35

corporate colonization   53

critical communication capacities   34

critical theory   42

cultural studies   45

culture industry   43

dialectical theory   42

economic determinism   42

Frankfurt School   41

hegemony   52

historical materialism   37

ideology   39

Marx (Karl)   35

surplus value   38

STUDENT STUDY SITE

Visit the student study site at **www.sagepub.com/mumbyorg** for these additional learning tools:

- Web quizzes
- eFlashcards
- SAGE journal articles

- Video resources
- Web resources

PART II

Studying Organizational Communication Historically

Fordism and Organizational Communication

Many political, cultural, and economic factors have led to the emergence of the modern organization.

The organizations and corporations that we know today have their origins in important economic, political, and technological changes that occurred in the 19th and early 20th centuries. In this chapter, we will examine those changes in the context of the historical emergence of Fordism—a set of organizational and societal arrangements (named after their principal architect, Henry Ford) that profoundly shaped 20th-century life. In addition, we will examine some of the early theories of management and organizational communication that—in conjunction with huge shifts in the way we live—emerged early in the 20th century to help manage the employees who worked in this new organizational form. It is important to recognize that these theories did not emerge in a vacuum but are closely connected to the kinds of social and political tensions society was experiencing. The most influential theories of this time were scientific management, bureaucratic theory, human relations theory, and human resource management. Each of these theories had a significant effect on the management of the dominant institution of the 20th century—the Fordist organization.

Overall, our goals in this chapter are to (1) examine the emergence and characteristics of the Fordist organization, (2) assess the impact of Fordism on 20th-century work and life, and (3) discuss the management theories that both shaped and were shaped by Fordism. First, let's explore the historical conditions that laid the grounds for the emergence of what became known in the 20th century as the modern, Fordist organization.

🎴 THE FORDIST ORGANIZATION

In both the United States and Europe, the decades from the mid-19th to early 20th century saw great social, political, and economic turmoil. Authoritarian and dangerous working conditions had led to increasing unrest amongst workers and a considerable rise in organized action against both factory owners and the political order of the day. In Britain, the working class Chartist movement (1838–1848) organized millions of citizens in an effort to produce political reform (only property owners could vote at this time) and improve pay and working conditions in factories. The movement culminated in the 1848 presentation to parliament of a People's Charter. In Germany in the same year, a radical working class movement demanded similar democratic reforms. In the United States between 1881 and 1905, there were 37,000 strikes involving 7 million workers in a total workforce of 29 million (Bederman, 1995, pp. 13–14). Unions became a major political force, with membership rising from 487,000 to 2,072,700 between 1897 and 1904 (Perrow, 1986, p. 57). The so-called Gilded Age (roughly 1870–1900) witnessed huge wealth created by industrialization but also extreme inequality and poverty. Tragedies such as the Ludlow massacre in 1915 (where a 7-month strike at a coal mine, owned by John D. Rockefeller Jr., ended with 10 men, 2 women, and 12 children being shot dead by government soldiers) and the 1911 Triangle Shirtwaist Factory fire in New York City (where 141 women and men working in sweat-shop conditions died) raised public awareness about unsafe and oppressive working conditions. See *The New York Times* commemoration of the 100th anniversary of this tragedy ("Triangle Shirtwaist Factory," 2011).

Moreover, capitalism as an economic and political system was itself on trial, with increasing awareness of corruption in both government and private industry. The Progressive movement—which lasted from the 1890s to the 1920s and was led by such diverse figures as Teddy Roosevelt, Upton Sinclair (author of *The Jungle*), and Ida B. Wells (cofounder of the NAACP)—was a loose coalition of politicians, scientists, and social activists who advocated for political and social reform. Issues such as antitrust legislation (to prevent monopolies and promote competition), women's suffrage, and the improvement of education were key to the Progressive movement's agenda. Its overall goal was to transform society by strengthening democracy and applying science to social problems.

In these relatively early days of capitalism, management as a social science was very much in its infancy. For example, Harvard Business School was established in only 1908 (the Wharton School at the University of Pennsylvania, established in 1881, was the first business school). But Wallace Donham, the second dean of Harvard Business School, summarized the plight of capitalism in the early 20th century when, in 1919, he stated,

> Capitalism is on trial, and on the issue of this trial may depend the whole future of western civilization. . . . Our present situation both here and in all the great industrial nations of the world is a major breakdown of capitalism. Can this

be overcome? I believe so, but not without leadership both in business and in government, a leadership which thinks in terms of broad social problems instead of in terms of particular companies. (as cited in O'Connor, 1999b, p. 125)

Donham's words draw sharp attention to the extent to which U.S. industrial leaders saw capitalism as under threat from a number of sources, including workers' movements for better pay and conditions, challenges from many in the Progressive movement to democratize organizations, and perhaps most significantly from the rise of communism, which had succeeded in Russia 2 years earlier and which was gaining political power in a number of European countries, including Italy, Germany, and Great Britain. In many ways, then, the rise of Fordism and the management theories that helped shape it have to be understood in the context of these challenges to capitalism. In an important sense, Fordism provided stability to an economic and political system that was experiencing threats to its legitimacy. What, then, is Fordism?

Describing organizations as Fordist captures in a shorthand way the dominant organizational form of the 20th century. Named after industrialist Henry Ford (1863–1947), Fordism is generally understood not only as the emergence and dominance of the large-scale, mass-production organization but also as the development of a whole set of work, organizational, and societal principles that would shape people's lives for most of the 20th century. Fordism was capitalism's response to the threats to its legitimacy addressed above. What were these principles, and why were they so important in re-establishing the legitimacy of capitalism?

If we want to establish a particular time for the invention of Fordism, we might choose October 7, 1913—the day that Henry Ford introduced the moving assembly line for the mass production of his Model T automobile. This technological innovation reduced production time for each car from 12 hours to 2.5 hours, and by 1918, half of the automobiles driven in the United States were Model Ts. This growth was remarkable in itself, but it is important to keep in mind that Fordism involved much more than simply the creation of a new technology for mass production. In discussing Fordism, then, we need to analyze its developments along two dimensions: (1) a technical-rational dimension that shaped the nature of work and organizing, and (2) a sociopolitical dimension in which the principles of Fordism shaped the wider society. Let's discuss each of these dimensions in detail.

Fordism as a Technical-Rational System

Fordism involved a technical revolution in which the very nature of work was transformed, going through what might be termed a process of rationalization—the application of rational principles to make work as efficient and productive as possible. As we shall see later in this chapter, both Frederick Taylor's principles of scientific management and Max Weber's principles of bureaucracy were key to this rationalization process. Before we discuss these thinkers, however, let's lay out some of the Fordist organization's basic technical features.

A Divided, Deskilled Labor Process

Work under Fordism was characterized by extreme division of labor; rather than have a skilled worker complete a number of tasks, many workers each completed a single, repetitive task. While this principle had been developed by Adam Smith more than 100 years earlier, the Fordist system greatly expanded it, dividing work into its most basic elements. For example, at a Ford factory, even the production of a car wheel was broken down into dozens of tasks. This enabled Ford and other large companies to hire thousands of unskilled workers who needed very little training for the work they performed. While this reduced labor costs (because workers needed minimal training and could be replaced easily), it also resulted in a very high turnover rate, given the boring and repetitive nature of the work. Indeed, Matthew Crawford states that according to one of Henry Ford's biographers, "So great was labor's distaste for the new machine system that toward the close of 1913 every time the company wanted to add 100 men to its factory personnel, it was necessary to hire 963" (Crawford, 2009b, p. 20). This quote gives some insight into the extremely alienating conditions under which workers often functioned in large, Fordist factories. Karl Marx argued that in order to feel connected to their work, workers needed to in some way see themselves in the finished product; when you are repetitively engaged in one task out of potentially several thousand, it's difficult to recognize that connection. We will address the question of deskilling in more detail when we discuss Frederick Taylor's principles of scientific management later in this chapter.

Direct, Technological, and Bureaucratic Forms of Control

In many respects, the classic Fordist, large-scale industrial organization was characterized by a highly centralized decision-making system, a strong hierarchical structure, and a low level of trust between workers and managers—a distrust that was rooted in part in class differences, with workers often coming from blue-collar, working class backgrounds and managers coming from white-collar, middle class backgrounds (Beynon, 1973; Collinson, 1992). Any gains in wages and benefits that workers achieved were hard-won, and as the 20th century wore on, unions played an increasingly important role in negotiating wages and benefits for workers. Certainly, in the early days of Fordism, management fought hard against worker efforts to unionize. Henry Ford was rabidly anti-union, and even went so far as to employ a private security firm that identified union organizers and even beat up striking workers. In 1937 at the Ford River Rouge plant, for example, a group of workers leading an effort to unionize the plant were severely beaten by Ford's Service Department (its internal security force)—an incident that came to be known in labor history as the "Battle of the Overpass."

In terms of the day-to-day operation of Fordist production, however, direct, technological, and bureaucratic forms of control were routine. Workers were often disciplined for talking on the production line, and their work was carefully monitored by supervisors (direct control). Technological control, of course, was embodied in the moving assembly line, which dictated the pace of work for the employee. This form of control also prevented the worker from moving around the factory, as the assembly line delivered the work to him or her, rather than he or she having to go to the work. Finally, bureaucratic control was used to create a vast administrative structure of rules and regulations that all employees had to follow. Breaking a rule could result in a sanction or firing. As we will see when we discuss Weber later in the chapter, bureaucracy also introduced a more rational form of organizing that was in many ways more democratic and meritocratic than the old, more traditional form of (often family-run) organization characteristic of the early days of capitalism.

Production-Oriented, With Large Economies of Scale

One of the main features of the Fordist organization was its ability to produce vast quantities of products. Everything was done on a large scale. Ford's River Rouge plant in Dearborn, Michigan, effectively captures the scale of this production. The plant had 93 buildings with a total area of 16 million square feet. It had its own docks where barges delivered the raw materials for making automobiles (iron ore, rubber, coal, etc.), its own steel mill, and 100 miles of railroad tracks around the plant. In the 1930s, it had over 100,000 employees working three 8-hour shifts. This plant is a prime example of what is called a vertically integrated production system, in which all of the processes necessary to manufacture a product are performed in one organization.

Fordism, then, was a system of mass production, in which the main purpose was to sell vast quantities of standardized products relatively cheaply. Thus, Henry Ford famously stated that people could purchase any color of Model T they liked as long as it was black (chosen because it was the only color that would dry quickly enough to keep up with the fast pace of production). Such large-scale production enabled costs to be kept down for both producers (because they could buy in bulk at reduced rates—a principle that companies like Walmart still use today) and consumers (because the profit margins could be smaller with such large quantities of goods produced). This system is important as we will see later; Fordism not only created an era of mass production, but also an era of mass consumption (it's no good producing mass quantities of goods if there is no one to buy them). Henry Ford himself realized this when, in January 1914, he introduced the then unheard of pay rate of $5 per day, which served the dual purpose of reducing worker turnover and providing workers with the money they needed to purchase consumer goods, including Model T's! Ford even made in-house propaganda films for employees that encouraged them to use Ford's employee savings plan to save up for their own automobiles.

Fordism as a Sociopolitical System

In addition to fundamentally changing the technical nature of work in the 20th century, Fordism was also the catalyst for a sociopolitical revolution that changed the way that most people lived their lives. In this sense, Fordism refers not simply to how corporations operated but also to a broader system of principles and societal values that shaped how people thought about themselves as both workers, citizens, and consumers. Under Fordism, capitalism was shaped by a political and economic philosophy that attempted to manage the boom and bust economic cycles of the early days of primitive capitalism and that also attempted to reduce some of the disparity between rich and poor that was a product of capitalism. For example, in the early days of capitalism, it was relatively rare for companies to provide employees with any remuneration beyond their wages. Work was often dangerous, and any efforts to develop a system of employee welfare were few and far between. In the first decades of the 20th century, however, a system of welfare capitalism began to emerge in which companies increasingly saw the importance of employee welfare for their bottom lines. For example, in the early 20th century, the Western Electric Company (a subsidiary of AT&T) in Hawthorne, Illinois, was a national leader in this welfare capitalism movement, providing workers with higher than average pay, as well as other forms of compensation such as health care, pensions, and even company housing (Hassard, 2012; see "Critical Research 3.1" later in the chapter). As we will see below, AT&T's Hawthorne plant would become part of management lore as the site of the famous Hawthorne Studies.

However, such welfare capitalism was largely dependent on individual companies and did not necessarily solve the larger societal problem of extreme wealth at one end of the system and extreme poverty at the other end. In addition, many of the companies often implemented welfare programs as a way of limiting the chances of union activism amongst employees. As the 20th century progressed, however, there was increasing recognition that political intervention was required to help to stabilize capitalism. Thus, over the course of several decades a number of laws were passed that institutionalized welfare capitalism. Some of the most important of these laws included the following:

- The Adamson Act (1916) establishing an 8-hour work day
- The passing of the Social Security Act (1935) that guaranteed income for retired people and the unemployed
- The passing of the G.I. Bill (1944) that provided hospital care, low-interest mortgages, and stipends for college tuition and living expenses for war veterans
- The establishment of universal health care in many industrialized countries (though not in the United States)
- The development of a mass system of education, providing citizens with increased access to education as a means of self-improvement

Moreover, rather than a completely laissez-faire market economy, Fordist capitalism was a politically managed mixed economy, in which the government would intervene directly when it needed to prevent economic recessions or depressions. This economic philosophy was referred to as Keynesianism, after its creator, the British economist J. M. Keynes. For example, class inequality was addressed in part through income taxes, whereby those who earned a higher income paid more in tax. In 1944 in the United States, for example, any income over $200,000 (about $2.75 million in today's dollars) was taxed at a 94% rate, compared with a top income rate in 2017 of 35%. This economic philosophy was dominant in the period between 1945 and 1975, after which it increasingly gave way to the political and economic philosophy of neoliberalism (which we will discuss in Chapter 6 on post-Fordism).

How, then, did Fordism as a sociopolitical system shape the character of work and organization? Some of its features are discussed below.

Stable, Lifetime Employment

One of the key features of Fordism was the creation of an economic system in which work was a relatively stable and secure part of many workers' lives. For perhaps the first time in human history, the idea of a career was available to the average worker. Many workers spent their entire working lives employed by a single company and on retirement received a company pension (and often a watch). There is a good chance that your grandparents experienced work in this way, and perhaps your parents. Such stable, lifetime employment was made possible in part by the fact that the period from 1945 to 1975 was one of unprecedented economic growth and high living standards. The United States during this period was the dominant economy globally and faced little competition from other countries, particularly as many industrial nations were rebuilding their economies in the wake of World War II. In comparison to the more turbulent period of worker-management relations during the early decades of the 20th century, the 1945–1975 period was characterized by a workplace social contract in which management agreed to provide employment stability (high wages, good benefits, long-term employment) in exchange for worker loyalty and high productivity.

Internal Labor Market

Corresponding with the often career-long connection between a worker and his or her company was the development by the latter of an internal labor market. This development meant that jobs were advertised in-house, and workers were able to get promoted through the ranks of a company. This development is consistent with the idea of the Fordist organization as a large bureaucracy with a complex job classification system that enabled employees to compete for jobs internally. It was not unusual, then, for an employee to begin his or her career in a shop-floor job and end in a white-collar management position as he or she developed seniority, experience, and expertise in the company. As we will see in Chapter 6 in our discussion of post-Fordism, such internal labor markets have largely disappeared as companies have increasingly outsourced many of the jobs that were previously performed in-house and have increasingly moved toward employing temporary workers.

Clear Work-Life Separation

Work in the Fordist organization was clearly separated from other aspects of life. There was a strong sense in which work was a 9 am to 5 p.m. task that could be left behind once the work day was over. In this sense, work was identified as a sphere of life that, while important and necessary for the reproduction of human life, was hardly more important than family or leisure time. In this sense, work was viewed as the means by which other aspects of life were made possible. This separation between work and life meant not only that work did not impinge on other aspects of one's life but also that other features of life should not enter the workplace. This reflected the heavily bureaucratic and hierarchical nature of Fordism, in which work and organizing were viewed as a sphere of rational management that precluded (at least theoretically) any intrusions from the private sphere of life. Any such intrusions were often viewed as damaging to productivity. Thus, companies might have prohibitions against coworkers dating or have strict limitations on the number of family photographs on one's desk. As we saw in Chapter 1, sociologist Huw Beynon (1973) reports the Ford company motto as follows: "When we are at work, we ought to be at work. When we are at play, we ought to be at play. There is no use trying to mix the two" (p. 25). Apart from being a pretty clunky motto, it does give some indication of how seriously many Fordist organizations took the work-life separation. Twenty years later, Ken Starkey and Alan McKinlay (1994) report that employees at Ford were being told by coworkers, "Don't smile, let alone laugh too much" (p. 979) in case your boss thought you were not devoted enough to your work. In Chapter 6, we will see how this careful separation of work and life has very much broken down under post-Fordism.

The Emergence of a Consumer Society

One of the most important aspects of Fordism was the creation of a consumer society. In many respects, the 20th century represents the first period in human history when people purchased and consumed goods for a reason other than subsistence living; the idea of living a consumer lifestyle in which goods were purchased for pleasure, prestige, and lifestyle enhancement first became widely available to people other than the elites during this period. As I indicated above, Fordist mass production made little sense without a public that had both the economic means and—just as importantly—the disposition to regard themselves as consumers. The Fordist period thus witnessed the development of mass media advertising as a means to sell consumer goods. Companies began to compete for this new mass audience, developing the idea of branding products and competing for brand loyalty among consumers. Moreover, at the same time that the large-scale mass-production factory emerged, so on the consumption side, we see the development of the large department store—huge shopping emporia containing thousands of products where customers (mostly women) could have a shopping experience (Turow, 2017). We thus see the beginnings of the idea that consumers could have a relationship with mass produced items—an issue that we will take up in much more detail in Chapter 10 on branding, work, and consumption.

The emergence of a consumer society is key to Fordism, then, not only because it provided a population to purchase the mass-produced goods but also because it provided a sense of connection among increasingly urbanized people. As the United States and other industrial nations become more urbanized and more fragmented (fewer people living in small communities where everyone knows one another), consumption became a means by which social solidarity could be developed. In other words, you may not know your neighbor, but everyone knows about the latest movie or fashion craze! Moreover, mass consumption was widely seen as having a democratizing function, providing people from every class with access to cheaper consumer goods (Turow, 2017).

In summary, then, we can say that Fordism was both a particular mode of work and organizing and a particular form of life that dominated much of the 20th century, particularly the period between 1945 and 1975. It was a period of high productivity and high employment in which society was characterized by efforts to limit the negative effects of capitalism and provide people with a social safety net. Organizations tended to be large, bureaucratic, and hierarchical, and work was divided between waged unskilled and semi-skilled blue-collar workers and a professional class of salaried white-collar workers. Of course, not everyone worked in this kind of Fordist organization, but it is a dominant organizational form that heavily shaped 20th-century life.

Having established these broad features of Fordist work and organizing, we now need to discuss in greater detail the management theories that helped to shape how the Fordist organization operated on a daily basis. We will thus examine, in turn, Taylor's principles of scientific management, Weber's bureaucratic theory, human relations theory, and finally, human resource management. Each of these is key to understanding evolution of work and organizing under Fordism.

🔹 FORDISM AND SCIENTIFIC MANAGEMENT

There is little doubt that the development of **scientific management** principles and their application to the work process was a key ingredient in the emergence of the large, mass production, Fordist organization. Indeed, part of Ford's initial success—and the organizational form that became a model for other industrial organizations—was the marriage of Taylor's principles and the moving assembly line. Below, we discuss the system of work organization that Taylor developed.

Frederick Taylor's Principles of Scientific Management

As an engineer at the Midvale Steel Company in Pennsylvania, Taylor spent his entire professional career attempting to develop more efficient ways to work. From moving piles of pig iron to the science of cutting metals in machine shops, Taylor was single-minded in his efforts to develop the "one best way" to perform various tasks. Starting in 1880, and continuing for 26 years, Taylor performed between 30,000 and 50,000 experiments on steel cutting alone (Taylor, 1911/1934, p. 106).

The development and implementation of the principles of scientific management, however, were by no means simply a technological issue. More than anything else, Taylor's system addressed the relations between employers and employees. In the late 19th and early 20th centuries, Taylor was confronted with a work environment characterized by high levels of antagonism between workers and managers. Much of this conflict revolved around efforts by employers to intensify the work process (i.e., get workers to work harder) and corresponding attempts by workers to restrict their output. Taylor referred to this deliberate restriction of output by workers as **systematic soldiering**—a problem he saw as the central problem in the workplace. While what he referred to as "natural soldiering" involved "the natural instinct and inherent tendency of men to take it easy" (Taylor, 1911/1934, p. 19), systematic soldiering resulted "from a careful study on the part of the workmen of what will promote their best interests . . . with the deliberate object of keeping the employers ignorant of how fast work can be done" (p. 21).

At first glance, systematic soldiering appears to defy logic. Why would workers wish to restrict their output and at the same time hide from their employers how fast a particular job could actually be done? This seems especially odd given that most workers in Taylor's time were paid according to a piece rate (i.e., a given amount for each piece produced) and thus, theoretically, would receive higher wages the more they produced. As Taylor shows, however, systematic soldiering is a rational response by workers to the logic of the workplace. For the most part, systematic soldiering occurred because in order to reduce labor costs, employers tended to reduce the piece rate as the workers' output increased. As such, workers had to work harder to earn the same amount of money. Thus, they would attempt to find the minimally acceptable output level that would both maintain wages and insulate themselves from employer attempts to reduce labor costs.

The process of systematic soldiering was not an act by individual workers; it involved collective decision making by groups of workers. Workers policed one another to make sure no one was engaging in rate busting—a practice that could jeopardize the piece rate (and potentially, coworkers' jobs). Indeed, such collective decision making was possible in part because many workers in the late 19th century were still organized into work groups within factories that reflected the old guild system. For example, Joanne Ciulla (2000) documents the case of iron rollers in the Columbus Iron Works who worked in 12-man teams, with each team negotiating with the employer how much iron they would roll and their fee. They then made a collective decision regarding what portion of the fee each member would receive. These groups worked according to a strong moral code, the most important element of which was an agreement to produce only as much as their union had agreed on. A constant struggle was waged between these workers and the owners, who wanted increased output. According to Ciulla, "Worker restriction of output symbolized unselfish brotherhood, personal dignity, and cultivation of the mind" (p. 92).

In developing his principles of scientific management, Taylor's objective was to replace this old system of **ordinary management**—a system he perceived as arbitrary and based on rules of thumb—with a rational system rooted in sound scientific principles. Such a system, he argued, demonstrated conclusively that the workplace did not have to be rooted in conflict and antagonism between mutually exclusive interests but instead could be based on cooperation and mutual benefit. From his perspective, scientific management turned a zero-sum game into a win-win situation. Taylor outlines four basic principles of scientific management:

1. *Scientific job design.* Each element of the work task is designed according to scientific principles, thus replacing the old rule-of-thumb method of ordinary management.

2. *Scientific selection and training of individual workers.* Each worker is matched to the job for which he or she is best suited and then trained in the necessary skills. This differs from the system of ordinary management, where workers chose their own work and trained themselves.

3. *Cooperation between management and workers.* In order to ensure that all the work being done corresponds to scientific management principles, managers supply a supportive supervisory environment that provides workers with a sense of achievement.

4. *Equal division of work between management and workers.* Under this principle, management assumes the responsibility for scientifically designing tasks and planning ahead. Under the old system, workers were responsible for both the planning and labor of work. Under the new system, managers develop the laws and formulas necessary to design and plan tasks scientifically.

Taylor argues that the only way in which these principles can be enacted is through what he calls a "complete mental revolution" in society in which both workers and managers fully recognize the benefits of working under the new system. Consistent with Adam Smith's idea of "enlightened self-interest," Taylor claims that scientific management simultaneously increases productivity, cheapens the cost of consumer goods, and raises the income of workers. As a result, the population's real income is greatly increased and the entire country's general standard of living improves.

In his book *The Principles of Scientific Management*, Taylor provides the reader with a series of vivid illustrations to make his case for "the one best way" to perform work tasks. In the most famous example, Taylor describes his effort to increase the productivity of a worker he calls "Schmidt" (real name Henry Noll), an employee at the Bethlehem Steel Company, whose job is to carry pig iron ingots to a railroad car. Schmidt is a good worker who works hard, moving 12½ tons of pig iron a day. After carefully analyzing his work, however, Taylor decides that, simply by redesigning the work along scientific management principles, Schmidt should be able to move 47 tons of pig iron. In this example, Taylor promised to pay Schmidt $1.85 per day instead of his usual $1.15. Thus, under Taylor's system, a 60% increase in wages is more than offset by an almost 300% increase in productivity.

From its inception, scientific management was an extremely controversial system. Indeed, in January 1912, Taylor was called to appear before a congressional committee set up to investigate the effects of his system on workers. While much of the opposition to scientific management came, not surprisingly, from labor unions, the system also encountered opposition from factory owners and captains of industry. From the latter's point of view, the idea that management skills were rooted in scientific principles rather than inherented by a superior class of men (captains of industry) was difficult to accept.

However, for Taylor, scientific management was more than just an efficiency system designed to improve productivity—it was something akin to a moral crusade. Historian Martha Banta (1993) has pointed out that *The Principles of Scientific Management* is written not so much like a typical scientific treatise but rather in a strong moral tone. As such, the principles of scientific management reflected Taylor's need "to eliminate immoral waste motion in the workplace and to replace dissonance with harmony in society at large" (Banta, 1993, p. 113). Indeed, Taylor's system was consistent with the progressive ideology of the time, in which science and efficiency were connected to social harmony (Fry, 1976, p. 125).

This connection between efficiency and societal harmony is a good indication of the extent to which many of the leading thinkers of the day saw the question of organization as the central issue facing society as a whole. At the turn of the century, mass immigration, African Americans moving north into industrial areas, women entering the workforce, and labor unrest were all seen as disrupting the smooth functioning of society. As such, the emergence of the scientific, machine model of organization appeared to provide a way to assimilate the new worker into the fabric of society. A formula to describe this historical period might be written as follows:

science → rationality → efficiency → moral virtue → social harmony

From a communication perspective, Taylor's principles encapsulate the idea that a progressive society rests on the clear and convincing communication of ideas. As becomes clear from reading Taylor's work, he was fully convinced that the only thing preventing full adoption of his principles is a lack of clear understanding of how his system operates. Thus, the provision of information in a clear manner and the use of vivid practical examples will ensure the wide acceptance of his system. Taylor even recommended that managers prepare job cards that gave workers precise instructions for their tasks; in this way, there could be no misunderstandings or ambiguities about the nature of the work.

A Critical Assessment of Scientific Management

Sociologist Harry Braverman provides perhaps the most systematic critique of Taylor's system. Writing from a critical perspective, Braverman (1974) argues that scientific management is an "attempt to apply the methods of science to the increasingly complex problems of the control of labor in a rapidly growing capitalist enterprise" (p. 86). According to Braverman, Taylor assumes a capitalist perspective, recognizing the antagonistic relations between capital (represented by the employers) and alienated labor. His basic goal is to adapt the workers to the needs of capital. However, workers are not adequately controlled because they maintain their hold over the labor process, generally knowing more about how the work is done than do managers. For Taylor, then, control over the labor process must be placed in the hands of management in order to realize the full potential of labor power.

Braverman (1974) claims that Taylor succeeds in his task by making a fundamental division between the conception of work and its execution. While in the old craft system, conception and execution were united in a single worker (for example, a shoemaker both designs a shoe and makes it), under Taylor's system, the unity of labor is broken in order to control it. By placing all knowledge about work in the hands of managers, workers lose control over how work gets done. This division between mental labor and physical labor serves to alienate workers from their jobs, insofar as they become mere appendages to the work process. Their autonomy and decision-making ability are minimized. Furthermore, as managers gain a monopoly over work knowledge and work is further divided into different tasks, workers become increasingly deskilled.

We can argue, then, that for Taylor the focal point of organizational control was the human body. In his effort to take control of the labor process from workers and place it in the hands of management, he advocated the development of a vast body of knowledge about work processes, the object of which was to discipline the worker's body so it performed work in precise and calculated ways (Foucault, 1979a). This legacy is still very much with us, as many of today's jobs carefully shape and monitor workers' movements. For example, Solon (2018) reports that Amazon has patented technology for a wristband that warehouse workers will wear; as the workers search for items consumers have ordered, the wristband will vibrate and nudge the worker's hand in the direction of the product they are looking for.

A second, related criticism of Taylor is that he viewed the individual worker as his basic unit of analysis and neglected the social dimension of work (an issue addressed by the human relations movement, as we will see shortly). Indeed, Taylor saw any kind of communication and cooperation among workers as problematic precisely because it led to such problems as systematic soldiering. For Taylor, then, group communication in the workplace was dysfunctional because it interfered with the "one best way" of performing tasks. In this sense, Taylor's conception of communication is rooted in one-on-one information transmission between manager and worker.

Third, Taylor had a rather limited view of workers, seeing them as motivated exclusively by economic incentives. Any notion that workers might fulfill higher order, psychological needs through satisfying work was completely absent from Taylor's model. Furthermore, his descriptions of the workers he studied suggested a rather paternalistic view of their abilities. For example, in his testimony to a Special Committee of the United States' House of Representatives set up to investigate scientific management, Taylor argued that "the man who is physically able to handle pig-iron and is sufficiently phlegmatic and stupid to choose this for his occupation is rarely able to comprehend the science of handling pig-iron" (Taylor, 1912/1926, p. 100)

Finally, as we have already suggested, Taylor operated with a very limited conception of communication, though it was consistent with prevailing views of his time. For him, communication was a largely transmissional, mechanical process compatible with the conduit model (Axley, 1984) discussed in Chapter 1. While Taylor talks about cooperation between management and workers, his conception of organizational communication seems limited to managers accurately transmitting information about work tasks to employees.

We will now turn to the second important management theory associated with the emergence of the Fordist organization—bureaucratic theory.

FORDISM AND BUREAUCRACY

The large bureaucratic organization is, in many ways, the defining institution of 20th-century Fordist capitalism. Max Weber (1864–1920)—pronounced "Vayber"—is an important figure in the social sciences whose work is wide-ranging, complex, and difficult to classify (Clegg, 1994). Indeed, Weber was not really an organizational theorist or researcher at all but rather a sociologist, economist, and philosopher. Weber was interested in studying organizations, but only to the extent that they were examples of the broader social, political, and economic processes he was interested in explaining.

In brief, most of his work sought to explain the historical development of various civilizations through the examination of political, legal, religious, and economic systems (Morrison, 1995). He asked questions such as "What is the connection between religious systems and the development of particular economic structures and organizational forms?" For example, his famous study titled *The Protestant Ethic and the Spirit of Capitalism* (Weber, 1958) analyzes the influence of protestant religious doctrine on the development of capitalism in the United States and Europe. In this study, he shows how work and the gain spirit were elevated in the 19th century to a moral duty in everyday life—accumulating wealth was seen as a means to acquire grace and salvation.

One of the issues that most interested Weber was the forms of power he identified as having emerged historically in various societies. Specifically, he was interested in how a particular form of authority emerged with the modern, capitalist state, replacing earlier forms of authority associated with monarchies and feudal systems. Below, we will discuss Weber's forms of authority and address their importance for understanding contemporary organizations.

Weber's Types of Authority

In Weber's (1978) terms, *authority* refers to a society's development of a system of rules, norms, and administrative apparatus to which people adhere. In such a system, leaders are legitimately able to exercise authority over others, who are expected to obey. Weber identified three forms of legitimate authority, which he identified as characteristic of three different forms of social order.

Charismatic Authority

Literally speaking, *charisma* means "gift of grace" and identifies a source of authority derived from the identification of a particular individual as having exceptional—perhaps even supernatural—abilities and qualities. History is full of charismatic figures—both good and evil—such as Adolf Hitler, Martin Luther King Jr., John F. Kennedy, and Nelson Mandela. Each of these figures had a charismatic presence that secured the allegiance of millions of people. **Charismatic authority** is also a significant feature of organizational life. In the late 19th and early 20th century, captains of industry such as John D. Rockefeller and J. P. Morgan were heroic figures of their day. In the 21st century, industry leaders such as Elon Musk, Mark Cuban, and the late Steve Jobs are identified as charismatic figures with magical abilities when it comes to making money.

One of the features of charismatic authority is that it tends to emerge in times of crisis and social unrest. For example, Hitler came to power as a result of the economic and political instability experienced in Germany in the 20 years after World War I. Dr. Martin Luther King Jr.—by virtue of his rhetorical powers—was able to unite diverse groups to pursue the goal of civil rights for all. Nelson Mandela (1995) was a charismatic figure even while in jail under the apartheid system, and in post-apartheid South Africa, he was a unifying force, appealing to both white and black South Africans.

Another feature of charismatic authority is its tendency toward instability and social chaos. Because such authority is rooted in a single individual, its potential for disruption is quite high. Perhaps the most extreme example of this danger is in the case of religious cults, where the actions of unethical and dangerous charismatic leaders have led to the deaths of many followers. For example, Jim Jones (the leader of a religious cult in the United States in the 1970s called The Peoples Temple) and Charles Manson in the United States were two examples of such leaders. Similarly, the assassination of Dr. Martin Luther King Jr. in 1968 contributed to a period of great civil unrest and political instability in the United States. Many organizations also experience instability when a charismatic leader is no longer in charge. For example, Steve Jobs' death provoked concerns about Apple's future, and his successor, Tim Cook, is viewed by many as less charismatic than Jobs.

Traditional Authority

In Weber's second form of authority, legitimacy is derived from tradition and custom. **Traditional authority** is rooted largely in the inherited right of an individual to expect obedience and loyalty from others. The legitimate exercise of authority, then, comes not from any kind of special powers of the person but from adherence to a tradition that may go back hundreds of years.

Monarchy is one example of traditional authority. Kings and queens derive their authority not from any specific skills or individual characteristics but by an accident of birth. While Weber associates traditional authority with a bygone age (mainly feudal systems), such authority still exists even in corporate life. For example, in family owned businesses,

© iStockphoto.com/EdStock

Steve Jobs met Weber's conception of a charismatic leader.

sons and daughters frequently inherit the reins of power from parents. Such appointments may have little to do with expertise; indeed, even when children are groomed for many years to inherit businesses, developing considerable skill, the organization is still operating within a traditional system of authority. For example, Australian media mogul Rupert Murdoch employs two of his children in prominent positions in his company, and Donald Trump has appointed his daughter and son-in-law to important positions in the White House.

Another good example of traditional authority is the operation of an "old-boy" or old-school-tie network in an organization. Employees gain power not based on their abilities but because they have gender and racial characteristics that fit the prevailing value system of the organization. Employees not exhibiting such characteristics tend to be marginalized. For years, women managers have fought against informal organizational structures where important decisions are made on the golf course or at private clubs—places from which women have traditionally been excluded. Indeed, the recent #MeToo movement not only brings to light the pervasiveness of sexual harassment of women but also clarifies the degree to which many men see themselves as being able to act with impunity in a system that has been built by, and serves, traditional male forms of authority. College fraternities and sororities might also be seen as structured along traditional systems of authority. Organizational structures and belief systems are rooted in age-old customs and values handed down from generation to generation, and potential members are closely vetted to make sure they fit the typical member profile (Bird, 1996; DeSantis, 2007).

Rational–Legal Authority

Weber's final system of authority is the most important and the one he argues is at the foundation of the modern form of Western democracy. **Rational–legal authority** is the form underlying the bureaucratic model. The term *bureaucracy* means "rule of the bureau [office]" and refers to a system based on a set of rational and impersonal rules that guide people's behavior and decision making. People owe allegiance not to a particular individual or set of customs and beliefs but to a set of legally sanctioned rules and regulations. Among the features of bureaucracy identified by Weber (1978, pp. 956–958), the following are the most important for our purposes:

1. A hierarchically organized chain of command with appropriately assigned responsibilities.

2. A clearly defined system of impersonal rules that govern the rights and responsibilities of office holders.

3. The development of written regulations that describe the rights and duties of organization members.

4. A clearly defined division of labor with specialization of tasks.

5. Norms of impersonality that govern relations between people in the bureaucracy. Employees behave and make decisions according to the rules of their positions rather than personal ties to others.

6. Written documentation and use of a file system that stores information on which decision making is based.

Weber argued that the bureaucratic system, with its foundation in rational–legal authority, was technically superior to the other forms of authority in a couple of ways. First, bureaucracy was democratic insofar as it treated everybody equally and impersonally. While at first glance an impersonal organizational decision-making system might seem lacking in human qualities, it remains an important feature of most organizations in the Western world and ensures that people are treated according to their merits and abilities. Second, Weber argued that the rational–legal authority system and its bureaucratic structure promoted the development of capitalism (Morrison, 1995) insofar as bureaucracy enhances the speed of business operations by maximizing efficiency and functioning according to a set of calculable rules. In addition, because of its impersonal structure, business people are increasingly encouraged to make decisions for economic rather than emotional reasons. As Morrison states, "When fully developed, bureaucracy adheres to the principle of *sine ira et studio*—without hatred and passion" (p. 299).

Weber's three authority systems do not represent three mutually exclusive forms of organization. Indeed, it is not unusual for all three kinds of authority to be found in a single organization. There are certainly plenty of examples of organizations that not only are highly bureaucratic but also employ charismatic figures and have strong traditions to which members adhere.

A Critical Assessment of Bureaucracy

Interestingly, Weber himself was not simply an uncritical advocate of bureaucracy and was skeptical about the direction in which a bureaucratized, rational society was heading (Clegg, 1994; Kalberg, 1980). Although he was not a critical theorist in the sense that Marx and the Frankfurt School researchers were (see Chapter 2), his model of society nevertheless had a strong critical element.

Much of this critical element centered on Weber's analysis of what he called the rationalization process in modern society. For Weber, rationalization referred to how the natural and social world was increasingly subject to planning, calculation, and efficiency. Such rationalization was an important hallmark of modernity, he argued. But while rationalization was an efficient process that helped fuel the massive growth of capitalism, it also led to a narrowing of human vision and limited appreciation of alternative modes of existence. While a rationalized world is a predictable, efficient, and calculable world, it is not necessarily a fulfilling world in which to live. In recognizing these negative consequences, Weber referred to the iron cage of bureaucracy in which everyone had become imprisoned.

Innumerable examples of this rationalization process are all around us. The shift from shopping at the local mom-and-pop store to shopping at department stores and malls is one example of everyday life being rationalized and stripped of enchantment. While department stores may be cheaper and more efficient and offer a wider selection of goods, they undermine our sense of community and destroy our connections to one another. Department stores try to compensate for this process of rationalization by employing greeters and instructing employees on how to be friendly to customers. Of course, the irony is that this kind of "emotional labor" (Hochschild, 1983) is itself a form of rationalization. Many businesses engage in the commercialization of human feeling and emotion in order to improve their efficiency and profitability. And of course, shopping at brick-and-mortar stores is rapidly being replaced by online shopping, increasing speed and efficiency but further degrading our sense of community and connection to others (and think about the poor Amazon warehouse employee working hard to locate your item with his or her vibrating wristband!).

The rationalization process is not confined to the corporate world, however. Any social context that can be subject to rational calculation exhibits such qualities. For example, universities are increasingly subject to rationalization as administrators look for ways to increase organizational efficiency and accountability. For instance, professors are under increasing pressure to provide quantitative assessments of their classroom performance. Whether such assessments provide actual evidence of classroom performance seems less important than the fact that these measures exist as data that administrators can use when lobbying state legislatures for funding. In the same vein, many students adopt a means–end approach to education, in which the actual process of learning is viewed as less important than the grades (and ultimately, the job) received. In this instance, the educational process is rationalized to fit within an instrumental worldview.

CRITICAL CASE STUDY 3.1

Rationalizing Emotions

Dennis's oldest brother, Ken, hates the service in U.S. restaurants. Sure, he thinks the service is fast and efficient, but he can't stand the way servers try to create a synthetic connection with the customer ("Hi, my name is Julie, and I'll be your server—how are you guys this evening?!"). He feels manipulated, arguing that it's simply an effort to sell more food and increase the size of the tip. He much prefers the service in Spain, where being a server can be a career, the pay is good, and service is discreet, knowledgeable, and professional.

But one of the legacies of both scientific management and bureaucracy is efforts to micromanage and rationalize social interaction, and emotional labor in the service industry is part of that legacy. In recent years, scholars have documented how for-profit organizations increasingly co-opt employees' emotional expressions as a way to increase profitability (Raz, 2002; Tracy, 2000, 2005). Sociologist Arlie Hochschild (1983) coined the term *emotional labor* to describe this process of putting emotion to work for profit. In describing Hochschild's study of flight attendants' use of emotional labor, Kathy Ferguson (1984) states:

> The flight attendant's smile is like her makeup; it is on her, not of her. The rules about how to feel and how to express feelings are set by management, with the goal of producing passenger contentment. Company manuals give detailed instructions on how to provide a "sincere" and "unaffected" facial expression, how to seem "vivacious but not effervescent." Emotional laborers are required to take the arts of emotional management and control that characterize the intimate relations of family and friends . . . and package them according to the "feeling rules" laid down by the organization. (p. 53)

In her ethnographic, participant–observation study aboard a cruise ship, organizational communication scholar Sarah Tracy (2000) describes similar control efforts, discussing in detail how she became a "character for commerce," largely forfeiting any rights to personal emotions not expressed in the service of the cruise line.

The reality is that in a 21st-century service economy we all expect efficient, friendly, and helpful service from employees. We generally give little thought to the stresses and strains the employee might be experiencing as we revel in the knowledge that the customer is "king." On the other hand, many of you have worked or currently work in such positions and so have intimate knowledge of the kinds of emotional labor employers expect of you to ensure that customers have a positive experience. You know what it's like to work a long shift, all the time having to maintain a sunny and positive disposition as you interact with customers who are often demanding and surly.

Discussion Questions

In class or group discussion, address the following questions related to emotional labor:

1. Discuss your own experiences both giving and receiving emotional labor in service contexts. What limitations, if any, should be placed on employers' ability to use employees' emotions as a way to sell their products and services? What are the limits of customer rights to demand friendly and attentive service from employees?

2. Discuss the following comment by Herb Kelleher, former CEO of Southwest Airlines, responding to the question, Aren't customers always right?: "No, they are not. And I think that's one of the biggest betrayals of employees a boss can possibly commit. The customer is sometimes wrong. We don't carry those sorts of customers. We write to them and say, 'Fly somebody else. Don't abuse our people.'" (Freiberg & Freiberg, 1996, p. 268).

FORDISM AND THE HUMAN RELATIONS SCHOOL

In this section, we will examine the **human relations school** of work and organization. In many ways, the studies conducted by the founding theorists of this school still provide the touchstone for many of the central questions that present-day organizational communication and management scholars are asking themselves. The human relations school was the first to establish the idea of the workplace as a social organization, in which "the intersubjective relations of the workplace" became a central concern of management (Rose, 1999, p. 70). In simple terms, the work organization became viewed as a context in which the individual worker had to be psychologically and socially adjusted to the (often alienating) conditions of industrial work. As sociologist Nikolas Rose (1999) has suggested, with the development of the human relations school, "The minutiae of the human soul—human interaction, feelings, and thoughts, the psychological relations of the individual to the group—had emerged as a new domain for management" (p. 72). This development is important because it establishes the idea that the worker requires more than economic motivation to work (as Taylor thought); rather, it becomes widely accepted that managing workers requires a detailed knowledge of individual workers—their psychology, emotions, attitudes, personality, and so forth. In other words, as Rose suggests, managing becomes a question of governing the worker's soul.

Let's now turn to a discussion of the founding of this human relations movement, focusing on the research of Elton Mayo and the famous Hawthorne Studies.

Elton Mayo and the Hawthorne Studies

In his early work on industrial relations, Elton Mayo (1880–1949) argued that the experience of the average worker in industry ran parallel to the experience of posttraumatic stress victims during wartime. In other words, the workplace produced an extreme sense of alienation in the worker, leading to a form of "negative reverie" and detachment from the work environment (O'Connor, 1999a, p. 226). Mayo's answer to this problem was to propose that, through counseling, the workers could be psychologically adjusted to their work and thus experience it as meaningful and worthwhile.

Following sociologist Emile Durkheim, Mayo saw the workplace—specifically one's occupational group—as the primary medium for the creation of human identity. However, Mayo argued that the industrialization process had destroyed the tight social bonds between workers, thus alienating individuals from the social world. For Mayo, workers did not have the time or ability to re-create these social bonds themselves. Instead, "social collaboration can be restored only through the creation of administrative elites trained in techniques of social organization and control coupled with a readiness to move away from a belief in simplistic political solutions" (J. H. Smith, 1998, p. 237). For Mayo, Western-style democracy was one such simplistic political solution.

Thus, just as Taylor saw his system of scientific management as having ramifications well beyond the workplace, we see the same with Mayo. For him, the development of a cooperative system in the industrial workplace had implications for the social system as a whole. He saw the widespread industrial and social conflict of his day as the product of political agitators and politicians who exploited class antagonisms. Mayo argued that the development of an administrative elite who could instill cooperative principles in the minds of agitation-prone workers would be superior to the existing system of democracy.

The Hawthorne Studies

The Hawthorne studies were conducted from 1924 to 1933 at the Western Electric (a subsidiary of AT&T) Hawthorne plant in Cicero, Illinois. In a series of experiments—some lasting many years—the researchers attempted to investigate the effects on employee behavior and attitudes of a variety of physical, economic, and social variables (Roethlisberger & Dickson, 1939).

The Illumination Studies (1924–1927)

The initial set of Hawthorne experiments was conducted closely along classic scientific management lines. Carried out by Hawthorne engineers, these experiments were intended to discover the effects of variations in lighting on employee productivity. Using two groups of workers, the researchers gradually increased the level of illumination in one group (the experimental group) while keeping illumination constant in the other (the control group). In all other ways, the two groups were identical. In keeping with their initial hypothesis, the researchers found that the productivity of the experimental group increased along with the level of illumination. Strangely, however, the productivity of the control group increased as well. Furthermore, even when the researchers began to decrease the level of lighting in the experimental group back to its original level, worker productivity continued to go up. It even continued to increase as the lighting fell below normal levels. Only at the point when lighting levels were extremely low did worker productivity drop (Perrow, 1986, p. 80).

The researchers were baffled by these results—clearly, some variable other than the level of illumination had caused the increased production levels. Some of the researchers speculated that participation in the experiment might be having some kind of psychological effect on the workers, thus encouraging increased output. To investigate this alternative hypothesis, a second set of studies was set up.

The Relay Assembly Test Room (RATR) Studies (April 1927–February 1933)

In this new experiment, five women were separated from the rest of the workforce and set to work in a special test room. The women were subject to a number of experimental changes in the conditions of their work, including a much less variable work task, shorter working hours, more rest pauses, freer and friendlier supervision, and a new wage incentive system. The women's output increased by 30% over the first 2 years of the study, and the researchers concluded that, although the physical changes and new incentive system had some effect on productivity, much of the increase in productivity could be explained by the new system of friendly, laissez-faire supervision (Roethlisberger & Dickson, 1939).

Two more experiments—the second RATR study (August 1928–March 1929) and the Mica Splitting Test Room study (October 1928–March 1930)—were conducted to further investigate the findings of the initial RATR study. Again, the researchers concluded that increased productivity levels could be attributed mainly to the new supervisory system. In later years, this phenomenon, in which workers respond to the personal attention paid to them by supervisors, became known as the **Hawthorne effect**. For the first time, social scientists seemed to have established the significance of the human element in the work process. Workers appeared to be motivated not merely by economic incentives (extrinsic motivation) but also by their experience of, and attitudes toward, the work process itself (intrinsic motivation). What workers were thinking and feeling while working became subject to intense scrutiny.

In addition to the set of experimental studies described above, the Hawthorne studies had two other components.

The Interview Program (September 1928–January 1931)

Armed with the knowledge that workers actually possessed a whole set of opinions, thoughts, and feelings about their work, investigators launched a massive interviewing campaign aimed at providing employees with the opportunity to express those thoughts and feelings (Bramel & Friend, 1981; Perrow, 1986; Roethlisberger & Dickson, 1939). This element of the Hawthorne studies was very much influenced by Mayo's philosophy and reflected his belief that such nondirective counseling (as he envisioned these interviews) provided a way for workers to become mentally well-adjusted to the workplace.

It should be stressed that the purpose of these interviews was not to collect information from workers in order for management to address their concerns but rather to allow workers to let off steam (they were called ventilation interviews) and thus experience psychological and emotional improvement in their attitudes toward work. Roethlisberger and Dickson (1939, p. 227) pointed out that the workers seemed to appreciate being recognized as individuals by the company.

The Bank Wiring Observation Room Study (November 1931–May 1932)

The last study at Hawthorne was one of the earliest examples of qualitative, naturalistic (as opposed to experimental) research in the workplace. Based on the observation of a group of male workers, the goal of the study was to examine the natural development of informal group relations without interference from researchers. The most important finding of this study was that the workers engaged in a classic case of systematic soldiering, developing a strong set of group norms aimed at restricting output.

At first glance, this discovery seems to contradict findings of the earlier studies regarding the importance of human relations for the development of productive workers. For Mayo and his colleagues, however, the significance of this study lay in its identification of workers as forming social groups and developing elaborate norms and sentiments to shape their relationship to the work process (see also Roy, 1952, 1959).

CRITICAL RESEARCH 3.1

John Hassard (2012). Rethinking the Hawthorne Studies: The Western Electric research in its social, political and historical context. *Human Relations, 65,* 1431–1461.

Critical management scholar John Hassard's important article questions the standard textbook history that the Hawthorne Studies discovered the importance of human relations at work. He does this by considering the wider cultural, social, and political context of those famous studies—something that the studies themselves neglected. Hassard's study asks a simple question: What kind of enterprise was Western Electric around the time of the Hawthorne Studies? In his analysis, Hassard undermines the myth that the company was an unexceptional reflection of the managerial philosophy of the time (deeply authoritarian and uncaring in its attitudes to workers), and he disputes the idea that the Hawthorne findings were a revelation for Western Electric managers.

Western Electric was a major U.S. company, and the Hawthorne plant had already developed a reputation as a champion of welfare capitalism early in the 20th century, well before the Hawthorne experiments. Indeed, many of the factory's 25,000 workers lived close to the plant and had developed a family culture outside work that spread to the plant itself. As such, the Hawthorne plant was a "social center" (p. 1439) of the surrounding community. Hassard suggests further that Hawthorne reflected the progressive era of the time, focusing on the human side of business and positioning itself as socially responsible and as early as 1913, implementing a Benefit and Insurance Plan for all workers. As Hassard argues, much of this effort at welfare capitalism was aimed at avoiding unionization efforts by workers (and Western Electric employed company spies to identify union organizers). Thus, managers at Hawthorne were already practicing "capitalism with a human face," and the company was already meeting human relations needs in practice, if not in theory: "The impression from this research is that Mayo and his team did not so much turn the sociological tide at Hawthorne as swim briskly with it" (p. 1447).

The most interesting part of Hassard's essay is his discussion of the SS Eastland disaster and its impact on the company. The disaster occurred on July 25, 1915, when the SS Eastland capsized on the Chicago River during the Hawthorne employees' annual picnic; 841 employees drowned, including 22 whole families. This disaster was the greatest loss of life in Chicago history, and America's worst maritime disaster. As Hassard states, "The social and cultural awareness of its workforce was impacted by a major human tragedy" (p. 1445) such that after this disaster, the company became even more focused on the quality of its employees' lives.

Hassard's study, then, counters "the traditional practice of explaining organizational behaviour at Hawthorne within a contextual vacuum" (p. 1445). His study is a great example of how context-based research can question or qualify textbook explanations and "deconstruct aspects of those hegemonic narratives so regularly embraced in explanations of the Hawthorne Studies in the organizational behaviour literature" (p. 1453).

Discussion Questions

1. In what ways is Hassard's study similar to or different from the account of the early history of management in this chapter?

2. Hassard's essay challenges the validity of textbook accounts of the Hawthorne Studies. What does this questioning tell us, if anything, about the role of textbooks in creating disciplinary knowledge?

3. Conduct a brief survey of organizational communication and management textbooks' accounts of the Hawthorne Studies. What are the elements of the hegemonic narrative that Hassard identifies?

Implications of the Hawthorne Studies

The significance of the Hawthorne studies and their findings cannot be overestimated. Although there is plenty to critique (and we will get to that next), the research of Mayo and his colleagues had a profound influence on the course of research in organizations for the next several decades. The findings produced many important implications for the further study of organizational life. These are summarized below.

1. *Discovery of the informal work group.* Unlike Taylor, who associated the work group with systematic soldiering, Mayo argued that group cohesiveness could, in the

right context, lead to a more cooperative and productive workforce, especially with appropriate attitude adjustment through counseling. This discovery of the informal workgroup was a catalyst for several decades of research on small-group relations (Perrow, 1986; Roy, 1959).

2. *Importance of informal communication.* While classical theories argued that informal communication was largely detrimental to the functioning of organizations, the human relations movement emphasized its positive social aspects and its contribution to worker satisfaction (Roy, 1959).

3. *The Hawthorne effect.* As a result of the Hawthorne studies, worker attitudes to work and feelings of satisfaction became a focus of organizational research. The Hawthorne effect seemed to suggest a great deal of untapped potential in terms of managers' abilities to motivate workers. "A happy worker is a productive worker" became a mantra for the human relations movement.

4. *Impetus for leadership research.* With Mayo's emphasis on the importance of administrative élites appropriately trained in techniques of social control, later researchers attempted to establish the criteria for "good" leadership, spawning numerous leadership models (Bass, 1990; Yukl, 2006).

5. *Use of qualitative methods.* The Hawthorne researchers were among the first to utilize naturalistic, qualitative methods in the workplace (J. H. Smith, 1998, p. 237). In this sense, they were considerably ahead of their time if we consider that, in management and organizational communication studies, qualitative research has only in the past 30 years been accepted into the mainstream of these fields.

6. *Solution to industrial conflict?* The Hawthorne studies, coupled with Mayo's political philosophy, seemed to provide a solution to the intense industrial conflict that was a pervasive feature of the workplace in the 1920s and 1930s. If Mayo's emphasis on the psychological adjustment of the workers to industrial life could be implemented, then industrial peace and cooperation between workers and managers would be the result. The preindustrial organic community could be reestablished in the workplace.

However, it quickly became apparent that there were a number of limitations to the Hawthorne Studies. We briefly discuss these below.

A Critical Assessment of the Human Relations School

We can divide the criticisms of the Hawthorne studies into two categories. First, the studies were critiqued on empirical grounds. A number of commentators argued that when the Hawthorne data were subject to close scrutiny, the researchers' claim of a connection between worker satisfaction and productivity did not hold water (Argyle, 1953; Carey, 1967; Francke & Kaul, 1978). For example, Alex Carey (1967) re-examined the original data and argued that in the second RATR study the implementation of a new group-incentive pay scheme (where the workers are paid based on total group output rather than individual output) accounted for much of the increase in productivity—much more, in fact, than the researchers' claims about the importance of the more laissez-faire, friendly system of worker supervision. This claim is given further credence by the fact that when the group incentive system was removed after 9 months of the study, the productivity of the workers dropped by 16%. However, such critiques did not prevent the main finding of the Hawthorne Studies being reduced to the rather simplistic (and not always correct) idea that "a happy worker is a productive worker."

Second, the Hawthorne findings have been critiqued on ideological grounds, as commentators have questioned the study's (or more accurately, Mayo's) highly conservative vision of worker–management relations. Management history typically views Hawthorne as a revolutionary paradigm shift in worker–management relations; scientific management's view of workers as purely economically motivated is replaced with a much more humane vision of the worker as part of an organic community. The reality, however, is somewhat different. For Mayo, human relations theory was never about changing the nature of work itself. He was not interested in making structural changes to organizations by, for example, making work more meaningful or participatory. Instead, his goal was to psychologically adjust workers to existing organizational forms. Mayo was deeply concerned about the rise of industrial unrest among workers and like his boss at Harvard Business School, Wallace Donham, he believed in the need for an administrative elite who could develop theories and strategies to help guide society out of its troubles. As such, Mayo maintained a clear ideological split between the rationality of the managerial elite and the nonrationality of the workers. On many occasions in the account of the Hawthorne studies (Roethlisberger & Dickson, 1939), workers are described as being ruled by the logic of sentiment. Mayo and his colleagues seemed convinced that, unlike managers, the average worker was unable to understand the nature of working conditions objectively. By definition, then, any resistance on the part of the worker was irrational and had nothing to do with the material conditions of organizational life.

Thus, the early human relations movement was heavily paternalistic in its view of the average worker, with little interest in making real changes in the quality of workers' lives. Rather, the goal was to adjust workers' attitudes to existing organizational conditions. As such, human relations theory did nothing to change the strongly hierarchical structure of existing organizations. Indeed, one can argue that human relations theory is simply the flip side of the scientific management coin. That is, while scientific management took the worker's body as the focal point of control efforts, human relations theory focused on the psychology of the worker—his or her attitudes and feelings about work. Thus, control practices shifted from body to mind, but with little or no change in the nature of work itself. Indeed, it might be said that human relations theory did not replace scientific management but rather complemented it with efforts to mentally adjust workers to the industrial labor process. As such, this theory was arguably a significant force in the affirmation of the status quo at a time of considerable industrial and political unrest.

❧ FORDISM AND HUMAN RESOURCES MANAGEMENT

The years following World War II (1939–1945) were boom years for the U.S. economy and in many ways, marked the institutionalization of the modern corporate organization. As markets expanded and a stable, growing economy and full employment became the norm, so the large-scale corporate bureaucracy came into its own. This was the age of the organization man (Mills, 1951; W. H. Whyte, 1956). The manager possesses the skills necessary (rationalizing work, long-term planning, marketing, product standardization, leading employees, etc.) to enable the corporation to maximize profits and grow.

However, this period of a stable, growing economy and full employment also created a problem from a managerial perspective. While in the early days of capitalism, coercion and threats were enough to motivate employees, this was no longer the case. The 1920s and 1930s had witnessed labor struggles, a Great Depression, and the creation of New Deal legislation that limited conflict between workers and management. The result of all these changes was that workers were in a more powerful position after World War II than before it. Stable, well-paid employment and strong unionization meant that management could no longer simply use coercion or the threat of firing to motivate workers.

This shift is the political context for the arrival of human resource management (HRM) on the organizational scene. HRM is usually framed as a genuine effort to motivate workers by recognizing their value to the organization—their human resources. And this idea is certainly true in part. But what is often overlooked is that HRM is also a response to a legitimacy crisis in management; that is, managers appeared to have little influence over the motivation and productivity of their workers. Employees saw work as the place where they took care of their lower-level needs (physiological and safety) but not as the place where their higher-order needs (love/belonging, esteem, self-actualization) were satisfied; these were reserved for life with friends and loved ones (Maslow, 1987). HRM, then, represents an attempt to tap into these higher-order needs and make work relevant to the achievement of human potential. In the rest of this section, then, we will discuss the work of two of the most important HRM theorists, whose work is still impacting management theory and practice today: Douglas McGregor and Rensis Likert.

Douglas McGregor's Theory X and Theory Y

In developing a model of work motivation, McGregor (1960) explicitly frames his theory in terms of influence and control. McGregor argues that managerial authority is still largely based on an outdated model of authority founded primarily on coercion of employees. This model is problematic because it ignores the fact that the means of enforcing authority is no longer available in the same way; workers do not have the same kind of dependence on managers that they once had.

McGregor (1960) terms this traditional philosophy of management control **Theory X** and describes its view of workplace control in the following way:

1. The average human being has an inherent dislike of work and will avoid it if he can.

2. Because of this . . . most people must be coerced, controlled, directed, threatened with punishment to get them to put forth adequate effort toward the achievement of organizational objectives.

3. The average human being prefers to be directed, wishes to avoid responsibility, has relatively little ambition, and wants security above all. (pp. 33–34)

McGregor claims that as long as Theory X continues to be the guiding philosophy behind management strategy, then organizations will fail to realize the full potential of workers as human beings. As such, he argues that management philosophy must shift from coercion to what he calls "selective adaptation," in which the power to influence workers is not a function of coercive authority but rather the selection of the means of influence that circumstances require. This alternative perspective recognizes the high degree of interdependence among managers and workers in achieving organizational objectives. If managers recognize this interdependence, then the philosophy of management they will adopt will reflect an effort to achieve the human potential of their employees.

McGregor (1960) calls this philosophy **Theory Y** and describes its assumptions in the following manner:

1. The expenditure of physical and mental effort in work is as natural as play or rest.

2. External control and the threat of punishment are not the only means for bringing about effort toward organizational objectives. Man will exercise self-direction and self-control in the service of objectives to which he is committed.

3. Commitment to objectives is a function of the rewards associated with their achievement.

4. The average human being learns under proper conditions not only to accept but to seek responsibility.

5. The capacity to exercise a relatively high degree of imagination, ingenuity, and creativity in the solution of organizational problems is widely, not narrowly, distributed in the population.

6. Under the conditions of modern industrial life, the intellectual potentialities of the average human being are only partially utilized. (pp. 47–48)

As you can see, the management philosophy of Theory Y reflects a very different view of human nature than Theory X. Theory Y situates work as providing the possibility for human growth and the realization of higher needs of esteem and self-actualization, as described by Maslow. Work becomes motivating, and not drudgery, precisely because workers recognize that their higher needs can be realized through the degree of autonomy and responsibility they are given.

Thus, while the central principle of Theory X is direction and control, the goal of Theory Y is integration, which McGregor (1960) defines as the "creation of conditions such that the members of the organization can achieve their own goals *best* by directing their efforts towards the success of the enterprise" (p. 49). In other words, Theory Y requires that both organizational and the individual needs be recognized if employees are to achieve their potential and organizations are to reach their objectives. Indeed, McGregor describes Theory Y as "an invitation to innovation" (p. 57). Ultimately, the goal is a higher degree of participation in decision making by lower-level employees. Importantly, McGregor argues that, unlike Theory X, Theory Y sees ineffective organizational performance squarely as a managerial failure to get the best out of employees—the organization's most important resource.

Rensis Likert's Four Systems Approach

Published a year after McGregor's book, Likert's (1961) *New Patterns of Management* picks up many of the same themes. Indeed, the book starts out with an explicit recognition that workers will not accept coercive forms of management as they had in the past. Likert puts his framework in a broader political context when he states, "The trend in America, generally, in our schools, in our homes, and in our communities, is toward giving the individual greater freedom and initiative" (1961, p. 1).

Based on research conducted at the Institute for Social Research at the University of Michigan beginning in 1947, Likert (1961) argues for what he calls "a generalized theory of organization" (p. 1) that reflects the management practices of the highest producing companies. Conducting a comparative analysis, he argues that all organizations can be classified into one of four systems, or leadership styles, that reflect the degree of employee participation in organizational decision making. The leadership styles in the **four systems approach** are as follows:

1. *Exploitive–authoritative*: Motivation occurs through fear and threats; information flows down the hierarchy; management communication is viewed with great suspicion by subordinates; decisions are concentrated with top management; orders issued and expected to be followed without question; high employee turnover; mediocre productivity.

2. *Benevolent–authoritative*: Motivation occurs through both rewards and threats; communication is mostly downward, with limited upward communication; orders are issued, with possible opportunity for comment at lower levels; moderately high employee turnover; fair to good productivity.

3. *Consultative*: Motivation occurs through rewards, with some low-level participation in decisions; goals are set or orders issued after consultation with subordinates; moderate employee turnover; good productivity.

4. *Participative*: Motivation occurs through rewards; there is group participation in setting organization goals; lots of communication occurs downward, upward, and with peers; decision making is distributed throughout the organization; employee turnover is low; excellent productivity.

Likert advocates adoption of the participative form, arguing that—like McGregor's Theory Y—it most effectively taps into human resources and is the most productive organizational system. From a communication perspective, Likert provides a fairly in-depth discussion of the relationship between formal and informal communication. He argues that in the exploitive–authoritative system, formal and informal communication are at odds; the level of suspicion between workers and organizational leadership creates an informal communication system that opposes the formal system. On the other hand, in the participative organization, informal and formal communication systems are one and the same, with a unified approach to organization goals. Likert's position thus supports early Hawthorne research that suggested the potentially productive nature of informal communication. Likert is also an early advocate of participative group decision-making processes, which have become a routine feature of 21st-century organizations.

Critically Assessing Human Resource Management

Perhaps the most important thing about HRM is that it represented a significant effort to address the top-down, hierarchical, and authoritarian features of the mid-20th-century corporate organization. Moreover, managers—not workers—were identified as the main obstacle in efforts to make organizations more productive. If managers could be taught to give up their tired old ideas about what motivates workers, then the hidden potential of employees could be released. Theorists such as McGregor and Likert thus rejected the idea that management's role was to psychologically adjust workers to existing organizational structures and argued instead that the structure of work itself needed to be changed.

Interestingly, the 1960s and 1970s saw the emergence of a quality of working life (QWL) movement (Miller & Rose, 1995) which involved a serious effort to develop more democratic and participatory organizational forms and to view employees as more than simply extensions of the machines at which they worked. Much of the research behind QWL occurred in Europe, and particularly in Scandinavian countries such as Norway and Sweden, where ideas about industrial democracy were quite advanced, even in the 1960s (Volvo's Kalmar plant in Sweden, for example, was already using a team-based work structure at this time). Research conducted under the socio-technical systems model (Trist & Bamforth, 1951; Trist, Higgin, Murray, & Pollock, 1963) explored how both increased industrial democracy and optimal production levels could be achieved by attending to the ways in which the social and technical features of work interacted in organizations. The result of this research was a shift away from viewing the individual worker as the primary unit of analysis (as was the case under scientific management, bureaucracy, and human relations theory) and toward the semi-autonomous work group that functioned quite differently from traditional top-down structures. However, while the group or "team" structure has become a common feature of today's organizations (and there is a very good chance that many of your jobs after college will involve your working in project teams) the development of democracy as a defining feature of organizational life never occurred in a systemic manner.

We've covered a lot of ground in this chapter. Table 3.1 below will help in providing you with a useful summary of the major features and points of contrast in each of the theories we have discussed.

⚬ CONCLUSION

Sociologists Luc Boltanski and Eve Chiapello (2005) argue that the period in which Fordism was dominant can be described as the second spirit of capitalism. The first spirit (the Gilded Age of the late 19th century) saw the dominance of the robber barons who created vast wealth. However, the lack of checks and balances in early capitalism created a system that was inherently unstable and which tended to lurch from crisis to crisis. Moreover, huge disparities between rich and poor combined with the lack of protection for the most vulnerable in society had increased the likelihood that capitalism's legitimacy would continue to be questioned and threatened.

Thus, Boltanksi and Chiapello (2005) argued the emergence of the Fordist, second spirit of capitalism was a response to the crisis about its legitimacy that primitive capitalism faced in the late 19th and early 20th centuries. As both a technical-rational and sociopolitical system, Fordism created changes that stabilized capitalism, introduced long-term planning (one of the main functions of managers under Fordism), and provided social stability for much of the population. Particularly in the three decades following World War II, Fordism provided a level of economic stability, growth, and job security that was unprecedented in human history. While in the first spirit of capitalism the captain of industry was the dominant, heroic figure, in this second spirit of capitalism the more staid and rational manager was the hero.

Thus, the classical theories of management that we have discussed in this chapter—scientific management, bureaucratic theory, human relations theory, and HRM—are all key to managing and maintaining Fordism at the organizational level; each of these theories reflects different efforts to construct and manage the Fordist worker. Thus, scientific management provides a set of principles that makes work more efficient and productive and, as importantly, shifts control over work to managers. Bureaucratic principles enable this control process to be depersonalized as a system of rules and procedures, while also creating possibilities for meritocracy and advancement. Human relations theory manages the alienating nature of industrial work by paying attention to the psychology of the worker. And, finally, HRM recognizes the iron cage of post–World War II Fordist bureaucracy as a potential threat to the ability of capitalism to fully utilize its human resources (Table 3.1 provides you with a summary of each perspective assessed in relation to a number of issues).

However, Boltanski and Chiapello (2005) argue that just as Fordism was a response to the legitimation crisis that the first spirit of capitalism faced, so we have now entered a third spirit of capitalism that is a response to the legitimation crises that—beginning in the 1970s—have increasingly beset Fordism. Indeed, by the mid-1980s, the Fordist organization with its strong bureaucracy and hierarchical structure was in serious decline as the dominant organizational form, and a new set of organizing principles—post-Fordism—was being implemented along with a new economic philosophy known as neoliberalism.

In the next three chapters, then, we are going to explore how this bureaucratic conception of organizations began to be challenged. As the economic and political environment became increasingly turbulent, organizational leaders and researchers alike began to develop alternative ways of both theorizing and enacting organizational communication. For our purposes, what is most interesting is that we see communication becoming increasingly central to these new perspectives. Thus in Chapter 4, we will discuss systems theory, which is an effort to both critique the idea that organizations are simply structures within which communication occurs and an attempt to capture the complexity of organizing. Then in Chapter 5, we will address the emergence of the cultural approach—a dominant model of the 1980s and 1990s—in which organizations are viewed as systems of meaning. Finally, in Chapter 6, we will discuss the emergence of post-Fordism. This is the organizational form that is most characteristic of the current 21st century workplace.

Table 3.1   Comparing Classic Theories of Management Under Fordism

Issue	Taylor's Scientific Management	Weber's Bureaucratic Theory	Human Relations Theory	Human Resource Management
Conception of communication	Transmission of information from supervisor to worker	Transmission of information along formal bureaucratic channels	Communication creates connection and enables social groups	Resource that generates worker participation, human growth, and innovation
Relationship to Fordism	Created deskilled work that enabled mass production	Created administrative structure for decision-making, planning, and career system	Psychological adaptation of worker to Fordist work	Effort to harness latent creativity of Fordist worker and create trust with management
Metaphor of organizing	Organization as machine	Organization as machine	Organization as organic community	Organization as creative community
Level of analysis	Micro-level focus on time and motion of work tasks	Macro-level focus on organization's role in society	Micro-level focus on individual psychology of worker	Autonomous group dynamics and collaboration
Main focus of critique	Ordinary management and rule-of-thumb decision making	Rationalization of life; iron cage of bureaucracy	Alienating nature of industrial work	Managerial models (e.g., Theory X) that don't utilize creative potential of workers
Focal point of control	Worker's body	System of impersonal rules and regulations; rule of the bureau	Psychology of worker; mentally adjust worker to work	Worker creativity; harness worker potential through participatory structures
View of the employee	Executor of work tasks; motivated by extrinsic rewards	Occupier of bureaucratically defined role; motivated by opportunities for promotion	Motivated by logic of sentiment	Site of creative potential that must be released by the organization
View of organization–society relationship	Complete mental revolution; organizations create wealth and maintain social harmony	Bureaucratic organization embodies democracy in Western industrial societies	Organization important site for development of societal harmony and cohesion	Organization important site for harnessing self-actualization and idea innovation
Current legacy	Defining element of many work processes and ways of thinking	Still defines many organizations, though challenged by the post-bureaucratic organizational form	Precursor to corporate culture movement and focus on worker feelings and identity	Impetus for focus on participative management and team-based organizing

CRITICAL APPLICATIONS

1. Reflect on your own relationship to time. As you think about your daily routine, how much of your time is dictated to you by external factors (work, school, etc.), and how much is under your control? What do your answers tell you about the nature of your daily life?

2. Make a field trip to a chain restaurant and take a notepad along with you. Observe how the restaurant operates and make a note of all the instances where you can detect scientific management and rationalization processes at work. Also make a note of your own feelings as you go through this dining experience. What are your expectations, and how do you feel at the end of the experience?

KEY TERMS

charismatic authority   72

division of labor   61

Fordism   59

four systems approach   86

Hawthorne effect   79

Hawthorne studies   78

human relations school   77

iron cage of bureaucracy   75

ordinary management   68

rationalization   75

rational–legal authority   73

scientific management   67

systematic soldiering   67

Theory X   84

Theory Y   85

traditional authority   72

STUDENT STUDY SITE

Visit the student study site at **www.sagepub.com/mumbyorg** for these additional learning tools:

- Web quizzes
- eFlashcards
- SAGE journal articles
- Video resources
- Web resources

Organizations as Communication Systems

A systems perspective focuses on the interdependence and connectedness of organizational life.

If there is a way to characterize the Fordist, bureaucratic organization discussed in Chapter 3, it is structure and stability. And the dominant metaphor for describing that organization would be machine. This bureaucratic machine, when working well, is well-oiled and running smoothly; it is efficient and productive. Such a view understands organizations by reducing them to their basic elements and examining how each element works. In the next three chapters, beginning with this one, we will see this dominant metaphor displaced by alternative ways of understanding organizations. The vision of the Fordist organization as a physical, tangible, bureaucratic structure will increasingly give way to views of organizing that attempt to capture its flux and fluidity. As we will see, theorists and practitioners increasingly view organizations not as things, but as complex processes that are characterized as much by disorder and change as they are by order and stability. And most importantly for our purposes, in each successive chapter communication will become increasingly important as a constitutive feature of organizing processes.

In this chapter, we will discuss the systems approach to organizational communication—a perspective that emerged in the 1960s and 1970s in the study of organizations and that has been an important perspective in our field ever since (Contractor, 1999; Monge, 1982;

Poole, 2014; Salem, 2002, 2017). In some ways, this perspective is the first to explore communication as more than simply the transmission of information within a physical organizational structure and to examine it as a defining feature of organizing. In this chapter, then, we will (a) place the systems perspective in its historical context, (b) lay out the basic premises of the systems approach, (c) examine how the systems perspective has been used to understand organizational communication, and (d) explore the "new science" of systems.

SITUATING THE SYSTEMS PERSPECTIVE

The emergence of the systems perspective represented a fundamental shift in the dominant metaphor for talking about both the natural and the social world (Skyttner, 2005; Wheatley, 1999). For three centuries prior to systems theory, the dominant explanatory metaphor had been the machine—the idea that everything in the universe can be understood mechanically. Starting in the 17th century, the ambition of the newly emerging sciences was to control, predict, and conquer nature. Everything in the universe—both natural and human—could be reduced to causal, linear relationships. In this model, humans and animals were seen as nothing more than elaborate mechanical beings that could be understood through dissection and examination of their individual parts. The human heart, for example, could be explained as a hydraulic pump that obeyed mechanical laws. Newtonian physics, with its unchangeable laws, best embodied this determinist, cause-and-effect model of the world.

Thus, determinism and reductionism together defined the pursuit of knowledge about both the human and natural world. Through the scientific method, reality could be reduced to basic, indivisible elements that provide the building blocks for higher-order explanations of phenomena: In physics, analysis revolves around the atom; in biology, the cell; in linguistics, the phoneme (the basic, indivisible unit of sound). This approach examines phenomena in isolation, controlling for or ignoring the effects of the surrounding environment. The laboratory experiment, with its careful control of experimental conditions, exemplifies this perspective on knowledge.

In an organizational context, Frederick Taylor's principles of scientific management are the best realization of this mechanistic, reductionist model. Taylor analyzed work by breaking it down into its basic, irreducible elements and then redesigning these elements into the one best way. In this sense, his methods were both deterministic and reductionist. And like the parts in a machine, workers could easily be replaced without affecting organizational efficiency. Similarly, Max Weber viewed organizations from this Newtonian, mechanical perspective, seeing them as stable bureaucratic structures that ideally functioned independently from the human office holders who occupied them.

The emergence of the systems perspective challenges all these assumptions about the way the world works. Early examples of this approach include Albert Einstein's theory of relativity, Werner Heisenberg's uncertainty principle, and Max Planck's quantum theory. Einstein, for example, showed how space and time are inseparable; a star millions of light-years away is distant not only in space but also in time. Moreover, he showed how two events separated in space that are judged to occur simultaneously by one observer can be seen as happening at different times by another observer. Each of these theorists shifted science away from studying objects and the immutable laws that governed them toward thinking of reality in terms of processes, transformations, and perspective. As a result, the determinism and reductionism of the mechanical age became the indeterminacy and perspectivism of the systems age. Such scientists work with probabilities, not certainties. This perspectivism is succinctly captured by Werner von Heisenberg—a famous theoretical physicist—who stated, "What we observe is not nature itself, but nature exposed to our method of questioning" (Heisenberg, 2000). Organizational communication scholar Scott Poole applies the same principle when he defines the systems approach as "a description of real world phenomena in terms of an abstract logic of explanation that is constructed by the observer" (2014, p. 49).

Importantly, then, the systems approach recognizes the role of the human observer in constructing the reality around us. In this sense, the world is not something out there, operating independently from us. Moreover, how we perceive the world has a profound effect on how we act toward it. For example, viewing the world as a machine predisposes us to think about and act toward it in terms of laws, predictability, efficiency, and so forth. Seeing organizations as impersonal bureaucratic machines predisposes us to do our jobs and follow the rules; it encourages us to understand our own function in making the machine operate. In the process, work becomes routine and often dehumanizing. Philosopher Zygmunt Bauman shows vividly how this 20th-century logic of bureaucratic rationalization made possible the extermination of 6 million Jews in the Holocaust: What is right is following orders, and a good bureaucrat does not worry about the content of the orders. Thus, a German officer was able to say, "I do not think I am in a position to judge whether [my commander's] measures were moral or immoral. I surrender my moral conscience to the fact I was a soldier, and therefore a cog in a relatively low position of a great machine" (Bauman, 1989, p. 22).

The systems perspective rejects this mechanical, bureaucratic view of the world. Ludwig von Bertalanffy (1968), considered one of the founders of what he called **general system theory** (GST), describes this alternative perspective in the following manner:

> We come, then, to a conception which in contrast to reductionism, we may call perspectivism. We cannot reduce the biological, behavioral, and social levels to the lowest level, that of the constructs and laws of physics. . . . The mechanistic world view, taking the place of physical particles as ultimate reality, found its expression in a civilization which glorifies physical technology that has led eventually to the catastrophes of our time. Possibly the model of the world as a great organization can help to reinforce the sense of reverence for the living which we have almost lost in the last sanguinary decades of human history. (p. 49)

In speaking of the world as a "great organization," von Bertalanffy references the interrelatedness and interdependence of all things, human and natural—the central principle of systems theory. You might note that his statement also holds a strong moralistic tone: The mechanistic worldview has brought us great technological progress but has also been catastrophic for the human race, encompassing two world wars and a nuclear arms race. Writing in the 1950s and 1960s, at the height of the Cold War, von Bertalanffy (1968) argued for both the scientific and moral superiority of systems theory, claiming that it represents "a way out of the chaos and impending destruction of our present world" (p. 52). The mechanistic worldview has undermined our sense of humanity and connection to one another; the systems approach restores and explores that connection, demonstrating that the individual is not "a cog in the social machine" (p. 53) but an important element of a wider, interconnected community. In some ways this position is quite similar to the philosophy expressed by the Frankfurt School theorists we discussed in Chapter 2.

🔅 THE PRINCIPLES OF THE SYSTEMS PERSPECTIVE

What, then, does it mean to adopt a systems approach to the study of the human and natural world? Von Bertalanffy (1968) defined GST as "the general science of wholeness" (p. 37). With this definition, von Bertalanffy argued that as a worldview, GST sees all systems as having characteristics in common, regardless of their internal structures. Thus, everything from the structure of biological cells to the social and economic structure of societies shares common features that explain its functioning. In this sense, von Bertalanffy viewed GST as a universal perspective that brings together all fields of study by providing them with a common language and shared set of principles. We can say, then, that with GST, von Bertalanffy attempted to provide a holistic framework that brings together research from various fields to produce a comprehensive view of human beings, nature, and society. Put simply, the systems approach represents a shift from the dominance of the machine metaphor in understanding human behavior (including organizations) to the dominance of the organism metaphor.

Given this framing, let's lay out the basic principles of systems theory. As we discuss them, however, keep in mind that, like a system itself, all the principles we will discuss should be seen as interconnected and interdependent, rather than as separate, mutually exclusive elements. In other words, the definitions are meaningful only in relationship to one another.

Interdependence

A system—biological or social—is made up of components that function, well, systemically. That is, a change in one component of the system can have an effect on the entire system. From a systems perspective, change is not linear and causal but rather affects the entire system. Similarly, one element of a system depends on many other elements of the system to function effectively. In this sense, a system is defined not by its parts (as a machine would be) but by the relationship between and among those parts.

The phenomenon of climate change is an example of this process at work on a global scale. As humanly created emissions increase and the greenhouse effect raises temperatures around the globe, there is no single, causal effect but rather, multiple effects across the ecological system: rapid melting of arctic ice, melting of glaciers and mountain snow, destruction of coral reefs around the world (which are highly sensitive to temperature change), and more extreme weather conditions, including wildfires, heat waves, and strong hurricanes. As an example of the lack of linearity and predictability in system relationships, a potential effect of climate change on Dennis's home country of the United Kingdom is falling temperatures due to the possibility that melting polar ice will push the Gulf Stream (a source of the United Kingdom's temperate climate) farther south, perhaps even producing another ice age.

Organizationally speaking, collective activity is difficult to imagine without interdependence of activities, people, and units. In a university setting, for example, students, faculty, administration, staff, and alumni function in an interdependent manner. Students rely on faculty for classes, on staff for various services (registration, counseling, food, degree processing, etc.), on alumni to fund fellowships and help maintain the university's reputation, and on administration to give the university direction, shape its mission, and provide a safe and dynamic learning environment. Faculty needs students to teach and to provide their *raison d'être*, staff to take care of organizational bureaucracy, and administration to uphold the system of tenure and promotion. Such interdependence means that changes in one part of a system can impact other parts of the system, or indeed the system overall. For example, a random remark by a team member in a meeting may resonate with other members of the team, get developed and formulated into a plan, and become part of the larger business strategy of a company.

Holism

When von Bertalanffy defines GST as "the general science of wholeness" (1968, p. 37), he is referring to the quality of **holism**. Holism involves the principle that when elements in a system combine and function interdependently, the result is different from the sum of the parts; in other words, a system is **nonsummative**. This quality distinguishes a system from a mere aggregate or collection of elements. The best illustration of this idea is the difference between weight and wetness. Weight is a summative state. If you add one brick to another, you have double the amount of bricks and double the weight; there is no change in the condition of the bricks. On the other hand, if you combine one atom of oxygen with two atoms of hydrogen, you get the nonsummative state of wetness. Oxygen and hydrogen are nonwet gasses, but combined they create a state that is different from the sum of its parts (Holland, 2014).

As a human, organizational example, a crowd and a congregation can be similarly distinguished. A crowd is an aggregate of individuals; a congregation is an interdependent organization of people defined by faith, values, customs, and rituals. A crowd has a summative quality; count the number of people present, and you have an accurate measure (recall President Trump's claim—and that of his press secretary Sean Spicer—that his inauguration crowd was the "biggest ever," despite photographic evidence to the contrary; Porter, 2018). A congregation has a nonsummative quality; a simple count of the number of people present does not capture the quality of fellowship, community, and so forth.

However, holism can also have negative qualities (note that previously we indicated that the whole is different from, not greater than, the sum of the parts). Psychologist Irving

Janis (1983) coined the term *groupthink* to describe these negative qualities, exploring how the holistic quality of groups leads to poor decision making. Such groups develop highly interdependent members, but in the decision-making process they eliminate dissenting opinions and consider only information that supports and confirms the group's worldview (Janis uses the term *mindguard*—a kind of information bodyguard—to describe a group member whose role is to protect the group from information that might challenge this worldview). Thus, groups with this dynamic function as relatively closed systems, limiting information input from their surrounding environments. Janis analyzes policy decisions such as President John F. Kennedy's decision in 1961 to send a group of CIA-trained Cuban exiles to invade Cuba in an effort to overthrow the government of Fidel Castro. The decision was ill-advised, and the invading force was defeated in 3 days.

Input, Transformation (Throughput), and Output of Energy

All open systems, both biological and social, exchange information and energy with their environments. This information and energy is taken into the system, transformed through various system processes, and put out as something different. For example, the human body takes in food, liquid, and oxygen and through various biological processes transforms these into heat, action, and waste products. An organization takes in money, people, information, and raw materials, and through various organizational processes, transforms these into products for consumption or services to a community.

Employees working interdependently in teams can be more creative and better problems solvers than employees working individually.

For example, a university system has numerous inputs, including state and private funds (including research grants), materials for building infrastructure, employees (faculty, part-time instructors, staff [clerical, custodial, food service], and administrators), and students (graduate and undergraduate). These various inputs interact in multiple ways and in the process are transformed into outputs that are quite different from the initial inputs. Raw materials are transformed into classroom and lab spaces where professors and students interact, ultimately (we hope!) creating more knowledgeable and experienced citizens and skilled employees; faculty interact with one another and use university resources (libraries, databases, grants, etc.) to produce original knowledge that in turn becomes a new system input, perhaps being taught in college classrooms worldwide or even winning a Nobel Prize (an event that transforms a university's reputation); graduate students interact with faculty and utilize university resources, ultimately earning the title Dr. and becoming inputs into other university systems.

Negative Entropy

One of the founders of systems theory, Kenneth Boulding (1985), states, "A system is anything that is not chaos." In this sense, an open system exhibits **negative entropy**. What does this mean? According to Isaac Newton's second law of thermodynamics, entropy is a universal condition by which all forms of organization naturally move toward disintegration and randomness. **Entropy**, then, is a measure of the relative degree of disorder that exists within a system at a given moment in time; the more disorder, the more entropy exists. Open systems have the ability to counter entropy, or disorder, and are thus negentropic. However, over time all systems, regardless of their degree of openness, move toward entropy and die; systems can arrest entropy, but they cannot eliminate it. Thus, biological systems grow and develop over time and then degrade, sometimes over decades or centuries. Organizations and societies thrive and grow but eventually deteriorate and succumb to entropy.

By virtue of their lack of interaction and information exchange with their environments, **closed systems** are, by definition, entropic and cannot resist disorganization and disintegration (McMillan & Northorn, 1995). Examples of such closed social systems are cults, which close themselves off from the rest of society in order to prevent contamination from unbelievers, and societies ruled by autocratic governments (North Korea, the former Soviet Union) that very carefully control the information their citizens receive (e.g., by limiting or banning access to social media). Closed systems often disintegrate spectacularly; the collapse of the Soviet Union almost overnight, the Jonestown massacre (Google this if you're not familiar with it—we get the phrase "drunk the Kool Aid" from this incident), and the battle between the Branch Davidians and agents from the Department of Alcohol, Tobacco and Firearms in Waco, Texas, are three examples of closed systems collapsing once they come under pressure from the outside environment.

It's important to point out, however, that open and closed are relative terms; no system is ever completely open or closed. A completely open system would have no structure or boundaries and would lack distinctiveness from its environment; as such, it would cease to exist as a distinct system. In this sense, openness is always a process of organizational selection—a process we will examine more closely below. Similarly, a completely closed system is unthinkable; even a cult needs to communicate with its environment to recruit new members.

Equilibrium, Homeostasis, and Feedback

Systems that are open and negentropic maintain equilibrium through a process of **homeostasis**. All systems maintain a degree of permeability with their environments, thus allowing information and energy to flow back and forth across the system's boundaries. Because of this permeability, organizations are able to receive information that provides intelligence about their own functioning in relation to their environments (which include other organizations). Such feedback enables system performance to be monitored and corrected if necessary. In this sense, open systems are able to adapt effectively to changes in environmental conditions, thus combating entropy.

The simplest (and most oft-cited) example of a system that maintains homeostasis (or a steady state) through feedback is a thermostat. A thermostat operates according to what is called negative feedback—that is, feedback that corrects a deviation from the norm and is therefore error activated (as you can probably tell, this sense of feedback isn't quite the same as our typical definition of the term). Thus, a thermostat detects variations in room temperature and sends signals to the heating and cooling system to adjust its performance; if the heating unit heats a room beyond the preset temperature (e.g., 70 degrees), an error signal will be sent to the heating system to turn it off. Anyone who has had class in a room where the thermostat is broken and the heating unit continuously blows hot air (thus creating a system lacking in equilibrium) will appreciate the thermostat's importance!

The system of feedback and regulation is obviously much more complex for social systems such as organizations, which receive information from multiple environmental sources and must make constant adjustments to maintain homeostasis. Indeed, a complex organizational system operates according to two kinds of feedback: negative (or deviation-counteracting) feedback and positive (or deviation-amplifying) feedback. For example, an automobile company must assess feedback from a variety of environmental sources, including parts suppliers, the economy (what is the price of raw materials, including oil?), customer tastes, and so forth. Currently, for example, U.S. automobile companies are shifting some of their production away from large, gas-guzzling vehicles and toward smaller, green (electric and hybrid) vehicles. However, such vehicles are still a very small part of the automobile market, and so car manufacturers will have to monitor their environments (including customer tastes, government mandates for more fuel-efficient vehicles, creation of more efficient technologies, etc.) and adapt to changes in order to maintain their competitiveness.

Systems can also combat entropy through deviation-amplifying feedback, in which systems engage in growth and expansion. Deviation-amplifying feedback is positive feedback in which more energy is taken into a system than is put out, and the system grows. However, systems cannot grow continuously and must return to a homeostatic, steady state if they are to survive. An organizational system in deviation-amplifying mode will often expand to take over parts of its environment, including other competing organizations. For example, in the last 10 years, the U.S. airline industry has experienced several mergers, with 9 major airlines being reduced to four—American, Delta, Southwest, and United (TWA, Continental, U.S. Airways, America West, and Northwest, have all been absorbed). The logic of such mergers is that market share increases and the larger system is less vulnerable to environmental changes.

However, deviation-amplifying feedback will destroy a system if that system does not return to a homeostatic, steady state condition at some point. For example, the dotcom boom and bust of the late 1990s to early 2000s is a perfect example of how a deviation-amplifying feedback loop creates a doomed system. The founding of the Internet and World Wide Web in the early 1990s stimulated the massive growth of Internet startup companies (dotcoms). Everyone wanted to get in on the act, and investment capital was available to anyone who had an idea for an online company. The problem was that most of these companies operated at a loss, expecting that market share (and, hence, profits) would come later. Thus, money was invested on the possibility of future earnings that, for the vast majority of these new companies, never materialized. Eventually, many companies used up all of their cash and could not attract more investors. In March 2000, the stock market crashed, with the NASDAQ (the tech stock index) losing 10% of its value in one day. Fifty percent of startups failed, with thousands of people losing their jobs. Companies and investors banked on the deviation-amplifying cycle continuing indefinitely—something that violates a basic system principle.

To stay competitive, companies must adapt to environmental changes

Hierarchy

One of the most important features of a system is its ordering into a **hierarchy**. Systems are not structured on a single level but rather process information and function dynamically across multiple levels. As such, any system is made up of interrelated and interdependent subsystems and is itself a subsystem within a larger suprasystem. In this sense, each level functions as a system in its own right (Poole, 2014). Moreover, all of these hierarchically ordered levels are interrelated, and any change in one level will produce changes throughout the system.

Tim's department at the University of Colorado, the Department of Communication, recently experienced a major change that illustrates the notion of system hierarchy. At most universities, departments are housed in colleges or schools, which are then overseen by a central administration. The Department of Communication had been part of the well-established College of Arts and Sciences. A few years ago, as part of a complicated administrative shake-up, a brand-new college—the College of Media, Communication, and Information, or CMCI—was created, and the communication department (along with one new and four existing departments) was given a new home. A department that was accustomed to students who were seeking broad liberal arts majors suddenly found itself in a more professional school environment, where the new dean (hired away from another university) saw CMCI's role as preparing students for careers in media, advertising, public relations, and the like. At the departmental level, being situated in this new system required attracting incoming students to these new departments, meaning that new courses needed to be added to the communication curriculum and the liberal arts stance of its existing courses needed to change. The interdependence and permeable boundaries across units in the system meant that these changes required coordination with the other departments in CMCI, as well as with the old partner units in College of Arts and Sciences as ties were severed.

Hierarchy at the college level was interesting as well: The dean's estimates for the number of students who would declare majors in CMCI in the first few years turned out to be overly ambitious, meaning that planned tuition money didn't materialize and the college didn't meet its budget. The dean appealed to the provost, the next level up in the university system—the level that created CMCI in the first place—for funds that would offset the shortfall. Taking funds from other programs (an interdependence those other programs didn't expect!), the provost agreed to eliminate the deficit, but required belt tightening by the CMCI dean. Unsurprisingly, this new fiscal discipline was then imposed on departments, including communication, which was forced to restrict its programs in response to the provost's conditions.

This case illustrates how the operations of a single system (we focused here on the Department of Communication) is always shaped by interactions with other systems connected to it (the other departments) and is always embedded in larger suprasystems (CMCI, the university) that influence, and are influenced by, its operations. And of course, we could have pursued this example further, examining implications for students, staff, faculty, and others. It's important, then, to understand systems hierarchically and to view them as both made up of subsystems and embedded within suprasystems.

Systems are hierarchical, consisting of subsystems and suprasystems.

Goals

All systems are goal oriented, and through the process of feedback (both positive and nega-tive), they are able to adjust their activities in order to maintain progression toward their goal. A simple example is the cruise control servomechanism on an automobile, which will con-stantly compare the set speed to the actual road speed, increasing road speed when it falls below the set speed and decreasing it when it goes above. This simple cybernetic feedback loop uses information to compare the actual performance of a mechanism with a preset goal, making appropriate adjustments to the mechanism's performance (Wiener, 1948).

Of course, in social systems such as organizations, **goal orientations** are far more com-plex; indeed, it is quite possible for organizations to have multiple and possibly competing goals. The research and development unit of a company, for example, might have a goal of creating the highest quality products, while the marketing division of the organization might want to get the product to market as quickly as possible to meet consumer demand. Similarly, a university might have the goal of being known as a top research institution, but this goal often competes with that of providing the best possible education for under-graduates (because research faculty don't teach as frequently as at teaching-oriented col-leges and class sizes are often bigger and more impersonal).

Equifinality

The principle of **equifinality** is the final property of an open system that we will discuss, and it reflects the dynamic, process-oriented, and interdependent character of a system. Equifinality refers to the fact that "a system can reach the same final state from differing initial conditions and by a variety of paths" (Katz & Kahn, 1966, p. 30). With a closed system, knowledge of the initial condition means that one can predict the final state; for example, the result of a chemical reaction in a test tube is known if one knows the composition of the initial substances. With an open system, however, the degree of complexity and interdependence means that no such prediction is possible. Indeed, the principle of equifinality captures the creativity and dynamism of an open system.

For example, organizational communication scholar Mike Pacanowsky (1988) has shown how Gore Company (the maker of Gore-Tex) uses a nonhierarchical lattice structure of organizing, in which employees are given autonomy to make connections with others in ways that will facilitate creativity in product creation and manufacturing. In such a system, equifinality rules, as there are literally thousands of permutations in terms of how employees interact and create functioning workgroups. And at Gore, employees are free to come up with new projects without managers' permission if they can attract interest and resources. And certainly over the past 30 years, equifinality has been a governing feature of organizational life, as companies have moved away from fixed, command-and-control structures toward more dynamic, processual organizing processes that attempt to maximize the creative and innovative capacities of their employees—creativity that can be easily suppressed in a mechanical model of work. Indeed, there is every chance that you will find yourself working in such an environment, where your job is not to follow a specific set of rules and procedures but to figure out how you fit into the organization and what relationships you can develop that will help the organization meet its goals.

In sum, when the systems perspective emerged in the 1960s, it represented a radical new approach to the study of both the biological and human social world. In this sense, the systems perspective rejects the individualistic approach of human relations and human resource management and instead looks at organizational behavior as interdependent systems. However, the early systems perspective has also been challenged by the emergence of what is sometimes called new systems theory, and we turn to that in the next section.

☙ THE "NEW SCIENCE" OF SYSTEMS THEORY: COMPLEXITY AND CHAOS

We're now going to throw you a bit of a curve ball. So far in this chapter we have been talking about systems theory as a way to think about organizations not as machines but as organic systems that maintain stability through adaptive processes. In this approach, order and equilibrium are the guiding principles. Environments may be volatile, but the most effective systems are able to manage this volatility and maintain stability and equilibrium.

The "new science" of systems theory (Salem, 2017) throws this approach out of the window. Chaos, complexity, disequilibrium, and disorder rule the day. Rather than seeing change as a background condition that organizations must deal with when it arises, change is approached as a defining, necessary feature of organizational life (Brown & Eisenhardt, 1997; Contractor, 1999; Orlikowski, 1996; Reuther & Fairhurst, 2000; Salem, 2002; Wheatley, 1999). In this perspective, organizations that are stable and orderly are likely to fail. As organization researcher Margaret Wheatley states, "The search for organizational equilibrium [is] a sure path to institutional death, a road to zero trafficked by fearful people" (1999, p. 76). On the other hand, organizations that welcome chaos and disorder recognize the possibilities that can emerge out of such apparent instability; chaos, then, becomes the catalyst for change, creativity, and a new order. In this context, managers shift from being the guardians of order and equilibrium to "equilibrium busters" (Jantsch, as cited in Wheatley, 1999, p. 108) who "thrive on chaos" (Peters, 1988).

The idea that chaos should be a defining feature of organizational life certainly strains our commonsense view of how organizations function. Everywhere we look there are stable, orderly organizations going about their business in a systematic manner. But chaos theorists argue that we see order only because we are still very much invested in the dominant Newtonian view of the universe, which causes us to see stable structures ("things") and causal events everywhere. We see individuals and buildings when we should be seeing relationships and processes. Thus, the idea that an organization is a structure is really a fiction in that it is only a momentary snapshot of an ever-changing process. Under quantum theory (the foundation for chaos and complexity theory), then, things disappear, and relationships and continuous motion are brought into focus.

Still with us? Let's unpack some of the basic principles of this new science of systems theory in more detail (keeping in mind that quantum theorists themselves are often perplexed by how life at the quantum level works). You will see some overlap with our discussion of old systems theory, but hopefully you will recognize that the two ultimately conceptualize systems (and hence organizations) quite differently.

Complexity

The first thing to understand about **complexity** is that it is different from complication. A phenomenon can be complicated without being complex (Holland, 2014; Poole, 2014). For example, a car engine is complicated but not necessarily complex. It can be understood by disassembling it into its basic components and examining how each component works. Moreover, the components have to be assembled in exactly the right way for the engine to work. In other words, a complicated phenomenon can be explained by the process of reduction. Complex phenomena, on the other hand, are characterized by nonlinear interactions and processes of emergence. In simple terms, nonlinearity means getting more than you bargained for. While under Newtonian theory, small causes lead to small effects, and large causes lead to large effects (Newton's Third Law of Thermodynamics), with complex, nonlinear systems there is no relationship at all between the strength of a cause and the consequences of its effect. Thus, the infamous butterfly effect is nonlinear; in meteorologist Edward Lorenz's famous example, a butterfly flapping its wings in Brazil results in a tornado in Texas (the *Butterfly Effect* is also the title of a terrible 2004 Ashton Kutcher film). The butterfly effect does not indicate that the world is completely unpredictable, but rather that small events can generate ripples in connected systems and eventually create larger systemic patterns over time—but because these systems are complex and the causality is nonlinear, it's impossible to predict when, and if, those flapping wings spawn treacherous weather a hemisphere away.

British journalist George Monbiot (2013) provides a great example of this process in his TED Talk on the phenomenon of rewilding (restoring an area to its natural, uncultivated state). Monbiot talks about the reintroduction of wolves into Yellowstone National Park in 1995 after an absence of 70 years. In a very real (not hypothetical) butterfly effect, the wolves changed the physical geography of Yellowstone National Park, actually altering the flow of the Yellowstone River. How? During the wolves' absence, elk had proliferated and had stripped large areas of the park of its tree foliage. The wolves' presence changed the behavior of the elk; they avoided areas (such as valleys and riverbanks) where they might be easy prey for the wolves. As a result, the trees on the valley sides began to regenerate, many quintupling in height in 6 years. As a result, many bird species returned to the park, as well as colonies of beavers, whose dams provided habitat for otters and other small mammals. Most significantly, however, the proliferation of trees in Yellowstone's valleys significantly diminished the amount of soil erosion that ended up in the Yellowstone River. Thus, rather than moving slowly with lots of twists and turns, the river began to flow faster and straighter. Thus, as the predator at the top of a complex ecological system, wolves literally changed the behavior of a river.

From an organizational perspective, an important lesson here is that complex systems (which all organizations are) cannot be managed by simple Newtonian, cause-effect efforts at control. One thing does not lead simply to another. Instead, organizations must be viewed as complex adaptive systems (CAS) in which many elements or agents interact, leading to emergent outcomes that are often difficult (or impossible) to predict simply by looking at the individual interactions. In such complex systems it is often difficult to figure out which is cause and which is effect; instead, it is necessary to look at the system (organization) as a whole (Poole, 2014).

Chaos

Complexity and chaos are closely connected. A system is chaotic when it is impossible to predict what it will do next. Why should organizations be interested in cultivating chaos? Surely chaos is the last thing organizations need? Complete chaos is a bad thing, but the argument of complexity theorists is that chaos is the generative force that enables innovation and creativity. Organizational communication scholar Kathy Miller (2002) gives some insight into this perspective in her study of a hospital patient care program when she quotes members of the program at a team support meeting:

Group leader: "How are you doing?"

Nurse: "I'm stressed out and don't feel like I know what I'm doing."

Group leader: "That's good! You're at the edge of chaos." (p. 112)

From a chaos theory perspective, early management theorists' efforts at control and maintaining constant equilibrium turned out to be dysfunctional. As management theorist Ikujiro Nonaka states, "Bureaucracy represents an organization form from which chaos has completely been eliminated" (1988, p. 64). Bureaucracy, in this sense, stifles the kind of creative destruction that chaos theory emphasizes.

From a chaos perspective, then, the function of management is to foment active, creative crises. Ryuzaburo Kaku, former President of the Canon camera company, states, "The first task of top management is to create a vision that gives meaning to employees' jobs. The second task is to constantly convey a sense of crisis to their employees" (as cited in Nonaka, 1988, p. 66). These two factors—organizational vision and constant crisis—neatly summarize many of the management initiatives that emerged in the 1980s and 1990s as organizations sought to innovate and become more competitive in turbulent markets. The idea is that to encourage innovation and change, management does not engage in the top-down enforcement of rules but rather encourages a few simple principles (organizational values and meanings) for which every employee is held accountable. Employees are given autonomy and agency to enact these principles but to do so in an environment where constant change and innovation is expected. Thus, we see here a dynamic tension between the stability of the core principles (what chaos theory would call fractals—simple structures that get reiterated at every system level) and the constant renewal of the chaotic process of self-destruction and renewal. As we will see in Chapter 5 on organizational culture, corporate values and vision will become a key focus of management theory in the late 20th century.

A good example of this kind of management practice can be seen in Amazon's management structure. Amazon has a reputation for rejecting equilibrium and looking for constant change and innovation. Employees are "encouraged to tear apart one another's ideas in meetings" (Kantor & Streitfeld, 2015), and the work culture is designed to push workers past what they thought were their limits. Conflict is cultivated as a way to bring about innovation and constant change and to constantly grow the company. Such a perspective is shared by many organizations that embrace a chaos philosophy. As a manager in Honda's research and development division stated, "I believe creativity is born by pushing people against the wall and pressuring them almost to the extreme" (as cited in Nonaka, 1988, p. 66). And Kiyoshi Kawashima, former president of Honda, is reported to have said, "I decided to step down as president because the employees began agreeing with me 70% of the time" (as cited in Nonaka, 1988, p. 65).

The promotion of innovation through the constant cultivation of instability is quite different, then, from the systems view that we explored earlier in this chapter, where instability was to be managed by restoring the system to homeostatic balance. From the new science perspective, instability is a constant presence, the only way that change and innovation can occur. However, change and innovation are not simply imposed on the system by the environment; rather, from a new science perspective systems are self-organizing. We address this final aspect of new systems theory below.

Self-Organizing Systems

The focus on **self-organizing systems** is an effort to understand how order emerges out of conditions of chaos (Contractor, 1999). Self-organizing systems are characterized by a lack of equilibrium (Poole, 2014), typically due to a large influx of new information or significant environmental shifts and are thus in the process of acting on this new information as a process of self-renewal. In this sense, self-organizing systems exhibit autocatalysis; that is, the catalysts for change and renewal occur in elements of the system itself as it seeks to renew itself. In order for this change and renewal to occur, the self-organizing system must also be self-referential in the sense that it must change in ways that are consistent with its sense of self (Wheatley, 1999, p. 88). In a self-organizing system, then, change is never random but is enacted in accordance with the core principles (the fractals) that guide system behavior.

Such self-organizing principles have become common in organizational life, particularly with the widespread implementation of autonomous organizational teams. Organizational communication scholar Jim Barker's (1993) study of an electronics company is a great illustration of how this self-organizing operates. The company that Barker studied transformed overnight from a traditional top-down bureaucracy with control tightly maintained by upper management, to a team-based organization in which hierarchy was eliminated and teams were given wide decision-making responsibility. The teams were thus presented with a highly chaotic information environment, out of which they had to create order. Over time, they engaged in a self-organizing, autocatalytic process in which they generated an internal system of behavioral and decision-making norms. Ironically, however, the workers found the degree of chaos so profound that they reinvented a quasi-bureaucratic system of decision making—a good sign, perhaps, of how difficult it is for us to give up the comfort and predictability of traditional Newtonian models of human behavior.

From a new systems perspective, however, self-organizing and self-referentiality are key to the ongoing process of organizational learning and change in turbulent environments. Organizations can never afford to be passive, reacting to environmental changes; rather, they must actively seek information from everywhere, even looking for information that might threaten its stability (but which will potentially open it to growth). Such information seeking leading to instability will, it is paradoxically argued, lead to longer-term stability and order as organizations strengthen and deepen the core principles on which they operate. Indeed, who could argue with the success of companies such as Amazon and Honda, who actively promote instability as a way to ensure long-term growth and stability? As Wheatley argues, "All life lives off-balance in a world that is open to change. And all of life is self-organizing" (1999, p. 89).

In the final section of this chapter, we want to explore in more detail an approach to organizations that, while not explicitly drawing on new systems theory, has much in common with this perspective. The work of Karl Weick has had considerable influence on the field of organizational communication and gets us to reconsider many of the Newtonian principles of organizational life that we have been critiquing in this chapter.

CRITICAL RESEARCH 4.1

Wanda J. Orlikowski (1996). Improvising organizational transformation over time: A situated change perspective. *Information Systems Research, 7*(1), 63–92.

Organization change and transformation is a key feature of new systems theory. Researchers apply the concepts of complexity and chaos theory in an effort to understand how change occurs at the level of everyday organizing. MIT management scholar Wanda Orlikowski provides an interesting early analysis of organization change using complexity theory. Orlikowski's goals are two-fold: (1) to show how existing models of change are inadequate in explaining how change occurs on the ground through everyday organizing processes and (2) to show how change is a dynamic and ongoing process, with each instance of change building iteratively on each other.

First, Orlikowski identifies three models of change, each of which fails to capture how change actually occurs. The first model is planned change, which problematically assumes that "managers are the primary source of organizational change, and that these actors deliberately initiate and implement change in response to perceived opportunities to improve organization performance or 'fit' with environment" (p. 64). The second model is the technological imperative model, which assumes that technology drives change, and social actors have little discretion in the implementation of change. Third, the punctuated equilibrium model of change opposes the idea that change is gradual and instead argues that it is rapid and radical with long periods of organizational stability punctuated by short and revolutionary periods of change.

Orlikowski rejects all three of these models, arguing that all operate on the assumption that stability is the norm and change is the exception in organizational life. In developing what she calls a "situated change perspective," Orlikowski argues that change should be viewed as "an ongoing improvisation enacted by organizational actors trying to make sense of and act coherently in the world" (p. 65). In this sense, she views organizations as "enacted"; that is, they are "constituted by the ongoing agency of organizational members, and have no existence apart from such action" (p. 65)—a view very consistent with the work of Karl Weick, discussed below.

Orlikowski's study focuses on the customer service department (CSD) of a software company, examining the 2-year period after the implementation of new software (the "Incident Tracking Support System") to improve customer service. Her findings show that while the organization of the CSD changed dramatically with the implementation of the new technology, the technology enabled the changes but didn't cause them. Instead, it occurred through the "ongoing, gradual, and reciprocal adjustments, accommodations, and improvisations enacted by the CSD members" (p. 69). Her findings are complex, but she shows how CSD members enacted five metamorphoses; that is, transformational changes that involved employee appropriation of the new technology, routine employee practices, and unanticipated consequences of the changes, which were then incorporated into routine behavior.

Thus, Orlikowski shows how the appropriation of the new technology by CSD members, combined with the adaptations and adjustments they made over time, enabled slow and subtle but extremely significant transformations of organizational practices and structure. Many of the changes were neither planned nor distinct events. Instead, they "revealed a pattern of contextualized innovations in practice enacted by all members of the CSD and proceeding over time with no predetermined endpoint" (p. 89). Change, then, is not gradual and linear but iterative and transformative.

Discussion Questions

1. How do you think about change? How have you made sense of change in your life? Do you see it as happening to you, or as something over which you have control?

2. What role does technology play in your life? How do you make sense of it? Do you see it as determining your behavior? How much are you tethered to your devices?

3. Have you ever been involved in a change initiative? What part did you play? To what degree did the initiative have a specific plan? To what degree did it simply evolve over time? What, if anything, did you learn about change processes?

KARL WEICK: ORGANIZING AND COMMUNICATING

Karl Weick is a bit of a maverick. While he spent his career in a business school, his writings constantly undermine the idea that organizations are places where people make rational decisions based on analysis of carefully gathered information. Management researcher John Van Maanen (1995) argues that Weick doesn't develop theories about organizations but rather engages in "allegorical breaching" (p. 135); that is, he tells stories to represent abstract ideas in ways that undermine our commonsense views of how organizations work. In this sense, he reflects Poole's view that "the quest of systems theory is to understand complexity and to turn mysteries that seem too difficult to grasp into verbal or formal models" (2014, p. 70)

To give you a sense of how Weick (1979) thinks, let's quote from the opening of his book *The Social Psychology of Organizing*:

> This book is about organizational appreciation. To understand organizing is to appreciate events such as these:
>
> A professor, named Alex Bavelas, often plays golf with other professors. Once, he took the foursome down to the golf course, and they were going to draw straws for partners. He said, "Let's do this after the game."
>
> The story goes that three umpires disagreed about the task of calling balls and strikes. The first one said, "I calls them as they is." The second one said, "I calls them as I sees them." The third and cleverest umpire said, "They ain't nothin' till I calls them." (p. 1)

In some ways, this quote captures all the elements of Weick's view of organizations. First, it's important to draw attention to the title of his book: *The Social Psychology of Organizing*. It deliberately invokes Daniel Katz and Robert Kahn's (1966) classic book, *The Social Psychology of Organizations*. Weick's shift from noun to verb form is significant, reflecting his view of collective activity as ongoing, process oriented, and dynamic. People don't work in organizations; they engage in organizing processes and continually try to make sense of the processes in which they are participating. As Weick (2001) states, "In the last analysis, organizing is about fallible people who keep going" (p. xi). Think about how different this idea is from most theories about organizations and how it implicitly draws on the idea of organizations as complex, chaotic, self-organizing systems. It captures an essential element of most people's organizational experience: Quite often, we don't know what the heck is going on, and so we spend a lot of our time figuring it out. Thus, "organizations are collections of people trying to make sense of what is happening around them" (Weick, 2001, p. 5).

This idea is well captured by the first story above about the golf outing. Think about the level of confusion that would be created if Bavelas's suggestion were taken up. First, as a member of the foursome, you wouldn't know whom to root for. If one of the other players sinks a long putt on the fifth green, does that hurt you or help you? Is he or she your partner or your opponent? Every shot played has a level of ambiguity that's almost too much to bear. Second, the game can be made sense of only in retrospect; that is, it's not until after the game when partners are revealed that the foursome can look back and reconstruct what happened over the previous few hours. Interestingly, Weick notes that none of the players were willing to take up Bavelas's suggestion—it created too much ambiguity and complexity for them.

Weick argues that the "crazy foursome" in this story actually epitomizes a lot of what happens in organizational life (no, not that a lot of golf gets played). That is, as they organize, people engage in lots of retrospective sense making, where they "reconstruct plausible histories" (Weick, 1979, p. 5) after the fact to provide rational accounts of their organizational behavior and decision making. But such retrospective sense making papers over the reality that, in the ongoing process of organizing, people rarely behave in such a rational manner. Let's give an example to illustrate Weick's perspective.

Every semester, instructors have to make decisions about which textbook to adopt for a particular course. Frequently, this decision is routine, especially if the instructor has taught the course before—in which case, he or she often adopts a previously used text-book. However, maybe the instructor is teaching the course for the first time or is fed up with the text currently being used. In an ideal world, and consistent with rational models of organizational decision making, the instructor would engage in a careful information search, reviewing all the available textbooks, and then decide which one best meets his or her instructional goals for the course. The reality is probably quite different. With the deadline for textbook orders looming, the instructor realizes it's impossible to review all the possible adoptions, especially with a large pile of papers that need grading. So he or she pulls a couple of texts from the bookshelf (complimentary copies from publishers), looks through the table of contents in each, and decides that one of them covers more topics with which he or she is familiar. An email is sent to the campus bookstore, and life becomes a little less chaotic and ambiguous. Indeed, it's possible that you're reading this textbook precisely because of this mode of decision making and not because of your instructor's recognition of its inherent genius!

Now, if you were to ask your instructor why he or she adopted this particular text, your instructor would probably tell you that it's the best one on the market and that it fits best with his or her own teaching philosophy for this course. Your instructor would probably not admit to ordering it at the last minute and might even describe the extensive information search conducted before choosing this text. Weick would say that this instructor is a perfect example of a "fallible person who keeps going" (2001, p. xi)—someone who lives in an organizational world that is inherently ambiguous but that demands rational behavior from everyone. Hence, the role of retrospective sense making—constructing rational accounts after an organizing process that is actually messy and ambiguous. People do this not because they are incompetent or liars but because it's impossible either to make sense of all the available information or to meet the expectations of the rational model of behavior by which organizations pretend they operate. Sometimes people can't make sense of what they do until after they have done it. Or, as Weick (1979) states, "How can I know what I think until I see what I say?" (p. 5).

In the second story, we have three philosopher umpires. The first believes that there's an objective world out there in which balls and strikes exist as facts, and it's just a question of describing that objective reality; a pitch is a ball or a strike. That's how most people view organizational life. The second umpire believes in a subjective, rather than objective, reality. Reality is determined by individual perceptions, and thus, there are as many realities as there are people to perceive them. However, if this were the case, how would people ever talk to each other and how would organizing as collective action ever take place, given that collective action requires at least some level of interdependent action and the development of a shared reality? In saying "They ain't nothin' till I calls them," the third umpire is the cleverest because he identifies an important element of organizational life; that is, people play a key role in creating the environments to which they then respond. By calling ball or strike, the third umpire enacts an organizational environment that everyone—players, managers, spectators—must make sense of. But until he makes the call, there's nothing to interpret. Moreover, with this story, Weick illustrates the central role of language and communication in organizing systems; communication does not function simply as a vehicle for information transmission but rather creates organizational possibilities. If a pitch is nothing until it's called, then naming brings a particular reality into being. Thus, the environment the organization worries about is put there, according to Weick, by the organization.

Here, we can identify an important sense in which Weick's perspective moves beyond the systems approach we discussed in the first part of the chapter and identifies more closely with the new systems perspective. While traditional systems research looks at how organizations as open systems adapt to changing environments, Weick argues that organizations actually create, or enact, their own environments, which they must then make sense of. His theory of organizing is therefore aimed at providing insights into the ways people organize—not to achieve predefined goals and make rational decisions but rather to cope collectively with the complex, uncertain, and equivocal information environments in which they find themselves. For Weick, then, organizing is about seeing everyday life as an ongoing sense-making accomplishment, in which people engage in the continuous process of making their situations rationally accountable to both themselves and others (like the instructor giving a rational account of his or her textbook choice) and in the process, reduce equivocality or uncertainty. For Weick, organizing is a process not of arguing about what's true but of figuring out what works best.

This perspective is reflected in Weick's model of enactment, selection, and retention, which we will discuss below.

Weick's Model of Organizing: Enactment, Selection, and Retention

Weick (1979) defines organizing as "a consensually validated grammar for reducing equivocality by means of sensible interlocked behaviors" (p. 3). He presents this equivocality (uncertainty) reduction process as a three-stage model of enactment, selection, and retention (see Figure 4.1). For Weick, equivocality reduction is the key function of organizing. As you try to make sense of this model, you should think about it not as a static thing but as an effort to depict an ongoing, dynamic, and never-ending self-organizing process that people collectively engage in as they go about their daily organizational lives. In this sense, it represents collective sense-making activity in which people who function interdependently (i.e., systemically) constantly engage.

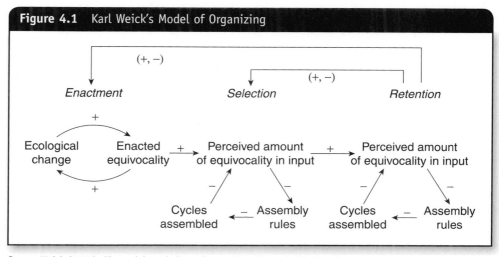

Figure 4.1   Karl Weick's Model of Organizing

Source: Weick (1979). *The social psychology of organizing* (Second ed.). Reading, MA: Addison-Wesley.

Again, Weick's model is unique in his attention to what he calls an enacted environ-ment. That is, organizations as systems not only respond and adapt to environmental (ecological) changes but also create their own environments by virtue of what they choose to pay attention to. As Weick (1988) states, enactment refers to the fact that "when people act, they bring events and structures into existence and set them in motion" (p. 306). Organizations inhabit communication environments that they selectively perceive, and this selective perception and creation of environments is subject to sense making.

Once an equivocal organizational environment is enacted, organization members must decide how to make sense of it and select sense-making processes. Weick argues that rules and cycles are the two principal mechanisms that organization members employ. Cycles are series of interactions made up of **double-interacts**, which Weick sees as the basic unit of organizing. A double-interact is actually three interrelated acts of communi-cation: A-B-A. For example, a supervisor (A) may say to a subordinate (B), "Can you get that report to me by 9 a.m. tomorrow?" This instruction may not be clear to the subordinate, thus increasing the amount of equivocality in her communication (i.e., sense making) environment. Because of this equivocality, she responds, "Do you mean the final version of the report, or just a first draft?" The supervisor (A) responds, "Just the first draft." Thus, through this double-interact (A-B-A), equivocality is reduced. Of course, this example is extremely simple, and Weick argues that daily processes of organizing actually consist of thousands of such interactions.

On the other hand, rules are established organizational practices for making sense of equivocality. Rules are employed in contexts that are less equivocal (often because there is a precedent for them and hence, the existence of rules), while cycles tend to be adopted more when equivocality is high. Selection processes that are successful in reducing equivocality are retained (retention stage) as organizational memory to be used should similar equivocal situations arise in the future; however, this retention doesn't guarantee that such rules will work at a later time, given the changing and dynamic nature of systems. Indeed, Weick argues that memory should be treated as a pest; too much retention of tried-and-tested rules often limits an organization's flexibility in responding to equivocal situations. Weick uses the term *requisite variety* to refer to the idea that complex enacted environments require similarly complex responses from the organization; in other words, complex situations do not lend themselves well to simple solutions (application of organizational rules) and vice versa.

Let's briefly explore an organizing context to which this model can be applied. Imagine that your professor sets a written assignment that requires you to team up with two other class members and write a 25-page research paper that analyzes an organization using two different theoretical perspectives. Your professor's only instructions are that the paper must be written like a scholarly article and must include a minimum of 15 different citations of scholarly research in addition to those assigned in class; also, it must conform to APA standards for style and format. Using Weick's model, we can say that your professor has enacted an organizational environment that greatly increases the level of equivocality you experience. In other words, your world (at least in terms of this class) has gone from relatively predictable (your level of coping is fairly high) to highly uncertain. The professor's enactment thus invokes a sense-making effort on the part of you and your classmates.

Pixland/Pixland/Thinkstock

Group assignments can suck, but they can also provide important insights into how teams make decisions and cope with equivocality.

In terms of selection (i.e., sense making) processes, you quickly realize that your existing recipes and rules (i.e., what's retained in your organizational memory from previous organizing experiences) for written assignments don't work. You've never written such a lengthy research paper before, never mind one that's written like a scholarly article, and you're not even sure what counts as scholarly research (do magazine or online articles count?). You kind of know what a citation is, but what the heck is APA? What's more, your friendly local fraternity/sorority doesn't have a copy of a similar assignment in its collection of papers and exams from other classes. None of the online paper-writing services is any help either (we're not condoning these, just acknowledging their existence).

So what do you do? Weick (1989) argues that "to understand organizing is to understand jazz" (p. 242). Jazz is an improvisational musical form in which "a little structure goes a long way" (p. 243); all the musicians in a jazz group work from a loose theme, or structure, and then improvise with one another in creating something original. Your group paper assignment can be addressed in the same way. Using the principle of requisite variety, any simple formula (organizational memory for paper writing) must be viewed with suspicion given the complexity of the assignment, and we can think of the professor's instructions as the loose structure around which the group can engage in improvisational double-interacts and cycles of communication to engage in sense making and equivocality reduction.

For example, your group might begin with a brainstorming session, throwing out ideas for the paper. A plan of action might be created as a result of this session, not necessarily as a solution to the identified problems but instead, as a way to motivate action. Weick (1995) indicates that plans are often useful less as rational, goal-oriented solutions to problems and more as a "binding mechanism" (p. 127) that brings people together and encourages collective activity. What action might the plan motivate? One (or all) of the group might go meet with the professor (a radical and scary notion, we realize) and ask him or her for more explicit instructions: What counts as a scholarly article? (In our experience, students sometimes have difficulty distinguishing scholarly and more popular publications.) What is APA, and why does it have to be used? Where can the 15 scholarly research publications be located?

Your professor might refer you and your group to some online scholarly databases and tell you to go to the library. Your visit to the library might involve some wandering around in the stacks (some of our best research discoveries have occurred through wandering and not because of any carefully planned search). Based on what your meanderings lead you to, you may have an actual conversation with a real, flesh-and-blood librarian who points you to some more resources and might even send you to another librarian who has specialized knowledge about the topic you're researching. Meanwhile, another member of your group has a conversation with a friend, who tells him about this great company he's just started working for and how it has this really interesting corporate culture that would be fascinating to study. Just like that, you have your study site.

And so it goes. This example is just one small illustration of how a relatively complex and equivocal communication environment can evoke an equally complex sense-making effort on the part of the organization members involved. As Weick (2001) points out, there is no single solution to this situation. Engaging in sense making and equivocality reduction is rather like being a mapmaker; an infinite number of plausible maps can be created of the same territory. However, the organizational sense-making problem is compounded because the terrain keeps changing; thus, the members' task is to carve out temporary stability in a continuous flow of behavior.

Similarly, there's no single answer to the paper-writing problem. Weick argues that part of the answer to effective organizing is to recognize that plausibility—not accuracy—is the goal. Plans are not really solutions, there are no simple cause–effect answers to problems, and Point B can be reached from Point A in an infinite number of ways (and, anyway, the location of Point B will change over time). Creating a group paper that is plausible rather than accurate is the goal; that is, it provides an interesting narrative account (among the many possible) of the organization studied, drawing on a small part of a vast scholarly literature.

From Weick's perspective, students (or any organization members) make the mistake of thinking that the vision of the organization's order that exists in their heads (often the Newtonian model) is actually how organizations operate. In fact, organizations act and then think, make sense of actions after the fact, create plans in order to have something for people to follow, and generally behave in a less-than-rational way. In other words, organizing is never tidy, despite the best efforts of management researchers to make it so. As Weick (2001) states,

> To appreciate organizations and their environments as flows interrupted by constraints of one's own making is to take oneself a little less seriously, to find a little more leverage in human affairs on a slightly smaller scale, and to have a little less hubris and a little more fun. (p. xi)

A Critical Perspective on Weick

Weick is generally classified as a systems theorist (hence, his appearance in this chapter), but he would fit just as well in Chapter 5 on the cultural perspective given his focus on the ways people organize through processes of sense making—a central issue in the next chapter, as you will see. Moreover, although Weick doesn't talk about power and control in a direct way, as would a critical theorist, he is critical of traditional models of organization that depict human beings as strategic, goal oriented, and rational in their decision making. As he states, "Efforts to maintain the illusion that organizations are rational and orderly in the interest of legitimacy are costly and futile" (Weick, 2001, p. xi). Indeed, Weick argues that, put into practice, such traditional models are actually detrimental to effective decision making, and even to personal health; his analyses of both the Mann Gulch firefighter tragedy (Weick, 1993) and the Tenerife air disaster (Weick, 1990) show how narrow definitions of organizational effectiveness based on hierarchy and formal organizational structure can cost people their lives (see Critical Case Study 4.1).

Weick's critics would argue that his perspective overemphasizes the nonrational features of organizational life and downplays the degree to which organizations can successfully implement plans that have been carefully and thoughtfully developed through rational decision making. But Weick might point out that, in some ways, his vision of organizational life has become more fully realized in recent years as organizations have shifted away from rational bureaucracies toward more fluid, decentralized structures that give employees more flexibility in decision making. And in a number of ways, Weick was an early practitioner of new systems and complexity theory, even if he doesn't talk about fractals and chaos. Either way, Weick provides us with an incredibly creative, insightful, and, moreover, practical view of organizational life. His aim is not only to contribute to abstract theorizing but also to get managers to think differently and creatively by thinking in circles, not straight lines, and by mutating metaphors—shifting from machine metaphors and cause–effect thinking to alternatives, like organizing as improvisational jazz. What do you think? Do you want to belong to organizations that deploy machine metaphors or to organizations that think like Weick?

CRITICAL CASE STUDY 4.1

Airlines and Equivocality

On March 27, 1977, two Boeing 747 jumbo jets collided on the runway at Tenerife airport, killing 583 passengers and crew. The planes, originating from New York and Amsterdam, respectively, had been diverted to Tenerife on their way to the Canary Islands because of bad weather. The crash occurred when KLM Flight 4805 commenced its takeoff run while Pan Am Flight 1736 was still taxiing on the takeoff runway and slammed into the side of the other aircraft; low clouds at Tenerife airport obscured the Pan Am plane from the KLM flight crew's view. Weick's (1990) analysis of the factors that led to the crash addresses a number of issues, including the small size of the Tenerife airport, the limited experience of the control tower crew in dealing with large aircraft, pressure on the aircraft to take off, and unpredictable weather conditions. However, much of his study focuses on the KLM cockpit crew's interaction immediately prior to takeoff:

> The communication from the tower to the [Pan Am plane] requested the latter to report when it left the runway clear. In the cockpit of the KLM, nobody at first confirmed receiving these communications until the Pan Am responded to the tower's request that it should report leaving the runway with an "OK, we'll report when we're clear." On hearing this, the KLM flight engineer asked, "Is he not clear then?" The captain did not understand him and he repeated, "Is he not clear that Pan American?" The Captain replied with an emphatic "Yes." Perhaps influenced by his great prestige, making it difficult to imagine an error of this magnitude on the part of such an expert pilot, both the copilot and flight engineer made no further objections. The impact took place about 13 seconds later. (Weick, 1990, p. 574)

Such was the system of hierarchy on the flight deck that neither the copilot nor the flight engineer felt free to challenge the pilot's decision to take off, despite not having received clearance from the control tower.

More than 30 years after this event, in late May 2011, Dennis was on an American Airlines flight from Boston to London. About a minute after takeoff, he noticed two flight attendants—sitting directly in front of and facing him—talking to each other in a rather animated way. Both had concerned looks

(Continued)

(Continued)

on their faces, and one of them kept looking out the window at the right engine. Then she picked up a phone and made a call. The next thing he knew, another flight attendant came rushing forward from business class and consulted with the two flight attendants. Then she rushed back to the front of the plane. As casually as he could, Dennis leaned forward and asked the flight attendants what was going on. "The noise of the right engine is much louder than it should be; we're recommending to the captain that he turn back to Boston," she said. Sure enough, a couple of minutes later the captain's voice came over the PA system, announcing that he was going to jettison fuel and return to the airport.

The next few minutes were a bit nerve-racking, to say the least, but the plane landed safely back at Logan airport. After taxiing back to the gate, Dennis sat and watched as a meeting took place right on the gangway (his seat was next to the exit door), involving the captain, first officer, flight engineer, two mechanics, and two flight attendants. They all stood in a circle talking. Dennis couldn't hear what was being said, but one of the flight attendants was pretty animated and clearly getting her point across. Eventually, the two mechanics came onboard and ran some tests on the engine. A few minutes later the captain announced that they couldn't find anything wrong but that they were going to change to another aircraft anyway. The plane took off again from Boston about 3 hours after the original departure time.

What's extraordinary about this incident is that it could not have happened 30 years ago. Why? Because in the wake of accidents such as the one in Tenerife, airlines have widely instituted a more team-based authority structure among flight crews. Now common sense tells us that the last place you need democracy and shared power in decision making is on the flight deck of a jumbo jet, where in critical situations you want to feel as though someone is in charge. And we're all used to the iconic father figure captain who is completely professional, highly competent, and fully in charge of the crew and passengers (Ashcraft, 2007). But as Weick's analysis shows, it's precisely this kind of strict hierarchy that creates a decision-making context in which challenging questionable decisions is almost impossible. On the Boston to London flight, the decision to turn back was ultimately the captain's, but he made that decision based on a flight attendant's perception that an engine sounded different from normal. If that same system had been in place 40 years ago, there's a good chance that 583 people would not have perished.

Developing a more flexible structure in which sense making and reducing equivocality is not just one person's responsibility but everyone's leads to a safer and more adaptive system. Who would have thought it? Think about that next time you fly somewhere.

Discussion Questions

1. How might Weick's model of enactment, selection, and retention be used to compare and contrast the two scenarios discussed above, in terms of both effective and ineffective organizing?

2. As you look at the interaction among the flight crew described by Weick, what strikes you most? How would you describe the language used by the crew, and why might it be problematic?

3. Using Weick's model, analyze an organization with which you are familiar. In what ways do the organization and its members enact environments? How is equivocality engaged with? How are rules and cycles invoked? To what degree is organizational memory (retention) relied on or treated with healthy skepticism?

⁂ CONCLUSION

The systems approach to organizational communication is a powerful and insightful perspective that represents a significant advance beyond earlier perspectives on organizational communication. However, it's often hard to grasp precisely because we are so used to breaking things down into individual elements (things) and looking for simple causes for events. The systems approach asks us to shift away from psychological, individual-focused explanations of organizational behavior (how can individuals be motivated more effectively?) to a perspective that attempts to explain organizational communication systemically and dynamically. In other words, it asks us to view individual behavior as meaningful only when understood as part of a set of a larger, interdependent system of dynamic processes. Thus, organizational communication behavior has to be understood contextually and holistically, not by dividing it up and looking at individual parts.

However, traditional systems theory has been criticized for its heavy focus on order, equilibrium, and stability, with a view of organizations as primarily engaged in processes of regulation and adaptation to environmental change. The development in the last 20 years or so of a new science of systems has overturned this early model, arguing instead that change is the norm for systems (and hence organizations) and that chaos is something not to be eliminated but rather to be encouraged as a way to foment organizational creativity and innovation. Working "on the edge of chaos" (K. Miller, 2002) is thus viewed as a normal condition for employees in successful and growth-oriented organization (e.g., Amazon). Moreover, the work of Weick also challenges us to rethink our conventional understandings of organizational life. Like complexity theorists, he suggests that organizations are not the stable structures they appear to be but rather are nonrational, precarious, and, most important, made up of complex communication processes that are the very stuff of organizing.

Finally, we can note that in many ways the idea of organizations as systems operating chaotically and in constant need of change and innovation was very much taken to heart by corporate strategists in the 1990s (and to a certain degree even today). Terms such as *re-engineering*, *downsizing*, *rightsizing*, and a number of other euphemisms were used to describe corporate efforts to constantly innovate, which typically meant cutting costs, reorganizing, and laying off thousands of workers. Innovation and change became a dominant ideology; a company that wasn't changing would see its stock price fall, even if change was not necessarily good for the organization. Thus, we should be careful about seeing chaos and change as an inherent good; often it is employed for strategic reasons that are less about the health of the organization and its employees and more about short-term profitability for shareholders.

In the next chapter, we will examine the emergence of the cultural approach to organizations—a perspective that swept the corporate world in the 1980s and 1990s, and very much put communication front and center as a defining feature of organizations.

CRITICAL APPLICATIONS

1. Using this class as your object of study, conduct a systems analysis of its organizing processes. What are its various inputs, transformations, and outputs? How does it function holistically?

Is it made up of subsystems? What processes of feedback and adaptation can you identify? In what ways might the class be analyzed as complex system that courts chaos and instability?

2. Watch the short animated film, *The Meatrix: Relaunched* (available at www.themeatrix.com) and discuss how it provides a critically oriented systems analysis of the food industry.

KEY TERMS

chaos   104

closed systems   97

complexity   103

double-interacts   111

enactment, selection, and retention   110

entropy   97

equifinality   101

equivocality (uncertainty) reduction   110

general system theory   93

goal orientations   101

hierarchy   100

holism   95

homeostasis   98

negative entropy   97

nonsummative   95

open systems   96

relationship   94

retrospective sense making   109

self-organizing systems   105

STUDENT STUDY SITE

Visit the student study site at **www.sagepub.com/mumbyorg** for these additional learning tools:

- Web quizzes
- eFlashcards
- SAGE journal articles

- Video resources
- Web resources

CHAPTER 5

Communication, Culture, and Organizing

The corporate culture approach seeks to create a shared reality for organization members.

The emergence of the cultural approach in the late 1970s and early 1980s represents what might be termed a paradigm shift in the field of organizational communication (Kuhn, 1970). This new perspective offered a radically different set of conceptual tools with which to examine organizations, creating a body of knowledge that stood in stark contrast to the dominant functionalist perspective. Moreover, it provided tools for management practitioners that offered a different philosophy of work and organizational life.

Why was the emergence of this new perspective so important? In brief, the cultural approach offered a radically different way to think about the relationship between communication and organization. For the first time, scholars began to take seriously the notion that organizations are communication phenomena that exist only because their members engage in complex patterns of communication behavior. Put another way, scholars viewed organizations as structures of meaning created through the everyday symbolic acts of their members (Keyton, 2011; Martin, 1992; Putnam & Pacanowsky, 1983). By studying communication phenomena such as stories (Boje, 1991; Browning, 1992; Martin, Feldman, Hatch, & Sitkin, 1983), metaphors (Koch & Deetz, 1981; R. Smith & Eisenberg, 1987), and rituals

(Trice & Beyer, 1984), researchers developed rich understandings of the ways members both constructed and made sense of their organizational realities.

In this chapter, we are going to examine that paradigm revolution and explore the 30 years or so of research that has significantly altered our understanding of organizations as humanly created phenomena. First, we will discuss a few of the reasons for the emergence of the cultural approach.

⚙ THE EMERGENCE OF THE CULTURAL APPROACH

By the 1970s, the large, bureaucratic, and homogeneous organizational form that had dominated the post–World War II era of unprecedented growth and stability had started to show its age. As such, a number of economic, political, and social factors came together that provided the impetus to look for new ways of approaching organizational life. First, the 1970s witnessed much greater economic instability, with high inflation and low economic growth. This instability was fueled in part by two energy crises (in 1973 and 1979), both of which were linked to political upheaval in the Middle East, with oil-producing countries limiting oil supplies to the United States. Related, management–labor relations were also in crisis, with frequent and widespread strikes in both the United States and Europe as unions fought to retain job benefits established in the 1950s. Moreover, U.S. corporations were facing increasingly strong global competition for markets, especially from Japan. For example, in the wake of the oil crises, Japanese automobile companies were quick to exploit U.S. companies' failure to produce fuel-efficient cars (we'll talk about these factors in more detail in Chapter 6 when we talk about the post-Fordist organization).

Furthermore, as we mentioned in Chapter 3, the large bureaucratic organization became seen as dehumanizing. While theorists such as Taylor and Mayo focused mainly on blue-collar workers and efforts to improve the experience of industrial labor, it became increasingly clear in the second half of the 20th century that white-collar, managerial work could be just as alienating. Classic texts such as C. Wright Mills's (1951) *White Collar*, William H. Whyte's (1956) *The Organization Man*, and Arthur Miller's (1949) play *Death of a Salesman* document struggles to maintain dignity in the face of a machine-like, impersonal organizational environment.

The employees who came of age in the 1970s, however, rejected the conformity of the megabureaucracy their parents accepted and adopted a more individualistic approach to work that sought something beyond a 9 to 5 job and a paycheck at the end of the week. In this sense, intrinsic rewards and meaningful work that produced personal growth (a phrase that would have been alien to the 1950s white-collar worker) became just as important as extrinsic rewards. The so-called me decade (Wolfe, 1976) that was part of the 1960s and 1970s cultural revolution (hippies, flower power, and all that) thus had a profound influence on organizational life.

In many respects, then, the rational manager who was the guardian of bureaucracy in the second spirit of capitalism (Boltanski & Chiapello, 2005) was losing his luster (in 1960s lingo, he was pretty square), and a movement was building for something new—an alternate way of organizing that was better able to tap into the greater complexities and aspirations of people's lives. While human resource management had begun this transformation, it really didn't take full hold until the cultural approach arrived on the scene.

This economic, political, and social transformation provides the frame for a number of research-related reasons why the cultural approach emerged as a new way of studying organizational life. Perhaps foremost among these is the very concept of culture itself, which provided a vivid and transformative way of examining organizations as communication phenomena. Put another way, researchers acquired a new metaphor with which to make sense of organizational life. Beginning in the late 1970s and early 1980s, there was a strong sense that the traditional forms of organizational research had become stagnant and were offering little in the way of new insights into organizational communication.

In particular, some researchers were becoming critical of that dominant paradigm, which attempted to show causal relationships between various communication variables and organizational outcomes, such as effectiveness and productivity (Mumby, 2015). Such an approach, it was argued, reflected a managerial conception of what was important to study in organizations. In other words, because managers were primarily interested in knowing how changes in organizational communication could lead to greater efficiency and productivity, that's what researchers studied.

The cultural approach, however, began from a different premise. As organizational communication researchers Mike Pacanowsky and Nick O'Donnell-Trujillo (1982) state,

> The jumping off point for this approach is the mundane observation that more things are going on in organizations than getting the job done. . . . People in organizations also gossip, joke, knife one another, initiate romantic involvements, cue new employees to ways of doing the least amount of work that still avoids hassles from a supervisor, talk sports, arrange picnics. (p. 116)

As such, the cultural approach started from the notion that one should study organizations not just to improve their efficiency and make people better employees but also because they are interesting and complex communication phenomena in their own right. Understanding how they operate thus provides greater insight into an important element of the human condition.

Of course, the idea of culture as a metaphor for the study of organizations did not originate in the field of organizational communication. Since the 19th century, anthropologists had been studying "exotic" cultures, partly as a way to understand those societies that were being colonized by Western nations. In the 20th century, anthropology turned its gaze closer to home and began to study the changing structure of U.S. society, particularly in the urban environment. Foremost in this movement was the University of Chicago School of Sociology, led by Robert Park. Much of this work was directed toward studying emergent social problems and social groups and giving voice to ordinary people as they dealt with these problems in their everyday lives (e.g., Liebow, 1967; W. F. Whyte, 1981).

Another source for the emergence of the cultural approach was the interpretive tradition that had been part of the human sciences since the early 19th century. This tradition focuses on language and communication as the principal medium through which human beings create social reality for themselves. In such a view, language and communication do not simply represent social reality but rather constitute it. In the field of communication, this interpretive focus started to have an impact in the mid-1970s as scholars began to draw on this tradition to provide alternative conceptions of communication processes (Deetz, 1973, 1982; Hawes, 1977).

However, the anthropological and interpretive traditions come together in the writings of Clifford Geertz, whose development of an interpretive approach to anthropology has significantly influenced organizational communication studies (Geertz, 1973, 1983). Indeed, Geertz's (1973) definition of culture is probably the most widely cited conception in organization studies:

> The concept of culture I espouse . . . is essentially a semiotic one. Believing, with Max Weber, that man [*sic*] is an animal suspended in webs of significance he himself has spun, I take culture to be those webs, and the analysis of it to be therefore not an experimental science in search of law, but an interpretive one in search of meaning. (p. 5)

There are a number of important elements to this definition of culture. First, Geertz argues for a semiotic conception of culture. As we saw in Chapter 2, semiotics is the study of the ways in which sign systems, or systems of representation, come to create social reality for people. In this sense, Geertz adopts a meaning-centered conception of culture—culture doesn't exist in people's heads but in the shared (i.e., public) rites, rituals, artifacts, conversations, and so forth, in which people engage.

Second, Geertz suggests that the "webs of significance" (1973, p. 5) that make up culture have a dual life. On the one hand, they are formed by people who actively participate in the creation of their culture. At the same time, culture acts back on its members, shaping and constraining their conceptions of the world. Just as a spider both creates and is limited by its web, so people create and simultaneously are limited by their culture.

Third, and related, the web metaphor emphasizes the notion that culture is not a thing; rather, it exists in the moment to moment—people spin their cultures in an ongoing and dynamic fashion as they go about their daily lives (Frost, Moore, Louis, Lundberg, & Martin, 1985).

Finally, Geertz describes the analysis of culture as an interpretive rather than experimental science. This difference is significant because it highlights another important element in the emergence of the culture paradigm in organizational communication studies: a shift away from the quantitative study of communication variables (and the search for laws of human behavior) toward the qualitative study of collective sense making in real-life settings. Geertz (1973) argues that the interpretive study of culture involves thick description—that is, the development of narrative accounts that provide rich insight into the complex meaning patterns that underlie people's collective behavior. We will examine examples of such thick description later in the chapter.

For several reasons, then, both corporate leaders and organization researchers were primed to rejuvenate their respective domains. The notion of culture appeared to provide just such a catalyst for rejuvenation. Books such as Tom Peters and Bob Waterman's (1982) *In Search of Excellence* and Terry Deal and Allan Kennedy's (1982) *Corporate Cultures* tapped into a desire by managers to rethink how organizations operated and, in many ways, to revive the flagging image of the manager as a dull bureaucrat. Thus, examining organizations from a cultural perspective seemed to provide managers with a new way to motivate employees, reinvigorate corporate productivity, and meet the challenges of a changing global economy. For organization researchers, the cultural approach provided a new frame that had the potential to revitalize their area of inquiry, making it more relevant to organization members.

In the next section, we will examine more closely the assumptions that underlie the different conceptions of the cultural approach to organizational communication.

⬢ TWO PERSPECTIVES ON ORGANIZATIONAL CULTURE

To understand the cultural approach, it is important to keep in mind that the notion of culture is a metaphor that provides us with certain insights into organizational communication processes (Morgan, 2006). Just as the machine metaphor of organizations highlighted issues of efficiency, predictability, and effectiveness, and the organism metaphor highlighted growth, adaptation, and complexity, so the culture metaphor highlights a particular way of examining organizations.

From the cultural perspective, organizations are systems of beliefs, values, and taken for granted norms that guide everyday behavior. The lens of culture enables us to focus on the ways in which people communicatively construct systems of meaning that shape and embody these beliefs and values. Adopting a cultural perspective, Charles Bantz (1993) defines organizational communication in the following manner:

> The collective creation, maintenance, and transformation of organizational meanings and organizational expectations. . . . Communication is the medium through which organizations, as symbolic realities, are constructed by humans. (p. 1)

Seen in this light, organizations exist only when our communication practices generate meanings (symbolic realities) that structure ongoing activity. From a cultural perspective, then, organizations do not exist independently from their members; rather, organizations are real only to the extent that their members engage in various communication activities.

Within the organizational culture literature, however, this basic principle is explored and conceptualized in a number of different ways. For our purposes, we will discuss in detail two prominent approaches: the pragmatist approach and the purist approach.

The Pragmatist Approach: Organizational Culture as a Variable

The conception of organizational culture as a variable has a distinctly managerial orientation to it. From a management point of view, interest lies in attempting to assess the impact of an organization's culture on its performance. Thus, in identifying culture as a variable, managers are interested in measuring how one feature of the organization (the culture) affects the larger organization. From this perspective, organization and culture are distinct entities. This distinction is important because one can show the effect of one variable on another only if they can first be shown as separate. Another way to think of this variable approach is that from this perspective, culture is seen as something that an organization *has*—it is one feature among others such as technology, structure, and environment.

Management scholar Joanne Martin (1985) refers to this variable perspective as the **cultural pragmatist** approach to organizations. Seeing culture as a variable means that scholars can examine how it varies (e.g., weak to strong, rigid to flexible) and how those variations are associated with other valuable organizational outcomes. If it is a variable, culture can—by definition—be manipulated and changed to create outcomes like employee commitment and productivity, which in turn improve company performance and profitability. Thus, from this perspective, one of the principal roles of managers is to diagnose and if necessary, change an organization's culture—in other words, to engineer the culture to meet corporate goals (Kunda, 1992; Sathe, 1983, 1985). The good manager is attuned to the cultural aspects of his or her organization and is able to manipulate that culture in the best interests of the organization. From a pragmatist perspective, then, there is a very strong means–end orientation at work; culture is a means by which particular ends (commitment, profit, etc.) are reached. As such, the pragmatist, variable approach assumes a causal relationship between culture and organizational performance—a strong, functional culture strengthens employee identification with their organization, while a weak, dysfunctional culture weakens that sense of identification.

The pragmatist approach also assumes that successful organizations possess a single, unitary culture that all employees buy into. Martin refers to this assumption as an integration approach to culture; that is, ideally, all organization members are integrated into a single worldview and set of values that guide their behavior and decision making (Martin, 1992). Such strong organizational cultures exercise the kind of ideological control we discussed in Chapter 1; when all members internalize a set of values, they can be counted on to act in the best interests of the organization without any direct control by supervisors.

Finally, we can say that the pragmatist approach adopts a strongly prescriptive orientation. By this, we mean that cultural pragmatists provide guidance for the shaping of strong, functional cultures. Peters and Waterman's (1982) *In Search of Excellence*, mentioned earlier, is a classic and widely read example of such a prescriptive approach. The basic premise of this book is that those companies identified as excellent (the authors discuss companies such as IBM, 3M, Disney, and McDonald's) have certain features in common (for instance, they stay close to the customer while they stick to the knitting and encourage employee autonomy and entrepreneurship in an environment characterized by a simple form and lean staff) and that companies wishing to emulate these exemplars of excellence need to adopt these features too.

The pragmatist, variable approach also adopts a distinctly functionalist orientation to organizational culture. That is, culture is seen as playing specific functions within the organization. These functions include the following:

1. *Creating a shared identity among organization members*. By developing a strong culture, members are more likely to share a single vision of the organization and its overall beliefs and values. Such a shared vision enhances the potential for members to make

decisions that are consistent with organizational goals. For example, Disney, which has a very strong corporate culture, carefully schools its employees (cast members) in the company vision, thus ensuring that each person identifies with the role he or she must play (Van Maanen, 1991). Subaru-Isuzu Automotive spends more time training new employees in the features of its culture than in teaching them the mechanics of their jobs (Graham, 1993).

2. *Generating employee commitment to the organization.* A strong, shared identity among employees also increases the possibility that those employees will be highly committed to the organization. Pragmatist research is full of stories about "organizational heroes" who exemplify the kind of commitment a strong culture can produce. For example, the sportswear company Nike has a relatively small (and somewhat secretive) group of expert employees who travel the globe proselytizing about the company's products. Called EKINs—that's Nike spelled backwards, purportedly because the company's founder and first EKIN, Phil Knight, said that the best traveling salespeople had to know the products backward and forward—these employees not only get special training but also receive early exposure to new technologies (for these people, that seems to be a major enticement). EKINs are expected to be deeply devoted brand ambassadors, and their passion is evidenced by the fact that most get a specially designed Nike swoosh tattoo, literally branding them as company disciples. An EKIN, in other words, is a particular sort of company hero, one who is committed to the company in the extreme (Katz, 1994).

3. *Enhancing organizational stability.* The creation of a strong culture, a shared identity, and high employee commitment minimizes organizational turnover, reduces the chances of distrust and worker–management conflict, and enhances the stability of the organization. Conversely, employees who do not buy into the corporate culture are likely to create conflict and organizational instability. Companies will frequently tolerate creative mavericks who behave in unconventional ways but nevertheless identify with the company's values; on the other hand, employees who deviate too far from corporate values are likely to be removed (Sathe, 1983). Similarly, in maintaining organizational stability, companies will look to hire employees who fit in with the corporate culture, such that measuring person–organization fit—the match between perceived and preferred organizational culture (Harris & Mossholder, 1996)—has become a key way to assess whether a given person belongs in, and will remain in, in the organization.

4. *Serving as a sense-making device.* Socializing employees into a strong organizational culture results in a highly internalized sense of the realities of organizational life. Employees develop a shared set of taken for granted norms and principles that help them negotiate the complexities of day-to-day organizing processes. Indeed, an important part of being socialized into any organization involves learning the culture of that organization. And the consequences for not quickly learning a culture can be severe. In his study of an Internet startup company, sociologist David Stark (2009) reports speaking to a new employee, recently recruited from IBM, who talked excitedly about working for a company that had an informal, laid-back culture (no more IBM suits!). However, he said, nobody had yet told him what his job was. This new employee was fired by the end of the week; he hadn't figured out that he was supposed to take the initiative and create a role for himself in the company—a very different culture from the one he was accustomed to at IBM.

The pragmatist approach to organizational culture thus represents an important body of research oriented to organizational intervention. Culture is defined as a tool that provides managers with a way to shape the organizational reality that employees experience. As a tool, it is a thing the organization has, one with variable characteristics, as mentioned above. When it entered management thinking in the 1980s, it presented a very different view of the human side of organization: Instead of eliminating or segmenting off the messiness of human behavior (as in both scientific management and human relations), the culture movement suggested that these elements of organizing could be shaped by managers. Peters and Waterman (1982) argued:

> What our framework has done is to remind the world of professional managers that "soft is hard." It has enabled us to say, in effect, "All that stuff you have been dismissing for so long as the intractable, irrational, intuitive, informal organization can be managed." Clearly, it has as much or more to do with the way things work (or don't) around your companies as the formal structures and strategies do. . . . Here, really, is the way to develop a new skill. (p. 11).

The primary motivation for the pragmatist approach is to explore the link between culture and organizational performance. If managers can successfully intervene in and shape organizational culture, then organizations can improve their effectiveness and competitiveness. Becoming an "excellent" company thus meant that the communicative and psychological elements of organizations had to receive explicit managerial attention. In the next section, however, we will discuss a very different approach to culture—one that rejects many of the primary assumptions of the pragmatist perspective.

The Purist Approach: Organizational Culture as a Root Metaphor

The assumptions underlying the cultural purist perspective stand in sharp contrast to those of the pragmatist approach. First, rather than viewing culture as one organizational variable among many, purists see culture as a basic, root metaphor for understanding organizations (Morgan, 2006; R. Smith & Eisenberg, 1987). In other words, culture is not something an organization has, or possesses; rather, from this perspective, an organization *is* a culture. In this sense, the notion of culture works as a basic framing device to shape our fundamental sense of organizational reality. Second, because an organization *is* a culture, it follows that organizations exist only insofar as members engage in the various communicative practices that make up the culture of the organization. Thus, where the pragmatist sees culture as one aspect of an organization among many, the purist argues that the organization can be understood as a meaning-based social collective only by viewing it through the lens of culture.

Third, cultural purists question the idea that organizational cultures can be manipulated to meet the needs and goals of the organization. They argue against the culture management approach for a number of reasons:

1. Organizational culture is emergent and not something shaped by managers. In this sense, culture evolves spontaneously, reflecting people's needs and experiences.

Purists argue that when pragmatist managers attempt to shape culture, they're targeting only surface-level manifestations, missing the deep and underlying character of culture.

2. Due to the complexity of organizational culture, it is impossible to establish any causal connections between culture and organizational outcomes, such as employee performance; culture is just too messy to quantify, measure, and make predictions about. As management scholar Mats Alvesson (1993) argues, "The general conclusion which can be drawn from . . . investigations of the link between organizational culture and performance is that the idea of culture very often promises more than it delivers" (p. 42).

3. Organizations do not have a single, unitary culture that all members share. Many organizations—especially large ones—are made up of a complex array of often competing subcultures that make it difficult to argue that employees share a single corporate vision (Martin, 1992). Management scholar Ed Young (1989) showed that even in organizational cultures where members share the same objects, sayings, rituals, and so on, interpretations of these cultural artifacts can vary across the various groups that make up the organization. In Young's study of a British clothing manufacturer, he shows how the meanings of important cultural manifestations, such as the Royalty Board (where workers posted anything related to the Royal Family), company outings, and the wearing of poppies on a special holiday, were interpreted very differently by two distinct groups of workers—one group consisting of older, married women and the other group consisting of younger, single women. However, managers in the organization saw the Royalty Board, the participation in the outings, and the poppies and believed these to be evidence of a single shared culture. The managers were largely unaware of the intense conflict on the shop floor that centered on the significance of these cultural expressions.

4. Attempts to manage organizational culture often manipulate employee feelings and emotions and are therefore, unethical. Alvesson (1993) argues that the pragmatist approach is based on a set of beliefs that prioritizes the interests of managers over those of employees. As such, employee desires are largely ignored in favor of bottom-line concerns. For example, an organization that emphasizes a team culture often places heavy pressure on individuals to come through for the team. Such pressure makes it difficult for workers to express anything but performance-related concerns. In such a culture, a single working mother who misses a day to look after a sick child would be expected to justify, to all the other team members, why she did something that demonstrated a lack of loyalty to the team (Mumby & Stohl, 1992).

For a number of reasons, then, cultural purists view the pragmatist approach as problematic. What, then, are the elements of the purist approach? We have already drawn attention to its conception of culture as a root metaphor for framing the study of organizations. Below, we explore its features in greater detail; but first, we describe a study that investigates the consequences of using the more typical pragmatist approach (the one discussed in the previous section) in organizational life.

CRITICAL RESEARCH 5.1

Sally Riad (2005). The power of "organizational culture" as a discursive formation in merger integration. *Organization Studies, 26*, 1529–1554.

Since the introduction of books such as *In Search of Excellence* (and others like it) in the 1980s, the notion of culture has assumed a central position in people's understandings of organizational life. But culture is key not merely within organizations; it is also seen as essential for relationships between organizations. One such interesting case would thus be organizational mergers and acquisitions, where management or ownership of two or more organizations are consolidated or combined. In fact, one of the central concerns often raised about potential mergers is whether the two organizations' cultures fit with one another, or whether the merger will experience a culture clash; in fact, the high rate of failure of mergers is often attributed to conflicting organizational cultures (Rottig, Reus, & Tarba, 2014).

Acknowledging these common assumptions about organizational culture, management scholar Sally Riad (2005) studied a merger that brought together two public sector organizations in New Zealand. She called these agencies TerraCorp and Argo and noted that these two were being privatized as the government sought bureaucratic efficiencies. Although Argo was the smaller of the two agencies, government authorities framed this transaction as a merger rather than an acquisition, emphasizing the equivalence of the organizations. The government authorities framed it this way in large part because Argo was seen as having a strong and hand-built (p. 1539) culture, one that was threatened by the consolidation with TerraCorp. Those authorities, moreover, appointed change management teams within each agency, as well as an inter-organizational transition team, designed to prevent cultural clashes between the agencies as they came together. Culture, in short, was a significant strategic concept guiding people's sense making about the merger.

The centrality of the notion of organizational culture played out in several interesting ways during the merger. Perhaps most telling was the use of an organizational culture audit, a survey-based measurement of the fit between Argo and TerraCorp, as well as the sort of new culture desired by employees. The transition team implemented this audit, but did not anticipate the degree to which the audit surfaced "torrents of passionate discussion on 'organizational culture'" (p. 1540). The debate around the audit concerned the validity of the culture measurement instruments used by the transition team but never challenged the premise that culture was a real, objective feature of organizational life—a variable that differed across (and thus separated) the two agencies.

Additionally, Riad observed that the notion of culture was used to exert power during the merger. Though it was the smaller agency, Argo was seen as having a much stronger and established organizational culture. TerraCorp members accused Argo of exploiting that reputation to blame Terracorp's inflexibility on its culture. Yet TerraCorp members also used Argo's culture against it. For instance, Argo preferred "open communication" (p. 1546), and thus shared merger information with all members, whereas TerraCorp restricted information sharing. TerraCorp managers were then able to portray themselves as outcome-oriented and thus better suited to a competitive marketplace.

In the end, the chief executive in charge of the merged agency decided how culture would be designed into the newly merged organization. Saying that "one culture had to dominate" and that "the government perceived the culture of [Argo] as wrong" (p. 1547), the die was cast for the dominance of TerraCorp's culture over that of Argo's. TerraCorp's change management team was better able to read the motivations guiding the merger and, in turn, to align depictions of its culture with those values. Though those engaged in mergers and acquisitions may express a desire to mesh cultures together, Riad's case shows not only how the notion of culture is framed as central and how culture clash is experienced in mergers but also how one side was able to win this particular culture game by appealing to encompassing values.

Discussion Questions

1. In this case, TerraCorp and Argo were each seen as having a culture (and a single, unitary culture at that). How do you think this merger might have gone if the people involved saw the possibility of multiple subcultures existing at these agencies, as in the purist approach? What events in the case would no longer make sense; what new possibilities for action might emerge?

2. In groups, reflect on the idea that TerraCorp "won" this culture clash. What sorts of talk, symbols, and artifacts do you imagine its change management team might have used in making the case for its alignment with the broader, surrounding culture? What might be some unintended consequences of TerraCorp's depiction of its culture in this way?

3. The story ends with the chief executive's decision about TerraCorp emerging victorious over Argo. But the actual merger had yet to occur. In groups, discuss what challenges (including, potentially, ongoing clashes) the merger would likely encounter following the case described here.

A Broader Conception of "Organization"

At the beginning of this chapter, we discussed how the cultural approach had broadened traditional understandings of what counts as an appropriate type of organization to study. While the pragmatist approach largely focuses on corporate organizations (which would make sense, given its managerial orientation), the purist perspective has included a large array of organizations in the scope of its studies. For example, Nick Trujillo and Bob Krizek studied baseball parks (Krizek, 1992; Trujillo, 1992); Dean Scheibel (1992, 1996) studied the socialization of medical students and communicative performances in bars; Sarah Tracy (2000, 2005) researched two very similar organizations—prisons and cruise ships; Alexandra Murphy (2003) studied strip clubs; Carrisa Hoelscher, Alaina Zanin, and Michael Kramer (2016) studied identification with values at farmers' markets; and Alan DeSantis (2003, 2007) studied campus Greek organizations and a group of smokers at a cigar store.

Because of this broad-based approach, cultural purists are generally uninterested in examining the relationship between culture and organizational effectiveness. Rather, their interest lies in understanding organizational life as complex, dynamic, and constituted in an ongoing fashion through communicative processes. They are committed to deepening our understanding of, and appreciation for, human experience and typically reject the drive to generalize knowledge about a given culture to a broader population. Moreover, purists are interested in understanding organizations "from the native's point of view" (Geertz, 1983)—in other words, from the perspective of the members of the culture being studied, allowing members' own sense making to emerge in the course of research. This method is very different from the pragmatist approach, where managerial definitions of organizational culture prevail.

The Use of Interpretive, Ethnographic Methods

Earlier in the chapter, we discussed the influence of anthropologist Clifford Geertz in the emergence of organizational culture research. Much of this influence is centered on his development of an interpretive approach to the study of culture. From the purist perspective, this approach has translated into an explosion of research that employs qualitative, field-based methods to develop thick descriptions of organizational cultures. When researchers employ the methods of **ethnography**, it means they are immersing themselves (often for a period of months, sometimes years) in a culture so they can become intimately familiar with the sense-making efforts of its members. Ethnographic research, then, does not set up experimental conditions but instead studies naturally occurring, everyday behavior and communication processes (Tracy, 2012). A number of implications are associated with this development, but perhaps the best way to explain it is by example.

Organizational communication researcher Bob Krizek (1992) gives an excellent example of thick description in an essay called "Goodbye Old Friend: A Son's Farewell to Comiskey Park." Krizek's goal in this essay is to provide the reader with a vivid account of the last baseball game in the Chicago White Sox's old Comiskey Park before it was closed and torn down. To accomplish this goal, Krizek draws on interviews with fans, detailed accounts of his own experiences and perceptions at the final game, and recollections of attending White Sox games as a child with his father (the friend in the title of the essay is a double reference to both the park and his father). The result is a powerful account that brings to life the sights, sounds, and emotions of that final game. Here's a brief extract from the essay to provide you with a sense of how an ethnographic thick description creates a vivid picture of a particular cultural context:

> Research was secondary on my mind that Thursday evening as I instinctively negotiated the ramps and stairways to those . . . upper deck seats. With all the Park renovations in the late seventies and the eighties (the years when ballparks were invaded by corporate skyboxes), the finding was based more on intuition than geographic certainty. Prompted by the climb to the upper deck, my twenty-pound equipment bag, and the anticipation generated by the moment, I arrived winded. I paused, filled my lungs with a few deep breaths, and then held one especially large mouthful of Comiskey Park air as I sank into the chair closest to the aisle. For one

brief moment, the confidence of adulthood drifted away, replaced by the feelings of a lost six-year-old boy. I began to cry. This may have been the first time I truly missed my dad or genuinely mourned his passing. (Krizek, 1992, pp. 88–89)

More than anything else, the account provides the reader with compelling insight into what the closing of the park means to the people in attendance. Krizek (1992) shows that the park is not just a place where baseball games happen but that, more important, it is a site of collective memory and a place where a strong sense of community and belonging has developed. For the fans in attendance, the tearing down of the park involves the destruction of that site of memory and community; indeed, as Krizek vividly demonstrates, it involves the destruction of part of their own identities.

Krizek's study is, thus, not objective in the sense of presenting a fair and balanced perspective. For example, he does not interview the owners or managers of Comiskey Park. Rather, he is emotionally invested in the fans' perspective and describes the closing through their eyes and sense-making efforts. Indeed, it is precisely because of his emotional involvement with the subject matter that he is able to provide such a rich and compelling account of the closing of Comiskey Park. As such, it provides powerful insight into the human condition—the ultimate goal of all research.

Of course, not every thick description requires Krizek's level of emotional involvement. Indeed, field research varies from a complete observer role, in which the researcher has no direct contact with organization members; through a participant-as-observer role, where the researcher participates in organizational life but members are aware of his or her status as a researcher; and to a complete participant role, where members are unaware of his or her status as a researcher (Bantz, 1993).

A classic example of this last type of study is Donald Roy's (1959) famous ethnography of a manufacturing company. Although Roy's study was written with a strong human relations orientation, it is actually one of the earliest examples of a full participant study of a specific organizational subculture. Roy took a job at a clicking machine in a room with three other workers and immersed himself in the workplace culture. Roy's status as a researcher was completely unknown to his workmates, and thus, he was able to participate fully in the daily rituals the workers developed to help offset the extreme tedium of the tasks they were performing. Roy shows how the daily rituals of "banana time," "coke time," "peach time," "fish time," and so forth gave meaning to the workday and helped time pass far more quickly in an extremely monotonous work environment. His findings showed that the social interaction among the workers increased their level of job satisfaction.

A more contemporary example is communication scholar Alan DeSantis's (2003) ethnographic, **participant-observation** study of a cigar shop. What we love about this study is that, as its title suggests, it is literally about a couple of white guys sitting around talking. DeSantis takes the most mundane and ordinary of circumstances (a group of men hanging out in a cigar shop, enjoying a cigar, and discussing issues of the day) and effectively illustrates how, through their everyday talk, they collectively construct a distinct social reality.

DeSantis (2003) focuses on one particular aspect of this communicative construction of reality—the men's collective rationalization regarding the health hazards associated with smoking. He shows how in the course of their interactions the men engage in "symbolic convergence" (Bormann, 1983); that is, their individual realities start to converge as they collectively create a social reality about smoking. DeSantis illustrates in great detail how the men construct a vision of their world that both denies and rationalizes away the health hazards of smoking. This rationalization contains five themes that arise routinely in the course of conversations among the men: (1) all things in moderation; (2) cigar smoking has health benefits; (3) medical research that shows smoking is hazardous to health is flawed; (4) cigars are not like cigarettes and don't have the same health risks; and (5) life is dangerous and smoking is a minor risk in the grand scheme of things.

DeSantis's (2003) study is particularly insightful in illustrating how, when confronted with a mountain of scientific evidence, the men have an amazing ability to construct communicatively a reality that essentially functions as an alternate universe (a process that has become all too common in today's political climate!). Even when one of the men dies from a heart attack at a relatively young age, they are able collectively to rationalize this event and construct the man's death as stress related, not smoking related. In sum, DeSantis's study is a perfect example of how "man is an animal suspended in webs of significance that he himself has spun" (Geertz, 1973, p. 5).

The Study of Organizational Symbols, Talk, and Artifacts

The purist approach to organizational culture places a heavy focus on the study of cultural expressions—that is, the various symbols, conversations, artifacts, and practices that are the visible manifestation of a given culture. The main difference between the pragmatist and purist approach to the study of these manifestations is that the former treats them as the outward expression of an objective culture that can be measured and quantified. The purist approach, however, argues that it is through these various communicative practices and processes that organizational culture actually comes into being. In this sense, the various symbolic forms do not represent something else but are the culture themselves. This idea is important because it points to the public character of both culture and the sense-making processes in which organization members collectively engage to create their social reality (Geertz, 1973, 1983).

Pacanowsky and O'Donnell-Trujillo (1982) argue that to understand the communicative accomplishment of sense making, culture researchers must try to answer the following two basic questions: (1) What are the key communication activities through which organizational sense making occurs? and (2) In any particular organization, what are the features of this sense-making process? (p. 124). The first question requires researchers to identify the public, communicative features of organizational culture; the second asks researchers to interpret these communication processes to understand how people make sense of the culture they inhabit.

What, then, are the various symbolic forms that culture researchers have tended to focus on in making sense of organizational culture? Pacanowsky and O'Donnell-Trujillo (1982) identify the following expressions of culture and sense making: (1) relevant constructs, (2) facts, (3) practices, (4) vocabulary, (5) metaphors, (6) rites and rituals, and (7) stories. Let's examine each of these cultural indicators separately, with a special emphasis on storytelling (which we'll give a whole section of its own).

Rites and rituals symbolically mark significant moments in organizations and the lives of their members.

Relevant Constructs. All organizations and social collectives identify objects, individuals, events, and processes that punctuate the daily life of the organization and allow members to structure their experiences. For example, the construct of meeting makes sense to most organization members as a relatively structured event that can be differentiated from more loosely scripted behaviors such as informal chats by the coffee machine. For students, **relevant constructs** are things such as grades, class meetings, assignments, partying, and so forth. All of these labels help students organize their experiences as members of a particular culture.

Similarly, subcultures within larger cultures have additional sets of constructs that differentiate their members' experience from the experiences of members of the larger culture. For example, members of Greek organizations identify with constructs such as brotherhood and sisterhood in a way that members of the larger student body likely do not. If you speak to your professors, many of them will tell you that the construct of tenure organizes much of their professional lives, especially at the beginning of their careers; in almost everything they do, they have to ask themselves the question "Will this help me get tenure?" The pursuit of tenure thus also creates a subculture within the faculty at a university, setting them somewhat apart from the broader culture.

Facts. Every organizational culture has a body of social knowledge, shared by members, that enables those members to navigate the culture. This social knowledge does not consist of facts in the sense of objective truths but rather consists of a shared understanding about what is significant and meaningful to the organization and its members. For example, the "fact," often propagated by college students, that "if your roommate dies you automatically get a 4.0 GPA for the semester" tells us something about the ways in which students collectively construct a shared social reality (Scheibel, 1999). Although objectively untrue, such a fact provides insight into several features of student sense-making activities, including (a) the intense pressure school frequently places on students, (b) the heavy focus on grades as an indicator of success, and (c) the ongoing search for ways to beat the system. DeSantis's (2003) study of cigar smokers, discussed earlier, is also an excellent example of a body of "facts" (e.g., smoking is not harmful) that are central to the creation of a particular organizational reality.

Practices. Organizational life is made up of a set of ongoing **practices**, situated and goal-oriented human activities, which members must engage in to accomplish organizing. From a cultural perspective, a focus on such practices provides insight into the routine features of everyday organizational life. In addition, this focus draws attention to the way the sense-making process is an ongoing, moment-to-moment, practical accomplishment for social actors. For example, a meeting is not only a significant organizational construct but also a set of practices in which members must engage in order to accomplish organizational business. Not only must members know their roles, rules for addressing agenda items, and so forth, but they also must be aware of the extent to which such meetings may embody cultural understandings of what can be said, what can't be said, what hidden agenda items are present, and so on.

In his study of a high tech engineering firm, management scholar Gideon Kunda (1992) shows how company meetings are places where people engage in a variety of behaviors, including grandstanding, attempting to belittle rival project groups, subtly criticizing the dominant culture of the organization, and making power plays and alliances. None of those sorts of issues are ever found on the official agenda, but they illustrate how being a member of a culture involves understanding and participating in the ongoing and practical accomplishment of everyday organizational life.

Vocabulary. Often one of the most distinctive features of a culture is members' use of a specific **vocabulary**, or jargon, which describes important aspects of the culture. Such jargon frequently serves as a kind of badge signifying membership of the culture, and anyone who doesn't know the jargon can be immediately identified as an outsider. For example, in his ethnographic study of mostly homeless men who sell used books and goods on the sidewalk in Greenwich Village in New York City, sociologist Mitch Duneier (1999) reveals a distinctive vocabulary that the men use to describe what they do. Phrases such as "table watcher," "laying shit out," "place holder," and "mover" signify a complex pattern of social roles and collective meanings that serve to impose order on the chaotic environment of the street.

Sometimes organization members' vocabularies are used as a way to denigrate nonmembers. In their study of a police department, Nick Trujillo and George Dionisopoulos (1987) show how police officers routinely use terms such as *scrote*, *dirtbag*, and *maggot* to describe members of the public. Not surprisingly, such terms framed the way the officers approached interactions with people they encountered on their patrols. Similarly, Tracy and Scott (2006) describe firefighters' routine use of the term *shitbum* to describe indigents who make 911 calls and *shitbox* to describe the ambulances that take those shitbums to the emergency room. Again, such terms do not simply describe a person or object but instead, communicatively organize the collective experience and professional identities of firefighters as they engage in routine interactions with members of the public. In other words, vocabularies don't just describe organizational realities—they shape them.

Metaphors. The study of organizational **metaphors** has become an important way for culture researchers to interpret the sense-making processes of organization members (Grant & Oswick, 1996; Kirby & Harter, 2002; Koch & Deetz, 1981; F. Smith & Keyton, 2001; R. Smith & Eisenberg, 1987). Researchers argue that metaphors are used not simply to describe the world but rather, as a fundamental part of our perceptions and experience of the world. Philosophers George Lakoff and Mark Johnson (1980) claim that "our basic conceptual system, in terms of which we think and act, is fundamentally metaphorical" (p. 1). By studying organizational metaphors, then, culture researchers can develop some important insights into how organization members experience and make sense of their organization (see Critical Case Study 5.1).

A good example of how metaphor analysis can provide such insight is Sarah Tracy, Pamela Lutgen-Sandvik, and Jess Alberts' (2006) study of workplace bullying. Through interviews and focus group meetings with targets of workplace bullying, the study analyzes victims' efforts to make sense of the painful experience of being bullied. Starting with the basic question "What does it feel like to be bullied?" Tracy, et al. (2006) identify a series of metaphors that interviewees articulate. In speaking about the experience of bullying, respondents described it variously as a game or battle, a waking nightmare, water torture, and a noxious substance. In metaphorically describing the bullies, interviewees used the metaphors of dictator, two-faced actor, and evil demon. Finally, in describing themselves as targets of bullying, respondents spoke of slaves or property, prisoners, children, and heartbroken lovers. Thus, for example, in describing bullies as two-faced actors, respondents made sense of how, while bullies made their lives miserable in one-on-one situations, around other employees or supervisors they played the role of the perfect organization member, making it difficult for targets of bullying to be taken seriously. Similarly, in using the metaphor of heartbroken lover respondents were attempting to address their experience of feeling betrayed in a job they loved.

Studies like this one illustrate the importance of the culture-as-root-metaphor approach in two ways. First, they allow researchers to enable organization members to make sense of their own reality, rather than their reality as shaped by managerial efforts to engineer culture. In this particular study, for example, the organization members' own metaphors provide a "linguistic shorthand to describe long, difficult-to-articulate, and devastatingly painful feelings associated with workplace bullying" (Tracy et al., 2006, p. 171). Second, these studies show how such research can be used to address real-world organizational issues. Workplace bullying is a widespread organizational problem that affects many employees (Lutgen-Sandvik, 2003), and Tracy et al. (2006) illustrate how this issue can be better understood by speaking directly to the people who experience it.

CRITICAL CASE STUDY 5.1

Organizational Culture and Metaphors

With the rise of the cultural approach to organizations and the more intense focus on communication, researchers started to pay much more attention to the kind of talk people use in making sense of their organizations. Because of this shift, metaphors became a particular focus for researchers.

(Continued)

(Continued)

Metaphors can be defined as understanding and experiencing one kind of thing in terms of another. For example, when someone says, "I won the argument," they are understanding one thing (having an argument) in terms of another (war or sport). As we have seen in this chapter, metaphors don't simply describe an already existing organizational reality but rather, function as fundamental ways for people to organize their experiences.

Organizational communication scholars Ruth Smith and Eric Eisenberg (1987) provide a fascinating example of the importance of metaphors in structuring organizational reality in their study of a management–employee conflict that resulted in a worker strike at Disneyland. In their study, Smith and Eisenberg (1987) argue that employees experienced Disneyland through two competing root metaphors: Disney as drama and Disney as family. The drama root metaphor constructed organizational experience as providing entertainment, putting on a show, wearing costumes (not uniforms), having onstage and backstage areas, and so forth. The drama metaphor also emphasized the business of show business, in which Disneyland was seen as a profit-making enterprise. While the management of Disneyland emphasized the drama metaphor, many of the employees experienced Disneyland as a family, in which employees were brothers and sisters, everyone looked out for one another, and Walt Disney (long since dead) was seen as the spiritual head of the family. As one employee stated, "The people who work here treat each other as a family, there seems to be a common cause. . . . We're family presenting family entertainment; it's like we're inviting someone to our home to entertain them" (Smith and Eisenberg, 1987, p. 374).

However, as Smith and Eisenberg (1987) show, these two root metaphors represent competing, and incompatible, worldviews—one representing Disney as a for-profit business, the other constructing Disney as a benevolent family where everyone pulls together and takes care of one another. Thus, when Disney management began to implement pay freezes, benefit cuts, and layoffs, employees regarded these acts as a fundamental violation of the principles on which Disney had been founded. As one employee stated,

> Walt Disney's philosophy was to bring families together so that they could have fun. The philosophy is now let's make as much money as [we] can. . . . We're numbers now, we're not people to [management] anymore. (Smith and Eisenberg, 1987, p. 374)

Such was the perceived conflict between the two competing metaphors that employees went on a 22-day strike in response to what they perceived as the poor treatment of family members. Interestingly, management responded by trying to reinterpret the family metaphor, arguing that during difficult times, families had to make sacrifices and tighten their belts if they expected to survive. However, this reinterpretation failed to catch on among employees.

Smith and Eisenberg (1987) argue that while the overt (first-order) conflict may have been focused on economic issues (pay freezes, etc.), a deeper, more far-reaching (second-order) conflict focused on the basic philosophy regarding what Disneyland was and how it should be run. The two competing metaphors of drama and family represented two largely irreconcilable perspectives on this philosophy. In this sense, then, we can see that the two metaphors are not just ways to describe an already existing organizational reality, but rather they fundamentally shape reality for organization members.

Discussion Questions

1. Think of organizations to which you belong. Can you identify metaphors that members use to describe the organization? How does this shape the experience of organization members?

2. In groups, brainstorm possible metaphors that might be used to describe organizations. Some common metaphors are organizations as family, team, machine, political system, prison, compass, tribe, and so on. For example, an organization as machine metaphor would emphasize efficiency, well-oiled parts, precision, impersonality, and so forth. Be as creative as possible in your brainstorming. What features are associated with each metaphor, and how would they shape organizational life?

Rites and Rituals. The fact that all organizations practice various kinds of **rites and rituals** suggests that, over time, organizational reality sediments into stable and patterned forms. Rites and rituals are repeated activities that are rendered particularly meaningful for members of a culture. These activities emerge partly from a need for organization members to experience order and predictability in their lives. Such rituals can be as informal as a daily greeting between two colleagues or as formal as the pomp and circumstance of a graduation ceremony. All such rituals contribute to the social order of an organization and aid members in the creation of a shared social reality in which they can invest their professional identities (Trice & Beyer, 1984). They can mark the passage into a new phase of one's life (such as a graduation ceremony or getting married), or they can serve to further integrate members into a culture. An office holiday party, for example, can serve as a rite of integration that increases common bonds and further commits members to their organization (Rosen, 1988).

Rites of enhancement (Trice & Beyer, 1984) can increase the status and power of organization members through public recognition of their accomplishments while at the same time placing the organization in a positive light. For example, at high-profile, high-energy ceremonies, the Mary Kay company gives awards to successful representatives, with the top sellers receiving pink Cadillacs (Waggoner, 1997).

In contrast, rites of degradation (Trice & Beyer, 1984) occur when organizations experience problems and top organization members must perform a customary acknowledgment of such problems in an effort to address them (or create the perception that they are being addressed). For example, in 2011 when News Corporation CEO Rupert Murdoch appeared before a British parliamentary committee in the wake of the *News of the World* phone-hacking scandal, he was engaging in a rite of degradation in an effort to limit damage to his global media empire. The fact that he stated to the committee "This is the most humble day of my life" served to mark the event explicitly as a ceremonial rite of degradation.

Organizational Stories and Power

Organizational storytelling has become one of the most extensively researched features of work and organizational culture (Boje, 1995; A. Brown, 1998, 2006; Czarniawska, 1998; Ewick & Silbey, 1995; Karlsson, 2012; Witten, 1993). Part of the reason for this popularity is that people like to both tell and hear stories, and so this form of cultural expression is a pervasive feature of everyday organizational life. Organizational culture researchers thus view storytelling as one of the most important ways in which humans produce and reproduce social reality. Rhetoric scholar Walter Fisher (1985) has gone so far as to argue that human beings are homo narrans—that is, storytelling beings. In other words, our identities as humans are largely dependent on our ability to construct coherent narratives about ourselves. Such stories can range from personal narratives that individuals tell about themselves to grand narratives that embody the identity of an entire nation. Thus, one might argue that the grand narrative of the United States is the American Dream—a story of individual freedom, opportunity, and an entrepreneurial spirit. Each new group of immigrants has attempted to find a place within this grand narrative.

As we saw in Chapter 1 in Kristen Lucas's analysis of working-class families and their stories about work, Lucas (2011) suggests that the working class promise is a narrative that operates as a moral imperative, much like the American Dream narrative. However, she argues that the two narratives operate in tension with each other, presenting paradoxical views of social mobility. On the one hand, the American Dream narrative argues that being working class "is a starting point, a social position one should strive to rise above"; on the other hand, the working class promise positions being working class as "an esteemed endpoint, a social position one should strive to maintain" (Lucas, 2011, p. 365). Thus, Lucas (2011) identifies a contradiction between the American Dream as a social structure that one can climb and the working class promise as a value system to which one feels connected, perhaps for life. These two narratives, existing in tension, are hard to reconcile if one has, at least socioeconomically, moved beyond one's working-class origins. Students who are members of the first generation in their families to go to college (like Dennis) may experience the same kind of tension between loyalty to the working class promise and the appeal of the American Dream. In other words, is it possible both to live the American Dream and to stay true to the values of the working class promise?

Management scholars Joanne Martin, Martha Feldman, Mary Jo Hatch, and Sim Sitkin (1983) provide a particularly interesting early example of research looking at organizational storytelling. In analyzing stories from a range of organizations, they discover that many of the stories exhibit common scripts. For example, stories might be told around such scripts as Can the little person rise to the top? How will the boss react to mistakes? Is the big boss human? Will I get fired? Martin et al. (1983) illustrate how stories with these same scripts occur across a range of organizations, often in both positive and negative versions. They dub this phenomenon the **uniqueness paradox** to get at the idea that stories intended to express an organization's uniqueness actually occur across a range of organizations (making them not at all unique—hence the paradox).

For example, in a frequently recurring script about the importance of following organizational rules, Martin et al. (1983) recount one version of the story in which a female security guard tells Tom Watson, CEO of IBM, that he can't enter a secure area because he isn't wearing the right ID badge; Watson reacts positively and sends one of his staff to get the ID. In a parallel story, a secretary at Revlon challenges CEO Charles Revson when he violates a rule about not removing the employee sign-in sheet from its location. In this instance, the secretary is fired for daring to challenge the big boss. Thus, the moral of the IBM version of the story is "Even the big boss follows the rules, so you should too." On the other hand, the moral of the Revlon version is that rules apply arbitrarily and capriciously; the more power you have in the company, the less the rules apply to you. Thus, two similarly structured stories provide diametrically opposite morals about organizational rule following.

Martin et al.'s (1983) idea of the uniqueness paradox is a widespread organizational phenomenon, and you may have seen this in action at your university. At many American universities, there are stories about statues or fixtures coming alive when a virgin comes walking by (it's probably not surprising that these stories are almost always about female students). At Missouri, Michigan, Cincinnati, and Purdue, stone lions will roar if a virgin should saunter by. At Rutgers University, "Willie the Silent" (a statue of William of Orange) will whistle. A statue of James Duke at Duke University will tip his hat. At Cornell, two statues facing each other will descend from their pedestals, walk to one another, and shake hands. At Nebraska, Penn State, and Arkansas, buildings or monuments will collapse. At the University of Maryland, a statue will rise during the commencement ceremony and fly over the crowd if a virgin ever graduates from the school. Needless to say, none of these enlivening events has been documented. Yet each story is intended to convey a unique feature of the university's culture while simultaneously being common to many campuses—hence, the uniqueness paradox.

From the perspective of a researcher wishing to understand the culture of an organization, the question is this: What does such an organizational story mean? What does it tell us about the ways members of these organizations make sense of their social reality? One simple reading might be to point out the obvious sexism and efforts to regulate female sexuality built into stories about (female) virgins, both on campus and in folklore more broadly (Dorson, 1959). Another simple surface reading might be "All the female students on this party-centric campus are sexually active." But of course, we know this isn't true; students and young people generally adopt a variety of orientations regarding their sexual activity, or lack thereof, regardless of the party image some students seek to create.

Instead, it's possible that the story is saying something about anxieties and tensions around sex on college campuses. Given the status of college life as a transition period to adulthood and independence, there is a great deal of pressure on students to figure out how sexually active, or inactive, they should be: Who's a friend? Who's a friend with benefits? What counts as a date, rather than just hanging out with someone? And of course, no one wants to appear sexually naïve or inexperienced, even if he or she is. In her study of student sexuality, Kathleen Bogle (2008) argues that on today's college campuses the idea of the traditional date has largely disappeared, replaced by the hook-up. Student stories about their sex lives suggest that first-year women are more likely to hook up than are their upper-class sisters. Again, this difference perhaps tells us something about the anxiety college students feel about their sexual identities—something they are maybe closer to figuring out by their senior year.

What concepts like the uniqueness paradox tell us about organizational stories is that they have a distinct moral imperative (Bruner, 1991); that is, through the story structure, they move us toward a particular moral conclusion about some aspect of organizational reality. Stories are not just random descriptions of events, but rather they perform a sense-making function in teaching us what is important to pay attention to. In other words, stories are told only about things that are worth having stories told about them. Such worthy events can range from "a funny thing happened at the office today" to stories about the fulfillment of the American Dream of wealth and prosperity. As a moral imperative, the American Dream narrative instructs us to value the individual over the collective, work hard, earn lots of money, and believe in a meritocratic system in which everyone, regardless of origin, can succeed.

This discussion of the uniqueness paradox suggests that scholars have been interested in stories and storytelling not merely because they help give us a picture of organizational culture. Beyond that, stories—along with the symbols, talk, and artifacts introduced in the preceding section—generate insight into the operation of power in organizational life. We will devote more attention to the dynamics of power in Chapter 7, but here we note that some researchers find the approaches to organizational culture covered above somewhat limited. For instance, management scholar Mats Alvesson (2002) notes that the purpose of the dominant approach to culture, the pragmatist approach, is enhancing prediction and control; the alternative stance, the purist approach, tends to be primarily concerned with improving mutual understanding. What is left out, he argues, is an **emancipatory approach** to culture, which works to expose the means by which organizational cultures dominate and exploit workers and then, in turn, to foster transformations in those cultures.

Emancipatory analyses of stories and storytelling can take several forms. One might be an attention to how managerial storytelling silences and marginalizes some narratives while privileging others (Boje, 1995), as in the case of the story of IBM CEO Tom Watson and the female security guard we mentioned earlier in this section. The story is typically offered to show how egalitarian IBM is, since everyone—even the CEO, surrounded by his entourage— is subject to the same rules. Yet there are other possible readings of this story, though those readings can get submerged when trainers trot out the official version in employee orientations. For instance, Mumby (1987) notes that IBM's rules, including the one employed here, are designed by the leaders (including Watson) to maintain and protect their own interests. In telling this story to indicate that no one is above the law, it tacitly acknowledges that Watson and his ilk are indeed above the law—otherwise the event would not be seen as remarkable. It also obscures the gender dynamics when it insists that the female guard is dressed in an ill-fitting uniform and that Watson doesn't need to talk: He raises his hand to gain the attention of his entourage, one of whom hisses to the guard, "Don't you know who he is"? Reading a story like this with an eye toward what it obscures, along with the alternative understandings of the story that get excluded in the telling, is a key contribution of emancipatory studies.

Emancipatory studies acknowledge that culture can be a valuable sense-making device for individuals, but authors in this tradition make it clear that culture is far from value-neutral. They worry that efforts to build strong corporate cultures (as in the pragmatist approach), extend management control over workers by colonizing their hearts and minds. Being a member of a strong corporate culture, like at Southwest Airlines, Disney, Google, or Zappos, requires that an employee internalizes particular values. It also tends to require that alternative values, goals, and employee identities—alternative in the sense that they are not aligned with the single dominant model of the culture—are seen as contaminants that must be eliminated. This organizational cleansing is often done by management, but researchers in the emancipatory vein have noted that, quite frequently, "employees come to *discipline themselves* with feelings of anxiety, shame and guilt that are aroused when they judge themselves to impugn or fall short of the hallowed values of the corporation" (Willmott, 1993, p. 523). In other words, strong cultures lead employees to shape themselves in the image given to them by the organization—they lose their autonomy. They are then more likely to suspend their critical reasoning abilities when managers seek their loyalty, or when they face decisions marked by competing values.

An interesting case of the effects of managers' efforts to shape culture can be seen in Peter Fleming's (Fleming, 2005, 2009; Fleming & Sturdy, 2011) research on an Australian call center called Sunray. Managers at Sunray tried to make the customer service reps' typically tedious and repetitive work more exciting. They did this not by changing the content of the work but by trying to both encourage authenticity and by making the workplace more fun. They decorated the workplace with *Sesame Street* characters, had team dress-up days, and emphasized diversity (especially sexual orientation) among employees. Sunray hired mostly young workers and told them to "just be yourself." The company encouraged workers to bring their whole, authentic selves to work and fostered a party environment, including open drinking on the job. As you might imagine, this approach ran into problems. When employees' desire to be themselves ran counter to the requirements of work, when their desire to have fun in the workplace threatened managerial authority or employee performance, and when the party atmosphere bordered on sexual harassment, the products of the culture escaped managers' control. Somewhat surprisingly, though, when certain expressions of workers' authenticity violated the culture's expectations (e.g., employees who didn't want to have fun at work), they were no longer accepted. As one employee put it, "It seems to me that individualism is forced here—to be yourself as the company wants you to be is not to be yourself at all really" (Fleming & Sturdy, 2011, p. 191). This example is a pointed illustration of the narratives about the organization that members tell themselves; it shows how efforts to manage culture through those narratives create challenging unintended consequences for employees.

In sum, narratives are important communication processes that can significantly shape organization members' sense-making efforts. We all love to hear a good story; indeed, we're happy to hear a story multiple times if it's good! This willingness suggests how much the narrative form resonates with us and how effective stories are in shaping realities. Stories are symbolically powerful not so much because of their relationship to reality (often they are fictional) but because of the way they provide us with a coherent and compelling reality. At an everyday level, they provide us with organizing scripts that tell us what to pay attention to; at a macrosocietal level (the American Dream, the working class promise) they shape and express value systems and overarching ideologies. Indeed, as management scholar Barbara Czarniawska (1997) compellingly states, "Organizational stories capture organizational life in a way that no compilation of facts ever can; this is because they are carriers of life itself, not just 'reports' on it" (p. 20).

Summarizing the Two Perspectives

The pragmatist and purist approaches represent two distinct ways of conceptualizing and studying organizational culture. The pragmatist approach is more managerially oriented, emphasizing the ways managers can intervene in and shape culture to fit the needs and goals of the organization; culture is viewed as an independent variable that can be manipulated to achieve particular organizational consequences. The purist perspective, on the other hand, rejects the idea that organizational culture can be manipulated and argues instead that one should adopt culture as a root metaphor, thus providing a powerful frame for understanding the complexities of organizational life. In this latter perspective, the notion of culture is used to get at the complex, precarious, and emergent features of daily organizational life. Heavy emphasis is placed on organizational actors as active and knowledgeable participants in the social construction of organizational reality. And as we noted, the purist approach is more amenable to thinking about emancipation.

Which of these approaches is better? The answer is that it depends on your particular interest in organizational culture. As a manager, you might well be interested in the link between culture and organizational performance (although, as we discussed earlier, this link is notoriously difficult to demonstrate and measure). On the other hand, as a culture researcher, you may have no interest in performance issues whatsoever, confining yourself to gaining insight into the endless complexities and nuances of human meaning-making processes. Thus, as with most theories, there is no absolute truth involved—just ways of seeing and not seeing. The two perspectives are compared and contrasted in Table 5.1.

Table 5.1 Comparing Pragmatist and Purist Approaches to Organizational Culture		
Issue	**Pragmatist Approach**	**Purist Approach**
Conception of culture–organization relationship	Culture as a variable; an organization has a culture	Culture as a root metaphor; organization is a culture
Role of communication	Means by which organization members are socialized into culture	Process through which members constitute organizations as cultures
View of culture	Unitary view: Ideally, organizations have a single culture with which everyone identifies	Pluralist view: Organizations consist of multiple, often competing subcultures
Orientation to knowledge	Functionalist: Allows intervention in organizational culture; promotes culture engineering	Interpretivist: Deepens understanding of human collective behavior and meaning construction
Research orientation	Managerial view: Engineers culture from top down; creates culture with which employee will identify	Native's point of view: Studies culture from bottom up, allowing members' meanings to shape findings
Research goals	Tie strong cultures to increased organizational effectiveness and competitiveness	Provide thick description of culture; increase understanding of complexity of organizational life

❧ CONCLUSION

In this chapter, we closely examined the cultural approach to the study of organizations. We laid out the origins of this body of research, showing how it emerged in response to particular economic, political, and social issues. In addition, we examined two of the main research traditions of the cultural approach: the pragmatist and purist perspectives on organizational culture. As we have shown, these two approaches adopt quite different assumptions about both the relationship between organizations and culture and the reasons for studying organizational culture.

Alvesson (1993) faults much research on organizations for being relatively uninteresting. He urges organizational communication researchers to counteract parochialism (narrow-mindedness or short-sightedness) and instead, develop perspectives that capture the full complexity of organizational life—what he calls eye-opening studies. Above, we examined some of those studies—research that gets us to think about organizations differently, moving beyond a purely managerial point of view (where efficiency and profit are the defining criteria) and to examine a vision of the complexities of the communicative character of organizational life.

What's interesting, however, is that in many respects the pragmatist approach to culture has itself come under scrutiny, as many organizations have moved away from the idea of developing strong cultures, which have often been accused of being "cult-like" and oppressive (Fleming, 2014b). In the next chapter on the post-Fordist organization, we will see that corporate culture has in many respects given way to a much more fluid notion of what the boundaries of an organization are. And communication and changing notions of work have a lot to do with this shift.

CRITICAL APPLICATIONS

1. Conduct an oral interview with someone who works full-time. Ask this person about what his or her work means. How is work tied to this person's sense of identity as a human being? Does the job require that this person bring an authentic self to the workplace? How is work related to other aspects of his or her life? Make extensive notes during the interview and/or ask your interviewee for permission to record the interview. What themes can you identify in the interview that provide insight into how your interviewee makes sense of his or her work life?

2. Conduct a participant–observation study of an organization to which you belong. This organization can be a place of work, a club, or any other social group. Provide an analysis of the organization's culture using Pacanowsky and O'Donnell-Trujillo's (1982) question as a starting point: What are the key communication activities through which organizational sense making occurs? Focus on members' use of stories, constructs, rituals, metaphors, and so forth. In other words, provide an analysis of the organization's culture—how do the members collectively produce meaning through communication processes?

KEY TERMS

cultural pragmatist   124

cultural purist   126

emancipatory
approach   140

ethnography   130

facts   133

metaphors   134

organizational
storytelling   138

participant-observation   131

practices   134

relevant constructs 133

rites and rituals   137

thick description   122

uniqueness paradox   138

vocabulary   134

STUDENT STUDY SITE

Visit the student study site at **www.sagepub.com/mumbyorg** for these additional learning tools:

- Web quizzes
- eFlashcards
- SAGE journal articles

- Video resources
- Web resources

PART III

Critical Perspectives on Organizational Communication and the New Workplace

CHAPTER 6

Post-Fordism and Organizational Communication

The gig economy can be a lonely economy.

In a recent article in *The New Yorker* magazine titled "The Gig Economy Celebrates Working Yourself to Death," author Jia Tolentino (2017) tells the story of Mary, a driver for Lyft, who was 9 months pregnant. About a week before her due date, Mary decided to work for a couple of hours to make some extra money. During her shift, she started to have labor pains and so she headed to the hospital. On her way there, however, she received a "ping," indicating a ride request. Rather than ignore the request, Mary picked up the passenger, took him to his destination, and then drove herself to the hospital where, shortly thereafter, she gave birth to a baby girl. As Tolentino indicates, this story appeared on the Lyft website and concluded by asking readers, "Do you have an exciting Lyft story you'd love to share?"

Depending on your perspective, there are a couple of different ways to interpret this story. Certainly, for Lyft, it was worth sharing because it's a warm human interest story that also illustrates how hard working and dedicated its employees are. Except for one important thing, of course: Mary is not a Lyft employee. In fact, in the new world of work—the so-called gig economy—no one who drives for Lyft, or Uber, actually can be called an employee. By defining their drivers as "independent contractors," companies like Lyft and

Uber (and many other companies that act as a platform for freelance services—AirBnB, Fiverr, etc.) do not have to provide benefits like health care, pension plans, vacation time, and so on. So Mary would not get health insurance to cover the cost of her pregnancy from the company that "employs" her. From another perspective, then, we can argue that Mary's story is less a warm and fuzzy tale of hard work with a heartwarming ending and more a story that reflects the way work and organizations have been transformed in the shift from Fordism (the dominant organizational and work model of the 20th century), to post-Fordism (and the neoliberal economic system that underpins it) in the early 21st century.

In this chapter, then, we are going to discuss neoliberalism, the post-Fordist workplace, and their implications for organizational communication and the world of work that you will soon be entering (or may have already entered); many of the things we will talk about are likely to be features of your own work experience—the gig economy, self-branding, entrepreneurship, knowledge work, decentralized decision-making structures, blurred work-life boundaries, and so forth. Each of you will, in one way or another, have to come to terms with the increasing complexity of work in the 21st century. Moreover, we will see that communication is a central feature of this new workplace, as it becomes an increasingly key feature of capitalism under neoliberalism and post-Fordism. First, however, let's provide a historical context for the shift from Fordism to post-Fordism.

🍂 THE FALL OF FORDISM AND THE RISE OF POST-FORDISM

In Chapter 3, we talked about how the large bureaucratic organization was, in some ways, the savior of 20th-century capitalism. It provided the basis for what Luc Boltanski and Eve Chiapello (2005) called the second spirit of capitalism, in which the rational manager was the iconic figure who engaged in careful, long-term planning that enabled stability and growth. Indeed, the three decades after World War II (from roughly 1945 to 1975) was an unparalleled period of high production, full employment, and mass consumption on a scale never seen before. By the late 1960s and early 1970s, however, the large bureaucratic organization was beginning to show signs of wear and tear. There is no single reason for this deterioration, but several are worth mentioning.

First, the 1970s witnessed a global economic crisis. The Bretton Woods Agreement (established in 1945 between the United States, Canada, Western Europe, Japan, and Australia), an economic monetary policy intended to create a stable global economy through the encouragement of free trade, came to an end in 1971 when President Richard Nixon withdrew the United States from the agreement. Without getting too technical, while the Bretton Woods Agreement tied the value of each nation's currency to the gold standard (thus stabilizing each nation's currency value), after the agreement failed, each currency's value was subject to fluctuation, thus creating greater global economic instability.

Second, there was a global energy crisis precipitated by the West's increased reliance on Middle East oil supplies—a supply that was unpredictable because of political instability in that region of the world. Oil shortages made energy much more expensive which, in turn, resulted in steep increases in the cost of consumer products, hence causing high levels of inflation (in March 1974, for example, the U.S. inflation rate was 10.4%, compared with 2.9% in July 2018). In addition to high inflation, there was also low economic productivity.

In 1974 and 1975 at the height of the economic recession in the United States, there was negative growth in Gross Domestic Product (GDP—the total value of goods and services produced by the economy) of −0.5% and −0.2% respectively. In other words, the economy shrank in each of those years. The situation was the same in many other Western countries, leading economists to coin a new term—*stagflation*—to describe a combination of stagnant (low or negative) economic growth and high inflation.

Third, during this time many nations saw a great deal of industrial unrest. The postwar social contract between companies and workers that guaranteed job security and good wages and benefits in exchange for high productivity and labor-management cooperation was breaking down. Real wages were falling as inflation increased, and workers went on strike for higher wages. But there was also something else going on here. Workers were not only dissatisfied with their pay but also with the working conditions they were experiencing. The large, bureaucratic organization was increasingly viewed as an autocratic institution where workers were treated poorly and job quality (i.e., its meaningfulness) was low. For example, in 1972 workers went on strike at the General Motors plant in Lordstown, Ohio. The Lordstown plant was the fastest in the world, producing 101.6 cars per hour (a car every 36 seconds). The workers there went on strike not for higher pay but in protest against what they viewed as their inhumane working conditions. In the wake of this strike, a 1973 report by the Department of Health, Education and Welfare called *Work in America* stated that "a significant number of Americans are dissatisfied with their working lives. Dull, repetitive, seemingly meaningless tasks, offering little challenge or autonomy, are causing discontent among workers at all occupational levels." The report went on to say that "having an interesting job is now as important as having a job that pays well" (as cited in Ross, 2003, p. 6).

Fourth, and related, political unrest increased in the 1960s, much of it directed at the government and large corporations. The anti-Vietnam War movement, the feminist movement, and the Civil Rights movement all critiqued large, entrenched bureaucracies as obstacles to social change. This political unrest came to a head in May 1968, with large demonstrations and confrontations with the authorities in countries around the world, but particularly in France, where at the height of the civil unrest 10 million French workers were on strike. Moreover, large corporations were critiqued not only as inhumane to their employees but also as damaging to consumers and the environment. Books like Rachel Carson's (1962) *Silent Spring* (which explored the effects of the chemical DDT on the environment) and Ralph Nader's (1965) *Unsafe at Any Speed* (which revealed dangerous design flaws in U.S.-made automobiles) had a significant impact on people's faith in large corporations. And important writers like Studs Terkel (1972) in his book *Working* and Huw Beynon (1973) in *Working for Ford* provided important insights into the damaging effects of unrewarding work (both bodily and spiritually) on people's lives.

In short, by the 1970s, capitalism faced a serious challenge to its legitimacy, largely due to the fact that it faced a crisis of capital accumulation. In other words, capitalism wasn't doing what it was supposed to do—create wealth (i.e., capital) and happiness! The great stabilizing factor in the post-World War II period had been that capitalism was creating wealth and opportunity for everyone—workers and capitalists alike. But now capitalism wasn't providing that sense of stability and opportunity. As a result, the economic elites faced increased political challenges, particularly from labor unions. Moreover, in the 1970s the share of wealth enjoyed by the top 1% of the population (which had remained fairly stable throughout the post-war years) began to fall. Thus, the economic and political elites had to do something if they were to retain their grip on economic and political power.

Their response to this crisis resulted in what Boltanski and Chiapello (2005) call the third spirit of capitalism. This third spirit had three elements: (1) a new economic system called neoliberalism, (2) an accompanying set of social and political developments that altered how we think about our relationship to the world—neoliberalism as a hegemonic discourse, and (3) the emergence of a post-Fordist organizational form that restructured work itself, enabled in part by new technologies (something we will talk about in detail in a later chapter). In the next three sections, then, we will examine each of these developments more carefully and explore their impact on the present-day workplace.

⚬ NEOLIBERALISM AS AN ECONOMIC SYSTEM

In defining **neoliberalism** (literally, "new liberalism"), let's first distinguish it from liberalism. While today in politics people might define themselves as liberal or conservative, historically speaking, liberalism has referred to a political and economic philosophy in which the freedom of the individual is the defining feature of a society. The role of government in such a system is both to protect these freedoms and limit its involvement in the lives of individuals. Classic liberal theorists of the 1700s, including Adam Smith, John Locke, and David Ricardo, argued that the common interest is served by enabling individuals to pursue their own economic self-interest, and hence, the primary role of government should be to allow the economic freedom of the individual to flourish.

Neoliberalism, on the other hand, constituted a reworking of classic liberalism for a 20th-century capitalist economy. Developed in the mid-20th century, neoliberalism was in part a response to concerns that the role of the state in people's lives was growing too large. The term *neoliberalism* was first coined in 1938 by the German economist Alexander Rüstow, but it did not become a coherent philosophy until after World War II when a group called the Mont Pelerin Society (named after the Swiss resort where it met in 1947) developed a set of economic and political principles that it hoped would provide an alternative to the Keynesian model that was increasingly dominant at that time. As we saw in Chapter 3, under Keynesian economics the state plays a central role in maintaining full employment, stimulating economic growth, and providing for the welfare of its citizens (e.g., by providing universal health care, state pensions, unemployment benefits, etc.). Under neoliberalism the state's role is significantly reduced, functioning largely to create and maintain economic policies that enable a free market to flourish. Central to neoliberalism, then, is individual freedom over collective interests, the protection of private property rights, and a free market unregulated by government intervention.

But how is neoliberalism different from the classic liberal model identified above? In brief, neoliberals argue that classic liberalism did not go far enough; it restricted itself to the creation of a political and economic system that enabled the individual to exercise his or her economic and political self-interest. Neoliberalism, however, argues that to maximize the social good, the model of the market must be extended to all realms of society. In other words, under neoliberalism, the market becomes the guide for all human action; it must become a way of life (we will unpack this idea further in the next section).

While the philosophy of neoliberalism was developed by members of the Mont Pelerin group—including, most famously, Friedrich Hayek (1944) and Milton Friedman (1982)— right after World War II, it remained a relatively obscure philosophy until the 1980s, when it was implemented as economic policy by President Ronald Reagan in the United States and by Prime Minister Margaret Thatcher in the United Kingdom. Both Reagan and Thatcher pursued policies that focused on limited government, breaking the power of unions (Reagan famously fired striking air traffic control workers, and the Thatcher government engaged in a protracted and often violent struggle with the National Union of Mineworkers), selling off publicly owned services (Thatcher sold off British Rail to private companies and allowed people in public housing to purchase their houses), and giving large tax breaks to the wealthy (in 1981, for example, Reagan cut the top individual income tax rate from 70% to 50%; today the highest rate is 37%). Indeed, Ronald Reagan identified the government itself as the main obstacle to economic growth, stating in his first inaugural address in 1981, "In our present crisis, government is not the solution to our problem; government is the problem" (Boyer, 1990, p. 31). For Reagan, individual entrepreneurship was the cure for the evils of big government.

Perhaps most famously, Margaret Thatcher commented in a 1987 interview on BBC Radio, "[W]ho is society? There is no such thing! There are individual men and women and there are families and no government can do anything except through people and people look to themselves first. . . . There is no such thing as society." In many ways, this quote captured neoliberal philosophy, with its reversal of the individual-society relationship. While Keynesianism saw society—maintained by government—as the system that provided individuals with a social safety net, neoliberalism views society as an impediment both to the efficiency of markets and to the ability of individuals to realize their full potential as enterprising beings. Under neoliberalism, then, the individual is sovereign.

What is interesting from an organizational communication perspective is that while neoliberalism began as an economic philosophy, it has evolved into a fundamental, taken for granted way of thinking about life in general (which again distinguishes it from classical liberalism). In this sense, we might say that neoliberalism is now a hegemonic discourse; that is, it is a common sense way for us to understand ourselves and the larger social and economic world in which we live (Hall & O'Shea, 2013). As such, communication plays a central role in neoliberalism in that (a) neoliberalism very much shapes how we communicate with each other and (b) organizations under neoliberalism (i.e., post-Fordist organizations) are increasingly communicative structures in that they are dependent on complex communication processes for their profitability. Let's unpack these ideas further in the next two sections.

⬡ NEOLIBERALISM AS A HEGEMONIC DISCOURSE

When we say that neoliberalism is a hegemonic discourse, we mean that it is a dominant way of thinking and talking about the world and our relationship to it (Harvey, 2005).

However, it is dominant not in the sense of being imposed on us but in the sense that we spontaneously and automatically think of ourselves and engage with the world in ways that reflect a neoliberal worldview. According to French sociologists Pierre Dardot and Christian Laval (2013), "At stake in neo-liberalism is nothing more, nor less, than the form of our existence—the way in which we are led to conduct ourselves, to relate to others and ourselves" (p. 3).

But what is the nature of this relationship? In simple terms, neoliberalism as a hegemonic discourse employs the logic of the market not only for the economic sphere but also for every sphere of life. The market becomes the principle through which human beings are both governed and govern themselves. In other words, the market provides the guide for all human action. Whether we are talking about our work, education, personal lives, or even our very sense of self and identity, we use a market logic to judge the quality and worth of our lives. For example, the quality of our education is assessed not in terms of the degree to which it provides us with critical thinking skills and makes us more engaged citizens (part of the classic liberal tradition) but in terms of how well it translates into a well-paid job. Many of you, we're sure, have frequently been asked by friends and family "What are you going to do with that major?" (particularly if you are a communication or humanities-related major!). Implicit in this question is "How on earth are you going to get a (well-paying) job with that major?" In this sense, the education system is understood via a market logic (Lair & Wieland, 2012).

At the center of this neoliberal logic of the market is the idea that each social actor must be viewed as **human capital** (Becker, 1976; Foucault, 2008); that is, we each possess a set of skills, knowledge, and abilities that we are responsible for maintaining and improving so that we accumulate more capital (and hence accrue more market value). While under Fordism, it was the role of capitalists to take the risks associated with raising and investing capital to create profit and wealth; under neoliberalism, individual workers become the risk takers and are encouraged to see themselves as forms of human capital—that is, permanent and ongoing commercial projects that compete with all other social actors for market share in order to increase their value. Under neoliberalism, then, each individual is a mini-enterprise in constant competition with other mini-enterprises for comparative advantage.

Importantly, then, we can say that under neoliberal discourse risk has become both pervasive and naturalized—something that is everywhere an accepted feature of daily life. In this sense, we are all—to a greater or lesser degree, "venture labor" (Neff, 2012), trying to manage and make sense of risk in our daily lives, particularly as it pertains to making a living. Communication professor Gina Neff coined the term **venture labor** as a play on the widely used "venture capital," which refers to the investment that "venture capitalists" make in startup firms in the hope of future profits on their investments (think *Shark Tank* here). Neff defines venture labor as "the investment of time, energy, human capital, and other personal resources that ordinary employees make in the companies where they work. Venture labor is the explicit expression of entrepreneurial values by nonentrepreneurs" (2012, p. 16). In simple terms, with this neoliberal discourse, society has shifted away from collective responsibility toward greater personal responsibility for economic well-being. We must all spend a lot of time and energy investing in ourselves as human capital, even though most of us work for others.

What, then, are the consequences of this hegemonic neoliberal discourse for how we think about ourselves in relationship to work and organization? Let's unpack some of the main issues below.

The Enterprise Self

As venture labor, we must all engage in forms of self-entrepreneurship and self-branding (we will talk about branding in more detail in Chapter 10). That is, because we are all mini-enterprises, we must learn how to develop a strong brand and constantly promote it in ways that differentiate us from all other brands in the marketplace. In other words, how do we develop a USP (unique selling proposition) as individuals who have something valuable to offer in the marketplace? As management guru Tom Peters (1997) states in his article "The Brand Called You," "Everyone has a chance to be a brand worthy of remark." But to do this, we must all be entrepreneurs of the self, willing to think of ourselves as commodities to be sold on the open market. Thus, "If you're going to be a brand, you've got to become relentlessly focused on what you do that adds value, that you're proud of, and most important, that you can shamelessly take credit for" (Peters, 1997). This idea is perhaps not new to you, as for many years you have been encouraged to do precisely this (M. Harris, 2017). Indeed, we suspect that many of you think of your résumés as summaries of your efforts to develop your own unique brands. Your extracurricular activities, leadership responsibilities, volunteer work, and so forth, are all ways to create for yourself a USP that will set you apart from the tens of thousands of other students who are trying to do the same thing. In other words, you think of yourself (at least implicitly) from an entrepreneurial perspective—as human capital that needs to create economic value. Thus, we can say that, under neoliberalism, enterprise has become a mode of subjectivation; that is, we are socialized into thinking and acting as individual enterprises that must compete against all other individuals/enterprises. As Jay Z puts it in Kanye West's "Diamonds from Sierra Leone (Remix)," "I am not a business man. I am a business, man." This quote not only nicely summarizes the enterprise self but also demonstrates the importance of correct punctuation!

Social theorist Nikolas Rose has argued that education itself now falls very much under the hegemonic discourse of neoliberalism, as the **enterprise self** becomes closely tied to what it means to be a citizen under neoliberalism: "The new citizen is required to engage in a ceaseless work of training and retraining, skilling and reskilling, enhancement of credentials and preparation for a life of ceaseless job seeking: life is to become a continuous economic capitalization of the self" (Rose, 1999, p. 161). Thus, when we talk about personal growth, we often mean this in the sense of accumulating our human capital, and thus as a move toward enhancing our employability. In this sense, "working on the self comes to coincide with job training" (Bröckling, 2016, p. 35). This shift is quite different from life under Fordism, when companies invested in their employees by providing them with on-the-job training that increased their value to the company; workers became a repository of knowledge and experience that maintained and increased the quality of a company's products.

Under neoliberalism, then, employees are expected to invest in themselves as a way to increase their value on the open market. One increasingly common way for people make this investment (in the hope of securing better jobs) is by enrolling in for-profit universities that saddle them with large amounts of debt that they are frequently unable to pay off. Sociologist Tressie McMillan Cottom (2017) reframes these for-profit colleges as sources of economic insurance: "The more insecure people feel, the more they are willing to spend money for an insurance policy against low wages, unemployment, and downward mobility." Ironically, the people most likely to enroll in such for-profit programs are at the lower end of the economic scale to begin with, thus increasing the levels of inequality in our society. Moreover, as discussed above, as individual enterprises we are socialized to engage in risk taking. Under neoliberalism, risk has become an ideology that can be used to explain inequality and social stratification. In other words, it is those who are prepared to take risks who will get ahead, and those who don't, will be left behind. Thus, running up extensive student debt (now $1.4 trillion in the United States) is a risk worth taking because it can be made sense of as investment in (potential) future success.

In an important way, then, we can say that under neoliberalism all workers have to become their own "micro-structures" (McRobbie, 2016, p. 18). In other words, because the social structures that typically provided security under Fordism (family, class, community, career, etc.) have been eroded, many people (particularly those in the gig economy) are expected to manage life and its uncertainties on their own. Cultural studies scholar Angela McRobbie (2016) argues, for example, that workers in the creative industries (advertising, design, fashion, PR, etc.) attempt to make up for the instability in their job situations (in which they typically move from gig to gig) by investing their work with romance and passion. Even though their work may be insecure, low paid, and involve long hours, they see it as meaningful, creative, and an escape from the boredom and alienation of traditional white-collar office work. Communication professor Brooke Duffy (2017) summarizes this condition of the contemporary neoliberal worker when she states, "The idealized neoliberal worker-subject is entrepreneurial, self-directed, flexible, and available to work incessantly" (p. 226).

Thus, under neoliberalism, society is experienced as much more atomistic, with individuals experiencing greater isolation and disconnection from others. While the Keynesian economy under Fordism might be described as a **WATT system** ("We're all in this together"), the neoliberal economy can be thought of as a **YOYO system** ("You're on your own"). As one of journalist Nathan Heller's respondents states, "The gig economy is such a lonely economy" (Heller, 2017). It's odd to think about, but the idea of colleagues and coworkers with whom one develops connections exists for a decreasing number of workers. If you are a gig worker, the chances are that you either work alone (as Heller's interviewee did) or never have the same colleagues for more than a few days or weeks at the most. And then it's on to the next gig. While gig workers are still numerically in the minority compared with permanent workers, economist Gerald Friedman (2014) points out that since 2005, 85% of job growth has been in the area of "alternative work arrangements" (i.e., contract-based gig work). There is a very good chance, then, that many of you reading this text will be part of the gig economy.

Management scholar Peter Fleming (2017) refers to this YOYO discourse as the **radical responsibilization** model of employment: each worker—as an enterprising self—is responsible for his or her success or failure. Thus, the securities of Fordist capitalism are disappearing as companies increasingly divest themselves of their traditional responsibilities toward workers. As we saw in the story that opened this chapter, as an independent contractor Lyft driver Mary must continue to work right up until the time she gives birth, knowing that she doesn't have the security of company health care.

Finally, it is important to point out that there is a strong aspirational quality to the idea of the entrepreneurial self. In other words, the hegemonic discourse of neoliberalism tells us what we ought to be, what we should aspire to. As sociologist Ulrich Bröckling (2016) argues, "The discourse of the entrepreneurial self does not tell people so much what they are; rather, it tells them what they have to become" (p. 21). Thus, we should never be satisfied with who we are or what we have; we should always be aiming to improve and strengthen our human capital. In this sense, our everyday lives become work, as we are constantly engaged in the work of constructing our identities as aspirational, entrepreneurial selves.

CRITICAL RESEARCH 6.1

Katie Sullivan and Helen Delaney (2017). A femininity that "giveth and taketh away": The prosperity gospel and postfeminism in the neoliberal economy. *Human Relations*, 70, 836–859.

Katie Sullivan and Helen Delaney's study is an excellent example of how the hegemony of neoliberal discourse produces particular forms of the entrepreneurial self. In their study of a network marketing company called Arbonne International (seller of personal care products like cosmetics and health supplements), they show how the company draws on two neoliberal discourses—the discourse of the "prosperity gospel" and the discourse of postfeminism—to articulate an image of their ideal, and typically female, consultant (as members are called). The prosperity gospel is a modern-day reworking of the Protestant Ethic (see Chapter 3) in which "the accumulation of capital and consumption are sold as the path towards spiritual enlightenment." (p. 840). In this discourse, God will bless you with health and prosperity if you have a positive attitude and unflappable belief in both God and yourself. The discourse of postfeminism, on the other hand, reframes certain feminist values (empowerment, equality, choice) through a neoliberal market lens; economic success is possible for anyone who "embodies and displays the right enterprising attitudes" (p. 839). In this version of feminism, success is about individual rather than collective empowerment.

In their analysis of a random sample of 42 out of several hundred "Eye On Arbonne Success Stories" provided on the company website, Sullivan and Delaney show how these two discourses appear consistently in these carefully crafted profiles. The authors state, "We quickly noticed a dominant rags-to-riches plot: each story has a beginning that captures an 'old' way of life rife with various struggles; a middle that depicts finding Arbonne and transforming into a 'new' life of

(Continued)

(Continued)

financial and personal abundance; and an ending where the [consultant] gives thanks and offers advice to others about how to succeed" (p. 845). Three themes emerge from their analysis that form the defining features of "evangelical entrepreneurial femininity": (1) a tension between empowerment and a higher power (the organization preaches female empowerment but only through following the path God has chosen for them), (2) a tension between breaking out of and staying within traditional gender identities (women are encouraged to break out in business as long as they continue to perform their gendered roles in the nuclear family), and (3) a mandate to conform to a hyper-feminine aesthetic of beauty and behavior (most of the women in the success stories conform to an ideal of hyper-femininity).

Most interesting, perhaps, is the hidden contradiction in these discourses that the study exposes: Only 10% of all consultants are actually active, and the average yearly earnings for a consultant is $515. Indeed, fully 90% of consultants are unlikely to earn enough to recoup what they initially invested in their products. Thus, what appears to be a discourse of individual empowerment turns out to be empowering for only a tiny fraction of consultants and, in fact, may leave many in a more precarious position than before they signed up with the company. As the authors state, "It is possible that organizations like Arbonne are promoting the evangelical entrepreneurial femininity in order to ideologically prime women to work in precarious employment conditions without complaint" (p. 854).

Discussion Questions

1. Go to the Arbonne International website at https://www.arbonne.com/discover/opportunity/whyarbonne.shtml and read some of the "success stories." To what extent do you agree or disagree with Sullivan and Delaney's analysis?

2. Have you or any friends ever participated in a direct selling network (or attended a direct selling event at someone's house)? What was your experience like?

3. In what ways does the study speak to the hegemonic discourse of neoliberalism and issues associated with the gig economy, the entrepreneurial self, and work insecurity?

Work Insecurity

A general sense of insecurity has rapidly become a defining feature of neoliberal discourse. While under Fordism, the assumption was that work was available even for people with few qualifications, under neoliberalism, everyone lives with a general sense of competition in which one's work status can never be taken for granted. Moreover, under welfare capitalism, society itself had structures in place intended to provide people with a broader sense of existential security, including things like universal health care (available in most developed nations, but not in the United States), pension plans, and so forth. However, neoliberalism argues that a "state of insecurity" (Lorey, 2015) promotes competition among people and hence leads to a more prosperous society in the long term. In this sense, Lorey argues, insecurity is not a condition only of those people on the margins, but it is a normalized condition of neoliberalism to which everyone is subjected.

What do we mean by work insecurity? In his book on precarious workers, Guy Standing (2011, pp. 10–13) argues that there are seven features of security that people are entitled to expect in their work:

1. **Labor market security** provides adequate income-earning opportunities to everyone, characterized by a government commitment to full employment

2. **Employment security** involves worker protection against arbitrary dismissal and regulations regarding hiring and firing workers

3. **Job security** provides stability once employed and enables opportunities for upward mobility in status and income

4. **Work security** provides workplace safety and health regulations, limits on working time, and compensation for workplace injury

5. **Skill reproduction security** involves the opportunity to gain skills at one's job through training, apprenticeships, and so forth.

6. **Income security** assures an adequate stable income (e.g., through minimum wage legislation)

7. **Representation security** enables workers to have a collective voice in the labor market through, for example, unionization and the right to strike.

By this definition, then, any work is considered insecure if it does not adhere to these features of security. Of course, precarity/security is not an either/or measure. For example, people may have labor market security at times of full employment when workers are in heavy demand but may have little employment or representation security if they work in industries (e.g., retail) that permit arbitrary dismissal and are hostile to union organization. However, there is lots of evidence to suggest that companies increasingly adopt an employment model in which they minimize the number of permanent employees and outsource those tasks that are seen as peripheral to the core competencies of the organization (see the section on the post-Fordist organization below). Thus, as sociologist Arne Kalleberg (2009, 2011) has shown, the United States is increasingly divided into "good jobs" and "bad jobs," with an elite core of workers in well-paying relatively secure employment and an increasing number of workers in poorly paid insecure employment. As Kalleberg points out, the shift from the Fordist model of work to post-Fordism has contributed to the disappearance of long-term unskilled or semi-skilled work that occupies the middle ground between these two poles.

The emergence of job insecurity has brought the notion of precarity to the fore, highlighting the idea that many people, even those with fairly well-paid jobs, operate under precarious, uncertain conditions where stable, long-term work is hard to find and short-term gigs have become the norm (Standing, 2011). Thus, the term **precariat** has been coined, referring to a global class of people whose default condition is to be either unemployed or moving continuously from one short-term job to another (or holding several low-paying, temporary jobs simultaneously).

Identity Insecurity

Another feature of neoliberalism as a hegemonic discourse is not only the emergence of insecure work but the emergence of insecure work identity. In other words, while under Fordism, work identity was relatively stable because most workers had a secure career path and a well-developed community of work colleagues; many workers under neoliberalism have a difficult time creating a coherent and stable sense of self. In Chapter 1, we referred to Diane Mulcahy's (2016) instructions to her MBA students that they should join the gig economy and look for work, not for a job. Mulcahy provides three reasons for telling her students this. First, full-time jobs are disappearing, with companies separating work from jobs. So, for example, the number of full-time jobs in journalism is decreasing, but the possibilities for freelance journalist work have increased given the explosion of media outlets. Second, employing full-time workers is a last resort for companies as they attempt to maintain flexibility and minimize costs. Full-time workers are expensive for companies, costing 30% to 40% more than free agent workers because of the benefits packages they must be paid. Third, Mulcahy argues that for most Americans traditional employment arrangements are not working, with 70% of full-time workers not engaged with their jobs. Mulcahy thus proposes that her students have a better chance of being engaged and satisfied in their work lives if they "focus on getting great work rather than a good job."

As Caza, Moss, and Vough (2018; Caza, Vough, and Moss, 2017) have noted, however, the gig economy presents challenges to people's sense of identity in relation to work. We have been socialized to believe that a stable and successful professional career is a defining feature of who we are as people. As Fleming (2017) states, "The objective necessity of a job—paying the bills—is conflated with our sense of individuality and social value" (p. 5). A stable work identity is difficult to maintain, however, when one is moving from one short-term job to the next, or even holding multiple gigs simultaneously. Moreover, this problem of an insecure work identity is compounded by the fact that the traditional anchors for a coherent and secure sense of self—family, class, community, and so on—have become fragmented for many people. This sense of insecurity is further compounded by the process of radical responsibilization (Fleming, 2017) that we discussed above. Because individuals are viewed as mini-enterprises, they are viewed as entirely responsible for their own economic fate; if someone fails to develop a successful skill set that makes them employable, then they have no one to blame but themselves.

Caza et al. (2017) provide three pieces of advice for those who participate in the gig economy but who don't want to lose their sense of self while doing so. Their advice is based on interviews with 48 gig workers who held between two and six jobs.

1. **Be selective in the feedback you get, at least at first.** People with multiple gigs often struggle with the judgments that friends and family make about them being

"uncommitted" or having "career ADD." Negative judgments about gig work can be detrimental to one's self-confidence, so at first explain your multiple jobs only to trusted others until you gain more self-confidence.

2. **Focus on each job until you gain confidence, but then forge connections.** At first, each job should be treated as a distinct role that needs to be developed; clear boundaries between jobs should be set to ensure you are meeting the expectations of each employer or client. Over time, however, you should look to establish common threads across your job portfolio. View each job as part of larger whole that captures your "brand" as a gig worker.

3. **Embrace yourself as being composed of multiple, sometimes distinct, identities.** Accepting that it's OK to hold multiple jobs, despite being contrary to social norms, allows you to forge a different sense of yourself that acknowledges that a multifaceted identity can be an important resource for future career development. As Caza et al. state, "For plural careerists, being authentic *does not* mean being the same across time and context."

Caza et al.'s (2017) advice is interesting in that it reflects both the anxiety that the gig economy creates for people ("How do I handle the absence of a steady job?") and the degree to which the relationship between self and work has become more complicated and problematic ("What does it mean to be authentic in the context of multiple work identities?"). Under Fordism, one did not have to think too much about the work-self relationship; work was something one did to support one's family and to have a sense of contributing to society. People tended to obsess about work only when they were unemployed. Work was important, but it was carefully segmented from other aspects of life. Under neoliberalism, on the other hand, work and self are interconnected in ways that make them almost impossible to separate. Work has to be meaningful and fulfilling; if it isn't, we are somehow failing ourselves. Thus, when Boltanski and Chiapello (2005) talk about the "new [third] spirit" of capitalism, they are in part talking about neoliberal efforts to enjoin people to constantly explore how the sense of self and work intersect, in part as a way to expand one's stock of human capital.

But of course, there is an important catch here. That is, the intimate connections among work, meaning, and identity have become a central pillar of neoliberal discourse precisely at a time when work itself has become more insecure. We must make work a defining element of our sense of self, but that very work is unpredictable and anxiety producing. This conflict produces constant and ongoing identity work in each of us as we seek a stable and coherent sense of self (hence, the kind of advice offered by Caza et al., (2017) above). The gig economy is often framed in positive, virtuous terms (it makes a free agent of everyone who has the autonomy to pursue work that makes one happy), but it is also at the root of many stresses and anxieties. Work under neoliberalism involves a constant process of managing the self in conditions of radical uncertainty (Gill, 2008).

CRITICAL CASE STUDY 6.1

Is Oprah a Neoliberal?

Everyone loves Oprah. Her personal story is truly inspirational: She grew up poor in the segregated Deep South, experienced sexual abuse as a child, but by sheer grit and determination became a truly global popular culture icon (measured by the fact that she doesn't need a last name) who today is one of the richest and most powerful women in the world. *The Oprah Winfrey Show* ran from 1986 to 2011 and was the top-rated show in its time slot for all of those 25 seasons. Her show has morphed into a media empire, bringing her a personal net worth of almost $3 billion as of 2018. She is a renowned philanthropist, supporting many causes (by 2012, she had given $400 million to educational causes) and funds the Oprah Winfrey Leadership Academy in South Africa. Her book club got millions of people to read. There's even been talk of her running for president. But a neoliberal? Let's make the case.

If there is one thing on which Oprah has focused throughout her career (through her show and her other media outlets including *O* magazine), it is the individual self. In the early years (1986–1994) of her show, her focus was on what has been called the "recovery paradigm" (Peck, 2016), in which family and relational dysfunction figured very prominently. Given the show's audience, many of Oprah's shows profiled women in dysfunctional relationships with men. "Women Who Love Too Much" (based on a popular book of the mid-1980s) was a common theme. Oprah would have lots of experts on her show (e.g., Dr. Phil) who would explain how these women failed to recognize (usually because of their psychological makeup) the problems in their relationships. As communication scholar Janice Peck (2016) argues, "The Oprah Winfrey Show's appropriation of a recovery framework of intelligibility served to depoliticize women's struggles by translating them into individual psychological defects. This psychologization process was also extended to the show's treatment of explicitly political-economic issues, such as poverty, homelessness, welfare, and unemployment" (p. 10). In this sense, Oprah's approach was to reduce the social to the personal and the political to the psychological, in many respects echoing the neoliberal themes of the Reagan era, in which an ideology of "pull yourself up by your bootstraps" was operant.

In 1994, Oprah announced that she was "done with negativity" and was embarking on a mission to "lift people up" (Peck, 2016, p. 130). Thus, she became an important part of the burgeoning happiness industry, which focuses on the idea that happiness depends on individual cognition and emotion rather than on political, social, or economic conditions. Psychologist Edgar Cabanas (2017) argues, "Happiness has become part of a commonsensical discourse through which the neoliberal ideology of individualism is rekindled, legitimized, and institutionalized" (p. 176). For Oprah, being happy is about turning one's gaze inward and engaging in processes of self-actualization. It's about "harnessing your power to your passion" (Winfrey, 2018) and discovering your authentic calling in life regardless of your societal position. Anyone can achieve self-actualization if he or she can liberate his or her true inner self. In this model, thoughts are destiny: Think positively, and you'll make it; think negatively, and you'll fail to realizes your inner potential.

Thus, one can make the case that Oprah's appeal is heavily based on her ability to tell stories about spiritual awakening and self-actualization that hide or obscure the function of larger social, political, and economic structures (Aschoff, 2015). In Oprah's worldview, structure and individual agency are synonymous. Her message is, you have choices, and external factors do not determine your life. However, the reality is that the amount of social capital (the network of relations you have access to), cultural capital (education, intellect, style of speech), and economic capital (wealth) to which you have access has a profound effect on life chances. But Oprah's message of self-fulfillment and self-actualization consistently obscures the functioning of social, cultural, and economic capital. For example, in a sample of 13 wealthy countries, the Unites States ranks highest on levels of inequality and lowest on intergenerational earnings mobility (the degree to which wealth is passed from generation to generation).

As we have illustrated in this chapter, the self is a particular focus of attention in neoliberalism. In this view, we are all independent, autonomous actors who meet and compete in the marketplace; we create our destinies, and in the process, construct society. We argue that Oprah reinforces and legitimates this neoliberal version of self. Consistent with the ethos of neoliberalism, Oprah draws on a self-help model of therapy in which we are expected to adapt to a changing world rather than change the world we live in. We must turn our gaze inward and reconfigure ourselves to adapt to neoliberalism. As Nicole Aschoff (2015) states in her analysis of Oprah, "We demand little or nothing from the system, from the collective apparatus of powerful people and institutions. We only make demands of ourselves. We are the perfect, depoliticized, complacent neoliberal subjects." In this worldview, the power of capitalism to create inequality and limit life choices is ignored.

Discussion Questions

1. Do you agree that Oprah is a neoliberal? Do you see this as a good or bad thing?

2. In her analysis of Oprah, Aschoff (2015) states, "Spirituality, self-actualization, and stuff are inseparable." What does this quote mean? How does this reflect the neoliberal moment?

3. Check out the TED talk by Gary Vaynerchuk at the link below. How does he reflect the Oprah model of neoliberalism? How is he different?

https://www.ted.com/talks/gary_vaynerchuk_do_what_you_love_no_excuses

Having discussed the broad features of neoliberalism as a discourse and the ways in which it shapes our relationship to ourselves and work, we can now talk about the specific features of work and organizational communication under neoliberalism—the post-Fordist workplace.

⚬ THE POST-FORDIST WORKPLACE: A NEW ORGANIZATIONAL MODEL

The emergence of neoliberalism as a hegemonic discourse over the last 30 years has led to some profound changes in the 21st-century work organization. As neoliberalism emerged as the dominant economic model for capitalism, so organizations began to restructure themselves to better take advantage of the more turbulent economic environment that characterized the post-Keynesian period. In this section, we look in more detail at the specific ways in which the structure and communication processes of organizations have changed as a result of the demise of Fordism and the rise of post-Fordism.

The "Fissured" Workplace

Labor researcher David Weil (2014) argues that in the last 30 years the very concept of the corporation as it was defined for most of the 20th century has been rethought, and we now live in the age of the **fissured workplace**. What does this mean? Weil argues that the emergence of the fissured workplace is a direct consequence of increasing pressure from capital markets (investors in companies) to improve returns. Thus, "companies who adopt fissured employment strategies aim to improve profitability by focusing attention and controlling the most profitable aspects of firm value while shedding the actual production of goods or provision of services" (Weil, 2014, p. 25). As examples of fissured workplaces, Apple does not employ anyone who actually makes iPhones or iPads, Nike does not employ anyone who makes sports attire, and (as mentioned above) Uber does not employ anyone who drives a taxi. In each case, these companies have adopted the following mantra: "Find your distinctive niche and stick to it. Then shed everything else" (Weil, 2014, p. 50). What Apple does best is design sleek and sexy personal devices, what Nike does best is design and market fitness and lifestyle products, what Uber does best is provide a digital platform that coordinates riders and drivers.

What characterizes the fissured workplace, then, is the idea that in order to maximize returns, companies need to figure out their core competencies (what provides greatest value to consumers and investors) and move every other aspect of their business outside the company. For example, once Nike recognized in the early 1980s that it was not a running-shoe manufacturer but a fitness and lifestyle company, their business model changed completely; its core competency thus became design and branding, and everything not connected to that core mission was outsourced, including the actual manufacturing of its products. The same is true across corporate life. For example, you might assume that when you stay in a hotel, the people who clean your room are employed by that hotel, but there's every chance that they come from a staffing agency. Similarly, when you call AT&T with a problem regarding your wireless account, the person you speak with will likely be working out of a call center in India and is not an AT&T employee at all. What are the consequences of this fissuring process?

Weil (2014) argues that the fissured workplace creates a precarious and unstable work environment for lots of workers. First, fissuring practices affect labor standards. For example, it's not uncommon for employment agencies to farm out their contracts to still other, smaller agencies. Because each level of a fissured workplace needs to be able to make money, the further down the chain one goes, the slimmer the profit margins become. The result is that companies often cut corners to maintain profits, including engaging in wage theft and nonpayment of overtime to workers. The U.S. Department of Labor's (n.d.) Wage and Hour Division, for example, reports that from 2012 to 2017 it recovered $1.2 billion in back pay (wages that should have been paid but weren't) for workers. This total amounts to $1,125 for every worker who was due back wages, or almost 4 weeks of work for a retail cashier, almost 3 paychecks for a security guard, and 3.5 paychecks for a maid or house-keeper. This amount is equivalent to 5 weeks of food, a month of rent, or 6 weeks of child care. This $1.2 billion, of course, does not account for all the wage theft that failed to ever get reported.

A second problem with fissured workplaces is that wages generally tend to be lowered and benefits often disappear when you are a contract worker. Furthermore, as temporary employees, contract workers don't get access to career and skills training or opportunities for promotion and pay increases. For example, someone working in IT or doing cleri-cal work as a contract worker will most likely be receiving lower pay than a permanent worker doing exactly the same work. Moreover, they will not be eligible for company health care, pension benefits, and so forth. It is also much more difficult to feel connected to your colleagues (and vice versa) when the chances are that you will be at the company for only a matter of days or weeks; the chance to learn from coworkers, or to create knowl-edge about how to solve problems, also dissipates. As we saw earlier, gig and contract work is frequently a lonely and dispiriting experience, and that loneliness has consequences for both individuals and organizations.

Finally, the fissured workplace can subject workers to greater health and safety risks. If someone is injured on the job, whose responsibility is that? Is it the staffing agency that officially employs the worker, or the company where the worker is actually working? Compounding this issue, the tighter profit margins further down the chain of fissured work often mean that companies are more likely to skimp on health and safety training for workers in order to cut costs and maintain those margins.

We raise these issues about the new organizational model of post-Fordism because there has been a lot of hype over the last few years about the brave new world of work in which we are living. In this vision, work is liberating, exciting, and full of opportuni-ties to improve oneself and lead a happy and fulfilling life. Titles like *Free Agent Nation* (Pink, 2001) and *The 4-Hour Work Week* (Ferriss, 2007) encourage the idea that we can all jettison boring 9 to 5 jobs and gain a (literally) rich and rewarding life of work and play if we can just get our acts together and put a plan into action (by of course, purchasing the latest how-to book and not coincidently, making the author of that book rich). In reality, many people live from paycheck to paycheck and are burdened with debt. For example, total consumer debt in the United States is projected to reach $4 trillion by the end of 2018 (Konish, 2018), and the class of 2016 is carrying an average student loan debt of $37,172 (Z. Friedman, 2018). Moreover, 69% of Americans have less than $1,000 in savings on average (McCarthy, 2016). The vision of the happy, fulfilled, well-compensated work-from-home or coffee shop gig employee is far from reality for most workers, many of whom may have to work multiple jobs to make ends meet (sometimes as many as six, as Caza et al. (2017) indicate above).

Thus, as we discuss the remaining features of the post-Fordist organization, it's important to keep in mind that this kind of organization and the work that it entails is often available only to the kind of core workers that Weil (2014) is speaking about—that is, the educated knowledge workers who are employed full-time in research and development, design, branding, and marketing. However, it is also true that actually being a highly educated knowledge worker does not automatically provide access to stable core employment; there are lots of knowledge workers (often those in creative industries such as digital media, design, PR, and advertising) who are part of the gig economy and experience unpredictable work lives (Duffy, 2017; McRobbie, 2016).

A Flexible Organizational Structure

As the notion of the fissured workplace indicates, one of the most frequently touted features of the post-Fordist organization is its flexibility as an organizational form. While the bureaucratic, hierarchical Fordist organization helped to provide stability and long-term planning during the heyday of capitalist economic growth in the post–WWII period, many economists and business leaders saw it as increasingly unable to adapt to the more turbulent economic environment that began to emerge in the 1970s, as global markets became more volatile and unpredictable. The transformation to a more flexible organizational structure, then, is a direct response to the need for businesses to be more adaptive to environmental change. What does greater flexibility mean? Geographer David Harvey (1991) has outlined three dimensions of flexibility that characterize the post-Fordist organization.

Flexibility in the work process itself. While Fordist organizations tended to involve large capital investments in heavy and costly machinery that made large quantities of the same product (think Henry Ford and the Model-T automobile), post-Fordist organizations put in place a labor process in which flexibility and adaptability are key. One way to think about this shift is to see Fordism as focused on the product (and lots of it) and post-Fordism as focused on the process of production. The focus on process is an innovation that began in the 1950s in Japan at Toyota (hence, the system is often referred to as Toyotism to contrast it with Fordism and Taylorism). Its introduction saved the company from the brink of bankruptcy and grew it into the world's largest auto manufacturer as of 2016.

The fundamental element of this process orientation is the philosophy of Kaizen (pronounced Ky-zen), a Japanese term that means continuous improvement. Rather than workers being instructed in the one best way to do their jobs, the flexibility of the production process means that workers are encouraged to continuously look for ways that the work itself can be improved. A good example of how this works in practice is provided by a company called FastCap (2011); two employees working on a fairly simple task are encouraged by their supervisor to work together and find creative ways to make the work more efficient; with little input from the supervisor, they are able to cut the time for the task from 45 seconds to under 15 seconds, simply by focusing on the process of the task itself. However, the Kaizen process not only makes work more efficient, but also enables manufacturing errors to be eliminated from the labor process (this benefit is one of the reasons why Japanese cars have historically been more reliable than American cars—because of U.S. automobile manufacturers' focus on the end product with a fixed production process).

Another important element in the flexibility of the labor process is the **just-in-time** (JIT) principle. Originally developed in the 1950s by Ohno Taiichi, who was in charge of production at Toyota, the JIT system is part of a lean production system in which a company increases efficiency and minimizes waste by maintaining a minimal level of inventory. Often, a company might maintain only enough stock to meet production for a single day, and inventory is maintained only to fill current customer orders. This system enables maximum flexibility as the production process can be changed to meet new customer orders as they are received. The JIT system requires a close relationship with suppliers, as a break in the company supply chain can create havoc in the production process if little inventory is maintained. Moreover, JIT also depends on relationships with customers; companies constantly seek feedback from their customer bases for information about products to be produced. Thus, instead of making a product and then creating customer interest (as under Fordism), a market is found and then a product is produced to fill the demand. The JIT system enables this flexibility, contrasting sharply with the Fordist just-in-case system where massive inventories are maintained (at great expense), thus minimizing the ability to adapt to changing customer demand (and also minimizing efficiency). Thus, we can say that while Fordism was strongly production-oriented with large economies of scale, post-Fordism is more heavily consumption-oriented with smaller economies of scale often aimed at specific niche consumer markets.

Flexibility in labor markets. In addition to flexibility in the labor process itself, post-Fordist organizations also depend on a flexible labor market through the extensive use of subcontracting and part-time and temporary employees. As we saw in the above discussion of the fissured workplace, many companies no longer employ a large, permanent workforce because (a) it is expensive and (b) it limits the organization's ability to maintain flexibility and adapt to changing market conditions. Thus, flexible labor markets reflect the new reality of the gig economy that an increasing number of workers experience. The service and retail industries employ large numbers of temporary and part-time workers, making them able to respond in real time to fluctuations in customer demand. But temporary, part-time, and subcontracted work is increasingly common in all areas of the economy as companies look to cut costs and maintain flexibility. There's a very good chance, for example, that the workers who clean dorm rooms or serve you food on your campus are employed by subcontractors and not by the university itself.

Greater geographic mobility. This final feature of post-Fordist organizational flexibility operates on two levels. First, geographic flexibility refers to the development and implementation of communication technologies that free workers up from being tied to a specific physical organizational site. Many employees these days practice **telework**, in which some or all of their work is performed from a remote location (typically at home or in a coffee shop somewhere). Many jobs, especially those involving digital labor (e.g., web design, graphic design, coding, etc.) do not require workers to be copresent and can be performed anywhere as long as there is Internet access. The advantage of such remote work is that, theoretically at least, employees can experience more autonomy and greater work-life flexibility (e.g., it's much easier to run errands or pick up a child from day care if your work day is flexible). However, two problems frequently emerge from telework. First, many employees report what communication scholar Melissa Gregg (2011) calls "presence bleed." This problem occurs when the boundaries between one's professional and personal identities largely disappear and work becomes ever-present, regardless of one's activity (e.g., replying to work-related emails late or night, or even while lying on the beach during a vacation). In this sense, for many employees, work mode is never fully turned off. The second problem associated with telework is social isolation. As we saw above, gig work is especially prone to this condition, but even full-time workers can experience isolation if they are rarely copresent with colleagues. Former Yahoo CEO Marissa Mayer caused quite a stir when, in 2013, she introduced a no-working-from-home policy. The memo her office issued to Yahoo employees stated, "To become the absolute best place to work, communication and collaboration will be important, so we need to be working side-by-side. That is why it is critical that we are all present in our offices" (Swisher, 2013).

The second form of geographical flexibility involves the increased use of outsourcing and the moving of production to wherever labor costs are cheapest. Thus, Apple outsources its production of iPhones, iPads, and Macs to a Chinese company called Foxconn, one of the world's largest electronics manufacturing companies with over one million workers at its various plants. Similarly, Nike contracts with 150 shoe factories in 14 different countries to manufacture its footwear, and with 430 different factories in 41 different countries for its apparel. While outsourcing significantly reduces costs and increases profit margins, it can also create significant problems. In 2010, for example, a series of employee suicides at Foxconn drew attention to the poor working conditions at many plants and created much negative publicity for Apple. Similarly, Nike has been criticized for the sweatshop conditions at many of the factories where its products are made.

A High Trust, "Dedifferentiated" Labor Process

A companion to the flexible organizational structure is the development of a high trust, dedifferentiated labor process. As we saw in Chapter 3, work under Fordism featured an extreme division of labor with deskilled workers. Moreover, workers were alienated from their work and little trust existed between management and employees (recall Collinson's "Engineering Humor" study from Chapter 2). Under post-Fordism, on the other hand, work is characterized by a high level of trust between workers and managers, and workers are given significant decision-making autonomy. Furthermore, the labor process itself is dedifferentiated; that is, work tends to involve higher levels of skill and is not divided into its most basic elements. In many ways, the knowledge worker is the archetypal employee of the post-Fordist organization. Such workers are not provided with a narrowly defined job description, as under Fordism; rather, they are encouraged to use their initiative to carve out their own sphere of responsibility and competence. David Stark's (2009) story about the former IBM employee who failed to adapt to his new job at a startup (reported in Chapter 5) is a good example of how this shift from Fordism to post-Fordism has changed the character of work for employees. The job of this worker was not to fulfill the responsibilities of the job to which he was assigned but rather to use his initiative to create a position for himself—that is, to figure out what added value he could bring to the company, given his knowledge and skill set.

This example brings up another important feature of the post-Fordist organization; that is, the management function is increasingly displaced onto the workers themselves. Practically speaking, this displacement has translated into the widespread use over the last 30 years of team-based organizing. In many respects, the emergence of work teams and the "team-based organization" under post-Fordism (Mohrman, Cohen, & Mohrman, 1995) is a throwback to an earlier period in the history of work when workers functioned together in skilled, self-organizing groups, largely determining how (and how quickly) work was performed. Indeed, if you recall our discussion of scientific management in Chapter 3, one of Taylor's principal goals in developing a new system of work was to break up the informal group that—through systematic soldiering—dictated the pace of work. Such work groups existed not only in factory settings but also in industries such as coal mining, where miners worked in teams not as a way to limit output but as the most effective way to perform a difficult, dirty, and dangerous job (Trist, & Bamforth, 1951; Trist, Higgin, Murray, & Pollock, 1963). Trist and Bamforth (1951) describe the organization of work in the traditional hand-got (nonmechanized) form of mining in the following manner:

> A primary work-organization of this type has the advantage of placing responsibility for the complete coal-getting task squarely on the shoulders of a single, small, face-to-face group which experiences the entire cycle of operations within the compass of its membership. For each participant the task has total significance and dynamic closure. . . . Leadership and "supervision" were internal to the group, which had a quality of *responsible autonomy*. (p. 6)

The management fascination with work teams has become even more intense given the shift to post-Fordism. As organizations have become more decentralized and less hierarchical, work teams are seen as the ideal decision-making structure in an economic environment that requires flexibility, adaptability, and innovation. From a management perspective, the advantages of work teams include the following:

- Empowerment of workers by enabling them to play a more direct role in organizational decision making
- Development of a workforce that is multiskilled rather than deskilled
- Development of holistic team synergies (think systems theory) that often result in more innovative decision making
- Subordination of individual employees' agendas to the collective task of the team
- Higher-quality decisions as a result of the pooling of team member talents
- Functional autonomy, with little need for direct supervision
- Greater commitment of employees to organizational goals
- Increased organizational productivity

iStock.com/tomazl

Team-building exercises are as much a feature of post-Fordist work as learning job skills.

As we will see in Chapter 7, however, work teams have been subject to considerable criticism because of the ways in which they frequently increase the amount of work stress that employees experience. Indeed, management scholar Amanda Sinclair (1992) has referred to the "tyranny of a team ideology" to describe some of these issues. Where teams are presented as the models of consensus building, issues such as power and conflict among team members often are underplayed.

Communication, the "Social Factory," and Immaterial Labor

So far in this chapter we have not talked in any detail about the centrality of communication to neoliberalism and the post-Fordist organization. However, in this section we will examine how fundamental communication has become not only to work itself but also to the way in which value is created under neoliberal capitalism. The emergence of the knowledge worker and the knowledge economy under neoliberalism and post-Fordism has in many ways changed not only the nature of work, but also the way in which economic value is created. As we saw in Chapter 3, under Fordism value was created through the mass production of physical goods within a particular, clearly defined workplace. Value was created by intensifying the labor process and converting the potential to labor (labor power) to actual labor productivity. Organizations made profit by creating surplus value (i.e., the difference between what workers were paid and the amount of value created by their labor) through the production process itself. Thus, the management theories we discussed in Chapter 3 were all focused on how the labor process could be intensified in order to produce more surplus value in the work setting itself. Under post-Fordism, however, three aspects of the labor process have changed. First, we have witnessed the emergence of the **social factory**. This refers to the idea that, under post-Fordism, the process of economic value production has escaped the walls of the factory and has become dispersed throughout society (Bohm & Land, 2012; Gill & Pratt, 2008; Kuhn, 2006; Lazzarato, 2004; Mumby, 2016). Second, much of the value production process in the social factory takes the form of **immaterial labor**, that is, "labor that produces the informational and cultural content of the commodity" (Lazzarato, 1996, p. 133). Third, this process of producing the cultural content of the commodity is fundamentally communication based. Let's unpack each of these ideas in turn.

First, the social factory tries to capture the changing nature of the value creation process under post-Fordism, and reflects the degree to which life itself is now going to work in the social factory (Fleming, 2014b). The best way to illustrate this is to provide an example. Critical management theorists Chris Land and Scott Taylor (2010) illustrate the operation of the social factory in the study of a company they call "Ethico." Ethico is a small clothing company employing about 25 workers, most of whom work in sales and marketing. The focus of Land and Taylor's analysis is on the various ways in which the distinction between work and life has largely broken down at Ethico. Indeed, the leisure activities of the employees are very much at the center of the company's value creation process. Thus, when one of the employees used her "too nice to work" voucher (awarded to staff for a good sales quarter) to take a day off and go sea kayaking, her day at the beach became a company branding opportunity, and she blogged about her day off on the company website. Thus, what was ostensibly a day of leisure away from work became a company marketing opportunity, and hence value creation. Another designer, Richard, wrote a blog entry called "Tattoos Can Be Bought, Scars Have to Be Earned," in which he talked about his love of skateboarding and the injuries he has sustained (the reference to tattoos is an implicit critique of inauthentic Nike employees who get Swoosh tattoos, as mentioned in Chapter 5). This blog stresses the idea that by purchasing Ethico products, consumers are also buying an authentic, active lifestyle. Thus, again we see how the leisure activities of employees become part of the value producing process of the company. In this sense, the distinction between work and life is largely erased. Work is life, and life is work. Rather than leaving their private selves at the factory gates (as under Fordism), their private selves become integral to the value creation process.

Second, immaterial labor involves the process by which the kind of activities discussed above are converted into grist for the value creation mill. Under post-Fordism, people are not so much consuming products as they are particular lifestyles and experiences (we will get into this issue in more detail in Chapter 10 on branding). The workers who are key to those experiences are those who are engaged in immaterial labor. Such workers are not making specific products per se but are engaged in creating the meanings and experiences associated with those products. Thus, the employees in Land and Taylor's (2010) study are immaterial laborers engaged in the production of the meaning encoded into the Ethico apparel. They don't make the T-shirts; they construct the meanings that consumers are actually purchasing when they buy those T-shirts with the cool logos and mottos (e.g., "Tattoos Can Be Bought, Scars Have to Be Earned").

Economist Robert Reich (1991) refers to such workers as symbolic analysts—people who engage in the processing of information and symbols for a living. He argues that in the era of global capitalism symbolic analysts constitute one of three categories of workers, the other two being production workers (i.e., workers who still actually make the physical stuff we buy) and in-person service workers (i.e., workers who have direct contact with consumers—servers, fast food workers, call center employees, and so forth). Reich's argument is that it is the symbolic analysts who will fare best and the production and in-service workers who will fare worst, given the shift in the global economy to information and meaning (through branding) as the drivers of economic value.

However, it is important to note that immaterial labor is widespread and not necessarily well compensated. Brooke Duffy's (2016, 2017) study of female fashion bloggers explores the efforts of women bloggers to turn doing what they love (wearing and blogging about the latest fashions) into an income-generating activity. Most, however, do not make a living out of it and are often expected by fashion brands to blog about their clothing for little or no compensation. Indeed, it is a common feature of immaterial labor that it is either poorly paid or free work, done with the hope that it will lead in the future to paying work. Duffy refers to this as aspirational labor which, as we saw earlier, is an important characteristic of the entrepreneurial self.

Third, communication is a central, arguably defining, element of immaterial labor and the social factory. Indeed, we might even argue that the production of economic value under post-Fordism is fundamentally communicative in character. Thus, we can claim that not only does communication constitute organization (see Chapter 1), but it also constitutes capital. It is the principal means by which capitalism creates more capital (i.e., economic value). Thus, while under Fordism communication was the process that greased the wheels, as it were, of organizational life (e.g., making sure that employees were instructed on their tasks properly, or that open channels of communication were maintained between different departments), under post-Fordism communication has become the principal medium through which value is produced, enabling the creation of meanings and experiences that are monetizable. Social theorist Maurizio Lazzarato summarizes this idea effectively when he states, "Contemporary capitalism does not first arrive with factories; these follow, if they follow at all. It arrives with words, signs, and images" (2004, p. 190). Lazzarato's statement takes us directly back to Chapter 1 and Sergio Zyman's claim that "everything communicates." Examined in the current light, we can say that this phrase captures the infinite potential of communication processes to be in the service of economic value production, capturing any aspect of everyday life as a means of economic value production. All it requires is for symbolic analysts, through their immaterial, communicative labor, to attach meanings to everyday activities (skateboarding, wearing fashionable clothes, etc.) in ways that capture the attention of a lot of people; that attention can then be translated into economic value—a phenomenon that is sometimes referred to as the attention economy (Marwick, 2013, 2015). We will look at the connection between communication and capitalism in more detail in the branding chapter.

As a way of summarizing our discussion over the last few chapters, below we provide a handy summary of the transition from Fordism to post-Fordism.

Table 6.1 Fordism vs. Post-Fordism	
Features of Fordism	**Features of Post-Fordism**
• Capitalism managed by political system; Keynesian economic model	• Neoliberalism; market forces as guide for all human action
• Culture of individual autonomy within social democratic welfare model; WATT system	• Human capital/enterprise model; YOYO system
• Production-oriented; large economies of scale & standardized production	• Consumption-oriented; limited production & niche markets
• Differentiated, deskilled labor	• Dedifferentiated, skilled knowledge work
• Low trust; direct, technological, bureaucratic control	• High trust; project-based work teams; ideological and biocratic control
• Vertical integration	• Externalization processes; retain core competencies
• Hierarchical structure; inflexible work	• Flatter, decentralized structure; flexibility of work processes, labor markets, geographic mobility
• Social contract; stable, lifetime employment	• Insecure, precarious employment; "gig" economy
• Clear work-life separation	• Blurring of work-life boundaries; social factory
• Stable identity; sense of ontological security	• Insecure identity; enterprise self
• Transfer of Fordism to society as a whole	• Market defines all spheres of life

CONCLUSION

In this chapter, we have done three things: (1) we have examined the emergence of neoliberalism as a new economic model that has emerged over the last 30 years, as the old Keynesian economic system began to falter; (2) we have explored how this new economic model was also accompanied by a hegemonic discourse that has significantly changed how we think about ourselves in relation to work; (3) we laid out the features of the new form of organizing—post-Fordism—that emerged as neoliberalism took hold.

This transformation from Keynesianism to neoliberalism and from Fordism to post-Fordism has had profound consequences not only for the nature of work and organizing but also for how we think about ourselves. The shift to an entrepreneurial, human capital model of the self means that, in many respects, we are never quite free of a market framework. The philosopher Michel Foucault (2008) argues that, under neoliberalism, the market is the "grid of intelligibility" through which we view everything in our lives: family (how can I juggle family around work?); education (is this course going to help me get a better job?); religion (the prosperity gospel has attracted millions of followers in the last two decades); and social life (am I meeting friends for a beer or am I networking?). The boundary between work and life has, in many respects, become blurred or even erased.

Some scholars have referred to this transformation as the new corporate enclosure movement (Boyle, 2003; Fleming, 2014a, 2014b). Under the first enclosure movement (which, as we saw in Chapter 2, was the impetus for the development of capitalism), common lands were privatized and turned over to wealth creation; the displaced commoners became the proletariat forced to sell their labor to factory owners. In the second enclosure movement, what is being enclosed by corporations is not land but life itself. Even the most basic, biological feature of human life—the human genome—has been corporatized, with companies selling us access to it. Have you noticed all those ancestry commercials on TV? For a small fee, a company will sell you the breakdown of your genetic ancestry: "I thought I was Irish, but then I discovered I was two-thirds German!"

Most important for our purposes, perhaps, is the fact that communication has become a central, constitutive feature of this new form of work and organization. Under post-Fordism and neoliberalism, communication is at the center of the value generation process. Indeed, most companies—regardless of what they produce—conceive of themselves as in the business of communication. For example, a few years back a Ford company executive stated the following: "The manufacture of cars will be a declining part of Ford's business. They will concentrate in the future on design, branding, marketing, sales, and service operations" (Olins, 2000, p. 51). While the executive might have been exaggerating slightly, his comment does speak to a widespread recognition by organizations that symbol analysis and manipulation is at the heart of what they do.

Finally, however, we must end on a note of caution. The emergence of the post-Fordist organization has not meant the end of Fordism. After all, the iPhone in your pocket may be designed by symbolic analysts, but it is manufactured by people working on a production line that, at least in its form of work, would not have been out of place in the 1950s. The main difference is that those people probably do not enjoy the same degree of job security and benefits that the average factory worker in the 1950s enjoyed. As we progress through the various chapters in this book, then, keep in mind that while the idea of the post-Fordist workplace is dominant in the popular business press, there are plenty of workers who toil away in routine service and production jobs that are both unfulfilling and insecure.

CRITICAL APPLICATIONS

1. In groups, share with one another your aspirations regarding your professional career. What do you want to be after college? Where did these ideas come from? With members of your group, share your hopes and anxieties about work. How confident are you about having a successful professional career? Relate this discussion to the elements of neoberalism and post-Fordism that we have discussed in this chapter.

2. Interview someone who has been in the workforce for a number of years. How many jobs has your interviewee had? How does he or she view work in relation to other aspects of his or her life (family, social life, etc.)? What does having a career mean to your interviewee?

KEY TERMS

enterprise self   153

fissured workplace   162

human capital   152

immaterial labor   169

just-in-time   165

Kaizen   164

neoliberalism   150

precariat   157

radical responsibilization   154

social factory   169

telework   165

Toyotism 164

venture labor   152

WATT system   154

work teams   167

YOYO system   154

STUDENT STUDY SITE

Visit the student study site at **www.sagepub.com/mumby.org** for these additional learning tools:

- Web quizzes
- eFlashcards
- SAGE journal articles

- Video resources
- Web resources

Power and Resistance at Work

Power is often associated with corporate symbols, such as a corner office.

In Chapter 1, we argued that power is a central and defining feature of organizational life, noting in the process Stewart Clegg, David Courpasson, and Nelson Phillips's (2006) claim, "Power is to organizations as oxygen is to breathing" (p. 3). In this chapter, we unpack what this analogy means. For much of the history of management thought, however, power has largely been ignored as an object of study. This neglect is at least in part because organizations have been treated as rational sites of decision making where the exercise of power (seen in this context as forcing choice and action) is viewed as a last resort. Early management theorists such as Frederick Taylor, Elton Mayo, and others rarely, if ever, mentioned power, instead talking about organizations in terms of cooperation, commitment, leadership, and so forth. As we saw in Chapter 1, however, organizations are made up of different stakeholder groups with often conflicting interests. In this sense, management is just as much about the exercise of power and control as it is about rational decision making. Indeed, management scholars John Van Maanen and Stephen Barley (1984) have argued that control is management's "most fundamental problem" (p. 290). Thus, power is a routine feature of everyday organizing, as various organizational actors bring different and competing interests and resources (economic, political, and symbolic) to the table.

However, such a claim belies the fact that power is a complex and slippery phenomenon that many social scientists in a number of different fields have attempted to explore. The exercise of power is not always obvious and visible. For example, superior–subordinate and professor–student relations are characterized by relatively overt differences in the power associated with each position. A professor has power over a student in the sense that he or she dictates course content, decides what will be talked about in class, and, most important from a student perspective, assigns grades. This authority places the professor in a clear position of power.

But what about cases when there isn't a clear "power over" granted by the surrounding system (such as an organization or the university)? In your previous classes, you've likely been on a team responsible for completing a project; these teams usually are made up of students who are peers in the course. Since these teams rarely allow any single member to have power *over* others, is power *absent* in such a team? Obviously not: You're probably well aware of the power that comes with particular forms of expertise (for instance, related to the topic or to navigating college course projects) or from the control over resources (such as the technologies or personal contacts the group needs to complete its task). Clearly, there is power operating in a project team, but it is decidedly not the same as that associated with the professor.

And then thinking further down this line, how would we characterize the power issues in a neoliberal, post-Fordist context, where the enterprise self is a prevailing theme? The discourse of the enterprise self emphasizes individual autonomy and independence, so in what sense is it possible to identify forms of power operating in such an environment? In contexts like these, we need to have available perspectives on power that look beyond the direct exercise of power of one person or group of people over another.

In this chapter, then, we will examine multiple conceptions and forms of power, as well as the ways that social actors respond to attempts to exercise power over them. In this sense, we can say that power is not a *thing* that someone in authority can possess. Rather, **power** is exercised through a dynamic process in which relations of interdependence exist between actors in organizational settings. Power, then, is not a thing that can be possessed; it *is* that relation between actors. Some actors have access to more resources than others, but such resources are useful only if others prize them and recognize that their relationship with the actor in question affects their ability to get those resources. Similarly, no one is ever without power; regardless of how limited or constraining a situation is, it is possible to act in the face of power. For example, even a prisoner can go on hunger strike; in this sense everyone, however limited, has some degree of **agency**. The sociologist Anthony Giddens (1979) refers to agency as the ability to "act otherwise" (p. 56), to choose a course of action different from the one prescribed by the situation or by another person. In other words, we are never simply billiard balls on a table reacting in a mechanical fashion to the pool cue of power; we can always push back against the exercise of power.

Thus, we are asking you to make a shift away from the commonsense perception of power as a thing that is tangible, quantifiable, and a human possession (much like the shift away from the Newtonian perspective we talked about in Chapter 4) and toward thinking about power as a dynamic, shifting, and complex process that is fundamentally communicative in nature. From this alternate perspective, power is closely tied to the ability of organizational actors to communicatively construct the lived realities in which people participate and that favor certain stakeholders over others. In this sense, communication is as important a resource as any other (economic, political, etc.). For example, President Trump's extensive use of Twitter is key to his ability to shape "truth" and maintain his base of support (and of course, negate alternative views of reality). Moreover, we will look at how the exercise of power is always a contested process; that is, people routinely resist efforts to shape meanings and often construct alternate meanings of their own. Examined through this lens, we can better understand organizations as dynamic phenomena that are key sites of human identity formation and decision making in society (Deetz, 1992).

First, let's look at one of the earliest debates about the nature of power—the so-called community power debate.

⚙ THE COMMUNITY POWER DEBATE

As we develop the idea of power in this chapter, we will examine increasingly complex understandings of power as a relational, dynamic, and meaning-based process. Debates about the nature of power became particularly focused in the 1950s, 1960s, and 1970s in the field of political science. During this time, scholars attempted to examine systematically the issue of who holds and exercises power in society (note the dominance of the thing or possession view of power here). Attempts to answer this question developed roughly into two camps: the pluralists (Dahl, 1957, 1958, 1961; Wolfinger, 1971) and the elitists (Bachrach & Baratz, 1962, 1963; Hunter, 1953; C. Mills, 1956). The debate between these two camps became known as the community power debate. The pluralists argued that power was equitably distributed throughout society and that no particular group had undue influence over decision-making processes. The elitists, on the other hand, claimed that power was concentrated in the hands of a privileged few who controlled political agendas. The pluralists adopted what can be called a one-dimensional view of power, while the elitists developed a two-dimensional view of power. Let's examine the two perspectives more closely.

The One-Dimensional Model of Power

As a member of the pluralist camp, Robert Dahl argued for a behavioral model of power. He defined power in the following way: "A has power over B to the extent that he [or she] can get B to do something that B would not otherwise do" (Dahl, 1957, pp. 202–203). Dahl thus defined power in terms of direct influence—for him, power is exercised when one person or group is able to influence directly (and measurably) the behavior of another person or group. For example, a boss exercises power over an employee when that employee chooses to forgo an evening out when instructed by the boss to deliver a report by 9 a.m. the following morning. The employee's behavior is directly influenced by her boss, who causes her to do something she would not normally do (stay at work to finish a report rather than go out with friends).

Dahl saw the presence of conflict as being a condition for the exercise of power. In other words, two people or groups bring two different perspectives or agendas to an issue, with each party having a preferred decision or course of action. The individual or group with the most power is the one that has issues resolved in its favor. Dahl used this model of power in his study of conflict and political decision making in New Haven, Connecticut, showing that no particular group exercised a disproportionate amount of power over decision outcomes (Dahl, 1961). In other words, a plurality of interests was represented (hence, the name of the perspective).

The Two-Dimensional Model of Power

The political elitists challenged Dahl's model of power, arguing that it was too simplistic and unable to capture the full complexity of how power actually worked in society. Thus, in response to Dahl, Peter Bachrach and Morton Baratz (1962, 1963) developed a model that captured what they called "the two faces of power." In this model, they argued that not only is power exercised when someone persuades another person to engage in behavior he or she otherwise *would not* have, but it is also exercised when someone *prevents* someone else from doing something he or she otherwise *would* have done. This model of power captures the exercise of power as involving both decisions and nondecisions. This view can be captured in the following statement: "A has power over B when A prevents B from doing something that B would otherwise do."

For example, imagine that you are the owner of a small retail store and you attend a public meeting of your city planning committee to complain about a plan to approve the building of a new Walmart on the outskirts of town. You feel that such a plan would hurt many small business owners in the downtown area. However, the meeting is dominated by Walmart representatives who present a barrage of facts and figures about why this new store would help revitalize the town's economy and provide 500 new jobs in the area. Under such circumstances, you feel intimidated and unable to state your own position and thus remain silent.

Bachrach and Baratz would argue that in this instance, Walmart's representatives exercise power because they are able to shape the discussion to serve their own needs and limit dissenting opinions. Borrowing a term from Elmer Schattschneider, Bachrach and Baratz (1962) refer to this process as "the mobilization of bias" (Schattschneider, 1960, p. 71). This term means that

> power is . . . exercised when A devotes his energies to creating or reinforcing social and political values and institutional practices that limit the scope of the political process to public consideration of only those issues which are comparatively innocuous to A. To the extent that A succeeds in doing this, B is prevented . . . from bringing to the fore any issues that might in their resolution be seriously detrimental to A's set of preferences. (p. 948)

To explain this concept, let's extend the Walmart example a bit further. Such mobilization of bias would exist if Walmart representatives were able to shape the discussion at the public meeting so that it addressed only issues that were relatively unthreatening to Walmart. For example, it would be in their best interests to minimize discussions about damage to local businesses, negative environmental impact, and increased traffic congestion. If such debate were minimized and Walmart representatives were able to restrict discussion to issues such as how big the store was going to be, how much the city's tax revenues would increase, or how many local people would be employed by the store, then one could argue that power was being exercised. Again, notice that no open conflict is occurring. Rather, the key issue is that mobilization of bias takes place, such that some (potentially conflictual) issues are organized out of public discussion, while others are strategically organized into the discussion.

Bachrach and Baratz's model of the two faces of power thus recognizes that overt conflict or difference between parties does not have to be present for the exercise of power to occur. Indeed, their model suggests that a more subtle exercise of power involves the ability to prevent potential conflict from being expressed in an overt fashion. Thus, they argue that power is not distributed evenly across different stakeholders, as the pluralists suggest, but is instead heavily skewed toward political elites; these elites are able to use their resources to mobilize bias and shape debates in ways that serve their own interests. For example, the Koch Brothers (two wealthy industrialists) donated almost $1 billion during the 2016 election in an effort to mobilize bias in favor of candidates who supported their conservative political agenda. They did not attempt to persuade voters directly but instead tried to create a political climate that favored their interests.

The Three-Dimensional Model of Power

Political scientist Steven Lukes (1974) added an important third perspective to the debate over the nature of power. Lukes argued that while both Dahl and Bachrach and Baratz provide useful conceptions of how power works in society, both are limited because they see power as a purely behavioral phenomenon. That is, power is exercised when people's behaviors are affected in some way (i.e., people are persuaded to do something or persuaded *not* to do something). Lukes suggests that both of these views of power presume some kind of conflict: in Dahl's case, overt conflict; in Bachrach and Baratz's case, covert conflict. This view is a problem, Lukes argues, because power can also be exercised in situations where no form of conflict—either overt or covert—exists.

Lukes thus developed a three-dimensional model that extends the conception of power. His position is summarized in the following quote:

> A may exercise power over B by getting him to do what he does not want to do, but he also exercises power over him by influencing, shaping, or determining his very wants. Indeed, is it not the supreme exercise of power to get another or others to have the desires you want them to have—that is, to secure their compliance by controlling their thoughts and desires? (Lukes, 1974, p. 23)

Lukes is not pointing here to some kind of mind-control program. Rather, he is highlighting a form of power that is widespread in society and that, in fact, functions as the very basis of modern capitalism. Capitalism is successful precisely because businesses spend large sums of money to convince us that we absolutely must have a particular product they just happen to manufacture. That is, they shape our very wants and needs, attempting to shape how we perceive our very sense of reality (an issue we'll look at in detail in the chapter on branding). In this sense, one could argue that many people see themselves as consumers before they see themselves as citizens. Such is the power of contemporary capitalism.

This form of power is very much a part of daily organizational life. Organizations spend a great deal of time and money getting employees to identify with organizational beliefs, values, and goals. Indeed, the pragmatist approach to organizational culture that we discussed in Chapter 5 is an excellent example of Lukes' third dimension of power in operation. Rather than simply telling employees to do something (one-dimensional view) or limiting opportunities for expressing alternative views (two-dimensional view), it is much better from a managerial perspective to cultivate in employees a way of thinking and acting that is consistent with the overall value system of the organization. One of the reasons why companies frequently use personality tests as part of the interview process is to collect data about how well potential employees may fit in with the culture of the organization and thus, whether their interests are likely to match existing organizational, or managerial, values (Holmer Nadesan, 1997).

It is perhaps the ultimate exercise of power for organizations to cultivate in employees a sense of identification that leads them to behave spontaneously in ways that serve the best interests of the organization (Barker, 1993, 1999; Casey, 1995; Cheney & Tompkins, 1987). For example, companies such as Disney and McDonald's have their own "universities" that not only provide employees with particular job skills but also socialize (perhaps indoctrinate) them into Disney's or McDonald's system of values. Once employees have internalized these values, their decision making and behavior are much more likely to be consistent with the larger organizational philosophy. McDonald's, for example, refers to such strongly identified employees as "having ketchup in their veins." And in Chapter 5, we talked about EKINs—highly committed Nike employees who live and breathe Nike values.

This three-dimensional view of power therefore argues that conflict (either overt or covert) is not a necessary condition for the exercise of power. The existence of a consensus amongst different groups does not mean that power is not being exercised. Instead, this view sees power operating at a deep-structure level, shaping people's very interests, beliefs, and values. But how does this happen? What is the mechanism by which large groups of people come to share a similar worldview? In order to understand this process more clearly, we turn to a discussion of the concept of ideology and its relationship to organizational communication and power.

⚬ POWER, IDEOLOGY, AND ORGANIZATIONAL COMMUNICATION

Ideology and power are closely connected. When Karl Marx and Friedrich Engels (1947) stated that "the ideas of the ruling class are in every epoch the ruling ideas" (p. 39), they recognized that those in power do not simply rule by coercion but, equally important, shape the ways in which people think about and experience the world. In this sense, ideology (as the term suggests) operates in the realm of ideas and meanings.

In this sense, a simple way to understand the concept of ideology is to see it as providing the link between meaning and power. That is, ideology functions as an interpretive lens through which people come to understand what exists, what is good, and what is possible (Therborn, 1980). In other words, ideology shapes people's sense of reality, provides them with a taken for granted frame for judging what is good and bad or right and wrong in that reality, and enables and constrains their thinking about what realities are possible. For example, as we discussed in Chapter 1, the widespread idea that women were suited to live in only the domestic sphere was maintained by the ideology of the "Cult of True Womanhood" (Welter, 1966), which naturalized the idea that women were incapable of participating in public and professional life. The fact that there is still a dearth of women in public life suggests how difficult it can be to overcome powerful ideologies.

Ideology, then, works to manage the relationship between communication and power by shaping the ways social reality is constructed. Returning to the above discussion of Lukes' work, we can say that ideology constructs a social reality in which potential conflicts between different groups are never allowed to rise to the level of full consciousness. In other words, people don't challenge or resist their social reality because they lack awareness of the contradictions on which it is based. For example, a woman who claims that a woman's place is in the home is, one could argue, under the sway of an ideology of patriarchy, in which men define the role of women as involving economic, political, and cultural servitude to men. Ideology, then, is accepted and actively upheld by both the dominant and subordinate groups, but only the former benefits from that ideology. Thus, it is in the best interests of the dominant group to maintain and reproduce that ideology.

However, ideology does not work that simply. Indeed, because it is largely about meaning and systems of signification, dominant ideologies are frequently challenged and vulnerable to change. Struggle always exists around ideologies, as different social groups compete to shape the meanings that make up social reality. As Stuart Hall (1985) states, "Ideology also sets limits to the degree to which a society-in-dominance can easily, smoothly, and functionally reproduce itself" (p. 113). While ideology functions to maintain the status quo, change is never far away. At various points in the past hundred years, for example, change has occurred through social movements challenging the dominant ideology: The women's suffrage movement in the 19th and early 20th centuries challenged the prevailing political status quo and won the vote for women; in the 1960s, the civil rights movement challenged racial discrimination and resulted in the passing of the Civil Rights Act; and in the 1960s and 1970s, the feminist movement challenged patriarchy and changed perceptions of what women can do. Today the #MeToo movement has highlighted and challenged the widespread sexual harassment of working women and brought attention to men's abuse of power. Think here about how sexual harassment is not just about men exercising power over women but about the existence of an ideology—a social reality—in which women fear they will not be believed if they speak out about harassment—an ideology that #MeToo has helped to change.

Scholars in the critical organizational communication tradition are therefore interested in studying organizations as sites of struggle (Fleming & Spicer, 2007). That is, they examine the complex relations between organizational efforts to shape employee behavior (Casey, 1995; Kunda, 1992) and employees' resistance to these methods of control (Courpasson & Vallas, 2016; Mumby, Thomas, Martí, & Seidl, 2017; Paulsen, 2014; Wilhoit & Kisselburgh, 2017). Critical researchers are particularly interested in the various ways struggles over meaning occur. In other words, how does organizational reality get defined, and who are the various groups and social actors that engage in this struggle? Such struggles over meaning occur through various kinds of everyday communication practices, including stories (Brown, 1998; Brown & Coupland, 2005; Mumby, 1987; Witten, 1993), rituals (Rosen, 1985, 1988), metaphors (Alvesson & Spicer, 2011; Fleming, 2005; Tracy, Lutgen-Sandvik, & Alberts, 2006), humor (Collinson, 1988; Mumby, 2009; Rhodes & Westwood, 2007) and everyday talk (Holmes, 2006), among other phenomena, to try to understand how power and resistance work at an everyday level.

Critical researchers also employ an additional concept in studying the relationships among communication, power, and resistance—the concept of **hegemony** (Gramsci, 1971). As we saw in Chapter 2, hegemony refers to the ways a dominant group is able to get other groups to consent actively to the former's conception of reality. Hegemony operates when the taken for granted system of meanings that everyone shares functions in the best interests of the dominant group.

Critical sociologist Michael Burawoy (1979) provides an interesting example of hegemony "at work" (bad pun intended) in his ethnographic study of a machine tool factory, which we also mentioned in Chapter 5. Burawoy begins his study by asking a question that upsets the taken for granted (i.e., dominant managerial) way of thinking about employees in the workplace. While a managerial orientation would start with the basic question, "Why don't workers work harder?" Burawoy begins with the question, "Why do workers work as hard as they do?" This simple shift in focus reorients our usual way of thinking about work. The hegemony of the managerial approach (i.e., a focus on efficiency, productivity, and profit) is so ingrained in all of us that it is hard for us to think any other way. Burawoy's question challenges our taken for granted sense of how the world works (i.e., that employees don't work as hard as they could and managers have the right to get them to work harder). His question makes the alternative assumption that employees already work harder than anyone has the right to expect them to; the real question is why is this the case?

Burawoy's (1979) answer to this alternative question is an interesting one that draws heavily on issues of power, ideology, and hegemony. He argues that the workers create for themselves a game called "making out" in which their workplace identities become strongly invested in their ability to maximize their output and hence, their pay (which is based on a piece-rate system). Different jobs in the plant have varying degrees of difficulty and thus vary in terms of workers' ability to "make out" (i.e., maximize pay) on a particular job. The workers thus engage in a process of negotiation for particular jobs, rates (how much they must produce to get a pay bonus), and information about how to maximize output on certain jobs. Thus, without management asserting any direct control at all, workers produce a culture in which all must adhere to the rules of the game of making out in order to be considered full-fledged members of that culture. In this sense, the game functions ideologically to produce a system of hegemony, creating a taken for granted organizational reality that serves the interests of the management (i.e., maximizing efficiency and profitability).

In a more post-Fordist context, management scholar Gideon Kunda (1992) details a high-tech company's efforts to instill the dominant corporate culture in every employee. Using the term normative control (similar to ideological control) to describe this process, Kunda shows how the strategic practices of the corporate culture are aimed at the employee's very sense of self. Kunda describes the process of normative control in the following manner:

> The attempt to elicit and direct the required efforts of members by controlling the underlying experiences, thoughts, and feelings that guide their actions. Under normative control, members act in the best interest of the company not because they are physically coerced, nor purely from an instrumental concern with economic rewards and sanctions. It is not just their behaviors and activities that are specified, evaluated, and rewarded or punished. Rather, they are driven by internal commitment, strong identification with company goals, intrinsic satisfaction from work . . . in short, under normative control it is the employee's self—that ineffable source of subjective experience—that is claimed in the name of the corporate interest. (p. 11)

Kunda (1992) illustrates how those aspects of the self that have traditionally been considered private are increasingly "coming under corporate scrutiny and domination" (p. 13). Kunda shows how the company co-opts personal emotions, values, and beliefs in order to get employees to identify strongly with corporate goals. For example, the company runs a culture boot camp—a 2-day workshop that indoctrinates new employees into the culture of the organization. The goal is not to teach employees about the formal structure of the company but how to make sense of the everyday organizational reality. Thus, new employees learn about the company's slogan, "Do what's right"—a phrase frequently uttered but never clearly defined. Indeed, it is the strategic ambiguity (Eisenberg, 1984) of this phrase and its multiple possible interpretations that aid in the process of normative control; the lack of a clear meaning leads employees to spend much time trying to figure out the corporation's expectations. As a result, employees invest a great deal of themselves in their work—working long hours, figuring out organizational politics, and taking work home—in the effort to be successful.

One of the ways ideology and hegemony work, then, is by creating a process of identification between employees and their organization. Organizational control is at its most effective when employees fail to differentiate between their own identities and the identity presented by their company; a strong sense of organizational identification exists and employees will actively pursue the interests of the organization, even putting the company's well-being above their own.

Much of the recent research on power and ideology has been conducted in post-Fordist organizations like the one in Kunda's study. As we saw in Chapter 3, Fordist organizations are characterized by strong hierarchies and low levels of trust between management and workers (in Burawoy's study, for example, the game of making out was a way for the workers to get around managerial rules about production levels). As such, power dynamics between managers and workers tend to be heavily conflict based. But as we saw in

Chapter 6, under post-Fordism, hierarchy and mistrust are replaced by flatter decision-making structures and trust-based work arrangements that heavily feature autonomous teams of workers. In this context, a lot of critical research has focused on work teams in post-Fordist organizations, particularly focusing on the power dynamics that emerge in this flatter organizational structure (Barker, 1993, 1999; Doorewaard & Brouns, 2003; Ezzamel & Willmott, 1998; Sewell, 1998; Sinclair, 1992; Vallas, 2003). In team-based systems, the power dynamics that develop are less between managers and workers and more among team members themselves. Indeed, many team members report that they feel more closely observed and subject to discipline in team contexts than they do in traditional hierarchical systems.

Thus, a fascinating contradiction emerges in which teams were introduced at least in part to provide workers with more autonomy and decision-making freedom but end up being more oppressive and stressful than traditional work arrangements. After all, you can find creative ways to avoid and/or resist your boss; it's more difficult to do that with team members with whom you work in close contact all day. As a respondent in organizational communication scholar Jim Barker's (1993) study of a team-based electronics company stated, "I don't have to sit there and look for the boss to be around. . . . Now the whole team is around me and the whole team is observing what I'm doing" (p. 408).

In terms of the connection between power and identification, then, we see that the identification process becomes less about identifying with the organization as a whole, and more about identifying with one's team. Cultural studies scholar Melissa Gregg (2011) shows that even virtual work teams can have a disciplinary effect on employees. Indeed, consistent with critical research on teams, she finds that members of online teams feel greater pressure to be in regular communication with other team members than they would with their managers in a conventional organizational hierarchy. For example, team members felt the need to be responsive to team members' emails, even when the messages arrived late at night. Team members felt they had to be responsive in order to maintain team solidarity (be a team player) and yet often were frustrated by the sheer volume of emails sent by some team members. In fact, online communication often seemed to function as a substitute for face-to-face interaction or was used to avoid dealing with an issue more directly with a phone call. Ultimately, Gregg argues that the work team "is one of several coercive dimensions of office culture exacerbated by new media technologies" (p. 74).

One might argue, then, that the shift to a team-based system under post-Fordism is a form of "management by stress" (Parker & Slaughter, 1990), as workers themselves engage in the surveillance of one another, with no intervention from management necessary. For example, in her ethnographic study of a Subaru-Isuzu automobile plant, sociologist Laurie Graham (1993) examines how the apparent increase in worker control and participation enabled by the Japanese system of Kaizen (see Chapter 6) actually resulted in tighter control and more stress on employees. Workers were assigned to teams of 12 that performed a specific set of tasks in the vehicle assembly process. Graham refers to "task time" as the time required for each worker to complete all the tasks assigned to him or her on each vehicle as it moved through the work station. At her station, Graham performed 22 tasks in the 5 minutes allotted (as the plant got more efficient, this time was cut to 3 minutes and 40 seconds). Stress arose from a number of sources, including workers who worked too slowly and then experienced peer pressure from teammates to speed up, team leaders putting pressure on members to work faster, management speeding up the work process, and arbitrary, last-minute requests from management to work overtime.

Although the philosophy of Kaizen is intended as a participatory model of work where employees are directly involved in the improvement process, Graham (1993) documents the amount of stress workers experience, indicating that the goal of Kaizen "was for workers to be working every second of every minute" (p. 160). Interestingly, in a study in the same plant some years later, organizational communication researcher Heather Zoller (2003) reported that tact time had shrunk to 1 minute and 54 seconds and that a number of workers were experiencing repetitive stress injuries as a result of their work.

CRITICAL RESEARCH 7.1

Alexandra Michel (2011). Transcending socialization: A nine-year ethnography of the body's role in organizational control and knowledge workers' transformation. *Administrative Science Quarterly,* **56, 325–368.**

Conventional wisdom has it that managerial efforts to control workers' bodies had their heyday with Frederick Taylor and scientific management, after which management focused on developing more subtle ways to motivate employees. However, management scholar Alexandra Michel shows how, even in a work environment where employee autonomy and work-life balance is baked into the corporate culture, employees' bodies are still very much a target of organizational control. Michel's study explores the autonomy paradox, in which employees work incredibly hard (sometimes 120 hours a week) even when they are not being coerced into doing so, to the point where they damage their health.

Michel's study is a 9-year ethnography of knowledge workers in two U.S. investment banks. Her focus is on how the banks' cultures not only shape attitudes toward work, but also target the employee's body. The study is particularly interesting and unusual because it is longitudinal, with data gathering occurring over multiple years. Michel used four data sources: 7,000 hours of observation over 2 years, over 600 formal interviews, 200 informal interviews, and analysis of company materials. In this sense, the study is not just a snapshot of a work culture at a particular moment in time; it examines employees' changing relationships to work, and, most importantly for this study, to their bodies.

Michel's findings show that employee recruits pass through three phases in their relationships to their bodies. In the first phase (years 1–3 of employment) employees view their bodies as objects their minds control. Employees are extremely devoted to their work and spend all their time and energy working. One interviewee sums up the body as object mentality when he states, "I totally believe in mind over matter. There are no such things as physical needs. Tell me one physical need and I can tell you a culture in which they have controlled it" (p. 341). In these early years of employment, control is high and the banks benefitted from their employees' devotion to work.

(Continued)

(Continued)

In year 4 onwards, the body becomes an antagonist, thwarting the completion of projects. Employees begin to develop addictions and eating disorders as they attempt to maintain the relentless pace of work. As one informant put it, "I'm at war with my body." Employees push harder to try and reassert control over their work, continuing to work 120 hours per week. However, many note that their creativity and judgment suffers.

Finally, Michel shows that from year 6 onwards around 40% of employees enter into a body as subject period of work, while the remaining 60% continue in the body as antagonist mode. The body as subject perspective is exemplified by the employee who states, "I have never before asked myself whether something actually feels good. That thought just never occurred to me. Just do your job. . . . If this firm had not rammed my body into the ground the way it did, my body might not have fought back and forced me to listen to it" (p. 342). In this mode, then, employees become more self-reflective and aware of the long-term damage they are doing to their health and find ways to work less and smarter; they question organizational control but also increase their creativity and judgment, ironically continuing to be just as productive for their employer as when they worked 120 hours a week.

Michel's study thus illustrates the importance of longitudinal studies of the workplace. As she states, "Tracking bankers longitudinally revealed that work also transformed them more fundamentally. It not only changed what they knew but also how they enacted essential aspects of being, namely, the relation between mind and body and action" (p. 355). Thus, while we tend to think of knowledge work as purely cognitive, it is important to remember that all forms of work are embodied and material in some fashion, often in ways that can be injurious to our health. Work can consume our entire selves, not just our minds.

Discussion Questions

1. Michel states, "Knowledge-based organizations achieve control's most elusive goal. They capture workers' hearts, minds, and energy" (p. 351). Reflect on your relationship to work. Can you imagine being as consumed by work as the bankers in this study? Why or why not? Can you think of anyone in your life whose body and mind seems to have been captured in this way?

2. In what ways do the bankers in Michel's study parallel how you work as students? Have you experienced any of these embodied work issues as students? Have you been through any of the three stages that Michel discusses? What strategies do you have for managing work-life balance?

♣ RESISTING WORKPLACE CONTROL

Employees often resist organizational control efforts, and critical scholars have increasingly focused on the various ways organization members engage in individual and collective acts of resistance (Ackroyd & Thompson, 1999; Ashcraft, 2017; Fleming & Spicer, 2003; Frayne, 2015; Gagnon & Collinson, 2017; Knights & McCabe, 2000; Mumby, 2005; Mumby et al., 2017; Murphy, 1998; Paulsen, 2014, 2015; Vallas, 2016). This research recognizes that employees have a great deal of insight into the daily routines and practices of organizational life, and organization members frequently make sense of their organizational lives in subversive ways that run counter to the dominant corporate ideology. Many of these activities cannot be classified as outright resistance to organizational power but frequently involve either undercover forms of resistance (Scott, 1989, 1990) or else subtle efforts to co-opt dominant meanings to serve alternative purposes (e.g., Knights & McCabe, 2000).

Of course, resistance to work is not a new phenomenon and has been a feature of organizational life throughout the industrial age. For example, the systematic soldiering among workers that Frederick Taylor set out to combat was a form of collective resistance to management efforts to increase production. Indeed, some scholars have argued that the entire history of management thought represents increasingly sophisticated responses to worker opposition to managerial efforts to intensify work and make it more productive (Fleming, 2015; Hardt & Negri, 2004; Tronti, 2012). And resistance runs the gamut from sabotage (Prasad & Prasad, 1998) to strike action (Cloud, 2005; Taylor & Moore, 2014) to whistle-blowing (Weiskopf & Tobias-Miersch, 2016) to more subtle acts such as loafing (pretending to work) (Paulsen, 2014), workplace humor (Collinson, 1988; Mumby, 2009), and identity work (Thomas, Mills, & Mills, 2004; Tracy, 2000; Trethewey, 1997)—that is, constructing work identities that are at odds with the prevailing corporate norms.

All of these forms of resistance point to various ways in which the process of corporate colonization can be undermined. Such resistance is important because it not only represents a different way of looking at organizational life but also suggests the ways organizations exist as sites of struggle where alternative sense-making processes can develop. Let's examine more closely an example of research that focuses on employee resistance to corporate hegemony.

Flight attendants are particularly subject to emotional labor.

The Hidden Resistance of Flight Attendants

A good example of an organizational environment that reflects the trend toward increasing levels of control over employees is the airline industry. As a service industry, airlines focus heavily on interactions between employees and customers because they know the profitability of their company depends on the success and pleasantness (for the customer) of such interactions. Sociologist Arlie Russell Hochschild (1983) examined the lengths to which airlines go to control the ways employees—particularly flight attendants—conduct themselves in interactions with customers. She showed that the demands of the job require flight attendants to engage in **emotional labor**—that is, "the management of feeling to create a publicly observable facial and bodily display" (p. 7). Flight attendants are required to employ their emotional expressions in the service of the company's need to please customers and make a profit. Thus, emotional labor "requires one to induce or suppress feeling in order to sustain the outward countenance that produces the proper state of mind in [passengers]" (p. 7).

Flight attendants are therefore trained to engage in a careful management of their public presentation of self, always exhibiting warmth and friendliness, even at times when their natural tendency might be to express very different emotions (e.g., when they are tired, frustrated, or dealing with the demanding jerk in seat 23C). This corporate management of emotions is a form of control that can have serious consequences for the psychological well-being of employees who regularly experience large differences between felt emotions and publicly expressed emotions.

Corporate ability to manage and control employee emotions and behavior, however, is not complete. In fact, employees can be amazingly inventive in their efforts to resist organizational control. For example, Hochschild (1983) illustrates how flight attendants respond to company efforts to get them to smile more often and more sincerely at more passengers. She states,

> The workers respond to the speed-up with a slowdown: they smile less broadly, with a quick release and no sparkle in the eyes, thus dimming the company's message to the people. It is a war of smiles.
>
> The smile war has its veterans and its lore. I was told repeatedly, and with great relish, the story of one smile-fighter's victory, which goes like this. A young businessman said to a flight attendant, "Why aren't you smiling?" She put her tray back on the food cart, looked him in the eye, and said, "I'll tell you what. You smile first, then I'll smile." The businessman smiled at her. "Good," she replied. "Now freeze, and hold that for fifteen hours." Then she walked away. In one stroke, the heroine not only asserted a personal right to her facial expressions but also reversed the roles in the company script by placing the mask on a member of the audience. She challenged the company's right to imply, in its advertising, that passengers have a right to her smile. (pp. 127–128)

This example brings into sharp focus one of the key ways employee resistance occurs. That is, rather than engage in direct confrontation with the corporation (through strikes, for example), employees organize their resistance around the inherent ambiguity of corporate meanings. In this case, flight attendants engage in resistance by playing with the definition of what it means to smile. While they follow the company's requirement to engage in frequent smiling, they invest their smiles with their own meaning rather than the company's intended meaning. Their smiles say "We resent company efforts to control our smiles!" rather than "I love my job, and I'll do everything I can to make your flight pleasant!" The flight attendant who confronted the businessman challenged the company more directly by questioning its right to control every aspect of her life. Nevertheless, her act of resistance is still rooted in the meaning implied in a smile or in its absence, and in her rejection of the dominant meaning of a smile. You might say that the flight attendants are engaged in a kind of emotional systematic soldiering.

Organizational communication scholar Alexandra Murphy (1998) has extended Hochschild's study by focusing more directly on flight attendants' resistance to corporate control over their expressed emotions. In her study, she is interested in the hidden transcripts (Scott, 1990) of flight attendant resistance—that is, discourse and behavior that occur "offstage," outside the immediate view of those in power in an organization. Murphy identifies three distinct forms of resistance in her analysis: (1) resistance to gender hierarchy and status, (2) resistance to the regulation of movement and space, and (3) resistance to the regulation of appearance.

1. *Resistance to gender hierarchy and status.* While part of the public role of flight attendants is to function in a feminized, nurturing role, Murphy shows how flight attendants frequently violate this role behind the scenes. For example, employing humor and irony, flight attendants often undermine the authority of the (usually male) pilot by making fun of company guidelines that require them to keep pilots fully hydrated during flights by bringing them drinks. As one flight attendant stated,

> When I ask the pilots if I can get them a drink, I always ask them, "So, do you need to be hydrated? I don't want you all to die of dehydration in the next hour and a half." And then I throw in that my father is a urologist, and perhaps they might want me to remind them to go to the bathroom so that they don't get a kidney infection, too! Usually I only have to go in there once. They get their own drinks after that. (Murphy, 1998, p. 513)

2. *Resistance to the regulation of movement and space.* Murphy shows that one of the ways in which the airline in her study attempts to control flight attendant behavior is by carefully restricting their movements during initial training. Female flight attendants are required to live on-site in a special training center where visitors (especially male ones) are not allowed and movements are carefully monitored with curfews and sign-in/sign-out procedures. There is also a resident "housemother," called "Momma Dot." The trainees describe this facility variously as the "convent" and "Barbie Bootcamp" (Murphy, 1998, p. 517). Murphy shows how this attempt to restrict trainee movement is by no means complete, however, as the women engaged in various strategies to maneuver around the efforts to control them. For example, they manipulated the sign-in/out system in order to subvert the curfew and set up a communication system that informed them when Momma Dot was in her room and the coast was clear for them to leave the premises. Similarly, when, as

qualified flight attendants, rumors of ghost riders (i.e., company supervisors who go undercover as passengers to check the quality of service) would circulate, the flight attendants shared information about ways to spot these "passengers." Thus, despite company efforts to regulate movement and space carefully, flight attendants became experts at circumventing control.

3. *Resistance to regulation of appearance.* In recent years, flight attendants have been less subject to the careful control of appearance-related factors such as age and weight. Female flight attendants no longer fall exclusively into the 120-pound, 20-something category. However, airlines still have tight regulations about such appearance factors as makeup, hairstyle, nail length and color, height of shoe heel, and so forth. Such regulations are an area of struggle for female flight attendants, who frequently rebel against the feminine image they are expected to project and opt for comfort and practicality instead. For example, some flight attendants wear shoes with heels only when a supervisor might see them. Others apply their makeup in a company-prescribed manner only for their yearly appearance checks. Thus, like the meaning of the smile, flight attendants resist company definitions of what it means to have a professional appearance. Again, because the meaning of the term *professional* is open to interpretation, flight attendants can strategically manipulate it for their own purposes.

It is certainly true that none of these examples of employee resistance is particularly profound or radical. Individually, they do little to challenge the existing power structure of the airline industry. However, it is worth noting that as a direct result of charges filed with the Equal Employment Opportunity Commission by a group of flight attendants against one airline, the practice of using standard weight tables to evaluate flight attendants was discontinued (In her study, Murphy [1998] states that many trainee flight attendants referred to Sunday evening as "Ex-Lax night" as they attempted to conform to the weight standards of the Monday weigh-in sessions). This is one example of the ways collective—rather than individual—forms of resistance to organizational power can lead to changes in working conditions for employees.

However, there is another way in which power and organizational communication intersect, and we will examine that in the final section of this chapter.

CRITICAL CASE STUDY 7.1

Steven Slater, Folk Hero?

An August 2010 flight from Pittsburgh to New York was Steven Slater's last as a JetBlue Airways flight attendant. During that flight, Slater had an altercation with a passenger. The story that ran in the *New York Times* the next day reported that a passenger had risen from her seat too early to retrieve her luggage as the plane was taxiing toward the gate, and Slater, given his responsibility dictated by the U.S. Federal Aviation Administration (FAA), told her to take her seat. She refused, and her suitcase fell from the overhead bin and hit Mr. Slater in the head. He angrily demanded an apology, but the passenger instead yelled a profanity at him.

When the plane arrived at the gate, Slater picked up the public address system. He returned the passenger's obscenity, and then announced to the roughly 150 passengers on board that, after 20 plus years as a flight attendant, he could take no more. He then grabbed two beers from the service cart, opened the exit door, activated the inflatable evacuation slide, and jumped out of the plane.

Though it's a dramatic (and perhaps deeply satisfying) way to quit a job, deploying an evacuation slide violates FAA policy and federal law—it's also potentially very dangerous had anyone been standing outside the plane. Slater retreated to his New York home, but police (and a throng of TV cameras) quickly tracked him down, charging him with several misdemeanors. It also cost JetBlue $10,000 to repack the slide, which Slater eventually agreed to repay.

Over the next several days, Slater became somewhat of a minor folk hero for his "take this job and shove it" moment (this expression was the name of a popular 1977 country song by Johnny Paycheck and has become a trope for cases where workers leave jobs they find abusive). His case appeared in media all across the country, making many lists for one of the top stories of the year. Slater was referenced on the TV show *30 Rock*, and on *The Tonight Show*, host Jimmy Fallon dedicated "The Ballad of Steven Slater" to the event. There were also reports that Slater had received an offer to host a reality TV show about disgruntled workers who leave their jobs in dramatic fashion, but it never materialized.

In the aftermath of the event, commentators (including members of the public writing in the comments sections on online newspaper articles) sought to explain this incident. Not surprisingly, they often thought of this event in psychological terms (interviewers regularly asked "What were you thinking?" questions), seeking to understand the personal stressors Slater experienced. It turned out that Slater was regularly caring for his terminally ill mother in Los Angeles and was suffering effects of HIV himself . He disclosed, too, that he was a recovering alcoholic and during an appearance on ABC's *Good Morning America*, said, "It was one of those days that drove me to drink, and I will admit that I had a little sip" (ABC News, 2010).

If this incident were viewed as an example of resistance to workplace control, however, different elements come to light. An analysis of the forms of resistance seen by Murphy (1998), discussed in this chapter, suggest that the appearance and emotional expressions of flight attendants are highly regulated, though the forms of control likely differ for males. Also, Murphy conducted her study before the September 11 terror attacks, and being a flight attendant on U.S. airlines post-9/11 requires flight attendants to provide pleasing service to customers (JetBlue calls its passengers *customers* to encourage its crewmembers to emphasize a service ethic), ensure safety in any possible emergencies, enforce FAA regulations, and then to clean the cabin in preparation for the next departure. The flight attendant is expected to manage the tensions across those roles and to do so in ways that keep those customers satisfied. And this expanded role is made even more challenging given airlines' incessant efforts to increase profitability in an environment that changed dramatically following airline deregulation in the 1980s and then in the wake of the financial strain airlines suffered after 9/11.

(Continued)

(Continued)

Slater himself noted in that *Good Morning America* interview that flight attendants bear the brunt of airlines' profit-seeking activity, saying,

> I think there's tremendous culpability in the airline industry as a whole. . . . At the end of the day, I'm accepting responsibility [for my actions], but I do believe that there were many, many contributing factors that came together to create this, and many of them are within the airlines' control. Why are we charging people to check their luggage? Obviously, everything in the world is going to come on board. (ABC News, 2010).

Discussion Questions

1. While Slater's case is clearly not one of hidden resistance as in Murphy's (1998) study, how might we understand this as a form of resistance to the ideological structuring of flight attendant work? In other words, how might we understand this as not merely about Slater's psychological state or his personal burnout but about the many forces that positioned him as having relatively little agency in a situation such as this?

2. There is little evidence that this episode had much impact on either JetBlue's or the wider airline industry's practices. JetBlue's CEO, in fact, called him a coward who didn't represent the company's values. As an act of resistance, then, can we call this act effective? Why or why not?

3. As mentioned above, Slater was celebrated after the event as a working-class hero. Do you agree with this sentiment? What does a response like that say about people's frustrations with work?

BIOPOWER AND ORGANIZATIONAL COMMUNICATION

In some ways, the configurations of power and resistance have changed with the emergence of neoliberalism and the post-Fordist organization. As we saw in Chapter 6, the hegemony of neoliberal discourse has significantly reshaped how we think about our relationship to work. Ideas like the enterprise self, the social factory, and immaterial labor mean that the relationship between organizations and employees has shifted. As the fissured workplace discussed in Chapter 6 has taken hold, organizations have become less concerned about developing strong, unified cultures and more concerned about how all aspects of life can be incorporated into work (the new corporate enclosure that we mentioned in Chapter 6). In this sense, organizational power is not simply concerned with shaping employee behavior *in* organizations, but rather in reconfiguring what counts as work and what counts as life. Indeed, as critical management scholar Peter Fleming (2014a, 2014b) has argued, under neoliberal capitalism the principal struggle is not between capital and labor (as under Fordist capitalism) but between capital and life itself. In other words, and as we saw in Chapter 6, any aspect of life—not just work—can be subject to corporate enclosure as a means to produce economic value. Thus, the strict separation between life and work that existed under Fordism has been largely eradicated, and any aspect of life becomes fair game for economic value creation. In this sense, we have entered the era of the social factory.

From a power perspective, one way to frame this shift is in terms of a change from managerial efforts to discipline people to get them to behave in specific ways (e.g., by ideologically shaping their reality) to what philosopher Michel Foucault (1979b, 2008) calls the exercise of **biopower**. Biopower refers to power over life (bios). Under neoliberalism, Foucault argues that the goal of power is not to make people docile and obedient but rather to encourage them to engage in competitive social relations, to view themselves as human capital in every sphere of life. As Peter Miller and Nikolas Rose (2008) state, "Individuals had to be governed in light of the imperative that they each conduct their lives as a kind of enterprise of the self, striving to improve the 'quality of life' for themselves and their families through the choices that they took within the marketplace of life" (p. 195).

Peter Fleming's (2014b) development of the concept of **biocracy** (which we first encountered in Chapter 1 as organizations that operate with biocratic control) is helpful in this context. Adopting the term *biocracy* to identify the exercise of biopower in work contexts, Fleming argues that post-Fordist workplace control is different from earlier forms of control such as Taylorism, bureaucracy, and even culture management. While Taylorism and bureaucracy both attempted to depersonalize work (with the goal of eliminating any expressions of the authentic self in work), and culture management molded workers to identify with the values of the organization (as we discussed in Chapter 5), biocracy promotes freedom of expression and lifestyle attitudes to work. This new form of power reflects the neoliberal conception of human beings not just as participants in an economic exchange relationship but as the living embodiment of capital (i.e., as human capital, introduced in Chapter 6).

Fleming (2014b) identifies four elements that distinguish biocracy from other previous forms of workplace power:

1. *Intersubjectivity*. Under biocracy, the social aspects of work are highly cultivated and viewed as an important source of value production. This view contrasts significantly with work under Fordism, where managers tried to eliminate any informal interaction, which was seen as having a negative effect on productivity. Under post-Fordism, workers are encouraged to bring creativity, spontaneity, and authenticity to their work. Indeed, the popular management literature often advises managers to simply get out of employees' way and allow them to self-organize and exercise their creativity. Such creativity, it is argued, also requires that organizations allow employees to bring their authentic selves to work in order to promote full engagement with work, thus emphasizing the lack of distinction between work and life (Fleming, 2009).

2. *Space*. Related, while Fordist organizations maintained a strict spatial separation of work and nonwork, post-Fordist organizations attempt to eliminate this distinction as a way to access life itself. In other words, aspects of the self traditionally associated with the nonwork realm (homelife, personality, sexuality, lifestyle activities, etc.) are increasingly incorporated into the official site of work as a way to draw on the cultural and social capital of employees. Moreover, the blurring of work and nonwork boundaries makes it increasingly difficult for employees to distinguish between their professional and nonprofessional

identities. For example, Chris Land and Scott Taylor's (2010) ethnography of a clothing company shows how the employees are encouraged to bring their recreational pursuits (surfing, kayaking, skateboarding) into the workplace by incorporating these interests into their design work. Moreover, activities on days off become opportunities for enhancing the authenticity of the company brand.

3. *Time.* Under Fordism, work was carefully and strictly punctuated; the beginning and end of the workday was calibrated to the minute or second, with strict enforcement of rules regarding breaks in the working day. Processes of control were premised on the ability of managers to intensify the labor process at the point of production (i.e., in the workplace itself). More direct forms of control such as scientific management and bureaucracy focused on the fixed amount of labor time (along with carefully controlled space) that potentially could be made more productive by intensifying work. Under post-Fordism, the blurring of the spatial boundaries between work and nonwork are accompanied by ambiguity between time at work and time away from work. Under biocracy, the pressure to work occurs well beyond official working hours, as post-Fordist organizations increasingly exploit the degree to which work, identity, and entrepreneurialism are linked. Melissa Gregg (2011), for example, documents how knowledge workers are increasingly unable to switch off from work, even during the most intimate moments of their lives as they interact with loved ones. Gregg identifies "presence bleed" (always being mentally at work) and "function creep" (increased time devoted to work; e.g., answering work emails while watching TV) as two of the most significant ways in which work is colonizing more and spheres of nonwork life (we also consider this issue in the chapter on communication technologies at work).

4. *Economic valorization.* This feature is perhaps the most interesting element of biocracy, as it draws attention to how post-Fordist organizations increasingly draw on unpaid labor as a way to increase surplus value. Unpaid labor refers not just to those employed directly by an organization (e.g., unpaid interns) but to forms of communicative labor that occur as people engage with company products and meanings, or socially interact via branded meanings and products. For example, companies now routinely create online discussion sites that enable customers to help one another solve technical problems; bloggers (typically women) blog about their daily lives, incorporating discussion of branded products (e.g., specific brands of clothing) into their accounts; and gamers provide innovations for new editions of online games. As we noted in Chapter 6, Brooke Duffy's research on fashion bloggers shows how these women attempt to turn "doing what they love" into a revenue stream, although most of the them are largely doing unpaid labor for fashion brands (Duffy, 2016, 2017).

How, then, do workers engage in resistance against biopower? Under this view, power is increasingly dispersed and diffuse, saturating most aspects of life through the creation of a social factory where all forms of interaction are monetizable. Just ask "Alex From Target": In 2015, he became a micro-celebrity (Marwick, 2013) and a marketable product simply because a teenage girl posted a photo of him on Twitter (Mumby, 2018); if you're not familiar with Alex, Google him and see what comes up! If biopower is everywhere, how does one resist it or escape it? After all, it's hard not to participate in the enterprise culture and think of oneself as human capital whose value must be maintained or increased. Some scholars have argued that we need to develop what they call a "post-work imaginary";

that is, think beyond the idea that all life revolves around or is made sense of in relation to work (Frayne, 2015; Livingston, 2016; Weeks, 2011). A post-work imaginary, these scholars argue, requires an act of refusal—a refusal to allow work to define who we are as human beings. As feminist scholar Kathy Weeks has said, "The refusal of work . . . comprises a refusal of work's domination over the times and spaces of life and its moralization, a resistance to the elevation of work as necessary duty and supreme calling" (2011, p. 124).

Such a view suggests that we try to rethink the relation between work and life, the result of which might be more nonwork time rather than less. If, as we mentioned above, the main struggle today is not between capital and labor (i.e., workers) but between capital and life itself, then the main focus of any form of resistance needs to be in preventing capitalism from completely enclosing and consuming life. In some ways, as critical management scholars Carl Cederström and Peter Fleming (2012) have argued, "self-exploitation has become a defining feature of work today" (p. 7). Under neoliberalism, life itself is a human resource to be exploited, and we happily participate in that exploitation, even pushing ourselves to ill-health, or even death, as we submit to the demand that we define ourselves through our work. IT worker Rob Lucas even writes about dreaming in code, such is the extent to which his work consumes his life. Poignantly, he states, "It is only when sickness comes and I am involuntarily rendered incapable of work that I really regain any extra time 'for myself'. It is a strange thing to rejoice at the onset of flu with the thought that, in the haze of convalescence, one may finally be able to catch up on things pushed aside by work [have you had this experience?] . . . But if sickness is all we have, it offers little hope for meaningful resistance" (Lucas, 2010, pp. 128–129).

⁂ CONCLUSION

This chapter has examined the dynamics of communication, power, and resistance as played out in organizational life. Starting from the premise that it is impossible to understand organizational communication processes without focusing on issues of power, critical scholars attempt to explore how organization members negotiate the complexities of organizational control processes. From a critical perspective, understanding organizational power involves gaining insight into how the struggle over the management of meaning occurs. Who has the resources to shape the meaning of the dominant organizational culture? In what ways are organization members subject to the hegemony of this dominant meaning system? How do organization members with fewer resources (e.g., flight attendants) create alternative, resistant meanings for themselves? What communicative resources (stories, rituals, metaphors, etc.) do organization members utilize in this struggle over meaning? All these questions are central to critical organizational communication researchers in their efforts to explore the complexities of everyday organizational life.

We hope the above discussion has illustrated to you the complexities of control processes in everyday organizational life. Organizations do not simply exert control over passive employees. Rather, organization members actively contribute to organizational sense-making processes and frequently resist corporate efforts to impose a particular reality on them. However, in addressing power and resistance processes in organizations, it is important to keep in mind that we are not examining two distinct and separate processes.

We oversimplify organizational life if we view some activities as reproducing the dominant organizational ideology and see others as resisting it. A more appropriate way of thinking about control and resistance is to see these activities as interdependent and mutually defining. Just as the meaning of communication can be ambiguous, so the ways in which communication behavior fits into the overall control processes of an organization can be too.

In the next chapter, we turn to an examination of the relationship between gender and organizing—a relationship that has important implications for how we understand the exercise of organizational power. If the #MeToo movement has taught us anything, it is that power, gender, and organizations are very closely linked.

CRITICAL APPLICATIONS

1. Conduct a power analysis of your day. How many different situations can you identify in which power is a contributing factor to your communication behavior? How many different perspectives on power can you identify in your analysis?

2. Can you think of work situations in which you have actively (or passively) resisted organizational control efforts? What was your motivation in these situations? What do you think should be the limits of the degree to which organizations can dictate or shape employee behavior?

KEY TERMS

agency   176

biocracy   193

biopower   193

community power debate   177

elitists   177

emotional labor   188

hegemony   182

hidden transcripts   189

ideology   180

normative control   183

one-dimensional view of power   177

pluralists   177

power   176

three-dimensional view of power   180

two-dimensional view of power   177

STUDENT STUDY SITE

Visit the student study site at **www.sagepub.com/mumby.org** for these additional learning tools:

- Web quizzes
- eFlashcards
- SAGE journal articles

- Video resources
- Web resources

CHAPTER 8

Communicating Gender at Work

Gender is not just a women's issue, but much of the early research equated women and gender.

Surgeon, nurse. Corporate executive, secretary. Airline pilot, flight attendant. All of these terms denote occupations, but if we are all honest with ourselves, for the first occupation in each pairing we typically think "man," and for the second occupation, we think "woman." How many of us are not at least still a little surprised when we hear a woman's voice coming from the flight deck on a commercial flight? These examples highlight the relationship between gender and work, illustrating how work and occupations are gendered. As organizational communication scholar Karen Ashcraft (2013) has shown, the gendering of work and occupations has little or nothing to do with natural distinctions between men and women, and everything to do with how certain professions and forms of work have historically been constructed as suited to either men or women, mainly as a way to preserve structures of advantage and disadvantage in society.

In this chapter, then, we are going to examine the relationship between gender and work, exploring how gender has historically played (and still plays) a central and defining role in structuring the nature of work and indeed, in providing occupational opportunities (or lack thereof) for men and women. In this sense, we will address the connections among gender, work, and power. In other words, the configuration of the gender-work dynamic that operates today did not occur spontaneously, but is the result of structures of power that date back to the beginning of industrial capitalism. As we saw in Chapter 2, the so-called Cult of True Womanhood (Welter, 1966) developed as an ideology to preserve the public sphere (including work) for men and confine women to the private sphere of home and hearth. As sociologist Steven Vallas (2012) indicates, we are still living with the legacy of that ideology more than 150 years later, as women still struggle to achieve parity with men in the workplace.

It's important, however, that when we think about gender and work, we don't immediately think women and work. This chapter is not simply about women's progress (or lack thereof) in the work sphere. Instead, it examines work, organization, and gender from a communication perspective. What does a communication perspective bring to the study of gender dynamics at work in the organizing process? First, it understands that both women and men have (or more accurately, do) gender; that is, both men and women engage in gendered communication behavior as they go about their everyday lives. Second, a critical communication perspective understands that power is a routine feature of the gender-work relationship, shaping workplace interaction. Third, a communication perspective recognizes that gender is fluid and dynamic; it is not located in people but emerges from the communication dynamics of particular social contexts. In other words, we *perform* gender. Finally, a communication perspective recognizes that gender identities are not fixed but historically variable; what counts as masculinity or femininity today has not always been the case, as social norms about appropriate gendered behavior shift over time.

Given the critical orientation of this text, we will also be adopting a feminist approach to the analysis of the gender-work relationship. This choice may seem a little odd for two middle-aged white males (Dennis being a bit more "middle-aged" than Tim), but as we hope to show, and as the title of one of feminist scholar bell hooks's texts says, *Feminism Is for Everybody*, especially if you believe in gender equality (hooks, 2000). In that book, hooks defines **feminism** as "a movement to end sexism, sexist exploitation, and oppression" (2000, p. 1). While this definition is a pretty broad, it does point to a key question common to all feminist approaches; that is, how do we understand, explain, and critique the relationship between gender and power? In other words, to what extent can the distribution of power in society be understood through the analysis of gender? While studying gender cannot account for all the ways power and oppression work in society, it provides a number of different insights into how social structures rest on gendered assumptions.

However, this picture is somewhat complicated by the fact that, historically speaking, multiple feminist perspectives have emerged that conceptualize the relationship between gender and power in different ways. In her overview of feminist thought, Rosemarie Tong (2009) identifies the following feminist perspectives: liberal, radical, socialist, psychoanalytic, care-focused, postcolonial, ecofeminist, postmodern, and third wave feminism. We're not going to review all of these here; our point is that thinking of feminism as a unified, homogeneous body of knowledge ignores its complexity. As an approach to the study of human behavior, it is much like any other area of study in its multiple and sometimes divergent efforts to understand how society works.

In this chapter, we are going to limit our discussion to three different feminist approaches to the study of gender and work: liberal feminism, radical feminism, and what we will call critical feminism. Each of these perspectives is particularly useful for exploring changing understandings of gender in the context of work and organizational life. However, while feminism has been around for 200 years, organizational communication and management scholars have been slow to systematically address gender issues at work. Indeed, it is really only in the last 25 years or so that organizational communication scholars have taken seriously the relationships among gender, power, and work (Ashcraft, 1998a, 1998b; Buzzanell, 1995; Mumby, 1996; Putnam, 1990; Putnam & Fairhurst, 1985). Let's turn, then, to a discussion of how different feminist perspectives have examined work and organization.

FEMINIST PERSPECTIVES ON ORGANIZATIONAL COMMUNICATION

The feminist movement is often referred to in terms of waves. The first wave of feminism from the mid-19th through the early 20th century defined oppression principally in terms of women's exclusion from voting and property rights. One might mark the beginning of an organized feminist movement by an 1848 conference held in Seneca Falls, NY, attended by over 300 men and women (including Lucretia Mott, Elizabeth Cady Stanton, Susan B. Anthony, and Frederick Douglass). The conference approved a "Declaration of Sentiments" (mirroring the Declaration of Independence) that included 12 resolutions regarding women's rights pertaining to property, child custody, marriage, and the franchise of voting. All 12 resolutions received unanimous approval except, ironically, Resolution 9 ("Resolved, that it is the duty of the women of this country to secure to themselves their sacred right to the franchise"). Many women delegates were concerned that the "extreme" nature of this resolution would result in all 12 being rejected (Tong, 2009, p. 22). It took a persuasive argument by Frederick Douglass to get the resolution passed: "In this denial of the right to participate in government, not merely the degradation of woman and the perpetuation of a great injustice happens, but the maiming and repudiation of one-half of the moral and intellectual power of the government of the world" (as cited in McMillen, 2008, pp. 93–94). It took more than 70 years after the Seneca Falls conference for women to receive voting rights in the United States.

The second wave of feminism that began in the early 1960s was a much broader movement. It was concerned with such issues as reproductive freedom, domestic violence, rape, and the participation of women in domains—such as upper management and politics—that were previously reserved for men (women have always been a significant portion of the workforce but until the last 30 years or so have been denied a significant presence in the upper echelons of organizations). Thus, as we will see below, the second wave viewed oppression in much more complex terms, identifying forms of exploitation (e.g., sexual harassment and domestic violence) that had not previously been brought into public consciousness (MacKinnon, 1979). A number of feminist perspectives emerged during this period, and debates swirled among feminists regarding the sources of women's oppression. Central issues included the following: Are women the same as men (i.e., have the same abilities), or do they offer different skills (e.g., empathy, nurturance, care, etc.) that have been marginalized under the ideology of male dominance in society known as patriarchy? Is capitalism or patriarchy (or both!) most responsible for women's oppression (Eisenstein, 1979)? Are the family and traditional sex-gender relations sources of women's oppression (Firestone, 1970)?

Finally, the past 30 years or so have witnessed a growing recognition that women are far from a homogeneous group and that oppression and exploitation are experienced in myriad ways. In fact, the second wave of feminism has rightly been criticized for privileging the voices of white, middle-class women and excluding working-class women and women of color from its agenda. In the early 1980s, for example, bell hooks (1981) wrote a book titled *Ain't I a Woman* (a phrase taken from a speech by 19th-century African American activist Sojourner Truth) that drew attention to the white middle-class worldview that dominated the second wave of feminism. Today, the project of feminism includes not only women of color but also men. As a result of efforts to capture the diverse experience of women, in recent years a feminist third wave has thus come to prominence. If the second wave could be summed up by the idea that women share similarities, particularly in their experience of oppression, the third wave of feminism emphasizes multiplicity and difference. Moreover, such multiplicity and difference can be fluid, as third wave feminists recognize that identities are not fixed but, instead, are ambiguous and characterized by "lived messiness" (Haywood & Drake, 1997, as cited in Tong, 2009, p. 288). The forms of empowerment that third wave feminists invoke are often individual rather than collective forms of empowerment including, for example, celebration of multiple forms of gender and sexual expression.

Given this historical context, let's turn now to a discussion of the three forms of feminism that we see as most effectively informing discussions of gender, work, and organizational communication. These perspectives are (1) liberal feminism, (2) radical feminism, and (3) critical feminism. While these perspectives overlap in some fashion, each presents us with different ways of examining issues such as patriarchy, domination, gender, equality, emancipation, and so forth. In addition, each perspective provides different ways of understanding and examining organizational life; indeed, the nature of societal institutions and organizations is very much a focal point of feminist analysis and critique. A summary of the three perspectives can be found in Table 8.1 later in this chapter.

Liberal Feminism: Creating a Level Playing Field

Liberal feminism is a product of late 18th- and 19th-century liberal political theory and is perhaps most associated in its early days with the writings of Mary Wollstonecraft (1792/1975), Harriet Taylor Mill (1851/1994), and her second husband, John Stuart Mill (1869/1970). Liberal feminism is both a critique and an extension of the Enlightenment tradition that focused on individual autonomy and rights. While this perspective firmly believes in Jean-Jacques Rousseau's "declaration of the rights of man," it critiques the fact that women were excluded from that declaration. Thus, while (male-oriented) Enlightenment liberal political theory developed the principles of liberty, fraternity, and equality, liberal feminism critiqued its failure to include women in this new conception of individual rights.

As we saw above, the early days of liberal feminism focused on voting and property rights, but the feminist second wave was a much broader movement. It emerged partly out of disenchantment with the emerging civil rights and student movements (which tended to marginalize the role of women activists) and partly in response to Betty Friedan's (1963) landmark book, *The Feminine Mystique*. In identifying what she called "the problem that has no name" (p. 15). Friedan gave voice to many middle-class, educated women who experienced a deep sense of malaise as a result of their limited opportunity for fulfillment through anything other than their roles as wives and mothers. The rallying cry "The personal is political" stressed the idea that what patriarchal society had traditionally defined as individual, personal issues (domestic violence, child care, relational abuse, etc.) actually had much more profound and far-reaching implications for the ways in which society defined women and their roles. In this sense, the second wave of feminism was a time of consciousness raising, in which feminists attempted to draw attention to the various institutional mechanisms that limited women's full participation in society.

In what ways can these concerns be related to organizational communication issues? From a liberal feminist perspective, the principal concern has been with expanding access to work and career opportunities for women. The past several decades have seen efforts on a number of different fronts to level the playing field in order for women to compete for jobs on an equal basis with men. For example, in 1964 Title VII of the Civil Rights Act was passed, prohibiting employment discrimination on the basis of sex, race, or religion. In addition, affirmative action programs and Equal Employment Opportunity laws have mandated equal access to job opportunities for women.

Despite these legislative efforts, women still lag behind men on a number of different organizational fronts. For example, many women continue to experience the **glass ceiling** phenomenon (Buzzanell, 1995), where they reach a certain level of the organizational hierarchy and then have great difficulty progressing any further. Indeed, the Center for American Progress, a public policy research institute, provides the following information regarding the movement of women into senior-level organizational positions (Warner & Corley, 2017):

Women are 50.8% of the U.S. population:

- They earn almost 60% of undergraduate degrees and 60% of all master's degrees.
- They earn 47% of all law degrees and 48% of all medical degrees.
- They earn 38% of MBAs and 48% of specialized master's degrees.
- They account for 47% of the U.S. labor force and 49% of the college-educated workforce.

However, despite holding almost 52% of all professional-level jobs, American women lag behind men when it comes to their representation in leadership positions:

- While they are 44% of the overall Standard & Poors 500 labor force and 36% of first- or mid-level officials and managers in those companies, they are only 25%

of executive- and senior-level officials and managers, hold only 20% of board seats, and are only 6% of CEOs.

- At S&P 500 companies in the financial services industry, they make up 54% of the labor force but are only 29% of executive- and senior-level managers and 2% of CEOs.

- In the legal field, they are 45% of associates but only 22% of partners and 18% of equity partners.

- In medicine, they comprise 37% of all physicians and surgeons but only 16% of permanent medical school deans.

- In academia, they are only 31% of full professors and 27% of college presidents.

- They were only 6% of partners in venture capital firms in 2013—down from 10% in 1999.

- In 2014, women were just 20% of executives, senior officers, and management in U.S. high-tech industries. As recently as 2016, 43% of the 150 highest-earning public companies in Silicon Valley had no female executive officers at all.

A 2017 *Fortune* magazine article celebrates the fact that the number of women CEOs increased by more than 50% over its 2016 figure (from 21 out of 500 to 32 out of 500)—a whopping 6.4% of Fortune 500 CEOs (Zarya, 2017). Moreover, only two women of color are Fortune 500 CEOs—Geisha Williams at PG&E, and Indra Nooyi at PepsiCo (Zarya, 2017). But as we point out in Chapter 11 on leadership, there are still as many male CEOs in large U.S. companies named John as there are women CEOs (Miller, Quealy, & Sanger-Katz, 2018).

One of the earliest and most important liberal feminist efforts to address the lack of women's progress up the corporate hierarchy was Rosabeth Moss Kanter's (1977) book *Men and Women of the Corporation*. In her 5-year-long investigation of a large corporation, Kanter identified a number of different factors that prevented women from advancing in this organization. Two phenomena in particular are significant for us in understanding how gender and organizational communication are closely linked: (1) tokenism and (2) homosocial reproduction.

Tokenism refers to a condition whereby a person finds himself or herself identified as a minority in a dominant culture. In Kanter's (1977) study, women were the tokens because of their minority status in the corporation, but anyone who is a member of a minority group can be given token status (e.g., African Americans, Latinos/as, individuals with disabilities, etc.). The important thing about tokens is that they are visible (because they look or behave differently from other organization members), and they come to be viewed as representatives of their minority groups rather than as individuals with particular traits and skills. This visibility means that any mistake they make tends to be amplified while, ironically, competent performance is overlooked. In other words, ability is often eclipsed by physical appearance, according to Kanter. As such, token organization members frequently have to work much harder than do dominant group members in order to get recognition and rewards. Thus, tokens are under tremendous pressure and are, in effect, set

Comstock Images/Comstock/Thinkstock

The glass ceiling limits women's ability to reach the highest levels of corporate life.

up for failure. Furthermore, any failure is taken as indicative of the performance of members of the token group, rather than as a failure of the individual person.

From a communication perspective, tokenism is a perceptual phenomenon created by the members of the dominant culture; people are not tokens unless others communicatively construct them as such. Kanter indicates that tokenism is a perceptual tendency characterized by high visibility, contrast, and assimilation. That is, a token (a) has a high organizational profile; (b) is perceived as contrasting significantly with the dominant culture, such that members of the dominant culture exaggerate both their differences from the token and commonalities amongst themselves; and (c) is assimilated into the stereotype of his or her token group and not allowed by members of the dominant group to function as an individual. In this sense, tokenism is a creation of the perceptual and communication practices of those who shape the dominant culture of the organization.

In such contexts, people who experience tokenism feel that all their actions and decisions are scrutinized in a manner that members of the dominant culture do not experience. As such, they can never afford to function merely adequately and often end up working much harder than the average organization member in order to be perceived as competent. As journalist Anna Quindlen (2003) has stated, "Women [and minorities] have won the right to do as much as men do. They just haven't won the right to do as little as men do" (p. 74).

Homosocial reproduction is a condition that functions in tandem with tokenism and describes an organizational context in which, to put it simply, "the men who manage reproduce themselves in kind" (Kanter, 1977, p. 48). In her interviews with male managers, Kanter discovered that they preferred to work with people who were like themselves, mainly because it facilitated a relatively predictable environment in which communication with colleagues was easy and comfortable. In this sense, women employees inserted a level of unpredictability that upset the smooth flow of communication and decision making. Put in the terms discussed in Chapter 5, we might say that male managers were comfortable being part of a single, coherent organizational culture that reflected their view of the corporate world. Women undermined that coherence.

Thus, phenomena such as "the old boys' network" and the "old school tie" are part of the process of homosocial reproduction, whereby men hire other men who look a lot like them and come from similar backgrounds—white, middle class, educated at particular schools, and so forth. In such a context, it becomes extremely difficult for women to assimilate into a culture where they do not immediately understand the taken for granted meanings at work, and where the in-group perceives them as alien before they have even had a chance to prove themselves. Silicon Valley, for example, is notorious for its gender inequity, with only 2% of women-led companies receiving venture capital funding (Corbyn, 2018). Indeed, the term *Brotopia* is often used to describe Silicon Valley, where women frequently experience the phenomenon of being the only woman in the room because of the dominance of a "Bro" culture (Chang, 2018).

Of course, much has changed in the 40 years since Kanter's study. But while it is no longer unusual for women to be in management positions, they still frequently experience barriers to advancement that limit their success when compared with similarly qualified men. Where women are able to move into particular occupations, they frequently tend to fill "occupational ghettoes"—professions that are defined as women's occupations. These include clerical work, nursing, pediatrics, social work, elementary school teaching,

Jupiterimages/Pixland/Thinkstock

As the #MeToo movement has shown, sexual harassment is still a widespread feature of organizational life.

temporary employment, and so forth. When women are able to move into a profession that has previously been dominated by men, the salaries in such professions tend to fall.

In the 1990s, researchers identified a phenomenon that complements women's glass ceiling experience—the **glass escalator** (Harvey Wingfield, 2009; Williams, 1992, 2013). This phenomenon is a different form of tokenism, in which men in female-dominated professions (e.g., nursing, grade school teaching, social work) experience a pressure toward upward mobility that sees them promoted more quickly than women. In other words, tokenism works negatively for women but positively for men. Thus, even in professions where women have a distinct numerical superiority, they still experience difficulty in their efforts to progress professionally. Interestingly, men entering female-dominated professions are generally welcomed by those women (because it raises the prestige of the profession), while women entering a male-dominated profession do not receive the same welcome, frequently having access blocked to professional social networks and possibilities for career advancement (Harvey Wingfield, 2009).

Recently, Christine Williams (who did the original research on the glass escalator) has revisited the phenomenon, arguing that her original conception failed to consider issues of race, sexuality, and class (Williams, 2013). In other words, her research failed to adopt what feminists refer to as an **intersectional approach**, where the combined effects of race, class, gender, and sexuality on people's positions in society are explored. Adopting an intersectional approach to the glass ceiling has interesting results, showing that the glass escalator effect works only for white men in traditional work organizations; it does not apply to minority men. For example, Adia Harvey Wingfield's (2009) study of African American men in the—heavily feminized—nursing profession shows that they do not experience a glass escalator effect. Indeed, it is often quite the opposite; while white male nurses are often mistaken by patients for doctors, minority male nurses are often mistaken for orderlies or janitors. Moreover, Williams points out that her original research took place in traditional occupations with high stability and career ladders, while today (and as we saw in Chapter 6) neoliberalism has drastically reshaped work, with more low-paying retail jobs than well-paid manufacturing jobs in the United States. As a result, glass escalators and glass ceilings have been replaced for many workers by revolving doors. Retail work has an incredibly high turnover rate and is notorious for gender pay disparities, with women earning only 75% of what men earn in retail work (often because men in retail get fast-tracked into managerial positions while women remain in frontline, customer service positions). The glass escalator, then, is a useful concept to explain some forms of gender discrimination, but it is also a good example of how treating gender in isolation (and limiting its application to traditional occupations) can be problematic.

A further glass metaphor has also been used to describe women's organizational experience, one that is often applied to women who do make it through the glass ceiling, or who are not overlooked by the glass escalator—the **glass cliff**. Developed by management scholars Michelle Ryan and Alex Haslam, the glass cliff refers to the precarious position women managers often find themselves in once they have succeeded in shattering the glass ceiling (Bruckmüller & Branscombe, 2010, 2011; Haslam & Ryan, 2008; Ryan & Haslam, 2007). Based on their analysis of the appointment and subsequent tenure of numerous women CEOs, Ryan and Haslam argue that companies are more likely to appoint men as

CEOs when the company is stable and thriving and more likely to appoint women as CEOs in times of crisis. Ryan and Haslam claim that companies tend to operate with the formula "Think manager—think male; think crisis—think female" (Ryan & Haslam, 2007). This trend means that women are often appointed to senior positions associated with a greater risk of failure. Thus, "women were more likely than men to be placed in positions *already associated* with poor company performance" (Ryan & Haslam, 2007, p. 556).

The glass cliff, then, refers to an additional form of discrimination that women may face once they have broken through the glass ceiling—successful women are more frequently placed in precarious positions and thus, potentially set up for a fall. They tend to be overlooked when safe or "cushy" positions are available. Susanne Bruckmüller and Nyla Branscombe (2011) argue that CEOs such as Carly Fiorina of Hewlett-Packard, Kate Swann of W. H. Smith, and Carol Bartz of Yahoo had all been subject to the glass cliff phenomenon, being fired once they had not delivered the expected company revitalization.

In general, then, we can describe liberal feminism as an entryist approach to organizational communication, in which efforts are aimed at providing ways for women to receive the same professional opportunities and support as men do. For example, at General Electric, the corporation's Women's Network—established to improve women's access to high-ranked GE positions—coaches women managers in public-speaking skills, in making effective presentations, and in "exuding leadership qualities" (Walsh, 2000, p. 13).

Many companies now have parental leave programs in place that permit women (and often men) to take paid leave around the birth of a child without compromising their professional status and career chances in the firm. However, the United States is years behind many other (particularly European) industrialized nations in providing adequate parental leave programs. For example, in a study examining the parental leave laws in 21 countries, the United States ranked 20th in the amount of protected job leave available to parents (Ray, Gornick, & Schmitt, 2008). Switzerland ranked last with 14 weeks of protected leave, while Spain and France ranked first with more than 300 weeks. The United States offers a combined 24 weeks of protected leave for a two-parent family. Moreover, while almost all countries provide direct financial (government-paid) support for parents (varying between 3 months and 1 year of full-time equivalent paid leave), the United States is one of only three countries that offers no paid parental leave (the other two are Lesotho and Papua New Guinea). Finally, "only about one-fourth of U.S. employers offer fully paid 'maternity-related leave' of any duration, and one-fifth of U.S. employers offer no maternity-related leave of any kind, paid or unpaid" (Ray et al. 2008, p. 1). Figure 8.1 provides information on all 21 countries in the study and certainly displays some interesting comparative data on the efforts of most of the top industrialized nations to provide parental leave for their citizens. The United States does not fare well in this comparison.

Often, when women do take advantage of such programs, they find themselves less competitive in terms of raises, promotions, job opportunities, and so on. As such, women (and men) are often loath to participate in company parental leave programs even when they are available, for fear it will indicate they are not serious about their careers. For example, in their study of one workplace with a parental leave policy, organizational communication scholars Erika Kirby and Kathy Krone (2002) discovered that employees often adopted an attitude of "the policy exists but you can't really use it," indicating a considerable gap between the official company leave policy and the ways employees made sense of it within the culture of the organization.

One final and influential effort to address the professional barriers that women face is Sheryl Sandberg's (2013) book, *Lean In: Women, Work, and the Will to Lead*. Sandberg argues that women's lack of access to upper-level management positions is largely self-imposed; she suggests that the route to workplace equality lies through individual women's ability to overcome their own psychological hang-ups that prevent them from recognizing their worth and "leaning in" (rather than sitting back) at the (literal and metaphorical) board-room table where the important decisions are made. She provides three pieces of advice for women: (1) Sit at the table, (2) don't leave before you leave, and (3) make your partner a real partner.

First, Sandberg (2013) argues that women face internal, self-imposed barriers to advancement, choosing to watch from the sidelines rather than get involved in decision making. Many women fall prey to the impostor syndrome in which they feel like a fraud, with it being only a matter of time before they are exposed as incompetent (both men and women experience the impostor syndrome, but women tend to experience it more intensely and frequently). Part of this, Sandberg argues, is because women consistently underestimate themselves, while men do not; women often judge their work performance as worse than it is, while men judge their performance as better than it is. Moreover, a man will attribute his success to his own abilities, while women attribute it to external factors like luck or help from others. Sandberg thus encourages women to feel more confident and less insecure and to seize opportunities when they come along; in other words, fake it 'til you feel it.

Second, Sandberg (2013) advocates that women "don't leave before they leave." This advice addresses the dilemma young women often face between a career and family. Sandberg argues that far too often women make decisions too prematurely, scaling back investment in their careers in anticipation of children (she tells the story of a young woman at Facebook who asked her questions about how to balance career and family, even though at the time of the conversation she didn't even have a boyfriend). Sandberg's point is that women often pass up career opportunities because they fear that they will get in the way of having a family. But Sandberg argues, "Anyone lucky enough to have options should keep them open. Don't enter the workforce already looking for the exit. Don't put on the brakes. Accelerate. Keep the foot on the gas pedal until a decision must be made. That's the only way to ensure that when that day comes, there will be a real decision to make" (p. 103).

Third, and related, Sandberg (2013) encourages women to "make your partner a real partner." Here her argument pushes back against traditional gender roles that reinforce the expectation that women will take on more parental responsibilities than men. As she points out, very few women who have made it to the top of their companies have done so without a supportive partner: "Of the twenty-eight women who have served as CEOs of Fortune 500 companies, twenty-six were married, one was divorced, and only one had never married" (p. 109). In contrast, the absence of a real partner, Sandberg argues, has a negative effect on women's careers, with fully 60% of women who leave the workforce citing their husbands as significant factors in their decisions (p. 110). As she states, "As

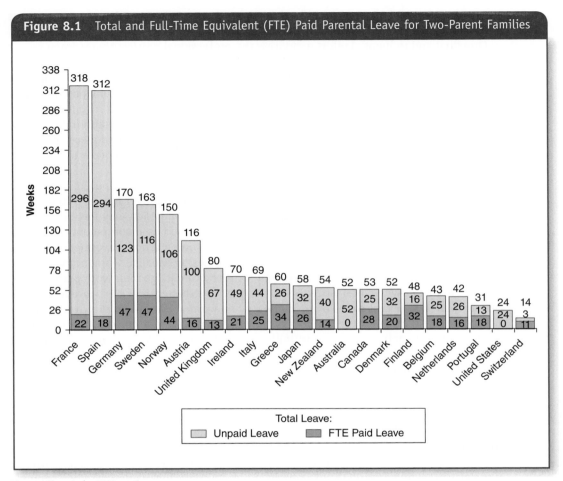

Figure 8.1   Total and Full-Time Equivalent (FTE) Paid Parental Leave for Two-Parent Families

Source: Ray et al., 2008, p. 6.

women must be more empowered at work, men must be more empowered at home. . . . We need more men to sit at the table . . . the kitchen table" (pp.108, 120).

Sandberg's argument is compelling and engaging, and it resonates with a lot of career-oriented women. Indeed, she provides a lot of useful and practical advice for women (and men too, particularly regarding how to help their partners be successful in their careers). However, it is also worth mentioning a couple of limitations in her argument. First, and consistent with lots of liberal feminist writings, she tends to treat women as a single, undifferentiated category, with little attention to how the structural conditions of race and class affect women's opportunities. Thus, it is difficult to explain women's relative lack of success in terms of internal, psychological barriers when one is comparing, for example, a single, working-class mother with two kids and an upper-middle class mother in a dual career situation (as was the case with Sandberg herself). The former can "lean in" as much as she wants, but she does not have the same starting point as the latter. Second, Sandberg's focus is very much on what individual women can do to empower themselves, rather than on the collective forms of empowerment that much of the feminist movement has focused on. In this sense, one can argue that Sandberg's perspective is neoliberal feminist (Fraser, 2013). That is, her focus is on enabling women to be more entrepreneurial within the existing corporate system; she has little interest in changing the structures of inequality that exist in the system itself.

In summary, the liberal feminist approach to work has done much to draw attention to the difficulties professional women often face in organizational settings, including pay inequities, lack of advancement opportunities, tokenism, and so forth. However, this approach also has certain limitations. First, in leaving unquestioned the basic structure and assumptions of contemporary organizational life, this perspective places the onus on women adapting to a male-dominated organizational environment. For example, Sandberg's (2013) focus on leaning in does not ask for change from men, just from the women who want to get ahead in their careers.

Second, the liberal feminist perspective can be described largely as a women-in-management approach to organizational issues (Calás & Smircich, 1996). As such, its focus has been on white, middle-class women, to the neglect of minority and working-class women. For example, while liberal feminism has drawn attention to the difficulties career women face in juggling work and home life, struggling against the glass ceiling, and developing support networks, it has often ignored the fact that many women (a) have little choice about whether to work or stay home, (b) are often in low-wage jobs with little or no hope of advancement, and (c) are more subject to sexual harassment than are women in higher-level positions. Thus, the research on women who make the choice both to have a career and a domestic life with children often overlooks the fact that many poor and working-class mothers have no option but to work, given the decline in real income over the past 30 years. Many of the blue-collar occupations that could support a family on a single income have largely disappeared from the American economic landscape, forcing many women into low-income jobs that are the only means of family survival.

Third, the liberal feminist perspective has tended to treat gender as a variable, regarding masculinity and femininity as unproblematic categories. As we will see in our later discussion of the critical feminist perspective, gender is more usefully understood not as an organizational variable but rather as a constitutive feature of organizational life that shapes everyday meaning and sense-making practices. From this perspective, gender is viewed not as a role one takes on or casts off depending on the social setting but, instead, as a quality intimately tied up with the ways we construct our identities.

Radical Feminism: Constructing Alternative Organizational Forms

Like the second wave of liberal feminism, **radical feminism** has its roots in the political movements of the 1960s and arose out of disenchantment with the sexism of those movements. However, it developed in a very different direction and is rooted in a different set of premises than liberal feminism.

Radical feminism is radical in the sense that it is woman centered (Calás & Smircich, 1996). That is, while liberal feminism seeks women's access to male-dominated institutions, radical feminism proposes alternative institutional forms rooted in women's values. In this sense, radical feminism takes feminine qualities that have traditionally been devalued in a patriarchal society and revalues them, placing them at the center of an alternative vision of society (Firestone, 1970). Thus, traditional feminine qualities such as emotion, nurturance, sensitivity, and connectedness—qualities that have occupied a secondary status to rationality, competitiveness, and independence in patriarchal society—are reframed as the basis on which an alternative vision of the world can be built. Radical feminism therefore emphasizes women's ways of knowing as an alternative to the perceived failure of men's stewardship of the world (which, radical feminists would argue, has led to wars, poverty, persecution, famine, etc.). Their argument is that patriarchal ideology has taken certain facts about male and female biology, exaggerated the differences, and built cultural constructions around them that (conveniently) empower men and disempower women. Some radical feminists, like Shulamith Firestone (1970), argued for the end of the traditional nuclear family because it created a false dichotomy between men and women, positioning women in their reproductive role as subservient to men.

Radical feminists are thus interested in the transformation of various features of society through the development of alternative ways of thinking, feeling, and acting. As radical feminist Audre Lorde (1984) stated in her critique of patriarchy:

> [Feminism] involves learning how to take our differences and make them strengths. *For the master's tools will never dismantle the master's house.* They may allow us temporarily to beat him at his own game, but they will never enable us to bring about genuine change. And this fact is only threatening to those women who still define the master's house as their only source of support. (p. 112; emphasis in original)

Thus, while liberal feminism generally tends to downplay the differences between men and women, arguing that women are just as competent as men and able to perform traditionally male-dominated roles, radical feminism—following Lorde—argues that the very assumptions on which patriarchal society is built are problematic and inherently oppressive to women. Thus, society needs to be built on a set of principles that reject patriarchy and embrace matriarchy.

Radical feminists argued that this could be done through the establishment of women-based groups and organizations structured according to a different set of values and operating principles. Beginning in the 1960s and 1970s, these organizations were aimed at providing contexts that were free from the oppressive conditions that frequently characterized male-dominated bureaucracies and thus provided women with a forum for consciousness raising—that is, a context in which women could come to a better understanding of themselves and others that was untainted by dominant patriarchal ideologies.

In many ways, this was very much a utopian project; it was a collective effort to develop alternative organizations and groups that provided women with spaces in which to create an alternative vision of what the world might be like based on a very different set of principles. For example, many of these women's organizations had no hierarchy, preferring to engage in decision making through developing consensus, and leadership roles tended to rotate regularly among members of the organization. Furthermore, many of these organizations described themselves as collectives, to distinguish themselves from the traditional bureaucratic forms of patriarchy.

Sociologist Joyce Rothschild-Whitt (1979) characterizes such collectivist organizations as having the following features:

- Authority resides in the collective as whole, not individuals who occupy an office.
- There is minimal stipulation of rules rather than the universal, formal rules of a bureaucracy.
- Social control is based on mutually shared values rather than supervision or use of impersonal rules and sanctions.
- Social relations are personal and of value in themselves, as opposed to the role- and rule-based relations of bureaucracies.
- Recruitment and advancement are based on friends and shared values rather than specialized training and formal certification.
- Individual incentives focus on furthering the organization's values and political goals, rather than securing economic rewards.
- Power is distributed in an egalitarian manner, rather than determined by the office one holds. Any individual's power is strictly limited by the collective as a whole.
- Division of labor is minimized, with members sharing many jobs and functions; the separation of mental and manual work is minimized. In the bureaucratic organization job specialization and division of labor are maximized.

As we can see, then, such collective organizations attempted to reject completely the bureaucratic model and the hierarchy and impersonal organizational environment it implied; such a model was seen as inherently patriarchal. Instead, radical feminist organizations valued an organizational structure and form that emphasized the opportunity for individual women to contribute to a larger vision of what life could be like in a non-oppressive, more egalitarian society where women could more fully realize their identities. While such an approach to organizing certainly has its merits, the utopian project of radical feminism remains unrealized for a number of reasons.

First, it adopts what might be described as an essentialist approach to gender issues. That is, women are valued because of what are seen as their natural characteristics—nurturance, emotionality, caring, connection, and so on—which are viewed as superior to masculine tendencies of rationality, independence, hierarchy, and individualism. Such an approach suggests that women have natural characteristics, and that men do also. This approach leads to a very bifurcated, bipolar view of the world, in which women and men live in different universes. In addition, the characterization of women and men as having natural characteristics suggests little possibility for change.

Second, radical feminism adopts a separatist philosophy, in which women can fully realize their possibilities only through the creation of social structures and institutions free from patriarchal values and ideologies. In other words, such feminist organizations often have a women-only rule. Under some circumstances, such a separatist philosophy makes good sense (e.g., women's support groups for victims of rape, domestic abuse crisis centers, etc.); in such contexts, the presence of men can provoke extreme anxiety in the women seeking support and counseling. On the other hand, we could argue that in many circumstances such a separatist philosophy simply reifies (or naturalizes) the differences between men and women.

Third, the very separatist philosophy of some feminist organizations frequently led to their demise, largely because, in reality, there is no such thing as an organization not inter-connected with many different organizations and its environment. As we saw in Chapter 4 on systems theory, organizations that cannot adapt to environmental changes tend toward entropy and disorder, and certainly this was the case with many of the feminist organizations of the 1970s: Their separatist philosophy proved to be their downfall, and many went out of existence. Those that did survive and thrive learned the importance of adaptation and interdependence with other organizations. Mariangela Maguire and Laila Mohtar (1994), for example, show how a feminist women's crisis center was able to remain true to its feminist values of advocacy for women while at the same time developing close ties with state funding agencies and the local police department. Furthermore, Ashcraft (2000, 2001) focuses on a contemporary feminist organization's efforts to adopt a hybrid structure that combines feminist values with the bureaucratic formalization of organizational goals and principles—a form of control Ashcraft describes as feminist-bureaucratic. Finally, management scholars Joanne Martin, Kathleen Knopoff, and Christine Beckman's (1998) study of The Body Shop international corporation demonstrates how even a large, multinational, for-profit organization can combine bureaucratic, post-bureaucratic, and feminist principles to create a progressive corporate structure that allows organization members to be expressive and emotional in their work.

In general, then, radical feminist principles in their pure form were typically unable to survive the realities of their social, political, and economic environments. Instead, radical feminist goals tended to adapt to the practicalities of everyday organizational life. While on the one hand this adaptation may seem like a compromise of basic principles, on the other hand, it recognizes the need for organizations and their members to address the changing character of the real world.

Critical Feminism: Viewing Organizations as Gendered

The last perspective we will consider is what we call critical feminism. We see this perspective as the one that is the most interesting and useful for understanding the relationship between gender and organizational communication. The critical feminist approach has a number of advantages.

First, it views gender as a socially constructed phenomenon that is subject to change. For example, in the past 100 years what counts as feminine and masculine has altered considerably as the norms for gender-appropriate behavior have shifted. For instance, the phrase "woman leader" is not the oxymoron it was 50 years ago (though it's interesting that we'd never think of saying "man leader"—an indication that the term *leader* is still heavily gendered).

Second, the critical feminist perspective views gender not as an organizational variable that can be isolated and studied separately from other organizational phenomena; rather, gender is seen as a defining, constitutive feature of daily organizational life. In this sense, we can think of organizations as gendered. Sociologist Joan Acker (1990) defines this term in the following manner:

> To say that an organization . . . is gendered means that advantage and disadvantage, exploitation and coercion, action and emotion, meaning and identity, are patterned through and in terms of a distinction between male and female, masculine and feminine. Gender is not an addition to ongoing processes, conceived as gender neutral. Rather, it is an integral part of those processes, which cannot be properly understood without an analysis of gender. (p. 146)

This definition gets at the idea that gender is not only a routine feature of daily organizational life but also impossible to escape because it lies at the very foundation of how we define ourselves, the world, and others. All of our identities, sense-making efforts, and organizational meanings are therefore gendered. Thus, many jobs and professions are gendered and hence coded as either masculine or feminine (Ashcraft, 2013). Secretarial work, nursing, and grade school teaching are gendered as feminine, while airline pilot, bank manager, and surgeon are coded as masculine. This gendering does not mean, of course, that men can't be nurses or that women can't be surgeons—many are. The point is that the organizational roles themselves are gendered such that the people occupying them have particular expectations placed on them by the organization and those around them. In other words, gender is a structural feature of organizations rather than simply a characteristic of individuals.

For example, a female airline pilot might have to work very hard in her organizational performance to be seen as equally competent as her male colleagues. As Ashcraft (2005; Ashcraft & Mumby, 2004) has shown, the airline industry historically has deliberately constructed an image of the airline pilot as coolly rational, professional, in control, and paternalistic—a gendered professional identity intended to make us feel safe while we are flying in a metal tube at 30,000 feet. Similarly, the role of flight attendant has been deliberately constructed in a gendered manner to convey warmth, nurturance, and attentiveness; this feminized role perfectly complements the masculine role of the pilot. Thus, the creation of an organizational reality that allows us to fly with at least some level of comfort and calm is heavily dependent on gendered organizational identities and scripts in which the man takes care of the rational, technical, mechanical aspects of flying and the woman tends to the emotional, bodily dimensions of the experience. To take the analysis one step further, we can say that the experience of flying as a safe activity depends on a mind–body split, in which the masculine is associated with the mind and rationality and the feminine is associated with the body and emotions. Thus, pilots are held accountable for performances that exhibit rational decision making, coolness under pressure, paternalism ("This is your captain [father] speaking"), and technical proficiency. Flight attendants, on the other hand, are held accountable (by passengers) for their gendered performance of emotional labor that keeps passengers feeling safe and cared for.

Third, and following from the idea of organizations as gendered, the critical feminist perspective focuses on the ways organization members do gender; that is, it is an ongoing, performative accomplishment of both women and men (Butler, 1990; West & Zimmerman, 1987). This notion enables us to understand how, as social actors, we are constantly engaged in performances of gendered identity that are highly context driven and for which we are held accountable by others on a moment-to-moment basis. This doing of gender encompasses everything from the way we dress to how we talk to the kinds of activities we engage in, as well as the meanings we construct. In other words, our very identities are involved in the process of doing gender.

The notion of **gender accountability** is extremely important in this process. As sociologists Candace West and Don Zimmerman (1987) argue, each of us is constantly being held accountable for our adequate performance of masculinities and femininities, with each performance judged in terms of the social context in which it occurs. Feminist scholar Jane Flax (1990), for example, argues that both men and women are "prisoners of gender" (p. 179) and that we need to examine how both masculine and feminine identities are constructed in modern society. The usefulness of this approach is that it does not simply isolate women and femininity as problems to be addressed. Instead, masculinity is examined as something that is every bit as socially constructed as femininity is. It also recognizes that, as Flax suggests, men are in many ways just as constrained by societal gender scripts as women are. For example, men are often held to standards of hypermasculinity and required to behave in macho and aggressive ways; such standards frequently limit how men are legitimately able to express emotion and tenderness.

For example, Karen Ho's (2009) study of the culture of Wall Street investment bankers shows a gendered performance in which employees are held accountable for their masculinity through working insane hours, earning lots of money, and pushing their (often drug-fuelled) bodies to the limit. Interestingly, the workers in Collinson's (1992) study of working class truck factory workers (see Chapter 2) would probably consider such work effeminate, given that it does not involve actual, physical labor in which one gets one's hands dirty—a good example of how the social construction of gender (masculinity or femininity) is contextual.

An interesting extension of the gender accountability notion is the challenges transgender people encounter in and around work. Although organizations have made strides in accepting workers who identify as lesbian, gay, bisexual, and queer, transgender identities still meet significant discrimination (Dixon & Dougherty, 2014), including an unemployment rate three times the national average. Curious about how identifying as transgender affects the search for employment, organizational communication scholar Elizabeth Eger's (2018) study of transgender jobseekers found that they often tried to keep their transgender identities closeted to avoid stigma and make themselves marketable but that potential employers enforced gender accountability without their consent. In many cases, interviewers "read" the jobseekers' bodies and/or their speech in interviews and directly questioned their identities; some even conducted background checks revealing interviewees' former names. Many trans people are thus reluctant to disclose their gender identities, fearful that managers and co-workers will enforce a restrictive two-category gender accountability on persons who problematize performances of masculinities and femininities.

Finally, the critical feminist perspective enables us to look closely at the relationships among gender, work, and power. While gender is socially constructed and changing, such constructions do not occur in a haphazard manner. Rather, they are the result of relations of power in organizations and society. Generally speaking, those groups who have the most power and resources have the most influence on the ways gender identities are constructed. Moreover, those groups in power construct these gendered identities in ways that benefit them the most (Ashcraft, 2013).

The simplest example of this process at work is the way that, historically, men have largely shaped the gendered identities available to both women and men, with feminine identities being constructed as inferior to masculine identities. Such constructions (e.g., women as emotional/irrational, subject to hysteria, maternal, etc.) were traditionally used as a means to justify women's exclusion from many spheres of society (government, industry—except in limited roles—law, etc.). In the airline industry, for example, the argument for excluding women from the cockpit included the claim that a woman who was menstruating might act emotionally and place passengers in danger! And of course, legally speaking, women historically were considered to have no rights and were viewed literally as the property of their husbands. Such a view of women in society is hard to sustain without discourses and sense-making practices that construct women as weak, emotional, needing paternalistic care, and so forth. In addition, the perspective of history allows us to see just how socially constructed these views of women were (although, of course, these social constructions had very real political and economic consequences).

In contemporary organizational life, the relationship between gender and power shapes everyday work and professional contexts. Angela Trethewey (2001), for example, shows how middle-aged professional women are subject to a societal master narrative of decline in which they are positioned as less attractive and less powerful by virtue of their aging bodies; professional women often experience aging as a time of loss and isolation. Such a narrative typically does not apply to male professionals, who are generally viewed as more experienced, distinguished, and powerful as they age. Trethewey's point is that women professionals inevitably have to confront and make sense of the narrative of decline, choosing either to reproduce it by buying in to the idea that they need to work out more, get plastic surgery, and so on, or to resist it and reject the idea of youth and beauty as superior to the aging process.

The idea that gender, work, and power are closely connected is effectively illustrated by another glass metaphor—that is, the **glass slipper** (Ashcraft, 2013). Ashcraft defines the glass slipper as "the alignment of occupational identity with embodied social identities as it yields systematic forms of advantage and disadvantage" (p. 16). Put simply, the glass slipper draws attention to the ways that certain forms of identity are deemed to fit more naturally with certain professions (like Cinderella and her glass slipper). Thus, as Cinderella's particular form of femininity eliminated the ugly sisters from contention for the prince's hand in marriage (because the slipper was made for her, and her only), so many occupations carefully construct the social identity that is to be seen as a natural fit for the work they perform. Ashcraft's point is that such constructions do not happen arbitrarily; they are the result of strategic efforts to construct occupational glass slippers that fit only certain kinds of social identities (white, male, heterosexual, etc.) and exclude others (black/brown, female, gay, etc.), even though there is no connection between the form of work performed and the social identity of the worker. Technical professions, for example, are often heavily male dominated, even though there is no natural or biological connection between the kind of work done and male bodies. Thus, the glass slipper "calls attention to systematic patterns of disadvantage and advantage" (Ashcrat, 2013, p. 26) by highlighting how taken for granted divisions among occupational identities are socially constructed.

An excellent example of the glass slipper is portrayed in the 2016 film *Hidden Figures*, which dramatizes the important role of African American women mathematicians in the NASA space program of the 1960s. The film draws attention to how, although essential to the success of the space program (Katherine Johnson, for example, calculated launch and re-entry trajectories for manned spacecraft), these women were excluded from the history of the space program precisely because the occupational glass slipper of mathematician/ NASA employee does not fit them (the title of the film alludes to how their black bodies ("figures") were written out of the official historical record of the NASA space program). Indeed, the film superbly portrays how, at every turn, they are socially constructed as "other," the "ugly step sisters," as it were, of the space program. As Ashcraft (2013), indicates, however, the glass slipper "is both solid and fragile; it can be shattered and refashioned" (p. 22), as occupations go through discursive struggles over their collective identity. The professional identities of occupations change, but often only through the efforts of those who are marginalized and deemed not worthy of wearing the glass slipper.

Table 8.1	Comparing Liberal, Radical, and Critical Feminist Perspectives		
	Perspective		
Issue	**Liberal Feminism**	**Radical Feminism**	**Critical Feminism**
View of organizations	Creates barriers to women's advancement (e.g., glass ceiling)	Inherently patriarchal; needs alternative organizations rooted in women's ways of knowing	Gendered forms that construct systems of power and meaning (e.g., glass slipper)
Conception of gender	Social roles played by men and women; gender as variable	Gender as essential features of women and men	We are always accountable for our gendered performances
View of communication	Communication as expression of gender roles; communication styles reflect gender	Built on patriarchal meanings; needs to create alternative, woman-centered forms of communication	Communication and power inextricably linked; communication creates gendered identities
Goal of emancipation	Creates equal opportunities for women and men	Creates a world based on feminist principles, free from patriarchy	Free both women and men from systems of power that make both prisoners of gender

❧ MASCULINITY AND ORGANIZATIONAL COMMUNICATION

When people think about gender and feminism, they typically think about women's issues. This tendency is partly because, for much of its history, feminism has been concerned with women's rights and advancement, but it's also because, from a commonsense perspective, women have gender and men do not. However, as we have already learned, masculinity is just as much a product of social constructions and power relations as femininity is. The case is simply that those groups possessing the most power tend to position themselves as the norm and therefore are relatively invisible (the glass slipper is not visible on men, for example). Hence, masculinity typically has not been held up to the same kind of scrutiny as femininity has. So, in this section, we will take a closer look at the relationship between masculinity and organizing.

Historian Gail Bederman (1995) shows that the term *masculinity* came into common usage only in the early 20th century and replaced the term *manliness* in describing appropriate male behavior and identity. From the early to mid-19th century, the term manliness was used to describe "honor, high-mindedness, and strength stemming from . . . self-mastery" (p. 12). Manliness had strong moral connotations, describing a virtuous form of life characterized by gentility and respectability; in complementary fashion, true womanhood involved the pious, maternal guardianship of virtue and the domestic sphere. This conception of manliness was seen as the foundation on which virtuous men could build their fortunes in an entrepreneurial society. Thus, "middle-class men were awarded (or denied) credit based on others' assessment of the manliness of their characters, and credit raters like Dun and Bradstreet reported on businessmen's honesty, probity, and family life" (p. 14).

In the late 19th century, however, this conception of manliness changed as the economic landscape shifted from small-scale businesses to the large-scale corporations of industrial capitalism; between 1870 and 1910, the percentage of middle-class men who were self-employed dropped from 67% to 37%. Moreover, middle-class male identity and authority were being challenged on two fronts: by women demanding universal suffrage and by working-class men and immigrants who were increasingly gaining political power through unions. If we add to this scenario a newly diagnosed medical condition called neurasthenia (a nervous disorder caused by excessive brain work in an increasingly competitive economy) from which doctors claimed middle-class businessmen were increasingly suffering, then manliness as a form of identity was under significant threat.

Bederman (1995) claims that in the face of this threat, middle-class men attempted to remake and revitalize their sense of manhood. For example, social contexts traditionally associated with working-class men, such as saloons and music halls, were increasingly adopted by middle-class men, and values such as physical prowess, aggressiveness, and strong sexuality were seen as desirable traits. Moreover, middle-class men began to take up activities such as sparring and adopted boxing as a spectator sport.

Interestingly, Bederman (1995) indicates that in the late 19th century, as men worked to reshape manhood, they adopted new terms used to denigrate behaviors seen as unmanly. *Sissy*, *pussyfoot*, and *stuffed shirt* were all coined "to denote behavior which had once appeared self-possessed and manly but now seemed overcivilized and effeminate" (p. 17).

In contrast, a new term increasingly emerged to refer to all behaviors that embodied the new, virile sense of manhood—masculinity.

In many ways this new form of masculinity (which Bederman, 1995, says was firmly established by 1930) is still hegemonic, or dominant, today. Aggressiveness, strong heterosexuality, assertiveness, independence, individuality, and so forth are probably terms that most men (and women) would use to describe what it currently means to be masculine. The important thing to keep in mind is that this form of hegemonic masculinity is not a natural feature of men but is the product of specific historical, economic, political, and social conditions and is open to change and transformation.

In studying workplace masculinity, the focus of many organizational researchers has involved, as management scholar Jeff Hearn (1996) puts it, "deconstructing the dominant—making the one(s) the other(s)" (p. 611). In other words, shining a light on masculinity means exploring how it is constructed as a dominant gender and also enables us to think about other ways in which masculinity might be performed (Connell, 1993, 1995; Connell, Hearn, & Kimmel, 2005). As Albert Mills and Peter Chiaramonte (1991) put it, organizations provide a gendered metacommunicative frame; that is, they communicate about the appropriate gendered communicative practices in which we should engage.

Of course, such frames do not dictate how we must enact our gendered identities—masculine or feminine—but as indicated above, we are always held accountable for our gendered performances, rendering us open to sanctions (punishment) if we do not perform adequately. Women are often sanctioned if they fail to act in an appropriately feminine manner (whatever that might mean), while men are often sanctioned for exhibiting behavior that is not appropriately masculine (again, the meaning of this varies from context to context).

CRITICAL RESEARCH 8.1

Kristen Barber (2008). The well-coiffed man: Class, race, and heterosexual masculinity in the hair salon. *Gender & Society, 22*, 455–476.

In her ethnographic study, the perfectly named Kristen Barber examines how the traditionally feminine space of a hair salon becomes a site for the management of professional heterosexual masculinity. While the salon (as opposed to the barber shop) is a space where women "create bonds and form friendships with each other" (p. 458), it is increasingly used by men as a resource to maintain their professional identities. Barber situates the study in the context of the historical shift from Fordist industrial work in which men's masculinity was judged in terms of their ability to perform manual labor, to late-Fordist and post-Fordist work in which there is a greater emphasis on appearance. As such, white-collar employees are increasingly required to interact with customers and develop strong interpersonal skills and elegant appearance. Thus, "it is no longer enough for men to work hard, they must also look good" (p. 460).

Barber's study focuses on the men's motivations for going to a hair salon rather than a barbershop and examines how these motivations reflect a particular construction of masculine identity. She identifies three motivations: (1) to enjoy the salon as a place of leisure, luxury, and pampering; (2) to form personalized relationships with their hair stylists; and (3) to obtain a stylish haircut that they view as reflecting a white, professional aesthetic. To address these motivations, Barber adopts an intersectional approach (considering how race, class, and gender come together) to address these questions.

First, Barber shows how the men construct the salon as a place where they can be pampered. They see it as a place where they can relax and take a pause from what they view as their hectic (read "professional") daily lives. They feel taken care of by the gendered body work of the female stylists. While they could never justify attending a spa, a 45-minute pause in their day is constructed as part of their professionalization process.

Second, and related, the men see the relationship with their stylists as personal, involving the sharing of intimate details about family and home life. Thus, the stylists perform both body and emotional labor in constructing personal relationships with the men. Interestingly, the men make sense of this personal attention as contrasting with the (male) barber–client relationship at a barbershop, where the barber "doesn't care about you" and is simply doing a job. Barber (the author!) argues that this distinction is not only gendered but classed, as the clients describe a distinction between "garage talk" at the barber's and "professional talk" at the salon. Again, we see how gender construction never occurs in isolation, but always in relation to other constructions of gender.

Finally, Barber suggests that while attention to looks can potentially threaten their masculinity, the men justify patronizing a salon by arguing that it is not for them but to maintain a professional appearance for others. In the process, they again distance themselves from the barbershop where, they argue, the haircuts are outmoded and not professional. Moreover, they suggest, the barbershop reflects a more aggressive (read working class) masculinity that does not fit with their professional identity.

In sum, the study is an interesting example of how gender construction often occurs through binary oppositions; in this case, the binary of professional white men and working-class white men. Note that the extent to which this opposition exists in reality (e.g., the Brooklyn-style barbershop has become hipster central in popular culture and thus contradicts this reality) matters less than the fact the opposition is used by a particular group to engage in identity work to resolve particular tensions (in this case, men attending a feminized space).

Discussion Questions

1. What kind of salon or barbershop do you use? Can you identify gendered performances (by both client and stylist) in this context?

2. To what degree do you agree with Barber's analysis? As a brief field study, visit a barbershop and a hair salon and see if you can identify the patterns of gendered behavior that Barber discusses. Do you see additional forms of gender expression at work?

3. Are there other forms of service or retail work that exhibit the same kind of gender binary that the hairdressing industry exhibits? What are they, and what kinds of gender performances do they entail?

It is important to note, though, that when we talk about masculinity, we are not referring to individual men or women and the ways they act. Instead, masculinity refers to a set of routines, scripts, and discourses that shape behavior. In this sense, masculinity is less a personality trait and more a set of meanings and institutional frames through which we are held accountable for our gendered performances. In addition, masculinity as a gendered practice makes sense only in relation to femininity; neither stands alone as a meaningful identity.

For example, author Joseph Finder (1987) provides an interesting account of his experience working as a secretary in a large corporation (the title of the article, "A Male Secretary," gives some insight into how gendered the traditional secretarial role is). He describes how everyone who visited the office where he worked would try to make sense of his role there by asking questions such as "Are you filling in for the regular secretary?" or "Are you working here temporarily?" Even his boss would try to avoid giving him certain tasks, such as photocopying and would frequently stop by his desk to talk sports ("How about those Red Sox?") in an effort to reassert a "normal" masculine relationship. Interestingly, even his female secretarial coworkers refused to accept his presence there or his claims that this position was his "real" job, choosing instead to encourage him to move on to better things (think about how this encouragement ties in to the notion of the glass escalator, discussed above).

This article is a great example of how gendered organizational structures and ideologies constantly reassert themselves and reify established power relations, with those in subordinate positions often working to reproduce such power relations, even when they are not in their own best interests. Thus, rather than see the presence of a male secretary as a possibility for challenging traditional gender roles and creating the potential for change, secretaries instead choose to hold Finder accountable for his gender violation, hence reproducing their own subordination to gender ideologies that limit their own professional mobility.

Masculinity, then, is worthy of our consideration because it is usually taken for granted in the wider culture and has profound implications for how we view men, women, and their relationships with each other. As we have seen, masculinity is every bit as socially constructed as femininity, and what counts as masculine behavior is dependent on a number of contextual factors, including historical precedent, economic conditions, class, race, organizational culture, and so forth. As we indicated earlier in the chapter, quoting Jane Flax (1990), both men and women are "prisoners of gender," and, as such, we need to understand how contemporary conceptions of masculinity (and the kinds of femininity that complement them) both enable and limit possibilities for personal growth and development in organizational life.

The idea that masculinity, like femininity, is socially constructed means it is potentially open to change and transformation. Thus, although one might argue that the kind of hegemonic masculinity Bederman (1995) describes is still dominant in organizations and society more broadly, it is certainly the case that competing, or alternative, masculinities exist. Eric Anderson's (2009) notion of inclusive masculinity, for example, challenges the idea that masculinity is always rooted in homophobia and antifemininity. His ethnographic study of members of fraternities and university sports teams such as soccer and rugby reveals a greater openness to alternative masculinities, such as gay and more feminine men, than has usually been seen as typical for such social contexts, where domination, aggression, competition, sexism, and homophobia are thought to prevail. Inclusive masculinity doesn't necessarily challenge or overthrow hegemonic or orthodox masculinity but instead, broadens the range of possibilities for legitimate expressions of masculinity. If we think back to our earlier discussion of gender and accountability, we might say that Anderson's study suggests that young men in the contexts he studied (university sports teams and fraternities) are less likely to hold one another to a narrow definition of what counts as appropriately masculine behavior. In your experience, do you agree with this assessment?

CRITICAL CASE STUDY 8.1

Performing Working-Class Masculinity

During his college summer breaks, Dennis worked for an agricultural contractor in the United Kingdom called Farmwork Services (FS) that provided crop-spraying services to local farmers (not many young adults have such romantic and rewarding summer employment!). Many of the men he worked with (and they were all men, apart from one female clerical worker in the office) were relatively uneducated (some never finished high school), and all were poorly paid, earning wages barely above the poverty line. It would be fair to say that all of them were very much working class. All, however, had strong mechanical and technical skills; one had trained as a JCB driver (a JCB is a large, earth-moving machine), another could fix any engine around, and another had extensive body shop experience. In one way or another, all had practical skills that Dennis most certainly did not have.

Much of the interaction among the men was rooted in, and expressive of, a particular kind of working-class masculinity, not dissimilar from that of the workers in David Collinson's (1988) "Engineering Humor" study discussed in Chapter 2. Of course, there was the usual banter and joking about sexual performance (questions like, "Did you get any [sex] last night?" abounded), as well as the ritual daily passing around of the "Page Three girl" in *The Sun*—a daily tabloid that always featured a topless model.

But beyond these more obvious expressions of masculine heterosexuality, working-class masculinity was also performed in more subtle ways. For example, there were informal, though strictly enforced, rules about who sat in which chair in the crew room. As a new employee, Dennis made the mistake of sitting in a senior employee's seat and was told in no uncertain terms to move, finally being allocated the least desirable seat by the drafty crew room door. Also, early in his employment he made the mistake of picking up and reading a newspaper sitting on the seat next to him. The owner of the newspaper berated him for this faux pas; what he quickly discovered was that a newspaper became

(Continued)

(Continued)

common property in the crew room only when its owner had read it to his satisfaction; opening a crisp, clean newspaper for the first time was the owner's prerogative and no one else's.

Finally, one of the most distinctive ways in which masculinity was performed was through employees' careful separation of book knowledge and white-collar work on the one hand, and practical knowledge and blue-collar work on the other hand. Much of the employees' identities as men was tied up in the practical skills they possessed, whether that involved working complex equipment, repainting company vehicles, or spraying crops with chemicals. Moreover, despite the fact that they were more poorly paid than the white-collar office workers and managers, they frequently compared themselves favorably with them, arguing that the managers knew little about the "real work" they did. In fact, one of the employees who had expertise in spray painting vehicles turned a 2-day job into 3 days of work because he knew his supervisor had no idea how such a job was done. Such resistance to managerial control is not unusual as workers attempt to maintain some degree of autonomy in work environments where they have little power.

Work at FS, then, was defined in part by the working-class masculine identities employees enacted in the workplace. These identities were constructed partly through identification with a particular kind of work—hard, physical labor that required engagement with and mastery of something tangible—and partly through opposition to other forms of identity that did not pass muster on the masculinity front. The latter included white-collar masculinity that involved paper pushing or book knowledge and any form of femininity (most of the men Dennis worked with placed women in two categories—sex objects and faithful or nagging wives—but either way they were placed in a subordinate position).

Thus, gender roles are not simply acted out in individualistic ways but rather are produced through interactions with others who hold us accountable for playing out those roles. Such accountability leaves us open to sanction when we fail to meet the standards of the organization or those around us—even if those other people occupy subordinate positions in the organizational hierarchy. For a longer discussion of Dennis's experience at FS, see Mumby (2006).

Discussion Questions

1. How would you describe your gender identity? In what ways do you express or perform this identity?

2. Have you ever been in a work context that was highly gendered? In what ways was it gendered? In what ways did you enact and/or resist this gender construction? How were you held accountable for your performance of gender?

3. In what ways do class and gender intersect? Can you identify different gender performances that are specific to particular class locations?

♣ SEXUAL HARASSMENT IN THE WORKPLACE

We did not want to end this chapter without drawing attention to the issue of sexual harassment. In many ways, this workplace phenomenon draws acute attention to the relationship between gender and power. As the #MeToo and #TimesUp! movements have powerfully illustrated, what most sexual harassers have in common is their ability to exercise power and control over the people they harass (e.g., Harvey Weinstein, Kevin Spacey, Mario Batali, and Matt Lauer). And while there are many cases of men being sexually harassed (Scarduzio & Geist-Martin, 2010), the vast majority of harassment cases involve men harassing women. Indeed, using a broad definition that covers everything from verbal harassment to sexual assault, a recent survey indicates that 81% of women and 43% of men have experienced sexual harassment (Chatterjee, 2018).

According to the U.S. Equal Employment Opportunity Commission (2002),

> Unwelcome sexual advances, requests for sexual favors, and other verbal or physical conduct of a sexual nature constitutes sexual harassment when submission to or rejection of this conduct explicitly or implicitly affects an individual's employment, unreasonably interferes with an individual's work performance or creates an intimidating, hostile or offensive work environment.

Sexual harassment is typically viewed as taking two different forms: (1) hostile environment and (2) quid pro quo. In the hostile environment form, sexual harassment involves contexts where conduct directed at a person because of her or his sex or sexuality unreasonably interferes with the person's ability to perform her or his job. The quid pro quo (literally, "something for something") form involves situations in which a harasser demands sexual favors with the promise of preferred treatment regarding employment or evaluation (Harvey Weinstein's assurances, and threats, that he would provide or eliminate movie roles for his victims would be a prime example of this sort of harassment).

Almost everyone would agree that sexual harassment is unacceptable and a significant problem in the workplace; however, it is surprisingly difficult for people to agree on when sexual harassment has occurred. Even organization members who have experienced sexual harassment are not always comfortable naming their experience as harassment. Furthermore, one person's perception of behavior as friendly banter can sometimes be framed by another as threatening and intimidating behavior. This difference in interpretation of behavior is especially true when there is a power differential between the parties involved. There is a much greater chance that a person in a subordinate position will view a particular behavior as harassing than a person in a more powerful position will. We are sure many of you—particularly the women in the class—have felt uneasy about behavior exhibited toward you by a superior or someone in authority, and we suspect that if you were to confront that person about his or her behavior, he or she would be shocked at your interpretation of the actions in question. Of course, such a response does not mean that person's behavior is not harassment (regardless of the intent) or that you are wrong to feel uncomfortable.

However, it is important to point out that harassment is not just an interpersonal issue, but an organizational one too. Institutionally speaking, organizations are often terrible at dealing with sexual harassment and often have bureaucratic procedures in place that do more to protect the organization than the individual who is experiencing harassment. Indeed, as organizational communication scholar Kate Harris (2013) argues, official organizational discourse on sexual harassment and violence is often written in ways that excuse those organizations from complicity with harassment and violence. Indeed, it is well worth reading engineer Susan Fowler's (2017) account of her time working at Uber, in which the company not only systematically failed to address her sexual harassment complaints (about a manager who had been reported by numerous women) but also punished her (by giving her poor performance reports and blocking a transfer) for reporting the issue. Fowler notes that when she joined Über, 25% of its workforce were women, but by the time she tried to transfer, that number had fallen to 6%.

Sexual harassment experiences of organization members, then, are often sequestered (i.e., hidden from public view and discussion) by the ways both the people who experience harassment and the institutions that create policies discursively frame (i.e., give meaning to) such behaviors (Clair, 1993a, b). Clair reports that in her interviews with women who had experienced workplace harassment, the women used some common discursive frames to make sense out of their experiences. These frames include, for example, simple misunderstanding, in which women who experience harassment frame it as an interpretive error on their part (thus shifting blame away from the harassers and to themselves), and reification, in which sexual harassment is accepted as part of the culture of the organization, as the way it is.

One might assume that, 25 years after Clair's (1993a, b) research, it has become easier for women to identify and confront forms of organizational discrimination, including sexual harassment—especially as women gain a stronger foothold amongst the managerial élite. However, recent research by psychologist Britney Brinkman and her colleagues suggests that this is not the case; women continue to struggle to confront instances in which they experience various forms of gender prejudice (Brinkman, Garcia, & Rickard, 2011; Brinkman & Rickard, 2009). Analyzing daily online diaries kept by 81 college-age women, Brinkman found discrepancies between what the women said they would do and what they actually do in dealing with gender prejudice. Thus, women seem readily able to identify gender prejudice (unlike some of Clair's respondents) but are often loath to confront it directly, expressing concerns about possibly escalating the situation or harming their careers. This evidence suggests, then, that women still struggle with how to deal with prejudice and harassment, fearing backlash from supervisors and peers. Indeed, as the #MeToo movement has shown, such concerns are very real, as many women have reported experiencing such backlash. In perhaps the most extreme (and scary) example, Harvey Weinstein is reported to have hired ex-Mossad (Israeli secret service) agents to spy on women who accused him of sexual harassment (Farrow, 2017).

CONCLUSION

In this chapter, we have examined the relationships among gender, power, work, and organizing. To begin with, we discussed three different feminist perspectives that provided us with three very different lenses for viewing the gender-power-organization perspective. While all three perspectives are useful in their own right, the critical feminist approach best captures the ways in which gender is a socially constructed, communicative phenomenon. Moreover, the critical feminist approach enables us to think of gender as an ongoing accomplishment of everyday organizational life that always occurs in the context of power relations; everyone is held accountable for the performance of gender, but some people are held more accountable than others. Finally, the critical feminist perspective enables us to see gender not as simply a characteristic of individuals but rather, as an endemic, defining feature of organizational life. In claiming that organizations are gendered, we are saying that the very meanings, structures, routines, and norms of organizing are rooted in particular understanding of male and female, masculine and feminine. By examining the relationship between gender and power in this way, we can develop a better understanding of how gender issues thread themselves in complex ways through everyday organizational life.

We also examined the relationship between masculinity and organizational communication. This examination is important in part because as a rule, men and masculinity are the neutral norm against which gender performances are measured. By unpacking masculinity and its meanings we better understand how what is "normal" and "natural" comes into being and thus how what complements the normal (femininity, alternative masculinities, etc.) is positioned in society and in organizational life. This discussion opens up the possibilities for thinking about what alternatives to hegemonic masculinity might look like.

Finally, we discussed the phenomenon of sexual harassment, noting that it needs to be understood as an extreme (though all too routine) example of the intersection of gender and power. Sexual harassment at work does not just involve one or more person's bad behavior, but it must be understood and addressed at the institutional, organizational level.

Overall, we have tried in this chapter to think about gender and organizational communication in more complex ways than it is typically discussed. Through this process we can better reflect on the role gender plays in everyday organizational life.

CRITICAL APPLICATIONS

1. Conduct a gender analysis of yourself. How would you describe your own gendered identity? Keep in mind that this is different from your sexuality; it refers to the ways you engage in a gendered performance as you engage with others in social situations. Do you see yourself as highly masculine/feminine? Metrosexual? Why? What is it about your gender identity that enables you to classify yourself in this way?

2. Think about some examples from your everyday organizational life that illustrate how gender is socially constructed. What consequences does this social construction process have for the way organizations operate and make decisions?

3. On a piece of paper, write down as many answers as you can to the following question: "When you have to walk home late at night from, for example, class or the campus library, what precautions do you take to protect yourself?" Once you have completed the list, pair up

with a man (if you are a woman) or a woman (if you are a man) and compare your lists. What do you notice. Discuss with your partner what these lists say about the relationship between gender and power. This exercise can be concluded with a full class discussion about the differences between men's and women's answers to this question.

KEY TERMS

critical feminism   212

feminism   198

gender accountability   214

glass ceiling   201

glass cliff   205

glass escalator   205

glass slipper   215

hegemonic masculinity   218

homosocial reproduction   203

hostile environment   223

intersectional approach   205

liberal feminism   200

quid pro quo   223

radical feminism   209

sexual harassment   223

tokenism   202

STUDENT STUDY SITE

Visit the student study site at www.sagepub.com/mumby.org for these additional learning tools:

- Web quizzes
- eFlashcards
- SAGE journal articles
- Video resources
- Web resources

CHAPTER 9

Communicating Difference at Work

iStock.com/photomorphic

Increased difference and diversity characterize the 21st-century organization.

Fear of difference is dread of life itself.

—Mary Parker Follett (1924, p. 301)

What are the differences that make a difference (Bateson, 1972)? Put another way, what differences matter? We will attempt to answer this question in this chapter. Today's workforce is more diverse than it has ever been, and it will continue to become even more so over the next several decades. Indeed, the U.S. Census Bureau (2018) predicts that the United States will likely become majority-minority within the next 30 years, while minority children will be in the majority by the time you read this textbook. As such, it is important to get an understanding of the complex dynamics of difference in current organizational life. More profoundly, however, as questions of identity become increasingly central to work life, we need to understand how difference plays a central role in human identity construction. While we will address identity and the meaning of work in Chapter 14, in this chapter we will focus on difference as a central organizing principle of the workplace.

Although it has traditionally been a neglected area of study, a number of organizational communication scholars have begun to examine the question of difference and to think about how it can be addressed from a communication perspective (Allen, 2000, 2011; Ashcraft, 2011, 2013; Ashcraft & Allen, 2003; Eger, 2018; Harris & McDonald, 2018; McDonald, 2015; McDonald & Kuhn, 2016; McDonald & Mitra, In press; Mumby, 2011; Parker, 2014; Sullivan, 2014). From this viewpoint, differences such as race, class, gender, sexuality, and so forth are not natural but are historical, political, and economic constructs that require a lot of communicative labor to maintain them (Dempsey, 2009). However, arguing that forms of difference are socially constructed does not negate their real-world consequences. Indeed, we will discuss the ways the communicative construction of difference shapes the material and economic realities of difference in its various forms. The organization of difference in the workplace, then, is very much a consequence of the communication processes that occur currently and historically. We will thus address difference by asking the question "How does communication organize work through difference?" (Ashcraft, 2011). In other words, rather than think of difference as a set of individual characteristics (natural or otherwise) or as something that exists in organizational settings (e.g., "We have a diverse workforce"), we will think of difference as an organizing principle that—through communication processes—shapes the meaning, structure, and very practice of work. First, let's define what we mean by difference.

DEFINING DIFFERENCE AT WORK

Borrowing a conception from communication scholars Mark Orbe and Tina Harris (2001) that they developed to define race as a category of difference, we can say that difference is a social construction "that has been used to classify human beings into separate value-based categories" (p. 6). A number of interconnected issues are associated with this definition:

1. Difference is connected to power; that is, those in power construct differences that create systems of enfranchisement and disenfranchisement. In this sense, differences are not benign or neutral in their effects.

2. All differences are not created equal. Each pair in a binary system of difference is characterized by a dominant, more highly valued pole and a subordinate, less-valued pole. In the following pairs, for example, the first item in the binary pair is historically dominant and valued, while the second is subordinate and less valued: man/woman, white/black, heterosexual/homosexual, able-bodied/disabled. All binary differences contain a positive and a negative element.

3. Related, difference contrasts with and complements what is defined as normal. That is, the dominant term in each of the pairs above is normalized and becomes the largely invisible (because it is the taken for granted norm) lens through which the lesser term is measured. A deviation from the norm is that which is different and hence targeted for classification and investigation. For example, as we will see

below, "whiteness" is the invisible, normalized racial category against which other racial categories are constructed, classified, and assigned value.

4. Difference is communicatively constructed. That is, differences are produced and maintained through various forms of talk, texts, and interactions. Racial differences, for example, are maintained and reproduced through something as mundane as a job application form or as significant as anti-miscegenation laws (basically, laws against interracial marriage) in the United States, which operated from the late 17th century until (in some states) the 1960s.

Thus, when we asked at the beginning of this chapter, "What are the differences that make a difference?" we were referencing the processes through which certain forms of difference get connected to judgments around value (what are those differences worth?) and power (who is it that gets to decide who is worthy of having value and who is not?). Historically speaking, the differences that make a difference include gender, race, class, and sexuality, with the more recent recognition of ability and age (Allen, 2011). These differences have been especially pivotal in the institutional construction of forms of value and systems of power. There are other forms of difference, of course, although their importance tends to be more situational. For example, Romo (2018) has investigated what it means to "come out" at work as a nondrinker. While the binary of drinker/nondrinker is not generally regarded as a difference that makes a difference, it can become so if an employee is a former alcoholic (the revealing of which may create stigma) or a nondrinker in a work culture that favors alcohol consumption (e.g., campus fraternities). Dennis's younger brother Neil (a former police officer in an anti-terrorist unit) once received a performance evaluation in which he was told that he wasn't enough of a team player. When he asked his superior officer what this comment meant, it turned out that the other members of his unit had noticed that he never went out drinking with them after a shift, preferring to go home to his wife. What is interesting here is how a particular behavior (not drinking) is interpreted as a form of difference that is incompatible with an informal work culture norm (regular drinking after work to create team unity).

Differences, then, are not naturally occurring; they are social constructions that get normalized and institutionalized in organizations. Such institutionalization serves the interests of the dominant group, who will often go to great lengths to preserve that dominance if it appears under threat by anyone regarded as different. Historically, dominant groups have organized in both formal and informal ways to marginalize difference, including, for example, opposition to women's suffrage, Jim Crow legislation in the U.S. South, and criminalization and demonization of homosexuality (including its classification as a mental disorder until the early 1970s).

But wait a second, we hear you say. How can you argue that differences are not naturally occurring when they clearly exist in the world? We have men and women, white people and people of color, straight people and gay people, and so on. This is, of course, true. However, it's also false. Race, for example, is a humanly constructed category (Gilroy, 2002). Society (well, the people in power in society) has taken an arbitrary difference between groups of people (one that makes up an infinitesimal part of our DNA) and has constructed a massive cultural, political, and economic edifice around it. In this sense, race as a category is a powerful ideological construct rooted in an arbitrary, insignificant biological variation among humans. Just because it is a mere construct, however, does not mean that race does not organize the world in ways that have genuine material and economic consequences for people. Similarly, homosexuality was not constructed as deviant until the Victorian age, when it became an intensive object of scrutiny of medical discourses and was subsequently criminalized precisely because of the way it had been constructed and classified by medical discourses (Foucault, 1980).

However, let's make a couple of further points before we move onto a discussion of specific forms of difference. First, it's important to think about difference intersectionally. That is, we should view differences not as existing independently but as combining together to create particular effects and structures of power (K. Crenshaw, 1991). For example, the differences of race and gender intersect in different ways for different people, affecting their career possibilities and life chances. A woman of color does not experience systems of power in the same way as a white woman, who does not experience them in the way as a white, gay man, and so on. This is not to say that differences determine outcomes; rather, it says that differences are made sense of and confronted by people differently, depending on how differences intersect to form particular social identities (Allen, 2011). A woman of color moves through (and is confronted by) the world differently than a white woman precisely because of the ways race and gender intersect to form her identity.

Second, it is important to understand that differences are not individual traits; rather, they are embedded in institutions and organizations, creating what feminist scholar Joan Acker (2006) refers to as inequality regimes. This statement is not to deny biological differences, but rather to recognize that what gets noticed and framed as desirable or undesirable is the product of social construction. What we typically take to be traits, then, are better understood as "loosely interrelated practices, processes, actions, and meanings that result in and maintain class, racial, and gender inequalities within particular organizations" (p. 443). Thus, just as organizations are gendered (see Chapter 8), so are they raced, classed, and so forth. Men of color have particular bodies and identities, but it is the way their difference is constructed and encoded in discourses and institutions that creates the regimes of inequality. For example, the arrest of two African American men who were waiting for a friend in a Starbucks in April 2018 shows how inequality regimes get enacted. Starbucks' closing of its stores in May 2018 to provide anti-bias training to its employees reflects the company's recognition that racial bias is an institutional rather than individual issue (see Chapter 11 for a more detailed discussion of the Starbucks case).

Given this framing of difference, we can argue that difference is not about the ways that people fit particular identity categories but about how normalization occurs through communication processes. A helpful way to think about this process is through queer theory (de Lauretis, 1991; McDonald, 2015, 2016; Sedgwick, 2008). Originally used as a pejorative term for gay people (or for anyone who was considered odd), in the last 20 years the term *queer* has been reclaimed in a positive way in an effort to critique how processes of normalization operate to marginalize certain groups of people. Communication scholar and queer theorist Gust Yep (2003) defines **normalization** as

the process of constructing, establishing, producing, and reproducing a taken-for-granted and all-encompassing standard used to measure goodness, desirability, morality, rationality, superiority, and a host of other dominant cultural values. As such, normalization becomes one of the primary instruments of power in modern society. (p. 18)

In this sense, queer refers to "whatever is at odds with the normal, the legitimate, the dominant" (Halperin, as cited in Yep, 2003, p. 36). Thus, queer scholars address how one can queer processes of normalization by showing how they are rooted in inequality regimes. Organizational communication scholar James McDonald suggests that rather than think in terms of the identity categories that people occupy, organizational communication researchers focusing on difference should "expose and critique the multitude of ways in which organizational members become normalized, as well as the consequences of those normalization processes" (2015, p. 322). Like Halperin above, McDonald defines queer broadly as "anyone or anything that goes against the norm and is considered deviant" (p. 322).

As we explore forms of difference below, then, we would like you to think about them through this queer lens; that is, in the context of work and organizations, how does normalization occur, and with what consequences for certain forms of difference? How does difference get organized into, and out of, organizational life through communication processes?

Let's now look more closely at two important forms of difference and examine their relationship to organizational communication: (1) race and (2) sexuality.

⚬ RACE AND ORGANIZATIONAL COMMUNICATION

Putting Race and Organization in Historical Context

It's very evident in reading books such as William H. Whyte's (1956) *The Organization Man* or Rosabeth Moss Kanter's (1977) *Men and Women of the Corporation* that for most of the 20th century, organizations were dominated by white males. As we saw in the previous chapter, this domination was functional if you were a white male, but it pretty much sucked if you weren't.

In fact, the idea that difference and diversity among employees was a good thing did not even register as an issue with mid-20th century managers. In the 1950s and 1960s (and even into the 1970s), managers did not walk around thinking "We really need to make our organization more diverse—if only I could attract lots of female and minority employees." The white maleness of most organizations was just a fact—the way things were and always had been, with no need for justification. In this sense, whiteness was the invisible, taken for granted norm against which everything was measured. Indeed, the presence of the occasional token woman or person of color in managerial positions often reaffirmed the white male norm, especially as these token employees often failed, hence providing justification for the natural order of the work world. Furthermore, this white male norm obscured the fact that while women and minorities were largely absent from managerial and professional positions, they have always been a significant presence at lower levels of organizations, occupying unskilled and semiskilled positions in factories and on production lines throughout the history of industrial capitalism (Vallas, 2012).

Management scholars Stewart Clegg, David Courpasson, and Nelson Phillips (2006) even argue that there was a strong racial element to the surveillance Henry Ford's Sociological Department imposed on Ford's employees. The department consisted of teams of investigators whose job was to make sure that workers at Ford were living a clean, sober, industrious, and thrifty private life worthy of their $5-a-day wage. Many Ford workers in the early 20th century were African Americans who had migrated North to purse work opportunities denied to them in the Jim Crow South. Clegg et al. argue that much of the motivation for the surveillance program was a larger, society-level moral panic that focused on the apparent connections among African American migration, alcohol, and jazz music. Such moral panics, they argue, were "barely coded concerns for the contagion of white society by black bodies and black culture" (p. 59). As a 1921 edition of *Ladies Home Journal* stated,

> The effect of jazz on the normal brain produces an atrophied condition of the brain cells of conception, until very frequently those under the demoralizing influence of the persistent use of syncopation, combined with the inharmonic partial tones, are actually incapable of distinguishing between good and evil, right and wrong. (as cited in Clegg et al., 2006, p. 59)

It is easy to see here how a form of culture originating with African Americans is constructed in the popular imagination as a threat to (white) social order. More recently, American Studies scholar Elizabeth Esch (2018) has explored the close connection between Fordism and race. While in the early 20th century the Ford Motor Company attempted to systematically "Americanize" its heavily European immigrant workforce (through English language schools, visits to their homes, etc.), it viewed its African American workforce as "more akin to colonized subjects" who "were to the company neither sufficiently American nor Americanizable" (p. 5). Thus, even though Ford employed 10,000 African American workers (and indeed, was the only automobile company that did so in the early 20th century), these workers typically did not have the high prestigious and well-paid production jobs. Instead, they were employed in the forge and foundry at the massive River Rouge plant in Detroit—work that was dirty and dangerous.

The relationships among race, ethnicity, and work are particularly fascinating when we examine U.S. history in the late 19th and early 20th centuries. While the United States is generally described as a nation of immigrants and a great melting pot, this period of massive immigration from Europe (and the intense competition for jobs) is also a period during which many debates took place about national identity and, more specifically, which immigrant groups counted as white. Such debates were hardly academic and had a profound effect on the ability of particular immigrant groups to find work.

For example, as labor historian David Roediger (2005) shows, Italian immigrants were discriminated against by being constructed as nonwhite and frequently as black. Roediger reports that the Italian diaspora in the United States was racialized both as "the Chinese of Europe" (a group historically barred by law from working in the United States after their work on the railroad system was completed) and linked closely to Africans. Indeed, in a fascinating insight into how Italian immigrants were othered (i.e., marginalized) through racial classification, Roediger states, "The one black family on the *Titanic* was until recently lost to history in part because 'Italian' was used as a generic term for all the darker skinned passengers on board" (p. 47). Roediger also indicates that in the Jim Crow South, Italians were sometimes assigned to black schools. When in 1911 a white Louisiana lynch mob killed 11 Italians, their perceived identity as nonwhite was a significant factor in the actions of the mob.

In a similar manner, Hungarians and Eastern Europeans more broadly were identified in the early 20th century as nonwhite. Known by the racial slur Hunky (a corruption of Hungarian) or Bohunk (Bohemian-Hungarian), the term shifted from a specific reference to Hungarian immigrants and became applied more widely to unskilled immigrant workers from central and Eastern Europe. One early 20th-century Texas planter worried that "Bohunks wanted to intermarry with whites," adding that, "yes, they're white but they're not our kind of white" (Roediger, 2005, p. 43).

From a 21st-century perspective, such a system of classification seems to defy logic. However, it provides important insight into the degree to which race as a difference that makes a difference has little to do with biology and natural divisions among racial groups and everything to do with the broader political, economic, and historical context that shapes human behavior and decision making. The strangeness of the classification system in operation here suggests how truly contextual efforts to construct difference can be; they are rooted less in natural or essential criteria and much more in efforts to construct systems of inclusion and exclusion that protect the interests of particular groups at particular points in history (in these instances, white males).

These examples also suggest to us how fluid and changeable identities can be and how such changes happen through political and economic factors. Thus, the fact that Italians, Hungarians, Irish, Greeks, Austrians, and so forth, are no longer othered (at least for the most part) has less to do with people simply becoming more enlightened and more to do with changing political and economic circumstances in which an expanding economy needed more workers to work in various industries as well as to contribute to economic well-being by purchasing consumer goods. Constructions of forms of difference such as race, gender, and sexuality, among others, then, have much to do with context—historical, cultural, economic, and political.

Race and the Contemporary Workplace

It is perhaps not surprising to learn that race is both widely examined and partly ignored in the study of work and organizations. For the most part, when race and ethnicity are taken seriously by theorists and practitioners it is usually in the context of **managing diversity** and cultivating a workplace that reflects the demography of the wider population in terms of race, gender, and ethnicity. Such claims are typically made in terms of a business case for diversity; that is, organizations that do not develop a diverse workforce are deemed to be hurting their bottom lines because they are not drawing on the full range of skill sets offered by the entire working population (Martino, 1999; Mease, 2012; Moss, 2010; R. Ross, 1992). As organizational communication scholar Jennifer Mease (2012) has indicated, such an approach to diversity is problematic in that it appropriates difference purely for market ends, hence dehumanizing people because it treats them as mere commodities leveraged to bring about particular outcomes. However, as she shows in her study of diversity consultants, sometimes the business case is used as means to gain access to corporations, after which consultants incorporate more humanistic approaches as they gain trust from members of the organizations where they work.

On the other hand, the heavy focus on managing diversity means that race is rarely treated as a central theme in research on organizations. In other words, race is a focus of study only under certain circumstances, typically involving a deviation from the white norm (as in the perceived need, for example, to diversify the workforce, or in investigating minority leadership styles). However, just as we saw in the previous chapter how a focus on gender issues is not synonymous with studying women employees (men do gender too), so a focus on race and ethnicity need not be exclusively about people of color; white people also do race, but mostly in an invisible manner by virtue of their taken for granted neutral status.

Thus, rather than think of race as relevant only in the context of minority issues, we would need to think about it as an everyday feature of organizational life. Moreover, a view of organizations as raced means that we need to explore the relationships among race, organizing, and power. It's less useful to think of race as being about individuals who possess a certain racial or ethnic identity and more useful to view race as a structural aspect of organizations and society that shapes meanings, values, and identities. In other words, how race is enacted through communication practices creates the process of normalization we discussed above. As we have seen, differences are produced by power (who controls what differences make a difference?), and so race is more fruitfully understood as a normalized system of meanings and practices that have differential effects on organization members, depending on their social locations.

Such a position enables us to go beyond seeing the race–organization relationship as simply about managing cultural differences between individual people in order to improve organizational effectiveness. Instead, we can think about how, from a critical perspective, power relations are created and sustained by the communicative production of difference. Let's briefly examine one area of research in organizational communication to provide a sense of how thinking about race as an everyday feature of organizational life might change our perceptions of work and organizing.

Organizational communication scholar Brenda Allen's (1996, 1998, 2000) analysis of organizational socialization shows how thematizing race can alter our understanding of how these processes work. For the most part, research on this topic has taken the white professional worker as the universal norm for explaining how new employees move through stages of organizational socialization. In perhaps the most famous and widely adopted model, Jablin (1987) lays out different stages of socialization: anticipatory socialization, assimilation, and exit. In the first stage, people gather information about work from friends, family, school, the popular media, and so forth, all of which create certain expectations about the nature of work. In the second stage, a worker enters an organization and goes through an assimilation process characterized by organizational efforts to integrate the worker into its formal and informal norms and values, and efforts on the part of the worker to tailor a position to his or her own goals, interests, and expectations. Jablin argues that at some point a metamorphosis occurs in which the worker adjusts his or her expectations, resolves organizational conflicts, and develops her or his own individualized job role. Finally, exit occurs when the worker leaves the organization for a different position.

Adopting feminist standpoint theory (Hill Collins, 1991) and writing from her perspective as an African American scholar, Allen (2000) provides a critique of Jablin's (1987) model, arguing that its supposedly universal principles do not very accurately capture the experience of many women and workers of color. Feminist standpoint theory argues that knowledge must be grounded in people's lived experiences (standpoints) and that differences between the lived experiences of men and women, white people and people of color, provide the opportunity for knowledge claims that reflect the situated experiences of women and minorities. Thus, Allen's life experience as an African American woman enables her to bring a different lens to the process of organizational socialization—a lens that does not unreflectively mirror the universal model of socialization.

Drawing on her experience of being socialized as a faculty member into a U.S. university setting, Allen (2000) describes how her socialization experience cannot be fully accounted for by Jablin's (1987) model. For example, Allen notes that a woman of color is likely to encounter negative experiences on a much more regular basis than the socialization literature suggests. As the only black woman faculty member in her department, and one of very few on campus, she was regularly confronted by everyday acts of stereotyping that required a great deal of energy for her to process and make sense of. A few of these socialization experiences included the following:

- During a conversation at a faculty reception, a white female faculty member asked her to sing a negro spiritual.

- After the first day of class, a white male student informed her that he was dropping her class because he had already fulfilled his ethnic studies requirement (even though the class was not about race or ethnicity).

- A colleague told her that another colleague was overheard telling a group of students she was not qualified for her job and was hired only because she is a black woman.

- She was called on to do a variety of tasks her white colleagues were not asked to do, such as serving on task forces on minority issues, having dinner with visiting minority job candidates, giving advice to minority students who were not in her classes, and so forth.

Note that these behaviors do not involve outright racism (though bullet points one and three do flirt with it) but rather point more to the ways in which the broader organizational culture in which Allen works institutionalizes and normalizes a white worldview. Allen's blackness is not only constructed as different and exotic but as over-determining who she is as an individual. Her socialization experience suggests that her white colleagues largely reduce her to her blackness. In this sense, everyday organizational communication processes construct Allen as an outsider within the professional culture into which she is being socialized (Hill Collins, 1991).

Such behaviors and comments are routinely experienced by people of color in organizational and work contexts. Indeed, the term *microaggression* has been coined to describe such behavior. A **microaggression** can be defined as "brief and commonplace daily verbal, behavioral, or environmental indignities, whether intentional or unintentional, that communicate hostile, derogatory, or negative racial slights and insults toward people of color" (Sue et al., 2007, p. 271). Psychologist Derald Wing Sue and his colleagues note three prominent forms of microaggression: microassaults, microinsults, and microaggressions. A microassault is an intentional action or slur, such as using a racial epithet or displaying a confederate flag; it is conscious and deliberate. A microinsult involves forms of communication "that convey rudeness and insensitivity and demean a person's racial heritage or identity" (p. 274). Microinsults typically involve subtle snubs that convey a hidden (but not necessarily intentional) meaning to the person of color who is the recipient. For example, when a minority employee is asked "How did you get your job?" the hidden meaning is that the person is either not qualified or got it only because of affirmative action or both. Finally, microinvalidations are forms of communication "that exclude, negate, or nullify the psychological thoughts, feelings, or experiential reality of a person of color" (p. 274). For example, when an Asian American is asked where they are really from, or a mixed-race person is asked "What are you?" (being mixed race doesn't make a person a "what"), those are microinvalidations. When a white person tells an African American woman that he or she doesn't see color, that is a microinvalidation of the African American woman's experience in that she doesn't have the luxury of not seeing her color.

Microaggressions are particularly powerful because they are invisible to the perpetrator, who doesn't perceive himself or herself as engaging in bias (because we view ourselves as decent human beings who couldn't possibly engage in discrimination). Of course, the recipient is placed in an extremely difficult situation because (a) there is often an alternative, reasonable explanation for the microaggression; (b) he or she does not want to be accused of being too sensitive; and (c) minimal harm is typically attached (by the perpetrator) to the microaggression. For example, it is quite possible to frame the examples of Allen's experience listed above as simply interpersonal differences and lack of cultural awareness on the part of the people involved (one could argue, for example, that the female faculty member who asked to hear a negro spiritual was simply trying to be welcoming and acknowledge Allen's cultural heritage). However, such a position ignores the degree to which Allen's experiences occur within a set of power relations rooted in white patriarchy. As such, the default way of thinking, talking, and sense making reflects white, patriarchal norms that regularly position Allen as an outsider within.

Because of the historically sedimented assumptions about organizational life and the predominantly white viewpoint they reflect, there is little that Allen can take for granted as she learns the ropes of the organization—stuff that many of us can take for granted: assumption of your competence until evidence proves otherwise (rather than the reverse); formal and informal ready-made networks that provide an instant support system (rather than having to seek out actively or perhaps create a network from scratch); relative anonymity that lets you get on with your job (rather than high visibility in which every mistake is noted); and mentors who share your experience (rather than no mentors, or mentors who have little in common with your life experience). Of course, if you are a person of color reading this book, you can probably instantly identify with Allen's experience and the ways microaggressions operate in an everyday manner, even beyond the workplace (and the cumulative effect they can have on one's sense of self).

Interrogating Whiteness and Organizational Communication

As we indicated earlier, if we are to take race seriously in studying and understanding organizations, then we need to treat it in a thematic way and not just as a problem that crops up under particular circumstances. Race should not only be an issue when, for example, instances of racial bias come to the fore or when organizations recognize the need for great workforce diversity. "Queering" the concept of race also means that we examine the ways that whiteness has become normalized as a (largely invisible) means of enacting power and assessing the value of others. As such, we can explore whiteness as a socially constructed racial category (Frankenberg, 1993; Grimes, 2001, 2002; Martin & Nakayama, 1999). In this context, whiteness is not the same as being a white person. Rather, we can think of whiteness as "a set of institutionalized practices and ideas that people participate in consciously and unconsciously" (Parker & Mease, 2009, p. 317). Thus, we can distinguish between the institutionalized practices and ideas that make up whiteness as a societal discourse or narrative, and the behavior, talk, and ideas of specific white people. From this perspective, we can explore the ways white people—either consciously or unconsciously—protect their own normal status by reproducing whiteness, or else challenge and interrogate the discourse of whiteness.

As a socially constructed racial category, whiteness is simultaneously taken for granted, largely invisible, and the yardstick for judgment. An example will perhaps help illustrate this point. Rhetoric scholar Carrie Crenshaw (1997) reports the following meeting with a white student from her communication and diversity course:

> [She] came to me in tears struggling with her beliefs about race. She volunteered her reluctance to return home because her family members were racist. We talked at length, and at the end of our conversation she thanked me with a smile and said, "I'm glad you're white. You're so much more objective than other professors." (p. 253)

Crenshaw finds this incident interesting (and disturbing to her own sense of identity) because it illustrates a pretty rare occurrence in everyday talk—white people talking about and naming whiteness. For the most part, whiteness goes unnamed while remaining the hidden-in-plain-sight norm against which deviations from that norm are judged. In explicitly naming Crenshaw as white, the student did a couple of things: (1) She equated whiteness with objectivity, thus suggesting that nonwhite people are unable to be objective about issues of race (because they have race, whereas white people do not), and (2) she placed Crenshaw herself in a position of privilege, better able to rule on matters of race precisely because she is perceived as having no race. In this sense, one might argue, the student's naming of Crenshaw as white is less about placing her in a specific racial category and more about imbuing her with the supposed objectivity that comes with her nonracial whiteness.

This example also nicely illustrates an earlier point we made about race—it is relevant not only when identifiable racial incidents occur but also when performed at the level of everyday life, in the moment-to-moment of routine organizing (such as a student meeting with a professor). In this sense, race is structured into everyday life through ideological struggles over meaning. Whiteness, then, "functions ideologically when people employ it, consciously or unconsciously, as a framework to categorize people and understand their social location" (Crenshaw, 1997, p. 253). Thus, the student (probably unconsciously) uses whiteness ideologically to position her professor in a specific social location—a neutral arbiter on racial issues. By implication, of course, such a position also does the ideological work of positioning professors of color as lacking objectivity because they are raced in a visible manner (at least as framed from the position of the invisible white norm).

One of the benefits of interrogating whiteness, then, is that it makes visible the ways that race and power come together in routine ways to reproduce the organizational status quo. Interrogating, or queering, whiteness is about "making the center visible" (Nakayama & Krizek, 1995, p. 294); that is, it highlights the processes through which whiteness itself is both obscured as a category and the norm against which organizational life is defined. A brief example will illustrate this point.

Recently there have been numerous cases of white people calling the police on people of color who are simply engaging in normal, everyday behavior, promoting the hashtag, #whileblack. These incidents have included a white woman calling police on a group of African Americans barbequing in a park in Oakland, CA ("barbequing while black"); a white woman calling the police after observing three African Americans (two women and one man) loading suitcases into the back of a car (they were checking out of their AirBnB rental after a conference—"Airbnbing while black"); in San Francisco, a white woman calling police to report an 8-year-old girl selling water bottles on the sidewalk to raise money for a trip to Disneyland ("selling while black"); in Chicago, two white CVS employees calling police when an African American woman presented a discount coupon they thought might be fraudulent ("shopping while black"); a white male pool manager in Winston-Salem, NC, calling the police when a woman with her son refused to produce ID to prove that they could use the pool, even though she had a pool access card ("swimming while black"); and a white woman calling campus police at Colorado State University because two Native American brothers on a campus tour looked suspicious ("walking around while black") (Victor, 2018). And of course, there are many more that we could have mentioned.

Now, we would argue that each of these incidents is not really about blackness at all; they are all about whiteness. That is, in each case we have a white person calling the police because they experience discomfort with the actions of a person of color who, in reality, is engaged in routine behavior that is not out of the ordinary at all. These feelings of discomfort led in each case to an immediate escalation of the situation. Each incident can be characterized as a misunderstanding, but what's troubling is that in none of these instances is the person of color given the benefit of the doubt; that is, they are presumed guilty of wrongdoing until proven otherwise (in each case the police are called to adjudicate the situation). We suspect that in each instance if the person engaged in "suspicious" behavior had been white, that behavior would either not have been visible to the other white person (and thus not classified as suspicious), or the person would have been politely engaged in conversation to ascertain his or her motives—misunderstanding cleared up, and no police intervention necessary. Thus, black and brown bodies are constructed as suspicious in spaces that are normalized as white (Silva, 2016); whiteness constructs blackness as threatening and dangerous until it is able to prove otherwise, while whiteness is constructed as benign until it proves otherwise.

The idea that whiteness carries privilege in terms of the ability to negotiate the world relatively free from evaluation by the gaze of others is captured by Peggy McIntosh (1990) idea of the invisible knapsack—a set of privileges and practices that white people carry around with them that largely protect them from everyday injustices. For example, because we are both white, we don't have to worry about students doubting our competence when we walk into the classroom on the first day (worrying about it halfway through the semester when students have had the chance to watch us in action is a different matter, but we're given the benefit of the doubt until we prove otherwise!). We go to meetings and see lots of people around the room who look just like us. We don't have to worry too much about the way we dress or style our hair (in one of our cases, styling hair is no longer an option anyway) and whether we look appropriately professional. When we express opinions in meetings or at public gatherings, the viewpoints we express are generally viewed as reasonable and rational, and people will not question whether our motives are race based. In other words, it's simply easier for us as two white men to negotiate daily organizational life because the organizations we inhabit are socially constructed in our image.

Finally, in talking about whiteness and white privilege our intention is to move us away from the idea that racism is mainly about uneducated individuals who hold and express racist beliefs. Rather, as we said above, the idea is to focus on a system of power and domination that we all, to a greater or lesser degree, participate in. This does not make all white people racist; instead, it suggests that we need to develop greater awareness and self-reflexivity about the ways that we—often unconsciously—participate in systems of inclusion and exclusion.

CRITICAL RESEARCH 9.1

Angela Trethewey (2001). Reproducing and resisting the master narrative of decline: Midlife professional women's experiences of aging. *Management Communication Quarterly, 15,* 183–226.

One of the differences that make a difference that we have not addressed in this chapter, but that is nevertheless important in the context of work and organization, is age. Ageism in the workplace is a serious problem, as corporations frequently forgo experienced workers in favor of younger, often cheaper, employees. In this context, Angela Trethewey's study is important because she focuses on white midlife professional women and their experiences of aging in the context of work. In an interview study, she is concerned with answering the question "What does aging mean to white professional women?"

(Continued)

(Continued)

Interestingly, Trethewey frames her study through the discourse of the enterprise self that we discussed in Chapter 6. In this discourse, aging is seen as entrepreneurial choice; that is, how one ages is all about lifestyle and attitude. If you don't age well, you only have yourself to blame. Of course, as Trethewey points out, there is a strong gender component to aging. While men who age are typcially seen as gaining maturity and experience (and even looks), women who age are viewed as in decline. Trethewey argues that professional women have to make sense of their aging in the context of a societal master narrative of decline that constructs women's aging as negative, against which they must struggle.

Thus, Trethewey's goal in the study is to critique "the discourses of decline and entrepreneurialism that work to 'fix' the meanings of aging for midlife professional women and to offer alternative narratives of aging" (p. 187). She builds the study around three research questions:

1. How is aging organized and experienced by white middle-class professional women?

2. How do white middle-class women reproduce the discourse of decline in their narratives and embodied identities?

3. How do white middle-class professional women resist the discourse of decline through their narratives and embodied identities?

First, the women interviewed addressed their concerns about discrimination, downsizing, and unemployment. "Digger," for example, reported being downsized three times in 12 years, resulting in diminished income. Moreover, the women spoke about the difficulty of filing discrimination complaints based on ageism, which are notoriously difficult to prove. Many women also reported leaving the corporate world because of numerous glass ceiling experiences.

Second, the women often reproduced the discourse of decline by talking about losing face; that is, the consequences of visible signs of aging. Some spoke of the sense of freedom that comes with no longer being perceived as sexually desirable. As Trethewey states, "It is undoubtedly liberating to be able to do one's job without being sexually harassed or reduced to a sex(ed) object" (p. 201). However, respondents also spoke about being erased (i.e., no longer visible) because of their aging, and some tried to compensate for aging by working out, wearing fashionable clothes, and carefully applying makeup. Respondents also addressed the sense of isolation they felt; many were trailblazers in their male-dominated professions, and few had female role models to look up to or system of social support to draw on.

Finally, some of the women resisted the master narrative of decline by speaking of the benefits of aging. These included shifting priorities to make them less work-focused, and thus experiencing a better work-life balance; being less concerned about the internalized male gaze ("what do my male colleagues think about me?"); and enjoying the respect and credibility that comes with experience. Thus, while the master narrative of decline suggests that aging professional women have less to offer,

"These women provide powerful reminders that midlife women have much to contribute and are still a force to be reckoned with" (p. 211).

Trethewey concludes her study with the following critique of how the discourse of the enterprise self positions midlife professional women:

Aging appropriately requires the enterprising management of identity, particularly for women. The findings of this study imply that aging successfully requires that midlife professional women make careful and considered choices, including passing as younger women. Yet, this entrepreneurial discourse effectively prevents us from looking at midlife as a social and political construct. Those who do not age "successfully," those who are downsized or left without the benefit of pensions, for example, can be explained away by their lack of "entrepreneurial" savvy or their inability to control their aging process. (p. 214)

Discussion Questions

1. While aging might not be an issue for you (yet!), the connection between professional identity and appearance is strong, particularly for women. To what degree do you agree or disagree with Trethewey about the internalized male gaze that women experience? Are there similar issues for men in the workplace?

2. Have a conversation with an older female friend or relative. Has she experienced any of the issues that the women in Trethewey's study faced? What were her responses?

3. Trethewey's study is about white women. To what degree is the relationship among age, appearance, and professionalism similar or different for women of color?

⚛ SEXUALITY AND ORGANIZATIONAL COMMUNICATION

In this section, we will explore the relationship between sexuality and organizational communication. Consistent with the perspective taken in this book, we will explore the ways that sexuality and sexual identity are tied to communication processes (Compton, 2016). That is, how do employees (gay, straight, and nongender-conforming) manage their sexual identities in work contexts? Moreover, how do organizations construct sexuality in the workplace? After all, people are sexual beings, and despite bureaucracies' best efforts to monitor and restrict its expression we do not check our sexuality at the door when we go to work. Organization members flirt, have romantic relationships, sometimes dress provocatively, and experience work at least in part through their bodies. Work, in this sense, has a very sensuous dimension. Because of this increasing recognition of organizations as sites of sexuality, a number of researchers have begun to take seriously the idea that organizations, sexuality, and the body come together in important ways (Brewis & Linstead,

2000; Brewis, Tyler, & Mills, 2014; Fleming, 2007; Hearn, Sheppard, Tancred-Sheriff, & Burrell, 1989; Pringle, 1989).

Furthermore, it's clear that over the last 20 years definitions of acceptable expressions of sexual identity have shifted, particularly in terms of both public and corporate attitudes toward people who identify as LGBTQ. Fortune 500 companies now routinely take concrete steps to ensure greater equity for LGBTQ workers and their families in the form of comprehensive policies, benefits, and practices. For example, the vast majority of Fortune 500 companies (91% as of 2018) now include sexual orientation in their non-discrimination policies—a figure that has risen considerably from the figure of 61% of companies in 2002. Even more striking is the shift in companies developing official policies regarding gender identity protections—in 2002 only 3% of Fortune 500 companies included such protection in their policies, while in 2018 83% provide it (Campaign, 2018). This is an encouraging sign that corporate America increasingly "gets it" when it comes to protections for LGBTQ employees. In some respects, societal mores and national legislation have lagged behind corporate efforts to be inclusive. Same-sex marriage was not approved by the U.S. Supreme Court until 2015, for example, and the United States lags behind other nations in enacting laws banning employment decisions based on sexual orientation. While 20 states plus the District of Columbia and Puerto Rico have enacted such laws (Wisconsin was the first to do so in 1982), there is still no federally mandated policy.

Of course, this progress in gay rights in the workplace and in the broader society comes in the wake of almost 50 years of struggle on the part of the modern gay rights movement, initiated by the 1969 Stonewall uprising (where patrons at a gay bar in New York City resisted constant harassment by police). For much of its history, the modern corporation has operated according to the principle of "compulsory heterosexuality" (Rich, 1980). Stuart Seidman (2002) argues that the period 1950 to 1980 was the heyday of the closet in the United States—a period that corresponds closely to the dominance of the formal, bureaucratic organizational form. During this period, workplaces were often actively homophobic in ways that demonized and stereotyped gay and lesbian workers.

However, progress in company policies and national legislation are one thing; understanding the ways that LGBTQ employees negotiate organizational life in contexts that are generally heteronormative is another. Following Lauren Berlant and Michael Warner, we can define **heteronormativity** as "institutions, structures of understanding, and practical orientations that make heterosexuality not only coherent—that is, organized as a sexuality—but also privileged" (1998, p. 565). Let's give a simple example of heteronormativity. A few years ago when Dennis was chair of his department, he met with a student who was visiting campus in anticipation of joining the graduate program. She mentioned that she had made the trip with her partner, who was checking out the job possibilities in the area. "What kind of work does he do?" Dennis asked. "*She's* in retail," was her response. This exchange is an example of heteronormative communication by Dennis, in which he assumes that the student is heterosexual. What's important here is that the presumption places the gay student in the position of having to negotiate the, albeit unintentional, faux pas by Dennis. While this is one simple interaction, it's important to understand that such interactions are often routine, even in gay friendly organizational environments. So below we'll examine some of the research that has examined how organizations communicatively construct sexuality and how LGBTQ employees negotiate those construction processes.

253Stock.com/mattjeacock

The success of the gay rights movement has helped create organizational climates that are more open to gay and lesbian workers. The rainbow flag (a symbol of gay pride, shown in this photograph) has become a more common sight in corporate contexts in the last few years.

Gay Workers and Heteronormativity

An early study of gay male identity in the workplace is James D. Woods and Jay H. Lucas's (1993) book, *The Corporate Closet*. They identify three different strategies that gay professional employees adopt in negotiating their workplace identity: (1) counterfeiting, (2) avoidance, and (3) integration. Counterfeiting involves efforts to pass as heterosexual. Avoidance involves efforts to provide as little personal information as possible to colleagues, hence concealing one's sexual identity. Finally, integration occurs when gay employees come out in the workplace, either by directly or indirectly disclosing information to colleagues or by enacting a gay identity that conforms to cultural expectations. In each strategy, gay male workers attempt to maintain control over the disclosure of their sexuality.

In the field of organizational communication, Anna Spradlin's (1998) essay "The Price of 'Passing'" focuses in more detail on communicative efforts to conceal one's gay identity. As the term **passing** suggests, Spradlin discusses the various communication strategies she used as a way to be identified by others as a straight woman at work and hence remain in the corporate closet (Woods & Lucas, 1993). Spradlin identifies six strategies she used when interacting with her colleagues at work:

- *Distancing*: Removing oneself from informal conversational situations where personal information might arise, including not attending department social events.

- *Dissociating*: Avoiding any interaction or association with other homosexual workers.

- *Dodging*: Using conversational topic shifts to steer discussions away from disclosure of personal information.

- *Distracting*: Employing identity messages that bolster one's image as heterosexual. For example, Spradlin would reference the fact that she was once married or that she came from a conservative, religious background.

- *Denial*: Withholding information about one's gay identity. For example, Spradlin listed her parents as her emergency contacts on employment forms rather than her partner and did not have photos of her partner in her office.

- *Deceiving*: Constructing deliberately misleading messages regarding one's sexual identity—for example, referring to one's partner as "he" rather than "she" or inviting a male friend posing as a boyfriend to a social event (what today is referred to colloquially as a "beard") to bolster one's heterosexual credentials.

Two issues are important here. First, Spradlin's (1998) essay provides considerable insight into the extensive effort (emotional, psychological, and communicational) required to engage in passing behavior. For example, Spradlin describes herself as learning to be a "hyper-attentive listener" so she can be constantly attuned to the need to redirect conversations away from "dangerous" topic areas. Such hyper-attentiveness can be extremely exhausting when practiced 24/7. Second, Spradlin's essay points to how identity is communicatively constructed. Her passing strategies rely on her colleagues' ability to make sense of her through the various verbal and nonverbal communication cues she exhibits. In this sense, Spradlin communicatively performs heterosexuality, but it works only because of the heteronormative frame within which people make sense of her behavior.

More recent research reflects the changing character of organizational life by focusing not as much on passing behavior but rather on the ways gay and lesbian workers manage their identities in workplaces that are either gay friendly or where LGBTQ workers are out to their colleagues (Compton, 2016; Compton & Dougherty, 2017; Dixon & Dougherty, 2014; Giuffre, Dellinger, & Williams, 2008; Rumens, 2008, 2010; Rumens & Broomfield, 2012; Rumens & Kerfoot, 2009). Again, this research is interesting because of its focus on how sexuality is communicatively constructed through the everyday interactions of gay and straight organization members.

For example, management scholar Nick Rumens and his colleagues focus on gay men's construction of professional workplace identity (Rumens, 2008, 2010; Rumens & Broomfield, 2012, 2014; Rumens & Kerfoot, 2009). They argue in part that the new, "gay friendly" workplace culture has provided gay men with the opportunity to "invent themselves afresh" as "respected and openly gay professionals," although expectations of heteronormativity promotes considerable identity struggle over what it means to be professional (Rumens & Kerfoot, 2009, p. 775). How do they enact a professional identity that incorporates their sexuality and is still recognized by colleagues as professional? Rumens and colleagues suggest that gay men are very conscious of the need to project a professional image while being open about their sexuality. For example, in interviews professional gay men indicated that they perceived being too "camp" in the workplace as unprofessional behavior (Rumens & Kerfoot, 2009). Moreover, they often viewed the body as a site where professionalism could be enacted. As Rumens and Kerfoot (2009) state, "Because the gay male body, rather like the female body, can be at risk of being interpreted as a site of sexual excess, fashioning the body to appear professional is critical" (p. 780). Thus, many gay men choose to project a professional image through the use of expensive, well-made clothes, as well as working out regularly to present a fit body to colleagues. Both of these strategies are used to project an image of workplace competence. In some ways this finding fits nicely with Ashcraft's (2013) glass slipper concept discussed in Chapter 8, in which only particular forms of embodied social identity are perceived as professional. Here, we see the connection between the glass slipper and heteronormativity as gay men struggle with the boundaries of what performing professionalism means in the context of their sexuality.

Two further studies by Rumens and Broomfield (2012, 2014) provide interesting insight into the management of gay workers' identities in two very different occupations: the performing arts and the police. Both studies were conducted in the United Kingdom. It is useful to contrast these studies because they involve two occupations (policing and the performing arts) that typically are seen as having divergent attitudes toward LGBTQ workers. Typically, lesbian and gay workers are viewed as representing a threat to the gendered characteristic of police work, which is seen as highly masculine and heteronormative (Dennis comes from a law enforcement family, with a father and two brothers who were police officers, and he can attest to this characterization). On the other hand, the performing arts are seen as stereotypically gay friendly, even encouraging "camp" behavior. In their police force study, Rumens and Broomfield (2012) find that, generally speaking, gay officers "anticipate and report positive disclosure experiences" (p. 284) as police forces increasingly attempt to divest themselves of a highly masculine culture. In their study, gay police officers articulate three reasons for disclosing their sexuality: personal integrity, developing and improving workplace relationships, and inspiring other gay officers to be out. Interestingly, respondents in the study argued that successful police work depended heavily on trust between officers and commitment to a team orientation. Thus, not disclosing one's sexuality could be viewed as undermining team cohesion. As one respondent in the study states,

> If I was your colleague and every day I was coming to work and I wasn't talking about my home life, how off putting would that be in terms of our working relationship? Police teams are very close teams, very intertwined and it needs to be that really cohesive entity . . . because you're reliant on each other in some really difficult situations . . . you've gotta be out and realise that team dynamics and the way your relationships gel within your team depend on it (Sean, Inspector). (Rumens & Broomfield, 2012, p. 289)

Thus, motivation to disclosure one's sexuality was seen as having a positive effect on team performance as well as on one's personal credibility. This effect is in stark contrast to arguments among opponents of gay members of the military who argue that the presence of gay soldiers undermines unit cohesion.

In their second study, Rumens and Broomfield (2014) examine a much more stereotypically gay friendly environment—the performing arts. Interestingly, despite the fact that performing arts professions have a high percentage of out gay members, often there are considerable pressures to conform to heteronormative expectations. For example, actors in drama school are often critiqued for being "too gay." One respondent, Zac, reported, "Because I'm camp, it was made clear to me that I might struggle going professionally" (Rumens & Broomfield, 2014, p. 374). Moreover, actors were often told that being "too gay" would limit the kinds of roles for which they would be cast. As Rumens and Broomfield state, "Participants felt that decisions to perform gay male sexuality in front of casting directors and agents were structured by a need to respect a conservatism which counsels that it is better not to offend heteronormative sensibilities about how homosexuality ought to be expressed" (2014, p. 375).

The studies that we've discussed so far look at the intersection of gender and sexuality in a fairly narrow manner; that is, how do gay men manage their professional identities in contexts that normalize particular performances of workplace masculinity? What happens when we shift the focus to a study that examines lesbian workers in a stereotypically heterosexual masculine context?

Amy Denissen and Abigail Saguy's (2014) study focuses on the intersection of gender, sexuality, and class, with an examination of women's experience in the building trades (e.g., construction workers). In interviews with tradeswomen (both lesbian and heterosexual), they show how the women's presence in a traditionally masculine occupation threatens the perception of that work as inherently masculine. As such, the male workers attempt to restore the gender order by either sexually objectifying the tradeswomen or labeling them as lesbians (and hence not "real women"), even if they are not. While viewing tradeswomen as lesbians neutralizes the threat to the masculine definition of the work, Denissen and Saguy argue that it also "threatens heteronormativity and the sexual and economic subordination of women to men" (p. 391), leading male workers to direct homophobic comments at lesbian tradeswomen, or else sexually objectifying all tradeswomen, hence attempting to undermine their professional competence. Thus, the women must engage in various behaviors and communication strategies to negotiate their place at work. Denissen and Saguy show how the women "skillfully mix performances of femininity and masculinity to resist being depicted as occupationally incompetent or sexually deviant and to assert their sexual autonomy" (p. 386). For example, the tradeswomen often adopt a "keep them guessing" strategy, in which they give out varying and contradictory cues about their sexual identity. Alex, a lesbian tradeswoman, deliberately mixes stereotypically heterosexually feminine behavior with traditionally masculine behavior as a way to keep her male coworkers off balance:

> I'd rather act feminine and friendly and cute than get harassed, ignored, or treated worse. But at the same time it's like I have to be careful that I don't act overly feminine because they'll think I can't work. Sometimes I'll say something that will totally throw them for a spin [or] make them raise an eyebrow because I'll say it in a masculine way. I'll say something that's really clear, concise, and to the point, and they don't expect that of me. They think I'm a bubbly person; they stereotype me as a female. (p. 394)

One of the important aspects of this study is that it illustrates the significance of the intersectional approach that we discussed earlier. In this case, gender, sexuality, and class intersect in a specific way in the building trades, where a hegemonic form of heterosexual masculinity prevails. Moreover, the presence of women in a male-dominated profession is perceived as a threat in a way that the presence of gay male workers in a middle-class profession is not.

Finally, some researchers have pointed out that, while workplaces have generally become more gay friendly, even those organizations identified as such can engage in forms of discrimination, albeit in ways more subtle than outright homophobia (Giuffre et al., 2008; Ward & Winstanley, 2003). For example, some heterosexual workers feel comfortable asking gay colleagues about aspects of their private lives—including their sex lives—that they would never ask straight coworkers. Sometimes this occurs because openly gay workers are treated as "tokens" and "exotic" creatures in the workplace and, thus, as figures of curiosity. And James Ward and Diana Winstanley (2003) have reported that gay and lesbian workers sometimes experience a workplace silence. That is, while heterosexual colleagues will happily talk about their home lives and weekend activities, they demonstrate little interest in hearing about the equivalent lives of their gay coworkers, in part because they define the latter largely through their sexuality and are afraid of getting details that may make them uncomfortable (even though, as several gay workers indicate, their home lives are every bit as boring and routine as those of their heterosexual colleagues).

Let's now examine some of the ways in which organizations have routinely (and historically) addressed sexuality in the workplace by treating it in an instrumental manner (to be controlled or used for profit).

Instrumental Uses of the Body and Sexuality

Critical management scholar Gibson Burrell (1984) argues that, with the growth of industrial capitalism, organizations sought actively to control employee sexuality because it was perceived to interfere with their productivity. Indeed, as mentioned above, Henry Ford's Sociological Department attempted to monitor his employees' behavior outside of work, including their sexual behavior and personal hygiene (Jeffrey Eugenides's 2002 novel, *Middlesex*—whose main protagonist is intersex—has a wonderful description of a Ford researcher visiting the home of a Greek immigrant Ford employee to check on his home life). More broadly speaking, the bureaucratic form generally functions to eliminate or suppress the idea of employees as sexual beings with bodies and desires. However, incorporating what traditionally has existed in the private sphere of home and relationships, companies are increasingly encouraging employees to "just be yourself" at work (Fleming & Sturdy, 2011), including expressions of sexuality. The idea here is to bring the energy and vitality of the private sphere to the workplace.

Thus, the body and sexuality are seen as organizational resources that can be exploited for the gain of the organization (Burrell, 1992). Organizations carefully monitor and control expressions of sexuality, as well as harness it as a commodity that has value to the organization (as was the case with the "business case" for diversity discussed earlier in the chapter). In some organizations, such harnessing of sexuality for profit is explicit and obvious. For example, advertisers have recognized for decades that "sex sells," and today many commercials have overtly sexual messages that attempt to connect the purchase of products with enhanced sexual prowess. But perhaps more significantly, organizations are increasingly encouraging and harnessing employee sexuality as a way to enhance customer "brand experience" and corporate profitability (Fleming, 2009).

Meika Loe (1996) provides an example of this kind of management of sexuality and the body in her ethnographic study of "Bazooms" restaurant (an entertaining pseudonym for Hooters). Loe shows how the female body is gendered (and sexualized) in a specific way to create an organizational environment that maximizes the sale of burgers and chicken wings. Loe took a job as a "Bazooms girl" to study the ways the women are sexualized through dress, mandatory choreographed performances, and deliberate corporate efforts to present them as dumb (e.g., a Bazooms calendar features the months out of order because "the Bazooms girls put it together"). The effect is to create an image of the Bazooms girl as an all-American girl-next-door type who is always smiling, always ready to have fun, non-threatening, and always attentive and approachable to the (mostly male) customers. Loe notes in her study how male customers felt free to make lewd, suggestive comments to the women and how the women employees had to develop strategies to fend them off. Of course, the idea is to sell menu items by suggesting to customers that the "girls" are sexually available; such a notion is ridiculous at one level, but the reality is that few customers actually go to Hoo—, er, Bazooms, for the food!

While this might be seen as an extreme example from the food-service industry, the service and retail economies frequently demand a great deal from employees and their bodies through the concept of emotional labor (Hochschild, 1983). Especially in the customer service arena, the interactions between employees and customers are often carefully managed in order to maximize profits. Companies attempt to harness and control employee expression of emotions (an intimate aspect of one's identity) in order to enhance customers' experiences and thus maintain their loyalty. While Hochschild's original study focused on flight attendants, the principles of control over emotions, the body, and sexuality are not that different from Loe's experience at Bazooms. And we suspect that anyone reading this book who has worked in a customer service position of any kind will recognize managerial efforts to control and shape emotional expression and performance of body and sexuality.

Sociologist Millian Kang (2010) provides an extremely interesting ethnographic study of the instrumental use of female employees' bodies in nail salons. Kang extends Hochschild's notion of emotional labor by examining the forms of body labor in which the mostly Asian (Korean and Vietnamese) nail salon workers must engage in their work. This study is interesting and compelling because it is written from the perspective of the nail salon workers and provides insight into how their bodies are placed on the line every day to provide a cosmetic service for the (mostly female) clientele. When Dennis assigned this book in one of his classes, many of the female students indicated that it profoundly changed their perception of workers in nail salons and made them think twice about using this service industry.

Finally, and in a somewhat different organizational context, Peter Fleming's (2007) qualitative study of a call center shows how the organization deliberately engineers a culture of fun in which flirting, dating, and wearing hip and sexy outfits are encouraged among the mostly 20-something employees. Here, there is an effort to link the sexuality of employees (including creating an organizational culture that is gay friendly) directly to the profitability of the company. Interestingly, some of the employees found this "fun" work environment oppressive because of the perceived sleaziness of the flirting culture and the constant pressure to dress in a hip manner in order to be considered among the "cool kids" in the workplace.

From an instrumental perspective, then, we can see that the body and sexuality are used by organizations as a resource that can be rationalized and submitted to various forms of control. Sexuality and the body are viewed positively and productively as long as their expression is consistent with the goals of the organization. In this context, they are carefully monitored and controlled, even to the extent of dictating what employees wear, how they comport themselves, even how they use facial expressions. See Critical Case Study 9.1 for an example of how one particular corporation—Abercrombie & Fitch—uses employee bodies and sexuality in instrumental ways.

CRITICAL CASE STUDY 9.1

Sexualizing and Racializing the Retail Experience

Employee sexuality is increasingly becoming an explicit, actively encouraged aspect of organizational life. One of the clearest examples of this trend is the clothing chain Abercrombie & Fitch's (A&F) use of its employees' sexuality and bodies to sell its line of clothes. A few years back, A&F gave itself a brand makeover and went from an outdoors-oriented store (think Eddie Bauer) to one that appeals strongly to a younger demographic. The new CEO, Mike Jeffries, adopted a new brand strategy that sexualized the retail experience, embodied (literally) by the shirtless male model at the entrance to every A&F store. Needless to say, you needed to have a particular body type to land this job. The A&F website also featured a section called "A&F Casting: Do You Have What It Takes?" The A&F "look" (as it's called in its "Look Book") is described as "natural, classic, and current, with an emphasis on style." As Dwight McBride (2005) argues in his essay, "Why I Hate Abercrombie & Fitch," such a look is racially coded in a way that makes whiteness the invisible norm against which other "looks" are judged—you can't be "natural" and "classic" and also look "ethnic." Thus, for example, according to the "Look Book" men and women must have a "neatly combed, attractive, natural, classic, hairstyle . . . dreadlocks are unacceptable for men and women" (McBride, 2005, pp. 69–70).

As Barbara Farfan (2017) points out, Jeffries' intent in this "brand makeover" was to create a retail experience that was akin to being part of an invitation-only clique, making an appeal to a young,

(Continued)

(Continued)

cool-conscious demographic. As Jeffries himself stated in justifying his refusal to sell plus-size clothing, "In every school, there are the cool and popular kids, and then there are the not-so-cool kids. Candidly, we go after the cool kids. We go after the attractive all-American kid with a great attitude and a lot of friends. A lot of people don't belong [in our clothes], and they can't belong. Are we exclusionary? Absolutely" (as cited in Mosendz, 2014).

The A&F brand began to fail when the millennials who were its target audience began to see through and rejected this (racially and sexually) exclusionary image. And when A&F refused to offer discount clothing (like other retailers) during the great recession, customers began to leave A&F in droves. In 2016, A&F received the lowest customer satisfaction rating ever on the American Customer Satisfaction Index, and it was dubbed "the most hated retailer in history," replacing Wal-Mart in this dubious honor. Needless to say, Mike Jeffries is no longer CEO of A&F.

As we will see in Chapter 10, brand image is essential to the success of a company, and when that brand is constructed on racial and sexual identities that are alienating to its target demographic, that company is doomed to failure.

Discussion Questions

1. Have you had any work experiences in which there was an effort by the organization to incorporate sexuality and the body into the work process? These might be retail or service positions but can be other kinds of work too.

2. Engage in a broad discussion of the increasing ways that the body, sexuality, and organizations intersect. What are some of the positive and negative consequences of this development?

3. In 2007 the performance group "Improv Everywhere" pulled a stunt in which 111 bare-chested men invaded an A&F flagship store in New York City. Watch the video of the event and discuss how the group attempts to critique A&F's use of the body as a retail strategy: http://improveverywhere.com/2007/10/17/no-shirts/

Such instrumental uses of sexuality and the body at work certainly appear to be on the rise, especially as organizations increasingly attempt to break down the barriers between employees' work and private lives and tie their identities more closely to the organization (we will discuss the relationship between personal identity and work in more detail in Chapter 14). In this sense, employees' bodies and sexuality are seen as untapped resources of energy that employers can access to create organizational brand value.

CONCLUSION

In this chapter we have tried to suggest to you the complexities of the relationships between difference and organizational communication. We have attempted to show that difference is communicatively constructed; this occurs through the development of discourses that shape the values and meanings that define particular forms of difference. From a communication perspective our interest lies not in the differences per se but rather, in the ways the differences that make a difference become taken for granted and institutionalized in everyday organizational life. It is only by exploring how certain differences become seen as "natural" that we can understand the processes through which they are communicatively constructed.

In this chapter, we looked at two forms of difference—race and sexuality. We might have looked at a number of others, including class, age, and able-bodiedness. Indeed, one of the dangers of focusing on race and sexuality is that we forget their connections to other forms of difference. For example, it is hard to talk about race without addressing issues of class as well; being a middle-class, professional black man is quite different from being a working-class or unemployed black man in terms of the dynamics of inclusion and exclusion.

Perhaps the most important issue to take from this chapter is that even though we commonly think of difference as individual (U.S. society does heavily emphasize individuality, after all), such individuality can be understood only in the context of the larger organizational and societal forces that shape us. Difference is socially constructed and also shaped by power. The goal, then, as organizational communication scholar Jennifer Mease (2011) has suggested, is to take difference personally *and* think about it institutionally. That is, we need to "develop a critically engaged consciousness that allows [us] to analyze and respond to social constructions of difference and associated power dynamics as personally relevant" (p. 153). This means thinking less about inequality as a function of prejudiced or unmotivated individuals and more about how we, as individuals, personally participate in maintaining, ignoring, or short-circuiting institutional inequalities in our everyday lives.

CRITICAL APPLICATIONS

1. Reflect on your own racial and/or ethnic background. How important has this been in shaping your sense of who you are as a person?

2. Share your interrogation with someone else in class. What are the points of commonality and difference in your respective racial/ethnic personal narratives? How do other types of difference (class, sexuality, ability, etc.) intersect with your story? Can you come to any conclusions about the ways difference is socially constructed?

3. What are the differences that make a difference that are important to you? Create a map of the differences that impact your life and show how they intersect with each other. How does this "difference map" shape how you experience the world?

KEY TERMS

difference 228

feminist standpoint
theory 235

heteronormativity 242

invisible knapsack 239

managing diversity 233

microaggression 236

normalization 230

outsider within 235

passing 243

queer theory 230

whiteness 237

STUDENT STUDY SITE

Visit the student study site at www.sagepub.com/mumbyorg for these additional learning tools:

- Web quizzes
- eFlashcards
- SAGE journal articles

- Video resources
- Web resources

Shopping malls are the "cathedrals of consumption" in the age of branding.

CHAPTER 10

Branding, Work, and Consumption

To begin this chapter, let's consider the following, seemingly unrelated, events:

- On May 29, 2018, Starbucks stores across the United States closed for a day of racial bias training for its employees. Earlier in the year the manager of a Starbucks in Philadelphia called the police on two African American men who were sitting in the store (before buying any coffee) waiting for a meeting. The video of the incident went viral and became a major national and international news event (see our Case Study in Chapter 11).

- In August 2017, the ride share company Uber appointed Dara Khosrowshahi as its new CEO, replacing its founder, Travis Kalanick. The change in CEO was precipitated by Kalanick's problematic personal behavior, which included a video of him berating an Uber driver from the back seat of the driver's vehicle.

- In March 2017, the banking and investment company Wells Fargo launched a new ad campaign with the slogan "Building better every day." The campaign was launched in the wake of a massive scandal in which Wells Fargo was found to have pressured its employees into creating 3.5 million bank and credit card accounts without customers' permission. In May 2018, the company launched another ad campaign with the slogan, "Established 1852, Re-established 2018," in an effort to rebuild trust with its customers.

On the surface, there seems little to connect these three events: an example of racial bias, a CEO behaving badly, and an instance of company fraud. What connects these events, however, is the phenomenon of corporate branding. In each instance, an event occurred that threatened to seriously damage the brand of the company involved. Each company had to act quickly to prevent its brand from being permanently damaged.

Why is this so important? In this chapter, we will argue that "brands are increasingly becoming the internal organizing principle of business" (Kornberger, 2010, p. 22) and are thus central to understanding the nature of organizational communication in the 21st century. While the topic of branding is not typically included in an organizational communication textbook, we believe that understanding the importance of branding to both organizing and everyday life is an essential element of organizational communication literacy.

In addressing the phenomenon of branding, we will discuss it as a primarily communicative process that involves the efforts of corporations to shape human identity and influence the cultural and social landscape. Our lives are saturated with corporate, manufactured meanings that, in many respects, lie largely out of our control. What is interesting about this corporate meaning management process is that companies have very much taken to heart the idea that communication is not about transmitting information from A (company) to B (consumer)—a process characteristic of early advertising and branding—but rather is about creating complex systems of meaning that shape social realities and people's identities. Corporations are incredibly sophisticated in their methods of meaning management. As such, it is extremely important that as consumers we are equally sophisticated in our ability to decode and critique the ways such meanings are constructed. In addition, it's important that we appreciate the extent to which we participate in this meaning construction process and how we engage in a dialogue with the brands we purchase (Fiske, 1989). We will show how Sergio Zyman's phrase, "everything communicates," which we first encountered in Chapter 1, truly comes into its own in the age of corporate branding, as companies use every opportunity to turn everyday processes of communication into economic value. Indeed, the idea that the main struggle in contemporary capitalism is not between capital and labor, but capital and life itself (Fleming, 2014b) has branding at its center.

In this chapter, then, we will do the following. First, we will provide a brief history of branding. Second, we will examine three branding strategies that emerged after World War II. Third, we will examine the ways in which branding has become an integral part of organizing, both for customers and employees; we will explore how the distinctions between work and consumption have become blurred.

✤ BRANDING AND CAPITALISM IN THE 20TH CENTURY

How might we define a brand? It is "the total constellation of meanings, feelings, perceptions, beliefs and goodwill attributed to any market offering displaying a particular sign"

Bettmann/Bettmann/Getty Images

In the early days of branding, the housewife was the target consumer for branded goods, especially household products.

(Muniz, 2007). A brand, then, is less about the product per se, and more about the constellation of meanings that a product embodies and the feelings and perceptions that such meanings invoke in the consumer. In this sense, branding is a fundamentally communicative process. As Phil Knight, former CEO of Nike, once famously said, "Brands, not products." In other words, people purchase the brand (and the meanings and feelings associated with it), not the product. Through Knight's leadership, Nike transformed itself from a company making running shoes for dedicated athletes to a fitness and lifestyle company whose brand anyone could feel good about purchasing (even those who have a completely sedentary lifestyle!). In the late 1980s, as neoliberalism was gaining speed, many companies similarly came to realize that the road to profitability was not about actually making stuff but about focusing on brand management and cultivating consumer relationships. However, before we explore these developments in the 21st century, we need to take a step back and briefly examine the historical development of branding by returning to the 20th century.

In the second half of the 19th century, branding emerged as a revolutionary way for companies to market their products to an increasingly literate working population (Olins, 2000). As capitalism and industrialization expanded and new markets developed, companies competed to secure shares of the newly emerging consumer class. Branding was the principal way to artificially distinguish functionally similar products and develop customer loyalty, especially during a time when there were few government regulations regarding product quality. Branding, then, provided consumers with a sense that they could trust the company from whom they were purchasing items.

The increased importance of branding also coincides with the rise of an increasingly urban population. In an agrarian economy, people made or grew most of the goods they consumed themselves (e.g., clothing, food, soap, etc.). As such, they developed close relationships with the local merchants from whom they purchased grain, cloth, and so forth. As people migrated to urban environments, however, this direct connection to merchants disappeared (products had to be transported over long distances), and brands became a substitute for these personal relationships. Late 19th-century brands such as Quaker Oats and Aunt Jemima were among the first to develop these personal relationships with the customer, using the happy, smiling faces of a Quaker and Aunt Jemima, respectively, on the packaging. Such branding made sense; in the early days of branding, the housewife was the primary audience for advertising, given her role in determining household purchases. In fact, according to brand expert Wally Olins (2000), for about the first 100 years of modern advertising, the very notion of the brand was intimately connected with perishable household items such as laundry detergent, soap, jam, butter, toothpaste, and so forth—precisely the products that women purchased.

As Olins (2000, 2003) indicates, companies developed a brand formula that highlighted what the advertising industry referred to as the **unique selling proposition (USP)** of a product—a uniqueness often rooted in highly questionable claims. Such USPs, however, were—and still are—an essential part of the effort to establish a distinct brand identity. According to Olins (2003, p. 53), USPs were based on the following formula, aimed at homemakers:

1. This product is better because it contains X (secret, magic, new, miracle) ingredient that will make it work more effectively.

2. If you use it, your home will look more beautiful or your food will taste much better or you will be even more glamorous than ever before.

3. This will leave you more time to remain even more desirable and attractive for your lovely husband and family.

Very early in the 20th century, however, branding became a way not only to create customer trust and loyalty but also to create customer needs. The expansion of capitalism depends on the creation of new consumer markets, as old and established markets become saturated and less profitable. Consumers need to be not only continually persuaded to fulfill their needs and desires through consumption but also must be continually convinced of new needs and desires they were previously unaware they had!

Edward Bernays, founder of the field of public relations, is a pivotal figure in this shift from satisfying existing consumer needs to creating new needs. Early in his career, Bernays used the term *propaganda* in a positive way to describe what he did. In his 1928 book of the same name, Bernays states the following:

The conscious and intelligent manipulation of the organized habits and opinions of the masses is an important element in democratic society. Those who manipulate this unseen mechanism of society constitute an invisible government which is the true ruling power of our country. We are governed, our minds are molded, our tastes formed, our ideas suggested, largely by men we have never heard of. (1928, p. 9)

Woodburn soap was one of the earliest brands to tap into the sexual desires of consumers.

Thus, Bernays makes close connections among propaganda, capitalism, and democracy (a connection that we might find strange today), arguing that propaganda must be used in the service of capitalism to both create profit for companies and promote social issues such as women's rights and education.

Bernays therefore saw himself as a practitioner of propaganda (he later used the term *consent engineering*) who knew how to unlock the unconscious, underlying motives beneath people's desires. This ability is perhaps nowhere better demonstrated than in his 1928 campaign to increase smoking among women. In the 1920s, and in the wake of the successful suffrage movement, women were increasingly becoming part of the public sphere; more and more women were employed outside the home and had their own disposable income. However, it was still socially inappropriate for women to be seen smoking in public. Bernays was hired by the American Tobacco Company to encourage women to smoke, and he developed a campaign called "Torches of Freedom" (Amos & Haglund, 2000; W. Christensen, 2012). As the centerpiece of this campaign, Bernays hired a group of young attractive women to light up at the Easter Day parade in New York City in 1928. The photographic images of these young women smoking in public had a dramatic effect on the percentage of female smokers, with figures increasing from 5% in 1923 to 12% in 1929 to 18% in 1935, peaking at 41.9% in 1965 (today about 15.3% of women smoke; Nursing@USC Staff, 2017). In this campaign, smoking was closely connected with democracy, freedom, and women's liberation, and clearly it was very successful!

Bernays, then, was a key figure in developing idea that branding is about more than selling a product; it is about creating an emotional response through the identification of unfulfilled, often hidden, desires (not coincidentally, Bernays was Sigmund Freud's nephew). Thus, Bernays moved branding beyond the idea that products are purely functional, introducing the idea that they can fulfill emotional needs or be part of a particular lifestyle that has little to do with product use or functionality. For example, sociologist Janette Webb (2006) points out that automobile companies such as Ford and GM long ago abandoned

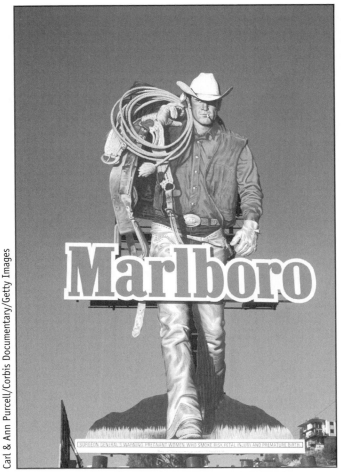

Carl & Ann Purcell/Corbis Documentary/Getty Images

Cigarette brands run the gamut of meanings from ruggedly masculine (Marlboro) to sexy and feminine (Virginia Slims).

the idea that they simply make cars and trucks (i.e., functional modes of transportation that get people from A to B). Instead, through marketing, advertising, and branding, they focus on "organizing social dependencies on the ownership of a car, and . . . creating the perception that car ownership symbolises status, independence, mobility and opportunity" (p. 56).

The process of branding thus involves the construction of a set of meanings around a particular product, person, company, town, city, or even a country (in other words, anything can be branded, including air, dirt, and water. The next time you're in an airport, pay attention to the ways the city markets itself to travelers.) Such meanings are extremely carefully constructed, and sometimes literally billions of dollars are spent on the development of such meanings. What's interesting about this process, however, is that the meanings associated with brands are often completely arbitrary, and frequently have little to do with any feature of the product itself; that is, there is little or no natural or intrinsic connection between a product and the way it is branded with meanings.

For example, cigarette brands run the gamut of meanings from rugged and masculine (Marlboro) to patriotic (American Spirit) to sexy and feminine (Virginia Slims); tobacco itself is none of these things in and of itself. It is only when millions of dollars are spent on branding cigarettes in these ways and creating emotional attachments between the product/brand and the consumer that these identities are associated with the products. Interestingly, Marlboro cigarettes were originally marketed to women in the 1930s but were rebranded (with great success) as a man's cigarette after World War II, again suggesting the extreme arbitrariness of the meanings associated with particular products. Brands are thus created through what is referred to as the floating signifier effect (Hall, 1985, 1997a). In other words, literally any meaning or quality can be attached to any brand (see Critical Case Study 10.1 below for an extended example of how the floating signifier effect works).

CRITICAL CASE STUDY 10.1

Diamonds Are Forever?

Perhaps the best and most interesting example we can provide of the floating signifier effect involves the diamond industry and in particular, the selling of diamond rings. Common sense tells us that diamonds are expensive because they are both inherently valuable and very rare. Surprisingly, this is not the case; diamonds are actually incredibly plentiful and have been since the discovery of extensive diamond fields in Southern Africa beginning in the late 19th century (Epstein, 1982a, 1982b). Furthermore, as a society we instinctively associate diamonds with romance, love, and marriage.

So how do these two facts come together—that is, the ready availability of diamonds and their connection to love and romance? First, when diamonds began to be discovered in great quantities in the late 19th century, the various mining companies quickly realized that if they didn't act fast, the price of diamonds would fall precipitously. In order to preserve the value of their commodity (and maintain the illusion of scarcity), they created a cartel of companies—called DeBeers—that could control the flow of diamonds onto the market and thus, their price. With the value and distribution of diamonds secured, DeBeers had to figure out how to sell its (now plentiful) product in a way that would not reduce its value. Indeed, despite the existence of the cartel, the price of diamonds had fallen steadily in the first part of the 20th century due to economic crises.

In the late 1930s, however, DeBeers hired an advertising firm—N. W. Ayer—to do two things. First, the firm branded diamonds in a way that created a strong tie with love and romance. They did this in part by employing the new medium of film to show movie idols symbolizing their love for leading ladies with diamonds. For example, N. W. Ayer wrote a memo to DeBeers suggesting that the cartel contact screenwriters to encourage them to write into movies scenes of men buying engagement rings for their girlfriends. The agency also recommended giving diamonds to public personalities and even to the Queen of Great Britain to cement the public's perception of diamonds as symbols of romance and indestructible love.

Second, it was extremely important for the stability of the diamond market that consumers were convinced diamonds should be kept as family treasures and keepsakes, not resold. An estimated half billion karats of diamonds are privately owned—about 50 times the yearly output of the diamond industry. Imagine what would happen to the market price of diamonds if this half billion karats (or even a portion of it) went back on the market? To prevent this flooding of diamonds, N. W. Ayer initiated a campaign around the phrase "A diamond is forever." This phrase, created in 1952 by an N. W. Ayer copywriter, is perhaps the most famous phrase in advertising history (even inspiring a James Bond novel and film!) and was incredibly persuasive in creating the image of diamonds not as a valuable commodity to be bought and sold but as a precious item that is eternal and should be kept for generations.

One final example from the diamond industry effectively demonstrates the power of branding to shape social realities. In the mid-1960s, the advertising firm J. Walter Thompson began a campaign

(Continued)

(Continued)

to sell diamond engagement rings in Japan. The interesting thing about Japan is that for 1,500 years, Japanese culture had followed the Shinto tradition of arranged marriage, with no real prenuptial courtship and romance as we would understand it in the West. In fact, in 1967, less than 5% of Japanese women wore engagement rings. So the Thompson agency began a campaign that branded engagement rings as a symbol of Western modernism. Print ads featured men and women dressed in European clothes, often driving European-model cars, and engaged in nontraditional (for Japan) activities such as hiking, camping, and swimming. The message of the ad campaign was clear—wearing diamonds is a symbol of entry into modern life and a break with the traditions of a premodern Japan. By 1972, 27% of Japanese women wore engagement rings; in 1978, this figure had risen to 50%, and by 1981 the figure was about 60%. So in the space of a mere 14 years, the advertising campaign had displaced 1,500 years of cultural tradition (Epstein, 1982a).

In summarizing the branding of diamonds, then, we want to reiterate two points about the floating signifier effect. First, the connection between diamonds and love and romance is an arbitrary, socially constructed relationship that is a result of the diamond industry's need to market what had become, by the 1930s, a plentiful commodity. Second, and related, in order to prevent the market price of this plentiful product from falling, diamonds had to be branded as precious heirlooms that signified eternity—"a diamond is forever." If you watch diamond commercials even today, you will see the same branding efforts in operation—diamonds are eternal; if you give a diamond to your loved one, your love will also be eternal. So that commonsense, almost instinctive association that most women (as well as men) make between diamonds and love/romance is a socially constructed association; it is the invention of an industry eager to preserve the illusion that diamonds are rare and precious and intrinsically valuable.

The branding of diamonds is an extremely successful example of how companies manage meanings for consumers, but the reality is that such corporate meaning management is such a routine feature of our everyday lives that we barely notice it.

Discussion Questions

1. What are the expectations, feelings, and sentiments that you associate with a diamond engagement ring? Where do these come from?

2. How many of you (men and women) have been involved in purchasing a diamond engagement ring? What were you told by friends, family, and diamond sellers about the rules and norms for purchasing diamond rings? Where do those rules and norms come from?

3. In groups, brainstorm other examples of consumer products that have been successful in constructing systems of meanings that have become part of our culture. How do these products use the idea of the floating signifier to create meanings? How have these products shaped our lives?

In the last 30 years, individual companies have increasingly come to understand the importance not simply of branding the products they make, but of creating a universe of branded meanings associated with the company itself (Klein, 2001). Companies are aware that consumers not only purchase particular products/brands but also "buy" the company behind the brand (Christensen, Morsing, & Cheney, 2008, p. 64). Many companies therefore rely on the strength of their corporate brands to engage in brand extension; that is, leveraging the meanings and emotions associated with the company to encompass a variety of different products—products that frequently bear little relationship to one another.

For example, the British company Virgin, which began in the 1970s as a record store, has extended its brand to include an airline (Virgin Atlantic), rail services, cell phones, and financial services, among many others. As you can see, there is little direct connection among these various products. But in the spirit of the floating signifier, these products are connected by the Virgin brand that, as Olins (2003) has described it, is "all attitude" (p. 95). Embodied in the maverick personality of its founder and CEO, Sir Richard Branson, Virgin brands itself as the cool, counterculture, upstart, renegade company that defends the little person against the corporate giants (even though Virgin is now a massive corporate empire!).

People are also branded. Michael Jordan is one of the earliest examples of a single individual becoming a brand that extends across a range of companies and products (Nike, Gatorade, Wheaties, Hanes, etc.). Donald J. Trump extended his personal brand beyond the business realm (real estate, Trump University, steaks, ties, bottled water, etc.) to include politics, branding himself as a nonpolitician who could "drain the swamp." Kim Kardashian is an example of a person who is almost all brand and no substance. While people like Michael Jordan and Serena Williams have built their brands on athletic prowess, Kim Kardashian's brand is based almost purely on her mere visibility; in other words, she is famous for being famous.

Universities and colleges have also entered the branding business in the last few years as a way to articulate their own USPs. As Ellen Wexler (2016) points out, a college is never just a college—it's an "experience," a "training ground," a "gateway," or (insert your own school's slogan here). Universities also use brief and punchy tag lines to capture their missions. The University of Colorado (Tim's school) uses "Be Boulder" (Get it?), and the University of North Carolina System of 17 campuses revealed a new motto in January 2018: "individually remarkable, collectively extraordinary" (not exactly the catchiest slogan ever!). Both our universities even have "Branding and Visual Identity Guidelines" that lay out in detail how brand consistency should be maintained (the worst thing a brand can do is fail to communicate a coherent and consistent image to its customers), including guidelines on font style and color usage). We suspect that your own college or university engages in similar branding activities, and you might think about to what degree these branding efforts reflect your decision to attend in the first place, as well as your actual experience on campus and in the classroom.

Social media, of course, has had a profound influence on the ability of people to develop personal brands, regardless of their level of fame. Indeed, we live in the age of the micro-celebrity, in which anyone with an Internet connection and a smartphone can generate a following and become Internet famous (see Case Study 10.2 below). With many micro-celebrities, their hope is to generate enough of a following that they will attract corporate sponsors who will pay them (or at least give them free stuff) to promote their brands. This effort to attract followers involves what some scholars have referred to as the attention economy, that is, if a micro-celebrity attracts enough followers (say, 100,000), then a company knows that those followers are potential consumers (Duffy, 2015; Marwick, 2015).

Companies have come to understand that wealth generation is very much about maintaining and growing the brand rather than the production of goods and services (though, of course, if the goods and services are not high enough quality, then the brand will suffer and lose value). Again, Nike, Apple, Uber, and the like focus their efforts on design and brand management, not on manufacturing the actual products or services they sell. Indeed, it is not unusual for the brand value of a company to be higher than its actual book value (the total of its tangible assets). For example, Apple's 2017 annual income statement showed total assets of about $375 billion, with total liabilities of $241 billion, giving it a net book value of about $134 billion. However, according to Interbrand (a brand strategy company that publishes an annual report of the top 100 brands worldwide), the value of Apple's brand is $184 billion. Thus, Apple's brand represents over 60% of its total value. This number means that "successful corporations are shifting their ground from making and selling to being—to representing a set of values" (Olins, 2003, p. 18).

The idea that much of the wealth of a company is located in its brand can be illustrated by looking at the example of Ford Motor Company. In 1989, Ford purchased the British car company Jaguar for $2.5 billion—twice the actual market value of Jaguar (Prokesch, 1989). How could such a deal be justified from a business perspective, especially when, at the time it was purchased, Jaguar was barely breaking even and making fewer than 52,000 cars a year? Ford executives made it clear that they were principally interested in the Jaguar brand, which is associated with luxury, elegance, and prestige.

After it purchased Jaguar, Ford radically altered the construction of its cars, building them with a Ford chassis and many Ford components, rendering a Jaguar, in many respects, no longer a Jaguar. But of course, in a branded world the actual physical makeup of the product is much less important than the image and meanings associated with it. Thus, if Ford were able to use its vast resources to construct large volumes of Jaguars, with some models in the price range of the average middle-class consumer, then many more people would be able to connect themselves to a luxury item (despite the decidedly blue-collar reputation of its parent company). In 2008, however, Ford sold Jaguar to Tata, an Indian automobile manufacturer, for $2.3 billion, having spent a further $10 billion trying to revive the Jaguar brand (Carty, 2008).

A 2008 report in *USA Today* provides a sense of how a company's efforts to extend its brand identity can sometimes result in failure and economic disaster:

> Ford spent a fortune acquiring Jaguar. . . . It paid $2.5 billion for Jaguar in 1990 after a bidding war of sorts with General Motors. Industry experts at the time estimated that was about $1.2 billion more than Jaguar was worth. Ford has since said the deal was worse than that. . . .
>
> Meanwhile, Jaguar's U.S. sales fell from 35,000 to a forecast 17,000 by the end of the year. . . . Despite current sales, Lindland says, both brands have strong images. "It's

the brands that make it worth the money. They're iconic brands with really storied histories." Still, she says, "It's a little bit like Wal-Mart buying Prada." (Carty, 2008)

The final sentence of this quotation puts company branding into sharp relief. If we know anything about consumption, we know that Wal-Mart and Prada are at opposite ends of the brand spectrum—the former is the dominant retailer in high-volume, low-cost items, while the latter is a high-end fashion company whose clothes and accessories are status symbols for its consumers. Wal-Mart, by definition, would never stock Prada items, and Prada customers would mutiny if its clothes were sold at Wal-Mart, even if the clothes/bags and their labels remained the same (it might hurt a Prada customer's *personal* brand to walk into a Wal-Mart!).

Thus, we can say that some brand associations are good, while others contaminate the brands with meanings that are deadly to the health of both brands. We can speculate that, among other factors, Ford's acquisition of Jaguar failed because it extended Ford's core brand identity too far away from its historical identity as a producer of cheap, reliable vehicles (remember that the Model T Ford was the world's first mass-produced car). It's interesting to note that Ford also purchased Volvo in the late 1990s but sold it to a Chinese auto manufacturer in 2010—another sign of its failure to extend brand identity. As a coda to this illustration, in May 2018, Ford announced that it would quit making cars (other than the Mustang) and focus on trucks and SUVs. This decision is yet another shift in the evolution of Ford's brand image and brings to fruition the quotation we first encountered in Chapter 6: "The manufacture of cars will be a declining part of Ford's business. They will concentrate in the future on design, branding, marketing, sales, and service operations" (Olins, 2000, p. 51). One wonders what Henry Ford would think of this shift if he were alive today. Whatever he might think, we can certainly say that Ford is now fully post-Fordist!

It's clear, then, that the branding process is murky and complex—something to be expected given that companies are dealing with the ways meanings and identities are constructed and communicated. Meaning, as we have discussed, is inherently ambiguous, and it is impossible fully to control and determine how customers take up brand meanings. Thanks to early practitioners of propaganda such as Edward Bernays, however, companies have long recognized the powerful connections among branding, consumption, and identity, fully understanding that the act of consumption goes well beyond simply purchasing a functional product. In this sense, in developing brands, companies are very consciously exploiting the human desire for affiliation and identification.

However, the brand–consumer relationship is not static and has undergone several transformations over the decades. One might argue that companies' understanding of branding as a fundamentally communicative processes has grown increasingly sophisticated during this time. In the next section, we will examine this evolution.

THE EVOLUTION OF BRANDING: THREE MODELS

The efforts of corporations to capture our sense of self and connect consumption to individual identity construction has undergone several transformations, particularly in the period since World War II. In this section, we will examine three periods of branding that, taken together, illuminate an evolving relationship between brand and consumer, in which communication plays a defining role. Following the work of communication scholar Sarah Banet-Weiser (2012) and critical management scholar Adam Arvidsson (2006), the three periods can be designated as (1) the Fordist period of mass marketing, (2) the period of niche marketing and appeals to authenticity, and (3) the (current) period of consumer engagement, or brand as institution. Let's discuss each below.

Fordism and Mass Marketing (Approx. 1945–1980)

In the 30 years following World War II, Fordist capitalism was at the height of its powers. The United States was the world's dominant economic system, and people had stable jobs and disposable income—income that could be spent on something other than food and shelter. It was during this period (roughly 1945–1970) that the mass marketing of consumer goods came into its own, catalyzed by the increasing presence of televisions in people's homes (television had been invented in the 1930s but was not widely available until the early 1950s).

In Chapter 3, we talked about the emergence of a consumer society under Fordism, and in many ways, the system of marketing and consumption that prevailed under Fordism mirrored the Fordist system of mass production. Goods were mass produced, and they were mass consumed. People watched the same TV shows (*I Love Lucy*, *Leave it to Beaver*, etc.) and went to the same movies. Women wore the fashion of the day, but for the most part all the men dressed the same (check out a street scene in a 1950s movie sometime), and there was no such thing as a teen market (the teenager wasn't invented until the 1950s as a specific demographic group to whom companies marketed products—it took rock and roll music to do that—and teenagers dressed mostly like small adults). Thus, companies did relatively little to target their products to specific demographic groups, other than by gender and broad socioeconomic status. The consumer, then, was constructed as relatively homogeneous. For example, with a few exceptions (Pepsi-Cola, for example, who marketed to African American consumers), companies did not see African Americans or other minority groups as worth marketing to, despite the existence of a growing black middle class. Banet-Weiser (2012) suggests that the two common themes in marketing at this time were "abundance and conformity" (p. 26); that is, minorities and the working class should aspire to be just like them (i.e., white, middle-class suburbanites) through conspicuous consumption. Aspiring to sameness, then, was seen as symbolizing capitalism and democratic freedom.

From a communication perspective, companies' marketing strategies during this period were not dissimilar from a sender–receiver model of communication, in which the goal was to get information out to potential consumers regarding the superiority of a company's products over its rivals. Moreover, while branding was important, branding efforts often focused on the functional superiority of a particular product (you see a lot of pseudo-scientific experiments in commercials in the 1950s and 1960s that "prove" the superior functionality of a product). A classic example is this Dove Soap commercial from 1957, where Dove with its one-quarter moisturizing cream ("it creams the skin while you wash!") is compared with regular soap: https://www.youtube.com/watch?v=jWD0co3qFpI.

Finally, it should be noted that while branding and marketing tended to be fairly functional and mass oriented during this period, there was also a strong aspirational quality to marketing efforts. There was a burgeoning middle class as income improved, and many people aspired to a better life through consumer goods (a new car every couple of years, new kitchen appliances, a home in the suburbs, regular vacations) and the idea of consumption as a way to participate in a particular lifestyle first came to the fore. Television in particular enabled the construction of a particular lifestyle around brands (the Dove ad mentioned above shows a beautiful woman in a penthouse apartment luxuriating in a bubble bath). For example, Hugh Hefner (creator of *Playboy*) saw his magazine, founded in 1953, not simply as a way to enable men to look at photos of naked women but as the purveyor of a particular (heterosexual) male lifestyle that included literature ("I only get it for the articles"), politics, fine wine, and music. Thus, even if a man lived a boring middle-class existence in the suburbs, he could purchase *Playboy* and read the latest short story by Norman Mailer while listening to jazz on his expensive stereo "Hi-Fi" system, transported— if only briefly—to another, more exciting life. Thus, companies were increasingly shifting from simply marketing products to articulating particular lifestyles around those products.

Niche Marketing and Authenticity (1980s–Late 1990s)

Companies and their branding strategies do not live in a social or political vacuum, and what was going on socially and politically in the 1960s and 1970s had a significant impact on the ways that companies marketed their brands to consumers. In the 1960s, we see the emergence of identity politics, particularly with the rise of the Civil Rights and feminist movements. The idea of a homogeneous society, with everyone aspiring to a white, middle-class life in the suburbs, gave way to a period of political and economic turbulence in which marginalized groups struggled for emancipation, in part by reclaiming a strong sense of identification with their cultural and racial heritage. In this sense, the idea of authenticity—being true to one's self and one's gender/race/class—became an important element of identity politics.

In response to the emergence of identity politics, companies recognized the need to develop authenticity as a market category. Consumers were increasingly unlikely to respond to mass marketing that failed to speak to their own sense of identity, and thus companies needed to develop a diverse and differentiated strategy that identified various niche markets. For example, Banet-Weiser (2012) explores how, beginning in the 1980s, Dove soap developed a branding strategy that made a direct connection between female empowerment and using Dove. The new strategy invoked second wave feminist discourse about the patriarchal repression of women's true selves (Banet-Weiser, 2012). Thus, being empowered meant being yourself. Different ads were targeted at different groups of women, focusing on the idea of allowing one's authentic, real beauty (as opposed to cosmetically enhanced beauty) to shine through by using Dove on one's skin. Thus, the marketing campaign rejected the idea of societally imposed, homogeneous beauty standards, focusing on the need for women to get in touch with their true selves. In this framing, women's pursuit of beauty was seen as an extension of the goal of feminism to empower women. One example of these ads (Shy, 2008) can be seen here: https://www.youtube.com/watch?v = FipEYhv3fEg.

In this era of niche marketing, then, we see how branding strategies respond to the changing cultural and political environment, in this instance involving the appropriation and commodification of anti-establishment discourses about personal expression, equality, and freedom. As Banet-Weiser (2012) argues, the shift in marketing strategy is from "you should buy this because everyone else has" under a mass consumption model, to "you should buy our product because it's different from everyone else's and is therefore authentic and real." The implication here, of course, is that buying an "authentic" product makes the consumer authentic too.

From a communication perspective, the branding strategy in this model shifts from a top-down, sender–receiver model ("you must buy this!"), to a more relationally oriented model in which there is a recognition by the company/brand that the consumer is a more active interpreter of media messages and thus may resist the way brand meanings are encoded (Hall, 2007). The idea, then, is that companies must strive to develop authentic brands that produce close relationships with their customers. As we will see below, the notion of marketing as involving a close brand–consumer relation will truly come into its own in the third period of marketing.

The Brand as Institution (Late 1990s–Present)

The third period of development in the brand–consumer relationship is the most significant. It began in the late 1990s and continues today. In this period, branding has moved beyond the idea of simply identifying niche consumer groups (although that certainly continues in an even more fine-grained way) and instead actually engages directly with consumers, viewing consumers as direct participants in the branding process. Thus, while the first two periods distinguished clearly between the processes of production (making and marketing goods and services) and the process of consumption (purchasing goods and services), the period of engagement blurs that distinction considerably. Consumers (or prosumers, as they are sometimes called) are now encouraged to interact directly with the brands and the companies who market them. Indeed, customers are even encouraged to be directly involved in brand management and strategy (see Critical Research 10.1 below for an example of this consumer involvement).

This shift to consumer engagement is a direct consequence of the emergence of neoliberalism and the recognition that we are now firmly in a period that we might call communicative capitalism (Dean, 2009, 2014; Mumby, 2016, 2018). Here, a strong connection exists between the creation of economic value and the construction of meanings through communication processes. If making meanings is more important for economic value production than making things, then the brand (where corporate meanings reside) becomes the most crucial element in the value production process. Thus, we can return to Maurizio Lazzarato's (2004) claim that we first encountered in Chapter 6: "Contemporary capitalism does not first arrive with factories; these follow, if they follow at all. It arrives with words, signs, and images" (p. 190). We can say, then, that while industrial capitalism exploited labor to make profits, contemporary capitalism exploits communication to the same end, with brands as the mechanism for that exploitation process.

We have therefore moved to the point where brands function as institutions; that is, just as bureaucracies used to be the most powerful organizational forms that guided our behavior, so brands have now taken on that role (Arvidsson, 2006). In this sense, companies engage with us through their brands in an effort to mediate our everyday experiences. Brands are institutions insofar as they attempt to provide us with the framework through which we experience our sense of self, others, and the world around us. In case you think we are being a little extreme here, let's quote Jez Frampton, the Global CEO of Interbrand (the company we mentioned earlier that annually ranks the top 100 global brands). In Interbrand's 2015 annual report, he writes about the relationship between brands and the individual, describing what he calls a branding mecosystem (a play on ecosystem, but with emphasis on the "me" at the center) in which each individual lives. In other words, just as in the natural world we are part of a delicate ecosystem, so in the world of branding we live in a complex system of meanings, emotions, and values that brands create for us. Frampton thus describes a mecosystem as,

> [A] select set of brands that create customized experiences around a single individual, where every brand in consideration slots in seamlessly, and where the most valuable micro moments are curated, connected, and choreographed. As people shape their mecosystems—as they explore and, just as importantly, edit— they are constantly being redefined, meaning that brands need to earn the right to stay in this set every minute of every day. (Jez Frampton, 2015, Global CEO of Interbrand)

This quote makes clear that brand strategists understand the intimate link between branding and identity. Indeed, it fits perfectly with Arvidsson's notion of the brand as institution. In other words, we do not simply purchase brands or develop relationships with brands; rather, brands provide the very social and cultural context that enable us to engage with the world. Brands, in this sense, become part of people's commonsense, taken for granted process of meaning making. Thus, we might say, following Celia Lury (2004) and Martin Kornberger, that "the brand involves the controlled reintroduction of meaning into market exchange" (Kornberger, 2015, p. 108). In other words, we must not forget that this entire process is about the creation of value and profit for companies. This is somewhat disguised, however, because brands have come to play a role in the production of culture itself, including the selves who make up that culture. Hence, brand strategies are framed not in economic or business terms, but as "the affective stuff of culture" (Banet-Weiser, 2012, p. 45). Thus, a company like Zillow (an online real estate database company) needs to make buying and selling houses more about affect and emotion than simply an economic transaction. Hence, the name/brand "Zillow" was chosen (meaning "zillions of pillows") as a way to tap into people's sense identification and emotional connection with home ownership. For brands like Zillow and others, then, "brand management is about making the becoming of subjects and the becoming of value coincide" (Arvidsson, 2006, p. 93).

One term that has been used to describe this process is the phenomenon of **murketing** (Walker, 2008). Whereas in traditional marketing strategies a fairly clear distinction exists between the programming of a particular medium and advertising (we know when we're watching a commercial break and when we're watching an actual program), with murketing the distinction is basically erased. At one level, murketing has been around for a long time; companies have used product placement in TV shows and movies to increase brand awareness (next time you go to a movie, see how many examples of product place-ment you can identify). In the past few years, however, the extent to which branding and everyday life have merged together has exploded. From a corporate perspective, the point is that if, indeed, consumers can exercise much greater freedom in choosing brands and integrating them into their lifestyles, then developing brand loyalty requires a much more sophisticated set of marketing strategies.

With murketing, the trick is to blend a brand seamlessly into everyday life and popular culture—to be successful, a brand must become an integral part of the way people express their identities. Again, we are back to the idea that consumers do not buy products but rather extensions of their own sense of self and relationship to the world and others. In murketing, then, the relationship between cultural expression and commercial expression is blurred.

We can illustrate this process by completing our analysis of Dove soap. As Banet-Weiser (2012) shows, in the 2000s, Dove launched the "Campaign for Real Beauty" and the "Dove Self-Esteem Project" in which the focus on the merits and functionality of the product basi-cally disappeared completely, and instead, consumers were enjoined to engage directly with social issues around women's and girls' body image. Dove made short documentary films, mostly shown on social media, in which girls talk about the societal pressures that they experience with body image. An example is available here: https://www.youtube.com/watch?v = 4ytjTNX9cg0. Dove's website also includes "Parent and Mentor Resources" cov-ering such topics as "family, friends, and relationships," "teasing and bullying," "respect-ing and looking after yourself," among others (www.dove.com/us/en/stories/about-dove/dove-self-esteem-project.html#). Mothers and daughters can also participate together in workshops that address body image issues.

Dove is one example (and there are many) of brands inserting themselves directly into political issues around processes of social change. In this sense, brands don't avoid political issues as they did in the past; instead, they embrace them and attempt to shape and define them. Thus, Dove attempts to shape debates around girls' and women's body issues, invit-ing consumers to participate in those debates themselves, through social media. Indeed, it is rare these days to find a brand that does not in some way take on a social or political issue; companies recognize that engagement with political issues through their brands is a way for them to develop long-term relationships with customers. For example, Starbucks recently committed to hiring 10,000 refugees by 2022—an effort to enter directly into the political debates around the global refugee crisis that involves 65 million people globally who have been forcibly displaced. Former Starbucks CEO Howard Schultz (2012) refers to these marketing strategies as "brand sparks," which he describes as "subtle, surprising, and rare marketing events—usually linked to cultural or humanitarian issues and devoid of a self-serving marketing pitch" (p. 216).

This co-opting of politics by brands led the late philosopher André Gorz (2010) to argue that, under branding and neoliberalism, the citizen has been turned into a consumer; that is, any engagement we have with politics is through the consumption process (again, one might attribute Donald Trump's success in the 2016 presidential election to his ability to brand himself through a strong emotional—rather than rational—appeal to voters). As such, Gorz (2010) argues, "The brand image effects a seizure of power by immaterial fixed capital over public space, the culture of everyday life and the social imaginary" (p. 100).

In other words, brands now mediate every sphere of life in an effort to exploit human interaction for profit.

If under neoliberalism, the brand is now an institution, then we can say, following Adam Arvidsson, "Life evolves entirely within capital; there is no longer any outside" (2006, p. 30). In other words, brands as institutions exist everywhere, and all social interaction has the potential to be incorporated into branding processes, and hence to produce economic value (Critical Case Study 10.2 below provides an excellent example of this process). Thus, one could argue that the branding process has become one of the most—perhaps *the* most—powerful mediators of everyday life. We are rarely, if ever, able to escape our own little mecosystem and experience the world in an unbranded, unmediated way.

Thus, in the next section, we examine more closely how branding and self-identity are intimately tied together.

CRITICAL CASE STUDY 10.2

Alex From Target

At 10 a.m. on Sunday, November 2, 2014, 16-year-old high school student Alex Lee began an 8-hour shift as a checkout cashier at the local Target store in Frisco, Texas. Early in the shift, Alex began to notice that his checkout line was longer than usual, and for some reason, giggling groups of teenage girls had started showing up to take his photograph. Things got so hectic that his supervisor had to reassign him to work in the stockroom. At the end of his shift at 6 p.m., Alex turned on his phone and discovered that his Twitter account had increased in a matter of hours from 144 to over 100,000 followers—a number that would jump to over 700,000 in the next few days. The sudden surge in followers prompted Alex to post the immortal tweet, "Am I famous now?"—a question that has since been retweeted 40,000 times and "favorited" by over 86,000 users (Bilton, 2014).

What made Alex such an object of attention? Early in his shift at Target, a teenage girl in the United Kingdom (@auscalum) came across a photograph of Alex (taken during his previous week's shift at Target) that had been posted on Tumblr. She thought Alex looked cute and immediately tweeted the photograph with the caption, "Yooooooooooo." The image quickly went viral, prompting the chaotic events at Target. Over the next few days, Alex would make guest appearances on *Ellen* and on CNBC's *Fast Money* show, the latter accompanied by his new agent, John Shahidi, CEO of the social media company Shots. Alex Lee, the ordinary 16-year-old boy, had become "Alex from Target," branded micro-celebrity in the attention economy (Marwick, 2015). Alex no longer works for Target, but he still has something of a celebrity status. After his newfound fame, he signed with Digitour, a company that holds public events to showcase social media stars from YouTube, Twitter, Vine, and

(Continued)

(Continued)

Instagram. He has an Instagram following of 1.5 million people and currently has his own YouTube channel with about 150,000 followers: https://www.youtube.com/watch?v=pM-sbalhZGU.

Alex's case is a perfect example of communicative capitalism in the current age of branding. Alex has no particular skills or expertise. In 2014, he was a 16-year-old kid working a part-time job and attending high school. But suddenly he had something that other kids his age did not have—hundreds of thousands of followers on social media. This popularity meant that he could be transformed from an ordinary boy to a brand with economic value, simply because of a photograph shared on social media. As such, it is easy to see how important and central communication is to the construction of economic value under neoliberal capitalism: Alex Lee is an ordinary boy; "Alex from Target" is a valuable, branded commodity that can make money for the companies and brands that want to associate themselves with him. Interestingly, shortly after "Alex from Target" became a media meme, a social media marketing company called Breakr claimed that the entire event was a marketing campaign created in order to demonstrate "how powerful the fangirl demographic was" (Levy, 2014). However, this origin story was immediately debunked by all parties involved, and Breakr had to withdraw its claim (H. Peterson, 2014). Thus, Breakr saw an opportunity to enhance its own brand value by co-opting the media attention "Alex from Target" was receiving.

Discussion Questions

1. What do you think of the "Alex From Target" phenomenon? Watch his interview on CNBC here and discuss how he is being branded during the interview: https://www.cnbc.com/2014/11/12/alex-from-target-fame-pretty-overwhelming.html.

2. What kind of social media presence do you have? How carefully do you curate what you post online? Do you consciously think about the online identity/brand that you are creating?

3. Do you have any aspirations to be a micro-celebrity? Do you consciously engage in efforts to increase your number of followers? How do you see your online identity as connected to your work and career aspirations?

WORK, BRANDING, AND THE ENTREPRENEURIAL SELF

So far in this chapter, we have spent a lot of time discussing the brand–consumer relationship, but we have not talked very much about the relationship between branding and work. After all, it is employees who are on the front lines, as it were, in the branding process; they are the ones who are expected to live the brand and embody the brand experience for customers. Talking about employees rather than consumers in a brand context is a little complicated, however, because of the blurred relationship under neoliberal capitalism between production and consumption. Consumers are actively involved in brand management; companies use their **brand public** as a source of innovation for their brands (e.g., Nike is famous for sending researchers into urban communities to find out what the latest fashions are, and Apple allows anyone to develop new apps). In other words, brands put consumers to work, resulting in a process of value co-creation (Zwick, Bonsu, & Darmody, 2008) between producers and consumers. Moreover, company employees are consumers of their company's brand, in that (at least ideally) they must internalize the brand to live it. In addition, and as we saw in Chapter 6, the growth of the gig economy means that workers are increasingly free agents who must constantly engage in efforts at entrepreneurship and self-branding; under such circumstances, it's hard to know when one is not at work. So how might we think about the relationships among work, branding, and the entrepreneurial self?

First, we can say that the brand changes the relationship between the individual and society (Kornberger, 2015). In Chapter 6, we talked about how, under neoliberalism, we saw the demise of the state and traditional institutions (class, family, community, etc.) as a mooring for a stable sense of self. Thus, we can argue that it is the brand that takes over to help provide that sense of stability. As brand strategists such as Jez Frampton (2015) would have it, we all need a branded mecosystem that we carry around with us and that enables us to feel connected to our brand communities. At the same time, however, we must all develop our own unique brand that is more than simply the amalgam of brands in our mecosystem. In other words, we all need to be enterprise selves who work hard to construct "a brand worthy of remark" (Peters, 1997).

We suspect that many of you reading this chapter have been asked on more than one occasion to think about ways you can brand yourselves in a way that's different from other college graduates in a competitive job market. Of course, there is nothing wrong with developing a distinct set of abilities that make you stand out from the crowd, but oftentimes such branding is less about particular skills and more about the packaging—just like consumer products, students are increasingly being asked to focus on image rather than on substance as a way to market themselves. In other words, they are being asked to engage in a discourse of enterprise where the focus is marketing and branding rather than engaging in an educational process. Our discussion in Chapter 1 of David Brooks's (2001) essay "The Organization Kid" is an example of how pervasive this discourse of enterprise has become among college students.

There is an important sense, then, in which the **enterprise self** is a central figure in the new era of branding. The enterprise self is, by definition, a branded self. We are not simply enterprise selves at work; we are enterprise selves all the time. If we live in the social factory (see Chapter 6) in which all of life is contained within capitalism, then every interaction that we engage in has the potential to be monetized (Willmott, 2010). Think back to Katie Sullivan and Helen Delaney's (2017) analysis of Arbonne International from Chapter 6. The business model of Arbonne is rooted in sociality (i.e., in connection and friendships among people) and enjoins Arbonne members to treat those friendships as enterprise opportunities. Moreover, Brooke Duffy's (2015, 2017) research on female fashion bloggers shows how quickly doing something that you love comes to consume individuals as they attempt to turn their passion into income through efforts to brand themselves as unique among the thousands of other bloggers. And communication scholar Alice Marwick's (2013) ethnography of high-tech startup workers in Silicon Valley explores the degree to which many are preoccupied with their status and attention, constantly engaging in self-branding efforts (including life-streaming!) and maintaining and increasing their niche online audience. The title of Marwick's book, *Status Update*, suggests how important it is for each enterprising self to constantly have something new to offer his or her audience, for fear that his or her brand might be devalued.

Branding thus functions as a form of biopower (see Chapter 7) that enables people to operate as free individuals within a market system. In this sense, branding is a way for the entrepreneurial self to make its activities as human capital meaningful. In other words, we're not only trying to increase our value as human capital through self-enterprising behavior; we are also adding meaning and connection to people's lives through our brands. For example, Alex from Target's agent, John Shahidi, talks constantly in his CNBC interview about how Alex is "doing great" and is "always very positive" and is "conveying his message to the world" (whatever that might be!), even though Alex has nothing particularly special about him from a branding point of view. Such meaning must be constructed, almost out of thin air, so that the emotional connection of teenage girls to Alex can be maintained.

Second, and related, it's important to draw attention to the degree to which employees have become an essential part of the corporate branding process. In examining the relationship between branding and work, Matthew Brannan and his colleagues have argued that "employee branding extends the frontier of control . . . beyond the physical boundaries of the organization" (Brannan, Parsons, & Priola, 2011, pp. 5–6). In Chapter 5, we saw how the corporate culture model kept a very tight rein on how employees identified with and expressed the culture (e.g., through intensive culture boot camps). In the contemporary branded organization, however, the goal is to draw on the cultural and social knowledge and forms of expertise that employees already possess (in contexts external to the organization) as a way to maintain and enhance the brand. This process is referred to as **branding from the outside in** (Kornberger, 2010); in other words, rather than try to get employees to conform to an imposed corporate culture, the corporate branding process mobilizes for its own purposes identities and lifestyles that are already preferred and expressed by employees (Endrissat, Karreman, & Noppeny, 2017). Instead of regulating employee identities in accordance with corporate values, employees are encouraged to be themselves at work (Fleming & Sturdy, 2011).

For example, as we saw in Chapter 6, Chris Land and Scott Taylor's (2010) study of the clothing company Ethico showed how the company didn't so much instill values in the employees as draw on the values, knowledge, and skills that the employees already possessed in their everyday lives. Thus, a preexisting expertise in skateboarding gets translated into slogans for T-shirts ("tattoos have to be bought; scars have to be earned"), and a love of kayaking and surfing quickly became incorporated into the company brand as a way to enhance its value.

In another study, Nada Endrissat and her colleagues (2017) explore how a "major international grocery chain," which they call "Genuine Groceries" (think "Whole Paycheck"), deliberately and strategically recruits art college graduates as a way to enhance its brand, giving these employees license to explore their creative talents in the store and providing wide latitude in terms of forms of personal expression like clothing styles and tattoos. As Endrissat et al. (2017) state, "From a branding perspective, GG has found a way to productively integrate the individual idiosyncrasies of creative people into a corporate context. Through association with different subcultures, the brand as alternative organization is built" (p. 505). Just like Ethico, then, GG is able to draw on alternate, nonmainstream lifestyles (in other words, forms of everyday life) as a way to increase its brand value and hence its profits (it will be interesting to see if GG, now owned by Amazon, will be able to maintain this counterculture brand image; early evidence is that a clash of cultures is developing, making many longtime GG employees unhappy and stressed out (E. Peterson, 2018)).

Both of these examples are interesting insofar as they show that not only are brands drawing on employees' real selves but that, in turn, the brands themselves provide employees with identity incentives (Endrissat et al., 2017); in other words, the brands provide an opportunity for employees to express and confirm their preferred sense of self. Thus, "employees derive identity from the brand they are working for, and the brand derives its meaning from the employees it incorporates" (Endrissat et al., 2017, p. 506). As Matthew Brannan and his colleagues show, this reciprocal relationship can also exist in mundane work (e.g., in call centers), where employees can use a strong brand as a kind of narrative promise, in which currently mundane work can be rationalized because it will lead to more exciting and fulfilling work opportunities in the future (Brannan et al., 2015).

Branding, then, is a form of organizational communication that extends beyond the employment relationship itself. Brands draw on the everyday lives of both workers and consumers, and workers and consumers draw on brands as a way of articulating their identities. Brands are a ubiquitous and defining feature of neoliberal capitalism because much of the value of a commodity resides in its "informational and cultural content" (Lazzarato, 1996, p. 133). In this sense, workers and consumers are immaterial laborers in the social factory, engaged in forms of meaning making that both produce and are mediated by brands. Brands are therefore part of the commonsense, taken for granted water in which we swim; they are, in this sense, hidden in plain sight (Mumby, 2016)—unnoticed, and yet indispensable to our sense of who we are. In the final section of this chapter, we take up the ethical implications of defining ourselves and the world through branding.

CRITICAL RESEARCH 10.1

Bernard Cova, Stefano Pace, & Per Skålén (2015). Marketing with working consumers: The case of a carmaker and its brand community. *Organization, 22*, 682–701.

As we have argued in this chapter, the distinction between workers and consumers has blurred considerably in the contemporary age of the brand as institution. In their ethnographic study of the Alfa Romeo (AR) automobile company, Bernard Cova and colleagues examine how this blurring of the worker–consumer distinction was strategically deployed by AR as a way to enhance its brand value. Using AR's 100th anniversary celebration as an opportunity for an ethnographic case study, Cova et al. explore collaborative marketing; that is, a process that "operates with blurred boundaries between

(Continued)

(Continued)

the producer and the consumer by considering the consumer as a partner and co-creator of value" (p. 685). The objective of collaborative marketing is to take the activities of a brand community (the people who are strongly invested in the brand) and turn them into brand value (i.e., monetize them).

Cova et al. focus their study on the Alfisti—AR enthusiasts who make up the core of its brand community. As part of it 100th anniversary celebrations, AR gave three managers the task of organizing a collaborative marketing program, in which they actively encouraged the input of Alfisti. The managers asked themselves the question: "What is the common goal or cause that could unite Alfisti?" Their answer was to invite Alfisti to plan "the biggest event in the history of the automobile celebrating the 100th anniversary of the brand" (p. 688). As such, they built an online platform in five languages (English, French, Swedish, Italian, German) to create "the biggest community in the automobile world" (p. 688). The launch of the platform took place in the wake of a 2-day seminar, involving AR executives and 80 Alfisti representing the biggest AR owners clubs in the world. At this meeting, the AR club representatives were asked by the AR president to work enthusiastically on behalf of the brand initiative and encourage other members to contribute to the platform discussion.

Discussion on the platform among the Alfisti focused mainly on the future of the brand, management strategy, and the range of AR models. One Alfista stated the following: "To understand what is important for an Alfista, we need to define what Alfa Romeo is . . . . Alpha is emotion and performance, nothing to do with transport. . . . You buy with the heart, you sell with the brain" (p. 692). Interestingly, Cova et al. report that the marketing team was not so much interested in the substantive contributions of the Alfisti (suggestions for defining the brand, marketing strategy, etc.) as it as in using them as brand evangelists rather than as partners in co-creative work.

Cova et al. conclude that the Alfisti's main function was as interactive service workers who contributed social and emotional skills to promoting the AR brand. However, they point out that the Alfisti saw themselves as able to make substantive creative contributions to the branding process. As Cova et al. state, "Like other brand community members, Alfisti claim ownership of the brand and, as a consequence, wanted to be involved in major issues and not merely in social and emotional work. They wanted to contribute technical skills and be involved in product development, marketing, design and similar tasks. In other words, they wanted to do what could be called traditional work rather than service work" (p. 696). All, of course, for no reward, except for their ability to express their love for and knowledge of the AR brand. In this context, we truly see the collapse of the distinction between production and consumption.

Discussion Questions

1. Do you consider yourself a member of a brand community? What is the brand? Why are you so enthusiastic about it?

2. Have you ever contributed to an online brand forum? What was your motivation for doing this?

3. Harley-Davidson also has a very strong brand community. Read the following article about Harley-Davidson's brand strategy: https://www.referralcandy.com/blog/harley-davidson-marketing-strategy/. What insights does it give you into how brands are created? Check out the "Harley Owners' Group" (HOG) online to get a sense of the strength of this brand community: https://members.hog.com/website/index.jsp;hogsessionid=gZKyq3UC3PfBbuRR YAWZS8S0?redirectUrl=https%3A%2F%2Fmembers.hog.com%2Fwebsite%2Fmain.jsp.

◦◦ THE ETHICS OF BRANDING

This chapter has provided a critical examination of corporate branding. However, is it fair to say that all branding is problematic or even unethical? Branding has been with us for 150 years, and there is little doubt that it will continue to define our relationships to organizations and corporations. One might argue that branding in and of itself is not unethical; rather, certain branding practices are. The reality is that in contemporary organizational life branding is an intrinsic element of what all organizations do on a routine basis. Any organization that needs to maintain a relationship with various stakeholder groups (customers, employees, shareholders, community members, etc.) has to articulate a set of meanings to those groups that enables them to identify with the organization in a particular way. Indeed, most corporations and their employees would probably argue that they believe strongly in the values embodied in their brand.

And of course, as we have discussed, branding is not limited to for-profit organizations. Nonprofit, volunteer, charitable, even government and public institutions engage in branding in an effort to cultivate stakeholder relationships. None of these branding efforts are intrinsically unethical; arguably, such efforts are unethical only when there is a contradiction between an organization's branding strategy and its everyday organizational practices. For example, if a university brands itself as student oriented, with frequent contact between faculty and students, and then new students discover that teaching is neglected in favor of faculty research, one might argue that such a university behaves unethically in trying to part students from their hard-earned tuition dollars. Or if a company brands itself as environmentally responsible as a way to increase its profits but then exploits nonrenewable resources (a practice described as greenwashing), one might legitimately accuse that company of unethical behavior.

However, not all ethical questions are quite so straightforward in the world of branding. Adopting a critical perspective, we are concerned with a broader set of ethical issues regarding the relationship between branding and the role of the modern corporation in everyday life, or with what we identified in an earlier chapter as the process of corporate colonization (Deetz, 1992). That is, to what extent should corporations play a role in defining who we are and how we see ourselves as connected human beings who are members of broader communities? Who gets to decide what is important and what is not in our lives?

As we discussed earlier in this chapter, the ultimate goal of corporate branding efforts is to mediate as many aspects of human experience and identity construction as possible. Certainly, the development of marketing suggests that the days of a relatively clear separation of corporate advertising and everyday life are long gone. We live in an environment that is completely saturated with mediated, branded meanings. It's almost as though nothing is meaningful until it is framed for us by a corporate sponsor. As such, corporations and the meaning systems they create play a disproportionately large role in defining who we are as people.

Some brand theorists have argued that branding and democracy are tied together in a positive manner (Gobé, 2002, 2007). Marc Gobé (2007), for example, argues that

> [branding] is not about money: branding is about life, it is about respect, it is about success, it is about love, freedom, and hope. It is about building bonds everyone can trust. . . . There is an economic and psychological divide that exists between

societies. If brands are the great equalizer, shouldn't they then inspire, motivate, problem solve? Shouldn't brands be part of the solution, not the problem? Shouldn't brands continue to foster freedom of choice? (pp. 65, 66)

Obviously, such a perspective makes a close connection between consumption and democracy. But do we really want to live in a society where freedom is defined in terms of the ability to purchase consumer goods that help us feel good about ourselves? Is having the choice among hundreds of different brands of soft drinks (a significant factor in obesity rates) or being able to choose how you want your burger prepared an appropriate litmus test for freedom and democracy? If, as Gobé (2007) suggests, Coca-Cola via its branding provides a message of optimism and freedom, even though it has a long history of exploiting local resources (see Elmore, 2015), and if Dove can frame the purchasing of soap as an act of feminist empowerment, then what does that say about the nature of democracy in the 21st century, especially when politicians themselves increasingly rely on branding and emotional (rather than rational) appeals to citizen–consumers?

One of the issues that brand theorists such as Gobé consistently ignore is that, ultimately, branding is about making profits for corporations and their shareholders. While it is possible to argue that brands embody principles of freedom and democracy, such a perspective adopts a very superficial view of democracy, overlooking at least two issues. First, because of the floating signifier effect, any meaning attached to a brand is purely arbitrary and, thus, the product of careful marketing—a brand signifies freedom only to the extent that its corporate parent wants it to! For example, Dove's parent company, Unilever, also sells Axe deodorant to men using a marketing strategy that frequently positions women as sexual objects whose agency disappears when men wear Axe—a further indication that branding is less about democracy and empowerment and more about profit margins. Second, in genuine democracies, ordinary people have a strong voice in the ways their political and civil interests are represented. As such, consumption is a form of pseudo-democracy that provides the illusion of participation and empowerment but is carefully mediated and managed by corporate interests.

Benjamin Barber (2007) has argued that consumer empowerment (a favorite phrase among brand managers) involves choice without consequences. We can feel empowered by our choice of a particular clothing brand, or by liking the latest social issue du jour on Facebook, but these activities are ultimately intensely private and isolated. Genuine democracy involves engaged, informed citizens participating with one another in the public sphere and vigorously debating the issues of the day (and not just in our own little self-contained social media silos!). The goal of branding is to get us to respond in emotional rather than rational ways to products. Indeed, the phenomenon of buyer's remorse, which we've all experienced, is a great illustration of how our rational faculties kick in once it's too late!

In many ways, such brand relationships stand in opposition to strong democracy, which requires careful and thoughtful examination of issues and active engagement with other members of our communities. As Barber (2007) argues, however, "shopping seems to have become a more persuasive marker of freedom than voting . . . and what we do alone in the mall [or online] counts more importantly in shaping our destiny than what we do together in the public square" (p. 37).

In sum, we would suggest that branding is not, by definition, unethical; all organizations have both the right and the responsibility to construct meaningful relationships with their various stakeholders, and branding is one part of that process. Branding does become ethically suspect, however, when organizations adopt communication and meaning construction strategies that (a) contradict their actual business practices, (b) deliberately exploit the vulnerabilities of less powerful members of society, or (c) present consumption as an empowering, defining feature of who we are as people. Consumption is a *dis*empowering act to the extent that it undermines our sense of ourselves as engaged citizens and makes a fetish out of our relationships to objects. Consumption makes us all a little more private, a little more isolated, and a little more disengaged from the world and the people around us.

CONCLUSION

In this chapter, we have examined the brand as a communication-based organizing device (Kornberger, 2015). That is, it is an institutional form that mediates our relationship to the world, shaping our sense of self. In Arvidsson's (2006) terms, the brand functions as a form a governmentality in that it enjoins us to develop our own mecosystem through which we participate as free subjects in the neoliberal enterprise. Indeed, we are subjects (i.e., active agents) under neoliberalism to the degree that we can brand ourselves in ways that enable us to accrue value and sell ourselves on the free market (the micro-celebrity and his or her constant efforts is a perfect example of this process). In this context, every social interaction (online or otherwise) is a potential opportunity to burnish one's brand.

If under neoliberalism, brands and identities are tied closely together, then the constantly shifting nature of the branding process leads to a constant sense of slippage and insecurity regarding our sense of who we are in the world. While brand managers can speak of empowering consumers through their brands, the reality is that it is a fleeting and superficial sense of empowerment that offers little in the way of a genuine connection to self, others, and the communities we inhabit. The branded identity that gave us a sense of security last year may not provide that same sense of security this year. As Rob Walker (2008) points out, such a relationship between branding and identity leads to terminal materialism as we engage in a constant, fruitless, and ultimately unsatisfying search for the next consumption high. Tying our identities to consumption practices pretty much guarantees we will be in constant search of an always elusive sense of security about who we are.

The same sense of insecurity about personal identity issues occurs in the workplace. In a post-Fordist organizational environment, the branding process goes beyond consumer products to include employees as well, who must constantly brand and rebrand themselves in a constantly changing, turbulent organizational environment. This notion of an enterprise self means that employees must constantly strive to be better, always have an edge over other employees, always be selling themselves. As a *Fortune* magazine article states, "Forget old notions of advancement and loyalty. In a more flexible, more chaotic world of work you're responsible for your career" (as cited in Holmer Nadesan & Trethewey, 2000, p. 228). Of course, such a sense of self is frequently unsustainable, leading to increased stress, a lack of work–life balance, and overall poorer life quality.

Of course, as educated people we would probably claim to be largely immune to the siren call of branding, but the reality is that we are all susceptible to it in some way. The important thing is that we are aware of the extent to which it shapes our lives and are thus able to be more reflective about our relationship to a world of images, symbols, and meanings mediated by corporate interests. As Walker (2008) states, "Considering yourself immune to advertising and branding is not a solution, it's part of the problem" (p. 68).

CRITICAL APPLICATIONS

1. What is your favorite brand? Perform an analysis of the brand identity it cultivates. Whom does the brand appeal to? What meanings do you associate with the brand? Why? What are the various communicative elements that make up the branding process? How does the brand appeal to elements of popular culture?

2. Conduct a brand analysis of your college or university. Examine its logos, slogans, online videos, and so on. What image does the branding process construct? How do you see yourself connecting (or not) to this branding process?

KEY TERMS

attention economy   262

brand   254

brand extension   261

brand public   271

branding from the outside in   272

brands as institution   266

communicative capitalism   266

consumer engagement   266

enterprise self   271

floating signifier effect   258

mecosystem   267

murketing   267

niche marketing   266

unique selling proposition   256

STUDENT STUDY SITE

Visit the student study site at **www.sagepub.com/mumbyorg** for these additional learning tools:

- Web quizzes
- eFlashcards
- SAGE journal articles

- Video resources
- Web resources

CHAPTER 11

Leadership Communication in the New Workplace

Digital Vision./Digital Vision/Thinkstock

What makes a good leader? It's more complex than you might think.

There's a long history of mythologizing "genius" company founders and powerful CEOs. People celebrate Mark Zuckerberg (Facebook), Elon Musk (Tesla), Steve Jobs (Apple), Bill Gates (Microsoft), Phil Knight (Nike), and Jeff Bezos (Amazon)—and in an earlier generation, Jack Welch (General Electric), Lee Iacocca (Chrysler), and Herb Kelleher (Southwest Airlines)—for their ability to lead their companies to incredible success. In the press, they're often presented as superheroes who wield magical powers over both employees and the culture. At the same time, however, people often loathe CEOs: Yahoo's CEO Marissa Mayer, for instance, made a list of "Most Hated CEOs" in 2017 (Kauflin, 2017) because after she arrived in 2012, she disallowed employee telecommuting to work (though she had worked from home at the end of her own pregnancy at the beginning of her tenure), built a separate room for her own child care needs next to the CEO suite, instituted a ranking system for employee performance, arrived late to meetings, and received a huge buyout ($186 million) when the company was sold—all despite failing to adapt Yahoo to the world of mobile computing (Vara, 2016).

Typically, we think of leadership as a trait of a special individual who, through the sheer force of his (and we usually think of strong leaders as male—it's telling that a key case of CEO failure is the only woman in the preceding paragraph) personality and charisma, is able to bring about his vision of the world. That leads us to link the success of organizations to specific individuals.

While these representations of leadership are appealing in their ability to simplify organizational performance, and for their ability to present leaders as colorful characters whose qualities can be distilled into some kind of formula (somehow just right for a best-selling business book), the reality of leadership as an everyday feature of organizational communication processes is quite different. So in this chapter, we will develop a more complex (and, we hope, more reality-based) conception of leadership—one that presents leadership not simply as a characteristic of gifted individuals but rather as a phenomenon that captures many of the issues we have addressed in earlier chapters—meaning, power, and communication.

First, let's look at some of the research that has emerged in leadership studies over the past several decades.

TRADITIONAL PERSPECTIVES ON LEADERSHIP

We suspect that for many of you, the concept of leadership plays quite a prominent role in your lives as college students. As you develop your credentials for the anticipated transition into a professional career, you probably hear regularly that you need to develop leadership experience and leadership skills. No doubt you have thought about how your résumé can be developed to reflect your leadership background, and we're sure you will hope that any letters of recommendation from your instructors will talk about how you have shown strong leadership initiative in your time in school. And universities cater to this desire to show leadership potential, both in majors and in extra-curricular activities. For instance, the University of Colorado Boulder (n.d.) has developed a minor in leadership studies, which claims that students will "learn new ways to think about leadership and discover your own leadership strengths. This includes learning skills such as leading project teams, managing conflict, speaking in public, and analyzing complex problems." While these skills are foundational to any communication degree, our point is that leadership is presented as not only essential to career success but also something that can be learned and then possessed by the learner (and in this case can be displayed by a line on the transcript).

What does it mean, however, to *possess* leadership skills or to *be* a good leader? Surprisingly, there is little consensus about the concept of leadership or the criteria for good leadership; indeed, there are almost as many definitions of leadership as there are scholars doing leadership research. Management scholar Andrew DuBrin (2016) estimated that there are about 35,000 definitions of leadership in the academic literature, which might make one wonder what's *not* considered leadership.

So how do we approach a phenomenon that is apparently so messy and ambiguous? From a critical communication perspective, we must start by recognizing that leadership is not simply an objective phenomenon, the facts of which need to be established so we know definitively how to be a good leader. Rather, we need to think of leadership as a socially constructed phenomenon, the study of which has its roots in particular social, political, and economic conditions. In this sense, leadership is a discourse that has been created by researchers, popular culture, the media, and industry, and that functions to frame the world for us in particular ways. As management scholar Simon Western (2008) claims, "Leadership is a growth industry and remains a 'sexy concept' and a buzz word in Business Schools, organizations, and social/political arenas. However, much of the mainstream literature is adapted and recycled theory; old news under a new headline" (p. 25). He argues that leadership ideas packaged into simple solutions are easier to sell in the "leadership industry."

From this critical perspective, we'd argue that leadership research is less about establishing a body of scientific evidence and more about perpetuating an industry that thrives on creating a culture where everyone is convinced that strong leadership skills are the answer to a lot of problems. Management scholar Keith Grint (2010, p. 1) gives an indication of the success of this industry when he points out that an October 2003 search for books on leadership on Amazon.com yielded 14,139 results; just over 6 years later, that number had risen to 53,121. When we did our own search in June 2018, the figure was over 80,000. Clearly, then, there is a sense that a lot of people have a vested interest in making sure that leadership is kept in the public eye!

One of the goals of this chapter, then, is to problematize the very idea of leadership as a coherent, clearly identifiable phenomenon (with essential features) and to explore it as complex, ambiguous, and uncertain (Alvesson & Spicer, 2011; Western, 2008). In this section, then, we will examine several different perspectives on leadership, looking at the historical context out of which these perspectives emerged. What does each of these perspectives tell us about the place of leadership in organization and society? In the following section, we will examine leadership as a communication phenomenon and aim to provide some useful guidelines about how you should approach questions of leadership in your own life.

First, let's provide a fairly generic, baseline definition of **leadership**. Almost 70 years ago, Ralph Stogdill (1950) defined leadership as "the process of influencing the activities of an organized group in its efforts toward goal setting and goal achievement" (p. 3). This definition contains three elements—influence, group, and goal—that are generally considered central to leadership. But this definition also raises the question of exactly how such influence occurs, why someone is considered influential, and if indeed, there is any measurable, causal connection between a leader and the behavior of followers (and as we will see later, the very idea of separating leaders and followers is problematic).

Below, we will examine three broad leadership perspectives that have developed over the past 100 years or so, each of which attempts to isolate the factors that explain leadership as a phenomenon. These three approaches are (1) the trait approach, (2) the style approach, and (3) the situational approach.

The Trait Approach

Leadership scholar Keith Grint (2010) argues that the modern study of leadership can be traced to Scottish philosopher and essayist Thomas Carlyle's (2001/1841) work *On Heroes,*

Hero Worship and the Heroic in History, which promoted the idea of the leader as a heroic figure who embodied the virtues of a society and stood head and shoulders above mere mortals. This idea was the "great man" approach to leadership. Although Carlyle was writing about historical figures, his work resonated with the emerging industrial society and its need for strong and larger-than-life leaders who embodied the values of entrepreneurial capitalism.

In its early decades, then, leadership research was dominated by an effort to establish the personal qualities, or traits, of these successful *captains of industry* (a term coined by Carlyle)—people such as J. P. Morgan, Andrew Carnegie, and John D. Rockefeller. From the perspective of the **trait approach**, leaders are born rather than made. Generally speaking, research focused on three main categories of personal characteristics: physical appearance, abilities (intelligence and fluency of speech), and personality (Bryman, 1996). For example, Grint (2010) uses the acronym THWaMP (tall, handsome, white alpha-males of privilege) to describe the archetypal leader in Western society. Certainly, there are exceptions to this rule, but the THWaMP is still very much a dominant figure in leadership roles. Grint (2010, p. 69) even cites research that correlates every extra inch of height with a 1 % increase in income (a finding that makes Dennis happy, given that he's 6 feet 5 inches tall! Tim, at 5'9", would like to object).

Other traits that research identified as important for successful leaders include intelligence (but there must not be too much of a gap between leaders and followers; otherwise the latter will feel inadequate and alienated from the leader), talkativeness (the gift of the gab is a skill many successful leaders possess), self-confidence, a willingness to take the initiative, and sociability/extroversion (not too many successful leaders are shy and retiring types). We suspect that most of us would recognize these traits as generally desirable and indicative of someone we might identify as a leader. And although paying attention to physical characteristics seems superficial, one has only to look at a list of CEOs of large corporations or heads of state to see that the nonwhite and/or female leader is still very much in the minority. In fact, as we mentioned in Chapter 8's discussion of gender at work, a 2018 *New York Times* investigation found that there are as many female CEOs among America's largest companies as there are male CEOs named John alone—a name that comprises 3.3 % of the population of U.S. males, compared with the 50.8 % of the population that are women (Miller, Quealy, & Sanger-Katz, 2018).

Trait research, however, proved to have too many limitations to provide an adequate explanation of successful leadership. Although it remained heavily influential until the early 1940s, Stogdill's (1948) review of that body of research and his outlining of its shortcomings largely signaled an end to programmatic research in that area. So what were its problems?

First, there was a huge amount of inconsistent and contradictory findings in trait studies; no consensus could be arrived at regarding the key traits of a successful leader. Second, the trait approach attempted to establish a universal set of leadership characteristics that were relevant regardless of the context in which they were applied. As we will see below, many researchers viewed the social and organizational context as a key issue in determining effective leadership. Third, trait research completely ignored the role of followers; in other words, leaders are leaders only when they have followers, and so understanding what works as effective leadership depends in good part on explaining the role of

Edward N. Jackson, *Popular Science Monthly* Volume 58, and William Ten Eyck Hardenbrook

19th-century captains of industry were the rock stars of their day—crowd surfing optional.

followers in the leadership process. Finally, from an ethical perspective, there's something rather unsavory about the idea that leaders are born rather than made. Such a perspective condemns people to the vagaries of their genes. Moreover, the fact that THWaMPs are identified as archetypal leaders is self-serving in its maintenance and reproduction of a system that privileges a white male view of the world.

Finally, it's worth noting that our old friend Frederick Taylor put something of a monkey wrench in the great man theory of leadership with his declaration that successful organizations were not dependent on heroic captains of industry but on decidedly unheroic managers trained to apply scientific principles to the work process. As we will see, as the idea of the rational, bureaucratic organization became the dominant institution in society, the careful, rational analysis of leadership as an acquired skill and set of behaviors took center stage.

The Style Approach

The **style approach** to leadership was the dominant mode of research from the late 1940s through the 1960s (Bryman, 1996). In this perspective, specific leadership behaviors became the focus of study, and emphasis shifted from selecting leaders who had "the right stuff" to training people in skills associated with good leadership. A number of theories emerged out of this approach, but we'll mention three very briefly.

First, in research at the University of Michigan, Kurt Lewin distinguished among three different styles of leadership—autocratic, laissez-faire, and democratic (Grint, 2010; Lewin & Lippett, 1938; Western, 2008). In a series of experiments with Boys' Clubs, Lewin discovered that laissez-faire (hands-off) leadership was ineffective, whether the leader was present in the task situation or not. On the other hand, with an autocratic (highly controlling) leadership style, followers would focus on tasks when the leader was present but slack off when he or she was not. Finally, Lewin argued that the democratic style was the most effective, as it promoted active involvement and group decision making and encouraged participation in tasks whether the leader was present or absent. However, while the democratic style promoted the most satisfaction, the autocratic style was most effective in terms of productivity.

This tension between satisfaction and productivity (a focus of research since the Hawthorne studies) was taken up in a couple of other style-based approaches. First, researchers at Ohio State University established two main components of leadership behavior: *consideration*, in which leaders demonstrate a concern for subordinates as people and are responsive to their needs, and *initiating structure*, in which leaders focus closely on the task, defining precisely what subordinates are required to do. Perhaps not surprisingly, research showed that leaders who emphasized consideration had subordinates with higher morale, while leaders who emphasized initiating structure had more productive subordinates. Further research came to the conclusion that leaders who demonstrated both kinds of leadership style tended to be the most effective.

This finding is elaborated in more detail by psychologists Robert Blake and Janet Mouton's (1964) well-known managerial grid. Blake and Mouton use the two dimensions of "concern for people" and "concern for production" (basically the same as the consideration and initiating structure styles) to create a grid that identifies five different leadership styles (see Figure 11.1). The five styles are (1) impoverished (low concern for both production and people), (2) country club (high concern for people, low concern for production), (3) authority compliance management—sometimes called produce or perish (low concern for people, high concern for production), (4) team leader (high concern for both production and people), and (5) middle-of-the-road (a compromise position that maintains the status quo by focusing on production without overlooking team morale). As Grint (2010) indicates, despite the lack of empirical evidence to support Blake and Mouton's model, their grid has enjoyed continued popularity, popping up in management and organizational communication textbooks (including this one!) to the present day.

Although the style approach to leadership is considered an advance on the trait approach, it still has important limitations. First, the emphasis is still very much on designated and formal leaders—a focus that ignores the fact that much organizational leadership occurs in an informal manner among employees who are not considered leaders in the formal sense. Second, once again the results of style research tended to be inconsistent. As with trait research, it proved incredibly difficult to demonstrate a consistent causal connection between specific leadership styles and increased performance by subordinates (Bryman, 1996). Finally, and perhaps most significant for leadership research, critics argued that it was difficult to establish universal leadership styles because this approach ignored the fact that effective leadership was often influenced by circumstances. These critiques led, in the 1970s, to the emergence of the situational approach to leadership.

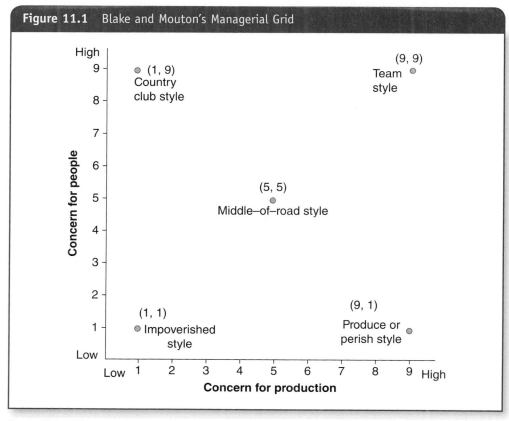

Figure 11.1 Blake and Mouton's Managerial Grid

Source: Blake and Mouton (1964).

The Situational Approach

The **situational approach**, or contingency approach, to leadership is an effort to move beyond a universal, one-size-fits-all perspective, answering the question "What makes a good leader?" with "It depends." In brief, the situational approach argues that contextual factors such as the structure of the task at hand, the power of the leader, and the size of the work group have a mediating effect on the leadership approach that different leaders adopt. Thus, no single leadership style or trait will be effective across different situations.

The most famous situational perspective is psychologist Fred Fiedler's (1967, 1997) contingency model of leadership. For Fiedler, a leader's effectiveness depends on two interacting factors: (1) the personality of the leader and (2) the extent to which the leadership situation provides the leader with influence and lack of uncertainty. Fiedler measures the personality of leaders along two dimensions: (1) leaders who are relationship oriented and strive to accomplish tasks through maintaining good relations with group members and (2) leaders who are task oriented and prefer tangible evidence of their competence (i.e., completion of tasks). The organizational situation is measured along three dimensions: (1) leader–member relations (the degree to which the leader feels supported by group members), (2) the structure of the task (how clear-cut or ambiguous it is), and (3) position power (the ability of the leader to reward or punish group members).

Fiedler (1967, 1997) determines leader personality through an instrument called least-preferred coworker (LPC), in which leaders are asked to think of the person they have been able to work with least well and to rate that person on numerous 8-point scales, such as friendly–unfriendly, gloomy–cheerful, backbiting–loyal, nasty–nice, and cooperative–uncooperative. Though these terms seem pretty biased, rating the LPC on these dimensions indicates whether a leader has a stronger orientation to tasks or relationships. Whether a task-focused or relationship-focused leader is more effective depends on how favorable the situation is to his or her personality. Fiedler argues that in uncertain situations, relationship-oriented leaders will first seek support from group members and then focus on the task once support is ensured. On the other hand, task-oriented leaders will deal with situational uncertainty by focusing primarily on the task and, once task accomplishment is ensured, will then focus on relational management with subordinates. Fiedler's research led him to conclude that task-oriented leaders are most effective in situations where they've got either high or low levels of control over the organizational situation and that relationship-oriented leaders do best in moderate-control situations.

Fiedler's (1967) model portrays leadership as a psychological process rather than a social process with his focus on leader personality types. Indeed, it served as the catalyst for a surge in psychological models of effective leadership. And to the extent it shifted attention beyond the leader's traits or style, it was an advance in our thinking. Yet there are numerous critiques of Fiedler's perspective (leading to its waning influence in the early 1980s), and three are worth mentioning briefly. First, his focus is exclusively on formal, designated leaders, so there is virtually no attention to informal, emergent leadership processes. Second, because his model focuses on leadership personality and since personality is notoriously hard to change, he appears to be suggesting that it is necessary to fit work situations to leaders rather than developing leaders who can adapt to various work situations. Third, there have been numerous critiques of the validity of contingency research due to inconsistent findings, including questions about the reliability of his LPC measure.

Summary

This section concludes the discussion of what, to be honest, we consider to be some of the more boring, tedious approaches to leadership—research that, despite decades of trying, has largely failed to demonstrate direct connections between specific kinds of leader behavior and employee performance (Perrow, 1986). By and large, this research operates with rather conservative, conventional notions about leaders, followers, and how communication operates. Leaders tend to be viewed as formally designated individuals who act in some official organizational capacity to influence subordinates in particular ways. For the most part, followers are missing from the analysis of leadership processes; while often surveyed regarding their preferred leader behaviors, they are generally not adequately accounted for in the leadership process itself. Moreover, when communication is examined, the model adopted is rudimentary, with communication conceived as the transmission of information between leaders and subordinates.

Finally, this research uncritically accepts the ideas of leader and leadership as objectively given features of organizational life that need to be empirically measured and explained (i.e., subject to prediction and control). These might have made sense when organizations looked like the hierarchical, bureaucratic forms of the mid-20th century but as we will see in the rest of this chapter, these very ideas have been increasingly questioned as organizations have evolved in post-Fordist directions.

Let's now turn to more recent leadership perspectives that reflect these changes.

NEW APPROACHES TO LEADERSHIP

Beginning in the early 1980s, **new leadership** (Bryman, 1996; Parry & Bryman, 2006) has been used as an umbrella term referring to a host of different orientations to leadership that emerged around some broad themes. These themes include the following, which encourage people to question the very idea of leadership as commonly understood:

- A view of leadership as symbolic action, where the leader is conceived as a manager of meaning.

- The emergence of transformational leadership and a neo-charismatic approach. This signals the return of the heroic great man, but in a different organizational context.

- A greater focus on followership, where the role of the follower in leadership processes is more thoroughly examined.

- A shift away from the formal aspects of leadership to a study of leadership as an everyday, informal process.

- A view of leadership as a socially constructed phenomenon rather than an objectively existing set of traits, behaviors, or personality types.

Let's examine some of these issues in more detail.

Leadership as Symbolic Action

The concept of **leadership as symbolic action** emerged largely at the same time as the corporate culture perspective we discussed in Chapter 5. This timing makes sense if you think about it, as the corporate culture approach—exemplified by Thomas Peters and Robert Waterman's (1982) *In Search of Excellence*—stressed the importance of strong, visionary leaders in implementing and maintaining the organization's strong culture and system of values. Historically speaking, this new approach to leadership emerged precisely when globalization was becoming an issue and the rise of Japan as an economic power was shaking U.S. companies out of their complacency regarding their preeminence in the global marketplace.

Given this context, many leadership researchers shifted from a narrow focus on controlled laboratory experiments and survey questionnaires that tried to establish key leadership behaviors and turned instead to developing a grander vision of leadership that portrayed leaders as shapers of symbolic realities. In some respects, we see a return of the heroic, visionary leader of the late 19th and early 20th centuries, but remodeled for a late-20th century economic and social reality.

Adopting this perspective, management scholars Linda Smircich and Gareth Morgan (1982) argue that

> leadership is realized in the process whereby one or more individuals succeed in attempting to frame and define the reality of others. . . . Leadership depends on the existence of individuals willing . . . to surrender, at least in part, the powers to shape and define their own reality. (p. 258)

It is thus the role of leaders to engage in sense making for others and to help develop a consensus among organization members around the resulting meanings (Pfeffer, 1981; Pondy, 1978; Smircich & Morgan, 1982). In this conception, leadership is socially constructed through interaction and emerges as a result of the sense making and actions of both the leaders and the led. A key feature of this approach, then, is that leadership is not a thing but rather a process that emerges and is reproduced in an ongoing manner through the daily sense-making activities of organization members.

For example, the IBM story we discussed in Chapter 5 involving a confrontation between Lucille Burger, a security guard, and CEO Tom Watson Jr. illustrates how leadership as the management of meaning can operate. The telling of this story to organization members does not command them to act in a particular way but instead operates as a sense-making device, constructing organizational reality around the issue of following rules at IBM. In this sense, the story can be used by leaders to shape organizational reality and in turn, influence the actions of members.

The conception of leadership as symbolic action thus fits well with the cultural, interpretive approach to the study of organizations: leaders engage in sense making on behalf of others and help create the reality they experience in the organization. From this perspective, "the key challenge for a leader is to manage meaning in such a way that individuals orient themselves to the achievement of desirable ends" (Smircich & Morgan, 1982, p. 262). Thus, managers and leaders not only play a central role in shaping the sense-making process but also in making sure the organizational reality that gets constructed serves the goals of the organization (or at least the powerful parties guiding the organization). Management scholar Edgar Schein (1992) puts this idea more bluntly when he claims that "the unique and essential function of leadership is the manipulation of culture" (p. 317).

For example, in Chapter 5 we saw how managers at Disneyland got into trouble because management lost control over the sense-making process of organization members and hence, the ability to shape the culture. While the official organizational reality utilized the drama metaphor, with its emphasis on show business and Disney as a profit-making company, the employees made sense of Disneyland through the alternative metaphor of family, which conflicted with the business approach. Thus, from a leadership as symbolic action perspective, managers at Disneyland failed in their efforts to define organizational reality for employees, with conflict and a strike being the result of their failure.

Transformational Leadership

Transformational leadership emerged in the 1980s as a response to the perceived need for visionary leaders in U.S. industry, partly because of increased economic threat from Japanese businesses (Bass, 1985; Bass & Riggio, 2006; Burns, 1978; Burns & Avolio, 2004). If vision and imagination were what American business needed, these scholars reasoned, management, as traditionally practiced, was the wrong place to look. As such, a number of scholars began to distinguish between a manager and a leader. According to Bryman (1996), the difference lies in the orientation of each to change. True leadership involves an "active promotion of values which provide shared meanings about the nature of the organization" (Bryman, 1996, p. 277). Management, on the other hand, concerns itself primarily with the here and now and is not concerned with broader issues of organizational purpose and identity, as leaders are. Gary Yukl (1989, p. 253) states this point in a slightly different way, arguing that leaders inspire, influence, and promote commitment in people, while managers simply direct subordinates' efforts and exercise authority over them. Leaders, then, create a vision of the future, and managers implement it.

James MacGregor Burns (1978), the originator of the notion of transformational leadership, distinguishes between two leadership approaches that reflect this distinction. First, *transactional* leadership involves exchanges between leaders and organization members in which the former sets goals and expectations and provides the latter with rewards (pay, recognition, etc.) when these goals are met—a model of leadership that reflects a managerial worldview. In the transactional model, "transactions [are] typically based on satisfying both the leader's self-interest and the self-interest of his or her followers" (Burns & Avolio, 2004). Transactional leadership thus entails a quid pro quo relationship between leader and follower; a psychological exchange occurs in that the leader clarifies the expectations and the follower delivers, receiving the appropriate reward.

On the other hand, *transformational* leadership involves binding the leader and members together in a higher moral purpose. The leader raises the aspirations of followers such that they think and act beyond their own self-interests. Followers are elevated from their everyday selves to their "better selves" (Yukl, 1989, p. 271). Transformational leaders are more concerned with the collective interests of the organization (or even society) rather than their own self-interests. As you can probably tell, there are a lot of what rhetorical theorist Kenneth Burke (1969) would have called "God Terms" operating here: who wouldn't want to be (or be seen as) a leader whose selfless vision inspired the best in her followers? Shouldn't everyone shun transactional leadership and become transformational? With such stark and value-laden distinctions, some clarification was needed.

Industrial psychologist Bernard Bass (1985, 1990) worked to do just that. In refining Burns's model of transformational leadership, Bass argued that this leadership style involves (1) charisma/inspiration, (2) individualized consideration, and (3) intellectual stimulation. First, a transformational leader is charismatic, commanding the attention of followers and inspiring them to carry out the vision of the leader. Second, the transformational leader must, through individualized consideration, get to know followers' needs, aspirations, abilities, and so forth, so they can be challenged to exceed themselves and take on leadership roles in their own right. Finally, a transformational leader must intellectually stimulate followers by challenging their basic assumptions and values; in this way, followers can be stimulated to think about work in novel ways. Bass thus views transformational leaders in terms of their effects on followers: If the leader is transformational, the follower becomes more aware of the importance of organizational goals, and he or she becomes more self-actualizing.

The transformational approach to leadership became dominant beginning in the mid-1980s and is still very influential today. Again, Peters and Waterman's (1982) study helped propel its popularity, as the excellent companies they profiled (Apple, Disney, IBM, etc.) generally had a transformational, visionary leader at their helms. Indeed, transformational leadership signals something of a return to the leader-as-hero approach, leading some researchers to label this perspective the neo-charismatic approach, given its focus on the larger-than-life leaders of corporations who inspire their followers to great deeds by articulating a higher moral purpose (e.g., Fairhurst, 2007). As such, it's worth noting that transformational leadership became popular during a time of crisis for U.S. corporations—consistent with Max Weber's (1978) view of charismatic authority as coming to the fore during crises in societies (see Chapter 3).

However, it should be noted that the charismatic leader and the transformational leader are not the same. Charisma is a necessary but not sufficient condition for transformational leadership to occur. While the charismatic leader can sometimes produce dependence among followers, the goal of transformational leadership is to give followers the skills to engage in their own forms of critical thinking and empowered behavior. Moreover, with charismatic leadership, the focus is on the individual leader as opposed to the leadership process itself; in transformational leadership, the idea is to share leadership among multiple leaders rather than keep the spotlight on a single leader.

Followership

Finally, under the broad umbrella of new leadership studies, there has been a significant and growing amount of research on what is called followership (Baker, 2007; Chaleff, Lipman-Blumen, & Riggio, 2008; Howell & Shamir, 2005; Kelley & Bacon, 2004; Manz & Sims, 2000; Meindl, 1995). This research takes seriously the idea that leaders do not exist without followers and that a dialectical relationship exists between the two; that is, leaders and followers mutually define one another.

This interest in followership arose in part because of the changed circumstances of U.S. businesses. In the post–World War II economic boom of the 1950s and 1960s and the global preeminence of U.S. businesses, the social contract prevailed and corporations promised employees lifelong employment in return for loyalty, obedience, and hard work. The stability of the economy left little need to empower workers by reframing the leader–follower relationship (Baker, 2007). However, the more unstable nature of the world economy over the past 30 years has generated an interest in exploring alternative leadership models.

In some ways, followership research is an effort to undermine the continued dominance of the leader both as a focus of leadership research and as a dominant construct in the media and popular culture. As we have already discussed, there is a common, widely accepted notion that organizations succeed or fail on the basis of high-profile leaders who impose their will and personality on the organization. For example, Jack Welch, former CEO of General Electric, typifies this kind of leader, and there is a veritable publishing industry devoted to packaging his leadership philosophy. A quick search turns up the following titles: *Jacked Up: The Inside Story of How Jack Welch Talked GE Into Becoming the World's Greatest Company* (Lane, 2008); *Jack Welch Speaks* (Welch, 2008); *Jack Welch and the 4Es of Leadership* (Krames, 2005); *29 Leadership Secrets from Jack Welch* (Slater, 2003); *Jack: Straight from the Gut* (Welch & Byrne, 2001); and *The Jack Welch Lexicon of Leadership* (Krames, 2002). The goal here is less to disseminate successful leadership skills to a broader public and more to create the image of Jack Welch as a corporate rock star whose very name on the cover of a book will guarantee sales. The image created in all this popular discourse is that Welch achieved his goals single-handedly and without the collaboration of thousands of employees!

Followership studies, on the other hand, take seriously the idea that "most of us are more often followers than leaders" (Kelley, 1988, p. 143). Management scholar Dennis Tourish and his colleagues have even suggested that business schools should stop marketing themselves as producers of transformational corporate leaders and focus instead on training enlightened followers who have a more critical orientation to business and leadership practices (Tourish, Russell, & Armenic, 2010). Such an approach would arguably provide better, more pragmatic, and more realistic training for students bound for the work world.

Of course, the problem with the idea of followership (at least in the individualistically oriented culture dominant in the United States) is that the term has quite negative connotations. For the most part, no one wants to be known as a follower, the implication being that one is a passive "yes person" who needs to be told what to do and never has an original or creative thought. Indeed, when was the last time you saw "strong followership skills" listed on someone's résumé?

What, then, are some of the elements of a followership approach? The initial stimulus for this perspective came from Robert Kelley's (1988) essay "In Praise of Followers" in the *Harvard Business Review*. Kelley developed a two-dimensional model that mapped out five different kinds of followership roles. The two dimensions are (1) independent critical thinking vs. dependent, uncritical thinking and (2) positive energy and active engagement vs. negative energy and passive engagement.

Kelley (1988) maps out five followership roles using these two dimensions (see Figure 11.2). First, "sheep" are both passive and uncritical, need to be told what to do, and avoid responsibility. Second, "yes people" or "conformists" are active and full of energy but are uncritical and need to be told what to do. Such people, Kelley argues, can be very deferential or even servile. Third, "alienated followers" have critical thinking skills but tend to be passive and have to be told what to do; they are often cynical and disgruntled and exhibit negative energy. Fourth, "pragmatic followers" or "survivors" cluster around the intersection of the two dimensions and adapt themselves to the prevailing conditions of the organization. They avoid taking strong positions and are constantly monitoring which way the wind is blowing in the organization. Kelley argues that they are the ultimate survivors, regardless of the level of organizational change. Fifth, and finally, "star" or "exemplary" followers are the ideal followers. These employees are highly committed to the organization; self-managing; willing to provide honest, independent, and constructive critique to leaders; and hold themselves to higher performance standards than others do, constantly working to upgrade their skills. Exemplary followers will also work proactively, looking to identify overlooked problems.

It's important to keep in mind that these five categories indicate followership roles and not personality types; thus, it is quite possible for the same person to exhibit different roles in different organizational contexts. An employee who takes on a star follower role in one context, for example, might become an alienated follower in another context if his or her boss or the tasks he or she performs do not make full use of his or her talents. Critical Case Study 11.1 provides a cute and funny example of how leadership is a social construction heavily shaped by other people's willingness to be followers.

Another interesting take on the concept of followership is provided by management researcher James Meindl and his colleagues in their development of a **romance leadership** perspective (Meindl, 1995; Meindl, Ehrlich, & Dukerich, 1985). In this approach, attention is placed squarely on followers, and in some ways, the actual activities of leaders are a secondary factor. Meindl is concerned primarily with how followers construct leaders (and

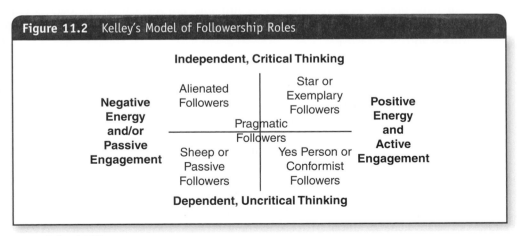

Figure 11.2 Kelley's Model of Followership Roles

Independent, Critical Thinking

Alienated Followers

Star or Exemplary Followers

Negative Energy and/or Passive Engagement

Pragmatic Followers

Positive Energy and Active Engagement

Sheep or Passive Followers

Yes Person or Conformist Followers

Dependent, Uncritical Thinking

Source: Kelley (1988).

not the other way around), arguing that leaders are romanticized so much that followers exaggerate their importance and influence. In this sense, Meindl focuses on the idea of leadership as a construct that helps organization members make sense of and comprehend the complexities of organizational life.

In Meindl's (1995) romance model, leadership is a product of the ways organization members interact with one another. While most of the leadership perspectives we have discussed attempt to provide empirical evidence for a causal connection between leader behaviors and follower attitudes and performances, Meindl argues that the relationship between leaders and followers is a constructed one; leadership emerges out of a form of social contagion in which the reputation of a particular person spreads amongst organization members, rather like an influenza virus. In this sense, the charisma of a leader is not necessarily an objective feature of his or her personality and behavior but rather exists in the sense-making processes of followers.

One important implication of Meindl's (1995) theory is that the behavior of followers is much less under the control of leaders than other perspectives suggest. Meindl indicates that while the media, business periodicals, and organization members romanticize the role and effectiveness of leaders, such effectiveness exists only as long as the network of relations around the leader constructs them as effective. Once the tide of public opinion turns against a leader, there's not much he or she can do about it.

A followership approach to leadership, then, has a couple of virtues in enabling us to think in different ways about leadership processes in the new workplace. First, as indicated earlier, it decenters the idea of the great, heroic leader and instead looks at leaders and leadership as a socially constructed process in which leaders and followers mutually constitute each other. As Brad Jackson and Ken Parry (2011) pithily state it, "Leaders keep on winning largely because their followers perceive them to be winners" (p. 52). Leaders can be effective only if followers construct them as such. Second, followership research decenters leadership in another way. If leaders are no longer positioned as the paragons of brilliance and "derring-do" (Google it!), then followers come to play a crucial role in organizational decision making. If followers played a role of "constructive dissent rather than destructive consent" (Grint, 2010, p. 29), then perhaps many of the corporate scandals that occurred over the past couple of decades (Enron, WorldCom, the bank mortgage crisis, the Wall Street bailout, the Wells Fargo scandal, and so forth ad nauseam) would have been less likely to occur.

CRITICAL CASE STUDY 11.1

Leadership Lessons From "Dancing Guy"

One of our favorite YouTube videos is about 2.5 minutes long. It doesn't involve cats or babies being cute but instead is a rather shaky video of a guy dancing enthusiastically in a field at a music concert.

(Continued)

(Continued)

Dancing on his own. Like a complete dork. The people around him are sitting around, chilled out, listening to the music, and completely ignoring him; they're probably embarrassed for him and his crazy gyrations. Then something weird and truly amazing happens. Suddenly another guy comes running up and starts dancing with him in a similarly dorky manner. Is he being ironic and making fun of him, or is he a fellow dorky dancer? It doesn't really matter. Within a few seconds several more people come rushing up and start dancing with Dancing Guy and his comrade. Now there's momentum. Pretty quickly, the people sitting around start to get up and get in on the act. Then, people are literally running over to join in the fun. In no time at all, anyone who's not up and dancing looks like a complete killjoy. A movement is born. You can watch the video at the link below. Make sure you have the sound turned up so you can hear the voice-over commentary: http://www.youtube.com/watch?v=fW8amMCVAJQ.

So what happened here? How did Dancing Guy go from an eccentric lone nut to the leader of a movement (however brief it might have been) in a few seconds? The video commentary talks about the importance of the first follower. That is, the first guy who comes and joins Dancing Guy creates the leadership context and hence, the possibility for more followers. In this sense, the video is a great example of the social construction of leadership in microcosm. There's no formal, designated leader and no followers—just a bunch of people sitting around with one eccentric guy following the beat of his own internal drummer (so to speak . . . since there was an actual drummer working in this case). There's not even a connection between "leader" and "followers," except the shared context of a music venue.

In essence, this event is about the management of meaning and a changing of the interpretive frame in operation. Once the first follower comes forward, then the frame is changed, and it's okay for others to become associated with Dancing Guy. As the video commentary suggests, it takes courage to associate yourself with the lone nut, but once that occurs, momentum develops and the "lone nut" becomes "cool Dancing Guy"—not because of anything he did but because of the shift in interpretive frame for the people around him. In this instance, leadership is indeed in the eye of the beholder. Dancing Guy doesn't attract followers by leading; he acts in a particular way and at a certain point gets defined as a leader engaged in behavior worth following. The rest is history.

Discussion Questions

1. Watch "Leadership Lessons From Dancing Guy" on YouTube. What's your reaction to what happens?

2. Think about your own ideas about leadership. Where do these ideas come from? What do you expect from a leader? Describe your experiences with both good and bad leaders. What differentiates them?

3. Think about your experiences as a follower. How would you categorize yourself in terms of Kelley's follower roles? What factors influenced your role behavior?

4. Compare this video with the following speech by Alec Baldwin's character in the 1990s film, Glengarry Glenross: https://www.youtube.com/watch?v=Q4PE2hSqVnk. What kind of leadership style does Baldwin's character reflect? How might you compare and contrast the leadership represented in the two videos from a communication perspective?

Gary Gemmill and Judith Oakley (1992) have gone so far as to argue that "the concepts of 'leader' and 'leadership' have become psychic prisons" (p. 114) and that much writing on leadership arises from a "deepening sense of social despair and massive learned helplessness" (p. 115). The return of neo-charisma and trait theories in transformational leadership has created the illusion that leaders are in control of events and allows followers to escape responsibility for their own actions. This acceptance of the leader myth and the resulting lack of responsibility "promotes alienation, deskilling, reification of organizational forms, and dysfunctional organizational structures" (p. 124). Gemmill and Oakley argue that rather than providing empirical support for the value of leadership, leadership research mainly offers ideological support for the existing social order. The followership perspective allows us to escape at least some of these problems by reskilling followers and reframing what leadership is. Let's address further this increasing skepticism about current leadership research by developing a critical communication perspective on leadership.

❀ A CRITICAL COMMUNICATION PERSPECTIVE ON LEADERSHIP

Most of the research we have discussed so far fits fairly comfortably into a managerial perspective on leadership. In other words, regardless of the theoretical approach—trait, style, contingency, new leadership, and so on—each perspective is interested in studying leadership as a phenomenon that can create more effective and efficient organizations and hence improve the organizational bottom line. But rather than ask the question "What is leadership, and how can we improve its outcomes?" what if we asked a different question? Following Mats Alvesson and Stanley Deetz's (2000) critical approach, we will address the question "What can we see, think, or talk about if we examine leadership from a communication perspective?" In other words, what if we abandoned the idea of leadership as a thing possessed by certain people and instead explored it as a dynamic communication process?

Let's briefly indicate the implications of this critical communication perspective on leadership and then explore them in more detail:

1. A communication approach rejects the traditional separation of leader and follower (Collinson, 2005). Both leader-centric and follower-centric approaches are rejected in favor of a view of leadership as coproduced among organization members.

2. A communication perspective is a post-heroic view of leadership that decenters the dominant and romanticized model of the "great man" as leader; instead, leadership is distributed throughout the organization. Understanding leadership doesn't require that we equate it with a single person in an organization.

3. From a communication perspective there is no essence of leadership to discover (as in traditional approaches); rather, leadership is seen as a socially constructed process in which people interdependently create what leadership means in specific organizational contexts (Fairhurst, 2007; Fairhurst & Connaughton, 2014; Fairhurst & Grant, 2010).

4. Communication is the way leadership is socially constructed; examination of various communication processes (talk, texts, stories, metaphors, etc.) enables us to see this construction process at work.

5. A critical communication perspective on leadership focuses on issues of power and control characterizing those social constructions. And because the exercise of power and control always implies the possibility of resistance (see Chapter 7), a critical communication stance encourages us to see that leadership can be a form of resistance (Collinson, 2011; Zoller & Fairhurst, 2007).

Given traditional research and popular conceptions of leadership, it's hard to give up (and hard not to write about!) the idea of leadership as a thing and leaders as specific people who exercise authority over others. However, we will discuss leadership not as something that is inevitable but rather as an ongoing process communicatively constructed by organization members (Fairhurst & Connaughton, 2014; Fairhurst & Grant, 2010). In this sense, we will adopt what management scholars Mats Alvesson and André Spicer (2011) refer to as an "ambiguity-centered" approach to leadership—one that focuses on leadership as a complex process that can be used in different ways by different people. In this way, we will challenge the idea that conventional ideas of leadership are inherently good and necessary for all organizations.

We will investigate three different areas within a critical communication approach to leadership: (1) leadership and disciplinary power, (2) resistance leadership, (3) and narrative and leadership.

Leadership and Disciplinary Power

In this book, we've spent a lot of time talking about organizational control processes, and for the most part, that has been framed in terms of managers and managerial systems of thought exercising various kinds of control over employees. The reality, however, is that managers and corporate leaders are subject to various forms of control as well. As we saw in Chapter 6, and as we will discuss in more detail in Chapter 14, one of the features of the new, postbureaucratic workplace is that white-collar and no-collar workers are increasingly subject to forms of control that focus on their identities as organization members—for example, the entrepreneurial self, in which employees see themselves as projects that need to be branded and sold like any other commodity. In a similar way, leaders and corporate executives are subject to forms of power in which they are constantly appraised and assessed in terms of their ability to lead employees and produce change. As organizational communication scholar Gail Fairhurst (2007) points out, in today's corporations, true leaders now have to be change masters.

When critically examining the relationship between leadership and disciplinary power, then, we need to think about the ways leaders and corporate executives are socially constructed by broader societal discourses. As we have already seen in this chapter, managerial discourse and research on leadership has constructed the leader differently in different historical and economic contexts, responding to the particular needs of organizations. The social construction of leadership has shifted from the "great man" to the rational planner to the symbolic manipulator and so forth. Today, as organizations exist in increasingly turbulent economic environments, executives are constructed as valuable intellectual capital, managing strategic change in the most difficult of circumstances; on the other hand, employees are often constructed as expendable through downsizing and cost saving (Fairhurst, 2007).

Because of their value to the company, these executives are subject to constant forms of appraisal and evaluation. In this sense, they are continuous objects of knowledge, through both formal tools for evaluation and their own self-scrutiny. Fairhurst (2007) has shown how three widely used technologies—performance appraisal, 360-degree feedback, and executive coaching—render the manager and executive constantly visible and subject to evaluation, thus inducing a constant sense of insecurity about their performances.

We see these technologies in our own leadership experiences. A few years ago, Dennis was selected to be a Leadership Fellow at UNC's Institute for the Arts and Humanities. As part of the fellowship, he attended a weeklong residential program at the Center for Creative Leadership in Greensboro, North Carolina. In preparation for that experience, he had to go through a battery of evaluations, including the FIRO-B, which measures interpersonal style; the MBTI (Meyers-Briggs Type Indicator), which measures personality and decision-making style; and 360-degree feedback, which provides evaluations of leadership effectiveness from subordinates, peers, and supervisors and also includes a self-assessment element. Thus, he was able to compare his self-assessment with others'.

In some ways, the 360-degree feedback evaluation is quite similar to Michel Foucault's notion of the Panopticon (discussed in Chapter 1). It's a tool that renders you visible to yourself, as seen through other people's eyes. It makes you incredibly self-conscious; you become an object of knowledge, both to yourself and to others. Obviously, such evaluations are not intrinsically bad and in fact, can be quite useful in identifying issues that one was not aware even existed. However, they are part of an increasing tendency to leave no stone unturned in constructing bodies of knowledge about organizational employees (Holmer Nadesan, 1997). And not coincidentally, a vast and very profitable industry has grown up around such evaluation processes, as companies seek a competitive edge.

If you haven't experienced any of these evaluation tools yet, you are likely to experience them at various points in your professional life. The results of such tests may well lead employers to draw conclusions about whether you have leadership potential or not. If we are to understand their disciplinary power, we should know that when these evaluations construct us as objects of knowledge, that knowledge is partial—there are several capacities that are ignored in the assessment. So we might want to examine the assumptions about leadership guiding the content of these evaluations and consider how these tools are used in shaping organizational practices and the people who carry them out.

Resistance Leadership

There is, however, another way to think about the relationship between leadership and disciplinary power. For the most part, critical scholars have tended to treat leadership as part of the system of domination, due largely to the fact that leadership research comes mostly from a managerial perspective that accepts the existing systems of power and authority in organizations. However, organizational communication scholars Heather Zoller and Gail Fairhurst have challenged this conception and made the case for what they call **resistance leadership** (Fairhurst & Zoller, 2008; Zoller & Fairhurst, 2007). They argue that leadership is not simply about managing dissent and getting people to coordinate their behavior; rather, dissent itself can be viewed as a form of organizational leadership.

Zoller and Fairhurst (2007) thus disconnect leadership from management and frame the former as a political act that contributes to the well-being of a community. They argue that "leadership is not about the person in charge but about the way one or more actors engages the community and its mores in collective action" (Zoller & Fairhurst, 2007, p. 1339). In this sense, leadership challenges both conventional assumptions and an organization's existing power relations. For example, from a traditional managerial perspective, an organizational whistle-blower (someone who, in the public interest, reveals information about organizational misdeeds) is a disloyal employee who needs to be managed and even disciplined or fired (there is a long history of whistle-blowers being treated extremely harshly by organizations, even in cases where they expose practices that hurt the organization as well as members of the public). From a resistance leadership perspective, however, a whistle-blower is reframed as someone who challenges existing power relations and engages organization members in thinking about and perhaps changing the way things are done. In this sense, a whistle-blower leads an organization to new practices.

For example, in the 1999 movie *The Insider*, Russell Crowe plays Jeffrey Wigand, a vice president for research and development at Brown and Williamson tobacco company who, at great personal risk, reveals documents showing how tobacco companies deliberately manipulate the ingredients in cigarettes to increase the amount of nicotine that smokers receive. In essence, Wigand's testimony revealed that the seven CEOs of Big Tobacco had perjured themselves before a congressional hearing in 1994 when each of them stated for the record that nicotine is nonaddictive. Wigand's act of whistle-blowing opened the door for massive lawsuits that resulted in a multibillion-dollar settlement by tobacco companies. Wigand's actions were a form of resistance leadership.

The idea of resistant leadership, then, gets at the way everyday organization members can challenge taken for granted realities and through communication and action, create possibilities for change. Leadership becomes a political act because dissenters engage with other organization members in a dynamic manner and potentially produce a new reality (Kassing, 2011).

Narrative Leadership

Earlier in this chapter we discussed the idea of leaders as managers of meaning, in which much of the art of leadership involves the ability to frame reality for organization members. In Chapter 5, we discussed the role of stories in creating organizational culture, and in recent years researchers have discussed how stories can be an important framing mechanism for organizational leaders to use with followers (e.g., Fairhurst & Sarr, 1996). Stories are useful because they make abstract ideas more concrete and can also provide organization members with guiding principles and morals regarding appropriate and inappropriate organizational behavior (e.g., Martin, Feldman, Hatch, & Sitkin, 1983). As we saw in Chapter 5, the famous IBM story about the security guard Lucille Burger confronting CEO Thomas Watson Jr. provides IBM employees with a lesson about the importance of following organizational rules and policies.

From a leadership perspective, the IBM story is a great example of a follower-based, or distributed, model of leadership in operation—what might be called **narrative leadership**. That is, although Lucille Burger is a low-level employee, she still demonstrates leadership in working to preserve the integrity of IBM rules about security, regardless of who is trying to circumvent the system. The fact that the story became part of IBM lore attests to its effectiveness in serving as a frame for employee sense making.

Another example of an organizational story that performs a similar framing function comes from FedEx:

> The FedEx courier did not intend to go swimming during the work day, especially with the harsh winds and rain covering much of Honolulu, Hawaii. However, when a gust of wind plucked a package from the back of his truck and flung it into the ocean, James did not think twice about diving in. James recovered the package and, soaking wet, delivered it to the customer. (Parry & Hansen, 2007, p. 281)

Again, this story depicts the leadership qualities of a regular employee as he takes ownership of a problem and deals with it himself. Stories such as these are common in organizational life: When Tim was studying a large U.S. airline in the 2000s, employees told tales about employees "going above and beyond" the call of duty to satisfy customers, including pilots sprinting from the airplane to the baggage claim area with carry-ons forgotten on a plane, flight attendants sitting with unaccompanied children when the plane hit patches of turbulence, and flight crews ordering pizza for all the passengers stuck on the tarmac during a weather delay. None of these activities, of course, appear in employee manuals, and when they become stories about the value of customer service circulating throughout the organization, they provide evidence of distributed leadership.

CRITICAL RESEARCH 11.1

Flemming Holm & Gail T. Fairhurst (2018). Configuring shared and hierarchical leadership through authoring. *Human Relations*, 71, 692–721.

Taking a communication perspective means that we see leadership no longer as a characteristic of a person, but as decentered and distributed. The differences between notions like teamwork or collaboration, on the one hand, and leadership on the other, can become blurry. Interested in this blurriness, management consultant Flemming Holm and communication scholar Gail Fairhurst set out to examine the tensions between traditional hierarchical leadership (where individuals' power is a

(Continued)

(Continued)

result of their rank in an organizational structure) and shared leadership (where power is an interactive process among team members). Most leadership scholars acknowledge that hierarchical and shared leadership are likely to occur together in organizations, and Holm and Fairhurst argue that authority is the notion that links them. Authority, here, is the perceived legitimacy to influence and decide on organizational matters, and this authority is tied not necessarily to organizational position but to a person's ability to be seen as an authentic translator of the organization's purposes. The authors suggest that we should pay close attention to the ways that authority is produced in communication because it is in communication that authority—and thus leadership—is claimed, granted, and resisted.

Holm and Fairhurst studied a city government in Denmark where several departments merged to create what the city called the "Organizational Advancement" (OA) department. Michael, previously the head of one of the merged departments, was appointed to lead the new 80-person unit; committed to shared leadership, he structured OA into six sub-teams. Structurally, the team leaders were considered hierarchically equal and composed a leadership team headed by Michael. Holm and Fairhurst studied the interactions of this seven-person leadership team in detail, recording four dozen meetings over roughly six months.

Efforts to "author" (i.e., to legitimately influence and decide) the OA leadership team's direction came through claims that used hierarchical position, expertise, and moves that advanced the task at hand. As might be expected, Michael tended to be the one to use hierarchical position, but many of the remaining team members used the other two types of claims in their authoring, including resistance to Michael's bids to use his hierarchical authority (e.g., through subversive humor in team meetings). Holm and Fairhurst saw this as evidence of shared leadership existing alongside hierarchical leadership, both within and across meetings. The authors also followed four topics that cut across many of the 48 meetings they observed and found that Michael used his position to bookend discussions on these topics, opening and closing meetings with a statement about the issue at hand but letting the group conversation go where it might in the middle. Michael saw this as evidence that he was a leader "who would much rather delegate and spur others to find shared solutions" (p. 714). What was particularly interesting about this technique is that the other group members saw his leadership very differently. They generally saw Michael's bookending as evidence that he was not assertive enough. In the words of one member, "Michael has to step a bit more into character.... Sometimes he puts himself too much on line with us and says, he has his opinions and such things, but sometimes he has to be more clear on his expectations regarding that we make some decisions" (pp. 713–714).

The result was that OA's restructuring of the workplace, a deliberate effort to enhance productivity through shared leadership, produced the opposite effect: "a sustained period of seemingly endless team meetings with Michael deliberately 'sitting on his hands'" (p. 714). The other team members were frustrated at a perceived lack of progress, and this seemed to be the result of doing neither hierarchical nor shared leadership to the members' satisfaction.

Discussion Questions

1. Have you ever been a member of a group that had "seemingly endless team meetings" that produced little outcome? (If you haven't yet, you're fortunate—you will at some point!) How might the mismanagement of the tension between hierarchical and shared leadership described by Holm and Fairhurst explain your experience? What would you add to the account here?

2. Holm and Fairhurst note that control-oriented hierarchical leaders can be accused of creating "discursive closure" (mentioned in Chapter 2), which is when people in positions of power find ways to suppress dissent and avoid genuine conversation. How might hierarchical leaders (people in positions of formal authority) promote the free and open exchange of ideas without being accused of being too heavy-handed?

3. If Michael asked you for advice about how to more successfully address the tension between hierarchical and shared leadership, what would you tell him? What resources does this chapter provide for such a conversation?

Management scholars Alan Parry and Hans Hansen (2007) argue that organizational stories are more than simply a tool that leaders can use to frame organizational reality; instead, stories themselves play a leadership role. In this sense, Parry and Hansen provide the ultimate example of a communicative model of leadership, in which leadership is no longer located in people at all but in the communication processes that constitute the organization. Of course, they do not mean that stories literally become leaders but, rather, that stories "exhibit the functions of leadership" (p. 287). Basically, Parry and Hansen argue that organizational stories get told and then are "set free to spread among the organizational community" (p. 292). As such, their position is much like the social contagion model of romance leadership discussed previously. If stories are powerful and charismatic, then they will be told and retold; in other words, they possess "followability." Thus, "leaders may come and go, but an enduring corporate story can last the life of the company, and just as everyone enacts their interpretation of a leader's vision, they enact the vision a story provides" (p. 290).

Consistent with the ambiguity-centered conception of leadership discussed earlier, this idea of stories as leaders encapsulates the ways organizational meanings and realities are often up for grabs. That is, there is never a single interpretation of a story (or indeed any organizational symbol or artifact), and thus the way a story performs a leadership function might vary, depending on how organization members make sense of it. Furthermore, it's quite possible that organization members will create counter-narratives—everyday organizational stories that resist the dominant corporate vision communicatively constructed in the officially sanctioned corporate narrative. For example, in Ruth Smith and

Eric Eisenberg's (1987) study of an industrial dispute at Disneyland, discussed in Chapter 5, the employees were able to generate a counter-narrative through the metaphor of family that challenged the official corporate vision of Disney as a business enterprise built on the enactment of a drama. We can therefore say that organization members are imaginative consumers of leaders' visions for an organization (Linstead & Grafton-Small, 1992).

CRITICAL CASE STUDY 11.2

Re-Imagining Leadership: Diversity Training at Starbucks

On April 12, 2018, two African American men were waiting in a Philadelphia Starbucks for a business associate (or maybe a friend; the reporting isn't clear) to arrive. One of the men asked to use the restroom, but the manager on duty declined because the men had not purchased anything while waiting. The store manager called 911, stating that the men refused to leave and were thus trespassing. Moments later, approximately eight police officers arrived and arrested the men, an arrest that quickly went viral on social media because few could imagine that white guests, whether purchasing coffee or not, would be treated with as much suspicion and disrespect by either the Starbucks manager or the police.

In the wake of the social media firestorm, Starbucks CEO Kevin Johnson, in a press release, issued an apology to the men and called the event "reprehensible," saying, "We have immediately begun a thorough investigation of our practices. In addition to our own review, we will work with outside experts and community leaders to understand and adopt best practices" (Johnson, 2018). At the beginning, then, this looked like yet another example of a corporation seeking to reduce the harm caused by an embarrassing event through the typical PR channels. But Johnson, along with Executive Chairman (and former CEO) Howard Schultz, did something surprising: They decided to close all 8,200 U.S. Starbucks locations for a 4-hour anti-bias training session in which all employees (they're called "partners" at Starbucks) were required to participate.

Critics lined up quickly. They asserted that the notion that an afternoon training session would erase many lifetimes' worth of bias was delusional at best. (Schultz contended that the training that occurred a month and a half later was to be only a first step in the company's long-term commitment to diversity. And Starbucks did change its policy to no longer require a purchase to use the shop's restroom.) But because Starbucks has used other public events to build its brand identity, it would be reasonable to see this reaction as a way to strengthen its brand. For example, in the wake of the civil unrest in Ferguson, MO, in 2014, Starbucks began a "race together" campaign, in which Starbucks employees were told to write #racetogether on coffee cups and initiate conversations with customers about race. For obvious reasons, this campaign was widely criticized and it was quickly withdrawn. Kelefa Sanneh, a reporter for *The New Yorker*, pursued this line of inquiry in an interview with Howard Schultz that aired on the public radio program, *This American Life* (which was conducted just before the training occurred). Schultz vehemently denied branding as the purpose of the training: "This is the antithesis of a marketing event. . . . it has nothing to do with trying to sell anything. Marketing is about creating awareness and selling your product. This is not—we're not trying to sell anything" (Glass, 2018).

Thinking differently about leadership in this case would start by framing the training as not merely about the Starbucks brand, its internal operations, or the leadership tactics of its executives. Instead of viewing this through the lens of its impact on the organization's culture or profitability, what if we see it as cultivating leadership of a different sort than is normally seen in the corporate world? Let's take Schultz at his word, from that same interview: "What kind of country do we want to live in? And what can we do as a company, what can we do as citizens, to enhance the lives of all Americans? And I think it's a courageous step on our part to talk about a difficult subject" (Glass, 2018).

In other words, whatever else the training is (e.g., a PR stunt), might it also be a set of resources to challenge dominant narratives about race in and around organizations in American life? If leadership is a dynamic communication process (as mentioned above), what in that process would provide evidence of the impact of those narratives?

Discussion Questions

1. After the interview with Schultz on the radio program mentioned above, the reporter attends one of the Starbucks training sessions on implicit bias. Listen to this segment (https://www.thisamericanlife.org/648/transcript; it ends at 27 minutes through the program), and then discuss your reactions with classmates. What was accomplished in the training? What impediments to confronting implicit bias were present? Is there hope that the Starbucks partners heard in this segment will change themselves or others?

2. Just a few days after the training session occurred, Howard Schultz resigned from Starbucks, and it was widely reported that he was considering a run for U.S. president. Does that information change your assessment of the case? Why or why not?

3. Above, we presented an ambiguity-centered approach to leadership, which suggests that the meanings of stories (and all other symbols) are up for grabs. What are the sources of influence over the meanings of the training? Imagine if Starbucks partners used the lessons of the training to reinforce (rather than challenge and change) implicit biases in themselves and others—would we still consider this leadership?

4. The Starbucks implicit bias training occurred in late May 2018. From your perspective at this point in time, can we say that it had any effect? Has it led to more talk about a difficult subject in the broader culture?

♣ CONCLUSION

In this chapter, we have addressed a number of perspectives on leadership, showing how research has evolved over the course of several decades (Table 11.1 provides a handy summary of the various approaches). Leadership research has tended to develop in ways that reflect the changing economic, political, and cultural climate in which organizations and corporations find themselves. In broad terms, theories have evolved from strongly leader-centric perspectives, in which the idea of the heroic leader is front and center; through follower-centric approaches, which recognize that leaders don't exist without followers; and finally to a dynamic, dialectical approach, which focuses on the social construction of leaders and followers, with the heroic leader completely decentered.

And this is perhaps one of the most important lessons to take away from this chapter: While many leadership approaches attempt to demonstrate a direct, causal relationship between leader behavior and follower attitudes, performance, and commitment, the reality is much more complex and ambiguous. Moreover, one can argue that many of the problems in corporations today can be traced to alpha-male leaders who truly believe they can control every aspect of organizational life around them. The kind of leaders depicted in anthropologist Karen Ho's (2009) ethnography of Wall Street are recruited from elite institutions and are told from Day 1 that they are special, the best and the brightest. Such socialization does not make for humility and fosters an absolute belief in one's decision-making ability.

Consistent with the critical communication perspective adopted in this chapter, perhaps the optimal approach to leadership is to recognize that one can manage meaning and empower people to a certain degree but that, ultimately, as meaning-making creatures, humans will always create a version of reality that fits with their own individual and collective experience. Given this situation, let's end the chapter with a critical-communication–oriented definition of leadership (drawing on several leadership scholars) that we hope provides some food for thought:

> Leadership is a coordinated social process through which people communicatively construct and experiment with new possibilities for thought and action. Such possibilities are recognized by the group or organization as moving beyond self-interest and meeting a collective, higher good. Within this communication process, individuals may be constructed as leaders who help guide and facilitate decision-making and action.

The question this definition raises is this: what kind of leader will you be? Do you have what it takes to be not only a good leader (in the broadest, ambiguity-oriented sense) but an enlightened follower too? In the course of your professional career you are likely to have several leadership opportunities and be confronted with many difficult decisions and scenarios. Do you have the courage of "Dancing Guy," as well as that of his comrade, the first follower?

Table 11.1 Comparing Leadership Perspectives

Approach	Trait	Style	Situational	Symbolic Action	Transformational	Followership	Resistance	Narrative
View of leadership	Innate property of "great men"; leader as charismatic	Set of skills that can be learned; focus on formal leaders	Determined by work context, situational factors; psychological model	Ability to frame reality for followers; leader as visionary; leadership as process	Ability to articulate higher moral purpose for followers; return of charisma	"Decenter" leader; leaders socially constructed by followers	Leadership as political act; resistance and dissent as leadership	Contained in the stories that organization members tell; distributed among many employees
View of communication	Means to impart wisdom to followers; use of persuasion through oratory	Provides direction; helps create supportive work context	Shaped by task and leader personality; use to provide direction and support	Process through which meaning and reality are created and framed	Frames reality and creates organizational vision	Process through which followers construct leaders	Use of communication to challenge taken for granted organizational realities	Narrates and constructs organizational values and reality
Leader–follower relations	Leader has hero status for followers	Balances concern for followers with productivity	Shaped by nature of task and personality of leader	Co-construct corporate reality, with leader framing employee sense making	Leader empowers followers to be leaders themselves; creates multiple leaders	Followers create leader success; followers play role of "constructive dissent"	Resistance leader engages his/her community in collective action	Leadership not in people but in the stories people tell
View of organization	Product of vision of "great man"	Sites of task accomplishment and work relations	Sites of task accomplishment and work relations	Cultural system of beliefs and values	System of beliefs and values where higher moral purpose is realized	Socially constructed through leader–follower relations	A moral community where freedom must be realized	Organization created and exists in stories members tell

CRITICAL APPLICATIONS

1. Interview someone in a position of leadership. Ask that person about his or her leadership philosophy and how he or she came to develop this particular perspective. Can you identify this philosophy in any of the leadership theories we have discussed in this chapter?

2. Think about your own experiences in positions of leadership. What are/were the particular challenges you faced? What is/was most rewarding and most frustrating about the experience? In what ways has this chapter helped you put these experiences in context?

3. Find a leadership consulting company on the Internet and read the description of the services it offers. With others in class, discuss the following questions: What does this firm seem to do? What does it promise? What expertise do the consultants claim to possess? What are the assumptions about leadership, and about communication, are they using—and what would happen if they took the sort of critical stance you've read throughout this book?

4. Skim a bestselling leadership book (you can find a good list at Amazon.com by searching for bestselling leadership books or the *New York Times'* list: https://www.nytimes.com/books/best-sellers/business-books/. What explicit lessons do you see? More importantly, what are the implicit lessons you're supposed to get?

KEY TERMS

critical communication perspective on leadership   295

followership   290

leadership   281

narrative leadership   299

new leadership   287

resistance leadership   298

romance leadership   292

situational approach   286

style approach   284

symbolic action   288

trait approach   282

transformational leadership   289

STUDENT STUDY SITE

Visit the student study site at www.sagepub.com/mumby.org for these additional learning tools:

- Web quizzes
- eFlashcards
- SAGE journal articles
- Video resources
- Web resources

CHAPTER 12

Information and Communication Technologies in/at Work

New information and communication technologies are not only transforming workplaces, but also how we experience our social world.

Modern technology has become a total phenomenon for civilization, the defining force of a new social order in which efficiency is no longer an option but a necessity imposed on all human activity.

—*Jacques Ellul*

Science and technology revolutionize our lives, but memory, tradition and myth frame our response.

—*Arthur M. Schlesinger*

Today's college students—perhaps you—are often told that they need to prepare themselves for the jobs of the future, including jobs that don't yet exist. When people think about those future jobs, technology is often a central player: The future means that digital communication tools, artificial intelligence, big data, algorithms, and even robots will radically change the face of work. Projections about technology's effects frequently conjure up fear: From self-driving cars replacing truck drivers, to computers making radiologists irrelevant, to algorithms making retail buyers obsolete, to artificial intelligence writing magazine articles, people worry about the rise of the machines.

Radical technological changes certainly caught Dan Lyons by surprise. In his book *Disrupted: My Misadventure in the Start-Up Bubble*, Lyons (2016) recounts his experience working in marketing at HubSpot (www.hubspot.com), a Boston-based startup that sold inbound marketing software to small businesses, allowing those businesses to attract and manage customers through blogs, websites, and online videos. His path to HubSpot was atypical: After working as a journalist for decades, the 52-year old Lyons was laid off by *Newsweek* and found a job posting for this position on the LinkedIn social networking site. The shift from old media to a software startup was rough for Lyons, and he narrates his discomfort with things the other HubSpot workers seemed to accept without question, such as the ambiguity of job responsibilities and reporting relationships, the proliferation of silly acronyms, the Nerf gun fights, the illogical performance reviews, the widespread belief that they're making the world a better place, and that they have an actual teddy bear seated in meetings to represent the customers they're serving.

Perhaps, Lyons (2016) speculates, HubSpot employees accept things he found absurd because the company seemed a relatively good bet: At the time of writing, it had just raised $100 million in venture capital funding, and people in the industry spoke highly of its long-term prospects; employees hoped that their ownership of a small piece of the company (which is given to them as compensation, since salaries are low) would bring hefty returns down the road. Or perhaps they accepted practices he saw as ridiculous because they were young and inexperienced (he was by far the oldest person working there) and lack comparisons. Or perhaps these practices are the norm in high-technology fields, and it is the old-timer whose expectations are out of place.

Lyons (2016) tells a fascinating and humorous tale (he had been a writer for the HBO program *Silicon Valley*) about his efforts to come to grips with a work world that he finds unrecognizable and illogical. But it also should lead us to pause and question the assumptions about technology operating here. In Lyons's account, technology drives organizations and their communication practices: Technology was responsible for a media environment in which *Newsweek* could no longer employ him, and HubSpot's marketing technologies were directly responsible for the culture that Lyons found so ridiculous. Technology didn't force HubSpotters to place a teddy bear in meetings or have Nerf gun battles, but he understood the technologies they sold and the technologies they used as driving the workplace practices he couldn't stomach (he ended up leaving, unceremoniously fired, after only 7 months).

Viewing technology as the driver of organizations and their practices carries with it a troubling assumption about what technology is and how it works. It portrays technologies like HubSpot's inbound marketing software as not only separate from the people using them but also as having power over them. This view of technology is a common one that portrays tools as imposing themselves on us, as if we have little choice in the matter. There are times when a view like this makes sense, like in Chapter 1's description of software algorithms that schedule workers to meet staffing needs in real time but which take a toll on low-wage workers' salaries and personal lives. Similarly, you've probably heard older people (like professors!) rail against smartphones that seem to be so addictive to "kids these days," rendering them unable to engage in face-to-face (FtF) communication (a friend of Tim's is a manager at one of the world's largest technology companies, a maker of products you probably use every day; this friend has outlawed laptops, tablets, and smartphones at team meetings because, he says, employees both young and old can't seem to resist the distractions offered by their screens). This vision of technologies wielding power over us can indeed be a useful stance because it allows us to think about how specific characteristics of technologies generate particular organizational outcomes, how persons and organizations will need to adapt to technological changes, and how the designs of these devices can be so alluring (see the quote by Ellul at the very beginning of the chapter).

We said that seeing technologies as imposing themselves on people was a troubling assumption—but what's wrong with it? As we'll discuss in this chapter, thinking of technology in this way makes it seem like our choices have little impact on organizational practices, compared with the influence of technologies. And it also makes it seem as if a few large companies—think Apple, Facebook, Google, and the like—are all-powerful. But as decades of research have shown, the impacts of technologies on the workplace depend on a host of factors, and communication practices are at the top of the list. And, in keeping with the critical stance in this book, it's important to ask about what (and whose) interests are served in those communication practices—in other words, our use of technology is always political. In this chapter, we're not going to review an array of theories about technology; instead, we'll examine developments in workplace use of technology as communicative (and thus political) practices. As a first step, we need to clarify what falls under the banner of technology.

UNDERSTANDING TECHNOLOGY

What do we mean by the term *technology*? When most people talk about technology, they're talking about the electronic tools Tim's friend prohibited at meetings: smartphones, tablets, and computers. But the notion of technology is much broader than that. If we think about technology in very basic terms, as the application of tools and techniques to extend the limits of the self in solving problems, we start to see how broad the category can be. Technology can be, as sociologist Read Bain (1937) portrayed it over eight decades ago, all the "tools, machines, utensils, weapons, instruments, housing, clothing, communicating and transporting devices and the skills by which we produce and use them" (p. 860). This classic definition means that almost any object—a rock, pencil, fork, shoes—can be understood as a technology depending on how it's used.

But this definition doesn't mean that everything (and anything) counts as a technology. We're referring here to devices that mediate and construct the relationship between the person and the world. A smartphone does that, but so does a bicycle. Thinking about technology in terms of extending human capabilities and shaping our relationships with the world around us means that a thing functions as a technology only when it intersects with our knowledge and activity in the pursuit of some aims (as expressed in the quote by Schlesinger that opens this chapter).

In this chapter, we're going to focus specifically on **information and communication technologies** (ICTs) and their use in, and at, work. When digital media saw its first widespread use in workplaces in the 1980s and 90s—starting with email, instant messaging, groupware (computerized collaboration, decision, videoconferencing, and documentation tools), websites, intranets, and computerized information systems—scholars predicted that these would make work largely unrecognizable as compared with the past (see Zuboff, 1988). Because ICTs offer the ability to easily send messages to anyone, to bridge geographical distances, and to interact more efficiently, many predicted that ICTs would reduce hierarchy, enhance productivity, generate better decisions, and remove barriers to collaboration. On all of these counts, however, evidence of a technological transformation of the workplace is mixed (Bar & Simard, 2002). The reason for the unclear results may be that analysts have treated the ICTs as independent causal forces that, in the language above, simply impose themselves on work.

But as we said, ICTs are never merely things. Technological objects are always tied to the techniques in which they're employed and the goals we pursue in using them. Another way of saying this is that ICTs are not merely the gadgets we hold in our hands but are the constant interplay of social and technical factors. Communication scholar Marshall Scott Poole and management professor Geraldine DeSanctis (1992) developed **adaptive structuration theory** to explain this social-technical interplay. In theorizing ICTs, they distinguish between the objective features designed into a technology (the things it's designed to do) and its spirit, the general goals and philosophy it promotes. So as users deploy an ICT in their work, they can draw upon it either faithfully or ironically, depending on whether the use aligns the features and the spirit. For example, when you use your smartphone to make a call, you're using it faithfully, since that feature was designed into the phone. But when you pretend to receive a call (or use one of the many fake call apps available to any user) to avoid talking with another person, you're using the phone in a way that it wasn't intended—but which its features make possible. Faking that you're receiving a call is not something people could have imagined with old corded phones!

Thus, if our communication shapes the meanings of the ICTs we use, it also shapes the users' future action. Management scholar Stephen Barley's (1986) study of medical technologies (CT scanners) introduced into two hospitals is a case in point. In both hospitals, radiologists had dominance over how medical imaging was done and how the results were interpreted. When the CT scanners were introduced, it created uncertainty because experienced radiologists were confronted with an object they didn't quite know how to use and with an inability to read outputs—so they had to rely on technical specialists to get their work done. One hospital hired experienced technical specialists and encouraged its younger radiologists to use the new technology, which threatened the dominance of the older, experienced radiologists and upended authority relations. In the other hospital, however, it hired novice technical specialists and relied on their experienced, knowledgeable radiologists to work with the new scanners—keeping the existing system of authority in place. The point is that the scanners became social objects whose meanings were defined by the contexts (the relations of expertise and authority) they entered, not by some objective features of the machines.

Adaptive structuration theory, then, is a way to show that ICTs' influence on the workplace is not a result of the technologies imposing themselves on people; instead, their effects always occur through communication, as the technology becomes part of a communication system. In other words, it is the meanings we create around technologies that shape how we use them. Those meanings are shaped by the design of the technologies but are not limited by design. What we take any technology to be—whether we're talking about bicycles, smartphones, CT scanners, or the newest social media app—is socially constructed as people interact with and through it and therefore might well have multiple meanings around it. And to reiterate a point made above, those meanings are political in that they usually privilege some interests over others.

NEW TECHNOLOGIES, NEW CHALLENGES

With the point about the importance of meanings, and not merely the devices themselves, in mind, we consider several ICT-oriented developments in the workplace. These are algorithmic management, mobile communication, and knowledge management. Across them, we show that these technologies may make work look different and occur in different locations, but they reinforce themes characterizing work and the workplace that you've seen all throughout this book.

Platform Capitalism

Before you read further, try a Google (or Bing, or whatever) search and type in "the Uber of" and see what its auto-fill feature brings up to complete the phrase. When we did this

Bloomberg/Bloomberg/Getty Images

Platform-based companies, like ride-sharing services, are changing the character of work.

search in summer 2018, the terms Google offered (which reflect users' frequent searches) were real estate, marijuana, private jets, massage, solar panels, trucking, and lawn care. (And this is not simply for low-skill work; white-collar work such as copyediting, radiology, computer programming, and even management are being "Uber-ized.") If you click on any of the links from one of those searches, you're likely to see companies trying to disrupt industries by creating a platform that allows the company to serve as an intermediary between different users. In the case of the ride sharing service Uber, drivers (sellers) and customers (buyers) get connected, but platforms can link a wide array of service providers (like delivery persons), advertisers, producers, suppliers, and consumers.

What, then, is a platform? In the simplest terms, a platform is digital infrastructure that enables two or more groups to interact. In this sense, a platform can be seen as something of a matchmaker, a way for parties to connect, especially if they were somehow unable to do so otherwise (Evans & Schmalensee, 2016). Some of the world's largest and most innovative companies are organized as platforms: Apple, Google, Microsoft, Amazon, Uber, Airbnb, Facebook, TaskRabbit, OpenTable, and Tinder. Platforms typically provide a set of tools that allow users to build their own products or presence associated with the platform (with rules set by the platform owner), depend on a critical mass of users to provide a valuable matchmaking service (and adding additional users is not costly once the infrastructure is in place), and engage in cross-subsidization: One part of the service is free (or cheap), but other revenue sources, like advertising, selling users' data, or taking a cut of each sale, generates profits from the free service (Srnicek, 2017). This approach to raising money means that platform companies need to attract a wide array of users and then figure out which ones will be subsidized and which will be the sources of profit, a model that is different from when the company focuses intensely on its one core competence.

Within the context of contemporary work, it's important to understand platforms for at least three reasons. First, platforms are foundations upon which the on-demand, sharing, and gig economies we've mentioned in this book are built. Understanding how platforms operate is important given the increasing popularity of these forms of work, but it's also important because the conception of the worker has changed under platform capitalism. Specifically, the drivers for Uber (or Uber Eats), the taskers for TaskRabbit, the masseuses for Zeel, the delivery persons for DoorDash, and the homeowners on Airbnb are not employees of these firms. Instead, they are independent contractors, a categorization that saves the companies millions in benefits, training, overtime pay, sick days, and tax and retirement contributions. The companies take a slice of each task or gig arranged through their sites, and because those monetary exchanges happen electronically (via credit cards), the companies' take looks invisible.

A second reason to understand platform-based work is that it makes us question a key theme running through this book: Control over employees. If the people doing the majority of work for a company are independent contractors, you may be wondering, How does management control them? The answer is that most platforms have built into them reputation systems, rating devices that allow users (as well as providers, in some cases) to assess the provider's service. You've no doubt seen this ability in ride-sharing services, on Amazon, or in any other of the sites of platform capitalism—usually represented by a five-star scale. Because there are no clear criteria for or checks upon these ratings, they tend to be about users' impressions of the provider—and not surprisingly, these ratings often encode the same biases around race, gender/sexuality, and class seen in other forms of labor (Rosenblat, Barocas, Levy, & Hwang, 2016). These are used, often in less-than-transparent ways, by the platform companies to discipline workers, which can perpetuate those biases while also feeling like always-on surveillance.

Finally, keeping with the theme of this chapter, we need not think of platforms as imposing themselves on us, as if we have no choice about their influence. As technologies, their impacts are neither straightforward nor inevitable. Critics have drawn attention to the working conditions promoted by platform capitalism, while politicians have railed against these companies' size and political power and have introduced new regulations (Morozov, 2013). In fact, some have argued for the need to develop platform cooperatives, democratically owned computing platforms governed by the stakeholders who use them most (Scholz, 2014). Although there are only a few small and scattered examples of this alternative to platform capitalism, their presence shows how technologies are always socially constructed as people interact with and through them.

Algorithmic Management

One of the unique differences between platform capitalism and other approaches to managing and organizing, then, is the approach to data. As we mentioned, platforms extract a great deal of digital data from the users and providers they bring together, and those data become a source of competitive advantage. Platforms bring us into the era of big data: Sets of digitally collected data, usually collected from a variety of sources that produce a high velocity of ongoing data streams, which are so vast that traditional approaches to processing and analyzing them (by people or software made for the personal computer) no longer work (De Mauro, Greco, & Grimaldi, 2016).

Of course, organizations have always analyzed data to make decisions. Yet something changes when datasets get big because individual human managers might not be able to handle the quantity of data available. Consequently, workplaces turn to algorithms. Algorithms are rules that specify operations to find trends in data; they can learn from patterns, as well as make decisions and predict the future. Algorithmic management, in turn, involves marrying algorithms' data processing power with advanced software to extract information from big data that allows managers to oversee workers in an optimized manner at a large scale. When organizations can represent employees' activity (behaviors, interactions, outputs, etc.) digitally, they seek ways of making sense of all those representations.

Under algorithmic management, some of the tasks conventionally done by humans are outsourced to computers and the algorithms they run. For instance, at Uber, the rates drivers receive for a ride are determined by the workings of algorithms that take into account a wide array of factors, including demand, traffic, past ratings, and willingness to accept driving shifts. The platform captures data on drivers, even when they are not receiving a fare: "Uber uses the data to ensure that its drivers are not working for other taxi platforms. . . . In China, Uber monitors even whether drivers go to protests" (Srnicek, 2017, p. 84). If the algorithm determines that a driver is undesirable, it—not a human manager—deactivates him or her (and informs him or her through a pop-up message on his or her smartphone). Should the driver seek to appeal this decision, it seems impossible to find a human to listen to the case. So while companies like Uber highlight the opportunity to be your own boss (Peticca-Harris, deGama, & Ravishankar, In Press), the real bosses seem to be faceless algorithms that can manage the glut of data the company collects (Schildt, 2017).

The attractiveness of algorithmic management is that it offers an ability to optimize operations in a way that has previously been unavailable to management. Algorithms can power through huge volumes of emails, credit scores, résumés, and photos in seconds, largely eliminating the need for human analysts (O'Neil, 2016). As suggested throughout this book, efficiency has long been a driving aim of management, but big data and analytics provide new ways to control costs, to detect patterns, and to make predictions. For instance, the sensors in technologies like smart watches collect data about a person's location, amount and type of movement, heart rate, sleep patterns, exercise goals, and the like; given the millions of users, the data could be overwhelming. This is where analytics comes in, since it refers to computerized techniques, including the algorithms mentioned above, to uncover and interpret meaningful patterns in these data. In the context of workplaces, a particular application of this called **people analytics** (also sometimes called workforce or human resources analytics; it is a specific application of algorithmic management) finds patterns in big data derived from employee behavior, allowing managers to optimize human resources and make evidence-based decisions about hiring, promotion, as well as the organization's strategy (McAfee & Brynjolfsson, 2012). In some cases, people analytics is being used to mine employee data for evidence of which employees may develop illnesses, a use that raises concerns about what managers might do to employees with such knowledge (Silverman, 2016).

But what is sacrificed as organizations use people analytics to seek optimization? One consequence can be that decisions that formerly were in human hands get delegated to algorithms, and the decisions become mysterious for the humans involved. This was the case when the state of Arkansas automated its provision of home health care in 2016: Neither the staff nor the clients could understand why cuts to assistance were being made to people who seemed to need more than they received (Lecher, 2018). Many other states have done the same, seeking an objectivity that human systems often fail to deliver and a rationality that seemed to be missing from bureaucratic systems, but as is the case with Uber's faceless bosses, figuring out how an algorithm operates and protesting the choices that have been made can feel like a futile task.

The concern about algorithmic management is not merely that decision-making authority is removed from humans or that power is hidden from view; it is also that those algorithms' effects are far from neutral. Though we have come to stop questioning computational systems since we all started carrying devices in our pockets (Finn, 2017), communication scholar Safiya Noble (2018) suggests that algorithms can generate a number of problematic consequences. In *Algorithms of Oppression*, she shows that the algorithms powering search engines like Google encode discrimination against marginalized groups, including women, people of color, and LGBTQ people. Though these results are usually the product of pattern recognition (and rarely intentionally inserted into the computations), Noble argues that algorithm designers' lack of education about, and reflection on, technological biases reproduces the divisions society has hoped to overcome. For instance, facial recognition algorithms, used in smartphones, computers, and ever-present security cameras, are trained using data sets composed mostly of white faces, which has led to some webcams' inability to recognize dark-skinned faces and to some photo-sharing sites auto-tagging black faces with the category "gorilla" (Couch, 2017). Further, Facebook's algorithm, which encodes its policy of forcing users to supply their real names, outlaws words or phrases in place of a middle name. This prevented several Native Americans from signing up for the service. Their names—Lance Browneyes, Robin Kills The Enemy, and Dana Lone Hill—were not seen as legitimate by the company's algorithm (Luxen, 2015).

These examples underscore our guiding claim in this chapter. The development and use of computational technologies in organizations is always deeply intertwined with the meanings we construct around them, including historical biases. When people treat algorithms and data analytics as merely tools to produce efficiency—and objective tools at that, one that doesn't suffer the same sorts of problems humans do—they risk losing the capacity to examine how these technologies influence organizations and those who depend on them.

CRITICAL RESEARCH 12.1

Joshua B. Barbour, Jeffrey W. Treem, & Brad Kolar (2018). Analytics and expert collaboration: How individuals navigate relationships when working with organizational data. *Human Relations, 71*, 256–284.

Big data and analytics have become hot topics in the management press, to the point where they have become seen as the holy grail for managers seeking to make their organizations optimally productive (Hobsbawm, 2017). These notions align with larger trends that have produced the "datafication" of work (where ever more elements of work are quantified and turned into data) and an overarching faith in the possibility of making fully rational decisions in the workplace. What the fascination with the computerization of management tends to ignore, however, is how these factors shape the doing of work in actual organizations.

Organizational communication scholars Joshua Barbour, Jeffrey Treem, and Brad Kolar (2018) wondered about this. Starting with a recognition that making use of big data and analytics in complex organizations requires the sharing and interpretation of data across many organizational experts (as well as the functions they represent), Barbour et al. studied an organization's implementation of analytics. They conducted interviews and administered questionnaires to 54 members of a Fortune 500 financial services company that was seeking to become a more data-driven company. The 54 members had been identified as people in leadership positions who would

(Continued)

(Continued)

be capable of undertaking special projects that would make novel and insightful uses of the company's developing collections of data. And these leaders had significant leeway in defining their projects: The plans had to relate only to their day-to-day work and to the person's specific expertise, with the aim of producing significant benefit for the organization. But in each case, these members needed to collaborate with experts in other parts of the organization to access and interpret data in their pursuit of their projects.

Barbour et al.'s respondents reported that getting data was relatively easy, especially after they learned of its location; what was more challenging was collaborating with those other experts to help with formatting and interpretation. Algorithmic management tends to overlook the fact that many obstacles to cross-unit projects like these exist in complex organizations, including "individual and organizational agendas, hierarchical divisions, and legal and regulatory constraints" (p. 275) that don't simply disappear when analytics arrives. What Barbour et al. found was that the members used informal communication to create the trust necessary to make those expert collaborations happen:

> Formal meetings were a space for rationalizing decisions, but informal interactions were central for gathering the data needed to make decisions. Informal communication with individuals early in projects . . . brought [experts] on board during preliminary conversations about the work with data and increased the likelihood they would be invested in the project. (p. 276)

The recognition of the centrality of informal communication processes led Barbour et al. to propose that expert relationships depended not merely on requesting data and collaborating but also on the communicative practice of commissioning: delegating analytical tasks to an expert only after conversations about the demands of the project and securing the other's commitment. Commissioning is not, therefore, simply about making a request (or an order); it depends on previous informal communication that created trust and connection between experts.

Discussion Questions

1. Barbour et al. found that people in this organization encountered challenges in collaborating, even after big data and analytics arrived on the scene. Using adaptive structuration theory, explain why those challenges remained.

2. In groups, consider how you might overcome the problems of "individual and organizational agendas, hierarchical divisions, and legal and regulatory constraints" noted in this study. Is there a technological solution to these challenges? Is there a social solution? What were the consequences of ignoring the informal communication that created trust between experts?

Mobile Communication and the Extension of the Workplace

One of the most attractive features of ICTs is that they allow us to overcome limitations on time and space. Email, for example, is an asynchronous medium, which means that parties to communication participate in an interaction at different times and in different places: We can send a message to another person, and that person can reply to it when it when it suits him or her. Synchronous media, like videoconferencing, telephone, or instant messaging, come closer to the FtF context because parties to an interaction are exchanging messages at (something close to) the same time but from different locations. Synchronous media can therefore support immediate feedback and tend to support the expression of verbal, nonverbal, and paralinguistic (rate, pitch, inflection) cues but generally do not support the storing and retrieval of messages.

When ICTs such as these first entered the workplace, scholars wondered about the impact they would have on work. Some reasoned, for instance, that these technologies reduced the cues available to interactants compared to FtF interaction and that computer-mediated communication thus could be useful for only some tasks. One version of this thinking was social presence theory, which addresses an ICT's ability to make people feel like they're together (co-present) even when they're separated in space and time (Short, Williams, & Christie, 1976). Researchers using this theory argued that text-based messaging offers less presence than video-based interaction, both of which are impoverished compared to FtF communication. If you want to merely interact about tasks, the theory goes, low-presence media are fine; developing relationships or dealing with interpersonally tricky issues, as in the Barbour et al. (2018) study from the Critical Research 12.1 box, requires more sophisticated technologies.

A related line of thinking about ICTs in the workplace is media richness theory. This perspective suggested that ICTs possess particular characteristics, regardless of how they're understood and used in a particular context (Daft & Lengel, 1986). The central claim of media richness theory is that people select (or should select) media that are rich enough to support the ambiguity and complexity of the topic they're discussing. Richness is a measure of a medium's ability to support complex communication and to aid a user to change another person's understanding of an issue. Richer media, then, are better able to handle multiple cues at the same time, facilitate rapid feedback, and establish a focus on the person. FtF communication is thus seen as very rich, videoconferencing would be slightly less so, and a medium like instant messaging is relatively lean. The main extension offered by media richness theory is that a lean medium can be appropriate for reducing uncertainty (when the issue in question has an objectively right answer, like when you remind a coworker of a meeting), but that reducing equivocality (determining which is the right question to ask and which of the many possibilities is best, like deciding on a complex strategic vision or conducting a performance appraisal) requires a rich medium.

As intuitive as these theories sound, they were not strongly supported by research (Rice & Gattiker, 2001) and not long after they were introduced, scholars argued against their assumptions. Janet Fulk, Joseph Schmitz, and Charles Steinfeld (1990), in their social influence model of media use, argued that social presence and media richness theories make it seem as if the choice of the appropriate medium is (or should be) a rational choice, one dictated by the objective features of the technology. Fulk et al.'s research suggested, however, that the meanings communicatively constructed around ICTs shape their use. Social influences such as the communication patterns in an organization, the practices of other organizations, the norms regarding how an existing medium is used, and changing understandings outside an organization can all shape how a given ICT is used.

These theories help explain why particular technologies are used for particular sorts of communicative tasks. But they tell us little about how the workers using these tools are affected. And given the widespread use of ICTs in the contemporary workplace, we should examine the research on the unintended consequences of ICT use. Some of the key consequences scholars have found are the product of how ICTs extend work well beyond the workplace.

The devices many of us carry around all the time, like smartphones, provide a range of ways to communicate in the service of work: Telephone, email, text, social media, video chat, data entry, and computer. On the one hand, this ability can be liberating: Work no longer is tethered to a particular organizational site, especially for those who do work that can be done anywhere, like professionals who do knowledge work or those whose work takes them to many sites, like salespeople. Visit any coffee shop during working hours and you're likely to see a slew of professionals hunched over laptops or chatting away on their phones. Alternative work arrangements can be tremendously helpful for those who provide care to others (such as children or elderly family members) or whose work doesn't require them to be physically around their coworkers at all times. And reducing required trips to a workplace can also decrease time wasted in commuting, not to mention the pollution and congestion relieved by fewer cars on the road. In other words, the extension of work beyond the traditional workplace can bring some important benefits.

On the other hand, extending the workplace can carry some harm for workers as well. Because these ICTs are always on our bodies, we might be expected to be always on—to be permanently accessible and available. This **constant connectivity** means that work can seep into every nook and cranny of our lives. We see four concerns for workers with constant connectivity.

First is what is known as the **autonomy paradox**. This paradox means that the professionals who do knowledge work tend to prize their autonomy at work, in that they exercise a decent amount of control over the content, procedures, and location of their activity. But with the constant connectivity offered by ICTs, these workers willingly limit that autonomy. A study of professionals' uses of ICTs for email found that these professionals

> choose to be technologically connected to work at all hours of the day and night. . . . Rather than feeling frustrated or trapped, they report that using the mobile email device offers them greater flexibility and capacity to perform their work, and it increases their sense of competence and being in control. (Mazmanian, Orlikowski, & Yates, 2013, p. 1337–1338)

If you have observed this paradox in others, or have personal experience with it, the autonomy paradox may not be completely surprising. But it is somewhat ironic that those who enjoy the most freedom in their work choose to curb their own independence.

What explains the autonomy paradox? This effect is not simply a result of the technology, nor is it merely a product of the jobs professionals perform. Indeed, in a study of "Crackberries" (BlackBerry smartphones), informatics scholar Melissa Mazmanian (2013) found that salespersons who weren't strongly dependent on their coworkers and who didn't have a strong sense of professional identity used the devices only to keep current on email, but not to make themselves always on; management scholars Donald Hislop and Carolyn Axtel (2011) found something similar in their study of service engineers whose work was mostly independent of other workers. This finding suggests that the professional workers who experience the paradox—who willingly restrict their own autonomy—do so because of the commitments they have. These commitments are both a sense of loyalty to their co-workers (and to the norms operating in their workplaces) and to the meanings of being a professional. To return to our overarching point about technology from the start of the chapter, the issue is not that technologies impose themselves on us; instead, the meanings we create around them shape our uses and in turn the effects they produce.

A second (and related) implication is that, in the Western world, ICTs lead us to feel more stress at work and to spend more time working (see Chapter 14) than we did in the past. Researchers Killian Mullan and Judy Wajcman (In Press), in a study where a large sample of workers in the United Kingdom recorded their activities throughout a day in 2000 and another large sample did the same in 2015, found that the increased use of ICTs was associated with both more work hours and a feeling of being rushed. Managers and professionals attributed significantly more work, and more time pressure, to ICT-based work extension, but the researchers found that, on the whole, workplace arrangements—the meanings and practices produced at work—produce these effects.

For those whose workplaces produce time pressures and the sense that the pace of work is constantly accelerating (Rosa, 2013; Wajcman, 2015), stress can be a constant

Information and communication technologies allow workers to be constantly connected to their workplaces.

Ariel Skelley/DigitalVision/GettyImages

companion. Email is a case in point: Because it is easy and almost costless to send, many more messages are exchanged (compared with letters and memos), and those messages distract and interrupt work, exacerbating communication overload.

However, knowledge workers frequently do not experience their work as fragmented. Indeed, Wajcman and Rose (2011) report that workers view interruptions and multitasking as an integral part of the workday. As two different knowledge workers in the study state, "It's the interruptions which form the genesis of the work," and "I view [interruptions] as actual workflow; it's work coming to me." Thus, rather than ICTs dictating work, this study suggests that knowledge workers adapt and integrate them into a work environment that is already complex.

Workplace stress, however, can be much more serious than a feeling of psychological anxiety. Jeffrey Pfeffer (2018), a management scholar, suggests in his book, *Dying for a Paycheck,* that poor management practices, including the extension of work, cause as many as 120,000 deaths per year in the United States (and may be five times that in China), and the stress costs employers $300 billion a year. The stress is distributed across industries, but it is especially acute in the high-tech startup realm like that described in Lyons's (2016) *Disrupted,* above. Pfeffer notes that in Silicon Valley, the epicenter of the startup world, a health clinic operating out of a mobile van serves the largest companies in the area because employees don't have the time to visit a physician. Employees' attachment to the devices that allow constant connectivity is pronounced, as Pfeffer quotes the mobile van company's representative: "Some patients don't even get off their mobile devices while being examined" (p. 121). We see yet again that ICTs do not act on their own; it is their capacities intersecting with organizational culture and professional norms that produce practices that are stressful and, clearly, unhealthy.

A third consequence of the ICT-led extension of work is that it threatens work-life balance. Many argue that ICTs allow work to colonize (i.e., occupy and redefine) the times and spaces previously reserved for family and leisure (Duxbury, Higgins, Smart, & Stevenson, 2014). Cultural studies researcher Melissa Gregg (2011) saw this colonization in her study of Australian professionals. She argues that the expansion of work has been produced by companies seeking to get more out of their workers. Home then became a place to catch up on work that cannot be completed during the regular workday. This experience was particularly the case for women, who are often unable to work the long stretches of time required in professional workplaces because they are tasked with child care and home maintenance roles. The expectation that work extends into the home and late in the evening is greeted with a grimace, but often with a smile: Gregg shows that online technologies (including social networking sites) enable employees to generate a sense of camaraderie that blurs distinctions between work and friendship. That blurring generates collegial "pleasures and intimacies [that] underwrite professional workers' willingness to engage in work outside paid hours" (p. 6). If colonization of life occurs, it is in no small part because workers derive satisfaction from the presence of these ICTs in their lives.

Gregg (2011) demonstrates that work and home are not fully separate spheres of our lives. Communication scholar Annis Golden (2013) would agree, portraying work and home as interconnected systems that shape one another. When ICTs extend the workplace, they mediate (they get in the midst of) the work-home relationship. But Golden holds that the workplace's colonization of life is not the only possible outcome because employees and their families can be active—they have agency. Employees are agents, meaning that they can set limits on technology use, and they can also use workplace resources for family needs, even at the workplace. Her study of workers at a high-tech firm found what she called a *norm of reciprocity*: If workers are expected to bring work home via ICTs, they feel empowered to bring their home into the workplace, particularly when family members initiate interaction. In other words, workers' ICTs extended the workplace into the home, but workers made the relationship go the other way as well, such that work and family suffused one another.

Once again, however, the influence of ICTs on work-life balance is complicated. Wajcman Rose, Brown, and Bittman (2010) suggest that rather than creating more stress in the work–home relationship, ICTs help employees better manage that relationship. Counter-intuitively, the study found that the more a worker uses mobile communication technologies at home for work purposes, the lower the worker's sense that work negatively impacts home life. This belief is because workers in the study viewed the ability to work from home as a way to connect better with family.

A fourth concern of constant connectivity and the extension of work is that we are always potentially monitored by our employers. In Chapter 1's discussion of technological control, we mentioned surveillance as a logical outgrowth of management's desire to monitor employee behavior and productivity. We presented the Panopticon not merely as a design for a prison, but as a metaphor for how surveillance is repositioned, moving from a managerial concern to one shared by groups and, ultimately, to a task carried out by the self. Advanced ICTs provide new, and ever more intrusive, ways of making sure employees are doing what they're supposed to be doing. In addition to seeing when employees log on to company computer systems, some employers track the location of workers' cell phones to ensure that they don't veer from approved routes, others use keystroke logging software to make sure that employees working remotely are actually sitting at their laptops working, and still others use software to assess that workers are making progress on to-do lists. As you might imagine, these forms of surveillance can threaten autonomy, as Karen Levy (2015) found in a study of truck-driving work. The extensive data gathered via an on-board computer allowed management to strengthen control over the workers. It did this primarily by challenging truckers' claims that weather or traffic made on-time deliveries difficult (which management never could have done with paper-and-pencil log books) but also by sharing data on all drivers' performances, which allowed them to compare with one another. Truckers now had to explain late deliveries in light of the increased information held by management, a threat to workers who prided themselves on their independence: "I've been driving truck 42 years. I'm not in the habit of explaining myself. Having to explain myself is really an insult" (Levy, 2015, p. 170).

We take up this theme a bit more in the section "Transparency and Surveillance" below, but the point here is to show how the extension of work created by ICTs raises four primary concerns (the autonomy paradox, increased stress on workers, the challenges for work-life balance, and pursuit of surveillance by management), which can impact workers' quality of life.

Managing Knowledge and Monitoring Workers

A final form of work influenced by ICTs is what has become known as knowledge work. As discussed in Chapter 6, the shift to a post-Fordist information society highlights how value is increasingly produced by manipulating data and shaping symbols (what we discussed in that chapter as immaterial labor), and less so by the machinery and physical labor altering material objects. Often, knowledge work is defined, following the title of a book on this topic, as *Thinking for a Living* (Davenport, 2005). Seeing knowledge work as "thinking for a living" means that we define knowledge work in terms of what is inside workers' heads and how those people get knowledge from their brains into behaviors. This conception of knowledge displays a cognitive focus, one that portrays knowledge as something possessed by an individual. We'll discuss an alternative stance on knowledge in the conclusion of this section. Understanding knowledge in cognitive terms also implies that knowledge is an entity, a commodity that can be treated like any other commodity: It can be bought and sold, it can be moved from place to place, and it can be lost. Professional workers (such as lawyers or physicians), those in the STEM fields, and marketers are seen as doing knowledge work because what makes them special is what they have in their heads. This knowledge is considered *explicit* when we can put it into words, when it exists as facts and propositions that can appear in books or manuals; it is *tacit* when the knowledge concerns skills or routines that are unconscious or implicit and which, therefore, can't be easily articulated or codified. The classic example is riding a bicycle: To say that some activity is "just like riding a bike" means that you know how to do it without necessarily being able to explain it in words. It means that your body knows, even if your attempts to describe it to someone who's never ridden a bike overlook the bodily skill involved (Polanyi, 1967).

When we see knowledge as cognitive, we also think of it as something that can be measured, extracted, and accumulated from its locations; it is intellectual capital stored in individual containers. When most people talk about knowledge, this cognitive view is what they use. Consider, for example, how we talk about college: You hear people talk about *getting* an education, *acquiring* or *gaining* skills, and that *the* education—typically understood as a noun, not a verb—is useful only if it is tradable for something of real value, such as a job and the income it brings (we also mentioned this in Chapter 1). And when knowledge is understood this way, it is only a small step to see organizations in similar terms, as systems whose productivity is a result of the knowledge they can bring to bear in their products and services. And if organizations' competitive advantage is understood as a result of having more knowledge, as well as a quicker way to access knowledge (a common assumption in the information economy), it makes perfect sense that knowledge is something that should be managed for organizational benefit. This management occurs when organizations mine it from its locations (e.g., extract it from individuals' minds), store it in a central location, share it widely inside the organization, protect it from leaking outside the system, and nurture the creation of new knowledge. These tasks form the essence of knowledge management (KM): the creation of systems to locate, produce, capture, curate, move, and capitalize upon knowledge for organizational benefit. These systems are typically understood in technological terms as "a collection of information technologies used to collect, transfer, and distribute knowledge among employees" (Offsey, 1997, p. 115).

The cognitive view of knowledge and KM described above may miss some important elements of practice, however. Organizational communication scholar Paul Leonardi (2011; Leonardi & Bailey, 2008) studied a large carmaker's engineering operations at a few locations around the globe. The work he studied involved engineers in the United States and Mexico sending tasks to engineers in India, which relied on digital representations of the cars on which they were working. Leonardi found that the North American engineers transmitted tasks (largely over a company intranet and email system) as if they were simple, straightforward, and objectively understood bits of engineering knowledge. But in visiting the Indian engineers, he found that they required a good deal of interpretation to make sense of these artifacts, including their interpretive leaps about the cultural differences separating the groups. In other words, while the North American engineers thought they were simply sharing and transmitting knowledge, they were unaware of the substantial interpretive work the Indian engineers undertook. And because the Indian engineers were of a lower status in the company than the North Americans, they felt unable to speak up to change matters. Knowledge, therefore, was generated in the communicative practice of interpretation; it was not merely in the directives sent to India. This case also shows that KM should be concerned not merely with mining, storing, sharing, and protecting knowledge but should also pay attention to the political dynamics in organizations that shape knowing processes. With this in mind, we discuss three themes of KM system implementation.

Storing Knowledge: KM Repositories

When it burst onto the scene in the 1990s, KM, along with the ICTs that made it work, were all the rage. Because knowledge was just starting to be understood as a (perhaps the) key resource for organizational action at that time, technologies that promised to deliver high performance were everywhere. The research on knowledge and KM swelled (Barley, Treem, & Kuhn, 2018), and many existing technologies were re-branded with the label KM to appeal to a new batch of customers (including tools mentioned earlier in this chapter, such as groupware, intranets, and information systems). Other technologies have come and gone with developments in digitalization, new media, and artificial intelligence, but the knowledge repository has remained a central component of KM over time.

A key problem for many organizations is finding ways for employees in different units to share knowledge when the boundaries separating them seem immense. Knowledge repositories can help in addressing this problem. As tools that store lessons learned, best practices, and expert profiles, knowledge repositories are more than merely databases or fancy libraries. Especially when paired with advanced software and tools for engaging in conversations with experts, they can help users figure out new approaches to problems and who in the organization might be a useful resource (Flanagin & Bator, 2011). For instance, a nonprofit that aids in community redevelopment after a natural disaster might create a knowledge repository that includes entries on strategies and tactics used over its history. When the organization enters a new community following a disaster, members would search the repository to access previous projects and the lessons members learned, even if the situation (as well as the staff) differs slightly from previous emergencies (say, a forest fire versus a hurricane, or a rural versus an urban setting). Additionally, a repository could allow users to run simulations to test different routes of action (which might also be used to train employees prior to a disaster response), locate people in the organization with particular expert knowledge, and provide insight on what went right and wrong in prior projects (Chewning, Lai, & Doerfel, 2012; Osatuyi & Andoh-Baidoo, 2014). You can think of this with respect to the projects you work on in college: If you've ever struggled to remember who in your personal network knows a particular item that would help you on that paper, or realized only too late that your old roommate worked on a similar topic in a different course last year, you have a sense for what a knowledge repository can provide. These ICTs offer the hope of overcoming memory challenges and other human limitations to improve efficiency and innovation in organizations.

Figuring out what we know is key to problem solving in any organization. And though knowledge repositories can include some advanced simulation and mapping tools (to visualize knowledge and to project the consequences of particular choices), repositories can only be as good as the information they contain (Flanagin, 2002). A key problem, then, is how to populate knowledge repositories with valuable information. People who are already busy may not feel as if they have the time to write up their experiences, they may feel reluctant to include valuable information about failed (in addition to successful) projects, they may not want to reveal their knowledge in a given domain because they worry about the additional work it could entail, or their humility about the notion of claiming expertise could keep them from contributing (Shumate, 2011). Compounding the potential problem is the concern that allowing one's knowledge to be extracted from one's mind or body and encoded in a repository makes the person redundant and easily eliminated.

These issues expose a key assumption operating behind the scenes in KM: That knowledge integration—sharing and combining knowledge between people and across boundaries—is desirable. Integration can occur when one collaborates with someone from another unit, when one contributes to a knowledge repository, or when management obtains one's specialist knowledge. As Barley et al. (2018) show, knowledge integration is not always good, nor is it necessary, in organizational life; the drive to integrate knowledge across people and units is based on a fairly simplistic conception of organizations and their activities. This more complex view of knowledge integration is a reminder that it is not the ICT imposing itself on activity, but the ways in which knowledge, expertise, and power are configured in the organization that shape how the knowledge repository is used.

Distributed Knowledge Creation: Crowdsourcing. A second theme in the KM literature is a recognition that complex problems are often solved not by a single organizational member, and often not even inside a given organization. Instead, work is increasingly drawing upon the crowd for answers to important challenges. The term **crowdsourcing** is fairly new, having been introduced in a *Wired* magazine article only in the mid-2000s (Howe, 2006), but the practice of acknowledging the wisdom of the crowd is not; what has changed is the ability of ICTs to expand the size of the crowd and the reach of the activity. Seen in terms of technology, crowdsourcing becomes a "participative online activity in which an individual, an institution, a non-profit organization, or company proposes to a group of individuals of varying knowledge, heterogeneity, and number, via a flexible open call, the voluntary undertaking of a task" (Estellés-Arolas & González-Ladrón-de-Guevara, 2012,

p. 197). Crowdsourcing, in other words, is a form of organizing. And as the definition notes, crowdsourcing is useful not merely for projects facing formal organizations; it also has been used to enhance public participation in cases of urban planning, crisis response, and public health (Brabham, Ribisl, Kirchner, & Bernhardt, 2014; Zhao & Zhu, 2014).

There are several approaches to crowdsourcing, though all rely on the presence of ICTs. As communication scholar Daren Brabham (2013, 2015) notes, these include (a) calling upon users to provide data that can be combined to produce an overall representation of some object (e.g., the damage caused by a flood or traffic backups); (b) breaking a large job into micro-tasks that can be completed by individuals, as is the case with people populating Amazon's Mechanical Turk who code hundreds of images, vote on slogans, or write product descriptions, all for pennies each (Irani, 2013); (c) offering a reward for anyone who can solve an intractable problem, as found on the platform InnoCentive for science and engineering challenges (https://www.innocentive.com/); or (d) providing consumer feedback on a company's proposed products and strategies. The tasks that fit with crowdsourcing tend to be those with objectively correct answers, those that can be decomposed and then re-assembled, or those where the voice of the majority matters. Obviously, this doesn't exhaust the tasks facing organizations.

Across those four uses and the tasks they serve, KM looks very different than in the intra-organizational use of knowledge repositories from the previous subsection. The last two versions (c and d) are particularly relevant for KM, since they enable organizations to tap into knowledge that resides outside organizational boundaries and, therefore, provide new possibilities for innovative problem solving. But ironically, crowdsourcing can actually narrow an organization's vision when it comes to innovative problem solving. How can it do this? Management scholars Henning Piezunka and Linus Dahlander (2015), in a study of over 900 organizations' uses of crowdsourcing, found that large pools of suggestions, ideas, and opinions become overwhelming, so organizations deal with the oversupply by paying attention to only a limited number. And perhaps unsurprisingly, the ideas that remain tend to be the ones closely aligned with management's existing thinking. So an approach designed to expand knowledge and broaden ideas can end up doing just the opposite. This ironic research finding returns us to our guiding theme in the chapter: The use of these technologies is shaped not merely by the features of the ICTs but, importantly, also by the meanings and communication practices surrounding these tools.

Transparency and Surveillance

A third and final theme is not so much about particular ICTs as it is about one of the often-overlooked consequences of their use in KM. Specifically, because organizations typically see these ICTs as promoting transparency—for both knowledge workers and KM practices—the ICTs also foster surveillance. KM practices that use ICTs, say Hans Krause Hansen and Mikkel Flyverbom (2014), are **disclosure devices**: practices (and not just the technologies) that make people and processes visible, disclosing every detail of what workers do when they're producing and using knowledge. Those disclosures can be part of surveillance practices in organizations, and whether that surveillance is used for good or ill depends on the meanings about the individual-organization relationship.

CRITICAL CASE STUDY 12.1

Working at Amazon

In a 2015 *New York Times* article, Jodi Kantor and David Streitfeld described the workplace at Amazon, the (mostly) online retail behemoth. (This article did not paint the most rosy of pictures, and Amazon executives, including former Obama administration press secretary Jay Carney, published responses in its wake.) Since its founding in 1994, CEO Jeff Bezos has infused Amazon with a love for data. Amazon tracks its customers' purchases, of course, but it also collects data on almost everything employees do: We mentioned in Chapter 3 warehouse workers' wristbands that nudge them in the right direction to efficiently fill orders, but Amazon gathers data on white-collar workers as well. This drive for data is all part of the company's continual push for performance improvement. And to re-work the old management adage that "you can only manage what you measure," at Amazon, when everything is measured, everything can be managed.

One of Amazon's leadership principles is that the company should "Hire and Develop the Best," which is taken to mean that employees should hold one another to the highest possible expectations—and eliminate employees who can't meet that standard. When continual measurement was turned on employees themselves (and combined with other management tools), it seemed, to one former employee, that "the company [was] running a continual performance improvement algorithm on its staff" (Kantor & Streitfeld, 2015, p. 8).

Amazon's techniques for "hiring and developing the best," and for dismissing anyone who doesn't fit, include using as much data about employee performance as possible. So in addition to a bundle of quantitative data, any employee's performance review takes into account the impressions of everyone who works around her or him—and the company intranet allows coworkers to confidentially comment on that employee's performance. Employees reported using that feedback tool to gang up on a single disliked employee, though they also collectively shower a high performer with praise. Serving the interests of efficiency also means the potential for surveillance, backstabbing, and unrelenting efforts to manage others' impressions. Gathering data on employees is paired with a "rank-and-yank" system for employee performance evaluation, where managers must meet a yearly quota for the number of lower-performing employees to be fired.

What are the consequences of these techniques? One is that the performance evaluation meetings become something of a blood sport. Knowing that a certain percentage of employees must be fired as a result of this meeting regardless of performance, managers "come armed with paper trails to defend the wrongfully accused and incriminate members of opposing groups" (Kanton & Streitfeld, 2015, p. 14). Alternatively, managers "adopt a strategy of choosing sacrificial lambs to protect more essential players. 'You learn how to diplomatically throw people under the bus,' said a marketer who spent six years in the retail division. 'It's a horrible feeling'" (p. 14).

Another consequence is the disciplining of the self. Kantor and Streitfeld (2015) quote one employee who said that "If you're a good Amazonian, you become an Amabot," a term meaning that the person has "become at one with the system" (p. 8). And Amabots sacrifice: One employee reported not sleeping for four days straight (and once used her own money to hire a freelance worker in India to enter data so she could complete more work); another spent a Florida vacation in a Starbucks to get her work done; a mother who had just delivered a stillborn child was told that her performance would be monitored to make sure her focus stayed on her job; and still others report feeling a need to reply to emails immediately and before coworkers, regardless of how late in the evening (or early in the morning) they're received. Parents with young children were told that they would not be able to compete with younger employees with fewer commitments, and that sense of competition affected even those without children: "40-year-old men were convinced Amazon would replace them with 30-year-olds who could put in more hours, and 30-year-olds were sure that the company preferred to hire 20-somethings who would outwork them" (p. 17). At Amazon, the name of the game is efficiency, pursued regardless of whether employee anxiety is a (not entirely unintended) by-product.

Discussion Questions

1. You've probably been on a group or team at some point in your life where a "freeloader" or a "slacker"—in other words, someone not pulling her or his weight—has hurt the team's performance. And you were probably frustrated by it. (If you haven't, you just may be the freeloader everyone else complains about!) Amazon's system is designed to eliminate the possibility of freeloading. Does it sound like an attractive place to work for that reason? What about the description of working at Amazon appeals to you, and what repulses you?

2. One former employee reported in the story said, "Amazon is driven by data . . . It will only change if the data says it must—when the entire way of hiring and working and firing stops making economic sense." Do you agree or disagree with this? Are there other ways to change a system like this?

3. Throughout this book (and particularly in both this chapter and in Chapter 7), we've seen how managerial efforts to discipline workers generate resistance. In groups, what sorts of resistance would you imagine would be likely at Amazon?

One interesting illustration of ICT-enabled surveillance (a theme we touched upon above in the discussion of constant connectivity and the extension of work) is WorkSmart (https://www.crossover.com/productivity), a tool to monitor remote workers' activity. WorkSmart oversees workers by remotely taking screenshots of their computers every 10 minutes, snapping sporadic photos of them with their computer's camera, tracking their keystrokes, scanning the computer's browser history, and reviewing their text messages, social media posts, and even private messaging apps. Though this act might seem like an invasion of privacy, the company's CEO says that workers get used to it: "The response is 'OK, I'm being monitored, but if the company is paying for my time how does it matter if it's recording what I'm doing? It's only for my betterment'" (Solon, 2017). Perhaps not surprisingly, managers can opt out of this monitoring when they're working from home, but lower-level workers have no such choice.

We mentioned surveillance as a common organizational practice in Chapter 1, but here we point to a concern specifically related to managing knowledge. In KM, social media use—(micro)blogs, wikis, social networking sites, and the like—is prevalent, both for organizations and individual employees. These ICTs are valuable for locating expertise, for exchanging ideas with others, and for engaging in conversations where new ideas might emerge. But as workers use these social media, the detectability of their activities increases: These ICTs "afford users the ability to make their behaviors, knowledge, preferences, and communication network connections that were once invisible (or at least very hard to see) visible to others in the organization" (Treem & Leonardi, 2013, p. 150). Through posts, status updates, comments, texts, pictures, or likes, workers make themselves visible to one another (and to anyone else connected through these media). This exposure means that people might be mindful of the impressions they make; it also means that social media activity in the workplace might be logically monitored by management. A company called Wiretap (https://wiretap.com) scours enterprise social networks (workplace-specific chat and social media sites, which tend to be collaboration tools blended with social networking platforms) to, they say, prevent problems such as human resource policy violations, leaking intellectual property, and noncompliance with regulations. Mircosoft claims that its workplace collaboration software, Yammer, can peruse workers' messages to uncover "trending emotions" among the workforce in real time (Simonite, 2012). It isn't hard to imagine how monitoring of this sort might create a big brother scenario where management patrols the workplace and punishes those found to be dangerous to the company, or perhaps not enthusiastic enough about their work. And at the same time, KM-related tools like this Wiretap, Yammer, and Worksmart might decrease employee trust (Ball, 2010), which could shrink the interactions occurring through ICTs and ironically reduce the quantity and quality of knowledge developed and transferred within the organization.

As the "Internet of Things"—the network of Internet-enabled "smart" physical objects, including thermostats, vehicles, appliances, and the like—develops, the number of possible sources of monitoring has jumped dramatically. Machinery, office supply cabinets, smartphones, wearable devices, shipments, and even refrigerators carry networked sensors that can collect and transmit a wide variety of data. In this subsection, however, our interest was in how KM practices use disclosure devices to engage in surveillance over work and workers. Generally, the debate over workplace surveillance sees it not only as a responsible management practice that protects valuable information and prevents dangerous violations but also as one that can occasionally cross ethical lines. Yet surveillance is frequently framed as inevitable, both because the costs of failing to monitor workers appears so high (see the fears mentioned in the Wiretap example) and because the technologies make it so easy. And because employees rarely protest (because many of us have come to accept surveillance as a regular part of contemporary work) about KM activities that rely on disclosure devices. Yet to reiterate the theme of this chapter, these tools, like all ICTs, are neither simply good nor bad but depend on the ways they're used in specific organizations.

✦ CONCLUSION

Discussions about the influence of ICTs on work usually start with the belief that these tools impose themselves on people and their practices—that their features determine particular organizational outcomes, as suggested in Lyons's (2016) description of HubSpot's culture in the illustration that opened this chapter. In contrast, we have been arguing that understanding ICT use in work is not simply a matter of knowing what these tools can do (or in the language of adaptive structuration theory, what their features are). Instead, we also need to know how workers interpret those features—how they recognize what is possible and impossible with respect to the technologies. As an analyst of the workplace interested in communication practices, you should thus wonder about the factors shaping workers' interpretations. In other words, if the meanings of ICTs are (more or less) open to interpretation, what makes particular meanings (more and less) likely?

What then becomes necessary for all us analysts of the workplace is first to recognize that these tools offer some important benefits to organizations. Companies that have used analytics, like Amazon, have experienced gains in efficiency and effectiveness that were simply not available in the world before big data. But it is not just companies: Churches across the United States, urged on by consultants, have found ways to use data to track individual members' (and visitors') attendance, giving, service, and participation in activities, allowing leaders to not only get a sense for trends and to make better decisions but also to target individuals who haven't attended (with text messages, emails, calls) to bring them back to the flock. The use of analytics, as well as mobile communication, is everywhere, and it's here to stay.

A second necessity is that we must seek to examine the struggles over meaning that emerge in relation to ICT use in organizations. We might, for instance, examine the modes of resistance employees use in response to their companies' ICT use. Some of these result in humorous stories about innovative techniques employees use to evade the watchful eye of the company, as when an employee placed a tracking device inside a bag of chips to make a "Farady Cage" that scrambled its signals (Dwyer, 2017). And others look more mundane, like the frustrated trucker with 42 years of experience mentioned above. Understanding resistance can highlight the agency and creativity workers exercise to evade ICTs' domination over their autonomy at work. The problem, however, is that looking for instances of resistance tends to reinforce the idea that individuals and organizations are distinct entities with conflicting interests, and it locks our thinking into assuming that organizations and individuals are fundamentally opposed.

CRITICAL APPLICATIONS

1. Find a relative, friend, or acquaintance who does knowledge work and present that person with the notion of the autonomy paradox mentioned in this chapter. Ask this person if this characterizes his or her work or if the person sees it in others at work. From this person's perspective, is the reduction of autonomy really a choice?

2. The Society for Human Resource Management recently published an article inviting organizations to consider technology-free days (even taking devices away from workers) in their companies because it would actually boost productivity (Wright, 2017). Do you agree that productivity would benefit? Do you think would be effective for dealing with some of the challenges for workers mentioned in this chapter? Why or why not?

3. In this chapter's section on "Mobile Communication and the Extension of the Workplace," we suggested that in some ways, ICTs can threaten work-life balance, but in other ways, they can be interpreted by workers as making the balance more likely. In groups, discuss how both could be the case at the same time. Then debate both stances, using concepts from this chapter to make your case.

KEY TERMS

adaptive structuration theory   310

algorithms   313

algorithmic management   313

analytics   314

asynchronous medium   317

autonomy paradox   318

big data   313

constant connectivity   318

crowdsourcing   324

disclosure devices   325

information and communication technologies (ICTs)   310

knowledge management   322

knowledge repositories   323

knowledge work   322

media richness theory   317

people analytics   314

platform   312

platform capitalism   312

reputation systems   312

social influence model of media use   317

social presence theory   317

synchronous medium   317

STUDENT STUDY SITE

Visit the student study site at **www.sagepub.com/mumbyorg** for these additional learning tools:

- Web quizzes
- eFlashcards
- SAGE journal articles

- Video resources
- Web resources

CHAPTER 13

Organizational Communication, Globalization, and Corporate Social Responsibility

Globalization has transformed the relationships among people, organizations, and communication processes.

Part-time barista wanted. Must speak Danish.

—Sign on the door of a café in Copenhagen, Denmark, 2011

There's an old saying, attributed to the Irish playwright George Bernard Shaw, that Britain and America are "two countries separated by a common language." When Dennis first arrived in the United States from the United Kingdom in the early 1980s to go to graduate school, he was constantly reminded of this phrase. Of course, part of this separation was due to differences in U.K. and U.S. vernacular for everyday objects: car bonnet, not car hood; chips, not french fries; potato crisps, not potato chips; a jumper is a sweater, not a dress; pants are underwear, not outerwear; and so on. His most embarrassing (and funny) moment came when, in his first semester of teaching, Dennis told students to bring to the midterm exam a pencil and a rubber (Britspeak for eraser). They must have wondered what kind of exam it would be!

But what most made Dennis feel like a fish out of water was a profound feeling of isolation from his native culture: TV was quite different (More than four channels? How does anyone navigate all this? And what's with the commercials every 5 minutes?), the supermarkets made no sense (Why does anyone need 50 different breakfast cereals to choose from? And why is milk in those massive 1-gallon containers?), and he had no way of keeping up with news back home, other than the 2-week-old British newspapers at the library and the weekly letters (yes, letters) from his mom (international calls cost about $1 per minute in the early 1980s, and he was living on a meager grad student stipend).

This picture of Dennis's early experiences in the United States now seems rather quaint; in the past 30 years, globalization processes have profoundly transformed our relationship to the world and one another. Indeed, the U.S.–U.K. relationship is very much one of cultural convergence, in which the two societies have grown increasingly similar in lots of ways, both profound and superficial. An American visiting the United Kingdom today would see many familiar consumer-culture landmarks: McDonald's, Pizza Hut, Domino's, The Disney Store, Gap, Abercrombie & Fitch, Starbucks, and so on. Similarly, British culture has migrated across the Atlantic in a big way; the British Invasion that started with The Beatles has become a veritable flood. It's hard to turn TV on these days without seeing a British personality (John Oliver on *Last Week Tonight*, James Corden on *The Late Late Show*, and so on), and there's even a TV channel called BBC America. And most important, at least to Dennis, two U.S. cable networks (and now Amazon!) broadcast live English Premier League football (i.e., soccer) games, so he can watch his beloved Liverpool.

Things have changed a lot over the past 30 years, then, and sometimes at a speed that's hard to comprehend. For much of your authors' lives, the Internet and World Wide Web did not exist; many of you reading this book have known nothing else. Three decades ago, we could never have imagined that university courses could be offered anywhere but in a classroom on a college campus; now, educational practices made possible by the Internet, such as MOOCs (Massive Open Online Courses) and online-only, for-profit universities, are changing the face of college education.

In this chapter, we will address, through the lens of globalization, many of the transformations that have occurred in the world around us. More specifically, we will examine the relationship between organizational communication and globalization. Indeed, one might argue that it is the organizational—mainly corporate—form along with revolutions in communication processes that have driven the processes of globalization. Some commentators even argue that the corporation has eclipsed the nation-state as the most significant institution in the world today, precisely as a result of globalization processes. Given this, an additional issue that will concern us in this chapter is the increasingly important phenomenon of corporate social responsibility (CSR): With corporations' expanding role in a global world, in what ways have they attempted to become responsible corporate citizens?

First, however, we will examine the idea of globalization, exploring definitional issues as well as some of the debates that have emerged out of the effects of globalization on our understanding of the world.

⚬ DEFINING GLOBALIZATION

The world is in a rush, and is getting close to its end.

—Archbishop Wulfstan, 1014 (as cited in Giddens, 2001, p. 1)

Trying to define globalization is like trying to pick up mercury with chopsticks—it's a slippery and complex concept that doesn't lend itself to easy categorization. Indeed, as organizational communication scholars Cynthia Stohl and Shiv Ganesh (2014) indicate, the term itself did not even appear in Webster's dictionary until 1961 and wasn't in widespread academic use until the late 1990s (p. 718). It's also a highly charged term that evokes a wide range of opinions and emotions—some people see globalization as a democratizing force that is making the world smaller and more interconnected, while others view it as a new form of cultural imperialism and economic colonization of indigenous cultures by Western corporations.

As you might guess, the picture is more complex than either of these positions suggests. So in this section, we will try to get a handle on some of the issues that are addressed by scholars across a number of different fields—communication, sociology, economics, geography, and political science, to name a few—as they grapple with globalization. Thus, because scholars from numerous disciplines have attempted to explain globalization, we will necessarily take an interdisciplinary approach in order to get a more complete picture of globalization.

First, it's important to recognize that globalization in not a thing; that is, it is not a structure or a condition with a stable set of characteristics that can be enumerated one by one. It is much too fluid and dynamic a process to be characterized in this way. Rather, following geographer David Harvey (1995), we can think of globalization as a process—an ongoing one, not one with an easily identifiable beginning, middle, and end. In this way, we shift the focus from addressing the question, "What is globalization?" and instead ask, "How is globalization occurring?"

A useful definition comes from sociologist Roland Robertson, who argues that "globalization as a concept refers both to the compression of the world and the intensification of consciousness of the world as a whole . . . both concrete global interdependence and consciousness of the global whole" (as cited in Waters, 2001, p. 4). This definition focuses not on specific features of globalization but rather, on the overall transformation of space and time on the one hand and changes in human consciousness of the world on the other hand. In other words, globalization has compressed the world through communication technologies and speed of travel, and as a result, our consciousness of other places and our place in the world as a whole has intensified.

Robertson expands this definition by focusing on how globalization generates two competing but related forces: "What is involved in globalization is a complex process involving the interpenetration of sameness and difference—or, in somewhat different terms, the interpenetration of universalism and particularism" (Robertson & Khondker, 1998, p. 28).

This conception captures many of the arguments that circulate around the globalization process. Advocates of globalization argue that the creation of an increasingly universal and homogeneous world with shared economic interests and values leads to a more stable and cosmopolitan global society (e.g., T. Friedman, 2005; Giddens, 2001). Yet critics of globalization argue that it is an all-consuming force that destroys unique, indigenous cultures and erases difference, while also increasing the gulf between the haves and the have-nots (e.g., Klein, 2001, 2007). Cynthia Stohl (2001) frames this central issue in a slightly different way when she states that in globalization, "the environmental and technical pressures on contemporary organizations to become more and more similar clash with the proprietary pull of cultural identifications, traditional values, and conventional practices of social life" (p. 326). Globalization, in other words, embodies a constant tension between homogenization (producing sameness) and marking the uniqueness of local cultures.

This idea of competing forces is taken up by other scholars as well. Sociologist Anthony Giddens (2001) argues that "the battleground of the 21st century will pit fundamentalism against cosmopolitan tolerance" (p. 4). Giddens claims that fundamentalism—which he defines as "beleaguered tradition" (p. 49)—is actually a product of globalization and did not exist prior to it. In other words, the rise in fundamentalism that we've witnessed in religious, cultural, and political life over the past few decades emerged as a response to the changes that modernity and globalization wrought in the world. In this sense, fundamentalism (which, for Giddens, is not reducible to religion, and can refer to any unquestioned system of values) is an effort to defend tradition by asserting ritual "truths" in the face of a globalized, modern world that "asks for reasons" (p. 49). Giddens thus sees fundamentalism as the enemy of cosmopolitan values (such as honoring cultural differences and developing a responsibility to those outside one's own tribe, including to future generations) and tendencies toward increasing democratization.

Benjamin Barber (1995) makes a similar case in arguing that globalization is characterized by two competing worldviews: Jihad and McWorld. However, his position is much more pessimistic than Giddens's regarding the relationship between globalization and democracy. Barber argues that McWorld is a global process that is increasingly dominant everywhere and that constructs the individual as a consumer. McWorld is an economic and cultural form that focuses on lifestyle, knowledge, and services rather than on material goods, and hence, the object of McWorld is human identity—a position consistent with our discussion of branding in Chapter 10. McWorld has helped create a media culture in which patience, careful analysis, and argument have given way to simplified debate and the dominance of visual imagery. Jihad, Barber argues, is the child of McWorld and represents a turn toward communalism, tribalism, and tradition (Giddens's notion of fundamentalism). Barber sees Jihad as a response to the consumerist, homogeneous, and shallow culture of McWorld.

A further complication in discussing and defining globalization, however, is that its processes are occurring in multiple interrelated realms of human activity. Understanding globalization requires that we explore each of these spheres more closely. In the next section, then, we will examine globalization processes in the spheres of (1) economics, (2) gender, (3) and politics.

⬡ SPHERES OF GLOBALIZATION

Globalization and Economics

The ideas of globalization and capitalism as an economic system have historically gone hand in hand. In the 19th century, Karl Marx showed how, in order to increase profitability and surplus value, capitalism, by its very nature, needed to expand its markets constantly, finding new domains to colonize. Indeed, much of the imperialist expansions of countries such as Britain, Spain, Portugal, and France in the 1600s, 1700s, and 1800s were not only about cultural imperialism and the spread of certain values but also about economic imperialism and the capture of working populations and raw materials.

Over the past 40 years, the emergence of globalization has been associated with the economic philosophy of neoliberalism. As we saw in Chapter 6, neoliberalism rejects Keynesianism as an economic philosophy and argues instead for the power and value of the free market. In a famous essay in *New York Times Magazine*, Milton Friedman (1970) argued that

> there is one and only one social responsibility of business—to use its resources and engage in activities designed to increase its profits so long as it stays within the rules of the game, which is to say, engages in open and free competition without deception or fraud.

From a neoliberal perspective, such a responsibility could be carried out only if the market were allowed to regulate itself, free from any kind of government intervention and restrictions on trade. Any kind of collectivism that requires corporations to be socially responsible is, according to Friedman, "fundamentally subversive" in a free society. In this sense, and as indicated by the title of his famous book *Capitalism and Freedom*, Friedman (1982) argued for an essential link between unrestricted capitalism and the ability of individuals to exercise free choice, unfettered by any restraints of the collective. This argument fit very nicely with the tenets of neoliberalism, which portray the individual, embedded in free markets rather than communities, as sovereign.

The result of neoliberal economics, many commentators have argued, has been the transformation of both global and national business conduct. The results have been a massive increase in global trade, the offshoring of production to countries where labor is cheaper, huge movements of migrants seeking work, and trillions of dollars in investments being traded around the world every day. It is estimated that transnational corporations (TNCs) account for 70% of trade globally and that 51 of the 100 largest economies in the world are corporations (El-Ojeili & Hayden, 2006, p. 65).

There is considerable debate about the benefits of neoliberalism. Commentator Thomas Friedman (2005)—no relation to Milton—argues that the combination of neoliberal economic policy and new communication technologies has created a "flat world" in which previously "backward" nations such as India have now become global players. The opening of a McDonald's in the early 1990s in Red Square in Moscow is often taken as an iconic example of the connections among capitalism, globalization, and democracy (And against that backdrop, it's interesting to note that the McDonald's restaurant within the company's Chicago headquarters features a rotating menu of specialty items found at the chain's locations around the world). Yet another—unrelated—Friedman (Benjamin) argues that the opening up of more and more countries to capitalism and free trade (e.g., countries of the former Soviet Union and China) has certainly created significant problems around the globe but on the whole has generated more democratic political structures and raised living standards where it has been introduced (B. Friedman, 2005).

On the other hand, critics of neoliberalism (e.g., Klein, 2007; Piketty, 2014) have pointed to how it has increased inequality—both between nations and within nations—as the gap between rich and poor has become wider and wider (see Figure 13.1). As we have seen in earlier chapters, in addition to increasing income disparities, globalization has created a U.S. workforce that is more subject to job insecurity through downsizing, outsourcing of jobs, reduction of benefits, and so forth, as companies move their business interests offshore.

The top 1% of earners have seen a 200% increase in average earning since 1970, while minimum wage earners have seen a 26% decrease during the same period, despite the fact that the average worker's productivity has almost doubled during this time. If the median household income had kept pace with the economy since 1970, it would now be nearly $92,000, not $50,000.

Figure 13.1 Change in Minimum Wage Versus Top Incomes, 1970–2015

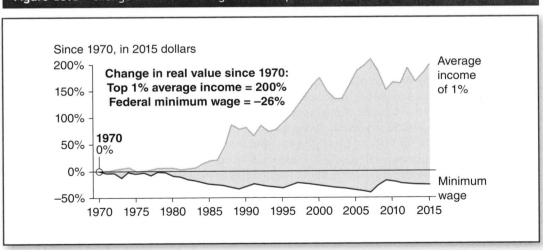

Source: "11 Charts That Show Income Inequality Isn't Getting Better Anytime Soon," *Mother Jones*, December 22, 2016.

At a global level, critics point to greater disparities between nations. Journalist Naomi Klein (2007), for example, provides a devastating critique of what she calls "disaster capitalism" as she explores the ways neoliberal economic policies, employed by the International Monetary Fund (IMF), have actually created greater poverty in many nations because of high-interest loans and the restrictions the IMF imposes on countries as a condition for receiving loans.

Critics of neoliberalism have also pointed to a number of other factors. Billionaire George Soros (2002), for example, argues that with fewer government restrictions, economic markets tend to spiral out of control because they are based largely on speculation rather than on knowledge—something we saw with the subprime mortgage crisis in 2008. In this sense, under neoliberalism, market speculation tends to function like the kind of deviation-amplifying system we discussed in Chapter 4—a type of system that always ends up crashing at some point. Moreover, Scholte (2000) claims that only about 5% of foreign exchange dealings involve transactions in real goods, with about 95% of all dealings being speculative in nature—greatly increasing the possibility of such crashes and bringing little or no economic benefit to anyone other than the market traders and stock owners.

Critics also point out that neoliberal policies create great human hardship for billions of people as the global flow of wealth creates mass migrations of people looking for work (something we discuss next). In addition, production gets relocated to free trade zones in developing countries where wages are low, work and environmental regulations are minimal, and conditions for workers are frequently terrible. For example, as recently as 15 years ago, Apple made its computers in the United States, but then the company outsourced this process to Southern China, to companies such as Foxconn, renowned for its oppressive labor conditions. In the first 6 months of 2010, 11 Foxconn workers committed suicide and 1 died after working a 34-hour shift (Daisey, 2011). Indeed, criticism of Apple's relationship with Foxconn has been so widespread that Apple CEO Tim Cook personally visited one of its factories in March 2012, perhaps more as a way of reassuring consumers than actually to examine its labor practices.

Finally, in case you think a discussion of economics is a long way from communication issues, it is worth noting that, in many respects, the social world we inhabit is largely written in economic and market language; we are now all framed as consumers first and citizens second. Indeed, in a real sense, economic consumption and democracy are equated. As we saw in Chapter 10, brand guru Marc Gobé (2002) even argues that brands themselves are citizens that can contribute to a consumer democracy. There is perhaps no clearer indication of how much economic discourse shapes us.

Gender, Work, and Globalization

The relationship among gender, work, and globalization is interesting in that it runs counter to the dominant narrative and media reports of globalization, which focus mainly on the "upper circuits of global capital" (Sassen, 2003, p. 254)—that is, the hypermobile capital, people, and investments in the fast-paced world of global finance. In contrast to this, the alternative narrative of gender and work in a global context tells the tale of southern, Third World women—a lower circuit of global capital and work—who provide the labor that enables that upper circuit to be maintained. Thus, although accounts of globalization tend to present it as gender neutral (Acker, 2004), the reality is that the globalization process has had a profound effect on the gender dynamics of work.

As Barbara Ehrenreich and Arlie Russell Hochschild (2003) state, as a result of globalization, "women are on the move as never before in history" (p. 2). But this movement is not the kind of upward mobility that has seen the movement of many women into managerial positions in the past 30 years. Indeed, as Ehrenreich and Hochschild point out, while an élite group of successful First World" women enjoy the benefits of a high-consumption, jet-set lifestyle, a much larger flow of migrant women is taking on the roles of nannies, maids, and even sex workers. This "female underside of globalization" (p. 3) involves a form of migration that sees women from poor southern countries taking on the child-rearing and home-maintenance tasks that many women from northern nations no longer perform. This shift is due in part to the fact that as household incomes in the United States have declined steadily in real terms since the 1970s, women have increasingly moved into the workforce to make up the income shortfall.

Ehrenreich and Hochschild (2003) argue, however, that this "feminization of migration" is largely invisible because unlike factory workers or taxi drivers, female migrant workers are often hidden away in private homes, working as maids and nannies to the children that professional dual-career couples don't have the time to look after. Moreover, the dominance of the ideology of individualism in U.S. society means that professional women are frequently loath to advertise their use of maids and nannies, instead perpetuating the myth of the superwoman and the idea of the CEO mom who can have it all.

In examining the relationship of gender, work, and globalization, then, we get a close-up view of the ways the economics and politics of the globalization process come together in the everyday lives of real people—in this case, mostly women who are providing (often invisible) support services that maintain the machinery of global capitalism.

Sociologist Saskia Sassen has written a great deal about the dynamics of gender, work, and globalization, focusing in particular on what she calls global cities (Sassen, 1998, 2000, 2003, 2005). Sassen argues that while much of globalization theory focuses on the capacity to overcome the limits of time and location, little attention has been paid to the fact that a whole infrastructure of activities and services has to be in place in order for the global economy to function. She advocates a focus on what she calls "counter-geographies of globalization" that shift the globalization lens to include not only the mobile professionals and knowledge workers but also the low-wage support workers who labor alongside them (Sassen, 2005).

Sassen (2005) argues that the global city reflects the fact that "the globalization of economic activity entails a new kind of organizational structure" (p. 28). Rather than nation-states functioning as the principal players in the global economy, global cities have become the primary "production sites for the leading information industries of our time" (Sassen, 2005, p. 109). Global cities such as New York, London, Paris, Tokyo, Amsterdam, Hong Kong, Zurich, and Sao Paulo are the new dominant financial centers that coordinate the flow of money and knowledge. These places are where the highly paid knowledge professionals work and communicate with one another across borders of time and space.

Sassen (2005) argues, however, that such time–space flexibility would be impossible without the reproductive work necessary to maintain this system. Thus, working right alongside the highly paid knowledge workers are the nannies, domestics, custodial staff, restaurant workers, and so forth, who engage in the labor that constitutes the service infrastructure of the global cities. Extending Sassen's argument, communication scholar Sarah Sharma (2014) has shown how "lived time" (how individuals experience time) in the global economy is closely connected to class position. For example, business professionals who travel the world experience a "temporal architecture" (commodities, services, technologies, etc.) that is dedicated to their "time maintenance" (2014, p. 35) and which makes business travel bearable (Sharma points out that there are even bras that won't set off airport metal detectors, designed for professional women so they can more quickly move through airports!). However, Sharma notes that this entire infrastructure is maintained by classes of people (taxi drivers, hotel workers, etc.) whose lived time is quite different. For example, taxi drivers are expected to accommodate the temporalities of others, working late hours or making time to catch flights that travelers are late for. Thus, "there is an expectation that certain bodies recalibrate to the time of others as a significant condition of their labor" (Sharma, 2014, p. 20). In this sense, the global city draws attention to issues of power and inequality, as the rich and the poor live side by side.

In examining the situation of women who migrate to the north from the south, Sassen (2003) argues that there are two sets of dynamics at work. First, in relation to the global city, globalization has created a demand for low-wage workers to take jobs that offer few opportunities for advancement—positions that native workers will typically not take. Given the increasing demand for high-level professional jobs in global cities, more and more women have entered the professions. In addition, high-income, dual-career couples often prefer urban living for family life, leading to an expansion of high-income residential areas in those global cities. One of the consequences is the "professional household without a wife" (Sassen, 2003, p. 259) and hence, the return of servant classes to global cities, working as nannies, maids, domestics, and restaurant workers to serve the consumption practices of high-income professionals (eating out regularly, weekends away, regular trips abroad, etc.).

Much of this labor is part of a large informal economy where many of the workers are illegal immigrants. As such, they have little recourse when it comes to poor treatment by employers, and in addition, much of the work tends to be temporary and unpredictable. Susan Cheever (2003), for example, provides a poignant depiction of the life of a nanny in New York City. "Dominique" emigrated from the Caribbean and was lucky enough to get a green card through one of the first families she worked for. However, she still has had eight jobs in 8 years and had to commute from her apartment in Brooklyn to Manhattan, where her various employers live. Cheever also describes nannies facing the attachment factor, in which both nannies and children become strongly attached to each other. However, nannies are often let go when children begin school, and both children and nannies can be devastated by the separation. As Nikki Townsley (2003) points out, the commodification of love is a basic feature of the global child care industry, where children are portrayed as gaining experience of another culture and nannies are portrayed as both exotic and maternal.

But as Sassen's description of the second dynamic indicates, this picture is not as rosy as suggested. Sassen (2003) argues that in conjunction with the global city, there is what she calls the dynamic of the "survival circuit." In this feature of globalization, there has been a feminization of survival in which households, communities, and even nations are increasingly dependent on women's migration and subsequent income for survival. Given the stagnation and shrinking of many southern economies, alternate ways of making a living and generating revenue become essential for the countries from which these women migrate. Frequently, the migration system is organized by third parties, including government and illegal traffickers (the latter specializing in trafficking women and girls for the global sex tourism industry). Governments frequently develop programs to encourage women to migrate to more affluent countries, reasoning that women are more likely than men to return their earnings to their home countries. Ehrenreich and Hochschild (2003) report on a Sri Lankan government program that even commissioned a song to encourage migration, the first two and the last lines of which are, "After much hardship, such difficult times / How lucky am I to work in a foreign land. . . . I promise to return home with treasures for everyone" (p. 7).

According to a 2015 United Nations International Migration Report, about 48% of the estimated 244 million migrants worldwide are women and girls, and women migrants outnumber men in developed countries (Anon, 2015). According to the United Nations, the most recent (2015) estimate of money sent home by migrants to developing countries is $436 billion (for more money than from official development assistance), although given the multiplier effect of this money on local economies, the total money sent home by migrants is equivalent to more than $1 trillion.

It is important to note that many of these women are typically forced to migrate because of conditions in their home countries. Sometimes this is because of war, but many times it is because of difficult economic situations often caused by debt-reduction programs put in place by the IMF. As Sassen (2003) indicates, often the first things to be cut in such austerity measures are education and health care programs, which heavily affect women and children. Women, then, frequently migrate to find work so they can provide for their families.

CRITICAL CASE STUDY 13.1

Work, Technology, and Globalization in the Call Center

In some ways the call center is the quintessential global worksite—it is the place where communication technology, organization, and globalization processes converge. There was even a short-lived TV situation comedy based in a call center. Called *Outsourced*, the "comedy" (one of the reasons you might not have heard of this show is that it wasn't particularly funny) focused on the trials and tribulations of a U.S. manager in an India-based call center and his efforts to navigate the intercultural pitfalls of life in a foreign country. While the call center was the primary location for the comedy, not much time was spent on the work itself, except when comic mileage could be extracted from conversations between operators and customers.

The reality of work in the global call center is, of course, quite different. Call centers "are emblematic of the uncertainties created by globalization" (Batt, Holman, & Holtgrewe, 2010, p. 454).

They are located in remote parts of the world, offer services via a combination of phone and computer technology, and have heavily displaced face-to-face service in local communities. Moreover, call centers require relatively little capital investment, other than a rented building and computer/phone equipment, so they can be relocated fairly easily in response to shifts in the global economy. Finally, call centers embody the post-Fordist shift to a service economy with a heavy use of emotional labor; while call centers do not involve face-to-face service, they depend on the ability of workers to provide customer satisfaction while handling a high volume of calls. In the United States alone, more than 4 million people (3% of the workforce) work in call centers. It's no wonder, then, that a number of organization and management researchers have focused on call center work (Brophy, 2011; Fleming, 2007; Taylor & Bain, 1999, 2003).

Call centers are an example of what some Marxist thinkers have called "cognitive capitalism" (Brophy, 2011), in which language is put to work and labor involves the production of knowledge and communication. In this sense, call centers are a classic example of "the production of communication by means of communication" (Virno, 2001, as cited in Brophy, 2011, p. 412). In other words, Brophy argues that call centers are an essential communication apparatus for managing the relationship between the corporations of cognitive capitalism and their consumers. Call centers act as the tools for selling various products, manage concerns and complaints about those products, and then act as long-distance digital debt collectors when consumers fail to maintain payments for those products.

But while call center work is often classified as knowledge work, it is also largely deskilled labor exemplifying the Taylorization of white-collar work. Workers are constantly monitored, have to follow scripts carefully in interacting with customers, and are under constant pressure to meet quotas and move on to the next customer in the queue on their computer screens. Indeed, Phil Taylor and Peter Bain (1999) have described call center work as "an assembly line in the head" (p. 109)—a phrase that fits nicely with the idea of cognitive capitalism and also captures how white-collar work can be every bit as soul destroying as factory work. Indeed, the image of the call center operator desperately trying to catch up with the callers stacked up in her or his queue is eerily reminiscent of the early scene in Charlie Chaplin's film *Modern Times*, where the little tramp flips out trying to keep up with the machine parts passing in front of him (later parodied in an episode of *I Love Lucy* set in a chocolate factory).

Taylor and Bain (1999) provide a compelling and poignant description of the typical call center employee:

> The typical call centre operator is young, female and works in a large, open plan office or fabricated building. . . . Although probably full-time, she is increasingly likely to be a part-time permanent employee, working complex shift patterns which correspond to the peaks of customer demand. . . . In all probability, work consists of an uninterrupted and endless sequence of similar conversations with customers she never meets. She has to concentrate hard on what is being said, jump from page to page on a screen, making sure that the

(Continued)

(Continued)

details entered are accurate and that she has said the right things in a pleasant manner. The conversation ends and as she tidies up the loose ends there is another voice in her headset. The pressure is intense because she knows her work is being measured, her speech monitored, and it often leaves her mentally, physically, and emotionally exhausted. (p. 115)

Discussion Questions

1. Have you ever worked in a call center? What was your experience of the work? How did it make you feel?

2. What are your experiences of calling a customer service center? Have you ever become angry with a customer service person? Why?

3. In 2014, Comcast got a lot of bad press when a recording of an interaction between a customer and service representative became public. Listen to the audio at the following link: https://www.youtube.com/watch?v=yYUvpYE99vg. What is your reaction? Why do you think the service representative acted the way he did?

Globalization and Politics

The politics of globalization has also been a significant point of debate among commentators (Banerjee, 2008; Beck, 2000; Giddens, 2001; Robertson, 1990; Waters, 2001). Much of this debate has revolved around the relationship between globalization processes and the nation-state. Put simply, a nation-state "possesses external, fixed, known, demarcated borders, and possesses an internal uniformity of rule" (Cochrane & Pain, 2007, p. 6). The nation-state has been a defining feature of modernity, providing stable political institutions and systems of government around the world, as well as functioning as a mediating mechanism between the individual and capitalist organizations. For example, it is at the level of the nation-state that, particularly in the first half of the 20th century, restrictions were placed on the more exploitive aspects of capitalism (e.g., by passing labor laws), worker unions were legalized, and a welfare system was put in place.

However, as sociologist Ulrich Beck (2000) and others have pointed out, the nation-state is a geographic, territorial state, while globalization is a deterritorializing process that transcends national borders. Thus, according to some, globalization undermines the importance of the nation-state because it is based on a multiplicity of communication networks, lifestyles, and financial systems, none of which are tied to a particular place. Given this, it is argued that TNCs have become more powerful global actors than nation-states. As Beck (2000) states, the globalization process has local political implications because it "permits employers and their associations to disentangle and recapture their power to act that was restrained by the political and welfare institutions of democratically organized capitalism" (p. 2). An example of the local implications of globalization is the plight of small farmers: As their profits are squeezed by corporate farming operations with better supply chains for seeds, fertilizer, pesticides, and water (as well as for selling their harvest), along with more efficient access to transnational markets, small independent farmers have become dejected, committing suicide in the United States at a rate five times higher than the general population (it's the occupation with the highest suicide rate—see W. L. McIntosh et al., 2016), and it's also bad in developing countries like India (Merriott, 2016; Pal, 2016).

Beck, then, sees dangers to democracy in the power that TNCs gain through globalization. Indeed, he goes even further, claiming that as the role of the nation-state declines and as corporations abdicate their role as citizens and "national champions" (El-Ojeili & Hayden, 2006, p. 64) for their home countries, they become "virtual taxpayers," paying a lower and lower percentage of the tax burden while simultaneously laying off more workers and demanding more and more perks from the countries in which they are located. Beck (2000) thus describes globalization as "capitalism without work plus capitalism without taxes" (p. 5). Certainly, Figure 13.2 below supports his position, showing the steadily declining share of U.S. federal tax revenue paid by corporations; in 2016, corporate income taxes made up only 9% of the U.S. Federal budget.

Anthony Giddens (2001) takes a somewhat different position from that of Beck, arguing that nation-states and the institutions that make them up "have become inadequate to the tasks they are called upon to perform" (p. 19). In this sense, they are "shell institutions" (p. 19). For Giddens, globalization provides opportunities for increasing levels of democracy around the world, fueled by developments in communication that compress the world and make it increasingly difficult for authoritarian governments to hide information from their citizens. Moreover, as the power of the nation-state weakens in the face of globalization, the demand for rights and autonomy of local cultures increases. Thus, Giddens argues that although globalization may threaten local cultures, this very threat "is the reason for the revival of local cultural identities in different parts of the world" (p. 13).

One of the outcomes of this revival of local cultural identities is the emergence of various forms of organizing against globalization. Below we look at a couple of examples of the forms this organizing has taken.

❖ ORGANIZING AGAINST GLOBALIZATION

Researchers who study political resistance to globalization—and recall that "political" here is the politics of everyday life, not Republicans and Democrats—examine collective responses to some of the effects of globalization around the world. Organizational communication scholars Shiv Ganesh, Heather Zoller, and George Cheney (2005) argue that it is critical to examine resistance "from the point of view of movements that work to resist and transform ideologies, practices, and institutions that support and constitute neoliberalism" (p. 170).

As Ganesh et al. (2005) indicate, this resistance is sometimes referred to as globalization from below (Ganesh et al., 2005). In other words, where globalization is often

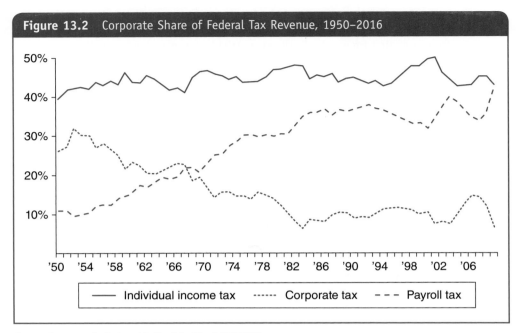

Figure 13.2   Corporate Share of Federal Tax Revenue, 1950–2016

Source: Center on Budget and Policy Priorities | CBPP.ORG

framed as various forms of imperialism from above in which TNCs are turning the world into one global marketplace, the globalization from below movement is conceived as a grassroots effort to resist these imperialist tendencies and provide possibilities for more democratic forms of life. In particular, globalization from below argues that the power of TNCs is undemocratic because it is not subject to the governance of nation-states or to popular will. In this sense, social movements against globalization are just as much opposed to the neoliberal economic policies we talked about earlier as they are to specific corporations (although corporations, as the beneficiaries and practitioners of neoliberalism, are frequently the target of anti-globalization protesters). Ganesh et al. (2005) thus argue that globalization from below involves "collective resistance efforts that aim for the transformation of power relations in the global economy" (p. 172). Here, transformation refers to the ability to "effect large-scale, collective changes in the domains of state policy, corporate practice, social structure, cultural norms, and daily lived experience" (p. 172).

A relatively recent example of collective efforts to resist the process of globalization is the Occupy movement, which began as an occupation of Wall Street to protest the unregulated excesses of financial capitalism that created the 2008 financial meltdown. The movement's protests, which quickly spread across the globe, focused on how, over the past 30 years, the forces of globalization have allowed the richest 1% of the population to increase its wealth by around 240%, while the income of the remaining 99% has stagnated (see Figure 13.1).

An alternative approach is less about overt resistance and instead seeks to capitalize on the market power of those typically seen as the victims of globalization. In the **Bottom of the Pyramid (BoP)** program developed by management scholar C. K. Prahalad (2006), the global poor, particularly those in underdeveloped nations, are understood not as passive recipients of wealthy countries' aid but as "resilient entrepreneurs and value conscious consumers" (p. 3). The claim of the BoP stance is that sustainable poverty alleviation can happen only when the poor are active participants in constructing new enterprises. One outcome of the BoP program is the development of microfinance organizations such as the Grameen Bank in Bangladesh (Papa, Auwal, & Singhal, 1995), which issues small loans with low interest rates to local entrepreneurs to aid in developing new businesses. Grameen Bank and its founder, Muhammad Yunus, have received great acclaim (including a Nobel Peace Prize) for their very promising work but have also received strong criticism because of the sometimes crushing debt assumed by the poor (also, in some versions of Islam, assuming debt is forbidden) and because forcing the poor in developing countries to become entrepreneurial can participate in the erasing of cultural differences mentioned above. In other words, assuming that Western-style business is the only way out of poverty frames the global poor as deficient and unenlightened and suggests that if they only learn Western ways, their problems will be overcome (Banerjee & Jackson, 2017; Chatterjee, 2016). And perhaps most importantly, the impact on BoP programs on poverty reduction has been limited at best.

iStock.com/tschuma417

The "microfinance" movement is an example of a Bottom of the Pyramid program.

A very different kind of resistance to globalization—one rooted in consumption practices—is the phenomenon known as **culture jamming** (Klein, 2001, 2005). Associated with the Canadian group Adbusters (which initiated the occupy movement), culture jamming is an effort to use the advertisements, billboards, and branding techniques of corporations against the corporations themselves by reworking their meaning. On its website, Adbusters describes itself as "a global network of culture jammers and creatives working to change the way information flows, the way corporations wield power, and the way meaning is produced in our society" (http://www.adbusters.org/abtv/occupy-wall-st-vs-fox-news.html).

Journalist Naomi Klein (2005) reiterates this sentiment, stating that "culture jamming baldly rejects the idea that marketing—because it buys its way into public spaces—must be passively accepted as a one-way information flow" (p. 438). Thus, the idea behind culture jamming is to seize back public space that has been colonized by advertising. Indeed, culture jammers describe what they do as a kind of semiotic jujitsu. Jujitsu is a Japanese martial art that uses the opponent's momentum to defeat him or her. Similarly, culture jammers use the power of corporate advertising against the corporations, creating new meanings that subvert the intended meanings. It's in this sense that they reverse the one-way flow of information from corporation to consumer, creating ads that enable consumers to critique corporations.

Numerous examples of culture jamming can be viewed at www.adbusters.org, but some of the more interesting ones include parodies of the "Joe Camel" ads, which show "Joe Chemo" in various settings, including in a hospital bed, hooked up to an IV machine, and so forth; a Marlboro billboard ad featuring two cowboys, with one saying to the other, "I miss my lung, Bob"; an American flag with the stars replaced by corporate logos; and hundreds of New York City taxicab rooftop ads selling "Virginia *Slime*" cigarettes. As Klein (2005) indicates, these ads don't just spoof the real ones; rather, they are "interceptions—counter-messages that hack into a corporation's own method of communication to send a message starkly at odds with the one that was intended" (p. 438).

⬡ GLOBALIZATION AND CORPORATE SOCIAL RESPONSIBILITY

In 1991, as an undergraduate student, Tim had an internship in the training and development arm of a very large agricultural company headquartered not far from the campus at the University of Minnesota. His main task was to aid one of the experienced trainers in developing a business ethics training program. As part of the preparation of the curriculum, Tim interviewed employees of this company all over the globe, asking them about the challenges of defining socially responsible behavior in settings that differed so dramatically from one another. Curious about these challenges, and doubting whether a training program could ever address the diverse concerns they encountered, Tim started asking his professors about how to proceed. As someone majoring in communication and management, he figured that his management courses in the business school would be the logical place to find insights on these issues. It turned out to be futile: The professors he asked largely repeated Milton Friedman's (1970) line about maximizing shareholder returns within the constraints of local laws. His communication professors, in contrast, were more interested in thinking about globalized corporate power, norms that could guide business activity across contexts, and the difficulty of training people to act in ways that might run counter to their workplace responsibilities. It showed, even back then, that CSR issues were understood by communication scholars as inherently communicative issues because they're centrally about how power and control are used to organize the social world. The communication scholars encouraged him to ask about the fundamental distinction under-lying the project; as management scholar John Roberts (2003) puts it, "What needs to be understood is how business and ethics got separated in the first place; how, in our minds, they became separate orders" (p. 250).

In the world before globalization, countries' governments were responsible for creating working markets, protecting property rights, and limiting the effects of business on others (e.g., reducing pollution). In this environment, Milton Friedman's (1970) argument, men-tioned above, made sense: The only social responsibilities of business are to maximize returns (i.e., profits) for shareholders and to follow the laws where the company is doing business. With the rise of globalization, those responsibilities have changed. Companies can shift operations and their bank accounts to other countries at will, reducing the legal power of governments over their operations. And the negative consequences of organiza-tional misconduct span boundaries too, as we've seen in recent cases of environmental disasters, health scares, and financial scandals. There is a recognition, in other words, that multinational corporations (MNCs) can fairly easily pursue profits across different coun-tries and that civil societies and nation states are fairly limited in their abilities to regulate those MNCs. And, since international governing bodies such as the United Nations and the World Bank have little formal authority over corporations' actions, the past several decades have seen calls for the development of norms—social expectations for proper behavior rather than laws enforced by government authorities—to which the world could hold corporations accountable (Scherer & Palazzo, 2011). These sets of norms, and the mechanisms to shape companies' behavior to align with them, are attempts to shape cor-porate behavior in ways nations can't.

This is **corporate social responsibility (CSR)** and seen from the perspective of a given organization, it is "the integration of an enterprise's social, environmental, ethical, and philanthropic responsibilities toward society into its operations, processes and core busi-ness strategy in cooperation with relevant stakeholders" (Rasche, Morsing, & Moon, 2017, p. 6). From the perspective of the broader society, CSR is an alternative (and pragmatic) way to regulate the conduct of private companies in a globalized economy. And for some scholars, CSR offers a way to encourage corporations to fill the gaps national governments can no longer play under globalization because it can "turn corporations into providers of public goods in cases where public authorities are unable or unwilling to fulfil this role" (Scherer, Rasche, Palazzo, & Spicer, 2016, p. 3). This corporate substitution for government can occur when companies join cross-sector partnerships to address pressing social prob-lems such as public transportation, education, poverty, and disease (Koschmann, Kuhn, & Pfarrer, 2012). A similar function can also occur when companies use their financial weight to advocate for (or against) particular causes, as when several corporations, includ-ing professional and collegiate sports associations and the CEOs of over 80 of the country's largest companies, threatened to pull operations out of the state of North Carolina after it passed what they saw as a discriminatory "bathroom bill" targeting LGBT persons in 2016 (Surowiecki, 2016).

Forms of CSR

What, then, does CSR look like? We'd suggest it takes several forms, and we underscore that because we're talking about norms rather than laws, each of these is a voluntary activity. First are corporate greening initiatives, which include companies' efforts to develop more environmentally friendly products and pledging to avoid causing environmental catastrophes like oil spills. Second, it can include social accounting, such as a model called the triple bottom line, which encourages companies to measure the costs and benefits of their activities in the pursuit of not merely economic outcomes but social and environmental interests as well (and which is advocated by international nongovernmental organizations such as the Global Reporting Initiative and the Organization for Economic Cooperation and Development). A third is the presentation of CSR ratings: evaluations and recognition by independent civic organizations, the business press, and consulting firms that assess companies on some criteria for ethical behavior.

The critical stance on communication running throughout this book should lead us to be suspicious about each of these (see Kuhn & Deetz, 2008). For instance, green initiatives are just as likely to be instances of greenwashing, one-off and insincere public relations efforts to make a corporation's routine operations look virtuous to an inattentive public—as well to its own employees, who tend to identify more strongly and express more satisfaction with responsible firms (Kim, Lee, Lee & Kim, 2010). Social accounting, critical theorists argue, tends to commodify CSR, making it into an object that can be purchased by companies willing to commit resources to it, ultimately turning CSR into yet another managerial tool (Shamir, 2005). Critics also assert that social accounting does little to alter a firm's profit-generating activities because decision-making processes are biased against CSR: People advocating for social accounting within corporations, like ethics officers, tend to be ignored when real decisions are made, especially if decision makers are insulated from the effects of their actions (Jackall, 1988; Kuhn, 2009). In other words, if social accounting only matters when the company's public image or its profitability are at issue, the only real influence it has is as a support for traditional financial performance. And by focusing attention on CSR awards, we run the risk of giving winners a pass when it comes to unethical practices. Moreover, we should also examine the bodies giving these awards because they are frequently granted by groups that "are established in order to disseminate and actualize corporate-inspired versions of 'social responsibility' while enjoying the aura of disinterestedness often bestowed upon 'civil society' entities" (Shamir, 2004, pp. 680–681). As you can probably tell, each of these critiques of CSR is about how power enter into communication processes. And because they're voluntary rather than legally required, they can be more likely eliminated when companies face economically tough times.

CRITICAL RESEARCH 13.1

Patrick Haack, Dennis Schoeneborn, & Christopher Wickert (2012). Talking the talk, moral entrapment, creeping commitment?: Exploring narrative dynamics in corporate responsibility standardization. *Organization Studies*, *33*, 815–845.

If, as mentioned above, globalization means that civil society develops norms to shape corporate behavior, it would make organizational activity very difficult if there were as many norms as there were business contexts. Haack, Schoeneborn, and Wickert wondered how standards for those norms develop. In other words, they asked how standards for desirable behavior spread across locations and over time and how those get incorporated into organizations' routine activity.

In a case study of the *Equator Principles*, a CSR standard in the field of international project finance, Haack et al. found the answer in the development of narratives. Aligning with what we've been arguing in this book, they see a narrative approach as "consider[ing] the possibility that the use of language does not merely reflect or transmit the material aspects of [CSR] standards but that language is constitutive of social reality" (p. 820). What this perspective means is that, as people engage in routine communication, they can develop a narrative (or set of narratives) that indicates what should be done, by whom, and for which purposes. Narratives, then, are not separate from the work being done—they are built in to the work and, at the same time, exercise authority over the work.

International project finance is a tremendously complicated realm, one that involves investments from financial institutions, located in many countries, in large public infrastructure projects like the construction of power plants, bridges, mines, and roadways around the world. As you might imagine, some of those projects attract activist protests, meaning that community and environmentally oriented NGOs (nongovernmental organizations) have an interest in shaping these projects. Haack et al. describe how, in the early 2000s, several NGOs came together to target the activities of a few large investment banks; the banks created the Equator Principles in response to the NGOs' challenge (which was also a move intended to protect their reputations).

Interviewing representatives from both banks and NGOs, and complementing these interviews with documents about the Equator Principles, Haack et al. located three distinct types of narrative. The first was a success narrative, which was employed mostly within banks and which portrayed the Equator Principles as a rational means of preventing project finance activities from damaging communities and the environment. These stories described how the Equator Principles were adopted by banks, made a business case for their ongoing use (framed them as ensuring a good return on investment), and saw the necessity for all banks to follow the same rules. Second was a failure narrative, which portrayed the Equator Principles as easy agreements for banks but because the principles

(Continued)

(Continued)

lacked enforcement mechanisms, they were also easy for banks to evade, often by releasing misleading information about a given project (Haack et al. call this sort of story greenwashing, as we did above). The message of failure stories is that evading responsibility means that banks' power cannot be challenged, and the community and environmental problems that led to the Equator Principles' development will be worsened. Finally, a commitment narrative is forward-looking, portraying banks who sign on to the principles as intending to make sustainability a key part of their operations, always in the future tense (and for some, these future developments were made more likely because the Equator Principles gave internal activists something to use in agitating for change.

Over the 6 years of this project, the failure narrative became more and more excluded, while the success narrative became more commitment oriented in the later years of the study. Interestingly, much of this effect is the result of NGOs' positive assessment of banks' actions: "The narrative shift in the discourse of financial institutions is accompanied by fading criticism, even praise for exemplary banks, by moderate NGOs" (p. 833). The authors concluded that the Equator Principles were relatively easy targets for banks in the early days, and the widespread adoption made the principles seem morally valid. And though at first the principles got more lip service than NGOs desired, banks learned to walk the talk over time.

Discussion Questions

1. As Haack et al. note, it was mostly moderate NGOs that found banks' actions adequate by the end of the 6-year study. How might a more militant NGO use the notion of narrative to advocate for more radical change? How could it ensure that alternative narratives gain traction?

2. Consider the narratives (regarding what should be done, by whom, and for which purposes) characterizing your work at the university. Is there a narrative you and the other students in this class can identify for the typical group or team projects in your courses? Have those differed across your years in college? Do they differ when group members come from different backgrounds (major, socioeconomic class, etc.)?

CSR as Communication

Our presentation of CSR thus far portrays it as a set of activities that corporations can either embrace or reject (and many suspect that a corporation's embrace is usually pretty phony—a way to distract critics from business as usual). But maybe it's more complicated than that. Of course, Milton Friedman (1970) would have suggested that all those types of CSR activities should be rejected because they're not in the immediate interests of the shareholders. However, some scholars following the same line see CSR as rational (in terms of the shareholders' financial interests) because it allows the company to create partnerships that will help the company in the long run. This sort of stance only deepens critics' cynicism: They see corporations as basically uninterested in doing the right thing, interested only in exploiting new ways to improve their ability to make profits.

Some research, however, suggests that if we understand communication as a struggle over meanings that constitute organizations, cynicism need not be the only stance we take on CSR (Kuhn & Deetz, 2008). One line of this work suggests that CSR talk within organizations can be aspirational, as was seen in Haack et al.'s (2012) commitment narrative: That while most CSR activities may be little more than window dressing now, making public pronouncements can be a form of **auto-communication** where the company communicates with itself about its commitment to a virtuous future identity—and that identity eventually gets performed into existence (Christensen, Morsing, & Thyssen, 2013; Schultz, Castelló, & Morsing, 2013). An alternative move is to see CSR as a dialogue across the corporate boundary with those most vulnerable to the effects of corporate conduct (Roberts, 2003). CSR, then, involves participation on the part of a multiple stakeholders (where a stakeholder is any group that has a stake, or an interest, in the actions of an organization, such as employees, communities, shareholders, governments, and so on).

One of the clearest depictions of how CSR dialogues can operate is Deetz's **stakeholder model** (Deetz, 1995; Deetz & Brown, 2004). Deetz's model starts by taking an explicitly political turn, recognizing that the framing of organizational and corporate life in largely economic terms severely limits our understanding of the ways corporations affect people's lives at an everyday level. Deetz's stakeholder model is thus an effort to rethink the role of the modern corporation in society. He expands the definition of the corporation to include not merely the interests of shareholders, but a wider array of stakeholders with wider outcome interests. Deetz (1992) argues that corporations are always political actors (again in terms of the politics of everyday life), which typically shape perceptions and interests through the money code—that is, as thinking about all stakeholders in terms of how they affect the bottom line—they frame every stakeholder group in economic terms. Taking an alternative tack, Deetz argues that "If modern corporations are political bodies that make significant decisions for the public, we must consider how they relate to the various groups that they affect and how, if at all, these groups are represented in decision making" (p. 43). Such a perspective is directly opposed to Milton Friedman's (1970) position, discussed earlier, that a corporation's only role is to make a profit for its shareholders.

Deetz (1995) argues that if we reframe the role of corporations in society, they can be seen as "positive social institutions providing a forum for the articulation and resolution of important social conflicts regarding the use of natural resources, the production of meaningful goods and services, and the development of individuals" (p. 36). But corporations won't become those positive social institutions if their interactions with stakeholders are seen as opportunities for each side to simply share its perspective about the topic at hand. Deetz argues that a far more radical rethinking is needed, one in which the various stakeholder groups (listed below) are seen as internal (rather than external) to the corporate system. This rethinking means that stakeholder interests are seen not as limits to the corporation but as part of its very existence and its goals. In this context, the development of strong dialogues—real, authentic conversations—positions managers as coordinators of conflicting stakeholder interests rather than controllers of organizational goals that stakeholders must adapt to or oppose. Thus, each stakeholder makes an important claim on the organization, in that each invests in and is affected by corporate decisions.

As you can see from Deetz's stakeholder model, depicted in Figure 13.3, the corporation is reconceived as a set of stakeholder groups whose conflicting interests are coordinated by a managing process, thus producing a set of potential outcomes that are much broader than the usual goods, services, and profits. According to Deetz (1995), these various outcomes can serve as an expanded measure of corporate success. In terms of the various stakeholders,

- *consumers* have an interest in companies producing needed quality goods and services at a fair price, as well as an expectation that these goods and services are produced using ethical, non-exploitive practices;

- *workers* desire a fair wage and safe working conditions, work that is meaningful, the chance to participate in organizational decision making, and a balance between work and private life;

- *investors* have a stake in a reasonable return on their investment and an expectation that corporations are ethically stewarding their investments;

- *suppliers* have an interest in a stable demand for their resources at a reasonable price;

- *host communities* have a stake in a strong quality of life, including fair taxation, creation of jobs, responsible integration of the company into the life of the community rather than destruction of public resources, and so forth;

- the *general society* has a vested interest in equitable treatment of its citizens, economic stability, the development of civility among its citizens, maintaining high-quality life, and so on; and

- the *world ecological community* has a stake in the extent to which corporate decision making has a global impact, particularly with regard to its effect on environments, global climate, and vulnerable communities.

For example, under this stakeholder model corporations would not exclusively determine income distribution. Rather, it would be determined through a process of deliberation and codetermination among various stakeholders. Given that CEOs of large corporations earn around 361 times what the average worker earns—$13.94 million to $38,613—and that many executives receive multimillion-dollar bonus packages even when their companies underperform or even fail (https://aflcio.org/paywatch), it is clear that the current unilateral decision-making model of managerial control is ineffective and counterproductive.

Deetz's stakeholder model can be understood as a form of CSR, outlined above. As suggested there, CSR communication is often understood as a corporation's efforts to display—to convey to audiences—its virtue to important decision makers (particularly consumers and government regulators), but there are other ways to imagine it. As Roberts (2003) notes, "There is a need, if there is serious corporate intent, for face-to-face dialogue

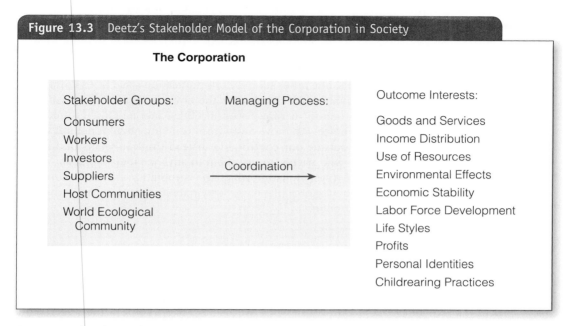

Figure 13.3 Deetz's Stakeholder Model of the Corporation in Society

The Corporation

Stakeholder Groups:	Managing Process:	Outcome Interests:
Consumers		Goods and Services
Workers		Income Distribution
Investors		Use of Resources
Suppliers	Coordination ⟶	Environmental Effects
Host Communities		Economic Stability
World Ecological		Labor Force Development
Community		Life Styles
		Profits
		Personal Identities
		Childrearing Practices

Source: **Deetz** (1995). *Transforming communication, transforming business: Building responsive and responsible workplaces.* Cresskill, NJ: Hampton Press.

with those different actors who are themselves most vulnerable to corporate conduct" (p. 264). CSR communication, then might take the form of dialogue with stakeholders, rather than speaking to them. Dialogue as a form of CSR, as imagined by Deetz and others, is a way for those in corporations (as well as other organizations) to not only understand the impacts of their actions on others but to construct alternative approaches alongside those affected groups (e.g., Barge & Little, 2002; Forester, 1999; Heath, 2007).

We should be cautious, however, about seeing dialogue as a simple remedy for a complex set of problems. As management scholar Bobby Banerjee (2018) notes in an analysis of dialogues in extraction industries (i.e., oil and gas) operating in developing countries, the interests of community groups are often fundamentally opposed to those of extraction companies, and dialogue (seen as finding agreement in deliberation) often masks corporate domination, particularly when corporations use the fact that they're engaging in CSR to get national governments on their side. Very much in line with Deetz, Banerjee argues for the need to think of CSR as a way to integrate leaders from local communities with finance and engineering specialists from corporations in an effort to "envisage organizations that are built on the basis of a nexus of relationships . . . relationships that are informed by reciprocity, cooperation, and an enduring commitment to land and community welfare" (Banerjee, 2018, p. 815). It was these sorts of consequential (and power-infused) communication practices that fascinated Tim's communication professors in 1991; in the ensuing decades, some management scholars have begun to ask similar questions.

A model like this one is clearly ambitious and utopian since it asks us to rethink completely the role of the corporation in contemporary society. But then, many ideas once considered utopian have come to pass, including democracy itself. If nothing else, it gets us to think in new ways about how we have multiple stakes in the way corporations function—not just as employees and consumers.

In addition to these concerns, one other serious communication issue faces CSR thinking. Across almost all CSR thinking is a concern for the environment. It's interesting to note, however, that the term "nature" is rarely seen in CSR. Banerjee (2003) thinks this selection of words reflects a choice: We move away from thinking about a natural world that existed before us and is outside our control and instead think in terms of a set of resources available to anyone who wishes to use them to advance their interests. When we think of the environment as a system within which the corporation exists, the concern, Banerjee says, becomes less about global planetary sustainability than with using the surroundings to sustain the corporation.

⚘ CONCLUSION

In this chapter, we have discussed the phenomenon of globalization, examining its relationships with the economic and political spheres, as well as some of the ways the globalization process has created gendered effects on work. We also examined some of the research on CSR, exploring some of the ways in which corporations have tried to position themselves as better citizens in a globalizing world in which they are having significant impact. If it is indeed true that neoliberal economic policies and processes of globalization have created more powerful corporations while at the same time weakening the role of national governments in people's lives, then it is important that we can understand, evaluate, and critique this expanding role of the corporation.

Anthony Giddens (2001) has argued that democracy is like a three-legged stool, with the government, corporations, and civil society (which includes family, education, the media, religion, public debate, etc.) each representing a leg. If one of those legs is broken, the stool isn't functional. In some ways we live in a period when the corporation wields more power than any institution ever has. It has colonized every aspect of our lives in ways that are in many ways detrimental to who we are as people, citizens, family members, and so forth. Perhaps it is time for us to make efforts—large and small—to regain our sense of self from the ever-expanding influence of the corporation.

Speaking of selves, in the final chapter we will address how work and organizations have a profound impact—both positive and negative—on our sense of identity. We will address the question, "How do we find meaning in the context of work and organizational life?"

CRITICAL APPLICATIONS

1. Visit the Slavery Footprint website at http://slaveryfootprint.org/. Take the survey on your slavery footprint and have a discussion about the ways we are connected in invisible ways to abusive labor practices around the world.

2. Read the story "Have We Had Our Fill of Water" on bottled water at the following link: www
.guardian.co.uk/society/2011/jul/22/had-our-fill-of-water. How does it influence your view of
bottled water consumption? What does this say about the relationship between the upper and
lower circuits of capital that Saskia Sassen talks about?

3. Find CSR statements of the corporations you're familiar with, interested in, or concerned
about (since we mentioned McDonald's above, its statements can be found at https://
corporate.mcdonalds.com/corpmcd.html). Compare what you find with other students in
class: What do these statements have in common, and what are the sources of differences?
Seeing the entire set of statements, are the concerns about greenwashing, social accounting
and corporate decision making, and CSR awards legitimate?

KEY TERMS

auto-communication   351

Bottom of the Pyramid
(BoP)   345

corporate social
responsibility (CSR)   347

CSR ratings   348

culture jamming   346

Deetz's stakeholder
model   351

deterritorializing   342

global cities   338

globalization   333

globalization from
below   343

greening initiatives   348

greenwashing   348

neoliberalism   335

social accounting   348

STUDENT STUDY SITE

Visit the student study site at www.sagepub.com/mumby.org for these additional learning tools:

- Web quizzes
- eFlashcards
- SAGE journal articles

- Video resources
- Web resources

CHAPTER 14

Communication, Meaningful Work, and Personal Identity

Our relationship to work shapes our identities as well as our sense of how meaningful our lives are.

We suspect that everyone reading this book has had the experience of meeting someone new and being asked the question "What do you do?" Of course, we all understand that the appropriate answer to this question is never "I read novels, hang out in coffee shops, and go running every day." Instead, we know that the person asking the question wants to know how we are employed; in other words, what do we do to earn a living? From your answer, the other person can deduce a whole host of other information about you, including likely social class, education level, and political leaning. A similar case holds for college students who meet each other for the first time: One of the first questions is usually "What's your major?" Followed closely by "And what are you going to do with that major?" The real interest is in figuring out what the person's career trajectory will be.

That these questions generally come pretty early in the conversation on first meeting someone provides a strong indication of the degree to which our identities—our senses of who we are as valued people—are closely tied to how we earn a living. It's also interesting that we all feel compelled to ask this question of people we meet; it's almost as though we are unable to categorize appropriately and make sense of someone unless we know how he or she is employed. As management professors, Blake Ashforth and Glen Kreiner

357

(1999) state, "Job titles serve as prominent identity badges" (p. 417). And there is plenty of evidence to suggest that work has an increasing grip over how we define our lives and our sense of selves. As philosopher Alain de Botton has stated, "All societies have had work at their centre; ours is the first to suggest that it could be something much more than a punishment or a penance" (de Botton, 2009, p. 106).

From a 21st-century perspective, it's hard for us to comprehend that work—or at least the kind of employment most of us experience—was not always closely tied to our sense of identity and the leading of a meaningful life. Indeed, one might argue that it was only with the emergence of the industrial age that such connections were made. Max Weber (1958), in his famous book *The Protestant Ethic and the Spirit of Capitalism*, argued that the capitalist economic system was undergirded by religious principles that made the pursuit of profit a calling that defined people's relationships to God. As Joanne Ciulla (2000) argues,

> The Protestants endowed work with the quest for meaning, identity, and signs of salvation. The notion of work as something beyond mere labor . . . indeed as a calling, highlighted its personal and existential qualities. Work became a kind of prayer. More than a means of living, it became a purpose for living. (pp. 52–53)

For the most part, this is the conception of work that remains with us. What we do for a living heavily shapes our sense of self, and thus, we want to do something that is fulfilling and feeds our perception of self-worth. From a young age we've been asked "What do you want to be when you grow up?" with a career, or job, as the desired response. Former Beatle John Lennon is reputed to have said, "When I went to school, they asked me what I wanted to be when I grew up. I wrote down 'happy'. They told me I didn't understand the assignment, and I told them they didn't understand life." If the Protestants were right about the need for work to be part of a calling, a purpose for living, it is an article of faith for us that we need to be engaged in meaningful work.

In the next section, we work through a definition of meaningful work. But we'd like to pause and acknowledge what this chapter hopes to accomplish. As the final chapter of a book advocating that we need to understand the theory and practice of working and organizing as always bound up with communicative processes of power and control, we hope that this chapter does two things for you. First, it should provide a vision of how we see the self in relation to work. In a sense, investigating the history of the individual–organization relationship is at the core of the critical communication project guiding this book, so the theory we present here will draw together several themes from the preceding chapters. And second, because you have no doubt been thinking, as you've read this book, about the choices facing you regarding the work you'll pursue after college—and because, as we've said, work is such a central part of our lives—we hope to provide a few resources to assess the significance, the meaningfulness, of that work.

❧ MEANINGFUL WORK

How, then, might we define meaningful work? One answer might be that such a thing is in the eye of the beholder—if work is meaningful to the person who is doing it, then, by definition, it is meaningful. However, it is perhaps possible to identify some general principles that apply broadly to work. After all, while meaningful work may not necessarily have any objective features, there are nevertheless social norms that define different kinds of work in different ways. Such norms are communicatively constructed; in other words, we can think of meaningful work as symbolically created by individuals and groups as well as by larger societal discourses that circulate through society in various media (Cheney, Zorn, Planalp, & Lair, 2008).

What, then, are some of the features of meaningful work that we can identify? Cheney et al. (2008—see also Bowie, 1998) suggest the following criteria that, while by no means exhaustive, provide a starting point for our discussion.

Enables a Sense of Agency

People experience work as meaningful to the extent that they have agency, or choice-making control, over the way their work is conducted. Using this first criterion, working on a production line would be less meaningful than, for example, working as a doctor. On a production line, machines dictate the tasks performed and the worker simply functions as an appendage to the machines. Like Charlie Chaplin's character in *Modern Times*, such work can lead to alienation because, as we saw in Chapter 3, the mind is disengaged from both the work itself and the worker's own body; the two function largely independently. On the other hand, when people experience a high degree of agency in their work, their sense of self is confirmed and they feel directly connected to the work being performed; mind and body tend to work as one.

However, we should be careful not to equate professional, white-collar work with agency (again, defined as a sense of self-determination) and blue-collar, manual labor with lacking such agency. Much white-collar work can be profoundly alienating and lacking in agency, while blue-collar work can provide significant experience of control and integration of mind and body. For example, the classic "pencil pusher" who spends all day completing forms and the data processor who mindlessly inputs numbers into a computer would probably not consider himself or herself as having much agency, while a skilled craftsperson who produces his or her own work would no doubt describe himself or herself as having considerable agency.

Indeed, in the past few years, there has been a renewed interest in the kind of work traditionally regarded as blue collar, especially that in which skilled workers grapple with difficult and complex problems. Writer Matthew Crawford, mentioned in Chapter 3, notes current media fascination with shows such as *The Deadliest Catch*, *Ice Road Truckers*, *Dirty Jobs*, and so on, all of which depict dangerous and grueling blue-collar work. He argues that such fascination stems in part from the fact that most of us occupy boring white-collar jobs in which we rarely see any tangible product of our labors and that, by comparison, the work on these shows seems downright exotic (Crawford, 2009a, 2009b). In referring to work that most Americans do, Crawford (2009b) asks the rhetorical question "What exactly have you accomplished at the end of any given day?" (p. 1). He suggests that shows such as *The Office* and movies such as *Office Space* ("We need to talk about your TPS reports") "attest to the dark absurdism with which many Americans have come to view their white-collar jobs" (p. 1).

Crawford argues that "the useful arts" (car mechanic, plumber, electrician, etc.) have been wrongly stigmatized as a career path and that most 18-year-olds are scared (by parents, counselors, friends) into believing that a prestigious college is the only path to career success. Trades suffer from low prestige, he says, because "dirty jobs" have been equated with stupidity and lack of education. However, speaking as the owner of a motorcycle repair shop, he makes a case for working with your hands, engaging directly with a material world problem that can be solved only by utilizing hands and brain together. Moreover, he argues that there is economic security in such jobs because they can't be outsourced, unlike many white-collar jobs (car repair can't be done over the Internet or by phone via a call center located in India).

Philosopher de Botton (2009) nicely captures what it means to exercise this kind of agency over one's work:

> How different everything is for the craftsman who transforms a part of the world with his own hands, who can see his work as emanating from his being and can step back at the end of a day or lifetime and point to an object . . . and see it as a stable repository of his skills and an accurate record of his years, and hence feel collected together in one place, rather than strung out across projects which long ago evaporated into nothing one could hold or see. (p. 182)

Furthermore, a sense of agency in one's work is tied to the distinction between clock time and task time that we discussed in Chapter 1. The more one's work is dictated by clock time, the less sense of agency one experiences. Indeed, the extent to which one is considered to be a professional (along with the autonomy that comes with that status) is determined in part by adherence to a task rather than to the clock. Thus, a surgeon would not quit an operation in the middle because her or his shift was over. As Ciulla (2000) states, "The defining moral aspect of what it means to be a professional is dedication to the task, not the clock" (p. 181).

Enhances Belonging or Relationships

A second characteristic of meaningful work is that it enhances our sense of connection to others. For the most part, work is not simply about the execution of tasks but also about developing relationships with other people in the process of accomplishing those tasks. In this sense, work is very much a communal affair where we gain a sense of identity and connection from our relationships with others. Of course, work varies considerably in this regard. For example, while working on a production line might allow little connection with others during work itself, a sense of connection can be created during breaks, on the company softball team, after work, and so forth. On the other hand, working in a cubicle along with dozens of other fellow employees in a so-called knowledge-intensive work environment can be a soul-destroying experience rather than a way to enhance connections with others.

However, it is also clear that for many people the relationships they develop at work are an important part of their lives. Many companies have recognized this and encourage the development of personal relationships in the workplace. This is a far cry from the old model of the formal, bureaucratic organization where personal connection was frowned on as a distraction from task accomplishment. Thus, even in contexts where the work itself is not intrinsically meaningful, companies spend a great deal of time and money attempting to make workers feel connected to one another and more important, to the company (Fleming, 2007). In this sense (and as we will discuss in more detail), meaningful work is at least in part connected to a sense of identification with what we do or the company for which we work.

Finally, Melissa Gregg's (2011) study of the meaning of work perhaps indicates the future of work relationships and personal connection for many people. She suggests that, for many workers (especially those who change jobs frequently), the main source of connection to others at work is via the Internet (e.g., through Facebook). With increasing amounts of work being conducted virtually and from home, the only stable work community that many people experience is that which exists online via social media. For workers who are free agents in the gig economy, their online communities move with them from job to job, providing a feeling of professional and personal stability.

Creates Opportunities for Influence

Third, work can also be meaningful if we are awarded opportunities to affect the organization for which we work, or to shape particular social issues that are important to us. In cases where we are simply subject to someone else's whims and unable to have an impact on others, chances are we will not find the work we do particularly meaningful or rewarding. If we toil away in jobs we know make little difference to the company or the lives of others, then we are unlikely to feel that our work is meaningful. For example, organizational communication scholar Charles Conrad (1985) describes the case of an employee who worked on an automobile production line and whose job was to monitor engine piston cases and discard those that weren't up to specifications. She was soon admonished for rejecting too many and told that she should not exceed a rejection rate of 1%. So even though she knew that many more did not meet the specifications, she simply rejected every hundredth piston case that passed in front of her on the conveyor belt and used the extra time to compose songs in her head. In other words, she recognized that the act of actually doing her job to the best of her ability had zero influence on her performance; indeed, she actually made her performance seem worse by working diligently. It's hard to imagine anyone feeling that his or her work is meaningful under such circumstances.

In general, opportunities for influence increase with one's rise up the corporate hierarchy. At one extreme, one could make the case that Steve Jobs engaged in incredibly meaningful work because he not only deeply influenced the direction Apple has taken as a company but also profoundly shaped the wider culture and society in which we all live with the production of the iconic Apple devices. However, most of us settle for a much more mundane and smaller sphere of influence in our work. For example, when Dennis was chair of his department, he exerted a stronger influence on the department and university than he had as a regular faculty member. Thus, one of the rewarding things about being in a position of formal authority is the ability to use the resources (economic and political) provided by the position to improve colleagues' quality of life. Of course, such influence also has a downside: you cannot always meet the expectations of those you want to help, and some people think they're getting comparatively less help than others.

Permits Use and Development of Talents

A fourth characteristic of meaningful work refers to the use of our skills in our work. We all want to be in jobs and careers where our talents are put to good use and allowed to flourish. We quickly tire of jobs that are easy to perform and don't really stretch and test us. Crawford, the motorcycle shop owner mentioned above, combined this criterion for meaningful work with the previous: "A good job requires a field of action where you can put your best capacities to work and see an effect in the world" (2009b, p. 10). Perhaps obviously, however, not all capacities are treated the same: As a boy, Tim liked to decorate his family's home and regularly rearrange its furniture; his aptitude for using colors, lighting, and space to create a mood was quickly quashed by family members who let him know that interior designer wasn't going to be an acceptable (read, appropriately masculine) career choice (Dennis was completely unaware of Tim's interior design talents!).

Of course, the nature of the post-Fordist economy we all inhabit means that frequent changing of jobs has become a normal part of the career cycle. Sociologist Richard Sennett (1998, p. 22) claims that the average worker with 2 years of education after high school will change jobs about 11 times during the course of his or her working life. And beyond merely switching jobs, there's evidence that people entering the workforce now will have five or more different careers—distinct occupations, professions, or categories of work—over their working lives (Barrett, 2017). Such a shifting and uncertain work environment does not necessarily lend itself to the kind of progressive skill development that is more typical when the employment landscape is more stable and long term. It suggests that those who can continually reinvent themselves, and who are more flexible with location, rank, and salary, will be more employable. Indeed, under such precarious employment conditions, movement from job to job can be lateral or even downward, rather than consistently upward.

On the other hand, sociologist Richard Florida (2003) has argued that it is precisely this kind of "horizontal hypermobility" (a fancy way of referring to frequent, lateral changing of jobs) that characterizes the creative class of workers (currently, he argues, around 30% of the population), who are much more interested in quality of place (What's there? Who's there? What's going on?) than in specific jobs. As such, identification and long-term employment with a specific organization are much less important than the quality of experiences provided by a particular geographical location.

Offers a Sense of Contribution to a Greater Good

We would all like to think that the work we do contributes to making the world a better place, even if only in a small way. Clearly, this fifth criterion is easier in some professions than in others. Doctors, teachers, nurses, and people in similar professions have a relatively easy time thinking of their work as meaningful in terms of the contributions they make to society. On the other hand (and going to the other extreme), someone who works as an account executive for a tobacco company and whose job is to market cigarettes might have a much harder time making such a case. Such a person may well meet the other criteria we have talked about, but how might he or she claim to be making a contribution to the greater good?

De Botton (2009) gives us some insight into how people in such professions might make sense of the work they do. His interview with the creator and account executive for cookies called Moments reveals the ways he sees himself contributing to a better life for people:

> Laurence had formulated his biscuit [cookie] by gathering some interviewees in a hotel . . . and, over a week, questioning them about their lives, in an attempt to tease out of them certain emotional longings that could subsequently be elaborated into the organising principles behind a new product. . . . [A] number of low-income mothers had spoken of their yearning for sympathy, affection and what Laurence termed simply, with aphoristic brevity, "me-time." The Moment set out to suggest itself as the plausible solution to their predicament.

> While the idea of answering psychological yearnings with dough might seem daunting, Laurence explained that in the hands of an experienced branding expert, decisions about width, shape, coating, packaging and name can furnish a biscuit with a personality as subtly and appropriately nuanced as that of a protagonist in a great novel. (pp. 72–73)

Of course, having read the chapter on branding and consumption, you should not be surprised at the ways something as mundane as a chocolate-covered cookie is invested with strong meanings (and backed by a $5-million development program). And interestingly, de Botton at first expressed disdain for people like Laurence, people spending (perhaps wasting) their limited lives and talents on items at the base of our pyramid of needs, on something so frivolous as constructing cookies' "personality." He accuses the work of exhibiting "a seriousness of means and a triviality of ends" (p. 103) and even says Laurence seems to know his work is meaningless because he seems "intelligent enough to be unable to fully believe in his own claims to significance" (p. 73).

De Botton stated his stance on the question of this section clearly: "When does a job feel meaningful? Whenever it allows us to generate delight or reduce suffering in others" (p. 78). By this measure, Laurence's claim of his work helping provide stressed, low-income moms with me-time could pass. De Botton was still skeptical, and it was only after he took a trip to one of the company's manufacturing plants in a small town in Belgium that he changed his tune. He saw how the work of mass-producing cookies supported an entire community through salaries (which were then spent on houses, clothes, food, and TVs), as well as through taxes that built infrastructure and contributed to government assistance programs. So while we might debate whether the activities of Laurence or workers on the cookie assembly line were using their best talents to full effect (see the preceding criterion), we can see the work as indirectly contributing to the development of the greater good through generating others' delight and reducing their suffering. Critical Research Study 14.1 offers an interesting take on the possibilities for, and consequences of, work that contributes to the greater good.

CRITICAL RESEARCH 14.1

Sarah E. Dempsey & Matthew L. Sanders (2010). Meaningful work? Nonprofit marketization and work/life imbalance in popular autobiographies of social entrepreneurship. *Organization, 17,* 437–459.

In a 2011 tweet, former Facebook director of market development Randi Zuckerberg (founder Mark Zuckerberg's sister) offered advice to entrepreneurs about tough life choices. Building a great company, maintaining friendships, spending time with family, exercising, and sleeping, she suggested, are fundamentally incompatible activities—and an entrepreneur can pick no more than three of these; the others have to go (Stillman, 2016). She later updated that in a bestselling book (of course), suggesting that you can pick a different three every day, though for an entrepreneur, working on the company should always be the top priority (Zuckerberg, 2018).

Many entrepreneurs believe, based on the Protestant work ethic mentioned above, that they have a calling, a spiritual command about their work serving a transcendent moral purpose. Serving the calling then justifies the sacrifices Zuckerberg mentions. This is especially the case for **social entrepreneurship**, which "involves the application of the tenets of capitalist entrepreneurship to nonprofit organizations, with the goal of creating meaningful alternatives to traditional corporate career paths" (Dempsey & Sanders, 2010, p. 438). We often think of working for nonprofit organizations as inherently more meaningful than work for profit-focused private sector firms, but Dempsey and Sanders wanted to understand the personal costs of such work. Therefore, they examined three popular autobiographies written by prominent social entrepreneurs to understand the consequences of being a social entrepreneur building an organization that contributes to the greater good. The books were these:

- *Leaving Microsoft to Change the World*: *An Entrepreneur's Odyssey to Educate the World's Children*, by former Microsoft executive John Wood, who founded the organization Room to Read

- *Three Cups of Tea: One Man's Mission to Promote Peace, One School at a Time*, by Greg Mortensen, who founded the Central Asia Institute

- *One Day, All Children*: *The Unlikely Triumph of Teach for America and What I Learned Along the Way*, by Wendy Kopp, founder of Teach for America

Each was a tremendously popular and influential narrative of founders' experiences in creating a nonprofit organization working on a pressing social problem. Each presented social entrepreneurship as meaningful work that responded to the founder's desire for something more, a desire that led each to have a visceral experience of a social problem of which he or she had been unaware (e.g., Wood's recognition that 450 students in a Nepalese village had no books in their school). These experiences led each to make a life-changing decision, as Kopp detailed while reflecting on what she and other

Princeton students sought: "It did seem that just about every Princeton senior was applying to a two-year corporate training program, most with investment banks and management consulting firms. . . . [Most] couldn't figure out what else to do. I sensed I was not alone—that there were thousands of other seniors like me who were searching for jobs that would offer them significance and meaning" (p. 446). Social entrepreneurship provided the possibility to fulfill a calling.

Dempsey and Sanders then explored two challenges of becoming a social entrepreneur. The first challenge was to make the developing nonprofit organization align with the demands of the market. Each of the books reports that an idealistic vision is not enough for success—that becoming more business-like became necessary. Wood, for instance, wanted to create "the Microsoft of nonprofits" (p. 448), acknowledging that he adopted many of the company's management techniques. The lesson, say Dempsey and Sanders, is that "non-profit organizations are best run like a business" (p. 448). A second challenge the social entrepreneurs encountered was a work-life imbalance. Their stories are populated with examples of sacrificing family and health to build the organization, as well as a good deal of unpaid labor. Mortensen, for instance, chose to become homeless for a stretch to put as much money as possible into the building of a school.

Based on their critical readings of these autobiographies, Dempsey and Sanders conclude that when we see our work as fulfilling a calling—something we choose to see—we run the risk of ignoring power relations. The three autobiographies provide justification for nonprofit work paying very low wages, failing to provide health care, and lacking job security (see also Bunderson & Thompson, 2009). They also fail to interrogate who can afford to pursue callings like these: Wood and Kopp had very privileged backgrounds and thus could "leverage their wealthy colleagues and former classmates at prominent universities to garner early financial support and attention for their projects" (p. 454). Moreover, these books don't question the dominance of neoliberal thinking in which the nation-state has no role to play in addressing social problems; they assume that individuals embedded in markets must make those changes.

Discussion Questions

1. Do you see yourself working in a nonprofit as a possible career? What benefits, and what drawbacks, are associated with that sort of work? More importantly, where do our beliefs about those benefits and drawbacks come from?

2. These books about successful nonprofit organizations contain recommendations that mirror those for operating businesses. Is it possible that nonprofits imitate for-profits because those techniques are simply the "one right way" to manage all organizations? If not, are there ways in which nonprofits should operate differently than for-profit firms?

3. Is it inevitable that workers who follow a calling will experience a work-life imbalance? In groups, brainstorm about how nonprofit work and nonprofit workers could change to eliminate work-life tensions.

Provides Income Adequate for a Decent Living

This criterion is clearly the most basic for making work meaningful; doing volunteer work feels good, but it doesn't put bread on the table. Of course, what counts as a decent living is very much in the eye of the beholder. The U.S. Census Bureau indicates that in 2015 the median household income in the United States was $56,516 (Proctor, Semega, & Kollar, 2016). On the other hand, in 2017 the U.S. Department of Health and Human Services placed the poverty threshold in the United States at $12,060 for one person, $16,240 for two people, and $24,600 for a family of four (Assistant Secretary for Planning and Evaluation, n.d.). Do you think you would be able to live on these figures?

Interestingly, this sixth criterion for making work meaningful is often the most difficult to talk about. When we ask our students what is important to them in a career, very few are willing to talk openly about "earning lots of money" as important, although a number will say that they want to earn enough not to have to worry about money. As we saw in the chapter on branding and consumption, however, we live in a society where the power to consume is viewed as a necessary prerequisite for a happy and meaningful life, and as a consequence, a large percentage of the population lives in perpetual debt with little or no savings. Thus, people are prepared to live well beyond their means in order to pursue what they define as a meaningful life.

All the criteria discussed above assume that in order for us to be happy, work must be a meaningful part of our lives. This is true for many people, but for a significant proportion of the population, work is simply a means to an end; that is, it is the thing they must do in order to earn the money that allows them to do other things in their lives. For such people, the idea of a career is not a defining feature of their lives. For example, Dennis's older brother Ken (now retired) had numerous jobs in his working life, including working in a steel foundry, serving as a police officer, driving a delivery truck, being a nontraditional student, being a postal worker, and working with special needs children. Looked at in total, it's hard to frame these jobs as a career. However, for Ken, they allowed him to pursue the things in life that are really important to him: supporting his family, spending time with his grandchildren, traveling, and so forth. In many respects, one might argue that Dennis's brother has a much healthier relationship to work than those of us who have devoted a lifetime to building a successful career. And Tim did a study (Kuhn, 2009) based on a conversation with his younger brother, Mike, that was in many ways the opposite of the case with Ken. As an undergraduate, Mike had an internship at a small law firm that did a great deal of work for the rural poor in Minnesota. He decided to enter law school intending to do the same sort of legal work, believing that practicing law to aid the poor would provide purpose and meaning to his legal career—and to his life more generally. Upon exiting law school, Mike instead took a job working for a very large law firm in Minneapolis doing corporate law, especially mergers and acquisitions. When confronted with what seemed to Tim to be a contradiction, Mike responded in a way consistent with de Botton's realization mentioned above; that is, he was contributing to the economic security of many people.

So the issue we need to address more closely is the relation between work and meaning in people's lives. Or as Ciulla (2000) puts it, "What is the relationship between meaningful work, a meaningful life, and happiness" (p. 208)? Addressing this relationship means two things. First, we're not suggesting that a job is something that exists externally to people and that we can assess it along these six criteria objectively. Instead, any assessment of meaningfulness requires that we make sense of the connections between the characteristics of the work and the identities of the people involved in it. Second, rather than thinking about the meaning of work as an individual and often idiosyncratic issue—we're not arguing that "whatever makes you happy, go do it"—we need to think about the larger social forces that shape not only the meaning of work itself but also other spheres of our lives (Kuhn et al., 2008). Therefore, we need to examine more closely the relationship between work and human identity; that is, how do we make sense of work as an integral part of who we are as human beings? How do we communicatively construct ourselves and others in relation to our work and professional lives? And how does work construct us? The next section presents identity as a concept to explore those questions.

MANAGING WORK IDENTITY: SOME HISTORICAL CONTEXT

The rather neat criteria for meaningful work that we laid out above get a lot more complex when placed in historical context. While it is fairly easy to think about the meaning of work in the context of stable, long-term employment and a relatively unchanging economic and political system, such a coherent picture becomes much more elusive in an environment where organizations are less stable, workers change jobs more regularly than they change their cars, and the relationship between work and other dimensions of our lives seems to get ever more complex and fuzzy.

A number of social commentators and theorists have argued that the changes in work and society over the past 50 years have led to a condition in which one's identity—"the conception of the self reflexively and discursively understood by the self" (Kuhn, 2006, p. 1340), or the story of the self that we tell to both ourselves and others—is much less stable than in the past, such that we are in a constant process of searching for a coherent and grounded sense of who we are (Bauman, 2000; Beck, 1992; Giddens, 1991). Many of these commentators have used the term **reflexive modernity** to describe this condition, in which traditional stability-maintaining structures of class, family, and industrial forms of production have waned, placing greater pressure on people to create their own sense of stability. The sociologist Anthony Giddens (1991) refers to this as a search for **ontological security**; people look for an experience of life that emphasizes order, continuity, and relative stability across time.

However, the current state of the global political and economic environment means that such stability and continuity are increasingly hard to achieve. Indeed, as sociologist Sennett (1998) points out, while uncertainty in people's lives used to be mostly the product of some kind of human or natural disaster (war, famine, destructive weather conditions, etc.), today it is woven into the everyday practices of vigorous capitalism. This uncertainty is in part because the demands of the market (see Chapter 6's discussion of neoliberalism) mean that long-term thinking is virtually impossible, and success is gauged in increasingly short time frames. Thus, organizations need to assess themselves constantly and make changes (e.g., in corporate structure, target consumers, branding, etc.) whenever deemed necessary.

The result is that long-term planning has been replaced by short-term thinking, frequently dictated by the quarterly report. Where the success of a company was previously connected to the quality of its products and services, these days it is more likely to be dictated by shareholder return on investment—returns that are measured on a quarterly basis. Indeed, CEOs will often attempt to influence quarterly reports by engaging in practices such as layoffs, reengineering, right-sizing, and so forth—activities that please shareholders but for which employees typically bear the brunt.

The sociologist Zygmunt Bauman (2000) uses the term liquid or light modernity to describe the social, political, and economic conditions that characterize life today and that shape how we relate to ourselves, one another, work, and consumption. He contrasts this condition with what he calls solid or heavy modernity, characteristic of the Fordist period. As he states:

> Fordism was the self-consciousness of modern society in its "heavy", "bulky", or immobile and "rooted", "solid" phase. At that stage in their joint history, capital, management, and labour were all, for better or worse, doomed to stay in one another's company for a long time to come, perhaps forever—tied down by the combination of huge factory buildings, heavy machinery, and massive labour forces. . . . Heavy capitalism was obsessed with bulk and size, and, for that reason, also with boundaries, with making them tight and impenetrable. (pp. 57–58)

Such heavy capitalism tied workers to one place and time, and to a career with a single organization (in Henry Ford's case, the introduction of the $5-a-day wage was the chain that helped secure workers to the labor process). On the other hand, liquid modernity is the era of disengagement and elusiveness; it is "those free to move without notice, who rule" (Bauman, 2000, p. 120). In contrast, "it is the people who cannot move quickly, and more conspicuously yet the category of people who cannot at will leave their place at all, who are ruled" (p. 120).

Because the disembodied labor of liquid modernity no longer ties capital to a specific location, it allows it to be free from spatial restraints; it can move anywhere, and very quickly: "Capitalism can travel fast and travel light and its lightness and motility have turned into the paramount source of uncertainty for all the rest. This has become the present-day basis of domination and the principal factor of social divisions" (Bauman, 2000, p. 121).

From an employee perspective, this means that the ontological security once provided by the social contract between workers and employers and its accompanying lifetime employment has largely disappeared, replaced by rules of the game that are constantly shifting. Career events such as promotions and dismissals are no longer grounded in clear and stable hierarchies and corporate rules but can occur in seemingly random and whimsical ways as the latest economic and/or cultural shift changes the way organizations do business (see Chapter 13's discussion of globalization).

In this context, more and more responsibility is placed on employees to be flexible and adapt to these changing conditions, or be considered dinosaurs and thus expendable. The problem is that there is frequently no way to know or understand what the next big thing will be, and so employees remain in a constant state of disequilibrium as they attempt to be "good employees" without necessarily knowing the criteria by which they are being judged. Such insecurity is intensified by a business climate in which the life cycle of management fads (you may have heard of programs like Six Sigma, Quality Circles, One-Minute Management, Matrix Management, and Business Process Re-engineering) has, in the past 30 years, shrunk from 10 years to 1 year (Mickelthwait & Wooldridge, 1996).

It is easy to see how such cycles of continuous change can have a corroding effect on any employee's sense of professional self and identity, particularly when such change cycles frequently contradict one another. Business rhetoric might stress the need for constant reinvention and reengineering, but the human consequences of such a philosophy can be far-reaching, with mass layoffs and the destabilization of families and even whole communities. A discourse of constant change that constructs successful people as always adapting undercuts the ability of employees to feel any real sense of stability and security in their work lives (and by implication, other realms of their lives).

Sennett (1998) has argued that the kind of short-term thinking and constant change that characterizes modern capitalism results in what he terms the **corrosion of character**. He claims that the strong influence of Wall Street and the stock market on corporate decision making means that companies are continually expanding and contracting to meet the demands of the market, and employees thus become much more expendable. Hence, the traditional corporate values of trust, loyalty, and commitment, shared reciprocally by employees and their organizations, have been discarded, to the detriment of both employees and the firms themselves. On the one hand, organizations lose the institutional knowledge that long-term employees develop; on the other hand, employees themselves are unable to engage in the long-term planning and organization that gives their lives a sense of stability and coherence. In other words, as Sennett states, it becomes difficult for people to develop a stable life narrative (another way of saying ontological security) around which their sense of character is built.

Indeed, one might argue that the stable, bureaucratic organization has been replaced by constantly changing institutional forms that value disloyalty, irresponsibility, and immediate gratification. As Sennett (1998) argues, "Detachment and superficial cooperativeness are better armor for dealing with current realities than behavior based on values of loyalty and service" (p. 25). As discussed in the chapter on branding, the rise of entrepreneurial and freelance (gig) work underscores the move away from a commitment to organizations (and the communities they're associated with) to a concern for self-interests (Bröckling, 2016). Short-term capitalism thus threatens to corrode those qualities that bind humans to one another and furnish a stable and sustainable sense of self.

Finally, it is worth noting that, according to Andrew Ross, there appears to be a negative relationship between job security and managerial efforts over the past 50 years to make work more meaningful and rewarding. One of the central, defining aspects of organizational life we have addressed in this book is the phenomenon of control and the ways theories of management have evolved from efforts to discipline and sanction workers directly to more recent attempts to exercise control through providing worker autonomy from rigid rules and bureaucratic structures. As Ross states:

> As the workplace became more inclusive, free or self-actualizing for employees, it became less just and equal in its provision of guarantees. This was as true

for production workers, reorganized into teams exercising a degree of decision-making around their modules, as for white-collar employees, encouraged to be self-directing in their work applications. In either case, the managerial program to sell liberation from drudgery was accompanied by the introduction of risk, uncertainty and nonstandard work arrangements. (Ross, 2008, p. 35)

Not surprisingly, risk hasn't been felt by all workers equally: Workers at the bottom of organizational hierarchies, those seen as disposable, and those in creative industries have been subject to greater levels of uncertainty. Returning to our Chapter 3 discussion of "spirits of capitalism" (Boltanski & Chiapello, 2005), it's somewhat ironic that a move promising to address a crisis of legitimacy in the capitalist system (attending to feelings of the meaninglessness of work) was purchased at the cost of workers' ontological security—generating an additional crisis. In the next section we turn to examine more closely the organizational environments in which people work and the ways they manage their organizational and professional identities in the face of this insecurity and instability.

✦ CREATING AND MANAGING WORK IDENTITIES

The crisis of identity we have discussed is further intensified because organizations have constructed a close link between employee identity and control (Alvesson & Willmott, 2002; Casey, 1995). As we have discussed throughout this book, corporations have shifted from behavioral forms of control (requiring the worker to act in a specific way) to control processes that focus much more heavily on the "soul" of the individual employee. As Stan Deetz (1995) has indicated, the modern business of management often involves managing "the 'insides'—the hopes, fears and aspirations—of workers, rather than their behaviors directly" (p. 87). At precisely the time that our own sense of identity is up for grabs, corporations step into the breach to create forms of control that exploit that insecurity.

In this sense, we can think about employees not simply as possessors of skill sets who perform specific tasks for the organization but, equally important, as identity workers who are asked to incorporate the latest managerial discourse into their own narratives of self-identity (Alvesson & Willmott, 2002, p. 622). As a simple example, corporate efforts to get workers to think and speak of themselves as team members, family members, or associates, rather than employees, reflects corporate efforts to encourage workers to construct a certain narrative of work identity—a narrative that fits with the goals of the organization.

However, such efforts to shape employee identity are by no means a simple case of employees uncritically accepting management discourses of work identity. As critical management scholars Mats Alvesson and Hugh Willmott (2002) argue, "The organizational regulation of identity . . . is a precarious and often contested process involving active identity work. . . . Organizational members are not reducible to passive consumers of managerially designed and designated identities" (p. 621).

There is, therefore, a more complex relationship between employee identity and forms of organizational control in the post-Fordist organization than in the traditional Fordist bureaucracy. Part of this complexity is due to the fact that we have shifted from a society in which selves are ascribed to one in which selves are achieved (Collinson, 2003). In other words, precapitalist societies tended to be characterized by institutional forms in which people's roles were fixed and assigned—serf, aristocrat, peasant, slave, and so on—with little or no room for movement to a higher place in the social order. (If you were born a boy, you'd likely end up in the occupation of your father; girls tended to do the housework and childrearing, just like their mothers.) Even well into the 20th century, the class structure in many societies left little room for maneuvering in the social and economic hierarchy. While ascribed identities limited social mobility, they nevertheless provided a sense of ontological security that enabled a more stable sense of self. Furthermore, work relationships between capitalists and labor, while often antagonistic, were long term. A strong sense of stability and security was gained through membership in a union and/or association with an occupational group—groups that traditionally have fought to protect the rights of their members.

On the other hand, achieved selves reflect more fluid social structures in which greater onus is placed on the ability of the individual to carve out a relatively stable, coherent identity. Thus, due to the precarious nature of contemporary life, much of our activity involves identity work, where we are "continuously engaged in forming, repairing, maintaining, strengthening or revising the constructions that are productive of a precarious sense of coherence and distinctiveness" (Alvesson & Willmott, 2002, p. 626). Identity work can be prompted by interactions that raise questions about, or threaten, our senses of self, such that we feel compelled to overcome a challenge, restore order, or even possibly create new identity possibilities (Alvesson, Ashcraft, & Thomas, 2008). However, the very fluidity of social structures means that individuals constantly reflect on and question their identity as the grounds of identity shift ("Am I successful enough?" "Does my boss like me?" "Should I change jobs?" "Do I have time for a social life?" "Does my butt look big in these jeans?" and so forth). In this sense, societies characterized by achieved selves are a double-edged sword: They provide the possibility of social mobility, but the choice making that this entails produces existential anxiety and the kind of ontological insecurity we discussed above. Under the conditions characteristic of liquid modernity and neoliberalism, we can say that identity work is about seeking stability within fluid social structures. How do people develop a coherent and stable sense of self under societal conditions that promote insecurity and instability?

Given the focus of this book on the relationship between communication and organization, we will examine such achieved work and organizational identities as communicatively constructed. In other words, identities will be examined not as some internal essence of each individual, or even as a cognitive (i.e., mental) phenomenon; instead, we will think about identity as meaning centered and rooted in social practices. That is, how do people reflect on and make sense of who they are, and how does this sense making get enacted through their communicative practices? In this sense, identity is personal ("Who am I?"), social ("How am I the same as or different from other people, and in what important or trivial ways?"), and societal ("What larger societal discourses and meanings make possible or limit the kind of person I experience myself as?"). Identities, therefore, are different from, and deeper than, roles. Roles refer to expected behaviors and obligations associated with positions (like accountant, sister, professor, waiter). Identities may draw upon roles but extend beyond them to deal with existential questions of personhood.

Identity, Identification, and Disidentification

Organization members, then, spend a lot of time engaged in identity work. However, as we indicated above, such work is a dynamic process that involves active negotiation and sense making on the part of employees. We are therefore not the passive recipients of the identities organizations present to us. What, then, are the elements of identity work?

1. *Identity is thoroughly social.* That is, we always develop identities and do ongoing identity work in relation to other people. We have no sense of self except as shaped by significant others around us. Identity is not a self-contained essence exclusive to any individual.

2. *Identity is always contingent and ongoing.* It is never fixed or finalized. Our identities change and adapt to the shifting social contexts in which we find ourselves. Indeed, multiple identities can be performed in a single day—even in a single conversation.

3. *Identity draws on various societal discourses that enable us to develop a self-identity that is meaningful and coherent.* For example, a societal discourse of enterprise can be drawn on to provide a sense of professional self that focuses on self-improvement and self-branding.

4. *Identity involves struggle.* That is, both employees and employers compete over the particular conception of workplace identity that will prevail. This struggle is primarily meaning based and involves competing interpretations and sense-making practices. For example, some workers may not buy into the family culture of an organization and choose to create a work identity that distances itself from many of the behaviors required of someone who is a family member. Identity, then, is a primary site of organizational control and resistance.

5. *Identity is a communication phenomenon.* Workers perform identities through daily communication practices, and companies attempt to shape workers' identities by developing strategic communication processes that attempt to provide a coherent work narrative in which workers can invest.

Given these elements of work identity, we can argue that there are three distinct but related processes: (1) managing identity, (2) identification, and (3) disidentification. In other words, in the process of (1) managing and negotiating their identities (i.e., doing identity work), workers will (2) develop differing levels of identification with their organizations and/or will (3) engage in various forms of disidentification in separating their sense of self from the work identity a company demands of its employees. Because of the complexities of the relationships among work identity, meaning, and organizing, it's quite possible that employees will experience both identification with and disidentification from various aspects of their work lives. For example, employees might identify strongly with a work subculture to which they belong (e.g., software engineers, or even an office bowling team) while disidentifying with the company's effort to engineer the workplace culture to improve commitment and productivity.

For our purposes, the importance of this tension between identification and disidentification is that it provides insight into how identity has become a focal point for both corporate control processes and employee efforts to maintain a sense of agency and autonomy. If, indeed, "the self" is the "last frontier of control" (Ray, 1986, p. 287), then it is important to understand how, particularly in post-Fordist conditions of relative insecurity, employees attempt to maintain a coherent and stable sense of self in the face of such control efforts. Management scholar David Collinson (2003) provides one way to think about this process, arguing that there are three principal (and intersecting) forms of work identity that people communicatively enact: (1) conformist selves, (2) dramaturgical selves, and (3) resistant selves.

Conformist Selves

Conformist selves involve efforts by organization members to portray themselves as valued objects in the eyes of those in authority. Under conditions of insecurity, one way to gain security is to demonstrate a level of performance that makes one indispensable to the organization. Under such conditions, the goal is very much to subordinate one's sense of identity to the needs and goals of the organization.

Anthropologist Karen Ho's (2009) ethnographic study of Wall Street investment bankers provides a fascinating example of a profession in which the need to perform a conformist self is extremely important to success. She shows how, first, Wall Street firms recruit from an extremely narrow demographic group, concentrating mainly on Ivy League schools—Harvard and Princeton in particular. Then she explores how new recruits are expected to devote their entire lives to their companies, sometimes working 100 hours a week in the quest to close deals and make lots of money for the company. As Ho suggests, what counts as acceptable and appropriate professional identity management is very carefully defined:

> In an investment bank the presentation of self is crucial. Not surprisingly, the range of possibilities for self-representation is extremely narrow . . . the limitation and boundaries on one's image repertoire are more onerous and the consequences of straying over them are much more dire for women and people of color. (p. 120)

What is fascinating, however, is that this remarkable level of commitment to work and careful cultivation of a Wall Street identity is not rewarded with job security. Wall Street investment banks are notorious for adopting short-term strategies (or as Ho points out, *no* business strategy at all) and hiring or firing people as they see fit and as investment fads come and go (the 2008 subprime mortgage fiasco is a great example of this). As a result, employees can make extreme levels of commitment to their employers but still find themselves with no job. Indeed, job insecurity is practically built into the culture of Wall Street.

As Ho (2009) points out, it is impossible to live a normal and balanced life under such work pressures. Wall Street employees are frequently young, single, and prepared to do anything to get ahead and make their fortunes by the time they are 40. As such, their commitment and development of conformist identities can frequently result in ill health and burnout due to the stress of work and the long hours, as well as an extremely skewed sense of life priorities.

Wall Street investment bankers are perhaps an extreme example of devotion (albeit self-interested) to a profession. However, it is not unusual for people outside of Wall Street banks to adopt such an approach to work. As we indicated above, many people are consumed with the idea of career success, and such an orientation to work often demands that every sphere of life become subordinated to the project of career. In his study of accountants, for example, management scholar Chris Grey (1994) shows how, as one becomes more successful,

> it becomes necessary to sublimate one's whole life to the development of career. Friends become transformed into "contacts," and social activity becomes "networking." . . . The transformation of the non-work sphere into a specific aspect of career development is seen as crucial to success. (p. 492)

Note that it is not simply the case that work takes over other realms of life; rather, all other realms get reframed and are made meaningful through a lens of career advancement and success. Grey even reports that the (mostly male) accountants he studied talked about their spouses in terms of how much they helped or hindered career progress. In Deetz's (1992) sense, the discourse of career colonizes the life-world of community and friendship, defining it in an instrumental manner.

Conformist selves thus often view their professional identities as ongoing projects that need to be constantly maintained and improved. In this sense, in the language of the post-Fordist organization, they are entrepreneurial selves whose focus is not only the work they do but also their own brands and professional images. Thus, such workers are their own projects (Du Gay & Salaman, 1992; Holmer Nadesan & Trethewey, 2000).

As Joanne Ciulla (2000) points out, however, one of the ironies of the modern organization is that "the less stability and loyalty companies have to offer employees, the more commitment they demand from them" (p. 153). Workers may perform the conformist self as their principal professional identity, but as we saw previously with Ho's (2009) Wall Street bankers, such conformism by no means guarantees job stability. The irony of the conformist self, then, is that the commitment and hard work they engage in is not reciprocated by the organization in terms of commitment to the employee.

Dramaturgical Selves

Dramaturgical selves frequently emerge in organizational contexts where employees "feel highly visible, threatened, defensive, subordinated, and/or insecure" (Collinson, 2003, p. 538). When employees employ the dramaturgical self, they engage in communicative performances aimed at enabling them to survive and prosper in the workplace. Frequently, such performances are a response to work environments where surveillance is high and the workers are highly visible—a common condition in the post-Fordist organization, as we discussed in Chapter 6.

In Karen Ho's (2009) study of Wall Street discussed above, for example, employees not only had to conform to a clearly defined work culture but also had to demonstrate—through their onstage performances—that they had fully internalized the work culture. This performance included fairly mundane activities such as wearing the regulation power suit but also involved more subtle elements such as eating lunch and dinner at their desks to demonstrate to others (and their bosses) that they were fully immersed in the intense work culture. It also involved the ability to employ the language of Wall Street fluently, thus demonstrating one's competence and immersion in the culture.

Similarly, in Fleming and Spicer's study of a call center, one way the mainly 20-something employees responded to management's introduction of a culture of fun was to dress in hip, sexy clothes at work and openly engage in flirting with coworkers (Fleming, 2007; Fleming & Spicer, 2007). In this context, conformity to the workplace culture was very much a matter of consciously and visibly performing a "trendy" self, thus bringing the nonwork self into the work environment.

However, the deployment of a dramaturgical self in the workplace does not necessarily mean that one is attempting to conform to the culture of the organization. It is also possible that dramaturgical selves can be used as a way to resist the dominant organizational culture. For example, in Taylor and Bain's (2003) study of a call center, they show how an openly gay and very theatrical employee used humor as a way to resist managerial control efforts. He satirized managers, using his campy persona as a way to undermine their authority. He was able to get away with this behavior "because he would exploit both his own popularity and managers' stereotypical expectations of a gay man" (p. 1503). Thus, this employee was able to engage in a very public performance of satirical gay employee as a deliberate strategy of resistance.

The dramaturgical self thus places a heavy emphasis on the public performance of particular work identities that can either demonstrate conformity and commitment to company norms or directly resist them. In either case, the dramaturgical self illustrates the extent to which "identity is a matter of claims, not character; persona, not personality; and presentation, not self" (Ybema et al., 2009, p. 306).

Resistant Selves

Finally, **resistant selves** are employed in organizational contexts where employees are attempting to resist managerial control efforts. As we have seen already, in the post-Fordist organization, the employee self and sense of identity are central to corporate efforts to develop commitment to and identification with the organization. Thus, rather than employing explicit and/or collective efforts at resistance (e.g., through strikes or work slowdowns), employees in such organizations respond by engaging with the organizational meaning system that undergirds corporate efforts to control employee identity. In this sense, resistant selves attempt to negotiate or subvert the dominant, or official, meanings that organizations attempt to foster.

Resistant selves use a number of different communicative strategies, including cynicism, humor, and irony—all tactics that operate at the level of meaning—in an effort to exploit the ambiguity that exists in all corporate efforts to shape organizational reality (Collinson, 1988; Fleming & Spicer, 2007; Karlsson, 2012; Mumby, Thomas, Martí, & Seidl, 2017; Paulsen, 2014, 2015; Vallas, 2016).

Resistant selves are interesting (especially from a critical perspective) because they demonstrate the extent to which employees engage in efforts to maintain a sense of personhood that is distinct and separate from the corporate self. If the self is the last frontier of corporate control, then it would seem important (if only from the perspective of personal well-being) that corporations not be allowed to colonize completely our sense of who we are. For this reason, employees will often act the part their employer expects them to play while at the same time holding on to feelings of cynicism and resentment and engaging in backstage acts of resistance through humor, irony, and so forth.

For example, management scholar Roland Paulsen (2014, 2015) has examined what he calls "empty labor"; that is, "everything you do at work that is not your work" (2015, p. 362), or "private activities at work" (p. 351). Empty labor involves the "simulation of work" (2015, p. 363) in which employees spend a good part of their work day pretending to work but actually engage in nonwork activities. Paulsen's study is interesting because it gives insight into the complexities of the work–self relationship. Most employees in his study do not avoid work simply because they are lazy. Some see the work they are assigned as meaningless, and private activities are more meaningful to them. Others even attempt to get more work to do, feeling an obligation to the company, but are confounded by managers who promise more work that never materializes (one employee found himself reduced to half-time employment after asking for more work, so clearly it was not in his self-interest to be diligent). Some see a balance between labor and empty labor as vital to physical and psychological well-being, given the intensity of the work they do. Paulsen's study thus provides insight not only into the work–self relationship, but also into the ways that workers attempt to reclaim an autonomous sense of work identity by reappropriating time; after all, as we saw way back in Chapter 2 in Karl Marx's analysis of capitalism, companies are not purchasing labor, per se, but labor time. Workers who engage in empty labor, then, are attempting to regain control over their work by refusing the forms of work intensification that are common in post-Fordism.

Resistant selves thus highlight the degree to which employees are able to pierce corporate efforts at control and self-consciously manage their identities, hence maintaining a degree of autonomy. However, as management scholars Peter Fleming and André Spicer (2003) have pointed out, it's quite possible that efforts at disidentification through communicative practices such as cynicism and irony simply serve to maintain organizational control. In other words, employees who practice cynicism (e.g., pinning up Dilbert cartoons in their cubicles) still engage in the daily activities of the workplace and maybe even perform their work with a high degree of competence. Cynics display their ability to see through managerial control strategies but do little to change them. In such cases, cynicism might be not so much a form of workplace resistance as an ideological device that enables employees to feel as though they are putting one over on their bosses while unwittingly reaffirming existing hierarchies of power.

There is some evidence for this view of irony and cynicism. Some management consultants suggest that cynicism is actually beneficial for organizations because it provides honest feedback to managers. Likewise, cynicism may ironically serve corporate interests because, as Fleming and Spicer (2008) point out, "The latest wave of management gurus invites employees to simply be themselves, even if that means being cynically against the values of the firm" (p. 303). In other words, it is precisely the mavericks and cynical, tattooed, counterculture types that bleeding edge companies want to hire! The philosophy here, of course, is that such employees are deemed to add value to the company precisely because they think outside the box and bring innovative ideas to the table. This philosophy is consistent with our discussion of the social factory earlier in the book and the idea that contemporary capitalism attempts to capture life itself (Fleming, 2014b).

In her research on temporary workers, organizational communication scholar Loril Gossett (2003) provides one final twist in this rather complicated picture. She suggests that with an increasingly unstable work environment, it is actually not in the best interests of organizations to cultivate strong feelings of identification in all of their workers. With the temporary workforce growing and companies increasingly relying on contract and freelance workers (see Chapter 6's discussion of the fissured workplace), it makes no sense for companies to encourage these workers to identify with them. Gossett shows how, through certain communication strategies, companies will actually actively work to keep such workers at arm's length. Strategies include denying temporary workers access to the symbolic artifacts that would identity them as members of the company culture (e.g., not allowing temp employees to have an internal email account even if they work at the company for several months) and denying temporary employees the opportunity to engage in any decision making or provide feedback to the company. Moreover, Gossett shows that temporary workers rarely experienced identification with their employment agencies, especially as they had little regular contact either with other temps or with employers at the agencies.

Thus, it is worth remembering that while millions of employees must negotiate the intricacies of identity management on a daily basis, there are also millions more for whom identification with their employers is not an option; indeed, many organizations employ a deliberate strategy of limiting employee identification in order to maintain organizational flexibility and simplify the hiring and firing process. Imagine, then, the quality of work life for those temporary employees who must suffer the indignities of being marginalized on a daily basis. No wonder—as Gregg's (2011) study, discussed earlier, suggests—such workers look to their online communities for a sense of identification and ontological security.

It is clear, then, that managing identities at work is a complex and sometimes contradictory process—conformist selves can sometimes turn out to resist corporate control processes, and resistant selves can inadvertently maintain the status quo. Much of this complexity arises from the fact that so much of the organizing process is concerned with the communicative construction and management of meaning. Companies are in the business of meaning production, both for consumers through branding of products and for employees through the internal branding of culture and the ideal employee. Because organization members are rarely simply passive recipients of such branding efforts, employees will work hard to create their own autonomous space within the complexities of organizational meaning systems. Managing work identity, then, is a key aspect of the negotiation of organizational meaning.

In the final section of this chapter, we'll take a brief look at the relationship between work and other aspects of people's lives.

U.S. workers work more hours and get less vacation time than workers in almost every other nation on earth.

NO COLLAR, NO LIFE

In her book *The Overworked American*, sociologist Juliet Schor provides some rather sobering statistics regarding Americans' relationship to work. She argues that the average employed person works an additional 163 hours (1 extra month) per year now than in 1969. Furthermore, there is a distinct gender gap in this increase—men work 98 hours more per year, while women work 305 hours more per year (Schor, 1993, p. 29). And there's a gender gap in leisure time as well: A 2013 Pew Research Center study found that men spend 4.7 more hours a week than women in activities such as watching TV, playing sports, and gaming (Drake, 2013). Moreover, a Families and Work Institute survey showed that the average workweek increased from 43.6 hours in 1977 to 47.1 hours in 1997 (Useem, 2000). By 2015, Americans were spending 173 more hours at work than they were in 1980. While accurately measuring the amount of time people work is notoriously difficult and some authors have challenged the claims of Schor and others (e.g., Robinson & Godbey, 1999), it is clear that many Americans are consumed by work, more so than citizens in other industrialized countries. And typically, the higher one goes up the socioeconomic ladder, the more consumed one is; thus, upper-middle-class, **no-collar workers** tend to report having less leisure time than do blue-collar workers (Robinson & Godbey, 1999).

A number of years ago sociologist Arlie Russell Hochschild's (1997) book, *The Time Bind,* addressed the question of why Americans seemed to be working more than workers in other industrialized nations, including the workaholic Japanese (on average, Americans work 137 hours more per year than the Japanese and 260 hours—6.5 weeks—more than the British; yes, Dennis's people are a lazy lot!). Interestingly, she discovered that this increase had little to do with companies requiring workers to put in lots of overtime; in fact, many companies reported having a hard time getting employees to go home at the end of the day. Rather, Hochschild put forward the counterintuitive explanation that people often preferred to be at work rather than at home because in many ways, work provided a sense of identity that home did not. At work, one does not have to worry about dysfunctional relationships and problems with children; rather, one can focus on the job and experience the camaraderie of workmates.

Whether one accepts Hochschild's thesis or not, it is clear that many people experience time famine (Robinson & Godbey, 1999). We never appear to have enough time, and our identities are very much tied up with managing time. We occasionally catch glimpses of students' daily planners in class and see how they are completely filled with work, activities, and appointments from early morning until late in the evening—recall the students at Princeton in Chapter 1 who made appointments with their friends to hang out! And in the no-collar, creative economy that many of you will join, time management seems to be a particularly pressing issue.

Florida (2003) reports that well-paid blue-collar workers appear to have the most leisure time while no-collar workers have the least. Why? Florida suggests that with the creative economy's focus on "novelty, variety, and customization" (p. 147), change is paramount; thus, there is constant pressure on no-collar workers to be flexible and adaptive and come up with ideas for new products. And here we are not simply talking about information technologies such as smartphones and laptops; even consumer products such as sneakers, cereal, and clothing are constantly being upgraded to ensure that consumers don't get jaded. And as was the case for Laurence (from the cookie company above) and other branding professionals, there is no end to coming up with new messages, checking measures of impact, and inspecting competitors' (or brand leaders') activities for inspiration. Such constant innovation and need for continual presence makes for long hours and pressurized work environments. Moreover, because no-collar workers generally earn salaries rather than wages, they are paid the same whether they work a 40-hour or a 60-hour week. Thus, companies have little incentive to hire more workers to create shorter workweeks, as the overtime of salaried workers is essentially free to the employers.

CRITICAL CASE STUDY 14.1

The Politics of Personal Branding

Throughout this book, we've paid attention to branding as a key form of value construction in post-Fordist work (see Chapter 10 in particular). Branding, of course, is not merely for products and

(Continued)

(Continued)

organizations; it has also become a task individuals are encouraged to undertake. The notion of **personal branding**, where people shape the emotions and impressions of others through intentional cultivation and reinforcement, is a key component of contemporary identity management. The idea took flight in 1997, when management guru Tom Peters (of *In Search of Excellence* fame) wrote an article for *Fast Company* magazine in which he claimed, "All of us need to understand the importance of branding. We are CEOs of our own companies: Me Inc. To be in business today, our most important job is to be head marketer for the brand called You" (Peters, 1997).

It didn't take long for personal branding to take hold. It's a common part of career services offerings on college campuses (check yours to see if it offers a session on this topic), it has spawned an abundance of consultants offering their expertise, and it has led to the development of several software programs to assess the brand's popularity. And even though it's called *personal* branding, it's almost exclusively geared toward making oneself marketable for work: for preparing for a job search or getting the next gig.

So it's popular, prevalent, and professionally oriented. Given this chapter's interest in identity, power, and meaningful work, what more can we see in personal branding? We see three things. First, personal branding is often presented as a journey of self-discovery, one in which people are told to reflect on their strengths, weaknesses, and desired career. And some versions carry instructions to interview former employers, parents, and friends to get a sense for how the person appears in the eyes of others. The implication is that the personal brand is something to be detected; it is something external to the person that, once located, can guide future action. The choice of sources to examine (and whom to bypass) for information about the self therefore becomes very important.

Second, the manifestation of personal branding is the reduction of identity complexity. Specifically, people are told to condense their identities into a mantra, "a quick, simple, and memorable statement describing who you are and what you have to offer" (Marrs, 2012). Attention then turns to the Internet: Personal branders are expected to curate their online presence, ensuring consistency across platforms and using social media to market themselves. Above, we claimed that identity management is a complex and contradictory process, and it's unlikely that the reduction of identity to a mantra aids people in working with those contradictions. Instead of bringing about an encounter with our real, authentic self, personal branding is more likely to be about commodification: reducing identity to a product (a commodity) to be consumed by others, potential employers in particular. And as was mentioned in Chapter 7's discussion of biocracy, companies are more likely to use these expressions of self as control devices than they are to foster people's unique individuality.

Third, Peters viewed personal branding as liberating, thinking that when people grab control of who they want to be and the work they want to do, they will be able to choose a series of projects that satisfy their personal ambitions. They'd be able to free themselves from corporate drudgery and, in that sense, be better able to find meaningful work. (He was writing in 1997, and there's little evidence that he knew that the freelance or gig economy was on the horizon.) But as we mentioned in our discussion of the post-Fordist world of work, gig workers' continual search for the next project can carry large threats to their ontological security. In this sense, personal branding might hinder the very meaningfulness Peters thought it would produce.

In the end, then, it's too simple to say that personal branding is either simply good or bad. But it's clearly tied to the post-Fordist world of work. And it's certainly all around us and not going away anytime soon.

Discussion Questions

1. Individually, complete the Personal Brand Workbook at https://www.pwc.com/us/en/ careers/campus/assets/img/programs/personal-brand-workbook.pdf, or watch the video by "Strategic Connector" (how's that for a branding move?) Amanda Rose at https://www .youtube.com/watch?v=bDNz3496abs. Focus on the five- or six-word exercises they encourage. Then, in groups, describe your five or six words, and then compare with others. What are the similarities? Differences? What do those similarities and differences tell you about your group and about the activity of personal branding?

2. If people are told to present themselves with a mantra, a simple phrase to signal their value, does it make it more likely that they will frame themselves as Collinson's conformist self? Why or why not?

3. Thinking of examples you've seen of personal branding outside of class (from celebrities, friends, politicians, classmates), does this activity inhibit or expand individuality? Explain your stance to a classmate.

4. What kinds of pressures do you feel, and do you think others feel, in articulating your/their personal brand? What choices are (im)possible?

There is also an interesting dimension to the ways we socially construct time for ourselves and its relationship to our personal and professional identities. In Chapter 1, we discussed the rise of industrial consciousness along with clock time, and in many ways, our 21st-century experience of time is that it is parsed into ever-smaller increments. We not only plan work but also plan our leisure and time with family and friends. Moreover, the blurring of work-life boundaries means that our relationship with time is more complicated. For example, in her book *Finding Time*, Leslie Perlow (1997) reports the case of a female project leader at an engineering firm who arranged to work from home 1 day a week. Even though the arrangement worked extremely well for both her and the company, she soon found herself moved to a less prestigious project that required her presence at the office every day, and she was passed over for an expected raise. Perlow explains this by noting that the firm granted time flexibility only in an ad hoc way and that a great deal of importance was placed on presence in the workplace. Hence, workers resorted to tactics such as leaving jackets and bags at their desks to give the appearance of being present.

So what does this all mean for your life after college? Let's try to pull things together below.

❧ CONCLUSION

In this chapter (and in this book as a whole), we have taken a close look at the relationships among communication, work, and identity. In our 21st-century organizational age, we are, to a large extent, defined by the work we do. As we have seen, however, the nature of our work identities and their relationship to other spheres of our lives is a complicated one; while work is a significant part of our identities, it can also pose a serious threat to a coherent sense of self—our ontological security—by colonizing other aspects of our lives. In addition, the likely continuing instability of the economic environment and the expansion of the gig economy means that the relationship between work and identity will be highly volatile for the foreseeable future. So as you think about your professional lives beyond college, how can the issues discussed in this chapter help you make sense of the world you can expect to face? Or as Sennett (1998) puts it, "How can a human being develop a narrative of identity and life history in a society composed of episodes and fragments?" (p. 26).

As you are already aware, your work life will not look like those of your parents or grandparents but will likely consist of "horizontal hypermobility" (Florida, 2003). But does this new, post-Fordist, postindustrial environment mean that young people just beginning their careers are inevitably facing a chaotic and insecure work environment? Is the corrosion of character that Sennett talks about an inevitable outcome of the passing of the Fordist era?

On the one hand, we will probably never return to a time when a career spent at one or two organizations was the norm—the global economy has changed too much for that to be the case. On the other hand, there are certainly possibilities for a different kind of coherence and stability—one perhaps less dependent on our relationship to particular organizations.

Florida (2003) argues that the age of organization is over and that place has become the key organizing factor in shaping people's lives. Based on an extensive study of numerous locations throughout the United States, Florida claims that for a significant minority of the working population (more than 30%), career decisions are influenced not by the quality of particular organizations but by the quality of the geographical location where organizations are based. How does Florida define quality? He argues that three criteria, or measures, are highly predictive of a high quality living and working environment—one that will attract talent and experience sustained economic growth. These criteria are (1) technology, (2) talent, and (3) tolerance. Technology refers to the amount of high-tech and innovative industry concentrated in a geographic region (e.g., Silicon Valley, Silicon Alley, Research Triangle), talent refers to the concentration of the creative class in a region, and tolerance refers to the extent to which a region welcomes gays and lesbians.

Florida argues that members of the creative class use these criteria in deciding where to live. With the criterion of tolerance, Florida is not saying that members of the creative class are predominantly gay but rather that the presence of a significant gay community in a region is a sign of diversity and a rich and interesting local culture (North Carolina's so-called bathroom bill—passed in 2016—that required transgender people to use public restrooms based on the gender they were assigned at birth was heavily opposed by corporations, precisely because it discouraged members of the creative class from locating to North Carolina and thus hurt the business climate of the state). Now, what these criteria say to us is that many people are developing lives and establishing a meaningful and coherent identity beyond the workplace, and in ways not characterized by retreat behind the fences of a gated community. Many urban areas are experiencing growth and transformation, and lots of people want to be part of that experience.

However, the dark side to Florida's vision is that such growth and transformation comes at a considerable cost, with an increasing divide between rich and poor in the kinds of urban areas that are the focus of his research (New York, San Francisco, Austin, Dublin, Barcelona, etc.). As the creative class has migrated to and gentrified urban areas, lower-paid workers in the service economy are increasingly squeezed out. For example, a recent *New York Times* article reports that an annual salary of $117,400 for a family of four officially qualifies as low income in the three counties that make up the San Francisco Bay Area, where fair market rent for a two-bedroom apartment is $3,200, and the median price for a home is over $1 million (Zraick, 2018). Florida (2017) acknowledges these concerns in his most recent book, *The New Urban Crisis*, where he talks about the emergence of an extreme divide between a creative class and a service class—a divide that, in many respects, is the product of neoliberal policies that have seen the erosion of the social safety net for many people (the United States has the lowest degree of upward social mobility amongst the world's affluent countries). And of course, as we discussed in Chapter 6, being a member of the creative class itself does not guarantee a prosperous life, as many creatives working in the gig economy hold multiple jobs and have little security (including access to health care and pension funds).

It seems to us, then, that a healthy balance between work and life depends not only on individual decisions about how each of us might manage that balance but also on social policies that help provide people with a stable foundation on which they can build a sense of ontological security. It does not seem reasonable, for example, that people can work 40 to 60 hours a week and still not be able to earn enough to live on, save for retirement, or have health care (40% of American have less than $400 in savings [Board of Governors, 2018, p. 2] and 69% have less than $1,000 [McCarthy, 2016]). A return to the Fordist, Keynesian model of social welfare is probably not possible in our current entrepreneurial, "brand you" environment, but a society that does not provide basic protections for its citizens (including its most vulnerable) does not seem like a society at all. Perhaps, as Margaret Thatcher (1987) once said, "There is no such thing as society, only individuals and their families" (and certainly neoliberalism has enshrined the idea that we are all individuals with little connection to each other, beyond our market value). We like to think, however, that we are better off when the (communicative) connections among us are the foundations upon which we build a society that enables everyone to thrive—economically, psychologically, emotionally, spiritually—regardless of social status. What do you think?

CRITICAL APPLICATIONS

1. Given our discussion of the meaning of work in this chapter, reflect on your own career desires and possible trajectory. In what ways did this chapter ring true for you? With what aspects of it do you disagree?

2. Return to the discussion on meaningful work above. Given the six criteria outlined there, is there anyone who would be unable to defend his or her work as meaningful? With a classmate, think of some work that you simply could not do because it's morally, socially, or physically dirty. How can such people account for the meaningfulness of their work? If they can, is the notion of meaningful work meaningless?

3. Writing during the Great Depression, the influential economist John Maynard Keynes (1932) predicted that, in the late 20th or early 21st century, people would be working just 15 hours per week. (Ironically, Keynes died from heart problems associated with his own habits of overwork.) As seen in the statistics in this chapter, that obviously didn't happen. Using concepts from this chapter, how and why could Keynes have got it so wrong—what didn't he understand?

KEY TERMS

achieved selves 371

ascribed selves 371

conformist selves 373

corrosion of character 369

dramaturgical selves 374

identity 367

identity work 370

identity workers 370

liquid or light modernity 368

no-collar workers 378

ontological security 367

personal branding 380

reflexive modernity 367

resistant selves 375

roles 371

social entrepreneurship 364

solid or heavy modernity 368

time famine 379

STUDENT STUDY SITE

Visit the student study site at **www.sagepub.com/mumby.org** for these additional learning tools:

- Web quizzes
- eFlashcards
- SAGE journal articles
- Video resources
- Web resources

Glossary

achieved selves: Achieved selves reflect more fluid social structures where greater onus is placed on the ability of individuals to create stable, coherent identities. Demands on the self are constantly changing and thus create precarious identities.

adaptive structuration theory: A theory of technology that addresses the interplay of the social and technical in organizational action; it explains that the effects of technologies always occur through communication as the technology becomes part of a communication system.

agency: The ability to act otherwise, to choose a course of action different from the one prescribed by the situation or by another person.

algorithmic management: Using algorithms' data processing power to extract information from big data to allow managers to oversee workers in an optimized manner at a large scale.

algorithms: Rules that specify operations to find trends in data, and can learn from patterns, as well as make decisions and predict the future.

alienation: A term coined by Marx to describe how, under capitalism, the workers feel separated from both their work and themselves.

analytics: Computerized techniques to uncover and interpret meaningful patterns in big data.

ascribed selves: Identity assigned at birth because of social or class position; largely unchangeable but providing a clear, stable sense of identity.

asynchronous medium: Enables people to communicate with one another at different times and in different places. A person can send a message to another person, and that person can reply to it when it when it suits him or her.

attention economy: A term used to describe the idea that, particularly in the context of social media, followers (attention) can be translated to economic value.

auto-communication: In the context of CSR, this is when an organization communicates with itself about its commitment to a virtuous future identity, which can eventually get performed into existence.

autonomy paradox: Although professionals generally value control over their work processes, with the constant connectivity offered by information and communication technologies (ICTs), they willingly limit their autonomy.

big data: Sets of digitally collected data, usually collected from a variety of sources that produce a high velocity of ongoing data streams, which are so vast that traditional approaches to processing and analyzing them are inadequate.

biocracy: Contrasted with bureaucracy, biocracy is an organizational form in which features of everyday life previously seen as irrelevant to organizations (e.g., emotions, lifestyle, sexuality) are increasingly viewed as central to the management of new, post-Fordist forms of work. Biocracy is an extension of organizational power rather than its relaxation.

biocratic control: A form of control characteristic of post-Fordist organizations in which the focus is on capturing "life itself" (bios) by erasing the distinction between work and life.

biopower: Power over life (bios). Under neoliberalism, the goal of power is not to make people docile and obedient but rather to encourage them to engage in competitive social relations, to view themselves as human capital in every sphere of life.

Bottom of the Pyramid (BoP): The thesis that the global poor are potential entrepreneurs and consumers, not merely passive recipients of wealthy countries' aid. According to BoP theorists, sustainable poverty alleviation can occur only when the poor participate in economic development by creating new business enterprises.

brand: "The total constellation of meanings, feelings, perceptions, beliefs, and goodwill attributed to any market offering displaying a particular sign" (Muniz, 2007). A brand is a carefully constructed set of meanings that a company attaches to a particular product, including the company itself.

brand extension: The process of leveraging the meanings and emotions associated with a particular company to a variety of different products that don't necessarily have any relationship to one another.

brand public: The community of people who are strangers to each but are connected through their identification and shared affinity with a particular brand.

branding from the outside in: The process of drawing on the cultural and social knowledge and forms of expertise that employees already possess (in contexts external to the organization) as a way to maintain and enhance the brand. In this sense, brands create organizations rather than organizations creating brands.

brands as institution: The role of brands in providing a framework through which we experience our sense of self, others, and the world around us. Companies engage with consumers through their brands in an effort to mediate their everyday experiences.

bureaucratic control: The use of formal systems of rules, structures, job descriptions, and merit systems to create routine employee behavior that is less subject to the arbitrary whims of supervisors.

capitalism: A mode of production in which owners of capital (capitalists) purchase labor power from workers at the market rate in order to produce surplus value and hence make profit. In this system, workers are expropriated; that is, because they do not own the means of production, they must sell their labor power in order to survive.

charismatic authority: The ability of a particular individual to exercise authority over others by virtue of his or her special abilities. Charismatic figures often emerge at times of instability and social unrest.

chaos: The condition of a complex system in which it is impossible to predict what it will do next.

clock time: A form of time developed through industrialization in which time is no longer passed but spent. Time is a valuable currency that defines the employer–employee relationship and over which struggles occur.

closed systems: A system is open or closed to the degree that it can exchange information and energy with its environment. A closed system cannot adapt to environmental changes and is more likely to move toward entropy.

communication: The dynamic, ongoing process of creating and negotiating meanings through interactional symbolic (verbal and nonverbal) practices, including conversation, metaphors, rituals, stories, dress, and space.

communicative capitalism: The idea that a strong connection exists between the creation of economic value and the construction of meanings through communication processes. In a brand economy, value is created through management of meanings.

community power debate: Debate in the field of political science about the nature of power that existed in society. The two camps in the debate were the elitists and the pluralists.

complexity: The quality of a system characterized by nonlinear, noncausal outcomes. One cannot predict the end point of a complex system from its starting point.

conformist selves: Efforts by organization members to portray themselves as valued in the eyes of those in authority. Under conditions of insecurity, one way to gain security is to demonstrate a level of performance that makes one indispensable to the organization.

constant connectivity: The expectation that, with information and communication technologies (ICTs) always available, workers will be always accessible and available for work.

consumer engagement: The branding strategy that involves consumers directly in the branding process, hence blurring the relationship between production and consumption.

corporate colonization: The spread of corporate ideologies and discourses to every aspect of our lives, including who we are as human beings. Corporate discourses have colonized other institutions such as the family and higher education, thus defining other, traditionally noncorporate spheres of our lives.

corporate social responsibility (CSR): Integrating a company's social, environmental, ethical, and philanthropic responsibilities toward society into its everyday operations and strategy for its future.

corrosion of character: The result of the shift to the new form of capitalism, in which loyalty and long-term employment are no longer key to professional success and a strong work identity. It is difficult for people to develop a stable life narrative on which to build a sense of character.

critical communication capacities: The ability to understand and analyze the ways that communication processes construct social realities that, over time, become common sense and taken for granted.

critical communication perspective (on leadership): Rejection of leader- or follower-centric view of leadership. Focus on leadership as dynamic communication process involving everyone. Leadership is socially constructed through communication. A post-heroic view of leadership, with a focus on power and control and possibilities for leadership as resistance.

critical feminism: A focus on the processes through which organizations and society are gendered. Gender is viewed as socially constructed and performed though power relations. How do both men and women do gender?

critical theory: A perspective that views the world as socially constructed through communication but sees underlying systems of power as shaping how this social construction process occurs.

crowdsourcing: Activity in which a large set of individuals, typically using information and communication technologies (ICTs), separately completes a task. The tasks best suited to crowdsourcing are those that can be decomposed into small units and then put back together, but it is also used to generate creative solutions to challenging problems.

CSR ratings: Evaluating companies on criteria for ethical behavior by civic organizations, government agencies, the press, and consulting firms.

cultural pragmatist: A view of organizational culture as a variable that can be manipulated to impact employee commitment and performance. Culture and organization are seen as separate. A managerial approach to organizational culture.

cultural purist: A root metaphor approach to organizations. Culture is not a thing an organization possesses; rather, an organization is a culture. A researcher approach to organizational culture.

cultural studies: The study of everyday popular culture and systems of meaning. How do people construct meaningful lives in the context of systems of power and control?

culture industry: The mass production of popular culture, administered from above, that creates needs in people that they would not otherwise have. The culture industry maintains the status quo and limits people's critical abilities.

culture jamming: Attempts to use the advertisements and billboards of large, multinational corporations against the corporations themselves by reworking their meanings; in other words, semiotic jujitsu.

Deetz's stakeholder model: A view of organizational decision making that sees organizations as consisting of multiple stakeholders, each of whom has a legitimate stake in the organization's actions. This is a model for how organizations might engage in dialogue as a form of CSR.

deterritorializing: The process of globalization in which money, information, and people flow around the world without regard for national boundaries. Globalization is based on virtual communication networks rather than geographic regions.

dialectical theory: An approach developed by the Frankfurt School to explore the complex relations between economics, culture, and politics. There is no one-to-one correspondence between these elements; instead, they interact in complex ways to create social reality.

difference: A social construction used to classify human beings into separate, value-based categories.

direct control: supervising employees in explicit ways and monitoring their behavior to make sure they are performing adequately.

disclosure devices: Practices and technologies that make people and processes visible, revealing details of what workers do when producing and using knowledge.

division of labor: Breaking down the labor process into its basic parts in order to improve productivity and decrease labor costs.

double-interacts: Karl Weick's notion of the basic unit of organizing (A-B-A) through which organization members reduce information equivocality.

dramaturgical selves: The employment of visible communicative performances aimed at enabling employees to survive and prosper in the workplace. They frequently emerge in organizational contexts where employees feel under constant surveillance, threatened, defensive, subordinated, and/or insecure.

economic determinism: A classic Marxist position that views the culture and ideas of a society as heavily shaped by the economic structure of that society.

elitists: A group of scholars involved in the community power debate who claimed that power is concentrated in the hands of a privileged few who controlled political agendas.

emancipatory approach: A mode of examining organizational culture, which exposes how organizational cultures dominate and exploit workers; it also promotes changes in those cultures.

emotional labor: The management of feeling to create a publicly observable facial and bodily display. Emotional labor functions in the service of organizations to increase profitability.

enactment, selection, and retention: Weick's model of the organizing process through which equivocality, or uncertainty, in organization members' information environment is reduced.

enterprise self: The condition of thinking and acting as individual enterprises that must compete against all other individuals/enterprises. The "enterprise self" is closely tied to what it means to be a citizen under neoliberalism. We are defined by our relationships to the market.

entropy: The second law of thermodynamics, whereby over time a system naturally moves toward chaos and disorder, and dissipates. An open system staves off entropy through adaptation to change and is hence negentropic.

equifinality: The ability of an open system to reach the same final state from differing initial conditions and by a variety of paths.

equivocality (uncertainty) reduction: The means by which, through the process of enactment, selection, and retention, organization members reduce the information uncertainty in their environments.

ethnography: The study of naturally occurring human behavior through a researcher's immersion into the culture of a group or organization; an exploration of how humans engage in meaning construction through communication processes.

facts: A body of social knowledge, shared by members, that enables them to navigate the culture on a daily basis.

feminism: According to bell hooks (2000, p. 1), feminism is "a movement to end sexism, sexist exploitation, and oppression."

feminist standpoint theory: A perspective that argues that knowledge must be grounded in people's lived experiences (standpoints) and that differences between the lived experiences of men and women, and white people and people of color, provide the opportunity for knowledge claims that reflect the situated experiences of women and minorities.

fissured workplace: An employment strategy that aims to improve profitability by focusing attention on and controlling the most profitable aspects of firm value while shedding the actual production of goods or provision of services.

floating signifier effect: The notion that the meaning of any particular brand is arbitrary. Literally any meaning or quality—any floating signifier—can be attached to any object, product, company, or person.

followership: A leadership approach in which leaders don't exist without followers; most people are followers most of the time. Exemplary followers are highly committed to the organization, self-managing, and willing to provide honest, independent, and constructive critique to leaders.

Fordism: The dominant mode of production and organization in the 20th century, characterized by a hierarchical, bureaucratic, centralized decision-making system; deskilled labor; large economies of scale; standardization of products; and lifetime employment.

four systems approach: Rensis Likert's classification of organizations into four systems (exploitative–authoritative, benevolent–authoritative, consultative, participative), with each representing an increasing level of worker participation in decision making.

Frankfurt School: A group of 20th-century German intellectuals interested in understanding capitalism not only as an economic system but also as a cultural and ideological system that had a significant impact on the way people thought about and experienced the world.

gender accountability: The process through which we are judged and evaluated (i.e., held accountable) on our appropriate performance of gender identities. Such accountability occurs in an everyday, ongoing fashion.

general system theory: Defined by Ludwig von Bertalanffy as "the general science of wholeness" (von Bertalanffy, 1968, p. 37); the study of living (including social) structures as interdependent, goal-oriented systems that are irreducible to their basic elements.

glass ceiling: An invisible institutional barrier that limits professional women's progress into the upper echelons of an organization.

glass cliff: The precarious position women managers often find themselves in once they have succeeded in shattering the glass ceiling. Women are often appointed to senior positions associated with a greater risk of failure and thus are often set up to fail.

glass escalator: The experience of faster upward mobility of men in traditionally female occupations.

glass slipper: The alignment of occupational identity with embodied social identities as it yields systematic forms of advantage and disadvantage. Occupations police what kinds of social identities are permitted to fit their occupational definitions.

global cities: The primary sites where the leading, global information industries are located. Global cities (London, New York, Paris, Tokyo, etc.) have become more powerful than nation-states in shaping global economies.

globalization: A political, economic, and cultural process that involves the intensification of consciousness of the world as a whole and an increased interdependence between nation-states and cultures.

globalization from below: Efforts by grassroots organizations and peoples around the world to resist the economic and cultural imperialism often associated with globalization; focus on transforming power relations and empowering local groups.

goal orientations: All systems are goal oriented, and through the process of feedback (both positive and negative), they are able to adjust their activities in order to maintain progression toward their goals.

greening initiatives: Efforts by companies to develop products that are environmentally friendly, along with pledges to avoid causing environmental disasters.

greenwashing: Public relations efforts, typically seen as insincere, intended to make a corporation's routine operations look virtuous to both the public and its own employees.

Hawthorne effect: The primary finding of the Hawthorne studies, suggesting a causal connection between the psychological state of a worker and his or her productivity ("A happy worker is a productive worker").

Hawthorne studies: A famous series of experiments, conducted from 1924 to 1933 at the Western Electric Hawthorne plant in Cicero, Illinois, that established the importance of social relations in work; inspired decades of group and leadership research.

hegemonic masculinity: The historically dominant, socially constructed form of masculinity—characterized by physical prowess, individuality, aggressive heterosexuality, and independence—against which other forms of masculinity are measured.

hegemony: The struggle over the establishment of certain meanings and ideas in society. A group maintains hegemony when it is able to create a worldview that other people and groups actively support, even though that worldview may not be in their interests. Hegemony operates when the taken for granted system of meanings that everyone shares functions in the best interests of the dominant group.

heteronormativity: "Institutions, structures of understanding, and practical orientations that make heterosexuality not only coherent—that is, organized as a sexuality—but also privileged" (Berlant & Warner, 1998, p. 565).

hidden transcripts: Employee discourse and behavior that occur offstage and outside the immediate view of those in power in an organization; a form of employee resistance to managerial control efforts.

hierarchy: Systems are not structured on a single level but rather process information and function dynamically across multiple levels. Any system is made up of interrelated and interdependent subsystems and is itself a subsystem within a larger suprasystem.

historical materialism: Marx's analysis of history according to the different modes of production used in a society (e.g., slave, feudal, capitalist, etc.).

holism: The systems principle of nonsummativity—the whole is different from the sum of its parts. The elements of a system, functioning interdependently, cannot be aggregated; they can be understood only through their dynamic interaction.

homeostasis: The ability of an open system to maintain a steady state by adapting to changes in its environment.

homosocial reproduction: The tendency of the dominant men in organizations to reproduce themselves in their own images through their hiring practices.

hostile environment: A form of sexual harassment where conduct directed at a person because of her or his sex or sexuality unreasonably interferes with the person's ability to perform her or his job.

human capital: The neoliberal idea that each person possesses a set of skills, knowledge, and abilities that he or she is responsible for maintaining and improving so that he or she accumulates more capital (and hence accrues more market value).

human relations school: A group of management researchers who focus on the social, interactional dimensions of work rather than its technical dimensions.

identity: "The conception of the self reflexively and discursively understood by the self" (Kuhn, 2006, p. 1340); the story of the self that we tell to both ourselves and others.

identity work: The process of continuously engaging in forming, repairing, maintaining, strengthening or revising the constructions that are productive of a precarious sense of coherence and distinctiveness.

identity workers: What most workers are required to become—in addition to performing work tasks—by developing a professional identity that meets the needs and goals of the organization.

ideological control: The corporate development of a system of values, beliefs, and meanings with which employees are expected to identify strongly.

ideology: The system of attitudes, beliefs, ideas, perceptions, and values that shape the reality of people in society. Ideology does not simply reflect reality as it exists but shapes reality to favor the interests of the dominant class.

immaterial labor: Labor that does not produce things per se but that produces the informational and cultural content of commodities.

information and communication technologies (ICTs): Computer-aided tools useful for overcoming communicators' separation in space and time through the electronic exchange of messages.

intersectional approach: A perspective that examines the combined effects of race, class, gender, and sexuality on people's position in society.

invisible knapsack: A set of privileges and practices that white people carry around with them that largely protects them from everyday injustices.

iron cage of bureaucracy: A term coined by Max Weber to critique the ways that bureaucratic systems often remove creativity and critical thinking from organizations and society.

just-in-time: Part of a lean production system in which a company increases efficiency and minimizes waste by maintaining a minimal level of inventory.

Kaizen: A Japanese system of continuous work improvement that focuses on the work process rather than the product (literally, "change for the better").

keynesianism: An economic philosophy that advocates a "mixed economy," in which government intervention creates a welfare system (unemployment benefits, pensions, health care, etc.) and a mixture of publicly (state) and privately owned companies. Its intent is to limit extreme economic cycles of "boom and bust."

knowledge management: The creation of systems to locate, produce, capture, curate, move, and capitalize upon knowledge for organizational benefit.

knowledge repositories: Tools that store lessons learned, best practices, and expert profiles; often used in conjunction with other knowledge management tools.

knowledge work: Work that tends to feature non-routine problem solving, accomplished through intellectual labor and information analysis.

leadership: "The process of influencing the activities of an organized group in its efforts toward goal setting and goal achievement" (Stogdill, 1950, p. 3).

liberal feminism: An approach to gender and power that focuses on creating equal opportunities for women in all spheres of life—work, home, and education.

liquid or light modernity: Bauman's view of the current state of capitalism in which change is constant, the social contract no longer exists between employers and employees, and the powerful are those free from geographical constraints.

managing diversity: A term used to describe efforts to create a workforce that reflects the gender, racial, and ethnic differences in the wider society.

Marx (Karl): A 19th-century philosopher and theorist who developed a systematic critique of capitalism as an economic, political, and cultural system.

mecosystem: A term used by brand strategists to describe how brands attempt to create customized experiences around a single individual (an individual brand ecosystem).

media richness theory: A theory suggesting that information and communication technologies (ICTs) possess features that make them "rich" or "lean" and that people select media appropriate to the needs of a given activity.

metaphors: The understanding and experiencing of one kind of thing in terms of another. Organizational cultures can be experienced as families, teams, machines, and so forth.

microaggression: "Brief and commonplace daily verbal, behavioral, or environmental indignities, whether intentional or unintentional, that communicate hostile, derogatory, or negative racial slights and insults toward people of color" (Sue et al., 2007, p. 271).

murketing: A marketing strategy that attempts to integrate brands into the expression of individual identities by blurring the distinction between marketing and everyday life and popular culture.

narrative leadership: A decentered model of leadership that sees stories as exhibiting a leadership function and playing a central role in shaping organizational vision.

negative entropy: A state that counters entropy, or disorder. An open system staves off entropy through adaptation to change and is hence negentropic.

neoliberalism: An economic philosophy that argues for the sovereignty of the free market without any government intervention. The sole responsibility of a company is to make a profit for its shareholders. To maximize the social good, the model of the market must be extended to all realms of society

new leadership: A broad term that describes innovations in leadership research, including leadership as symbolic action, followership, transformational leadership, and a view of leadership as socially constructed.

niche marketing: The development of brand strategies that appeal to specific social identity groups through a focus on the authenticity of the brand.

no-collar workers: A "free agent" worker with a nontraditional career path who engages in creative, "knowledge work" and rejects the idea of stable, long-term employment at a single company; creation of ideas ("symbol manipulators"), not things.

nonsummative: The idea that the whole is qualitatively different from the sum of its parts. For example, the difference between weight (summative) and wetness (nonsummative).

normalization: "The process of constructing, establishing, producing, and reproducing a taken-for-granted and all-encompassing standard used to measure goodness, desirability, morality, rationality, superiority, and a host of other dominant cultural values. As such, normalization becomes one of the primary instruments of power in modern society" (Yep, 2003, p. 18).

normative control: The attempt to elicit and direct the required efforts of members by controlling the underlying experiences, thoughts, and feelings that guide their actions.

one-dimensional view of power: Power is exercised through direct influence of one person or group over another. Overt conflict is necessary for power to be exercised. "A has power over B to the extent that A can get B to do something that B would not otherwise do."

ontological security: The creation of a personal narrative that provides a coherent sense of the self. An individual's impression that the world is stable, continuous, and predictable, which is often produced through routinized activity.

open systems: A system is open or closed to the degree that it can exchange information and energy with its environment. A more open system can adapt to environmental changes.

ordinary management: Management by rule of thumb and use of arbitrary principles to regulate the labor process; the system of management Frederick Taylor was attempting to eliminate.

organizational communication: The process of creating and negotiating collective, coordinated systems of meaning through symbolic practices oriented toward the achievement of organizational goals.

organizational control: The dynamic communication process through which different organizational interest groups struggle to maximize their stake in an organization.

organizational storytelling: A symbolic, narrative representation of an organization's culture that provides members with a moral imperative about appropriate and inappropriate organizational behavior.

outsider within: The experiences and perceptions of a person with minority status from a position within a dominant culture.

participant-observation: A form of ethnography in which the researcher studies an organization while participating in its everyday cultural practices.

passing: The various communication strategies adopted by minority group member (e.g., by sexuality, race, or class) in order to gain social acceptance within a majority group.

people analytics: Locating patterns in big data derived from employee behavior to shape human resources decisions.

personal branding: Individuals' intentional efforts to shape the emotions and impressions of others, usually with respect to making one a marketable commodity.

platform: Combinations of digital software and hardware that form an infrastructure facilitating connections between producers (sellers) and consumers (buyers) and also allow sellers to establish an enterprise linked to the larger business.

platform capitalism: The use of digital infrastructure that enables two or more groups (typically, users and providers of a service) to interact, which is the basis of the on-demand, sharing, and gig economies.

platform cooperatives: Democratically owned computing platforms governed by the stakeholders who use them.

pluralists: A group of scholars involved in the community power debate who argued that power was equitably distributed throughout society and that no particular group had undue influence over decision-making processes.

post-Fordism: The late 20th century successor to Fordism, characterized by flatter structures; decentralized decision-making systems; small economies of scale; niche production; increasing commodification of everyday life; more insecure, unstable employment; and a blurring of the distinction between work and life.

power: A dynamic process in which relations of interdependence exist between actors in organizational settings.

practices: The everyday behavior that enables members to accomplish the process of organizing and enacts the organizational culture.

precariat: Workers in all segments of the workforce who are in extremely precarious economic environments and are constantly under threat of losing their jobs.

queer theory: A perspective that works to critique how processes of normalization operate to marginalize certain groups of people.

quid pro quo: A form of sexual harassment in which the harasser demands sexual favors with the promise of preferred treatment regarding employment or evaluation.

radical feminism: A "woman-centered" approach that revalues feminine qualities that have been devalued in patriarchal society; focuses on the creation of alternative, women-centered organizations that attempt to operate independently from patriarchal society.

radical responsibilization: A system of employment in which each worker is responsible for his or her own success or failure.

rationalization: The process by which all aspects of the natural and social world become increasingly subject to planning, calculation, and efficiency. We are all subject to the "iron cage of bureaucracy."

rational–legal authority: Exercise of authority through the impersonal system of rules and responsibilities that come with the holding of a bureaucratic office; rule of the bureau.

reflexive modernity: A new period of modernity in which the traditional stability-maintaining structures of class, family, and industrial forms of production have waned, placing greater pressure on people to create their own sense of stability and identity.

relationship: A systems term used to describe the idea that systems are defined not by their parts but by the relationship between them.

relevant constructs: Important terms and phrases that help organize the experience of members of a culture; differentiate what is important from what is less important.

reputation systems: Rating devices that allow users to assess a provider's service; the aggregation of these ratings comprises the provider's reputation.

resistance leadership: A nonmanagerial approach to leadership that views acts of resistance as a form of leadership that can contribute to the well-being of a community or organization.

resistant selves: Employed in organizational contexts where employees are attempting to resist managerial control efforts. Resistant selves attempt to negotiate or subvert the dominant, or official, meanings that organizations attempt to foster.

retrospective sense making: Weick's view of how people construct rational accounts of organizational behavior after the fact—"how do I know what I think until I see what I say?"

rites and rituals: Regular, repeated organizational symbolic practices that create order and predictability in organization members' lives and produce a shared reality.

roles: Expected behaviors and obligations associated with a position in a social system.

romance leadership: A perspective that focuses on how leaders are socially constructed by followers. Leaders are romanticized such that followers exaggerate their importance and influence.

scientific management: Development of the "one best way" to engage in a work process using the scientific principles established by Frederick Winslow Taylor.

self-organizing systems: Systems characterized by a lack of equilibrium typically due to a large influx of new information or significant environmental shifts and are thus in the process of acting on this new information as a process of self-renewal. Self-organizing systems exhibit autocatalysis; that is, the catalysts for change and renewal occur in elements of the system itself as it seeks to renew itself.

sexual harassment: Unwelcome sexual advances, requests for sexual favors, and other verbal or physical conduct of a sexual nature constitutes sexual harassment when submission to or rejection of this conduct explicitly or implicitly affects an individual's employment; unreasonably interferes with an individual's work performance; or creates an intimidating, hostile, or offensive work environment.

situational approach: Rejects the idea of a universal leadership style or trait; views contextual factors such as the structure of the task at hand, the power of the leader, and the size of the work group as shaping the leadership approach adopted.

social accounting: Bookkeeping techniques that assess the economic, social, and environmental outcomes of a company's activities.

social entrepreneurship: Seeking to engage with pressing social problems through nonprofit and nongovernmental organizations but applying traditional (for-profit) entrepreneurship principles to their practices.

social factory: The idea that, under post-Fordism, the process of economic value production has escaped the walls of the factory and has become dispersed throughout society.

social influence model of media use: A reaction to media richness theory and social presence theory, this perspective argues that the meanings people construct around technologies, produced in communication patterns, norms, and general cultural beliefs, affect how technologies are used.

social presence theory: A theory describing the degree to which information and communication technologies (ICTs) foster feelings of co-presence even when people are separate in space and time.

solid or heavy modernity: The old, Fordist style of modernity based in the social contract, where relations between management and employees were clearly defined. Solid modernity was rooted in bulk and size and mass production of solid goods.

style approach: A leadership approach that argues there is a specific set of skills managers can learn to become effective leaders.

surplus value: The difference between the value of the labor power as purchased by the capitalist and the actual value produced by the laborer; the source of profit for capitalists.

symbolic action: A conception of leadership that focuses on the ways the leader is able to frame and define reality for others. Leadership is conceived as a process of interaction rather than a thing.

synchronous medium: Parties to an interaction exchange messages at (something close to) the same time but from different locations.

systematic soldiering: The deliberate and coordinated effort of workers to restrict output by limiting the speed at which they perform work. Workers engage in systematic soldiering to prevent piece rates being cut.

task time: An organic sense of time in which work is shaped by the demands of the task to be performed. For example, work in a farming community is shaped by the seasons.

technological control: The use of various forms of organizational technology to control worker productivity.

telework: A work system in which some or all of an individual's work is performed from a remote location, via communication technology.

Theory X: McGregor's term for the dominant management philosophy that sees workers as having an inherent dislike of work and needing to be coerced to be productive.

Theory Y: McGregor's own philosophy of management, which treats workers as motivated, creative, engaging in self-direction, and enjoying work as much as play.

thick description: The writing of narrative accounts that provide rich insight into the complex meaning patterns that underlie people's collective behavior; associated with ethnographic research.

three-dimensional view of power: Conflict (either overt or covert) is not a necessary condition for the exercise of power. Power operates at a deep-structure level by shaping people's interests, beliefs, and values.

time famine: The increasing sense that time is at a premium, requiring that we constantly engage in managing time. Our identities, including leisure activities, become tied up with effective time management and getting the most out of our time.

tokenism: A condition in which a person is visibly identified as a minority in a dominant culture. These people are identified as representative of their minority groups, and any failure is viewed as a failing of the minority group to which they belong. Tokenism is a creation of the perceptual and communication practices of those who shape the dominant culture of the organization.

Toyotism: A system of production invented in the 1950s by the Toyota automobile company in which focus is placed on the process of manufacture rather than on the products. Toyotism contrasts with the production system under Fordism.

traditional authority: The inherited right of individuals to expect loyalty and obedience from others; authority based in custom and tradition.

trait approach: A leadership approach that argues that the qualities of a leader are embodied in his or her innate personal characteristics—physique, intelligence, and personality. Leaders are born, not made.

transformational leadership: The active promotion of values to provide a shared vision of the organization. Leader and members are bound together in a higher moral purpose. The leader raises the aspirations of followers such that they think and act beyond their own self-interests.

two-dimensional view of power: Power is exercised by setting agendas and mobilizing bias to support one's position. Covert, but not overt, conflict is necessary for power. "A has power over B when A prevents B from doing something that B would otherwise do."

uniqueness paradox: The idea that stories intended to express an organization's uniqueness actually occur across a range of organizations.

unique selling proposition: A branding principle that enables a brand to distinguish itself from its direct competitors (regardless of whether any unique quality actually exists).

venture labor: "The investment of time, energy, human capital, and other personal resources that ordinary employees make in the companies where they work. Venture labor is the explicit expression of entrepreneurial values by nonentrepreneurs" (Neff, 2012, p. 16).

vocabulary: The use of a specific jargon that is exclusive to members of a culture and functions as a badge of identification, distinguishing members from other cultures.

WATT system: The system of social welfare capitalism that existed under Fordism, in which a social safety net is provided to all citizens ("We're all in this together")

whiteness: A socially constructed racial category that consists of institutionalized practices and ideas that people participate in consciously and unconsciously. Whiteness is simultaneously taken for granted, largely invisible, and a yardstick for judgment of behavior and ideas.

work teams: A collection of individuals who are interdependent in their tasks, who share responsibility for outcomes, and who see themselves and are seen by others as an intact social entity embedded in one or more large social systems.

YOYO system: The system under neoliberalism in which everyone is responsible for their own outcomes; any success is individual success and any failure is individual failure ("You're on your own").

References

ABC News. (2010, Oct. 27). Former JetBlue attendant Steven Slater's story [Video file]. Retrieved from https://www.youtube.com/watch?v = NBMWhMEGsNw.

Acker, J. (1990). Hierarchies, jobs, bodies: A theory of gendered organizations. *Gender and Society, 4,* 139–158.

Acker, J. (2004). Gender, capitalism and globalization. *Critical Sociology, 30,* 17–41.

Acker, J. (2006). Inequality regimes: Gender, class, and race in organizations. *Gender & Society, 20,* 441–464.

Ackroyd, S., & Thompson, P. (1999). *Organizational misbehaviour.* London: Sage.

Adorno, T. (1973). *Negative dialectics* (E. B. Ashton, Trans.). New York: Continuum.

Adkins, A. (2016). Employee engagement in U.S. stagnant in 2015. Retrieved from https://news.gallup .com/poll/188144/employee-engagement-stagnant-2015.aspx.

Alderman, L. (2017, February 9). Feeling "pressure all the time" on Europe's treadmill of temporary work. *The New York Times.* Retrieved from https://www.nytimes.com/2017/02/09/business/ europe-jobs-economy-youth-unemployment-millenials.html?hp&action = click&pgtype = Hom epage&clickSource = story-heading&module = photo-spot-region&region = top-news&WT .nav = top-news&_r = 0.

Allen, B. J. (1996). Feminist standpoint theory: A black woman's (re)view of organizational socialization. *Communication Studies, 47,* 257–271.

Allen, B. J. (1998). Black womanhood and feminist standpoints. *Management Communication Quarterly, 11,* 575–586.

Allen, B. J. (2000). "Learning the ropes": A black feminist standpoint analysis. In P. M. Buzzanell (Ed.), *Rethinking organizational and managerial communication from feminist perspectives* (pp. 177–208). Thousand Oaks, CA: Sage.

Allen, B. J. (2011). *Difference matters: Communicating social identity* (2nd. ed.). Long Grove, Ill.: Waveland Press.

Alvesson, M. (1993). *Cultural perspectives on organizations.* Cambridge, UK: Cambridge University Press.

Alvesson, M. (2002). *Understanding organizational culture.* London: Sage.

Alvesson, M., Ashcraft, K. L., & Thomas, R. (2008). Identity matters: Reflections on the study of identity scholarship in organization studies. *Organization, 15,* 5–28.

Alvesson, M., & Deetz, S. (2000). *Doing critical management research.* Thousand Oaks: Sage.

Alvesson, M., & Spicer, A. (2011). Theories of leadership. In M. Alvesson & A. Spicer (Eds.), *Metaphors we lead by: Understanding leadership in the real world* (pp. 8–30). London: Routledge.

Alvesson, M., & Spicer, A. (Eds.). (2011). *Metaphors we lead by: Understanding leadership in the real world.* London: Routledge.

Alvesson, M., & Willmott, H. (2002). Identity regulation as organizational control: Producing the appropriate individual. *Journal of Management Studies, 39,* 619–644.

Amos, A., & Haglund, M. (2000). From social taboo to "torch of freedom": The marketing of cigarettes to women. *Tobacco Control, 9,* 3–8.

Anderson, E. (2009). *Inclusive masculinity: The changing nature of masculinities*. New York: Routledge.

Anon. (2015). *International migration report*. Retrieved from: http://www.un.org/en/development/desa/population/migration/publications/migrationreport/docs/MigrationReport2015_Highlights.pdf.

Argyle, M. (1953). The Relay Assembly Test Room in retrospect. *Occupational Psychology, 27*, 98–103.

Arvidsson, A. (2006). *Brands: Meaning and value in media culture*. London: Routledge.

Aschoff, N. (2015). *The new prophets of capital [Kindle edition]*. London: Verso.

Ashcraft, K. L. (1998a). *Assessing alternative(s): Contradiction and invention in a feminist organization*. University of Colorado, Boulder, CO. Unpublished Doctoral Dissertation.

Ashcraft, K. L. (1998b). "I wouldn't say I'm a feminist, but . . .": Organizational micropractice and gender identity. *Management Communication Quarterly, 11*, 587–597.

Ashcraft, K. L. (2000). Empowering "professional" relationships: Organizational communication meets feminist practice. *Management Communication Quarterly, 13*, 347–392.

Ashcraft, K. L. (2001). Organized dissonance: Feminist bureaucracy as hybrid form. *Academy of Management Journal, 44*, 1301–1322.

Ashcraft, K. L. (2005). Resistance through consent?: Occupational identity, organizational form, and the maintenance of masculinity among commercial airline pilots. *Management Communication Quarterly, 19*, 67–90.

Ashcraft, K. L. (2007). Appreciating the "work" of discourse: Occupational identity and difference as organizing mechanisms in the case of commercial airline pilots. *Discourse & Communication, 1*, 9–36.

Ashcraft, K. L. (2011). Knowing work through the communication of difference: A revised agenda for difference studies. In D. K. Mumby (Ed.), *Reframing difference in organizational communication studies: Research, pedagogy, practice* (pp. 3–30). Thousand Oaks, CA: Sage.

Ashcraft, K. L. (2013). The glass slipper: "Incorporating" occupational identity in management studies. *Academy of Management Review, 38*, 6–31.

Ashcraft, K. L. (2017). 'Submission' to the rule of excellence: Ordinary affect and precarious resistance in the labor of organization and management studies. *Organization, 24*, 36–58.

Ashcraft, K. L., & Allen, B. J. (2003). The racial foundation of organizational communication. *Communication Theory, 13*, 5–38.

Ashcraft, K. L., Kuhn, T., & Cooren, F. (2009). Constitutional amendments: "Materializing" organizational communication. *The Academy of Management Annals, 3*, 1–64.

Ashcraft, K. L., & Mumby, D. K. (2004). Organizing a critical communicology of gender and work. *International Journal of the Sociology of Language, 166*, 19–43.

Ashforth, B., & Kreiner, G. (1999). "How can you do it?": Dirty work and the challenge of constructing a positive identity. *Academy of Management Review, 24*, 413–434.

Assistant Secretary for Planning and Evaluation. (n.d.). 2017 proverty guidelines. Retrieved from U.D. Department of Health Human Services: https://aspe.hhs.gov/2017-poverty-guidelines#guidelines

Axley, S. (1984). Managerial and organizational communication in terms of the conduit metaphor. *Academy of Management Review, 9*, 428–437.

Bachrach, P., & Baratz, M. (1962). Two faces of power. *American Political Science Review, 56*, 947–952.

Bachrach, P., & Baratz, M. (1963). Decisions and nondecisions: An analytical framework. *American Political Science Review, 57*, 641–651.

Bain, R. (1937). Technology and state government. *American Sociological Review, 2*, 860–874.

Baker, S. D. (2007). Followership: The theoretical foundation of a contemporary construct. *Journal of Leadership and Organizational Studies, 14*, 50–60.

Ball, K. (2010). Workplace surveillance: An overview. *Labor History, 51*(1), 87–106. doi:10.1080/00236561003654776

Banerjee, S. B. (2003). Who sustains whose development?: Sustainable development and the reinvention of nature. *Organization Studies, 24*, 143–180.

Banerjee, S. B. (2008). Necrocapitalism. *Organization Studies, 29*, 1541–1563.

Banerjee, S. B. (2018). Transnational power and translocal governance: The politics of corporate responsibility. *Human Relations, 71*, 796–821.

Banerjee, S. B., & Jackson, L. (2017). Microfinance and the business of poverty reduction: Critical perspectives from rural Bangladesh. *Human Relations, 70*, 63–91.

Banet-Weiser, S. (2012). *Authentic: The politics of ambivalence in a brand culture*. New York: New York University Press.

Banta, M. (1993). *Taylored lives: Narrative production in the age of Taylor, Veblen, and Ford*. Chicago: University of Chicago Press.

Bantz, C. R. (1993). *Understanding organizations: Interpreting organizational communication cultures*. Columbia: University of South Carolina Press.

Bar, F., & Simard, C. (2002). New media implementation and industrial organization. In L. Lievrouw & S. Livingstone (Eds.), *The handbook of new media* (pp. 254–263). London: Sage.

Barber, B. (1995). *Jihad vs. McWorld*. New York: Ballantine.

Barber, B. (2007). *Con$umed: How markets corrupt children, infantilize adults, and swallow citizens whole*. New York: W. W. Norton & Company.

Barber, K. (2008). The well-coiffed man: Class, race, and heterosexual masculinity in the hair salon. *Gender & Society, 22*, 455–476.

Barbour, J. B., Treem, J. W., & Kolar, B. (2018). Analytics and expert collaboration: How individuals navigate relationships when working with organizational data. *Human Relations, 71*, 256–284.

Barge, J. K., & Little, M. (2002). Dialogical wisdom, communicative practice, and organizational life. *Communication Theory, 12*, 375–397.

Barker, J. R. (1993). Tightening the iron cage: Concertive control in self-managing teams. *Administrative Science Quarterly, 38*, 408–437.

Barker, J. R. (1999). *The discipline of teamwork: Participation and concertive control*. Thousand Oaks, CA: Sage.

Barley, S. R. (1986). Technology as an occasion for structuring: Evidence from observations of CT scanners and the social order of radiology departments. *Administrative Science Quarterly, 31*, 78–108.

Barley, W. C., Treem, J. W., & Kuhn, T. (2018). Valuing multiple trajectories of knowledge: A critical review and research agenda for knowledge management research. *Annals of the Academy of Management, 12*, 278–317. doi:10.5465/annals.2016.0041

Barnard, C. (1938). *The functions of the executive*. Cambridge, MA: Harvard University Press.

Barrett, H. (2017, September 4). Plan for five careers in a lifetime. *Financial Times*. Retrieved from https://www.ft.com/content/0151d2fe-868a-11e7-8bb1-5ba57d47eff7.

Barthes, R. (1972). *Mythologies*. London: Cape.

Bass, B. M. (1985). *Leadership and performance beyond expectations*. New York: Free Press.

Bass, B. M. (1990). *Bass and Stogdill handbook of leadership: Theory, research, and managerial applications* (3rd ed.). New York: The Free Press.

Bass, B. M., & Riggio, R. E. (2006). *Transformational leadership*. Mahwah, N.J.: Lawrence Erlbaum Associates.

Bateson, G. (1972). *Steps to an ecology of mind*. New York: Ballantine.

Batt, R., Holman, D., & Holtgrewe, U. (2010). The globalization of service work: Comparative institutional perspectives on call centers. *Industrial and Labor Relations Review, 62*, 453–488.

Bauman, Z. (1989). *Modernity and the Holocaust*. New York: Cornell University Press.

Bauman, Z. (2000). *Liquid modernity*. Cambridge, UK: Polity Press.

Beck, U. (1992). *Risk society: Towards a new modernity*. London: Sage.

Beck, U. (2000). *What is globalization?* (P. Camiller, Trans.). Cambridge, UK: Polity Press.

Becker, G. (1976). *The economic approach to human behavior*. Chicago: University of Chicago Press.

Bederman, G. (1995). *Manliness and civilization: A cultural history of gender and race in the United States, 1880–1917*. Chicago: University of Chicago Press.

Beech, N. (2011). Liminality and the practices of identity construction. *Human Relations, 64*, 285–302.

Berlant, L., & Warner, M. (1998). Sex in public. *Critical Inquiry, 24*, 547–566.

Bernays, E. (1928). *Propaganda*. New York: Routledge.

Beynon, H. (1973). *Working for Ford*. London: Allen Lane.

Bilton, N. (2014, November 14). Alex from Target: The other side of fame. *The New York Times* Retrieved from http://www.nytimes.com/2014/11/13/style/alex-from-target-the-other-side-of-fame.html?_r = 0.

Bird, S. R. (1996). Welcome to the men's club: Homosociality and the maintenance of hegemonic masculinity. *Gender & Society, 10*, 120–132.

Blake, R. R., & Mouton, J. S. (1964). *The managerial grid: Key orientations for achieving production through people*. Houston, TX: Gulf Publishing Co.

Board of Governors of the Federal Reserve System. (2018). Report on the economic well-being of U.S. households in 2017. Retrieved from Federal Reserve: https://www.federalreserve.gov/publications/files/2017-report-economic-well-being-us-households-201805.pdf

Bogle, K. A. (2008). *Hooking up: Sex, dating, and relationships on campus*. New York: New York University Press.

Bohm, S., & Land, C. (2012). The new "hidden abode": Reflections on value and labour in the new economy. *The Sociological Review, 60*, 217–240.

Boje, D. (1991). The storytelling organization: A study of story performance in an office-supply firm. *Administrative Science Quarterly, 36*, 106–126.

Boje, D. (1995). Stories of the storytelling organization: A postmodern analysis of Disney as "Tamara-Land." *Academy of Management Journal, 38*, 997–1035.

Boltanski, L., & Chiapello, E. (2002). *The new spirit of capitalism*. Paper presented at the The Conference of Europeanists, Chicago, IL.

Boltanski, L., & Chiapello, E. (2005). *The new spirit of capitalism* (G. Elliott, Trans.). London: Verso.

Bormann, E. G. (1983). Symbolic convergence: Organizational communication and culture. In L. L. Putnam & M. Pacanowsky (Eds.), *Communication and organizations: An interpretive approach* (pp. 100–115). Beverly Hills, CA: Sage.

Boulding, K. (1985). *The world as a total system*. London: Sage.

Bowie, N. E. (1998). A Kantian theory of meaningful work. *Journal of Business Ethics, 17*, 1083–1092.

Boyer, P. (Ed.) (1990). *Reagan as president: Contemporary views of the man, his politics, and his policies*. Chicago: Ivan R. Dee.

Boyle, J. (2003). The second enclosure movement and the construction of the public domain. *Law and Contemporary Problems, 66*(1/2), 33–74.

Brabham, D. C. (2013). *Crowdsourcing*. Cambridge, MA: MIT Press.

Brabham, D. C. (2015). *Crowdsourcing in the public sector*. Washington, DC: Georgetown University Press.

Brabham, D. C., Ribisl, K. M., Kirchner, T. R., & Bernhardt, J. M. (2014). Crowdsourcing applications for public health. *American Journal of Preventive Medicine, 46*, 179–187. doi:dx.doi.org/10.1016/j.amepre.2013.10.016

Bramel, D., & Friend, R. (1981). Hawthorne, the myth of the docile worker, and class bias in psychology. *American Psychologist, 36*, 867–878.

Brannan, M. J., Parsons, E., & Priola, V. (Eds.). (2011). *Branded lives: The production and consumption of meaning at work*. Cheltenham, UK: Edward Elgar Publishing.

Brannan, M. J., Parsons, E., & Priola, V. (2015). Brands at work: The search for meaning in mundane work. *Organization Studies, 36*, 29–53.

Braverman, H. (1974). *Labor and monopoly capital: The degradation of work in the twentieth century.* New York: Monthly Review Press.

Brewis, J., & Linstead, S. (2000). *Sex, work and sex at work: Eroticizing the organization.* London: Routledge.

Brewis, J., Tyler, M., & Mills, A. (2014). Sexuality and Organizational Analysis—30 Years On: Editorial Introduction. *Organization, 21*, 305–311.

Brinkman, B., Garcia, K., & Rickard, K. (2011). "What I wanted to do was . . ." Discrepancies between college women's desired and reported responses to gender prejudice. *Sex Roles, 65*, 344–355.

Brinkman, B., & Rickard, K. (2009). College students' descriptions of everyday gender prejudice. *Sex Roles, 61*, 461–475.

Bröckling, U. (2016). *The entrepreneurial self: Fabricating a new type of subject* (S. Black, Trans.). London: Sage.

Brooks, D. (2001, April). The organization kid. *Atlantic Monthly*, 40–54.

Brophy, E. (2011). Language put to work: Cognitive capitalism, call center labor, and worker inquiry. *Journal of Communication Inquiry, 35*, 410–416.

Brown, A. (1998). Narrative, politics and legitimacy in an IT implementation. *Journal of Management Studies, 35*, 35–58.

Brown, A. (2006). A narrative approach to collective identities. *Journal of Management Studies, 43*, 731–753.

Brown, A., & Coupland, C. (2005). Sounds of silence: Graduate trainees, hegemony, and resistance. *Organization Studies, 26*, 1049–1069.

Brown, S. L., & Eisenhardt, K. M. (1997). The art of continuous change: Linking complexity theory and time-paced evolution in relentlessly shifting organizations. *Administrative Science Quarterly, 42*, 1–34.

Browning, L. D. (1992). Lists and stories as organizational communication. *Communication Theory, 2*, 281–302.

Bruckmüller, S., & Branscombe, N. R. (2010). The glass cliff: When and why women are selected as leaders in crisis contexts. *British Journal of Social Psychology, 49*, 433–451.

Bruckmüller, S., & Branscombe, N. R. (2011). How women end up on the "glass cliff". *Harvard Business Review, 89*(1/2), 26.

Brummans, B. (2007). Death by document: Tracing the agency of a text. *Qualitative Inquiry, 17*, 711–727.

Brummans, B. H. J. M., Cooren, F., Robichaud, D., & Taylor, J. R. (2014). Approaches to the communicative constitution of organizations. In L. L. Putnam & D. K. Mumby (Eds.), *The SAGE handbook of organizational communication: Advances in theory, research, and methods* (3rd. ed., pp. 173–194). Los Angeles, CA: SAGE.

Bruner, J. (1991). The narrative construction of reality. *Critical Inquiry, 18*, 1–21.

Bryman, A. (1996). Leadership in organizations. In S. Clegg, C. Hardy, & W. R. Nord (Eds.), *Handbook of organization studies* (pp. 276–292). London: Sage.

Bui, Q. (2017, February 17). A secret of many urban 20-somethings: Their parents help with the rent. *The New York Times*. Retrieved from https://www.nytimes.com/2017/02/09/upshot/a-secret-of-many-urban-20-somethings-their-parents-help-with-the-rent.html?hp&action = click&pgtyp e = Homepage&clickSource = story-heading&module = second-column-region&region = top-news&WT.nav = top-news

Bunderson, J. S., & Thompson, J. A. (2009). The call of the wild: Zookeepers, callings, and the double-edged sword of deeply meaningful work. *Administrative Science Quarterly, 54*, 32–57.

Burawoy, M. (1979). *Manufacturing consent: Changes in the labor process under monopoly capitalism.* Chicago: University of Chicago Press.

Burke, K. (1969). *A grammar of motives.* Berkeley: University of California Press.

Burns, J. M. (1978). *Leadership.* New York: Harper & Row.

Burns, J. M., & Avolio, B. J. (2004). *Transformational and Transactional Leadership. Encyclopedia of Leadership. SAGE Publications.* Thousand Oaks, CA: Sage.

Burrell, G. (1984). Sex and organizational analysis. *Organization Studies, 5,* 97–118.

Burrell, G. (1992). The organization of pleasure. In M. Alvesson & H. Willmott (Eds.), *Critical management studies* (pp. 66–89). Newbury Park, CA: Sage.

Butler, J. (1990). *Gender trouble: Feminism and the subversion of identity.* New York: Routledge.

Buzzanell, P. M. (1995). Reframing the glass ceiling as a socially constructed process: Implications for understanding and change. *Communication Monographs, 62,* 327–354.

Cabanas, E. (2017). "Psytizens," or the construction of happy individuals in neoliberal societies. In E. Illouz (Ed.), *Emotions as commodities: Capitalsim, consumption and authenticity* (pp. 173–196). London: Routledge.

Calás, M. B., & Smircich, L. (1996). From "the woman's point of view": Feminist approches to organization studies. In S. R. Clegg, C. Hardy, & W. R. Nord (Eds.), *Handbook of organization studies* (pp. 218–257). Thousand Oaks, CA: Sage.

Campaign for Human Rights. (2018). *Corporate equality index* 2018. Retrieved from https://www.hrc .org/campaigns/corporate-equality-index

Carey, A. (1967). The Hawthorne studies: A radical criticism. *American Sociological Review, 32,* 403–416.

Carlone, D., & Taylor, B. (1998). Organizational communication and cultural studies. *Communication Theory, 8,* 337–367.

Carlyle, T. (2001/1841). *On heroes, hero worship and the heroic in history.* London: Electric Books [Original publication date, 1841].

Carson, R. (1962). *Silent spring.* New York: Houghton Mifflin.

Carty, S. S. (2008). Tata motors to buy Jaguar, Land Rover, for $2.3 billion. *USA Today.* Retrieved from http://www.usatoday.com/money/autos/2008-03-25-ford-sells-jaguar-land-rover-tata_N.htm

Casey, C. (1995). *Work, self and society: After industrialism.* London: Sage.

Caza, B., Moss, S., & Vough, H. C. (2018). From synchronizing to harmonizing: The process of authenticating multiple work identities. *Administrative Science Quarterly.* doi:10.1177/0001839217733972

Caza, B., Vough, H. C., & Moss, S. (2017). The hardest thing about working in the gig economy? Forging a cohesive sense of self? *Harvard Business Review.* Retrieved from https://hbr.org/2017/10/the-hardest-thing-about-working-in-the-gig-economy-forging-a-cohesive-sense-of-self

Cederström, C., & Fleming, P. (2012). *Dead man working.* Winchester, UK: Zero Books.

Chaleff, I., Lipman-Blumen, J., & Riggio, R. E. (2008). *The art of followership: How great followers create great leaders and organizations.* San Francisco: Jossey-Bass.

Chang, E. (2018). *Brotopia.* London: Penguin.

Chatterjee, R. (2018). A new survey finds 81 percent of women have experienced sexual harassment [Press release]. Retrieved from https://www.npr.org/sections/thetwo-way/2018/02/21/587671849/a-new-survey-finds-eighty-percent-of-women-have-experienced-sexual-harassment?t = 1530891687165.

Chatterjee, S. (2016). Articulating globalization: Exploring the Bottom of the Pyramid (BOP) terrain. *Organization Studies, 37,* 635–653.

Cheever, S. (2003). The nanny dilemma. In B. Ehrenreich & A. Hochschild (Eds.), *Global woman* (pp. 31–38). New York: Metropolitan Books.

Cheney, G. (1991). *Rhetoric in an organizational society: Managing multiple identities.* Columbia: University of South Carolina Press.

Cheney, G. (1999). *Values at work: Employee participation meets market pressure at Mondragon*. Ithaca, NY: Cornell University Press.

Cheney, G., & Tompkins, P. K. (1987). Coming to terms with organizational identification and commitment. *Central States Speech Journal, 38*, 1–15.

Cheney, G., Zorn, T., Planalp, S., & Lair, D. (2008). Meaningful work and personal/social wellbeing: Organizational communication engages the meanings of work. In C. Beck (Ed.), *Communication yearbook 32* (pp. 137–185). Thousand Oaks, CA: Sage.

Chewning, L. V., Lai, C.-H., & Doerfel, M. L. (2012). Organizational resilience and using information and communication technologies to rebuild communication structures. *Management Communication Quarterly, 27*, 237–263. doi:10.1177/0893318912465815

Christensen, L., Morsing, M., & Cheney, G. (2008). *Corporate Communication: Convention, Complexity, Critique*. London: Sage.

Christensen, L. T., Morsing, M., & Thyssen, O. (2013). CSR as aspirational talk. *Organization, 20*, 372–393.

Christensen, W. (2012). Torches of freedom: Women and smoking propaganda. *Department of Sociology, University of Minnesota*. Retrieved from https://thesocietypages.org/socimages/2012/02/27/torches-of-freedom-women-and-smoking-propaganda/.

Ciulla, J. B. (2000). *The working life: The promise and betrayal of modern work*. New York: Times Books.

Clair, R. P. (1993a). The bureaucratization, commodification, and privatization of sexual harassment through institutional discourse. *Management Communication Quarterly, 7*, 123–157.

Clair, R. P. (1993b). The use of framing devices to sequester organizational narratives: Hegemony and harassment. *Communication Monographs, 60*, 113–136.

Clegg, S. (1989). *Frameworks of power*. Newbury Park, CA: Sage.

Clegg, S. (1994). Weber and Foucault: Social theory for the study of organizations. *Organization, 1*, 149–178.

Clegg, S., Courpasson, D., & Phillips, N. (2006). *Power and organizations*. Thousand Oaks, CA: Sage.

Cloud, D. (2005). Fighting words: Labor and the limits of communication at Staley, 1993 to 1996. *Management Communication Quarterly, 18*, 509–542.

Cochrane, A., & Pain, K. (2007). A globalizing society. In D. Held (Ed.), *A globalizing world? Culture, economics, politics* (2nd ed., pp. 5–46). London: Routledge/Open University.

Collinson, D. (1988). "Engineering humor": Masculinity, joking and conflict in shop-floor relations. *Organization Studies, 9*, 181–199.

Collinson, D. (1992). *Managing the shop floor: Subjectivity, masculinity, and workplace culture*. New York: De Gruyter.

Collinson, D. (2003). Identities and insecurities: Selves at work. *Organization, 10*, 527–547.

Collinson, D. (2005). Dialectics of leadership. *Human Relations, 58*, 1419–1442.

Collinson, D. (2011). Critical leadership studies. In A. Bryman, K. Grint, D. Collinson, B. Jackson, & M. Uhl-Bien (Eds.), *The Sage handbook of leadership* (pp. 181–194). Los Angeles, CA: Sage.

Colt, S. (2014). Tablets are making waiters obsolete—and Chili's is leading the way. *Business Insider*. Retrieved from http://www.businessinsider.com/tablets-are-making-waiters-obsolete-2014-6

Compton, C. A. (2016). Managing mixed messages: Sexual identity management in a changing US workplace. *Management Communication Quarterly, 30*, 414–440.

Compton, C. A., & Dougherty, D. S. (2017). Organizing sexuality: Silencing and the push–pull process of co-sexuality in the workplace, *Journal of Communication, 67*, 874–896.

Connell, R. W. (1993). The big picture: Masculinities in recent world history. *Theory and Society, 22*, 597–623.

Connell, R. W. (1995). *Masculinities*. Berkeley: University of California Press.

Connell, R. W., Hearn, J., & Kimmel, M. (2005). *Handbook of studies on men & masculinities*. Thousand Oaks, CA: Sage.

Conference Board (2016). Job satisfaction: 2016 edition: Tightening labor market means more opportunity, more satisfaction. Retrieved from https://www.conference-board.org/publications/publicationdetail.cfm?publicationid = 7250.

Conrad, C. (1985). *Strategic organizational communication: Cultures, situations, and adaptation.* New York: Holt, Rinehart, and Winston.

Contractor, N. S. (1999). Self-organizing systems research in the social sciences: Reconciling the metaphors and the models. *Management Communication Quarterly, 13,* 154–166.

Cooren, F. (2000). *The organizing property of communication.* Amsterdam: John Benjamins.

Cooren, F. (2015). *Organizational discourse: Communication and constitution.* Cambridge, UK: Polity Press.

Corbyn, Z. (2018, March 17). Why sexism is rife in Silicon Valley. *The Observer.* Retrieved from https://www.theguardian.com/world/2018/mar/17/sexual-harassment-silicon-valley-emily-chang-brotopia-interview.

Corman, S. R., & Poole, M. S. (Eds.). (2000). *Perspectives on organizational communication: Finding common ground.* New York: Guilford.

Cote, M., & Pybus, J. (2011). Learning to immaterial labor 2.0: Facebook and social networks. In M. Peters & E. Bulut (Eds.), *Cognitive capitalism, education and digital labor* (pp. 169–193). New York: Peter Lang.

Cottom, T. M. (2017). The coded language of for-profit colleges. *The Atlantic.* https://www.theatlantic.com/education/archive/2017/02/the-coded-language-of-for-profit-colleges/516810/

Couch, C. (2017, October 25). Ghosts in the machine. Retrieved from http://www.pbs.org/wgbh/nova/next/tech/ai-bias/

Courpasson, D. (2006). *Soft constraint: Liberal organizations and domination.* Copenhagen: Copenhagen Business School Press.

Courpasson, D., & Vallas, S. P. (Eds.). (2016). *The SAGE handbook of resistance.* London: Sage.

Cova, B., Pace, S., & Skålén, P. (2015). Marketing with working consumers: The case of a carmaker and its brand community. *Organization, 22,* 682–701.

Crawford, M. B. (2009a). The case for working with your hands. *The New York Times.* Retrieved from www.nytimes.com/2009/05/24/magazine/24labor-t.html

Crawford, M. B. (2009b). *Shop class as soulcraft: An inquiry into the value of work.* New York: Penguin Press.

Crenshaw, C. (1997). Resisting whiteness' rhetorical silence. *Western Journal of Communication, 61,* 253–278.

Crenshaw, K. (1991). Mapping the margins: Intersectionality, identity politics, and violence against women of color. *Stanford Law Review, 43,* 1241–1299.

Czarniawska, B. (1997). *Narrating the organization.* Chicago, IL: University of Chicago Press.

Czarniawska, B. (1998). *A narrative approach to organization studies.* Thousand Oaks, CA: Sage.

Daft, R. L., & Lengel, R. H. (1986). Organizational information requirements: Media richness and structural design. *Management Science, 32,* 554–571.

Dahl, R. (1957). The concept of power. *Behavioral Science, 2,* 201–215.

Dahl, R. (1958). A critique of the ruling elite model. *American Political Science Review, 52,* 463–469.

Dahl, R. (1961). Who governs? *Democracy and power in an American city.* New Haven, CT: Yale University Press.

Daisey, M. (2011, October 6). Against nostalgia. *The New York Times.* Retrieved from http://www.nytimes.com/2011/10/06/opinion/jobs-looked-to-the-future.html?emc = eta1.

Dardot, P., & Laval, C. (2013). *The new way of the world: On neoliberal society.* Brooklyn, NY: Verso.

Davenport, T. H. (2005). *Thinking for a living: How to get better performances and results from knowledge workers.* Boston: Harvard University Press.

de Botton, A. (2009). *The pleasures and sorrows of work.* New York: Vintage Books.

de Lauretis, T. (1991). Queer theory: Lesbian and gay sexualities. *Differences: A Journal of Feminist Cultural Studies, 1*(2), 3–18.

De Mauro, A., Greco, M., & Grimaldi, M. (2016). A formal definition of big data based on its essential features. *Library Review, 65*, 122–135. doi:10.1108/LR-06-2015-0061

Deal, T. E., & Kennedy, A. A. (1982). *Corporate cultures: The rites and rituals of corporate life.* Reading, Mass.: Addison-Wesley.

Dean, J. (2009). *Democracy and other neoliberal fantasies: Communicative capitalism and left politics.* Durham, NC: Duke University Press.

Dean, J. (2014). Communicative capitalism: This is what democracy looks like. In J. S. Hanan & M. Hayward (Eds.), *Communication and the economy: History, value, and agency* (pp. 147–164). New York: Peter Lang.

Deetz, S. (1973). An understanding of science and a hermeneutic science of understanding. *Journal of Communication, 23*, 139–159.

Deetz, S. (1982). Critical interpretive research in organizational communication. *The Western Journal of Speech Communication, 46*, 131–149.

Deetz, S. (1992). *Democracy in an age of corporate colonization: Developments in communication and the politics of everyday life.* Albany: State University of New York Press.

Deetz, S. (1995). *Transforming communication, transforming business: Building responsive and responsible workplaces.* Cresskill, NJ: Hampton Press.

Deetz, S., & Brown, D. (2004). Conceptualising involvement, participation and workplace decision processes: A communication theory perspective. In D. Tourish & O. Hargie (Eds.), *Key issues in organizational communication* (pp. 172–187). London: Routledge.

Dempsey, S. E. (2009). NGOs, communicative labor, and the work of grassroots representation. *Communication and Critical/Cultural Studies, 6*, 328–345.

Dempsey, S. E., & Sanders, M. L. (2010). "Meaningful work? Nonprofit marketization and work/life imbalance in popular autobiographies of social entrepreneurship. *Organization, 17*, 437–459.

Denissen, A. M., & Saguy, A. C. (2014). Gendered homophobia and the contradictions of workplace discrimination for women in the building trades. *Gender & Society, 28*, 381–403.

DeSantis, A. D. (2003). A couple of white guys sitting around talking: The collective rationalization of cigar smokers. *Journal of Contemporary Ethnography, 32*, 432–466.

DeSantis, A. D. (2007). *Inside Greek U.: Fraternities, sororities, and the pursuit of pleasure, power, and prestige.* Lexington: University Press of Kentucky.

Dixon, J., & Dougherty, D. S. (2014). A language convergence/meaning divergence analysis exploring how LGBTQ and single employees manage traditional family expectations in the workplace. *Journal of Applied Communication Research, 42*, 1–19. doi:10.1080/00909882.2013.847275

Doorewaard, H., & Brouns, B. (2003). Hegemonic power processes in team-based work. *Applied Psychology: An International Review, 52*, 106–119.

Dorson, R. (1959). *American folklore.* Chicago: University of Chicago Press.

Drake, B. (2013). Another gender gap: Men spend more time in leisure activities [Press release]. Retrieved from http://www.pewresearch.org/fact-tank/2013/06/10/another-gender-gap-men-spend-more-time-in-leisure-activities/.

Du Gay, P. (2000). *In praise of bureaucracy: Weber, organization, ethics.* Thousand Oaks, CA: Sage.

Du Gay, P., & Salaman, G. (1992). The cult[ure] of the consumer. *Journal of Management Studies, 29*, 615–633.

Dubrin, A. J. (2016). *Leadership: Research findings, practice, and skills* (8th ed.). Boston, MA: Cengage Learning.

Duffy, B. E. (2016). The romance of work: Gender and aspirational labour in the digital culture industries. *International Journal of Cultural Studies, 19*, 441–457.

Duffy, B. E. (2017). *On (not) getting paid to do what you love: Gender, social media, and aspirational work*. New Haven, CT: Yale University Press.

Duffy, B. E., & Hund, E. (2015). "Having it all" on social media: Entrepreneurial femininity and self-branding among fashion bloggers. *Social Media & Society*, 1–11.

Duneier, M. (1999). *Sidewalk*. New York: Farrar, Straus and Giroux.

Duxbury, L., Higgins, C., Smart, R., & Stevenson, M. (2014). Mobile technology and boundary permeability. *British Journal of Management*, *25*, 570–588. doi:10.1111/1467-8551.12027

Dwyer, C. (2017). Foiled! Electrician used a snack bag as a faraday cage to sneak off the job. Retrieved from https://www.npr.org/sections/thetwo-way/2017/11/27/566764082/foiled-this-faraday-cage-made-from-snack-bag-couldnt-save-electrician-s-job

Edwards, R. (1979). *Contested terrain: The transformation of the workplace in the twentieth century*. New York: Basic Books.

Eger, E. K. (2018). Transgender jobseekers navigating closeting communication. *Management Communication Quarterly*, *32*, 276–281. doi:10.1177/0893318917740226

Ehrenreich, B., & Hochschild, A. (2003). *Global woman: Nannies, maids, and sex workers in the new economy*. New York: Metropolitan Books.

Eisenberg, E. (1984). Ambiguity as strategy in organizational communication. *Communication Monographs*, 51.

Eisenstein, Z. (Ed.) (1979). *Capitalist patriarchy and the case for socialist feminism*. New York: Monthly Review Press.

El-Ojeili, C., & Hayden, P. (2006). *Critical theories of globalization*. Basingstoke, UK: Palgrave Macmillan.

Elmore, B. J. (2015). *Citizen Coke: The making of Coca-Cola capitalism*. New York: W. W. Norton.

Endrissat, N., Karreman, D., & Noppeny, C. (2017). Incorporating the creative subject: Branding outside-in through identity incentives. *Human Relations*, *70*, 488–515.

Epstein, E. J. (1982a, February). Have you ever tried to sell a diamond? *The Atlantic*. https://www.theatlantic.com/magazine/archive/1982/02/have-you-ever-tried-to-sell-a-diamond/304575/

Epstein, E. J. (1982b). *The rise and fall of diamonds: The shattering of a brilliant illusion*. New York: Simon and Schuster.

Esch, E. D. (2018). *The color line and the assembly line: Managing race in the Ford empire*. Berkeley, CA: University of California Press.

Estellés-Arolas, E., & González-Ladrón-de-Guevara, F. (2012). Towards an integrated crowdsourcing definition. *Journal of Information Science*, *38*, 189–200. doi:10.1177/0165551512437638

Evans, D. S., & Schmalensee, R. (2016). *Matchmakers: The new economics of multisided platforms*. Boston, MA: Harvard University Press.

Ewick, P., & Silbey, S. S. (1995). Subversive stories and hegemonic tales: Toward a sociology of narrative. *Law & Society Review*, *29*, 197–226.

Ezzamel, M., & Willmott, H. (1998). Accounting for teamwork: A critical study of group-based systems of organizational control. *Administrative Science Quarterly*, *43*, 358–396.

Ezzamel, M., Willmott, H., & Worthington, F. (2001). Power, control and resistance in "the factory that time forgot." *Journal of Management Studies*, *38*, 1053–1078.

Fairhurst, G. (2007). *Discursive leadership: In conversation with leadership psychology*. San Francisco: Jossey-Bass.

Fairhurst, G., & Connaughton, S. (2014). Leadership communication. In L. L. Putnam & D. K. Mumby (Eds.), *The SAGE handbook of organizational communication: Advances in theory, research, and methods* (3rd ed., pp. 401–433). Los Angeles: Sage.

Fairhurst, G., & Grant, D. (2010). The social construction of leadership: A sailing guide. *Management Communication Quarterly*, *24*, 171–210.

Fairhurst, G., & Sarr, R. A. (1996). *The art of framing: Managing the language of leadership*. San Francisco: Jossey-Bass Publishers.

Fairhurst, G., & Zoller, H. M. (2008). Resistance, dissent and leadership in practice. In S. P. Banks (Ed.), *Dissent and the failure of leadership* (pp. 135–148). Cheltenham, UK: Edward Elgar.

Farfan, B. (2017, July 12). Brand image vs brand reality in Mike Jeffries' led Abercrombie & Fitch. *The balance small business*. Retrieved from https://www.thebalancesmb.com/abercrombie-brand-image-reality-2891857.

Farrow, R. (2017, November 6). Harvey Weinstein's army of spies. *The New Yorker*. Retrieved from https://www.newyorker.com/news/news-desk/harvey-weinsteins-army-of-spies.

FastCap. (2011, Dec. 12). *Lean manufacturing—Kaizen methodology—lean FastCap style* [Video file]. Retrieved https://www.youtube.com/watch?v = su9CulCZTBg.

Ferguson, K. (1984). *The feminist case against bureaucracy*. Philadelphia: Temple University Press.

Ferriss, T. (2007). *The 4-hour work week: Escape 9–5, live anywhere, and join the new rich*. New York: Harmony Books.

Fiedler, F. E. (1967). *A theory of leadership effectiveness*. New York: McGraw-Hill.

Fiedler, F. E. (1997). Situational control and a dynamic theory of leadership. In K. Grint (Ed.), *Leadership: Classical, contemporary, and critical approaches* (pp. 126–154). Oxford, UK: Oxford University Press.

Finder, J. (1987, February 22). A male secretary. *The New York Times Magazine*. Retrieved from https://www.nytimes.com/1987/02/22/magazine/about-men-a-male-secretary.html.

Finn, E. (2017). *What algorithms want: Imagination in the age of computing*. Cambridge, MA: MIT Press.

Firestone, S. (1970). *The dialectic of sex: The case for feminist revolution*. New York: William Morrow.

Fisher, W. R. (1985). The narrative paradigm: An elaboration. *Communication Monographs, 52*, 347–367.

Fiske, J. (1989). Shopping for pleasure: Malls, power, and resistance. In J. Schor & D. B. Holt (Eds.), *The consumer society reader*. New York: The New Press.

Flanagin, A. J. (2002). The elusive benefits of the technological support of knowledge management. *Management Communication Quarterly, 16*, 242–248.

Flanagin, A. J., & Bator, M. (2011). The utility of information and communication technologies in organizational knowledge management. In H. E. Canary & R. D. McPhee (Eds.), *Communication and organizational knowledge: Contemporary issues for theory and practice* (pp. 173–190). New York: Routledge.

Flax, J. (1990). *Thinking fragments: Psychoanalysis, feminism, and postmodernism in the contemporary west*. Berkeley: University of California Press.

Fleming, P. (2005). Metaphors of resistance. *Management Communication Quarterly, 19*, 45–66.

Fleming, P. (2007). Sexuality, power and resistance in the workplace. *Organization Studies, 28*, 239–256.

Fleming, P. (2009). *Authenticity and the cultural politics of work: New forms of informal control*. New York: Oxford University Press.

Fleming, P. (2014a). *Resisting work: The corporatization of life and its discontents*. Philadelphia: Temple University Press.

Fleming, P. (2014b). When "life itself" goes to work: Reviewing shifts in organizational life through the lens of biopower. *Human Relations, 67*, 875–901.

Fleming, P. (2015). *The mythology of work: How capitalism persists despite itself*. London: Pluto Press.

Fleming, P. (2017). The human capital hoax: Work, debt and insecurity in the era of Uberization. *Organization Studies, 38*, 691–705.

Fleming, P., & Spicer, A. (2003). Working at a cynical distance: Implications for power, subjectivity, and resistance. *Organization, 10*, 157–179.

Fleming, P., & Spicer, A. (2007). *Contesting the corporation*. Cambridge, UK: Cambridge University Press.

Fleming, P., & Spicer, A. (2008). Beyond power and resistance: New approaches to organizational politics. *Management Communication Quarterly, 21*, 301–309.

Fleming, P., & Sturdy, A. (2011). "Being yourself" in the electronic sweatshop: New forms of normative control. *Human Relations, 64*, 177–200.

Florida, R. (2003). *The rise of the creative class: And how it's transforming work, leisure, community and everyday life*. New York: Basic Books.

Florida, R. (2017). *The new urban crisis: How our cities are increasing inequality, deepening segregation, and failing the middle class—and what we can do about it*. New York: Basic Books.

Follett, M. P. (1924). *Creative experience*. New York: Longmans, Green.

Forester, J. (1999). *The deliberative practitioner: Encouraging participatory planning processes*. Cambridge, MA: MIT Press.

Foucault, M. (1979a). *Discipline and punish: The birth of the prison* (A. Sheridan, Trans.). New York: Vintage.

Foucault, M. (1979b). Governmentality. *Ideology and Consciousness, 6*, 5–21.

Foucault, M. (1980). *The history of sexuality: An introduction* (R. Hurley, Trans., Vol. 1). New York: Vintage.

Foucault, M. (2008). *The birth of biopolitics: Lectures at the Collège de France, 1978–1979* (G. Burchell, Trans.). Basingstoke, UK: Palgrave MacMillan.

Fowler, S. (2017). Reflecting on one very, very, strange year at Uber. Retrieved from https://www.susan jfowler.com/blog/2017/2/19/reflecting-on-one-very-strange-year-at-uber.

Frampton, J. (2015). *Brands at the speed of life*. Retrieved from https://www.interbrand.com/best-brands/best-global-brands/2015/articles/brands-at-the-speed-of-life/.

Francke, R. H., & Kaul, J. D. (1978). The Hawthorne experiments: First statistical interpretation. *American Sociological Review, 43*, 623–643.

Frankenberg, R. (1993). *White women, race matters: The social construction of whiteness*. Minneapolis: University of Minnesota Press.

Fraser, N. (2013, October). How feminism became capitalism's handmaiden—and how to reclaim it. *The Guardian*. Retrieved from http://www.theguardian.com/commentisfree/2013/oct/14/feminism-capitalist-handmaiden-neoliberal

Frayne, D. (2015). *The refusal of work: The theory and practice of resistance to work*. London: Zed Books.

Freiberg, K., & Freiberg, J. (1996). *Nuts! Southwest Airlines' crazy recipe for business and personal success*. New York: Broadway Books.

Freelance Union & Upwork. (2017). *Freelancing in America: 2017*. Retrieved from https://s3.amazonaws.com/fuwt-prod-storage/content/FreelancingInAmericaReport-2017.pdf.

Friedan, B. (1963). *The feminine mystique*. New York: Dell.

Friedman, B. (2005). *The moral consequences of economic growth*. New York: Knopf.

Friedman, G. (2014). Workers without employers: Shadow corporations and the rise of the gig economy. *Review of Keynesian Economics, 2*(2), 171–188.

Friedman, M. (1970, February). The social responsibility of business is to increase its profits. New York *Times Magazine*. Retrieved from https://www.nytimes.com/1970/09/13/archives/article-15-no-title.html.

Friedman, M. (1982). *Capitalism and freedom*. Chicago: University of Chicago Press.

Friedman, T. (2005, April 3). It's a flat world after all. *The New York Times*. Retrieved from http://www.nytimes.com/2005/04/03/magazine/03DOMINANCE.html?pagewanted = 1%27s%20a%20 flat%20world%20aftre%20all&sq = It&st = cse&scp = 1&adxnnlx = 1317903299-jlh/RxVLC6 VhgT%20uRxvu%20w.

Friedman, Z. (2018, June 13). Student loan debt statistics in 2018: A $1.5 trillion crisis. Forbes. https://www.forbes.com/sites/zackfriedman/2018/06/13/student-loan-debt-statistics-2018/#67e1e957310f.

Frost, P. J., Moore, L. F., Louis, M. R., Lundberg, C. C., & Martin, J. (Eds.). (1985). *Organizational Culture*. Beverly Hills, CA: Sage.

Fry, L. W. (1976). The maligned F. W. Taylor: A reply to his many critics. *Academy of Management Review, 1*(3), 124–129.

Fulk, J., Schmitz, J., & Steinfeld, C. (1990). A social influence model of technology use. In J. Fulk & C. Steinfeld (Eds.), *Organizations and communication technology* (pp. 117–140). Newbury Park, CA: Sage.

Gagnon, S., & Collinson, D. L. (2017). Resistance through difference: The co-constitution of dissent and inclusion. *Organization Studies, 38*, 1253–1276.

Gallup. (2013). Employee engagement. Retrieved from https://www.gallup.com/services/190118/engaged-workplace.aspx.

Ganesh, S., Zoller, H. M., & Cheney, G. (2005). Transforming resistance, broadening our boundaries: Critical organizational communication meets globalization from below. *Communication Monographs, 72*, 169–191.

Geertz, C. (1973). *The interpretation of cultures* New York: Basic Books.

Geertz, C. (1983). *Local knowledge: Further essays in interpretive anthropology*. New York: Basic Books.

Gemmill, G., & Oakley, J. (1992). Leadership: An alienating social myth? *Human Relations, 45*, 113–129.

Giddens, A. (1979). *Central problems in social theory: Action, structure and contradiction in social analysis*. Berkeley: University of California Press.

Giddens, A. (1991). *Modernity and self-identity: Self and society in the late modern age*. Stanford, CA: Stanford University Press.

Giddens, A. (2001). *Runaway world: How globalisation is reshaping our lives* (2nd ed.). London: Profile Books.

Gill, R. (2008). Culture and subjectivity in neoliberal and postfeminist times. *Subjectivity, 25*, 432–445.

Gill, R., & Pratt, A. (2008). In the social factory? Immaterial labour, precariousness and cultural work. *Theory, Culture & Society, 25*(7–8), 1–30.

Gilroy, P. (2002). *Against race: Imagining political culture beyond the color line*. Cambridge, MA: Harvard University Press.

Gini, A. (2001). *My job, my self: Work and the creation of the modern individual*. New York: Routledge.

Giuffre, P., Dellinger, K., & Williams, C. L. (2008). "No retribution for being gay?" Inequality in gay-friendly workplaces. *Sociological Spectrum, 28*, 254–277.

Glass, I. (2018). Unteachable moment. *This American Life*. Retrieved from https://www.thisamericanlife.org/648/transcript.

Gledhill, C. (1997). Genre and gender: The case of soap opera. In S. Hall (Ed.), *Representation: Cultural representations and signifying practices* (pp. 337–384). London: Sage/Open University Press.

Gobé, M. (2002). *Citizen brand: 10 commandments for transforming brands in a consumer democracy*. New York: Allworth Press.

Gobé, M. (2007). *Brandjam: Humanizing brands through emotional design*. New York: Allworth Press.

Golden, A. G. (2013). The structuration of information and communication technologies and work-life interrelationships: Shared organizational and family rules and resources and implications for work in a high-technology organization. *Communication Monographs, 80*, 101–123. doi:10.1080/03637751.2012.739702

Gorz, A. (1999). *Reclaiming work: Beyond the wage-based society* (C. Turner, Trans.). Cambridge, UK: Polity.

Gorz, A. (2010). *The immaterial: Knowledge, value and capital*. London: Seagull Books.

Gossett, L. (2003). Kept at arm's length: Questioning the organizational desirability of member identification *Communication Monographs, 69*, 385–404.

Graham, L. (1993). Inside a Japanese transplant: A critical perspective. *Work and Occupations, 20*, 147–173.

Gramsci, A. (1971). *Selections from the prison notebooks* (Q. Hoare & G. N. Smith, Trans.). New York: International Publishers.

Grant, D., & Oswick, C. (Eds.). (1996). *Metaphor and organizations*. London: Sage.

Gregg, M. (2011). *Work's intimacy*. Cambridge, UK: Polity Press.

Grey, C. (1994). Career as a project of the self and labour process discipline. *Sociology, 28*, 479–497.

Grimes, D. S. (2001). Putting our own house in order: Whiteness, change and organization studies. *Journal of Organizational Change Management, 14*, 132–149.

Grimes, D. S. (2002). Challenging the status quo? Whiteness in the diversity management literature. *Management Communication Quarterly, 15*, 381–409.

Grint, K. (2010). *Leadership: A very short introduction*. Oxford, UK: Oxford University Press.

Haack, P., Schoeneborn, D., & Wickert, C. (2012). Talking the talk, moral entrapment, creeping commitment?: Exploring narrative dynamics in corporate responsibility standardization. *Organization Studies, 33*, 815–845.

Hall, S. (1985). Signification, representation, ideology: Althusser and the poststructuralist debates. *Critical Studies in Mass Communication, 2*, 91–114.

Hall, S. (1997a). The work of representation. In S. Hall (Ed.), *Representation: Cultural representations and signifying practices* (pp. 13–64). London: Sage/Open University Press.

Hall, S. (Ed.) (1997b). *Representation: Cultural representations and signifying practices*. London: Sage/Open University Press.

Hall, S. (2007). Encoding, decoding. In S. During (Ed.), *The cultural studies reader* (pp. 90–103). London: Routledge.

Hall, S. (2016). *Cultural studies 1983: A theoretical history* (J. D. Slack & L. Grossberg Eds.). Durham, NC: Duke University Press.

Hall, S., & O'Shea, A. (2013). Common-sense neoliberalism. *Soundings: A Journal of Politics and Culture* (*55*), 1–18.

Hansen, H. K., & Flyverbom, M. (2014). The politics of transparency and the calibration of knowledge in the digital age. *Organization, 22*, 872–889. doi:10.1177/1350508414522315

Hardt, M., & Negri, A. (2004). *Multitude: War and democracy in the age of empire*. New York: Penguin.

Harris, K. L. (2013). Show them a good time: Organizing the intersections of sexual violence. *Management Communication Quarterly, 27*, 568–595.

Harris, K. L., & McDonald, J. (2018). Introduction: Queering the "closet" at work. *Management Communication Quarterly, 32*, 265–270.

Harris, M. (2017). *Kids these days: Human capital and the making of millennials*. New York, NY: Little, Brown and Company.

Harris, S. G., & Mossholder, K. W. (1996). The affective implications of perceived congruence with culture dimensions during organizational transformation. *Journal of Management, 22*, 527–547.

Harvey, D. (1991). Flexibility: Threat or opportunity. *Socialist Review, 21*(1), 65–77.

Harvey, D. (1995). Globalization in question. *Rethinking Marxism, 8*(4), 1–17.

Harvey, D. (2005). *A brief history of neoliberalism*. New York: Oxford University Press.

Harvey Wingfield, A. (2009). Racializing the glass escalator: Reconsidering men's experiences with women's work. *Gender & Society, 23*, 5–26.

Haslam, S. A., & Ryan, M. K. (2008). The road to the glass cliff: Differences in the perceived suitability of men and women for leadership positions in succeeding and failing organizations. *The Leadership Quarterly, 19*, 530–546.

Hassard, J. (2012). Rethinking the Hawthorne Studies: The Western Electric research in its social, political and historical context. *Human Relations, 65*, 1431–1461.

Hawes, L. (1977). Toward a hermeneutic phenomenology of communication. *Communication Quarterly, 25*(3), 30–41.

Hayek, F. A. (1944). *The road to serfdom*. Chicago: University of Chicago Press.

Haywood, L., & Drake, J. (Eds.). (1997). *Third Wave agenda: Being feminist, doing feminism*. Minneapolis: University of Minnesota Press.

Hearn, J. (1996). Deconstructing the dominant: Making the one(s) the other(s). *Organization, 3,* 611–626.

Hearn, J., Sheppard, D., Tancred-Sheriff, P., & Burrell, G. (Eds.). (1989). *The sexuality of organization.* London: Sage.

Heath, R. G. (2007). Rethinking community collaboration through a dialogic lens. *Management Communication Quarterly, 21,* 145–171.

Hebdige, D. (1979). *Subculture: The meaning of style.* London: Routledge.

Heisenberg, W. V. (2000). *Physics and philosophy: The revolution in modern science.* Harmondsworth, UK: Penguin.

Heller, N. (2017, May 15). Is the gig economy working? *The New Yorker.* Retrieved from https://www.newyorker.com/magazine/2017/05/15/is-the-gig-economy-working.

Hill Collins, P. (1991). *Black feminist thought: Knowledge, consciousness and the politics of empowerment.* New York: Routledge.

Hislop, D., & Axtell, C. (2011). Mobile phones during work and non-work time: A case study of mobile, non-managerial workers. *Information and Organization, 21,* 41–56. doi:10.1016/j.infoandorg.2011.01.001

Ho, K. (2009). *Liquidated: An ethnography of Wall Street.* Durham, NC: Duke University Press.

Hobsbawm, A. (2017). Harvesting big data: Is this the holy grail of 2030. *Business Reporter.* Retrieved from https://www.business-reporter.co.uk/2017/12/22/harvesting-big-data-holy-grail-2030/#gsc.tab = 0.

Hochschild, A. (1983). *The managed heart: Commercialization of human feeling.* Berkeley: University of California Press.

Hochschild, A. (1997). *The time bind: When work becomes home and home becomes work.* New York: Metropolitan Books.

Hoelscher, C. S., Zanin, A. C., & Kramer, M. W. (2016). Identifying with values: Examining organizational culture in farmers markets. *Western Journal of Communication, 80,* 481–501.

Holland, J. H. (2014). *Complexity: A very short introduction.* Oxford, UK: Oxford University Press.

Holm, F., & Fairhurst, G. (2018). Configuring shared and hierarchical leadership through authoring. *Human Relations, 71,* 692–721.

Holmer Nadesan, M. (1997). Constructing paper dolls: The discourse of personality testing in organizational practice. *Communication Theory, 7,* 189–218.

Holmer Nadesan, M., & Trethewey, A. (2000). Performing the enterprising subject: Gendered strategies for success. *Text and Performance Quarterly, 20,* 223–250.

Holmes, J. (2006). *Gendered talk at work: Constructing gender identity through workplace discourse.* Malden, MA: Blackwell.

hooks, b. (1981). *Ain't I a woman: Black women and feminism.* Boston: South End Press.

hooks, b. (2000). *Feminism is for everybody: Passionate politics.* Boston: South End Press.

Horkheimer, M., & Adorno, T. (1988). *Dialectic of enlightenment* (J. Cumming, Trans.). New York: Continuum.

Howe, J. (2006, June 1). The rise of crowdsourcing. *Wired.* Retrieved from https://www.wired.com/2006/06/crowds/.

Howell, J. M., & Shamir, B. (2005). The role of followers in the charismatic leadership process: Relationships and their consequences. *Academy of Management Review, 30,* 96–112.

Hunter, F. (1953). *Community power structure.* Chapel Hill: University of North Carolina Press.

Irani, L. (2013). The cultural work of microwork. *New Media and Society, 17,* 720–739. doi:10.1177/1461444813511926

Jablin, F. M. (1987). Organizational entry, assimilation, and exit. In F. M. Jablin, L. L. Putnam, K. H. Roberts, & L. W. Porter (Eds.), *Handbook of organizational communication: An interdisciplinary perspective* (pp. 679–740). Newbury Park, CA: Sage.

Jablin, F. (2001). Organizational entry, assimiliation, and exit. In F. Jablin & L. L. Putnam (Eds.), *The new handbook of organizational communication: Advances in theory, research, and methods*. Thousand Oaks, CA: Sage.

Jackall, R. (1988). *Moral mazes: The world of corporate managers*. New York: Oxford University Press.

Jackson, B., & Parry, K. W. (2011). *A very short, fairly interesting and reasonably cheap book about studying leadership*. London: Sage.

Jacques, R. (1996). *Manufacturing the employee: Management knowledge from the 19th to 21st centuries*. London: Sage.

Janis, I. L. (1983). *Groupthink: Psychological studies of policy decisions and fiascoes*. Boston: Houghton Mifflin.

Jay, M. (1973). *The dialectical imagination*. Boston: Little & Brown.

Jeffries, S. (2016). *Grand hotel abyss: The lives of the Frankfurt School*. London: Verso.

Johnson, K. (2018). Starbucks CEO: Reprehensible outcome in Philadelphia incident. Retrieved from https://news.starbucks.com/views/starbucks-ceo-reprehensible-outcome-in-philadelphia-incident.

Kalberg, S. (1980). Max Weber's types of rationality: Cornerstones for the analysis of rationalization processes in history. *American Journal of Sociology, 85*, 1145–1179.

Kalleberg, A. L. (2009). Precarious work, insecure workers: Employment relations in transiition. *American Sociological Review, 74*, 1–22.

Kalleberg, A. L. (2011). *Good jobs, bad jobs: The rise of polarized and precarious employment systems in the United States, 1970s to 2000s*. New York: Russell Sage Foundation.

Kang, M. (2010). *The managed hand: Race, gender and the body in beauty service work*. Berkeley: University of California Press.

Kanter, R. M. (1977). *Men and women of the corporation*. New York: Basic Books.

Kantor, J. (2014, August 13). Working anything but 9 to 5: Scheduling technology leaves low-income parents with hours of chaos. *The New York Times*. Retrieved from http://www.nytimes.com/interactive/2014/08/13/us/starbucks-workers-scheduling-hours.html?_r = 0

Kantor, J., & Streitfeld, D. (2015). Inside Amazon: Wrestling big ideas in a bruising workplace. *The New York Times*. Retrieved from http://www.nytimes.com/2015/08/16/technology/inside-amazon-wrestling-big-ideas-in-a-bruising-workplace.html?_r = 0

Karlsson, J. (2012). *Organizational misbehaviour in the workplace: Narratives of dignity and resistance*. Basingstoke, UK: Palgrave Macmillan.

Kassing, J. W. (2011). *Dissent in organizations*. Cambridge, UK Polity Press.

Katz, D. (1994). *Just Do It: The Nike spirit in the corporate world*. New York: Random House.

Katz, D., & Kahn, R. L. (1966). *The social psychology of organizations*. New York: Wiley.

Kauflin, J. (2017, May 26). The most loved and hated CEOs in America. *Forbes*. Retrieved from https://www.forbes.com/sites/jeffkauflin/2017/05/26/the-most-loved-and-hated-ceos-in-america/#793fc17446c9.

Kelley, R. E. (1988). In praise of followers. *Harvard Business Review, 66*(6), 142–148.

Kelley, R. E., & Bacon, F. (2004). Followership. *Encyclopedia of leadership*. Thousand Oaks, CA: Sage Publications.

Kellner, D. (1989). *Critical theory, marxism, and modernity*. Baltimore: Johns Hopkins University Press.

Kenny, K., Whittle, A., & Willmott, H. (2011). *Understanding identity & organizations*. Thousand Oaks, CA: Sage.

Keynes, J. M. (1932). Economic possibilities for our grandchildren. In J. M. Keynes (Ed.), *Essays in persuasion* (pp. 321–327). London: Palgrave Macmillan.

Keyton, J. (2011). *Communication & organizational culture: A key to understanding work experiences* (2nd. ed.). Thousand Oaks, CA: Sage.

Kim, H.-R., Lee, M., Lee, H.-T., Kim, N.-M., & Sources, V. (2010). Corporate social responsibility and employee-company identification. *Journal of Business Ethics*, 95, 557–569. doi:10.1007A10551 -010-0440-2

Kirby, E., & Harter, L. (2002). Speaking the language of the bottom-line: The metaphor of "Managing Diversity." *The Journal of Business Communication*, 40(1), 28–49.

Kirby, E., & Krone, K. (2002). "The policy exists but you can't really use it": Communication and the structuration of work-family policies. *Journal of Applied Communication Research*, 30, 50–77.

Klein, N. (2001). *No logo*. London: Flamingo Press.

Klein, N. (2005). Culture jamming. In L. Amoore (Ed.), *The global resistance reader* (pp. 437–444). London: Routledge.

Klein, N. (2007). *The shock doctrine: The rise of disaster capitalism*. New York: Metropolitan Books/ Henry Holt.

Knights, D., & McCabe, D. (2000). "Ain't misbehavin"? Opportunities for resistance under new forms of "quality" management. *Sociology*, 34, 412–436.

Koch, S., & Deetz, S. (1981). Metaphor analysis of social reality in organizations. *Journal of Applied Communication Research*, 9(1), 1–15.

Konish, L. (2018, May 21). *Consumer debt set to reach record $4 trillion by the end of the year*. Retrieved from https://www.cnbc.com/2018/05/21/consumer-debt-is-set-to-reach-4-trillion-by-the-end-of-2018.html.

Kornberger, M. (2010). *Brand society: How brands transform management and lifestyle*. Cambridge, UK: Cambridge University Press.

Kornberger, M. (2015). Think different: On studying the brand as organizing device. *International Studies of Management and Organization*, 45(2), 105–113.

Koschmann, M. (2012, May 8). What is organizational communication? [Video file]. Retrieved from www.youtube.com/watch?v = e5oXygLGMuY.

Koschmann, M., Kuhn, T., & Pfarrer, M. (2012). A communicative framework of value in cross-sector partnerships. *Academy of Management Review*, 37, 332–354.

Krames, J. A. (2002). *The Jack Welch lexicon of leadership*. New York: McGraw-Hill.

Krames, J. A. (2005). *Jack Welch and the 4E's of leadership: How to put GE's leadership formula to work in your organization*. New York: McGraw-Hill.

Krizek, R. L. (1992). Goodbye old friend: A son's farewell to Comiskey Park. *Omega*, 25(2), 87–93.

Kuhn, T. (1970). *The structure of scientific revolutions* (2nd. ed.). Chicago: University of Chicago Press.

Kuhn, T. (2006). A "demented work ethic" and a "lifestyle firm": Discourse, identity, and workplace time commitments. *Organization Studies*, 27, 1339–1358.

Kuhn, T. (2009). Positioning lawyers: Discursive resources, professional ethics, and identification. *Organization*, 16, 681–704.

Kuhn, T. (2017). Developing a communicative imagination under contemporary capitalism: The domain of organizational communication as a mode of explanation. *Management Communication Quarterly*, 31, 116–122.

Kuhn, T., Ashcraft, K., & Cooren, F. (2017). *The work of communication: Relational perspectives on working and organizing in contemporary capitalism*. New York: Routledge.

Kuhn, T., & Deetz, S. A. (2008). Critical theory and corporate social responsibility: Can/should we get beyond cynical reasoning? In A. Crane, A. McWilliams, D. Matten, J. Moon, & D. Siegel (Eds.), *The Oxford handbook of corporate social responsibility* (pp. 173–196). Oxford, UK: Oxford University Press.

Kuhn, T., Golden, A., Jorgenson, J., Buzzanell, P., Berkelaar, B., Kisselburgh, L., Kleinman, S., Cruz, D. (2008). Cultural discourses and discursive resources for meaning/ful work: Constructing and disrupting identities in contemporary capitalism. *Management Communication Quarterly*, 22, 162–171.

Kunda, G. (1992). *Engineering culture: Control and commitment in a high-tech corporation*. Philadelphia: Temple University Press.

Lair, D., & Wieland, S. (2012). "What are you going to to with that major?": Colloquial speech and the meanings of work and education. *Management Communication Quarterly*, *26*, 423–452.

Lakoff, G., & Johnson, M. (1980). *Metaphors we live by*. Chicago: University of Chicago Press.

Land, C., & Taylor, S. (2010). Surf's up: Work, life, balance and brand in a new age capitalist organization. *Sociology*, *44*, 395–413.

Lane, B. (2008). *Jacked up: The inside story of how Jack Welch talked GE into becoming the world's greatest company*. New York: McGraw-Hill.

Lazzarato, M. (1996). Immaterial labour. In P. Virno & M. Hardt (Eds.), *Radical thought in Italy: A potential politics* (pp. 133–147). Minneapolis: University of Minnesota Press.

Lazzarato, M. (2004). From capital-labour to capital-life. *Ephemera*, *4*(3), 187–208.

Lecher, C. (2018). What happens when an algorithm cuts your health care. *The Verge*. Retrieved from https://www.theverge.com/2018/3/21/17144260/healthcare-medicaid-algorithm-arkansas-cerebral-palsy

Leidner, R. (1993). *Fast food, fast talk: Service work and the routinization of everyday life*. Berkeley: University of California Press.

Leonardi, P. (2011). When flexible routines meet flexible technologies: Affordance, constraint, and the imbrication of human and material agencies. *MIS Quarterly*, *35*, 147–167.

Leonardi, P., & Bailey, D. (2008). Transformational technologies and the creation of new work practices: Making implicit knowledge explicit in task-based offshoring. *MIS Quarterly*, *32*, 411–436.

Levy, K. (2014). "Alex from Target," the teen who went viral on social media, was all a marketing ploy. *Business Insider*. Retrieved from http://www.businessinsider.com/alex-from-target-a-marketing-ploy-2014-11.

Levy, K. E. C. (2015). The contexts of control: Information, power, and truck-driving work. *The Information Society*, *31*, 160–174.

Lewin, K. (1951). Problems of research in social psychology. In D. Cartwright (Ed.), *Field theory in social science: Selected theoretical papers* (pp. 155–169). New York: Harper & Row.

Lewin, K., & Lippett, R. (1938). An experimental approach to the study of autocracy and democratic leadership. *Sociometry*, *1*, 292–300.

Liebow, E. (1967). *Tally's corner: A study of Negro streetcorner men*. Boston: Little, Brown

Likert, R. (1961). *New patterns of management*. New York: McGraw-Hill.

Linder, M., & Nygaard, I. (1998). *Void where prohibited: Rest breaks and the right to urinate on company time*. Ithaca, NY: ILR Press.

Linstead, S., & Grafton-Small, R. (1992). On reading organizational culture. *Organization Studies*, *13*, 311–355.

Livingston, J. (2016). *No more work: Why full employment is a bad idea*. Chapel Hill, NC: University of North Carolina Press.

Loe, M. (1996). Working for men—at the intersection of power, gender, and sexuality. *Sociological Inquiry*, *66*, 399–421.

Lorde, A. (1984). *Sister outsider*. Trumansburg, NY: The Crossing Press.

Lorey, I. (2015). *State of insecurity: Government of the precarious* (A. Derieg, Trans.). London: Verso.

Lucas, K. (2011). The working class promise: A communicative account of mobility-based ambivalences. *Communication Monographs*, *78*, 347–369.

Lucas, R. (2010). Dreaming in code. *New Left Review*, *62*, 125–132.

Lukes, S. (1974). *Power: A radical view*. London: MacMillan.

Lury, C. (2004). *Brands: The logos of the global economy*. London: Routledge.

Lutgen-Sandvik, P. (2003). The communicative cycle of employee emotional abuse: Generation and regeneration of workplace mistreatment. *Management Communication Quarterly, 16,* 471–501.

Luxen, M. (2015). Facebook challenges legitimacy of some Native names. Retrieved from https://www.bbc.com/news/blogs-trending-31699618.

Lynch, O. H. (2002). Humorous communication: Finding a place for humor in communication research. *Communication Theory, 12,* 423–445.

Lyon, A. (2011). Reconstructing Merck's practical theory of communication: The ethics of pharmaceutical sales representative-physician encounters. *Communication Monographs, 78,* 53.

Lyons, D. (2016). *Disrupted: My misadventure in the start-up bubble.* New York: Hachette Books.

MacKinnon, C. A. (1979). *Sexual harassment of working women: A case of sex discrimination.* New Haven: Yale University Press.

Maguire, M., & Mohtar, L. F. (1994). Performance and the celebration of a subaltern counterpublic. *Text and Performance Quarterly, 14,* 238–252.

Mandela, N. (1995). *Long walk to freedom: The autobiography of Nelson Mandela.* Boston: Back Bay Books, Little, Brown.

Manz, C. C., & Sims, H. P. (2000). *The new superleadership: Leading others to lead themselves.* San Francisco: Berrett-Koehler Publishers.

Marrs, M. (2012, February 14). The first step to building your personal brand. *Forbes.* Retrieved from https://www.forbes.com/sites/dailymuse/2012/02/14/the-first-step-to-building-your-personal-brand/.

Martin, J. (1985). Can organizational culture be managed? In P. Frost, M. Louis, J. Martin, & C. Lundberg (Eds.), *Organizational culture* (pp. 95–98). Beverly Hills, CA: Sage.

Martin, J. (1992). *Culture in organizations: Three perspectives.* New York: Oxford University Press.

Martin, J., Feldman, M., Hatch, M. J., & Sitkin, S. J. (1983). The uniqueness paradox in organizational stories. *Administrative Science Quarterly, 28,* 438–453.

Martin, J., Knopoff, K., & Beckman, C. (1998). An alternative to bureaucratic impersonality and emotional labor: Bounded emotionality at The Body Shop. *Administrative Science Quarterly, 43,* 429–469.

Martin, J. N., & Nakayama, T. K. (Eds.). (1999). *Whiteness: The communication of social identity.* Thousand Oaks: Sage.

Martino, J.-M. (1999). *Diversity: An imperative for business success.* New York: Conference Board.

Marwick, A. (2013). *Status update: Celebrity, publicity and attention in the social media age.* New Haven, CT: Yale University Press.

Marwick, A. (2015). Instafame: Luxury selfies in the attention economy. *Public Culture, 27,* 137–160.

Marx, K. (1961). *Economic and philosophic manuscripts of 1844.* Moscow: Foreign Languages Publishing House.

Marx, K. (1967). *Capital* (S. Moore & E. Aveling, Trans.). New York: International Publishers.

Marx, K., & Engels, F. (1947). *The German Ideology.* New York: International Publishers.

Maslow, A. H. (1987). *Motivation and personality.* New York: Addison Wesley Longman.

Mazmanian, M. (2013). Avoiding the trap of constant connectivity: When congruent frames assume heterogeneous practices. *Academy of Management Journal, 56,* 1225–1250.

Mazmanian, M., Orlikowski, W. J., & Yates, J. (2013). The autonomy paradox: The implications of mobile email devices for knowledge professionals. *Organization Science, 24,* 1337–1357. doi:10.1287/orsc.1120.0806

McAfee, A., & Brynjolfsson, E. (2012). Big data: The management revolution. *Harvard Business Review,* 1–9.

McBride, D. (2005). *Why I hate Abercrombie & Fitch: Essays on race and sexuality.* New York: NYU Press.

McCarthy, N. (2016, September 23). Survey: 69% of Americans have less than $1000 in savings. *Forbes.* Retrieved from https://www.forbes.com/sites/niallmccarthy/2016/09/23/survey-69-of-americans-have-less-than-1000-in-savings-infographic/#6be93d341ae6.

McDonald, J. (2015). Organizational communication meets queer theory: Theorizing relations of "difference" differently. *Communication Theory, 25,* 310–329.

McDonald, J. (2016). Occupational segregation research: Queering the converstion. *Gender, Work and Organization, 23,* 19–35.

McDonald, J., & Kuhn, T. (2016). Occupational branding for diversity: Managing discursive contradictions. *Journal of Applied Communication Research, 44,* 101–117.

McDonald, J., & Mitra, R. (Eds.). (In Press). *Movements in organizational communication research: Current issues and future directions.* New York: Routledge.

McGregor, D. (1960). *The human side of enterprise.* New York: McGraw-Hill.

McIntosh, P. (1990). White privilege: Unpacking the invisible knapsack. *Independent School, 49*(2), 31.

McIntosh, W. L., Spies, E., Stone, D. M., Lokey, C. N., Trudeau, A. T., & Bartholow, B. (2016). MMWR: Morbidity Mortality Weekly Report. *Suicide Rates by Occupational Group: 17 States, 2012, 65,* 641–645. doi:10.15585/mmwr.mm6525a1

McMillan, J., & Cheney, G. (1996). The student as consumer: The implications and limitations of a metaphor. *Communication Education, 45,* 1–15.

McMillan, J., & Northorn, N. A. (1995). Organizational codependency: The creation and maintenance of closed systems. *Management Communication Quarterly, 9,* 6–45.

McMillen, S. G. (2008). *Seneca Falls and the origins of the women's rights movement.* New York: Oxford University Press.

McRobbie, A. (2000). *Feminism and youth culture.* New York: Routledge.

McRobbie, A. (2016). *Be creative: Making a living in the new culture industries.* Cambridge, UK: Polity Press.

Mease, J. (2011). Teaching difference as institutional and making it personal: Moving among personal, interpersonal, and institutional construction of difference. In D. K. Mumby (Ed.), *Reframing difference in organizational communication studies: Research, pedagogy, practice* (pp. 151–171). Thousand Oaks, CA: Sage.

Mease, J. (2012). Reconsidering consultants' strategic use of the business case for diversity. *Journal of Applied Communication Research, 40,* 384–402.

Meindl, J. R. (1995). The romance of leadership as a follower-centric theory: A social constructionist approach. *Leadership Quarterly, 6,* 329–341.

Meindl, J. R., Ehrlich, S. B., & Dukerich, J. M. (1985). The romance of leadership. *Administrative Science Quarterly, 30,* 78–102.

Merriott, D. (2016). Factors associated with the farmer suicide crisis in India. *Journal of Epidemiology and Global Health, 6*(4), 217–227. doi:10.1016/j.jegh.2016.03.003

Michel, A. (2011). Transcending socialization: A nine-year ethnography of the body's role in organizational control and knowledge workers' transformation. *Administrative Science Quarterly, 56,* 325–368.

Mickelthwait, J., & Wooldridge, A. (1996). *The witch doctors.* New York: Crown Business.

Mill, H. T. (1851/1994). Enfranchisement of women. In A. P. Robson & J. M. Robson (Eds.), *Sexual equality: Writings by John Stuart Mill, Harriet Taylor Mill* (pp. 178–203). Toronto: University of Toronto Press.

Mill, J. S. (1869/1970). The subjection of women. In A. S. Rossi (Ed.), *Essays on sex equality* (pp. 123–142). Chicago: University of Chicago Press.

Miller, A. (1949). *Death of a salesman: Certain private conversations in two acts and a requiem.* New York: Viking Press, 1968.

Miller, C. C., Quealy, K., & Sanger-Katz, M. (2018, April 24). The top jobs where women are outnumbered by men named John. *The New York Times*. Retrieved from https://www.nytimes.com/interactive/2018/04/24/upshot/women-and-men-named-john.html

Miller, K. (2002). Nurses at the edge of chaos: The application of "new science" concepts to organizational systems. *Management Communication Quarterly*, *12*, 112–127.

Miller, P., & Rose, N. (1995). Production, identity, and democracy. *Theory and Society*, *24*, 427–467.

Miller, P., & Rose, N. (2008). *Governing the present*. Cambridge, UK: Polity.

Mills, A. J., & Chiaramonte, P. (1991). Organization as gendered communication act. *Canadian Journal of Communication*, *16*, 381–398.

Mills, C. W. (1951). *White collar: The American middle classes*. New York: Oxford University Press.

Mills, C. W. (1956). *The power elite*. Oxford: Oxford University Press.

Mohrman, S. A., Cohen, S. G., & Mohrman, A. M. (1995). *Designing team-based organizations: New forces for knowledge work*. San Francisco: Jossey-Bass.

Monbiot, G. (2013). For more wonder, rewild the world [Video file]. Retrieved from https://www.ted.com/talks/george_monbiot_for_more_wonder_rewild_the_world.

Monge, P. R. (1982). Systems theory and research in the study of organizational communication: The correspondence problem. *Human Communication Research*, *8*, 245–261.

Morgan, G. (2006). *Images of organization*. Thousand Oaks, CA: Sage.

Morozov, E. (2013). *To save everything, click here: The folly of technological solutionism*. New York: PublicAffairs.

Morrison, K. (1995). *Marx, Durkheim, Weber: Formations of modern social thought*. London: Sage.

Mosendz, P. (2014, Dec. 10). With Abercrombie sales falling, CEO Michael Jeffries quits. *Newsweek*. Retrieved from https://www.newsweek.com/michael-jeffries-abercrombie-ceo-steps-down-290858.

Moss, G. (Ed.) (2010). *Profiting from diversity: The business advantages and the obstacles to achieving diversity*. Basingstoke, UK: Palgrave Macmillan.

Mulcahy, D. (2016). Why I tell my students to stop looking for a job and join the gig economy. *Harvard Business Review*. Retrieved from https://hbr.org/2016/10/why-i-tell-my-mba-students-to-stop-looking-for-a-job-and-join-the-gig-economy

Mullan, K., & Wajcman, J. (In Press). Have mobile devices changed working patterns in the 21st century? A time-diary analysis of work extension in the UK. *Work, Employment and Society*. doi:10.1177/0950017017730529

Mumby, D. K. (1987). The political function of narrative in organizations. *Communication Monographs*, *54*, 113–127.

Mumby, D. K. (1996). Feminism, postmodernism, and organizational communication: A critical reading. *Management Communication Quarterly*, *9*, 259–295.

Mumby, D. K. (1997). Modernism, postmodernism, and communication studies: A rereading of an ongoing debate. *Communication Theory*, *7*, 1–28.

Mumby, D. K. (2000). Common ground from the critical perspective: Overcoming binary oppositions. In S. R. Corman & M. S. Poole (Eds.), *Perspectives on organizational communication: Finding common ground* (pp. 68–88). New York: Guilford.

Mumby, D. K. (2005). Theorizing resistance in organization studies: A dialectical approach. *Management Communication Quarterly*, *19*, 1–26.

Mumby, D. K. (2006). Constructing working class masculinity in the workplace. In J. T. Wood & S. Duck (Eds.), *Composing relationships: Communication in everyday life* (pp. 166–174). Boston: Wadsworth.

Mumby, D. K. (2009). The strange case of the farting professor: Humor and the deconstruction of destructive communication. In P. Lutgen-Sandvik & B. D. Sypher (Eds.), *Destructive organizational communication: Processes, consequences, and constructive ways of organizing* (pp. 316–338). New York: Routledge.

Mumby, D. K. (Ed.) (2011). *Reframing difference in organizational communication studies: Research, pedagogy, practice.* Thousand Oaks, CA: Sage.

Mumby, D. K. (2015). Organizing power. *Review of Communication, 15,* 19–38.

Mumby, D. K. (2016). Organizing beyond organization: Branding, discourse, and communicative capitalism. *Organization, 23,* 884–907.

Mumby, D. K. (2018). Targeting Alex: Brand as agent in communicative capitalism. In B. H. J. M. Brummans (Ed.), *The agency of organizing: Perspectives and case studies* (pp. 98–122). New York: Routledge.

Mumby, D. K., & Stohl, C. (1992). Power and discourse in organization studies: Absence and the dialectic of control. *Discourse & Society, 2,* 313–332.

Mumby, D. K., Thomas, R., Martí, I., & Seidl, D. (2017). Resistance redux. *Organization Studies, 38,* 1157–1183.

Muniz, A. (2007). Brands and branding. In G. Ritzer (Ed.), The Blackwell encyclopedia of sociology. Oxford: Blackwell Publishing. Retrieved from http://www.blackwellreference.com.libproxy.lib .unc.edu/subscriber/tocnode?id = g9781405124331_chunk_g97814051243318_ss1-47.

Murphy, A. G. (1998). Hidden transcripts of flight attendant resistance. *Management Communication Quarterly, 11,* 499–535.

Murphy, A. G. (2003). The dialectical gaze: Exploring the subject-object tension in the performances of women who strip. *Journal of Contemporary Ethnography, 32,* 305–335.

Nader, R. (1965). *Unsafe at any speed.* New York: Grossmann Publishers.

Nakayama, T., & Krizek, R. (1995). Whiteness: A strategic rhetoric. *The Quarterly Journal of Speech, 81,* 291–309.

Neff, G. (2012). *Venture labor: Work and the burden of risk in innovative industries.* Cambridge, MA: MIT Press.

Nink, M., & Schumann, F. (2018). German workers: Satisfied but not engaged. Retrieved from https:// news.gallup.com/opinion/gallup/228893/german-workers-satisfied-not-engaged.aspx? g_source = link_NEWSV9&g_medium = TOPIC&g_campaign = item_&g_content = German % 2520Workers % 3a % 2520Satisfied % 2c % 2520but % 2520Not % 2520Engaged.

Noble, S. (2018). *Algorithms of oppression: How search engines reinforce racism.* New York: NYU Press.

Nonaka, I. (1988). Creating organizational order out of chaos: Self-renewal in Japanese firms. *California Management Review, 30*(3), 57–73.

Nursing@USC Staff. (2017, March 17). A century of smoking in women's history. Department of Nursing. Retrieved from https://nursing.usc.edu/blog/womens-history-smoking/.

O'Connor, E. (1999a). Minding the workers: The meaning of "human" and "human relations" in Elton Mayo. *Organization, 6,* 223–246.

O'Connor, E. (1999b). The politics of management thought: A case study of the Harvard Business School and the human relations school. *Academy of Management Review, 24,* 117–131.

O'Neil, C. (2016). *Weapons of math destruction: How big data increases inequality and threatens democracy.* New York: Broadway Books.

Offsey, S. (1997). Knowledge management: Linking people to knowledge for bottom line results. *Journal of Knowledge Management, 1,* 113–122.

Olins, W. (2000). How brands are taking over the corporation. In M. Schultz, M. J. Hatch, & M. H. Larsen (Eds.), *The expressive organization: Linking identity, reputation, and the corporate brand* (pp. 51–65). Oxford, UK: Oxford University Press.

Olins, W. (2003). *Wally Olins on brand.* London: Thames & Hudson.

Orbe, M., & Harris, T. M. (2001). *Interracial communication: Theory into practice.* Belmont, CA: Wadsworth.

Orlikowski, W. J. (1996). Improvising organizational transformation over time: A situated change perspective. *Information Systems Research, 7*(1), 63–92.

Osatuyi, B., & Andoh-Baidoo, F. K. (2014). Towards a community-centered knowledge management architecture for disaster management in sub-saharan Africa. In K.-M. Osei-Bryson, G. Mansingh, & L. Rao (Eds.), *Knowledge management for development: Domains, strategies, and technologies for developing countries* (pp. 17–41). New York: Springer.

Pacanowsky, M. (1988). Communication in the empowering organization. In J. Anderson (Ed.), *Communication yearbook* (Vol.11, pp. 356–379). Thousand Oaks, CA: Sage.

Pacanowsky, M., & O'Donnell-Trujillo, N. (1982). Communication and organizational cultures. *The Western Journal of Speech Communication, 46*, 115–130.

Pal, M. (2016). Organization at the margins: Subaltern resistance of Singur. *Human Relations, 69*, 419–438.

Papa, M. J., Auwal, M. A., & Singhal, A. (1995). Dialectic of control and emancipation in organizing for social change: A multitheoretic study of the Grameen Bank in Bangladesh. *Communication Theory, 5*, 189–223.

Parker, M., & Slaughter, J. (1988). *Choosing sides: Unions and the team concept.* Boston: South End Press.

Parker, M., & Slaughter, J. (1990). Management-by-stress: The team concept in the US auto industry. *Science as Culture, 1*(8), 27–58.

Parker, P. S. (2014). Difference and organizing. In L. L. Putnam & D. K. Mumby (Eds.), *The SAGE handbook of organizational communication: Advances in theory, research, and methods* (pp. 619–642). Los Angeles, CA: Sage.

Parker, P. S., & Mease, J. (2009). Beyond the knapsack: Disrupting the production of white racial privilege in organizational practices. In L. Samovar, R. Porter, & E. McDaniel (Eds.), *Intercultural communication: A reader* (12th ed., pp. 313–324). New York: Wadsworth.

Parry, K. W., & Bryman, A. (2006). Leadership in organizations. In S. Clegg, C. Hardy, T. B. Lawrence, & W. R. Nord (Eds.), *The Sage handbook of organization studies* (2nd ed., pp. 447–468). London: Sage.

Parry, K. W., & Hansen, H. (2007). The organizational story as leadership. *Leadership, 3*, 281–300.

Paulsen, R. (2014). *Empty labor: Idleness and workplace resistance.* Cambridge, UK: Cambridge University Press.

Paulsen, R. (2015). Non-work at work: Resistance or what? *Organization, 22*, 351–367.

Peck, J. (2016). *The age of Oprah: Cultural icon for the neoliberal era.* New York: Routledge.

Perlow, L. A. (1997). *Finding time: How corporations, individuals, and families can benefit from new work practices.* Ithaca, N.Y.: ILR Press.

Perrow, C. (1986). *Complex organizations* (3rd ed.). New York: Random House.

Peters, T. (1988). *Thriving on chaos: Handbook for a management revolution.* New York: Harper & Row.

Peters, T. (1997). The brand called you. *Fast Company.* Retrieved from https://www.fastcompany.com/28905/brand-called-you.

Peters, T., & Waterman, R. M. (1982). *In search of excellence.* New York: Harper & Row.

Peterson, E. (2018, February 1). "Seeing someone cry at work is becoming normal": Employees say Whole Foods is using "scorecards" to punish them. *Business Insider.* Retrieved from https://www.entrepreneur.com/article/308395.

Peterson, H. (2014). Alex from Target might not be a marketing stunt after all. *Business Insider.* Retrieved from http://www.businessinsider.com/alex-from-target-not-a-marketing-stunt-2014-11.

Peticca-Harris, A., deGama, N., & Ravishankar, M. N. (In Press). Postcapitalist precarious work and those in the "driver's" seat: Exploring the motivations and lived experiences of Uber drivers in Canada. *Organization.* doi:10.1177/1350508418757332

Pew Research Center. (2015, December 9). The American middle class is losing ground: No longer the majority and falling behind financially. Retrieved from http://www.pewsocialtrends .org/2015/12/09/the-american-middle-class-is-losing-ground/.

Pfeffer, J. (1981). Management as symbolic action: The creation and maintenance of organizational paradigms. *Research in Organizational Behavior, 3*, 1–52.

Pfeffer, J. (2018). *Dying for a paycheck: How modern management harms employee health and company performance—and what we can do about it.* New York: Harper Business.

Piezunka, H., & Dahlander, L. (2015). Distant search, narrow attention: How crowding alters organizations' filtering of suggestions in crowdsourcing. *Academy of Management Journal, 58*, 856–880. doi:10.5465/amj.2012.0458

Piketty, T. (2014). *Capital in the twenty-first century.* Cambridge, MA: Harvard University Press.

Pink, D. (2001). *Free agent nation: The future of working for yourself.* New York: Warner Books.

Polanyi, M. (1967). *The tacit dimension.* Garden City, NY: Anchor Books.

Pondy, L. (1978). Leadership is a language game. In M. W. McCall & M. M. Lombardo (Eds.), *Leadership: Where else can we go?* Durham, NC: Duke University Press.

Poole, M. S. (2014). Systems theory. In L. L. Putnam & D. K. Mumby (Eds.), *The Sage handbook of orgaeniztional communication: Advances in theory, research, and methods* (3rd ed., pp. 49–74). Los Angeles, CA: Sage.

Poole, M. S., & DeSanctis, G. (1992). Microlevel structuration in computer-supported group decision-making. *Human Communication Research, 19*, 5–49.

Porter, T. (2018, July 24). Sean Spicer admists he "screwed up" by claiming Trump had biggest-ever inauguration audience. *Newsweek.* Retrieved from https://www.newsweek.com/sean-spicer-admits-he-screwed-claiming-trump-inauguration-crowd-biggest-ever-1039439.

Prahalad, C. K. (2006). *The fortune at the bottom of the pyramid.* Philadelphia, PA: Wharton School Publishing.

Prasad, A., & Prasad, P. (1998). Everyday struggles at the workplace: The nature and implications of routine resistance in contemporary organizations. In P. A. Bamberger & W. J. Sonnenstuhl (Eds.), *Research in the sociology of organizations, 15: Deviance in and of organizations* (pp. 225–257). Stamford, CT: JAI Press.

Pringle, R. (1989). *Secretaries talk: Sexuality, power and work.* London: Verso.

Proctor, B. D., Semega, J. L., & Kollar, M. A. (2016) Income and poverty in the United States: 2015 (Report no. P60-256). Current population reports. Retrieved from U.S. Department of Commerce Economics and Statistics Administration, U.S. Census Bureau: https://www.census.gov/content/ dam/Census/library/publications/2016/demo/p60-256.pdf

Prokesch, S. (1989). Ford to buy Jaguar for $2.38 billion. *New York Times.* Retrieved from http://www .nytimes.com/1989/11/03/business/ford-to-buy-jaguar-for-2.38-billion.html?pagewanted = 1

Putnam, L. L. (1983). The interpretive perspective: An alternative to functionalism. In L. L. Putnam & M. Pacanowsky (Eds.), *Communication and organizations: An interpretive approach* (pp. 31–54). Beverly Hills, CA: Sage.

Putnam, L. L. (1990). *Feminist theories, dispute processes, and organizational communication.* Paper presented at the Arizona State University Conference on Organizational Communication, Tempe, AZ.

Putnam, L. L., & Fairhurst, G. (1985). Women and organizational communication: Research directions and new perspectives. *Women and Language, 9*(1/2), 2–6.

Putnam, L. L., & Nicotera, A. M. (Eds.). (2009). *Building theories of organization: The constitutive role of communication.* Oxford, UK: Routledge.

Putnam, L. L., & Pacanowsky, M. (Eds.). (1983). *Communication and organizations: An interpretive approach.* Beverly Hills, CA: Sage.

Quindlen, A. (2003, October). Still needing the F word. *Newsweek*, 1. Retrieved from https://www .newsweek.com/still-needing-f-word-138627.

Rasche, A., Morsing, M., & Moon, J. (Eds.). (2017). *Corporate social responsibility: Strategy, communication, governance*. Cambridge, UK: Cambridge University Press.

Ray, C. A. (1986). Corporate culture: The last frontier of control? *Journal of Management Studies, 23*, 287–297.

Ray, R., Gornick, J., & Schmitt, J. (2008). *Parental leave policies in 21 countries: Assessing generosity and gender equality*. Washington, DC: Center for Economic Policy and Research. Retrieved from http:// www.lisdatacenter.org/wp-content/uploads/parent-leave-report1.pdf.

Raz, A. E. (2002). *Emotions at work: Normative control, organizations, and culture in Japan and America*. Cambridge, MA: Harvard University Asia Center and Harvard University Press.

Redding, W. C. (1988). Organizational communication. In E. Barnouw (Ed.), *International encyclopedia of communications* (Vol. 3, pp. 236–239). New York: Oxford University Press.

Reich, R. (1991). *The work of nations*. New York: Vintage Books.

Reuther, C., & Fairhurst, G. (2000). Chaos theory and the glass ceiling. In P. Buzzanell (Ed.), *Rethinking organizational and managerial communication from feminist perspectives* (pp. 236–253). Thousand Oaks, CA: Sage.

Rhodes, C., & Westwood, R. (Eds.). (2007). *Humor, organization, and work*. London: Routledge.

Riad, S. (2005). The power of "organizational culture" as a discursive formation in merger integration. *Organization Studies, 26*, 1529–1554.

Rice, R. E., & Gattiker, U. E. (2001). New media and organizational structuring. In F. M. Jablin & L. L. Putnam (Eds.), *The new handbook of organizational communication* (2nd ed., pp. 544–584). Newbury Park, CA: Sage.

Rich, A. (1980). Compulsory heterosexuality and lesbian existence. *Signs, 5*, 631–660.

Ritzer, G. (2015). *The McDonaldization of society* (8th ed.). Los Angeles, CA: Sage.

Roberts, J. (2003). The manufacture of corporate social responsibility: Constructing corporate sensibility. *Organization, 10*, 249–265.

Robertson, R. (1990). *Globalization*. London: Sage.

Robertson, R., & Khondker, H. H. (1998). Discourses of globalization: Preliminary considerations. *International Sociology, 13*, 25–40.

Robinson, J. P., & Godbey, G. (1999). *Time for life: The surprising ways Americans use their time*. University Park, PA: Pennsylvania State University Press.

Roediger, D. R. (2005). *Working toward whiteness: How America's immigrants became white*. New York: Basic Books.

Roethlisberger, F. J., & Dickson, W. J. (1939). *Management and the worker*. New York: Wiley.

Romo, L. K. (2018). Coming out as a non-drinker at work. *Management Communication Quarterly, 32*, 292–296.

Rosa, H. (2013). *Social acceleration: A new theory of modernity*. New York: Columbia University Press.

Rose, N. (1999). *Governing the soul: The shaping of the private self* (2nd. ed.). London: Free Association Books.

Rosen, M. (1985). "Breakfast at Spiro's": Dramaturgy and dominance. *Journal of Management, 11*(2), 31–48.

Rosen, M. (1988). You asked for it: Christmas at the bosses' expense. *Journal of Management Studies, 25*, 463–480.

Rosenblat, A., Barocas, S., Levy, K., & Hwang, T. (2016). Discriminating tastes: Uber's customer ratings as vehicles for workplace discrimination. *Policy and Internet, 9*(3), 256–279. doi:10.1002/ poi3.153

Ross, A. (2003). *No-collar: The humane workplace and its hidden costs*. New York: Basic Books.

Ross, A. (2008). The new geography of work: Power to the precarious? *Theory, Culture & Society, 25*(7–8), 31–49.

Ross, R. (1992). *From equality to diversity: A business case for equal opportunities.* London: Pitman.

Rothschild-Whitt, J. (1979). The collectivist organization: An alternative to rational bureaucratic models. *American Sociological Review, 44,* 509–527.

Rottig, D., Reus, T. H., & Tarba, S. Y. (2014). The impact of culture on mergers and acquisitions: A third of a century of research. In C. L. Cooper & S. Finkelstein (Eds.), *Advances in mergers and acquisitions* (Vol. 12, pp. 135–172). Bingley, UK: Emerald.

Roy, D. (1952). Quota restriction and goldbricking in a machine shop. *American Journal of Sociology, 57,* 427–442.

Roy, D. (1959). "Banana time": Job satisfaction and informal interaction. *Human Organization, 18,* 158–168.

Rumens, N. (2008). Working at intimacy: Gay men's workplace friendships. *Gender, Work and Organization, 15,* 9–30.

Rumens, N. (2010). Workplace friendships between men: Gay men's perspectives and experiences. *Human Relations, 63,* 1541–1562.

Rumens, N., & Broomfield, J. (2012). Gay men in the police: Identity disclosure and management issues. *Human Resource Management Journal, 22,* 283–298.

Rumens, N., & Broomfield, J. (2014). Gay men in the performing arts: Performing sexualities within 'gay-friendly' work contexts. *Organization, 21,* 365–382.

Rumens, N., & Kerfoot, D. (2009). Gay men at work: (Re)constructing the self as professional. *Human Relations, 62,* 763–786.

Ryan, M. K., & Haslam, S. A. (2007). The glass cliff: Exploring the dynamics surrounding the appointment of women to precarious leadership positions. *Academy of Management Review, 32,* 549–572.

Salem, P. (2002). Assessment, change, and complexity. *Management Communication Quarterly, 15,* 442–450.

Salem, P. (2017). New science systems theories. In C. R. Scott & L. Lewis (Eds.), *The international encyclopedia of organizational communication.* New York: John Wiley.

Sandberg, S. (2013). *Lean in: Women, work and the will to lead.* New York: Alfred A. Knopf.

Sassen, S. (1998). *Globalization and its discontents: Essays on the new mobility of people and money.* New York: The New Press.

Sassen, S. (2000). Women's burden: Counter-geographies of globalization and the feminization of survival. *Journal of International Affairs, 53,* 503–524.

Sassen, S. (2003). Global cities and survival circuits. In B. Ehrenreich & A. Hochschild (Eds.), *Global woman* (pp. 254–274). New York: Metropolitan Books.

Sassen, S. (2005). The global city: Introducing a concept. *Brown Journal of World Affairs, 11*(2), 27–44.

Sathe, V. (1983). Implications of corporate culture: A manager's guide to action. *Organizational Dynamics, 12*(3), 5–23.

Sathe, V. (1985). *Culture and related corporate realities: Text, cases, and readings on organizational entry, establishment, and change.* Homewood, IL.: R.D. Irwin.

Saussure, F. d. (1960). *Course in general linguistics.* London: Peter Owen.

Scarduzio, J. A., & Geist-Martin, P. (2010). Accounting for victimization: Male professors' ideological positioning in stories of sexual harassment. *Management Communication Quarterly, 24,* 419–445. doi:10.1177/0893318909358746

Schattschneider, E. E. (1960). *The semi-sovereign people.* New York: Wadsworth.

Scheibel, D. (1992). Faking identity in clubland: The communicative performance of "fake ID." *Text and Performance Quarterly, 12,* 160–175.

Scheibel, D. (1996). Appropriating bodies: Organ(izing) ideology and cultural practice in medical school. *Journal of Applied Communication Research, 24,* 310–331.

Scheibel, D. (1999). "If your roommate dies, you get a 4.0": Reclaiming rumor with Burke and organizational culture. *Western Journal of Communication, 63,* 168–192.

Schein, E. H. (1992). *Organizational culture and leadership* (2nd ed.). San Francisco: Jossey-Bass.

Scherer, A. G., & Palazzo, G. (2011). The new political role of business in a globalized world: A review of a new perspective on CSR and its implications for the firm, governance, and democracy. *Journal of Management Studies, 48,* 899–931.

Scherer, A. G., Rasche, A., Palazzo, G., & Spicer, A. (2016). Managing for political corporate social responsibility: New challenges and directions for PCSR 2.0. *Journal of Management Studies, 53,* 273–298.

Schildt, H. (2017). Big data and organizational design: The brave new world of algorithmic management and computer augmented transparency. *Innovation: Organization and Management, 19*(1), 23–30. doi:10.1080/14479338.2016.1252043

Scholte, J. A. (2000). *Globalization: A Critical introduction.* Basingstoke, UK: Palgrave MacMillan.

Scholz, T. (2014). Platform cooperativism vs. the sharing economy. In N. Douay & A. Wan (Eds.), *Big data & civic engagement* (pp. 47–54). Rome: Planum.

Schor, J. (1993). *The overworked American: The unexpected decline of leisure.* New York: Basic Books.

Schultz, F., Castelló, I., & Morsing, M. (2013). The construction of corporate social responsibility in network societies: A communication view. *Journal of Business Ethics, 115,* 681–692.

Schultz, H. (2012). *Onward: How Starbucks fought for its life without losing its soul.* Emmaus, PA: Rodale Press.

Scott, J. C. (1989). Everyday forms of resistance. *The Copenhagen Journal of Asian Studies, 4,* 33–62.

Scott, J. C. (1990). *Domination and the arts of resistance: Hidden transcripts.* New Haven, CT: Yale University Press.

Sedgwick, E. K. (2008). *Epistemology of the closet.* Berkeley: University of California Press.

Seidman, S. (2002). *Beyond the closet: The transformation of gay and lesbian life.* New York: Routledge.

Sennett, R. (1998). *The corrosion of character: The personal consequences of work in the new capitalism.* New York: W.W. Norton.

Sennett, R. (2006). *The culture of the new capitalism.* New Haven, CT: Yale University Press.

Sewell, G. (1998). The discipline of teams: The control of team-based industrial work through electronic and peer surveillance. *Administrative Science Quarterly, 43,* 397–428.

Shamir, R. (2004). The de-radicalization of corporate social responsibility. *Critical Sociology, 30,* 669–689.

Shamir, R. (2005). Mind the gap: The commodification of corporate social responsibility. *Symbolic Interaction, 28,* 229–253.

Sharma, S. (2014). *In the meantime: Temporality and cultural politics.* Durham, NC: Duke University Press.

Short, J. A., Williams, E., & Christie, B. (1976). *The social psychology of telecommunications.* London: Wiley.

Shumate, M. (2011). Knowledge management systems and work teams. In H. E. Canary & R. D. McPhee (Eds.), *Communication and organizational knowledge: Contemporary issues for theory and practice* (pp. 191–208). New York: Routledge.

Shy, J. (2008). Dove soap commerical [Video file]. Retrieved from https://www.youtube.com/watch?v = FipEYhv3fEg.

Silva, K. (2016). *Brown threat: Identification in the security state.* Minneapolis: University of Minnesota Press.

Silverman, R. E. (2016, February 17). Bosses tap outside firms to predict which workers might get sick. *Wall Street Journal*. Retrieved from https://www-wsj-com.cdn.ampproject.org/c/s/www.wsj.com/amp/articles/bosses-harness-big-data-to-predict-which-workers-might-get-sick-1455664940

Simonite, T. (2012). Microsoft's workplace social network becomes emotionally aware. *MIT Technology Review*. Retrieved from https://www.technologyreview.com/s/428735/microsofts-workplace-social-network-becomes-emotionally-aware/.

Sinclair, A. (1992). The tyranny of a team ideology. *Organization Studies*, *13*, 611–626.

Skyttner, L. (2005). *General systems theory: Problems, perspectives, practice* (2nd ed.). Singapore: World Scientific Press.

Slater, R. (2003). *29 leadership secrets from Jack Welch*. New York: McGraw-Hill.

Smircich, L., & Morgan, G. (1982). Leadership: The management of meaning. *The Journal of Applied Behavioral Science*, *18*, 257–273.

Smith, A. (1776/1937). *An inquiry into the nature and causes of the wealth of nations*. New York: Random House.

Smith, F. L., & Keyton, J. (2001). Organizational storytelling: Metaphors for relational power and identity struggles. *Management Communication Quarterly*, *15*, 149–182.

Smith, J. H. (1998). The enduring legacy of Elton Mayo. *Human Relations*, *51*, 221–249.

Smith, R. (1992). *Images of organizational communication: Root-metaphors of the organization-communication relation*. Paper presented at the International Communication Association, Washington, DC, June.

Smith, R., & Eisenberg, E. (1987). Conflict at Disneyland: A root metaphor analysis. *Communication Monographs*, *54*, 367–380.

Solon, O. (2017, November 6). Big Brother isn't just watching: Workplace surveillance can track your every move. *The Guardian*. Retrieved from https://amp-theguardian-com.cdn.ampproject.org/c/s/amp.theguardian.com/world/2017/nov/06/workplace-surveillance-big-brother-technology.

Solon, O. (2018, January 31). Amazon patents wristband that tracks warehouse workers' movements. *The Guardian*. Retrieved from https://www.theguardian.com/technology/2018/jan/31/amazon-warehouse-wristband-tracking.

Soros, G. (2002). *On globalization*. New York: Public Affairs.

Spradlin, A. (1998). The price of "passing": A lesbian perspective on authenticity in organizations. *Management Communication Quarterly*, *11*, 598–605.

Srnicek, N. (2017). *Platform capitalism*. Cambridge, UK: Polity Press.

Standing, G. (2011). *The precariat*. London: Bloomsbury Academic.

Stark, D. (2009). *The sense of dissonance: Accounts of worth in economic life*. Princeton, NJ: Princeton University Press.

Starkey, K., & McKinlay, A. (1994). Managing for Ford. *Sociology*, *28*, 975–990.

Stillman, J. (2016, February 3). Work, sleep, family, fitness, or friends: Pick 3. *Inc*. Retrieved from https://www.inc.com/jessica-stillman/work-sleep-family-fitness-or-friends-pick-3.html.

Stogdill, R. M. (1948). Personal factors associated with leadership: A survey of the literature. *Journal of Psychology*, *25*, 35–71.

Stogdill, R. M. (1950). Leadership, membership and organization. *Psychological Bulletin*, *47*, 1–14.

Stohl, C. (2001). Globalizing organizational communication. In F. Jablin & L. L. Putnam (Eds.), *The new handbook of organizational communication: Advances in theory, research, and methods* (pp. 323–375). Thousand Oaks, CA: Sage.

Stohl, C., & Cheney, G. (2001). Participatory processes/paradoxical practices: Communication and the dilemmas of organizational democracy. *Management Communication Quarterly*, *14*, 349–407.

Stohl, C., & Ganesh, S. (2014). Generating globalization. In L. L. Putnam & D. K. Mumby (Eds.), *The SAGE handbook of organizational communication: Advances in theory, research, and methods* (3rd. ed., pp. 717–742). Los Angeles: Sage.

Sue, D. W. S., Capodilupo, C. M., Torino, G. C., Bucceri, J. M., Holder, A. M. B., Nadal, K. L., & Esquilin, M. (2007). Racial microaggressions in everyday life: Implications for clinical practice. *American Psychologist, 62*(4), 271–286.

Sullivan, K. (2014). With(out) pleasure: Desexualization, gender and sexuality at work. *Organization, 21*, 346–364.

Sullivan, K., & Delaney, H. (2017). A femininity that "giveth and taketh away": The prosperity gospel and postfeminism in the neoliberal economy. *Human Relations, 70*, 836–859.

Surowiecki, J. (2016, April 25). Unlikely alliances: When North Carolina's legislators tried to limit L.G.B.T. rights, big business was their toughest opponent. *The New Yorker*. Retrieved from https://www.newyorker.com/magazine/2016/04/25/the-corporate-fight-for-social-justice.

Sward, K. (1968). *The legend of Henry Ford*. New York: Russell and Russell.

Swisher, K. (2013). "Physically together": Here's the internal Yahoo no-work-from-home memo for remote workers and maybe more. Retrieved from *All Things Digital* website: http://allthingsd.com/20130222/physically-together-heres-the-internal-yahoo-no-work-from-home-memo-which-extends-beyond-remote-workers/.

Taylor, F. W. (1911/1934). *The principles of scientific management*. New York: Harper & Brothers [originally published 1911].

Taylor, F. W. (1912/1926). *Testimony of Frederick W. Taylor at Hearings before Special Committee of the House of Representatives*, January, 1912. Taylor Society. [originally published 1912].

Taylor, P., & Bain, P. (1999). "An assemblyline in the head": Work and employee relations in the call centre. *Industrial Relations Journal, 30*, 101–117.

Taylor, P., & Bain, P. (2003). "Subterranean worksick blues": Humour as subversion in two call centres. *Organization Studies, 24*, 1487–1509.

Taylor, P., & Moore, S. (2014). Cabin crew collectivism: Labour process and the roots of mobilization. *Work, Employment and Society, 29*, 79–98.

Terkel, S. (1972). *Working*. New York: Ballantine.

Thatcher, M. (1987, Sept. 23). Interview for "Woman's Hour" ("no such thing as society"). *Thatcher Foundation*. Retrieved from https://www.margaretthatcher.org/document/106689

Therborn, G. (1980). *The ideology of power and the power of ideology*. London: Verso.

Thomas, R., Mills, A. J., & Mills, J. H. (Eds.). (2004). *Identity politics at work: Resisting gender, gendering resistance*. London: Routledge.

Thompson, E. P. (1967). Time, work-discipline, and industrial capitalism. *Past and Present, 38*, 56–97.

Tolentino, G. (2017, March 17). The gig economy celebrates working yourself to death. *The New Yorker*. Retrieved from https://www.newyorker.com/culture/jia-tolentino/the-gig-economy-celebrates-working-yourself-to-death.

Tong, R. (2009). *Feminist thought: A more comprehensive introduction* (3rd ed.). Boulder, CO: Westview Press.

Tourish, D., Russell, C., & Armenic, J. (2010). Transformational leadership education and agency perspectives in business school pedagogy: A marriage of inconvenience? *British Journal of Management, 21*, S40–S59.

Townsley, N. C. (2003). Love, sex, and tech in the global workplace. In B. J. Dow & J. T. Wood (Eds.), *The Sage handbook of gender and communication* (pp. 143–160). Thousand Oaks, CA: Sage.

Tracy, S. (2000). Becoming a character for commerce: Emotion labor, self-subordination, and discursive construction of identity in a total institution. *Management Communication Quarterly, 14*, 90–128.

Tracy, S. (2005). Locking up emotion: Moving beyond dissonance for understanding emotion labor discomfort. *Communication Monographs, 72*, 261–283.

Tracy, S. (2012). *Qualitative research methods: Collecting evidence, crafting analysis, communicating impact*. New York: John Wiley.

Tracy, S., Lutgen-Sandvik, P., & Alberts, J. (2006). Nightmares, demons, and slaves: Exploring the painful metaphors of workplace bullying. *Management Communication Quarterly*, *20*, 148–185.

Tracy, S., & Scott, C. (2006). Sexuality, masculinity, and taint management among firefighters and correctional officers: Getting down and dirty with "America's heroes" and the "scum of law enforcement." *Management Communication Quarterly*, *20*, 6–38.

Treem, J., & Leonardi, P. M. (2013). Social media use in organizations: Exploring the affordances of visibility, editability, persistence, and association. *Annals of the International Communication Association*, *36*, 143–189. doi:10.1080/23808985.2013.11679130

Trethewey, A. (1997). Resistance, identity, and empowerment: A postmodern feminist analysis of clients in a human service organization. *Communication Monographs*, *64*, 281–301.

Trethewey, A. (2001). Reproducing and resisting the master narrative of decline: Midlife professional women's experiences of aging. *Management Communication Quarterly*, *15*, 183–226.

Triangle shirtwaist factory fire (1911). (2011, March 11). *New York Times*. Retrieved from http://topics.nytimes.com/top/reference/timestopics/subjects/t/triangle_shirtwaist_factory_fire/index.html.

Trice, H. M., & Beyer, J. M. (1984). Studying organizational culture through rites and ceremonials. *Academy of Management Review*, *9*, 653–669.

Trist, E. L., & Bamforth, K. W. (1951). Some social and psychological consequences of the longwall method of coal-getting: An examination of the psychological situation and defences of a work group in relation to the social structure and technological content of the work system. *Human Relations*, *4*(1), 3–38.

Trist, E. L., Higgin, G. W., Murray, H., & Pollock, A. B. (1963). *Organizational choice: Capabilities of groups at the coalface under changing technologies*. London: Tavistock.

Tronti, M. (2012). Our Operaismo. *New Left Review*, *73*, 119–139.

Trujillo, N. (1992). Interpreting (the work and talk of) baseball: Perspectives on ballpark culture. *Western Journal of Communication*, *56*, 350–371.

Trujillo, N., & Dionisopoulos, G. (1987). Cop talk, police stories, and the social construction of organizational drama. *Central States Speech Journal*, *38*, 196–209.

Turow, J. A. (2017). *The aisles have eyes: How retailers track your shopping, strip your privacy, and define your power*. New Haven: Yale University Press.

United States Department of Labor. (n.d.). Wage and Hour Division (WHD). Retrieved from https://www.dol.gov/whd/data/index.htm

University of Colorado Boulder. (n.d.). Leadership studies minor. Retrieved from https://www.colorado.edu/lsm/,

Useem, J. (2000, January 10). Welcome to the new company town. *Fortune*, 62–70. Retrieved from http://archive.fortune.com/magazines/fortune/fortune_archive/2000/01/10/271757/index.htm.

Vallas, S. P. (2003). The adventures of managerial ideology: Teamwork, ideology, and worker resistance. *Social Problems*, *50*, 204–225.

Vallas, S. P. (2012). *Work: A critique*. Cambridge, UK: Polity Press.

Vallas, S. P. (2016). Working class heroes or working stiffs: Domination and resistance in business organizations. *Research in the Sociology of Work*, *28*, 101–126.

Van Maanen, J. (1991). The smile factory: Work at Disneyland. In P. J. Frost, L. F. Moore, M. R. Louis, C. C. Lundberg, & J. Martin (Eds.), *Reframing organizational culture* (pp. 58–76). Newbury Park, CA: Sage.

Van Maanen, J. (1995). Style as theory. *Organization Science*, *6*, 133–143.

Van Maanen, J., & Barley, S. R. (1984). Occupational communities: Culture and control in organizations. In B. M. Staw & L. L. Cummings (Eds.), *Research in organizational behavior 6* (pp. 287–365). Greenwich, CT: JAI Press.

Vara, V. (2016, February 9). Why Yahoo couldn't adapt to the smartphone era. *The New Yorker*, 92. Retrieved from https://www.newyorker.com/business/currency/why-yahoo-couldnt-adapt-to-the-iphone-era.

Vaynerchuck, G. (2008). Do what you love (no excuses!) [Video file]. Retrieved from https://www.ted.com/talks/gary_vaynerchuk_do_what_you_love_no_excuses

Victor, D. (2018, May 11). When white people call the police on black people. *The New York Times*. Retrieved from https://www.nytimes.com/2018/05/11/us/black-white-police.html?action = click&module = RelatedCoverage&pgtype = Article&region = Footer.

von Bertalanffy, L. (1968). *General system theory*. New York: George Braziller.

U.S. Census Bureau. (2018, March 13). Older people projected to outnumber children for first time in U.S. history. Retrieved from https://www.census.gov/newsroom/press-releases/2018/cb18-41-population-projections.html.

U.S. Equal Employment Opportunity Commission. (2002). Facts about sexual harrassment. Retrieved from https://www.eeoc.gov/facts/fs-sex.html.

Vintage Dove commercial [Video file]. (1957/2011). [Original published 1957]. Retrieved from https://www.youtube.com/watch?v = jWD0co3qFpI.

Waggoner, C. E. (1997). The emancipatory potential of feminine masquerade in Mary Kay Cosmetics. *Text and Performance Quarterly*, *17*, 256–272.

Wajcman, J. (2015). *Pressed for time: The acceleration of life in digital capitalism*. Chicago: University of Chicago Press.

Wajcman, J., & Rose, E. (2011). Constant connectivity: Rethinking interruptions at work. *Organization Studies*, *32*, 941–961.

Wajcman, J., Rose, E., E., Brown B. J., & Bittman, M. (2010). Enacting virtual connections between work and home. *Journal of Sociology*, *46*, 257–275.

Walker, R. (2008). *Buying in: The secret dialogue between what we buy and who we are*. New York: Random House.

Wallace, D. F. (2005). "This Is Water." Retrieved from http://bulletin-archive.kenyon.edu/x4280.html.

Walsh, M. W. (2000). Where G.E. falls short: Diversity at the top. *The New York Times*, pp. Section 3, 1, 13.

Ward, J., & Winstanley, D. (2003). The absent presence: Negative space within discourse and the construction of minority sexual identity in the workplace. *Human Relations*, *56*, 1255–1280.

Warner, J., & Corley, D. (2017). *The women's leadership gap*. Washington, DC: Center for American Progress. Retrieved from https://www.americanprogress.org/issues/women/reports/2017/05/21/432758/womens-leadership-gap/.

Waters, M. (2001). *Globalization* (2nd. ed.). London: Routledge.

Webb, J. (2006). *Organisations, identities and the self*. Basingstoke: Palgrave Macmillan.

Weber, M. (1958). *The protestant ethic and the spirit of capitalism*. New York: Scribner's Press.

Weber, M. (1978). *Economy and society: An outline of interpretive sociology* (G. Roth & C. Wittich, Trans.). Berkeley: University of California Press.

Weeks, K. (2011). *The problem with work: Feminism, marxism, antiwork politics, and postwork imaginaries*. Durham, NC: Duke University Press.

Weick, K. E. (1979). *The social psychology of organizing* (Second ed.). Reading, MA: Addison-Wesley.

Weick, K. E. (1988). Enacted sensemaking in crisis situations. *Journal of Management Studies*, *25*, 305–317.

Weick, K. E. (1989). Organized improvization: 20 years of organizing. *Communication Studies*, *40*, 241–248.

Weick, K. E. (1990). The vulnerable system: An analysis of the Tenerife air disaster. *Journal of Management Studies*, *16*, 971–993.

Weick, K. E. (1993). The collapse of sense-making in organizations: The Mann Gulch disaster. *Administrative Science Quarterly*, *38*, 629–652.

Weick, K. E. (1995). *Sense-making in organizations*. Thousand Oaks, CA: Sage.

Weick, K. E. (2001). *Making sense of the organization*. Oxford, UK: Blackwell Publishers.

Weil, D. (2014). *The fissured workplace*. Cambridge, MA: Harvard University Press.

Weiskopf, R., & Tobias-Miersch, Y. (2016). Whistleblowing, parrhesia and the contestation of truth in the workplace. *Organization Studies*, *37*, 1621–1640.

Welch, J. (2008). *Jack Welch speaks: Wisdom from the world's greatest business leader*. Hoboken, N.J.: Wiley.

Welch, J., & Byrne, J. A. (2001). *Jack: Straight from the gut*. New York: Warner Business Books.

Welter, B. (1966). The cult of true womanhood: 1820–1860. *American Quarterly*, *18*(2), 151–174.

West, C., & Zimmerman, D. (1987). Doing gender. *Gender and Society*, *1*, 125–151.

Western, S. (2008). *Leadership: A critical text*. Los Angeles, CA: Sage.

Wexler, E. (2016, May 4). A campus by any other brand. *Slate*. Retrieved from http://www.slate.com/articles/life/inside_higher_ed/2016/05/diverse_college_branding_campaigns_rely_on_the_same_tried_and_true_cliches.html?via = gdpr-consentl.

Wheatley, M. J. (1999). *Leadership and the new science: Discovering order in a chaotic world* (2nd ed.). San Francisco: Berrett-Koehler.

Whyte, W. F. (1981). *Street corner society: The social structure of an Italian slum*. Chicago: University of Chicago Press.

Whyte, W. H. (1956). *The organization man*. New York: Simon and Schuster.

Wieland, S. (2010). Ideal selves as resources for the situated practice of identity. *Management Communication Quarterly*, *24*, 503–528.

Wiener, N. (1948). *Cybernetics or control and communication in the animal and the machine*. New York: John Wiley.

Wilhoit, E. D., & Kisselburgh, L. G. (2017). The relational ontology of resistance: Hybridity, ventriloquism, and materiality in the production of bike commuting as resistance. *Organization*. doi:10.1177/1350508417723719

Williams, C. L. (1992). The glass escalator: Hidden advantages for men in the "female"professions. *Social Problems*, *39*, 253–267.

Williams, C. L. (2013). The glass escalator, revisited. *Gender & Society*, *27*, 609–629.

Williams, R. (1983). *Culture and society, 1780–1950*. New York: Columbia University Press.

Willis, P. (1977). *Learning to labor: How working class kids get working class jobs*. New York: Columbia University Press.

Willmott, H. (1993). Strength is ignorance; slavery is freedom: Managing culture in modern organizations. *Journal of Management Studies*, *30*, 515–552.

Willmott, H. (2010). Creating value beyond the point of production: Branding, financialization, and market capitalization. *Organization*, *17*, 517–542.

Winfrey, O. (2018). Speeches, Oprah Winfrey's speech at Standford's commencement: Part 2. Retrieved from https://www.lingq.com/lesson/oprah-winfreys-speech-at-stanfords-comm-39220/.

Witten, M. (1993). Narrative and the culture of obedience at the workplace. In D. K. Mumby (Ed.), *Narrative and social control: Critical perspectives* (pp. 97–118). Newbury Park, CA: Sage.

Wolfe, T. (1976, August 23). The "me" decade and the third great awakening. *New York Magazine*. Retrieved from http://nymag.com/news/features/45938/.

Wolfinger, R. E. (1971). Nondecisions and the study of local politics. *American Political Science Review*, *65*, 1063–1080.

Wollstonecraft, M. (1792/1975). *A vindication of the rights of woman*. New York: W. W. Norton.

Women's suffrage. (n.d.). *In Wikipedia*. Retrieved from http://en.wikipedia.org/wiki/Women%27s_suffrage.

Woods, J. D., & Lucas, J. H. (1993). *The corporate closet: The professional lives of gay men in America.* New York: The Free Press.

Wright, A. D. (2017). *Want to boost productivity? Consider "no-tech: days.* Society for Human Resource Management. Retrieved from https://www.shrm.org/resourcesandtools/hr-topics/technology/pages/5-tips-for-preventing-smartphone-and-e-mail-related-distractions.aspx.

Wrzesniewski, A., LoBuglio, N., Dutton, J., & Berg, J. (2013). Job crafting and cultivating positive meaning and identity in work. *Advances in Positive Organizational Psychology, 1,* 281–302.

Ybema, Y., Keenoy, T., Oswick, C., Beverungen, A., Ellis, N., & Sabelis, I. (2009). Articulating identities. *Human Relations, 62,* 299–322.

Yep, G. A. (2003). The violence of heteronormativity in communication studies. *Journal of Homosexuality, 45*(2–4), 11–59.

Young, E. (1989). On the naming of the rose: Interests and multiple meanings as elements of organizational culture. *Organization Studies, 10,* 187–206.

Yukl, G. (1989). Managerial leadership: A review of theory and research. *Journal of Management Studies, 15,* 251–289.

Yukl, G. (2006). *Leadership in organizations.* Upper Saddle River, NJ: Pearson/Prentice Hall.

Zarya, V. (2017, June 17). The 2017 Fortune 500 includes a record number of women CEOs. *Fortune.* Retrieved from http://fortune.com/2017/06/07/fortune-women-ceos/.

Zhao, Y., & Zhu, Q. (2014). Evaluation on crowdsourcing research: Current status and future direction. *Information Systems Frontiers, 16,* 417–434. doi:10.1007/s10796-012-9350-4

Zoller, H. M. (2003). Working out: Managerialism in workplace health promotion. *Management Communication Quarterly, 17,* 171–205.

Zoller, H. M., & Fairhurst, G. (2007). Resistance leadership: The overlooked potential in critical organization and leadership studies. *Human Relations, 60,* 1331–1360.

Zraick, K. (2018, June 30). San Francisco is so expensive, you can make six figures and still be low income. *The New York Times.* Retrieved from https://www.nytimes.com/2018/06/30/us/bay-area-housing-market.html?hp&action = click&pgtype = Homepage&clickSource = story-heading&module = first-column-region&region = top-news&WT.nav = top-news.

Zuboff, S. (1988). *In the age of the smart machine: The future of work and power.* New York: Basic Books.

Zuckerberg, R. (2018). *Pick three: You can have it all (just not every day).* New York: Dey Street Books.

Zwick, D., Bonsu, S. K., & Darmody, A. (2008). Putting consumers to work: "Co-creation" and new marketing govern-mentality. *Journal of Consumer Culture, 8,* 163–196.

Zyman, S. (2002). *The end of advertising as we know it.* New York: John Wiley.

Index

About the Authors

Dennis K. Mumby is the Cary C. Boshamer Distinguished Professor of Communication at The University of North Carolina at Chapel Hill, United States of America. His research focuses on the communicative dynamics of organizational control and resistance. He is a fellow of the International Communication Association, and a National Communication Association Distinguished Scholar. He has authored or edited seven books and over 60 articles in the area of critical organization studies, and his work has appeared in journals such as *Academy of Management Review*, *Management Communication Quarterly*, *Organization Studies*, *Organization,* and *Human Relations*. He is past chair of the Organizational Communication Division of the National Communication Association, and an eight-time winner of the division's annual research award. He has also served as chair of the Organizational Communication Division of the International Communication Association, and is a recipient of the division's Fredric M. Jablin Award for contributions to the field of organizational communication.

Timothy R. Kuhn is professor of communication at the University of Colorado Boulder, United States of America. His research addresses the constitution of authority and agency in organizational action, with particular attention to how knowledge, identities, and conceptions of value emerge in sociomaterial and power-laden communication practices. He has authored or edited three books and more than 50 articles, which have appeared in journals including *Communication Monographs*, *Organization Studies*, *Academy of Management Review*, *Academy of Management Annals*, *Organization*, *Management Communication Quarterly*, and *Human Communication Research*, among others. He is former chair of the Organizational Communication Division of the National Communication Association, incoming chair of the same division at the International Communication Association, and co-coordinator of the Standing Working Group Organization as Communication at the European Group of Organizational Studies.